FRAMING THE SACRED

FRAMING THE SACRED

The Indian Churches of Early Colonial Mexico

Eleanor Wake

University of Oklahoma Press : Norman

Publication of this book has been made possible by a grant from the
Scouloudi Foundation in association with the Institute of Historical Research,
University of London.

Library of Congress Cataloging-in-Publication Data

Wake, Eleanor, 1948–
Framing the sacred : the Indian churches of early colonial Mexico / Eleanor Wake.
        p.   cm.
Includes bibliographical references and index.
ISBN 978-0-8061-4033-9 (hardcover : alk. paper)
1. Church architecture—Mexico.   2. Architecture, Spanish colonial—Mexico.
3. Decoration and ornament, Architectural—Mexico.   4. Christian art and symbolism—
Mexico—Modern period, 1500–   5. Symbolism in architecture—Mexico.
6. Indian art—Mexico.   7. Architecture and society—Mexico—History—16th century.   I. Title.
NA5253.W35 2009
 726.50972'09031—dc22

                                                                                                2008047270

The paper in this book meets the guidelines for permanence and durability of the committee
on Production Guidelines for Book Longevity of the Council on Library Resources, Inc. ∞

1 2 3 4 5 6 7 8 9 10

To the memory of Constantino Reyes-Valerio, whose passion for the Indian churches of early colonial Mexico was of such inspiration to us all

In memory of my parents

And for Rosie, Joan, Jeanne-Marie, and Tlilhua, with love

Contents

List of Illustrations *ix*

Acknowledgments *xix*

Abbreviations *xxi*

Introduction *3*

CHAPTER 1. *Ritual Manifestations and the Search for the Sacred* *35*

CHAPTER 2. *Colonial Ritual and the Accommodation of the Christian Sacred* *55*

CHAPTER 3. *Indoctrination and the Building of Churches* *77*

CHAPTER 4. *Native Perception of Churches* *101*

CHAPTER 5. *Architectural Detail: Embedded Stones* *139*

CHAPTER 6. *Painting and Sculpture in an Indo-Christian Context* *171*

CHAPTER 7. *Framing the Sacred* *235*

Appendix A. *Churches, Chapels, Monastery Complexes, and Other Religious Buildings Visited by the Author (1991–2007)* *257*

Appendix B. *Sample of Native Maps and Their Representations of Churches Cited in Chapter 4* *263*

Notes *265*

Glossary of Frequently Used Nahuatl or Nahuatl-Derived Terms *299*

Bibliography *301*

Index *323*

Illustrations

Color Plates

1. The festival of Atamalqualiztli, Códice Matritense del Palacio Real *12*

2. The mountain of sustenance, from mural paintings at Tepantitla, Teotihuacan *13*

3. Tlaloc, god of rain, Codex Borbonicus *14*

4. Chalchiutlicue, goddess of terrestrial waters, Codex Borbonicus *14*

5. Red and blue temples as replica water-mountains,
    Codex Nuttall and *Historia tolteca-chichimeca* *15*

6. Hiding the idols of Tenochtitlan *16*

7. The 1569 map of Tlahuelilpa, Hidalgo *17*

8. The 1578 maps of Coatlinchan, México *18*

9. The 1580 map of Acapixtla, Morelos *19*

10. The 1571 map of Tezontepec de Aldama, Mixquiahuala, Hidalgo *20*

11. An early mural painting, Asunción Tecamachalco, Puebla *21*

12. The Crucifixion, lower cloister, San Juan Evangelista Culhuacan, D.F. *22*

13. The Augustinian *Tebaida*, lower cloister, Culhuacan *22*

14. The Augustinian *Tebaida* at San Nicolás Tolentino Actopan, Hidalgo *23*

15. Crucifixion, upper cloister, Actopan *24*

16. Maize plant at Cacaxtla, Tlaxcala *25*

17. Birds sip flowers, open chapel, La Concepción Atlatlauhca, Morelos *26*

18. Birds seek songs, lower church nave, Los Santos Reyes Meztitlan, Hidalgo *27*

19. A bird seeks its song, lower cloister, San Guillermo Totolapa, Morelos *28*

20. Birds forage for songs, San Juan Bautista Cuauhtinchan, Puebla *29*

21. "Feather down butterflies" descend *30*

22. Crimson and blue flowers announce the presence of the Indo-Christian sacred *31*

23. A mythical beast sings flowers, San Miguel Arcángel Ixmiquilpan, Hidalgo *32*

24. A Mexican grotesque frieze, Los Santos Reyes Meztitlan, Hidalgo *33*

Figures

1.1.   The creation of the cosmos *38*

1.2.   Mural painting at Tlacuilapaxco, Teotihuacan, depicting flowery words and flowery water *41*

1.3.   The four directional tlaloque holding up the sky *43*

1.4.   Song and dance, Codex Magliabechiano *48*

1.5.   "I cut the blossoms . . .": preparation for a framing ritual, Florentine Codex *50*

1.6.   Mayahuel-Ayopechtli beneath her flower-bower, Codex Laud *51*

1.7.   Common species of psychoactive Mexican flora *52*

3.1.   Imaginary reconstruction of the "pantli-nochtli" writing system *78*

3.2.   Native glyphic inserts in the picture catechisms *79*

3.3.   The reuse of prehispanic masonry and sculpture *95*

4.1.   Layout of a typical sixteenth-century monastery complex *101*

4.2.   Title page of Codex Féjérváry *106*

4.3.   The architectural tepictoton, Códice Matritense del Palacio Real *107*

4.4.   Altepetl signs, Codex Osuna *109*

4.5.   West face of the Pyramid of the Sun, Teotihuacan *110*

4.6.   Architectural characteristics of prehispanic temples *112*

4.7.   Detail from the 1580 map of Huejutla, Hidalgo *116*

4.8.   Detail from the 1579 map of Suchitepec, Oaxaca *116*

4.9.   Detail from the 1579 map of Tlamacazcatepec, Oaxaca *117*

4.10. The ca. 1580 map of Huapalteopan, México *118*

4.11. Rooftop merlons on the sixteenth-century parish church of Tlaxcoapan, Hidalgo *119*

4.12. The name-glyph of Michimaloyan, "Place of Fishing" *120*

4.13. The merlon-like, stepped churches represented on Mapa de Cuauhtinchan No. 4 *123*

4.14. The 1572 map of Almolonca and Maxtlatlan, Veracruz *124*

4.15. The 1580 map of Cuzcatlan, Oaxaca *124*

4.16. Detail from the 1580 map of Huaxtepec, Morelos *125*

4.17. The ca. 1595 map of Mixtepec, Chicaguastla, and Cuquila, Oaxaca *125*

4.18. The 1591 map of Jocotitlan and Atlacomulco, México *126*

4.19. Drawing of the 1580 map of Atlatlauhca, México, with local patron-mountains and quincuncial layout of cosmic trees *127*

4.20. Franz Tichy's proposed system of radial sightlines across the northern sector of the Valley of Mexico *131*

4.21. The 1595 map of Nopaluca and Santa María Ixtiyuca, Puebla *132*

4.22. How the 1595 map of Nopaluca and Ixtiyuca was constructed *133*

4.23. The geography of the 1571 map of Tezontepec de Aldama *133*

4.24. The relationship of the church of Cempoala, Hidalgo, and surrounding mountains *135*

4.25. Line drawing of the 1590 map of Cempoala, Hidalgo *135*

4.26.   The 1581 map of Cholula, Puebla *136*

4.27.   View from the portal of the church of San Francisco Tlahuelilpa, Hidalgo *135*

5.1.   Embedded chalchihuitl, San Juan Tlaltentli Xochimilco *142*

5.2.   Embedded chalchihuitl and flower, Los Santos Reyes Meztitlan, Hidalgo (with inset) *142*

5.3.   One of a series of carved stones covering the wall faces of the prehispanic yácatas at Tzintzuntzan, Michoacán *143*

5.4.   Carved stones embedded into the east wall of the prehispanic temple platform at Tlatelolco, D.F. *143*

5.5.   The chalchihuitl as a colonial embedded stone *146*

5.6.   Flowers as colonial embedded stones *146*

5.7.   Colonial embedded stones with vegetal motifs *147*

5.8.   Chalchihuitl and flower together as embedded stones, Nuestra Señora de los Dolores Xaltocan Xochimilco *150*

5.9.   Chalchihuitl and flower combined as an embedded stone, open chapel of San Esteban, Tizatlan, Tlaxcala *150*

5.10.   "Mushroom" flower stone, San Luis Obispo Tlalmanalco, México *150*

5.11.   Flower-stars as embedded stones *151*

5.12.   Lizard stone, Santiago Tilantongo, Oaxaca *151*

5.13.   "Peacock" stone, Santiago Tilantongo, Oaxaca *151*

5.14.   Tenoned skull stone, Santo Domingo Chimalhuacan (Atenco), México *152*

5.15.   Native head and chalchihuitl, San Juan Tlaltentli Xochimilco *152*

5.16.   Spiral stones, San Bernardino Xochimilco *152*

5.17.   Mixtec ñuhu stone, Santiago Tilantongo, Oaxaca *152*

5.18.   Xihuitl stone, San Antonio Moyotla Xochimilco *152*

5.19.   Oyoalli motifs flanking a chalchihuitl, San Juan Tlaltentli Xochimilco *153*

5.20.   The oyoalli motif in prehispanic meaning *153*

5.21.   Embedded stone bearing the pierced-heart insignia of the Augustinian order, Los Santos Reyes Meztitlan, Hidalgo *154*

5.22.   Embedded stone bearing the star of the Dominican order, San Juan Bautista Coyoacan, D.F. *154*

5.23.   Horizontal bar of an atrial cross embedded into the church facade, San Matías Tepetomatitlan, Tlaxcala *154*

5.24.   Conch insignia of Quetzalcoatl and flower flanking a Latin cross, San Juan Tlaltentli Xochimilco *154*

5.25.   Latin cross mounted on a flower, San Francisco Tepeapulco, Hidalgo *155*

5.26.   Examples of the orientational relationship of embedded stones with important topographical features, political centers, and/or neighboring villages *166*

6.1.   The tequitqui carved door panel of the old cabildo, Tlaxcala, Tlaxcala *173*

6.2.   Modifications made by native artists to a grotesque frieze *178*

6.3.   A grotesque frieze with a native insert, San Juan Bautista Cuauhtinchan, Puebla *178*

6.4.   The native slipknot used on the reins of a galloping horse, San Gabriel Cholula, Puebla *179*

6.5.   The remains of two different mural programs, San Miguel Huejotzingo, Puebla *180*

6.6.   Painting local landscapes: San Agustín Acolman, México   *181*

6.7.   Painting local landscapes: San Andrés Epazoyucan, Hidalgo   *181*

6.8.   A large feline, lower cloister, San Juan Evangelista Culhuacan, D.F.   *186*

6.9.   Cerro Los Frailes and the twin crags as viewed from the site of Actopan's monastery complex   *188*

6.10.   A mural painting at San Nicolás Tolentino Actopan, showing the two native patrons of the monastery complex   *189*

6.11.   The portrait of Saint John the Good of Mantua at the base of Actopan's stairwell   *189*

6.12.   View of the stairwell at Actopan   *189*

6.13.   Lunette at the top of Actopan's stairwell depicting Saint Nicholas of Tolentine   *190*

6.14.   Lunette at the top of Actopan's stairwell depicting a hybrid Saint Monica/Mary Magdalene   *190*

6.15.   The monastery church and open chapel at Actopan   *191*

6.16.   Actopan's geography and toponymy in relation to the stairwell murals   *191*

6.17.   Cerro Xihuingo, Tepeapulco, Hidalgo, as viewed from the monastery complex of San Francisco   *193*

6.18.   The mural of the Holy Family, chapter hall, Tepeapulco   *194*

6.19.   Adoration of the Magi, chapter hall, Tepeapulco   *194*

6.20.   A mural painting in the chapter hall, Tepeapulco   *194*

6.21.   Portrait of Saint Lawrence, upper cloister, Tepeapulco (with inset)   *195*

6.22.   The Crucifixion, upper cloister, Tepeapulco (with inset)   *196*

6.23.   The star of Bethlehem, chapter hall, Tepeapulco   *196*

6.24.   The atrial cross at Taximaroa, Michoacán   *202*

6.25.   The atrial cross at Natividad de Nuestra Señora Tepoztlan, Morelos   *203*

6.26.   Side "A" of the atrial cross at San Martín Alfajayuca, Hidalgo   *203*

6.27.   The ixiptla of Tezcatlipoca at the festival of Toxcatl, Florentine Codex   *203*

6.28.   Portrait of Saint Clare, lower cloister, San Luis Obispo Tlalmanalco, México (with inset)   *204*

6.29.   Xochipilli, "Flower Prince"   *204*

6.30.   The tequitqui carved portal at Santo Tomás Tetliztaca, Hidalgo   *205*

6.31.   Indian "angels" on the church portal at Nuestra Señora de Loreto Molango, Hidalgo   *205*

6.32.   Indian "angels" on the church portal at San Francisco Apasco, México   *205*

6.33.   The pulque god Tepoztecatl, Codex Magliabechiano   *206*

6.34.   Leaping angels, Santa María Magdalena Amatlan, Morelos   *207*

6.35.   Pulque-imbibing (?) cherubs, portal arch of the monastery church at Natividad de Nuestra Señora Tepoztlan, Morelos   *207*

6.36.   The goggle-eyed, fanged face of the rain deity, Tlaloc, Codex Nuttall   *208*

6.37.   Indian "angel," church facade, Santo Tomás Tetliztaca, Hidalgo   *208*

6.38.   Cherub, cloister capital, San Francisco Tlahuelilpa, Hidalgo   *208*

6.39.   Ocelocoatl at the House of the Dean, Puebla, and at prehispanic Cacaxtla, Tlaxcala   *209*

6.40.   Tripod eagle-talon bowl and Christian symbolic fruits, mural of the Holy Family, chapter hall, San Francisco Tepeapulco, Hidalgo   *209*

6.41.   Pulque goddess Mayahuel, Codex Magliabechiano   *210*

6.42.   Mayahuel, with flowering maguey quiote, Codex Vaticanus B   *210*

6.43.   Mayahuel suckling a child, Codex Féjérváry   *210*

6.44.   The sculpted Virgin of the Seven Sorrows, San Agustín Acolman, México   *211*

6.45.   Mayahuel, with a circular pectoral, Codex Borgia   *211*

6.46.   Maguey spines and hayball, Codex Magliabechiano   *211*

6.47.   Maguey cactus and shooting quiote   *212*

6.48.   The head of Christ, atrial cross, San Agustín Acolman, México   *212*

6.49.   Xuchimitl in a decorative frame, Acolman   *212*

6.50.   A stylized maguey plant framing the choir loft window, San Andrés Calpan, Puebla   *213*

6.51.   The portal of the monastery church, Calpan   *213*

6.52.   A maguey quiote column, Calpan   *213*

6.53.   The *Ecce Homo* at San Andrés Epazoyucan, Hidalgo   *215*

6.54.   Maize plant   *215*

6.55.   The atrial cross at Asunción Tlapanaloya, México   *215*

6.56.   The atrial cross at San Buenaventura Cuauhtitlan, México   *215*

6.57.   Tlaloc, Lord of Rain and Sustenance, Codex Magliabechiano   *216*

6.58.   Frieze, lower cloister, Los Santos Reyes Meztitlan, Hidalgo   *218*

6.59.   The prickly-pear cactus/cross, refectory, Los Santos Reyes Meztitlan   *218*

6.60.   One of three surviving stone crosses at San Francisco Tepeapulco, Hidalgo   *219*

6.61.   The original atrial cross at San Miguel Huejotzingo, Puebla   *219*

6.62.   Side "B" of the atrial cross at San Martín Alfajayuca, Hidalgo   *219*

6.63.   The atrial cross at Santiago Tecali, Puebla   *219*

6.64.   The atrial cross at San Matías Tepetomatitlan, Tlaxcala   *220*

6.65.   Reverse side of the atrial cross at Santiago Anaya (Tlachichilco), Hidalgo   *220*

6.66.   The atrial cross at San Mateo Huichapan (Hueychiapan), Hidalgo   *220*

6.67.   The churchyard cross at San Miguel Huejotzingo, Puebla   *220*

6.68.   The second stone cross at San Martín Alfajayuca, Hidalgo   *221*

6.69.   The atrial cross at Santo Tomás Ajusco, D.F.   *221*

6.70.   The original atrial cross at San Martín Huaquechula, Puebla   *221*

6.71.   Base of the atrial cross at Nativitas Zacapa, D.F.   *222*

6.72.   The atrial cross at San Pedro Topiltepec, Oaxaca, compared to the "Bloody Path of the Sun" of Codex Vienna   *222*

6.73.   Upper section of the atrial cross at San Agustín Acolman, México   *225*

6.74.   The church rooftop cross at San Francisco Tlahuelilpa, Hidalgo   *225*

6.75.   The atrial cross at Todos Santos Cempoala, Hidalgo   *226*

6.76.   Four tlaloque and ritual trees, Codex Borgia   *226*

6.77. The four directional world trees, with the fifth at the center, Codex Borgia *227*

6.78. Relief carving of the maize deity, Temple of the Foliated Cross, Palenque, Chiapas *230*

6.79. Franciscan insignia, San Juan Bautista Acapixtla, Morelos *231*

6.80. Maize cobs (cintli), Florentine Codex *231*

7.1. The singer and his songbook, Florentine Codex *238*

7.2. Sacred flower-song, Codex Borbonicus *238*

7.3. Giant self-supporting flower chains invading the ritual arena, Codex Borbonicus *239*

7.4. Doorjambs carved with numerically adjusted foodstuffs, Los Santos Reyes Meztitlan, Hidalgo *239*

7.5. Portal bearing two tiers of ritual foodstuffs, San Agustín Acolman, México *240*

7.6. S-shaped xonecuilli, northwest posa, San Andrés Calpan, Puebla *241*

7.7. An example of the way in which the native calendar dictates the "formal" decoration of the churches, portal arch, Asunción Chiconcuac, Hidalgo (with inset) *241*

7.8. Configurations of "mushroom" flowers taking up their place in the framing ritual *242*

7.9. Toadstool caps or *Solandra* buds *243*

7.10. Mexica stone drum of Xochipilli-Macuilxochitl *243*

7.11. The hallucinogenic poyomatli in Indian religious artwork *244*

7.12. Sinicuiche, San Gabriel Cholula, Puebla *244*

7.13. The psychoactive huacalxochitl and ritual dancers, Florentine Codex and Codex Tlatelolco *245*

7.14. The huacalxochitl in Indian religious artwork *245*

7.15. Whirling flowers on Indian church carving *246*

7.16. The church portal at Santa Mónica, Hidalgo *246*

7.17. The church portal at Santiago Tequixquiac, México *247*

7.18. The church portal at Santa María Tulpetlac, México *247*

7.19. The tequitqui carved church portal at San Francisco Apasco, México *247*

7.20. The tequitqui carved church portal at San Martín Huaquechula, Puebla *247*

7.21. Flowers rain down in the interiors of Indian churches *248*

7.22. Flowers "dawn," upper cloister, San Miguel Arcángel Ixmiquilpan, Hidalgo *249*

7.23. Birds sing flowery and leafy songs on Indian churches *249*

7.24. Humans and leafy anthropomorphs sing flowers inside Indian churches *250*

7.25. The musical accompaniment at San Miguel Huejotzingo, Puebla *250*

7.26. Church walls resounding with the rhythm of drums *251*

7.27. The painted song scroll at Purificación y San Simón Malinalco, Morelos *251*

7.28 The painter-scribe, Codex Mendoza *252*

7.29. The church at San Mateo Xoloc, México, labeled as a place of song *252*

7.30. Santa Cecilia Atlixco, Puebla, labeled as a place of song *253*

7.31. A Mexican grotesque frieze, San Francisco Tepeapulco, Hidalgo *253*

7.32. The narrower the frieze, the faster its perceived rhythm   *253*

7.33. A painted song at the Hospital de Jesús, D.F.   *254*

Map

Map of New Spain (ca. 1600)   *xvii*

Tables

Table 3.1. Recorded building activity at monastery sites, 1520–1620   *85*

Table 5.1. Documented examples of known embedded stones on sixteenth-century religious structures by motif, site, and number of occurrences   *148–49*

Table 5.2. Location, positioning, and total numbers of embedded stones on sixteenth-century religious structures by site   *156*

Map of New Spain (ca. 1600)

NUEVA VIZCAYA

● Monterrey

NUEVO LEON

● Durango

GULF OF MEXICO

● Zacatecas

NUEVA GALICIA

● Mérida

Querétaro ● Meztitlan
Actopan ●
Acolman ● Tlaxcala
Toluca México ● ● Veracruz
● Puebla
Tepoztlan

Coixtlahuaca
Tilantongo ●
● Oaxaca

PACIFIC OCEAN

N E W   S P A I N

Acknowledgments

I am indebted to the Instituto Nacional de Antropología e Historia, Mexico, for its generosity in permitting the reproduction of all photographs of prehispanic and colonial monuments, images, and objects under its authority included in this book.

Unless stated otherwise, all photographs and line drawings are by the author.

Publication of this book has been made possible by a grant from the Scouloudi Foundation in association with the Institute of Historical Research at the University of London.

There are many others to be thanked for their involvement in the research and writing of this book, and I apologize now for any serious omissions. I remain indebted to Valerie Fraser at the University of Essex for her support from the inception of my doctoral research to this book, its final product; and to Gordon Brotherston, formerly at Essex, for nurturing my studies of pre- and postconquest Mexico and always being willing to discuss or clarify any areas of doubt on my part. I also thank Anthony Aveni of Colgate University for reading through the draft of chapter 5 and pronouncing it to be at least a testable hypothesis. It goes without saying that I take full responsibility for any errors or lacunae that may have crept in.

In addition, I acknowledge the generosity of the Arts and Humanities Research Council of Great Britain, for funding a period of leave from teaching and administrative duties to concentrate on writing; and Birkbeck College, University of London, for a series of travel grants that enabled me to update my fieldwork and documentary sources. The continuing cooperation of the Mexico-based Instituto Nacional de Antropología e Historia and the Archivo General de la Nación has also greatly facilitated my work. In Mexico, thanks also go to Beatriz Albores, Abraham Broca, Johanna Broda, Druzo Maldonado, Hildeberto Martínez, Andrés Medina, Andrew and Carmen Morris, Guilhem Olivier, Eugenio Reyes Eustaquio, Constantino and Carolina Reyes-Valerio, Francisco Rivas, Ethelia Ruiz, Nazario and Gabriela Sánchez, Keiko Yoneda, and Rafael Zimbrón, for their time, interest, and friendship.

Last but never least, I thank the people of rural Mexico who have welcomed me into their communities and sometimes their homes, have shown me their churches, and have treated me with such courtesy. It is in great part due to the devotion and pride with which they and their forebears have cared for the churches that so many survive today. Let us never abuse that devotion or the privilege afforded to us in being able to visit and study such a unique heritage of the Indian past.

Abbreviations

AGN	Archivo General de la Nación (Mexico City)
CDHM	*Colección de documentos para la historia de México*
CM	*Cantares mexicanos*
CMPR	Códice Matritense del Palacio Real
CMRAH	Códice Matritense de la Real Academia de Historia
DIHM	*Documentos inéditos del siglo XVI para la historia de México*
FC	Florentine Codex
HM	*Histoyre du Méchique*
HMPP	*Historia de los mexicanos por sus pinturas*
HTC	*Historia tolteca-chichimeca*
INAH	Instituto Nacional de Antropología e Historia (Mexico City)
INEGI	Instituto Nacional de Estadística, Geografía e Informática (Mexico City)
LS	*Leyenda de los soles*
MNAH	Museo Nacional de Antropología e Historia
RSNE	*Romances de los Señores de la Nueva España*

FRAMING THE SACRED

Introduction

In 1524 the first authorized mission of twelve "apostolic" Franciscans arrived on the shores of the recently conquered territory that was to be called New Spain. They were followed in 1526 and 1533 by members of the Dominican and Augustinian orders, respectively.[1] Further arrivals over the following decades (in the name of the three original orders and the secular clergy) gradually but firmly spread across this new land, preaching the word of the Christian god to millions of inhabitants in every valley and on every hillside through which they traveled. The task was enormous, but the initial response was positive. The native peoples flocked to be baptized and with equal enthusiasm set to the task of raising God's name in perpetuity across a landscape once inhabited by the deities of old. New Spain was soon dotted with the chapels, churches, and monasteries of Christ. This book is about those edifices and the native peoples who built them, decorated them, and worshiped in them during the first century of colonial rule.

A number of scholarly works on the religious conversion of native Mexico and its art and architecture have been published in the past and also more recently. Others will undoubtedly follow. Although some of the earlier studies are classics in their own right, at the level of historical enquiry they have been largely displaced today.[2] In terms of the conversion, their authors often relied too heavily on the sometimes subjective reporting and/or misinterpretations of European eyewitness accounts of native reactions to Christianity and related activities. Early studies on the art and architecture of the conversion also tended toward a biased viewpoint. Comparisons with Old World equivalents were particularly intrusive: if there was anything good about this art, it was because it was European. What was Indian—if recognized at all—was distinctive only in its lack of technical expertise or the appearance of an occasional prehispanic glyph or motif. The ease with which the native peoples assimilated the trappings of the new culture and its religion was explained away as resigned recognition of the invader's cultural superiority, while traditional motifs or glyphs were brushed aside as the "last gasps" of a retarded and dying culture (Kubler 1964).

Within a variety of academic disciplines, fresh methodological and intellectual approaches to both old and new material have since brought us a much greater understanding of both the prehispanic and colonial native world. As a result, a vast area of study has been opened up, exposing the multiple and very dynamic responses of Mexican indigenous peoples to the European religious and cultural invasion. Crucial to the findings of this new school of thought is not only the resounding intellect on which the native world was structured but also that world's capacity for adaptation or resistance in the face of change. Scholars working on the colonial codices and/or areas of day-to-day secular and religious life are showing all too clearly how the native world accepted certain aspects of the European culture while rejecting others.[3] Essentially, it pursued what it understood to be interesting, advantageous, or necessary in order to make a place for itself in colonial society—in order to survive as a cultural group. But what it adopted from the invading culture it also made its own. Despite the trauma of the political conquest, around 1550 we see "a picture dominated in so many aspects by patently untouched preconquest patterns," a people "going about their business, seeking the advantage of their local entities, interpreting everything about the newcomers as some familiar aspect of their own culture" (Lockhart 1993: 5). As I hope to show, the same process also occurred in regard to the "new" religion.[4]

In the specific area of religious art and architecture, John McAndrew (1965) was perhaps the first to discern a certain native "accent" in the Indians' treatment of the forms newly introduced from Europe. The pioneering work of Constantino Reyes-Valerio (1978, 2000) opened our eyes to the overwhelming Indian contribution in the art of the period and to the real extent of native inserts, in both a traditional and reworked form.[5] In her analysis of the sixteenth-century mural program at Malinalco, Jeanette Peterson (1993) highlighted the curious mix of Indian and European iconography, while at the same time drawing our attention to the possible ambiguities inherent in its socio-religious projections. With massive participation of native painters and sculptors now established and a more purposeful intervention on their part recognized, Samuel Edgerton (2001) offered a richly illustrated study, extending his material to the much neglected areas of the Yucatán Peninsula and what is today the U.S. Southwest. His argument, insightful although overly hasty in dismissing the work of others, nevertheless hinges on the ways in which native artisans were encouraged to manipulate the art and architecture of Europe as part of a strategy of evangelization devised and directed by Europeans. Again, any autonomy of native thought and action is denied. The erudite study on the same art and architecture by Jaime Lara (2004) is therefore refreshing. Although heavily focused on the Euro-Christian aspects of iconography and its meaning, it does acknowledge that a native interpretation might also obtain.[6]

My own study concentrates precisely on this angle of interpretation. While not rejecting the work of others, I try to move away from the idea that the whole artistic and architectural product of sixteenth-century New Spain tells a uniquely Euro-Christian story.[7] While this art and architecture is overwhelmingly Euro-Christian in iconography and form at a visual level it is more complex at the level of meaning and function. To this end, my study examines the way in which the native peoples actually perceived Euro-Christian art and architecture and how they came to relate it to the religion that they understood it to represent. While it is true that some accepted or assimilated Christianity and its signs and symbols as the evangelization mission intended, there is considerable evidence to argue that many more did not. That is the focus of the present work.

This line of enquiry begins with a series of more general factors that have not always been considered in studies of this type. The most obvious, perhaps, is the imbalance between the now well-documented native reactions and responses to the colonial presence in other areas of the cross-cultural experience—including their "reconstruction" (Clendinnen 1990) of Christianity—and the area of religious art and architecture. If the Indians adopted and adapted certain of the invader's cultural mores within the parameters of their own world—and let us also not forget the reformulated iconic script that they developed from the invader's own art forms—why should religious art and architecture be an exception? In other words, why should religious art and architecture, as executed by native artisans, be exclusively expressive of Euro-Christian (or Euro-Christian–sponsored) ideas and ideals? Albeit under the supervision of (principally) the three regular orders, and possibly with more than a dash of compromise on their part, the Indian churches of Mexico were physically raised and decorated by the Indians and for the use of the Indians. If they were reconstructing Christianity to suit their own needs, then it is not unreasonable to question whether, consciously or unconsciously, they also adapted its art and architecture to complement or express those needs. What the evangelization body saw and approved of was not necessarily what it was looking at.

In this context, the issue of the transculturative processes taking place also arises. The religious art and architecture of sixteenth-century Mexico was certainly intended to announce the presence and symbolize the permanence of the new cultural master, not to mention the new god: in style, from Gothic to Renaissance, Spanish Plateresque, and Moorish-influenced *mudéjar*; in technique, from arched portals to great vaulted interiors ("nuestra arte," as the Europeans insisted: our culture, our achievement);[8] and in iconography, from thematic representations of Christian figures to the decorative motifs of the grotesque. We understand today, however, that from a very early stage the new and very different circumstances in which this art and architecture was created were already impinging on its cultural exclusivity. In order to accommodate the sheer numbers of native proselytes, the three orders greatly extended church atria (or *patios,* as they called them) and introduced freestanding or annexed outdoor chapels (the so-called open and *posa* chapels). Here the Indians congregated to receive indoctrination, to worship, and to take part in other religious activities. Due to the low numbers of religious missionaries and their new (very full) timetable of teaching and ministration, cloisters were also reduced in size. In effect, such architectural innovation and modification meant that from the outset New Spain's religious architecture no longer carried the mark of its mainstream European equivalent: it became a New World architecture in both concept and function.

At the same time, however, while the evangelizers' endeavors adhered to a longstanding conversion strategy of building over the sites of pagan temples and shrines or other sacred sites—symbolically occupying pagan space—they seemingly also defied accepted Christian traditions of the West. As the pioneering work of geographer Franz Tichy has shown, the churches of sixteenth-century Mexico inherited the alignments of the prehispanic sites they covered (Tichy 1992). Thus, where the apse and high altar usually lie to the east (the direction of Jerusalem) in Europe, the churches in Mexico offer a whole series of "irregularities" of alignment. My point at this juncture is not so much who made the decision to use the prehispanic alignments, or why, but that Euro-Christian architecture in Mexico also took on one of the most singular aspects of prehispanic religious construction. As my study shows, the Indians occupied in building and decorating these edifices and representing them on their "maps" acknowledged this in a number of ways.

My research on the religious art and architecture of sixteenth-century Indian

Mexico has also pinpointed a series of consistencies in details and ideas expressed through architectural fabric or painted and sculpted décor. These are discussed throughout the study. It is worth emphasizing, however, that such consistencies are far from being arbitrary or out of context within an otherwise Euro-Christian whole. Rather, they complement one another to build up a composite picture of the way in which Christian architecture was perceived and Christianity interpreted over a relatively wide geographical area and among different ethnic groups. Such perceptions and interpretations also show themselves to be firmly rooted in the cosmovision that underpinned the native religious system.[9] While consistencies of this type may have arisen from the attempts of the evangelization body to make Christianity "familiar" to the Indians, they could not have resulted directly from its suggestions or directions. At a cultural level they are too strong. At a religious level they also exhibit a coherence of thought that the evangelizers, in their self-acknowledged ignorance of the native religious system and their own often intractable internal differences, could not have fostered as a body (nor, in certain cases, would they have wanted to). This is perhaps the clearest evidence that so many of the churches and their surviving iconography can also offer an indigenous interpretation of Christianity.

A final point, although circumstantial, relates to the impact of these churches on Western cultural perception today. In effect, when working with them, we cannot help noting how alien they are in respect to the European architectural product on which they were modeled. Whether acknowledged or not, this surely is part of the fascination they hold for those of us who choose to write about them. But their strangeness has nothing to do with their innovative or modified features; it is not because, as some have concluded, they are poor or curious copies of mainstream European architecture, designed from memory or word of mouth rather than from mastered expertise ("nuestra arte" again, twentieth-century stance). The churches of sixteenth-century Mexico stand still further from Europe in their very being, as if they have been stripped down and dispossessed of their cultural packaging and their shells reoccupied by an "other." Indeed, only after many years of fieldwork did I realize that the slightly uncomfortable feeling that still overcomes me in their presence is because I am now the "other."

Thus the aim of this book is to show that—despite protracted European intention—a greater part of the religious art and architecture of Indian Mexico expressed not only native religious responses to the conversion program but also native cultural responses to its introduction and imposition. The churches are Indo-Christian— to use the terminology of Reyes-Valerio (1978, 2000)—in that their iconography reflects the outcome of the conversion program in the sixteenth century, which gave root to the religious beliefs and practices that still characterize Mexico's traditional and near-traditional groups today. But the churches also narrate the dynamics of cultural change and continuity through which, I believe, the origins and underpinnings of Indo-Christianity and its artistic product can be more clearly explained. In this, the churches and their iconography tell a very Indian story.

My angle of approach to the conversion program and Indo-Christianity as a concept first dismisses the assumption (of the evangelizers but also of others in more recent times) that the introduction of Christianity into the native world initiated an encounter between two "religions." In the broadest terms, the outcome of that encounter is often understood to have resulted from deficient teaching on the one side, which led to a poor or confused assimilation on the other. This was exacerbated by the efforts of the evangelizers to appropriate the more "acceptable" aspects of native religious belief in the name of the Christian god and the efforts of the native peoples to cling to the "unacceptable" (their deities and other objectionable beliefs and practices)—in other words, to pursue the path of "idolatry." The underlying contradictions here (the ease with which the Indians assimilated the new secular world with no formal "teaching"; the persistence of what was judged to be idolatry in the face of an apparent enthusiasm for so many aspects of Christianity) can be clarified considerably by working on the hypothesis that Christianity was not understood to be either a new or a different religion.

Although the native peoples were no strangers to religious change at the level of social, political, and economic circumstance or aspiration (what I call here the "subreality"), their religious *system,* developed and practiced over millennia,[10] was nevertheless adhered to by all social, political, and historical groups alike. Underpinned by a shared cosmovision that explained the natural world in terms of its forces (the "gods") and cycles (the calendar), and the control they wielded over humankind, this system focused primarily on the temporal world and its continuing regeneration. For the sedentary and semisedentary societies that made up the greater part of Mesoamerica at the time of the European arrival, the key elements (or deity complexes) of water, sun, and the fertility of the earth that nurtured the growth of foodstuffs—above all, maize—were of paramount importance. This was the "reality" of the Indian religious world. Any changes that the religious system underwent at a local, regional, and national level (like the culture it embraced, it could not have been static) were in response to the *impact* of social, political, and economic changes, not to those changes in themselves. It is not the reality that changes but human responses to it. Thus, with the new subreality that the European intrusion supposed (an intrusion that also left the reality intact), the native religious system needed to be placed within a different cultural context once again. In other words, if at a religious level Christianity was "Indianized," at a cultural level the native religious system was "Christianized."

Turning now to the art and architecture that so well expresses this interactive process, my study attempts to show how its reformulation in Indian hands fell under the cultural traditions and perspectives of the Indian world. My concern is not only the way in which native builders, stonemasons, painters, and sculptors perceived the art and architecture of Europe but also the way in which they reproduced it. They did so in accordance with an analogous system of text inscribed and text performed—an integral part of the reflexive system of verbal-visual transmission that, as Gordon Brotherston (1992: 45) observes, was the crux of the Mesoamerican literary tradition.

Where "art" (the term so often applied to Mesoamerican graphic expression) is in fact script, the painters, sculptors, goldsmiths, and others were scribes who wrote—communicated textually—on their medium of specialization, or "sign carriers" as Walter Mignolo (1994: 227) prefers to call them. Writing took the form of a visual language of signs, symbols, and glyphic constructs, among other iconic conventions (see Brotherston 1992: 7–127 and Boone 2000: 31–61, among others). Readings were made through a process that Elizabeth Hill Boone (1998b: 158) calls "visual thinking," in which "the images themselves encode, structure, and present knowledge graphically," although *tlacuilolli,* as this writing system is known today,[11] can also register sound concepts in Nahuatl, Mixtec, and other Mesoamerican languages (Brotherston 1992: 50).

Even with the assimilation and wide usage of alphabetics, after the conquest the native peoples continued to think in visual terms in the preparation and reading of their pictorial literary output (Boone 1998b: 158). In my approach to the religious art of the same period, I therefore question to what extent native artisans, charged with decorating the churches and monastic complexes, understood the European images they were to reproduce as script. Did they attempt to "read" them, and then "rewrite" them on the walls of these edifices? In other words, where the walls of Indo-Christian edifices must also fall into the category of "sign carriers," at what point—if at all—do we draw a line between the iconic script of the postconquest codices and native-executed religious painting and sculpture? Would postconquest native mural painters and sculptors have understood such a Westernized distinction of their work? If they did, would they have adhered to it when it came to communicating Indo-Christianity (or even Christianity proper) to a native audience on an already established "sign-carrier"? In addition, where "decoration" (in the sense of imagery that does not carry a meaningful message or narrative) was also not a concept embraced by the native world, what in the "art" that they produced is in fact "decorative" and what is not? The transformation of two ornamental European grotesque friezes into the celebrated battle narrative on the walls of the church nave at San Miguel Arcángel Ixmiquilpan (Hidalgo) is instructive in both these respects.

But the writing and reading of the image carries with it a further dimension: its ritualization and reenactment, which I refer to throughout in terms of the native perceived inseparability of "ritual and the image." Ritualization of the image entails, at one level, the ritualization of the physical act of producing an image (or constructing a church), which finds its response in the empathic mode of reading that image back—not only visually thinking it but also "living" its narrative (see Johansson 1997). Closely linked in concept to this mode of writing and reading iconic text is the reenactment of its narrative. In addition to human voice, human action (dance and its movements, coordinated processing, the manipulation of carefully configured artifacts), costume and accouterments (their color, form, numeration, and material fabric), and even what we understand to be the settings and décor of performance (architecture, floral coverings) together also write text visually. And these images in performance are also visually thought out, and lived, by an audience.[12] The concept of ritual and the image, of performance and text, pervades the religious architecture of Indo-Christianity too, from its building and decoration to the reenactment of its iconography *by* its iconography. In other words, the text of the Indo-Christian sacred that is this art and architecture was written by native artist-scribes in paint and stone as the ritualized act of its own "framing."

In order to analyze the churches from the indigenous perspective that I am proposing, the present study also diverges from the works of others in terms of documentary sources. The chronicles of the evangelization body and its lay contemporaries are there, of course; once we can read beneath the religious, political, or cultural circumstances that often clouded their authors' objectivity and interpretations, their enormous value cannot be denied. But I also make use of two important native sources hitherto not included in a study of this kind: the "maps" or cartographically based texts produced by indigenous artists across the sixteenth century and beyond and the devotional songs of the *Cantares mexicanos* and *Romances de los señores de la Nueva España* series, which were written down in alphabetized Nahuatl in the first century of colonial rule. Together, these texts offer a much wider picture of what Christianity came to be in native thought. They also offer striking visual corollaries that not only complement each other but are repeated in the art and architecture under analysis.[13]

To extend my angle of enquiry still further, I have also consulted a series of modern-day ethnographical studies on Mexico's traditional and near-traditional communities. These have proved useful, for they offer considerable insight into syncretic religious beliefs and practices that have persisted since the time of the conquest.[14] Such beliefs and practices have not remained unchanged, of course, often having being distorted further through the more intrusive contact imposed on traditional communities by the modern technological world.[15] Nevertheless, the social, political, and cultural marginalization of these communities from the seventeenth through the mid-twentieth centuries has also meant that much has remained intact. As a result, a number of strong associations can be found between their current beliefs and practices and those of their ancestors, as witnessed and reported by the friars in the early colonial period or expressed by the indigenous population itself.

The core material presented in this book is drawn directly from my doctoral dissertation (Wake 1995). It has undergone considerable reorganization as a result of expanding on original ideas and omitting some of the more tedious analyses and background detail that the reader will probably already be familiar with. In addition, subsequent trips to Mexico have also yielded much to include in the area of visual evidence. A listing of early colonial religious edifices visited and documented between 1991 and 2007, on my own or with the assistance and guidance of others, can be found in appendix A. The "old favorites" are included, of course, along with many more, especially in the category of the small *visita* (that is, without resident clergy) chapels and churches so often ignored in studies of this kind. Weathered or boasting bright new coats of paint, some of these retain their original form. Others have undergone considerable renovation or remodeling over time, while still others are in the advanced stages of decay. All nevertheless have contributed in their own way to providing me with a much greater understanding of Mexico's early religious architecture and the people who worshiped, and still worship, within its physical boundaries.

Material for this book has also been drawn from other studies, especially those of Constantino Reyes-Valerio, whose indefatigable trail across Mexico I attempted to follow as part of my doctoral research. Despite this, the analysis and the interpretation of his finds remain very much my own, and I take full responsibility for them. Other sources are also duly acknowledged, whether or not they coincide with ideas originally presented in my dissertation.[16]

Finally, some of my interpretations might appear speculative, especially for the reader working outside the discipline of art history or Native American studies. But, as observed, interpretation also rests on an awareness of the historical and cultural contexts in which the churches were built and decorated and the consistent manifestation of certain patterns in the art and architecture under scrutiny, which cannot have been the product of Western thinking at the time. To put it another way, I understand the churches to be documentary evidence in their own right and attempt to "read" them as such.

FRAMING THE SACRED

Color Plates

PLATE 1. The festival of Atamalqualiztli, as narrated on Códice Matritense del Palacio Real f. 254r. © Patrimonio Nacional (Spain).

PLATE 2. Detail from the mural paintings at Tepantitla, Teotihuacan, depicting the mountain of sustenance (replica, MNAH).

PLATE 3. Tlaloc, god of rain, seated on his chromatically inverted mountain abode
(Codex Borbonicus 7). © Bibliothèque de l'Assemblée Nationale; photo Irène
Andréani.

PLATE 4. Chalchiutlicue, goddess of terrestrial waters, seated on her cave-womb bench
(Codex Borbonicus 5). © Bibliothèque de l'Assemblée Nationale; photo Irène
Andréani.

a

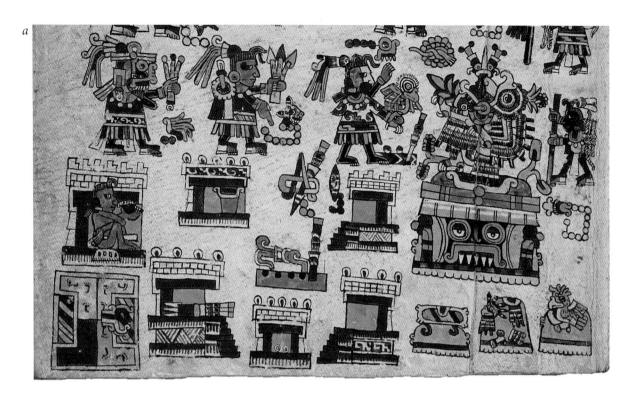

b

PLATE 5. Red and blue temples as replica water-mountains: *a,* Codex Nuttall 2.
© The Trustees of the British Museum. *b, Historia tolteca-chichimeca,* f. 14r.
Bibliothèque Nationale de France.

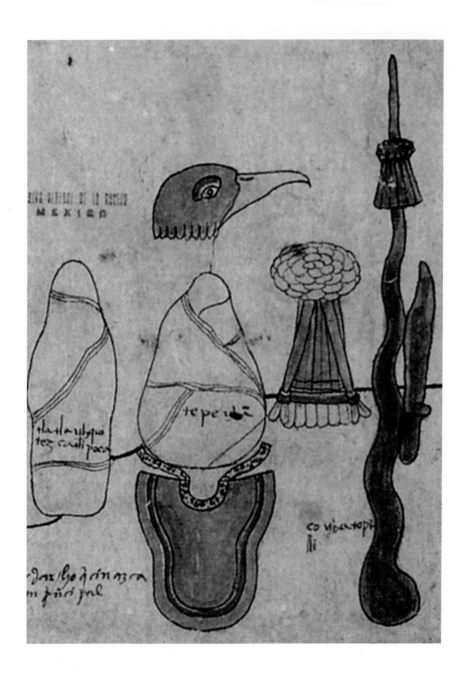

PLATE 6. Hiding the idols of Tenochtitlan (detail of the idol Tepehua secreted within a mountain cave). Archivo General de la Nación, *Inquisición* 37.

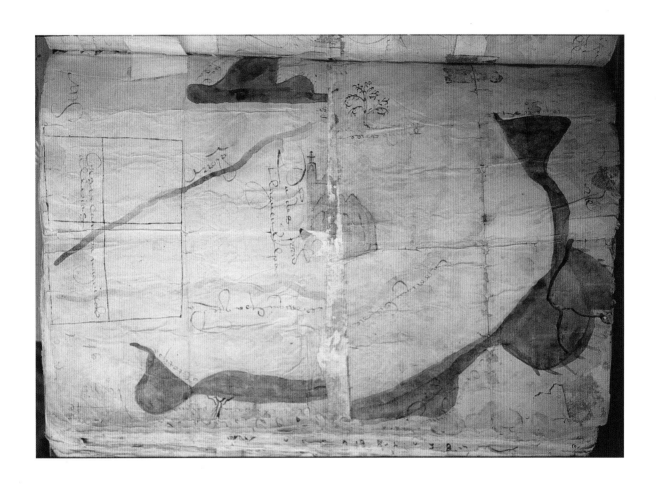

PLATE 7. The 1569 map of Tlahuelilpa, Hidalgo. Archivo General de la Nación 1147.

18

a

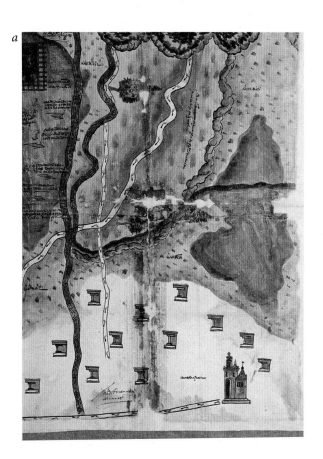

b

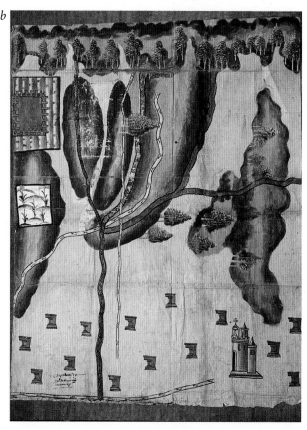

PLATE 8. The 1578 maps of Coatlinchan, México: *a,* pink church with a blue bell and blue interior; *b,* church with a pink exterior and interior. Archivo General de la Nación 1678, 1679.

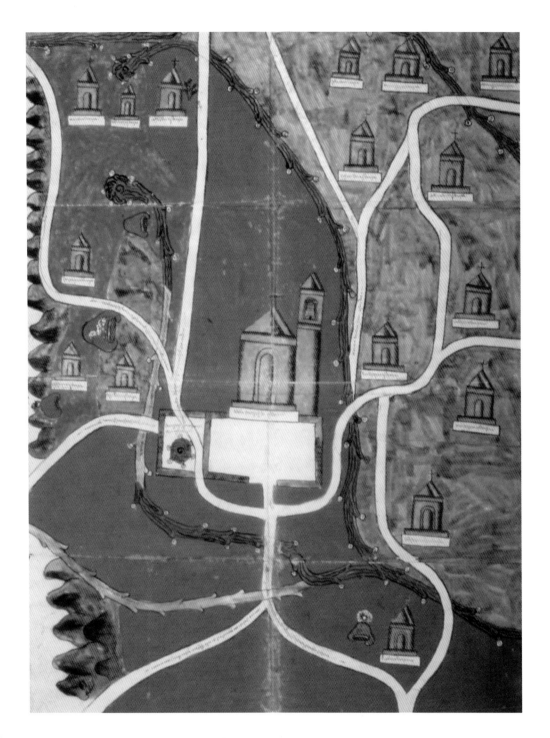

PLATE 9. The 1580 map of Acapixtla, Morelos (UTX JGI xxiii-8). Nettie Lee Benson
Latin American Collection, University of Texas Libraries, The University of
Texas at Austin.

PLATE 10. The 1571 map of Tezontepec de Aldama, Mixquiahuala, Hidalgo. Archivo General de la Nación 1240.

PLATE 11. Fragment of an early mural painting, nave wall of the monastery church of
Asunción Tecamachalco, Puebla.

PLATE 12. Detail from the Crucifixion, lower cloister, San Juan Evangelista Culhuacan, D.F.

PLATE 13. Detail from the Augustinian *Tebaida,* lower cloister, Culhuacan.

PLATE 14. The Augustinian *Tebaida* at San Nicolás Tolentino Actopan, Hidalgo.

PLATE 15. Lunette in an upper cloister chamber at Actopan, depicting a Crucifixion flanked by Saint Augustine *(left)* and Saint Nicholas of Tolentine *(right).*

PLATE 16. Maize plant with cob "heads" at Cacaxtla, Tlaxcala (replica, MNAH).

PLATE 17. In a field of turquoise, pink and crimson birds sip flowers: detail from a frieze in the open chapel, La Concepción Atlatlauhca, Morelos.

PLATE 18. In a field of gold, turquoise birds seek songs among the foliage: detail from a
frieze in the church nave, Los Santos Reyes Meztitlan, Hidalgo.

PLATE 19. In a field of crimson, a turquoise bird seeks its song, lower cloister,
San Guillermo Totolapa, Morelos.

a

b

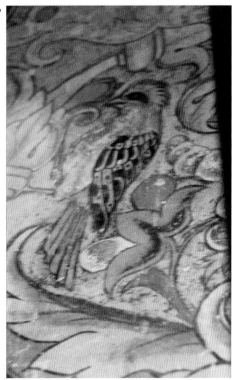

PLATE 20. Birds forage for songs in the flowery realm of turquoise, crimson, and gold
covering the apse wall at San Juan Bautista Cuauhtinchan, Puebla: *a,* a bird with
a turquoise crest and wing and crimson beak and legs (photo: John Castillo); *b,* a
"yellow bird blackened about the eyes," named resident of the home of the sun.

a

b

PLATE 21. "Feather down butterflies" descend: *a,* ceiling of the open chapel,
La Concepción Atlatlauhca, Morelos; *b,* vaulting below the choir loft,
Los Santos Reyes Meztitlan, Hidalgo.

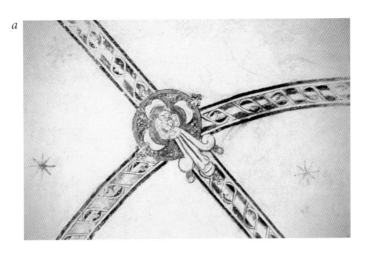

PLATE 22. Crimson and blue flowers, like sentinels, announce the presence of the
Indo-Christian sacred: *a,* on the monastery portada, Los Santos Reyes Meztitlan,
Hidalgo; *b,* on the church portal, San Juan Bautista Cuauhtinchan, Puebla.

PLATE 23. A mythical beast sings flowers: south wall of the monastery church of San Miguel Arcángel Ixmiquilpan, Hidalgo.

PLATE 24. A Mexican grotesque frieze beneath the choir loft, Los Santos Reyes Meztitlan, Hidalgo.

Ritual Manifestations and the Search for the Sacred

Ritual in prehispanic Mesoamerica undoubtedly touched all aspects of life. Based primarily on myth, ritual expressed native understanding of the reality of the world and humankind's place within it: religious ideology, or the explanation of religious theory contained in myth, propagated a system of action that was symbolically enacted—transformed into reality—through ritual (Broda 1982: 104). As Evon Vogt (1976) observes, ritual was (and is) also a system of communication and a system of meaning. Ritual messages are from and often about the "gods" and are thus charged with mythical efficacy. Verbal and nonverbal performance in ritual (myth and sequences of behavior that fit together into ceremonial dramas) constitutes the communicative behavior that serves to perpetuate knowledge essential for the survival of a culture. The symbols employed in ritual contain a periodic reinstatement of meaning, because they are models both for and of reality (Vogt 1976: 8–10).

The perceived "reality" of the Indian world was determined by the past, present, and future actions of the sacred conceptualized. At the very broadest level, that world was made up of the celestial, terrestrial, and subterrestrial planes, the four directions, and their center, all inhabited by a myriad of inter- and intra-acting supernatural forces, some benign and some utterly malignant. These forces, the essence of the meaning of the Nahuatl word *teteo* (sing. *teotl*), focused on and were the focus of the cycles of human existence, which in their turn were eternally sandwiched between them and dependent on them. *Teotl*, which the Spaniards insisted on translating as "god," may mean anything beyond the reach of usual experience. The terms "numinous," "mana," and "sacred" all suggest its significance, in that it explains a life-force present in greater and lesser measures in minerals, plants, animals, and humans as well as in ritual objects and buildings (Townsend 1992b: 173–74).[1]

Theocratic innovations and/or political manipulations imposed on Mesoamerican religious beliefs over space and time most evidently account for the complexity of ritual manifestations at the time of the Spanish invasion. But such impositions must be seen to represent the "subreality" of the temporal world, forged by the ever-changing historical makeup of human society. The evolution of the subreality also brought variations in ritual expression, but these do not denote the existence of different religious beliefs. Beneath a complex facade of social and economic structures, power and control, the exclusivity of warrior and priestly cults, pomp and pageantry, and loyalty and enmity resided the fundaments of a religious *system* to which all sedentary groups—commoners and nobility, rural and urban populations alike—had always adhered. Its primary focus throughout millennia had been to ensure the fertility of the earth, the flow of water to germinate new life, and the warmth of the sun to nurture that life.[2] In short, Mesoamerican religious endeavor directed itself toward the successful production of food and thus the survival and perpetuity of humankind. This was the basis on which the Indian religious reality was constructed, and its givers and takers (the teteo) were the essence of the Indian sacred: "they give us our sustenance, our food, everything we drink, and eat, that which is our flesh, maize, beans, amaranth, *chía*. They are the ones we ask for water, rain, by means of which things on earth are produced" (Sahagún 1986: 150–51).[3]

As a first step to understanding native interpretations of Christianity expressed in the art and architecture of sixteenth-century Mexico, this chapter and the following chapter trace the most basic native ritual manifestations focused on the Indian sacred, from the eve of the Spanish conquest through the early colonial period. At that point such manifestations came to be viewed by the evangelization body as evidence of the ongoing problem of "idolatry" or the persistence of prehispanic religious practices and beliefs. Paradoxically, the same rituals also came to serve as the fundamental expression of native worship of the Christian god and in an approved—but, it turns out, little changed—form were accepted by the evangelizers as a mark of successful conversion. The apparent contradiction here is partly explained by the cultural limitations of the invaders, who judged or interpreted native activities and behavior in accordance with Euro-Christian values. These basic rituals, they believed, were external manifestations of devotion. Where devotion was evidently directed toward the Christian god, the rituals were acceptable; where it was apparently not directed toward him, they were not. For the native men, women, and children who participated in them, however, the expression of devotion was not a primary objective. The Christian presence may have imposed a new subreality on their world, but the Christian sacred now formed part of its unchanging reality. Theirs was a quest for the sacred transformed.

Myth and Reality

As handed down to us by native and non-native sources at the time of the conquest, Mesoamerican myth focuses most strongly on four previous creations (or Suns) and that of the present era: the Fifth Sun, which opened the Age of Agriculture. The inordinately complex content of these myths of course permits multiple readings, but much of their symbolism nevertheless refers to the development of the calendar, the domestication of maize, and the move from a nomadic to sedentary lifestyle that the acquisition of such knowledge permitted. Additionally, the myths lay out sets of basic rules for ritual activities and the main impetus behind them.[4]

The creation of the Fifth Sun, recorded in greatest detail by the Nahua peoples in *Leyenda de los soles* (1992: 121–22) and by Bernardino de Sahagún (1981, 2:258–62), tells how the gods met in the primordial darkness at Teotihuacan following the destruction of the previous world age. After a dramatic self-sacrifice by fire on the part of the humble, pustule-covered god Nanahuatzin and the proud, ostentatious Tecuciztecatl (who hesitated so many times that Nanahuatzin eventually overtook him), both emerged from the flames to become the Sun and the Moon, respectively. All around, the horizon turned deep red. The other gods waited to see where the new celestial bodies would appear in the sky. Some looked north, some south, and some east, where the two finally rose one after the other but with equal brilliance. Perplexed at the thought that the Sun and the Moon would give off the same light, one of the gods, named Papaztac, hurled a rabbit at the Moon, thus forever dimming its face (*LS* 1992: 122). But the Sun and the Moon remained immobile in the sky. The gods therefore decided to sacrifice themselves. The Wind deity (Quetzalcoatl-Ehecatl) took charge of the killing and then blew the Sun and the Moon into motion.

In terms of the dawn of the agricultural age, one of the main themes of this myth alludes to the observation of celestial bodies and the structuring of a calendar that would serve to coordinate agricultural cycles. The gods watched the horizon for the point at which the Sun and the Moon would rise; day and night came into being through the dimming of the Moon; the calendar commenced when the Wind set the celestial bodies into motion. The Wind heralds the rain needed to germinate and nurture the newly planted seeds, and the role of its patron deity in the creation also refers to this early and crucial stage in the agricultural calendar itself.

The same myth speaks of the construction of ceremonial architecture: two tall pyramid-platforms, like towers or mountains (Sahagún 1981, 2:259),[5] were constructed where Nanahuatzin and Tecuciztecatl did penance and made offerings. Monumental architecture denotes not only permanence of residence but also cultural advancement. And, as is well understood today, architecture in Mesoamerica also served as a primary tool for the observation of celestial bodies and the computation of time.[6] Architecture thus becomes a major symbol of the Age of Agriculture.

During Quetzalcoatl's pursuit of the gods, one of them named Xolotl escaped to the maize fields, where he disguised himself as a two-stalked maize plant.[7] When discovered, he fled to the maguey patch, changing into a double maguey cactus. After being routed from there, he hid himself in water as an *axolotl* (a type of edible salamander). Xolotl's escape route defines the three major areas of importance for permanent settlement. The cultivation of maize as a staple was a primary factor in the social and cultural development of the Mesoamerican peoples. Waterside dwelling provided fish and fowl (and salt in the Valley of Mexico) and also gave rise to the development of the *chinampa* system of water-based agricultural plots. The maguey cactus, the sap of which had played a vital role in the hydroeconomy of early hunter-gatherers as well as being an important source of nutrition,[8] also came to be cultivated. The plant offers a variety of other uses for a sedentary lifestyle: for fuel, domestic construction materials, medicinal remedies, thread for sowing and fiber for weaving, footwear, and paper. In addition, an important cult focused on the fertility of the earth grew up around the maguey and its fermented sap, *octli* (or pulque, as the Spaniards labeled it and as it is commonly known today), with the rabbit and a crescent moon as major symbols of reference. Closely associated with the water deities, the pulque deities were agrarian gods and the protectors of agricultural labors (Gonçalves de Lima 1986: 119). By dimming the Moon with a rabbit the pulque deity Papaztac not only set the lunar cycles in motion but also inscribed rabbit as moon, where the twenty-nine nights of the rabbit's gestation cycle correspond to the average number of days in one synodic lunar cycle (Gordon Brotherston, pers. comm.). The same count also measures the human menstrual cycle, which is why the Moon is female.[9] Lord 2 Rabbit was a generic name for the 400 *totochtin* ("revered rabbits" or avatars of the pulque deities) (Nicholson et al. 1997: 82, nn. 7 and 8, 96, n. 15). Mayahuel, a virgin goddess from whose bones the maguey cactus was created by the Wind deity (*HM* 1979: 106–107), was an important female counterpart; 1 Rabbit was her calendrical name (Caso 1967: 193).

The version of the creation of the Fifth Sun by Jerónimo de Mendieta (1973) records that as the gods departed they all left a mantle in memory of their self-sacrifice. With the use of twigs and other objects such as precious stones and serpent skins, the devotees of the gods rolled up the mantles into bundles (Mendieta 1973, 1:50–51). That is, they symbolically reconstructed their gods, and these became their individual idols. Both Mendieta (ibid.) and *Histoyre du Méchique* (1979: 111) name Tezcatlipoca as the giver of song and the *huehuetl* and *teponaztli* drums to the newly created world, thus enabling humans to hold festivals and dances in honor of their gods. Together with the gods' gift of music and song, myth also tells how pulque was given to mortals to make them happy on earth and to permit them to praise their gods better through song and dance (*HM* 1979: 106–107). Herein lie the basic instructions to attract the attention of the deities of the Age of Agriculture.

Knowledge of the calendar and related wisdom imparted by the gods at the Creation is symbolized in the contrast between the blackness of the primordial night and the redness of the first dawn that sets the new age into motion. Carried by the wise ones in the *teoamoxtli*, "divine book," the sacred cosmic knowledge, or things difficult to understand, came to be expressed as the dual Nahuatl metaphor *in tlilli in tlapalli* ("the black, the red," often referred to as "the black ink, the red ink" and meaning writing and wisdom). References to this duality of colors occur throughout Nahua mythology in the same context (León-Portilla 1982: 11–12, 22, 23).

The next stage was the creation of the terrestrial plane: the sacred landscape where humans would dwell. One particularly vivid account tells how the body of Tlaltecuhtli, a dual-gendered, flesh-eating monster, was squeezed in half by the gods Quetzalcoatl and Tezcatlipoca in the guise of two giant serpents. The male half became the sky and the female half the earth. It was from her body that everything required for human sustenance would issue. Trees, flowers, and herbs were fashioned from her hair; grasses and smaller flowers rose from her skin. Her eyes became the sources of wells, springs, and small caves; her mouth, great rivers and caverns; her nose, mountain ridges and valleys. Related myth tells how the two parts were kept separate by posts in the form of trees or gods or beings that inhabited another dimension at the moment of creation, placed at the four corners of the earth. The posts or trees became the pathways of the teteo, the divine opposing essences contained in the monster's two parts flowing through them from the deepest part of the earth and the highest part of the sky. In this way time began to pass: the constant movement of the sacred forces between the monster's two parts created the cycles of the calendar and the perpetual regenerative union between male and female (*HM* 1979: 108; *HMPP* 1979: 32; López Austin 1994: 19–21, 1996b: 7). In glyphic representation (fig. 1.1), the flow of these opposing forces is understood to be symbolized by the two entwined elements of the twisted *malinalli* grass glyph, which run simultaneously up and down the trunks of the cosmic trees (López Austin 1994: 91, 99–100).

The creation of the first humans took place within a cave at a place called Tamoanchan. Quilaztli-Tlaltecuht-

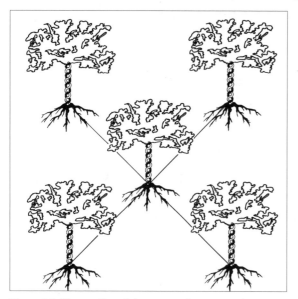

Figure 1.1. The creation of the cosmos: four trees at its corners separated the earth from the sky, with the axis mundi at the center (based on drawings in López Austin 1994).

li, as the earth monster also came to be called, ground up the bones of the ancestors carried out of the underworld of Mictlan, "place of the fleshless," by Quetzalcoatl. To give the bones life he pierced his penis and sprinkled blood on them. In order to feed the first humans Quetzalcoatl, disguised as a black ant, was led by a red ant to the *tonacatepetl,* "mountain of sustenance," within which the seeds of all the food needed for human nourishment were sealed. Taking the first maize grains from its interior, he returned to Tamoanchan, where the gods ground them up and placed them in the first humans' mouths (*HM* 1979: 106; *LS* 1992: 120–21).[10] But the first humans needed more food to survive, so Quetzalcoatl then made a failed attempt to carry off the whole mountain of sustenance. Nanahuatzin (the god who became the Sun) nevertheless succeeded in breaking it open, although it was the *tlaloque* (water deities) who retained the foodstuffs, distributing them each year for human use (Bierhorst 1984: 30; *LS* 1992: 121).

In these myths we see humans created as maize is cultivated: just as the dry bones of the ancestors are sprinkled with blood inside the cave, so the maize seed is germinated beneath the earth by the life-giving rains. In addition, it is the sun and the rain deities together who make the final assault on the mountain of sustenance. Sun and rain—at the right time and in the right quantities—are needed to cultivate maize; by extension, both sun and rain are primary elements for human survival.

The reference to the black and red ants that extracted the first seeds from the mountain of sustenance appears again to relate directly to the black ink and red ink, the metaphor for the sacred written knowledge. But the first humans were also given practical knowledge. Quetzalcoatl's failure to remove the entire mountain of sustenance taught them that they should not consume all their food at once and thereafter face hunger. The symbolic placing of the first maize in the first humans' mouths by the great teacher also denoted cultural advancement in Mesoamerican thought. In the annals of one group of previously nomadic Chichimecs, the eating of maize enabled them to speak Nahuatl (*HTC* 1989: 169) or to integrate into the "civilized," sedentary lifestyle of agriculturalists. Migration narratives in central Mexico most often commence with a cave emergence, a symbolic "rebirth" for those who set off to join the Age of Agriculture.

A second myth that merits comment here is the little-cited Creation of Flowers, as recorded in Codex Magliabechiano. Quetzalcoatl allowed semen from his member to fall on a stone, and from this a bat was born. The creature was sent by the gods to bite a piece of flesh from the goddess Xochiquetzal's genitals. The gods washed this piece of flesh, and from the water came the flowers that have little or no scent. The bat then took the piece of flesh to Mictlantecuhtli, Lord of the Underworld. When he washed it again, sweet smelling flowers poured forth. In this way, the myth tells us, sweet-smelling flowers came from the underworld, while flowers with no perfume grew on earth at the beginning of time (Boone 1983: 206).[11]

Native preoccupation with the scent of flowers is well illustrated in the texts of Sahagún's informants. Consider, for example, the *cacahuaxochitl:* its dense aroma penetrates the nose: "The tree, the blossoms, its foliage, all are of pleasing odor, all perfumed, all aromatic. . . . [The perfume] spreads over the whole land, swirls, constantly swirls, spreads constantly swirling, spreads billowing" (Florentine Codex, Book 11, Anderson and Dibble 1963: 202).[12] Equally desirable was the fragrance of the popcorn-like *izquixochitl* (ibid.). The perfume of the *acuilloxochitl* tears at the nose: "it spreads, stands constantly blossoming. It stands spreading an aroma, raining [blossoms]" (ibid., pp. 206–207). In contrast, the *tlalcacaloxochitl, tzompanquauitl,* and *teoquauhxochitl* have no fragrance, no perfume: they are "useless" (ibid., pp. 198–99, 204). On f. 7r of the postconquest Codex Ríos, we see Xochiquetzal descending from a red sky as the Age of Agriculture dawns. She is framed by a blue and red twisted rope from which large yellow and white flowers sprout, perhaps the "pleasing . . . fragrant, aromatic" *yolloxochitl* or the densely scented *eloxochitl* (ibid., p. 201), the mythical product of her own body.

The piece of Xochiquetzal's genital flesh fertilized with the semen of Quetzalcoatl by means of a bat (itself born from a stone) is an agricultural analogy for the means of human reproduction. From this union, the first flowers were born from water but smelled of nothing. As I interpret this imagery (which may also incorporate a moral or social lesson), the seed fell on stony ground; it fell outside the womb. Thus it could not grow properly. The plant rotted before maturation, and no child came of the union: the seed was wasted. When the seed was taken to the underworld—to the womb of the earth—the second fertilization produced the flowers that all desired: a healthy plant, a perfect child, a deliriously heart-gladdening aroma of life. Perfumed flowers bring life. In this sense the flower creation narrative also appears to refer to the development of improved agricultural techniques, to the process of learning through trial and error: the seed should not be scattered but planted, for many seeds will rot or be washed away before germinating; the harvest will not succeed.

A second reading of this complex myth pertains to the imagery of flowery water. One of the best sources in prehispanic graphic expression that may help us to explain its meaning is found in the mural paintings of Teotihuacan. At Tepantitla, for example, irrigator-priests stand at either side of a great goddess who straddles the seed-filled earth in the traditional birth position. The priests pour flower-laden streams from flower-laden volutes, which are now well understood to antecede the late Postclassic metaphor for sacred words spoken or sung: *in xochitl in cuicatl,* "the flower, the song." At Techinantitla elite figures perform the same task with similar flower-filled water and volutes, while at the Tlacuilapaxco compound a further figure wearing a coyote headdress walks between rows of maguey spines piercing the earth and spilling more flowery water from his hands as he speaks flowery words (fig. 1.2). These examples may well depict rituals focused on the earth at the time of sowing and petitions for rain to germinate the seed, where the maguey spines acknowledge the earth's own self-sacrifice as her body is pierced to accommodate the seed. Although the flower was a predominant symbol in Mesoamerican culture, with a multiplicity of meanings (Heyden 1983; Miller and Taube 1993: 88), it is from these images and the flower creation myth itself that we can perhaps understand how flowers represent the essence of the fertilizing properties of water. In this context, they are symbols of the sacred union of earth and water. Generically, flowers are symbols of the essence of life.

The lesson that perfumed flowers—those created in the place of the dead—were the only useful flowers must also pertain directly to their ritual use in attracting the attention of the supernatural. The prehispanic cult of the dead focused on the role of those who, in the afterlife, served as intermediaries with the gods; it was they who interceded with the teteo in order to secure favorable outcomes for the labors of the living. In modern-day festivals for the dead among traditional groups, flowers still constitute an important ritual element deployed to summon souls to return briefly to the land of the living and receive thanks for their endeavors. While the smell of food offerings also serves this purpose (Nutini 1988: 312), the floral arrangements on graves, the household *ofrendas* (tables of offerings), and the flower paths contain large quantities of heavily scented flowers, especially the native *cempoalxochitl* (golden marigold), today the flower of the dead *par excellence*. Their smell must also serve to guide the departed back from their dark world.

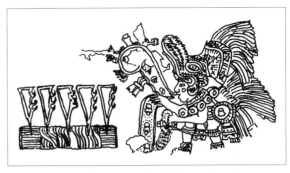

Figure 1.2. Detail from a mural painting at Tlacuilapaxco, Teotihuacan, depicting flowery words and flowery water (redrawn from Berrin 1988).

The Nahua peoples believed in three principal afterworlds, depending on the manner of death. Warriors who died in battle and women who succumbed in childbirth went to Tonatiuh Ilhuicac, the realm of the Sun. Those who drowned, were struck by lightning, or met a similar watery death found themselves in Tlalocan, the home of the rain deities. Most, however, went to the underworld, Mictlan. Apart from the locations of these afterworlds, each representing one of the three cosmic planes, it is striking how they also relate to the elements necessary for the cultivation of maize: earth, water, sun, and the stages of its cycle.

According to native sources, Mictlan was a dark, cold, barren place of cacti and brambles, a place of much work. In Mictlan the dead eat everything that is not eaten on earth: "there is great want in Mictlan" (CMRAH, f. 84r; Nicholson et al. 1997: 177).[13] Applied to the earth, these characteristics correspond well to the barren months between the end of one agricultural cycle and the beginning of the next, when nothing grows but brambles, which must be cleared before the new maize seed can be sown. Mictlan, however, was not only the dark place in the depth of the earth where humans found their origins in the bones of the ancestors but the place where sweet-smelling flowers were created. It was here also that the newly sown seeds must lie before their own fertilization, germination, and growth, which would carry them upward to be reborn on the surface of the earth. Mictlan was no paradise, but it was a place where all life found its origins and to which all life ultimately returned.

Bernardino de Sahagún's informants described the realm of the Sun as a desert, a place of mesquite groves, maguey, and other cacti (FC3, 1978: 49). Francisco Hernández, Philip II's physician, who studied native medicinal plants in New Spain between 1571 and 1577, reported that it was referred to as a beautiful woodland with various species of trees (Hernández 2000: 88). Sahagún's informants complemented this description by adding that there were also flowers from which the warrior dead, transformed after four years into precious birds and butterflies, would suck honey dew (FC3, 1978: 49). Turning from a place of dryness to a place of abundance, the realm of the Sun echoes the two dry seasons of the year: the hot, barren period, between the end and beginning of the agricultural cycle, and the later hiatus in rainfall before the harvest, when the warmth of the sun brings the water-swollen crop to maturation.

Described as a terrestrial paradise (FC6, 1969: 35; FC7, 1953: 68), Tlalocan was a place of absolute abundance and perpetual growth: "there was great wealth, there was great riches. Never did one suffer. Never did the ears of green maize, the gourds, the squash blossoms, the heads of amaranth, the green chillies, the tomatoes, the green beans, the *cempoalxochitl*, fail" (FC3, 1978: 47). To Tlaloc and his emissaries, the tlaloque, "were attributed rain and water. Thus they said he [Tlaloc] made that which we ate and drank—food, drink, our sustenance, our nourishment, our daily bread, our maintenance. All that which grew in the summer [he made]—sprouts, fresh green sprouts, trees, amaranth, *chía*, squash, beans; the maguey, the tuna cactus; and still others, not edible—flowers, herbs" (FC7, 1953: 17). Tlalocan stands as the cosmic and metaphysical link between the earth and the sun in the cycles of growing food, the source of water to germinate—to fertilize—the seed of the earth, giving succor to the growing plant and swelling its fruits before ripening.

But Tlaloc and the tlaloque were also lords of the mountains and of the caves (FC6, 1969: 40). Chalchiutlicue, "Jade Skirts," goddess of terrestrial waters, was likened to a mountain full of water (FC11, 1963: 247); she was the sacred volcano Matlalcueye, "Blue Skirts." Remembering the self-appointed role of the tlaloque as guardians of the mountain of sustenance, Tlalocan was therefore not just the source of water that gave life to everything that grew; it was also the mountain from which all food originated. Indeed Tlaloc, from the Nahuatl *tlalli*, "earth," was also Tlaltecuhtli, "Earth Lord," created as the supreme water deity with Chalchiutlicue as his consort (*HMPP* 1979: 26). Chicomecoatl, goddess of ripened maize, also resided at Tlalocan (FC6, 1969: 35), as did—on a part-time basis—Centeotl, the male aspect of Chicomecoatl and god of maize proper (CMPR, ff. 250v, 277r; 1997: 58 n. 12, 140).

Both Diego Durán (1984, 2:493) and Hernando Alvarado Tezozómoc described a paradise called Cincalco, "Place of the House of Maize Cobs," in much the same terms as Tlalocan.[14] Native sources tell us that Centeotl was born in Tamoanchan, the home of the earth deity but also a region of water and mist. The Song of Xochiquetzal refers again to Tamoanchan in the same way (CMPR, ff. 277, 279r; 1997: 140–41, 145). The conflation of Tamoanchan-Tlalocan (and probably Cincalco) has been amply discussed by Alfredo López Austin (1994), who also ascribes Tamoanchan (and, by implication, Tlalocan and Cincalco) a location at the center of the terrestrial plane. A "realm of flowers" (*xochitlicacan*) characterized by a great tree that bled from its broken trunk (Codex Telleriano-Remensis, f. 19r), Tamoanchan was the axis of the cosmos and the union of its four parts. Its tree was perceived as the total of the four cosmic trees or posts separating the sky from the earth (fig. 1.1) (López Austin 1994: 101, 225). From this explanation, we may also understand that the bleeding tree was the terrestrial outlet of the divine essences of cyclical creation and re-creation that circulated through the cosmic levels (ibid., p. 93). And, with Centeotl having been born in Tamoanchan, the central tree must also be seen as symbolic of the maize plant, the primary source of food to give life to humankind. Along much the same lines, the home of the water deities was described in myth as a dwelling of four rooms around a great courtyard where four great water containers stood. The tlaloque used these to distribute rain of different types—good and bad— over the earth (*HMPP* 1979: 26).

The spatial layout of Tamoanchan-Tlalocan also defines the conceived horizontal structure of the terrestrial plane. It is square or rectangular in form, with each corner occupied by a cosmic tree. The diagonal links between them create a quatrefoil configuration. With the great tree of life and the divine source of water at its center, the cosmos is also quincuncial. Both forms nevertheless allude to the basic cosmic diagram of four world directions and the center. The directions are clearly referred to in the myth of the Creation of the Fifth Sun as the gods search each quarter of the horizon for the appearance of the Sun and Moon: the new creation is ultimately symbolized in the *nahui ollin* or "4 Movement" date glyph (Galarza and Maldonado 1990: 96), the day on which the age of the Fifth Sun will end. The cosmic scheme may also derive from the position of solsticial risings and settings (Tichy 1990: 183), that is, the farthest points on the horizon north and south of the east-west axis between which the sun is perceived to move during the course of the year.

Prehispanic representations of the principal presiding deities of Tamoanchan and Tlalocan assist in our understanding that these mythical places were viewed as a single concept. Tlaloc, Chalchiutlicue, and the tlaloque did not just reside within the mountains—they were mountains and, as such, part of the body of the earth deity and her interior. During the festivals of Tepeilhuitl and Atemoztli, named images of sacred rain-giving mountains were made from amaranth seed dough called *tzoalli* (FC2, 1981: 131, 152). Depicted on Códice Matritense del Palacio Real f. 267r as five humanized figures, the *tepictoton,* "little molded ones," "belonged among the Tlalocs . . . were reckoned among the Tlalocs" (FC1, 1970: 47).[15] In his account of the festival of Tepeilhuitl, Durán (1984, 1:165) records that one of the mountain images was called Cihuacoatl, yet another name for the Quilaztli-Tlaltecuhtli earth deity. A clearer image of the fusion of the attributes of Tlaloc and Cihuacoatl-Quilaztli-Tlaltecuhtli comes in a carving on the inside of a Mexica stone lid (fig. 1.3), where four goggle-eyed tlaloque, complete with the mountain-crag headdress so typical of Tlaloc, link up symmetrically to support a center defined as the circle of the sky (López Austin 1996b: 13). Echoing the naming of a mountain image after Cihuacoatl, these tlaloque also represent the earth mother herself, for the lower half of their bodies is depicted in the squatting birth position characteristic of images of Tlaltecuhtli (Broda 1997b: 130–31). The presentation of mountain idols as groups of five, or four around a center, evokes the numbering and arrangement of the cosmic trees that make up the configuration of the terrestrial plane (López Austin 1994: 179). Mountains are therefore interchangeable with trees in the explanation of native configurations of space, a vision of geography that prevails today in many traditional communities.[16]

Figure 1.3. The four directional tlaloque holding up the sky (redrawn from López Austin 1994).

One further salient aspect characterizes the descriptions of mythical places of origin and destiny: the preoccupation with nourishment (or lack of it) always seems to give way to the presence of flowers, as if to say that there could be no nourishment without them. The logic behind this notion is perhaps evident: the return of springtime, when the earth's regenerative powers are resumed, is marked by the return of flowers over the land, "small flowers . . . which spread out blossoming, spread out bursting, spread out popping into bloom—the flowers of spring" (FC2, 1981: 57). But this interpretation is perhaps too easy; for within the complex system of spirituality in Mesoamerica and among Uto-Aztecan speakers in today's southwestern United States, flowery places are metaphors for the Spirit Land (Hill 1992: 117). The Spirit Land is likened to a beautiful landscape or more precisely to the deeds of creator-beings in their offering of such flowery abundance (ibid., pp.

117, 120). It is thus a place and an entity, which together encompass the notion of "sacred." In sixteenth-century Nahua devotional song, the Mesoamerican equivalent is referred to as "corn-tassel place," "rain place," "flower house," "flower mat," "green time" or "green place" (the perpetual season of Tlalocan), and so on (Bierhorst 1985b: 398).[17] As a conceptualized locus and abstract entity, the flowery and watery abundance of the native sacred embodied all that was desired in the temporal world, and the search for its presence was made through its re-creation in ritual.

Ritual Manifestations

Ritual in prehispanic Mexico was directed toward the sacred. Favors were petitioned and debts were paid through self-sacrifice and the sacrifice of humans, animals, food, feathers, and flowers, all of which constituted items of personal and economic value and/or were prized for their beauty and perfection. As the gods had also demanded, singing and dancing invariably accompanied these acts. Ritual venues echoed the sacred places where mythical events had occurred and continued to occur: mountains, caves, fields, or their constructed equivalents in the form of the pyramid-platform, the "artificial mountain with levels, with steps" (FC11, 1963: 269), the dark cave-temple of Cihuacoatl (Durán 1984, 1:125–26; FC2, 1981: 181–82), and the great courtyards stretching out before these structures, so often scattered with reeds, grasses, and flowers.

With few exceptions, the early sources describing ritual activities at Tenochtitlan tend to focus on the grim extravagances of Azteca-Mexica ceremony: long files of victims toiling up the steps of the pyramid-platforms to meet their death; quagmires of blood covering patio floors; walls or temple rooftops encrusted with thousands of skulls (Hernández 2000: 133); sinister priests; and hideous images of the gods who forever demanded more blood. But the rituals were also magnificent: the color of the processions; the throng of the crowds; the incessant beating of drums; the exquisitely fashioned feather headdresses and richly embroidered mantles of the nobles. Between the proud dashes of the eagle and jaguar warriors, the carefully and often delicately dressed *ixiptla* (the gods' impersonators) were paraded amid exotic paraphernalia such as precious quetzal plumes, gems, rare shells, jaguars, and alligators.

Ritual activities at Tenochtitlan dominated life across most of the year. Precisely co-ordinated by means of the 360-day solar calendar of 18 periods, or festivals, of 20 days plus the 5 "dead" days, together with a series of movable feasts based on the 260-day calendar (which might fall once or twice during a solar year), ritual periods were divided up into groups of days, usually 4, 5, and 10, as multiples of 20 days (cf. Sahagún 1981, 1:109–227). Most activities were also defined within the three parts of the day: midnight to dawn, dawn to midday, and midday to midnight (Shelton 1991: 7).

Emphasis on the qualitative and quantitative excesses of ritual and ritual imagery at Tenochtitlan and to a certain extent at other major centers nevertheless detracts greatly from the projection of the rituals themselves. In addition (but closely related) to warrior and sun cults, Azteca-Mexica ritual, often defined by its increasing ceremonial violence,[18] functioned as a public display of wealth and power to friends, enemies, and Tenochtitlan's own populace alike. Similarly, the city's public art, renowned today for its monumentality and stunning expressiveness, also reflected the grandeur with which its creators sought to project themselves to the world. Yet, beneath the facade of power and domination, they and their neighbors continued to recognize the fundaments of a religious system that demanded the reenactment of time-honored and established ritual to ensure success in agricultural pursuits. If the gods were not called on, entreated, and rewarded, the great life cycles could easily end as abruptly as they had begun. Indeed, as so many surviving examples of Aztec public sculpture attest, the signs, symbols, and glyphs that inscribe their texts (the sun and moon, the earth and water deities, symbols for blood and water [precious liquid], shells, skulls, bones, serpents, butterflies, birds, rabbits, reeds, maize cobs, cacti, flowers) all echo the imagery evoked in the myths of creation and the places of origin and destiny. And in the style of *horror vacui* in which they were configured, they effectively resemble a writhing, seething, fluttering mass of life. Aztec art and ritual reflected the monstrous proportions of the Aztec subreality that enveloped the reality, but they never smothered—never could be permitted to smother—the entities and beings of the reality itself.

The ritual calendars were also adhered to outside the large ceremonial centers; but, in contrast, ritual activities were less frequent and less elaborate, although by no means less meaningful in efficacy or terms of value. The fairly detailed sixteenth-century accounts of prehispanic ritual cycles at Acolman to the northeast of Tenochtitlan (Acuña 1986: 226–30) and Teutitlan (now Teotitlan del Camino) to the far south in the modern-day state of Oaxaca (Acuña 1984b: 198–201), together with their outlying villages, indicate that only the twentieth day of each ritual period was acknowledged and even then not always celebrated: "there was no ceremony other than to burn incense for the idol";[19] "there was no ceremony."[20] Whatever ritual took place was usually in the form of dancing, eating and drinking, incensing, self-sacrifice, and the scattering of fresh flowers and foliage. This was also the pattern adhered to elsewhere: the gods were worshiped with penitential piercing, dancing with flower garlands, and heavy drinking at Tututepetongo in the Mixteca Alta; dancing was the "custom" at nearby Xaltepetongo, and "ordinarily" they became very drunk (ibid., pp. 53, 150). Although the calendar dictated the timing of these rituals, for the populations who practiced them it was essentially an agricultural tool. Community ritual of this type was directed almost exclusively toward the fertility of the earth, the arrival of the rains, the growth and harvest of the maize crop, and the success of the hunting season that followed the end of the agricultural cycle. Community ritual was founded on the religious reality, not on the subreality created by dominant groups to further their own political or economic purposes.[21]

While the agricultural calendar marked the timing of reenactments of public rituals at both large ceremonial centers and smaller rural communities, acknowledgment of humankind's dependency on the sacred forces that structured and controlled the cosmos was also an integral part of the individual's daily life. Toribio de Benavente Motolinía (1990: 26), for example, noted how the Indians kept idols and altars at water sources, at crossroads, on mountain tops, and in the barrios of the villages, while oratories were found in "many other parts": "[A]nd those that passed by drew blood from their ears and tongues, or scattered a little incense . . . ; others [scattered] flowers that they had gathered on their way, and when they had nothing else, they threw down a little green grass or straw, and there they rested."[22]

There were apparently so many of these special, sacred places that after the conquest the friars had considerable difficulties in locating them; even when destroyed, they were immediately repaired or replaced (Motolinía 1990: 26). Similar private rituals were conducted on a continuous basis behind the scenes at Tenochtitlan. Food was offered to the gods every morning in the *calpulli* (wards), and family members were roused from sleep for this purpose. Inside homes incense was offered to the four directions twice a day; again, all family members were obliged to participate. Nobody drank pulque without first pouring some onto the four corners of the hearth (Sahagún 1981, 1:242–43). Frequently throughout the ritual calendar year, and on movable feast days, small mammals, birds, reptiles, insects, and flowers were also sacrificed at Tenochtitlan and elsewhere, as offerings to the gods from the populace in general (Las Casas 1992: 1162; Sahagún 1981, 1:103–227), that is, the "lowly and poor" (Durán 1984, 1:140; see also Codex Ramírez 1979: 140–41).[23] We cannot doubt that the same rituals were also performed in the homes or barrios of the villages.

Framing the Sacred

One constant in ritual activities remains. It was adhered to by rich and poor and in the towns and cities and the countryside alike and permeates all descriptions of ritual to such a degree that it often becomes commonplace. As a result, it goes unnoticed as we struggle to disentangle the more "challenging" symbolism inherent in action and artifact or is viewed as a secondary manifestation or just a celebratory act. Echoing Inga Clendinnen's (1991: 253–59) own observations on the "liminal zone" of Aztec ritual, I have chosen to call these activities framing rituals: the creation of a ritual arena to which the sacred could be called or enticed, in which its presence could be indulged, albeit for only a fleeting moment. In this definition, however, framing is not exclusively the construction of ritual space through symbolic action or image;[24] it also concerns the simultaneous summoning *and* reenactment of the being of the sacred itself.

The preparation and offering of food was an integral part of rituals carried out everywhere. The most detailed descriptions are found in the writings of Sahagún.[25] In most cases it was the commoners (*los populares*) who took on the task of food preparation. For example, at Tenochtitlan at the end of the festival of Tlaxochimaco, they occupied themselves all night in the making of tamales and the killing and cooking of fowls and dogs (Sahagún 1981, 1:183). We can only speculate that these preparatory tasks were also ritualized in some way, perhaps, as still happens in today's more traditional communities, by working together in public groups.[26] Mass ritual eating certainly did take place. In Tlacaxipehualiztli, for example, all spectators at the gladiatorial sacrifice carried little backpacks of uncooked tortillas that they ate as the *farsa* (live drama, in sixteenth-century Spanish terminology) took place (Sahagún 1981, 1:147).[27]

But ritual foodstuffs are interesting for other reasons. The general rule seems to have been to offer grain foods in precisely numbered groups, four, five, or seven being the most common. At the special feast of Xochilhuitl, celebrated in honor of Macuilxochitl-Xochipilli, "Five Flower–Flower Prince," five tamales pierced with an arrow (the metaphorical *xuchimitl* or pierced heart, literally "flower-arrow") were the principal offering among a variety of other foodstuffs of unspecified quantities (Sahagún 1981, 1:59). Over the twenty festivals of the solar year we can cite many other examples. In Hueytozoztli five baskets of tortillas and one each of *chía* flour and toasted maize with beans (5 + 2) were placed before the image of Centeotl. In Etzalqualiztli the priests offered four dough balls or four tomatoes or four chiles. For Teotleco lumps of honey mixed with amaranth seed were quartered and offered to the "young god" on a plate. Five small maize breads (*panecillos*) stuffed with beans were placed at the base of the statue of Xiuhtecuhtli in Izcalli. (ibid., pp. 150, 163, 197, 221–22). Three, nine, eleven, and so on also appear in the pictographic sources. These numerals correspond to the basic notations and multiples of the solar and divinatory calendars, the "ordering principle" (Brotherston 1979: 129) of the native world, and the explanation of the cosmos that gave them being. Three, for example, invokes the basic cosmic levels and the stones of the nuclear fire hearth; four and five, the quatrefoil and quincuncial configurations of the terrestrial plane; five, the quarter days of each of the eighteen ritual feasts. Nine corresponds to the number of Night Lords; seven (5 + 2), the midway point between one and thirteen, to the "metamorphic heart" (the butterfly) of the constituent numbers or sacred flyers (Brotherston 2005: 13); eleven, to the zodiac sky phases associated with the pulque cult (Brotherston 1992: 63, 66–67, 2005: 28); and so on.

In addition to preparing different foods for each specific ritual or ceremony (Durán 1984, 1:291), offerings made from the staples of maize and amaranth were often molded into or decorated with specific images. Sahagún (1981, 1:50) related how offerings to the women who died in childbirth included little "breads" called *xonecuilli* in the shape of butterflies and flashes of lightning. Toasted maize grains (popcorn) were also offered, seen as resembling pure white flowers. Butterfly and S-shaped xonecuilli appear again at the feast of Xochilhuitl, alongside *tlacuiloatolli* ("painted" maize gruel) on which a real flower was placed (that is, "painted") and amaranth seed cakes in the form of shields, arrows, and, as Sahagún put it, "swords." A mixture of amaranth seeds and honey (*tzoalli*) was used to make the effigy of Huitzilopochtli in the festival of Toxcatl and the images of the rain mountains in Tepeilhuitl; both were accompanied by tzoalli in the shape of bones (ibid., pp. 59, 60, 155–56, 199).

Food being the principal preoccupation behind ritual manifestations, offerings of this type not only acknowledged the source of human sustenance but also represented the desired abundance of the otherworlds. The manipulation of numbers and the shaping of symbols injected both those actions and the food itself with magical undertones. The conjuring had commenced.

According to the account of Sahagún (1981, 1:103–227), public pulque drinking took place in nine feasts over the year, although a number of surviving ritual codices suggest that this was extended to eleven (Brotherston 2005: 61). The discrepancy perhaps points to differentiation between priests and the public in general; at the Azteca-Mexica capital it was only in Izcalli, the last festival of the annual ritual round, that everybody was officially permitted to join in, to the point that they dropped senseless on top of each other (Sahagún 1981, 1:226). Mexica restrictions on pulque drinking are well known and may have been implemented as a measure of both social and religious control. Public rituals in the villages were almost always accompanied by heavy drinking, but such rituals were few compared to the never-ending round of activities at Tenochtitlan. If mass drunkenness had been permitted at the capital as an integral part of ritual, then the Aztec supremacy factor in ritual display would sooner or later have come up against serious problems of public order, not to mention the social and economic consequences of a permanently inebriated population. Regardless of the severest of punishments, however, drinking laws were often ignored, as the practice went on in secret (Sahagún 1981, 1:226; Durán 1984, 1:115). While f. 71r of Codex Mendoza might acknowledge that alcohol abuse did exist in prehispanic society, secret drinking was not necessarily a symptom of it. I see it rather as a (very risky) denial of regulations imposed on time-honored ritual expression by a ruling class with more compelling reasons to ban it on all but a few occasions or, to put it another way, as an imposition of the subreality. As we shall see, objections to this particular activity on the part of the colonial subreality that was to follow were also ignored. The excessive consumption of pulque acknowledged its divine origins and its divine function of honoring the gods. In addition, Sahagún's informants tell us that the imbiber of pulque became "like his rabbit," that is, one or more of the rabbit-pulque deities entered him (FC6, 1969: 230).

Coupled with the mind-altering properties of alcohol, the effects of self-sacrifice should also be considered. The practice was widespread among both commoners and the nobility and took place at regular intervals. Body parts included the legs, arms, tongue, chest, and genitalia (Sahagún 1981, 1:202; Durán 1984, 1:287). It is not apparent in the records whether designated body parts related to status, age, or specific rituals (penis-piercing, for example, might echo Quetzalcoatl's self-sacrifice in the creation of the first humans), to the levels of pain produced, or to other factors.[28] It is only clear that different types of instruments were employed. Coral and stingray spines were luxury commodities and therefore probably restricted to the ruling classes; bone and maguey spines were available to all. Possible penance aside, however, the loss of blood and pain incurred in self-sacrifice would undoubtedly have provoked degrees of delirium that enhanced the process of contact with the sacred.

Figure 1.4. Song and dance. Note the distinctive blossom of the huacalxochitl at the top left and top right (Codex Magliabechiano 82).

The sacred was also conjured up through song and dance (fig. 1.4). Every twenty-day period saw the playing of musical instruments such as drums, flutes, bells, and conch shells, usually accompanied by singing and dancing that lasted for several hours. The Franciscan Jerónimo de Mendieta (1973, 1:85) observed that song and dance was one of the principal activities of the land: every village had a space reserved for its singers to compose dances and songs. They danced everywhere—in the plazas, in the houses of nobles—and had special repertoires for each occasion: the commemoration of ancient deeds, the memory of dead lords, and the festivals of the gods. And "the songs they sang in those dances they understood to be prayers, performing them with uniformity of tone and movement, mind and body alike, without variance in voice or in step" (ibid., p. 51).[29] The role of song and dance in invoking the presence of the sacred is implicit in a report from Juan de Torquemada. In Teotleco, and in order to *receive* the "arriving" gods, "they drummed and sang throughout the night vigil and ate and drank as was their custom on all other occasions" (Torquemada 1975–83, 3:399–400).[30]

Dance was also choreographed to reenact the sacred otherworlds. In the eight-yearly festival of Atamalqualiztli, "Eating of Water Tamales," when the maize was allowed to rest, the gods danced around the image and temple of Tlaloc, alongside human participants dressed as birds, animals, hummingbirds, butterflies, bees, flies, and beetles. Others wore garlands of tamales around their necks, and maize bins were filled with the same victual. Still others swallowed live frogs and snakes (Sahagún 1981, 1:231). Whereas, for the Tlaxcallans at least, the souls of lords and rulers became mist, clouds, and exotic birds or precious stones and the souls of commoners became weasels, beetles, and rats (Torquemada 1975–83, 3:128), in this reenactment we seem to find the gods, the lords, and the commoners together in a veritable paradise filled with food and happiness. Only the elderly who would not live to see the festival again wept (Sahagún 1981, 1:231), perhaps in the knowledge that their chances of reaching this paradise were now very small. The description of this same festival on Códice Matritense del Palacio Real f. 253r tells how dancing continued for two days, at the end of which, at sundown, participants processed four times around the temple of Tlaloc (Nicholson et al. 1997: 67–69). The accompanying pictographic text (plate 1) also describes how four deities, including Chicomecoatl and Mayahuel in her aspect as Ayopechtli,[31] converge onto a tall, bright green flowering tree around which crimson- and turquoise-feathered birds flutter, sipping nectar from its flowers. These colors identify them as *quecholli,* birds found near springs and water holes (Torquemada 1975–83, 3:403), otherwise defined as the sacred flyers of the calendar, or *ipalnemoani,* "the ones through whom we live" (Brotherston 1992: 319). Footprints around the ritual enclosure echo the complex steps of the dance, with prolonged right-footed hopping before the tepictoton, who were "reckoned among the Tlalocs" (FC1, 1970: 47), who float on a vast expanse of turquoise water.

Colorful and entertaining as the dances may have been, they also had more finite aims in the search for the sacred. The dancers, it seems, drank pulque during the performances. The heat of the day (exacerbated by incessant movement) and the imbibing of the divine liquor eventually took their toll: the dancers fell, only to be removed by onlookers until they had recovered their senses and could return to the dance (Codex Tudela 1980: f. 66v).[32] In addition to the incessant drumming and the trancelike state that hour upon hour of rhythmically coordinated movement created in each participant, alcohol was therefore also a major contributor to the increasing frenzy of the performance. The sacred was being incited to enter the hearts and souls of those who danced for and in its presence.

The most striking aspect of any framing ritual was the almost perpetual use of flowers and vegetation. This occurred all year round, with a break during four festivals at the height of the dry season. It also took place everywhere and, together with dancing, was understood to be very ancient in origin.[33] When fresh flowers or greenery were scarce, food and popcorn flowers were substituted; paper flowers were also fashioned and attached to ritual garments (Sahagún 1981, 1:147, 166). Overall, the accounts of the chroniclers point toward five main ritual actions involving flora: spreading, decorating, covering, embowering, and dancing. In addition, the ingestion of certain flora provided a more powerful coordinate in the search for the sacred. Closer consideration of these actions suggests that their objective was basically the same: whether carried, spread, or ingested, fresh, sweet-smelling flowers and vegetation and their derivatives created an environment of dizzying perfumed abundance, the central element in the quest for union with the sacred.

Maize shoots, *zacate* grass, bulrushes, reeds, laurel branches, and flowers were spread out in front of temples and beneath the feet of ritual participants; even the steps of the pyramid-platforms were strewn with "flowers and roses" in different patterns (Tezozómoc 1943: 105). "I cut [the blossoms], spread them out, arrange them, cover them with leaves, thread them, make a flower mat of them, make a bed of flowers with them, spread them over the land" (FC11, 1963: 202) (fig. 1.5). For the festival of Etzalqualiztli the priests spread out reed mats and scattered them with incense made from the aromatic herb *yiauhtl* (powdered sweet-scented marigold: Nicholson et al. 1997: 83, n. 19), while another sowing of popcorn flowers was made in honor of the *tlaloc* Opochtli (Tezozómoc 1943: 73–74). For rituals in honor of Huitzilopochtli during the reign of Axayacatl, the ground was strewn with laurel leaves from Chapultepec to Tenochtitlan (ibid., p. 45). In Tlaxochimaco, and also in honor of Huitzilopochtli, everybody went out into the fields and woods to gather flowers of every possible species.[34] Then, in a manner that recalls Xochiquetzal's flower rope, "they stacked them in the house of the pyramid-platform where this feast was held. There they were kept overnight, and at dawn they threaded them onto strings or twine. Having threaded them, they made thick ropes of them, twisted and long, and they spread these in the patio of the platform" (Sahagún 1981, 1:183).[35]

Figure 1.5. "I cut the blossoms . . .": preparation of the floral "protagonists" for a framing ritual (Florentine Codex, Book 11).

Durán (1984, 1:42, 151) mentions several "decorative" rituals not included in Sahagún's descriptions. In Toxcatl the idol of Tezcatlipoca was brought from its temple into a courtyard whose walls were "adorned" with fresh branches and flowers. After the crowd had circled around it, the idol was returned to the temple and itself "adorned" with multicolored flowers. During the festival of Xochilhuitl, when the farewell to flowers was made and Xochiquetzal was honored, everything—people, temples, streets, and houses—was "adorned" only with flowers.

Flower and vegetal covering was undoubtedly directed at the gods, but these actions were neither decorative nor offerings as such. Sahagún's description of an enflowering that took place during the festival of the arrival of the gods provides a more interesting motivation, although he himself did not see the connection: "*After they had been covering for three days,* the god called Telpochtli arrived. . . . On the following day the god of merchants called Yacapitzauac or Yiacatecutli arrived, and another god called Ixcozauhqui or Xiuhtecutli" (Sahagún 1981, 1:197–98; my emphasis).[36] It seems clearer that the prolonged ritual covering was aimed specifically at attracting, or guiding, the gods to the ritual arena. Coverings, however, also served a further purpose.

Flowers, foliage, and other types of vegetation were used to construct *ramadas* (bowers). The act of embowering was most specifically directed toward the promotion of fertility (Nicholson 1971: 432). Again it is Durán (1984, 1:65) who refers to these structures, although his terminology is inconsistent. For the festival of Quetzalcoatl at Cholula, a "theater" of flowered and feathered arches was constructed within which to reenact the ritual. A ramada of zapote leaves at Tenochtitlan was raised to house the priests who were to perform the sacrifice of the day. Elsewhere a structure of reeds and flowers in front of a temple is described as a "roof terrace" (*azotea*) to shelter spectators (Durán 1984 2:173, 442). His choice of words evidently rests on his own perception of the structures' function, but all were more specifically flower-bowers constructed for a ritual purpose. We know from Tezozómoc (1943: 104–105), for example, that the lords seated beneath the embowered canopies were understood to be not spectators but part of the ritual paraphernalia. In addition, the example that Durán (1984, 1:193) gives on the occasion of a special dance for Huitzilopochtli suggests that this bower was yet another reconstruction of a flowery otherworld: a "house of flowers" (*una casa de rosas*) was set up, around which artificial trees laden with scented flowers were erected. Here sat the goddess Xochiquetzal (she of Tamoanchan, as we recall). In this flowery paradise, ritual participants danced in her honor: young men dressed as birds and butterflies descended from the temple, climbed the trees, and swung from branch to branch, sucking nectar (ibid.).

Bowers made from flowers and foliage are often seen in ritual settings in the codices, as part of the paraphernalia of deities. Most interesting are those found on pages 9–16 of Codex Laud, where nine figures of deities are depicted beneath flowery shelters, displaying different elements in their frames. Tlaloc, for example, sits beneath a mist cover, and Mayahuel beneath a maguey cactus (fig. 1.6). In front of each are laid out various ritual artifacts: cups of foaming pulque, bones, plates of food, and copal incense balls. Nectar-sucking birds flutter around the flowers. These flower-bowers can only be meant to depict the sacred regions of abundance that each deity inhabits or presides over. Earth deities are seated within the curving body of the earth monster; Tlaloc resides in the cavelike depths of a water mountain; Mayahuel is the maguey. But the types of blossoms on these sacred bowers are not consistent and do not represent the flowers of specific trees or plants. Different flowers sprout from the same bower. No flower on Mayahuel's bower corresponds to the maguey cactus. Thus the bowers were not intended to be specific ideographic representations of actual abodes but conceptual frames that denoted the sacred nature of the god or force in question. It was these frames that prehispanic native ritual tried to re-create, and within which it was perceived to be placed. López Austin (1994: 94–95) interprets the Codex Laud bowers as representations of the great tree of Tamoanchan, with the various flowers representing the different forces present in the divine cosmic essences flowing through it. In this sense, the elaborate flower-bowers constructed in the ritual arena also emulated the place of the source of all life.

Figure 1.6. Mayahuel-Ayopechtli beneath her flower-bower (Codex Laud 9).

Use of flowers and plants in framing rituals extended to the ingestion of psychotropic and hallucinogenic varieties. At Tenochtitlan this activity may have been restricted for the same reasons as pulque drinking, although it is perhaps clearer that the practice remained the domain of rulers, priests, and shamans. Diego Muñoz Camargo (1984: 191), for example, observed that in Tlaxcala it was more the nobility than the commoners who followed the practice, that is, those endowed with or trained in the knowledge to receive and interpret the visions induced. In traditional communities today the practice still lies with the shamans (see, for example, Schultes and Hoffmann 1982; Wasson 1983; Furst 1994): again, those gifted or trained in use and purpose. The continuing importance of this aspect of the native belief system cannot be overestimated. It is perhaps for this reason that native informants did not offer their interrogators detailed information: the reaction would have been all too predictable.

In prehispanic Mexico psychoactive plants were associated with the rain deity, Tlaloc, because most of them grow and flower during the rainy season (Garza 2001: 92). Principal Mexican sources include the button crown of the peyote cactus; certain species of fungi of the genus *Psilocybe* (*teonanacatl,* "flesh of the gods"); seeds such as *ololiuhqui,* "round thing," from the morning glory plant (fig. 1.7a), or the related, inordinately potent, *tlililtzin,* "revered black thing" (Schultes and Hoffmann 1982: 66–67, 74–75, 158–63); and *picietl* (raw tobacco), which "intoxicates one, makes one dizzy, possesses one" (FC11, 1963: 146).[37] Psychotropic blossoms include the *tlapatl* flower of the thorn apple, which, taken with pulque or a fermented maize drink, served as an added intoxicant (Schultes and Hoffmann 1982: 78–79, 109–11). According to Sahagún (1981, 3:292), "those that eat it lose their appetite, and it perpetually inebriates them and sends them mad."[38] Included in the preparation of smoking tubes, the very distinctive blossoms of the *huacalxochitl* (*Phyllodendrum affine* Hemsl.) (fig. 1.7b) or the *poyomaxochitl* or *poyomatli,* the calyx of the sweet-smelling *cacahuaxochitl* (*Lexarza funebris*), which "deranges one, provokes one," were employed to increase the narcotic properties of tobacco (fig. 1.7c) (FC10, 1961: 88; FC11, 1963: 212). The flower of *Datura ceratocaula* Ort., known today as *tornaloco,* was also a powerful narcotic and greatly venerated in prehispanic Mexico as the "sister of *ololiuhqui*" (Schultes and

Figure 1.7. Common species of psychoactive Mexican flora: *a,* morning glory (redrawn from Wasson 1983), *b,* huacalxochitl (Florentine Codex, Book 11), *c,* poyomatli (redrawn from Wasson 1983), *d,* the whirling toloatzin flower, a species of *Datura* (after a photograph in Schultes and Hoffmann 1982), *e,* sinicuiche (redrawn from Wasson 1983).

Hoffmann 1982: 78–79, 109–11). The curious "spinning" effect of the *toloatzin* or *totohuaxihuitl* blossom (another species of *Datura*: ibid., p. 109) as it opens (fig. 1.7d) recalls the heart-spinning, "whirling," "narcotic" flowers of the flower-songs of old (*CM*, f. 11v; Bierhorst 1985a: 166–67).[39] Last but not least among many, the mountain flower known as *sinicuiche* (*Heimia salicifolia*) served as an effective auditive hallucinogen (fig. 1.7e) (Schultes and Hoffmann 1982: 76–77; Wasson 1983: 100).

The association of seeds with flowers needs no explanation, but peyote crowns (which take many different forms) greatly resemble flowers. Mushrooms were called *xochitl* by the Aztecs and are still referred to as "little flowers of the gods" in traditional communities (Schultes and Hoffmann 1982: 144). Thus some references to *xochitl* in native sources may not always have to do with "flowers" as such.

As if to draw the sacred ever nearer, flowers and vegetation were carried by participants in processions and dances. The *huacalxochitl*, also a powerful fertility symbol (Peterson 1993: 93), was frequently employed. On Codex Magliabechiano 82 it is held in a dance as a penis (fig. 1.4, top left).[40] In the festival of Xochipaina, "Run for the Flower" (Siméon 1997: 773), which took place in Hueytecuilhuitl, the lords and nobles with their wives and women sang and danced all day, laden with flowers and carrying posies in their hands. At the end they took their flowers to Huitzilopochtli (Durán 1984, 1:128–29). In Etzalqualiztli, and in honor of Tlaloc, all those present at the sacrifice carried cuttings of the (also psychoactive) sagebrush in their hands, "and with them they went shooing, like those who shoo flies from their face . . . others put this plant in their ears. Also by way of superstition others brought this plant in their hands, squeezed inside their fists" (Sahagún 1981, 1:170).[41] On another occasion the impersonator of the goddess Huixtoccihuatl danced and sang for ten days with the women who made salt, their heads crowned with garlands made of sagebrush. All who watched the dance carried strong-scented marigolds or sagebrush in their hands (ibid., pp. 172–73). Torquemada (1975–83, 3:386–87) also commented on the lavish use of flowers in this particular dance and the strong smell of the sagebrush. But in honor of the goddess Toci nobody sang or danced. They marched to the rhythm of the drums, raising and lowering their flower-filled hands: "All those who danced [*sic*] looked like flowers" (Sahagún 1981, 1:194–95).[42]

The descriptions of these flower-laden ceremonials alone are vivid enough for us to imagine today. For those reenacting the flowery world of the sacred—their minds and bodies numb with the endless drumming and synchronized movement, heads dizzy from an excess of pulque or spinning with the effect of ingested flowers, and hearts pounding with physical exhaustion and mental anticipation—such activities must have created an intense atmosphere of communal delirium.

While the perfume of plants and flowers, copal incense, and sweet-smelling pastes made from crushed blooms (Muñoz Camargo 1984: 61, 126) are frequently mentioned in the works of the chroniclers, few attempted to understand their role in ritual; most believed it was for human pleasure (Durán 1984, 1:51). Francisco Hernández (2000: 134; my emphasis) nevertheless observed that "[t]hey *perfumed the statues* [of the gods]" with those same "herbs, flowers, powders and with various scented secretions from trees and with extremely pleasant smelling gum,"[43] suggesting rather more clearly that the specific act of enflowering the gods was also directed at attracting their attention through smell.[44] They filled the temple of Huitzilopochtli with yolloxochitl and eloxochitl and cacahuaxochitl; they offered mixtures of flowers, arranged in different ways, and with varied patterns: shield-shaped, rounded, in sprays, "all sweet-scented flowers, and that temple was filled with the perfume and sweetness of flowers" (Sahagún 1981, 1:348).[45]

In this manner the flower-scattering, the flower-houses, the flower-carrying, the flower-dancing, the flower-singing, and the flower-smelling brought the sacred directly to the human heart: "I pick flowers. I pick different flowers. I remove flowers. I seek flowers . . . I smell something. I cause one to smell something. I cause him to smell. I offer him flowers. . . . When I incite just with words, when I am beguiling him, it is said: 'I caress him with flowers. I seduce one'" (FC11, 1963: 214–15). Whirling, intoxicating, perfuming, beguiling, seducing, it comes nearer. Suddenly, and for the briefest of moments, the sweet-scented presence of the sacred brushes a hand, caresses a neck, opens a heart, and explodes inside a head with a roar of color and light and song: "I exalt him, rejoice him with heart-pleasing flowers in this place of song. With narcotic fumes my heart is pleasured. I soften my heart, inhaling them. My soul grows dizzy with the fragrance, inhaling good flowers in this place of enjoyment. My soul is drunk with flowers" (*CM,* f. 3r; 1985: 140–41).

CHAPTER TWO

Colonial Ritual and the
Accommodation of the Christian Sacred

During Holy Week in 1536 the Indians of Tlaxcala were preparing to celebrate Christ's Resurrection. From Thursday onward the Franciscan friar Toribio de Benavente—or Motolinía, as he chose to be called—had observed a continuous procession of Indians visiting the church and bearing gifts. By Saturday evening the flow of gifts had increased, including mantles, embroidered cloths, feathers, copal incense, cooked foods on plates, a lamb, and two live pigs, which, to the amusement of the Spanish onlookers, were cradled in the Indians' arms as they were presented at the altar. "They also offered hens and doves, and all this in great quantities; so much so that the friars and the Spaniards were amazed, and I myself went many times to view this, *and I was astonished to see such a new thing in such an ancient world*" (Motolinía 1990: 58; my emphasis).[1]

Motolinía (1990: 57) insists that what he saw at Tlaxcala he had not seen in any other part of New Spain; nor did he believe that it existed. For him, such offerings were a new thing in the Indian world, thereby implying that they expressed an early, and perhaps divinely inspired, acceptance of Christianity. But his remarks are highly problematic. By 1536 the Franciscan had been in New Spain for twelve years, had traveled widely, and must have witnessed reenactments of traditional rituals. Certainly in his *Memoriales* (1970, written about 1549) and *Historia* (1990, written about 1550) he shows an awareness of the types of rituals that had taken place in the native religion. Yet, and perhaps in a moment of what James Lockhart (1992) has called "double-mistaken-identity,"[2] he failed to see that there was nothing original about the activities of the Tlaxcallan Indians during this important Christian festival. What they were doing was, in fact, *a very ancient thing in a very new world.*

Motolinía's assessment is also symptomatic of what was to develop into a significant oversight with respect to the nature of Indian religious expression. Sixteenth-century chroniclers always emphasized the more gruesome aspects in their descriptions of prehispanic native rituals, and Motolinía was no exception. His comments focus almost exclusively on acts of human and self-sacrifice, ritual drunkenness, ingestion of hallucinogens, figures of idols, and blood (Motolinía 1990: 19–20, 32–49): "This land was like hell on earth" (ibid., p. 19).[3] It is also true that none of the chroniclers were, or could have been, cultural relativists, so elements of Indian culture and actions inevitably tended to be classified within the terms of a European worldview. Part of what the Spaniards saw in the ritual practices was—perhaps understandably—to remain ingrained in their minds, but it also led them to believe that the native religion was based exclusively on the fearsome idols housed in the blood-spattered temples, where the strange priests practiced their barbaric crafts. The gods also pranced across the folded pages of the incomprehensible—but clearly sinister—books (the *pinturas* or "paintings," as the Spaniards referred to them) demanding mass bloodshed and drunken orgies in return for questionable favors. By obliterating these horrors, they believed that the "religion" they underpinned could also be wiped out. Temples were therefore razed to the ground, idols smashed, books burned, and the old native priests dispatched from this world—to roast in hell, undoubtedly, along with their pinturas.

These acts were not exclusively one-sided. The native peoples often participated willingly in the destruction of the temples (Motolinía 1990: 22) and burned their own books in what now appears to have been a conscious effort to reaccommodate their world within the very different circumstances of the colonial experience (see Navarrete 1998). It is perhaps in this context that we can see why the Indians accepted the Christian equivalents imposed on them: the churches, the images of the Holy Family and the saints, Bibles and prayer books, and the usually kindly friars defined the new subreality in which they were living.

Much to the irritation of the evangelizers, however, certain prehispanic ritual activities persisted; and as a result it did not take the church authorities long to conclude that what they had destroyed of the native religion was only the tip of the iceberg. Although writing in defense of the Indians in the mid-sixteenth century, Bartolomé de las Casas (1992: 1256) admitted that "of a thousand or ten thousand parts, we have not understood one concerning the religion and its characteristics that these people had."[4] Despite the efforts of men like Sahagún and Durán to get to the root of the problem, some seventy years later the issue was still no clearer. The Indians believed that gods lived in all parts of the land: on hills, in valleys, ravines, rivers, lakes and springs. "[H]aving resolved to ascertain the fundaments [of their beliefs] and what they all are, we find as little to lay our hands on as if trying to squeeze smoke or wind in our fist" (Ruiz de Alarcón 1984: 43). Compared to the time of Las Casas this was progress; but if the object of worship was now apparent, its meaning was not.

The failure of investigations to have any impact on continuing Indian religious beliefs was as much due to the limited circulation of early observations (Sahagún's work on the Indian past was ultimately confiscated; Durán's descriptions were never published) as to the nature of the observations themselves. The colorful accounts of prehispanic ritual activities such as the dressing of idols, the scattering of flowers and vegetation, the offerings of food and drink, and singing and dancing were seemingly viewed as secondary elements. Even in the seventeenth century, when offerings of food, drink, and copal incense were well understood to be native ritual practices, song, dance, and flowers were still seen to be incidental. They represented the external aspects of religion in much the same way as the church in New Spain promoted elaborate processions, richly adorned altars, and choral extravaganzas.[5] The impulse behind such activities, which were viewed as an expression of worship rather than of belief, was never seriously questioned.

It is certainly true that some took exception to singing and dancing, but for reasons that had more to do with their timing, content, and mode of expression than with the acts themselves. During the very early years Indians in large groups took to singing the Christian prayers and chants that they had been taught, everywhere and at all times (Mendieta 1973, 1:137; Torquemada 1975–83, 5:76). Ritualization of the Christian word, it would seem, had already been absorbed into daily life. As a direct result, in 1526 members of the Dominican and Franciscan orders requested that "the songs be [sung] during the day, and only on Sundays and Christian feast days" (*CDHM* 1980,

2:550).[6] Evidently it was felt that the new converts might lose sight of the religious focus of the songs if they were adopted as part of daily life. The first Mexican Provincial Council of 1555 ordered that dance and song be closely watched. Dancing, it observed, carried an unpleasant aftertaste of the Indian past; if the native peoples were going to dance, then they should not sing ritualized songs at the same time without the songs first being examined by a member of the clergy well-versed in the native language (Lorenzana 1981: 146–47). This was not an outright ban; lapses into profanity appear to have been the main issue here.

Writing in the second half of the sixteenth century, Sahagún was of the opinion that the devil himself was lurking in the songs and dances. But his objections seem mainly directed toward the obscurity of meaning of native song (Sahagún 1981, 1:255): the extensive use of metaphors and interchangeable sets of images found in the collections of native compositions that have survived to our day (the twenty prehispanic songs of the Florentine Codex or the later *Cantares mexicanos* and *Romances de los Señores de la Nueva España* manuscripts, for example). To remedy this, and assisted by four native scholars from the Franciscan school at Tlatelolco, he wrote his 1583 *Psalmodia Christiana* (Sahagún 1993), a collection of fifty-four new songs in Nahuatl that attempted to follow the traditional style, although with a content now focused exclusively on Christian referents. Although acknowledging that dancing was elaborated rather differently for Christian purposes, he was still reminded of his informants' descriptions of prehispanic festivals. Dancing was therefore "the wood of idolatry that has not been pruned" (Sahagún 1981, 1:63).[7] Here again, however, the *meneos* (jerking movements) to which he refers suggest that his protests were more keenly focused on the issue of moral conduct. While Francisco Hernández (2000: 125) objectively noted that some of the dances took on erotic undertones, the religious body nevertheless regarded this particular aspect of native choreography as bordering on lewdness (Durán 1984, 1:193). Sahagún and his contemporaries also classed lewdness as idolatry, which betrays the ambiguity of the meaning of the word as it was employed in respect to the native peoples. As so many of the sixteenth-century records of idolatry trials reveal, acts of social immorality and even political defiance often overrode accusations of non-Christian activities. Anything deemed offensive to Christian morals and the Spanish presence was defined as "idolatrous."[8]

Like song and dance, flowers were an essential part of native religious ritual. Objections to the continuing tradition were rare and were only based on practicalities or—very occasionally—on an underlying suspicion that all was not as it should be. In the 1560s *visitador general* (inspector general) Jerónimo de Valderrama remarked on the excessive use of flowers in Christian activities, attributing it to unnecessary demands on the part of the priests and friars (Codex Osuna 1947: 178). In turn, a 1569 report from the (secular) priest of Tizayuca (México) blamed native leaders for these excesses: for their festivals they sent the commoners as far as the "hotlands" for flowers, grasses, and other things (*Descripción del arzobispado* 1976: 65). Commenting on the task allotted to young Indian men of decorating the churches with branches, flowers, and reeds, Durán (1984, 1:55) recognized that the tradition was prehispanic in origin but believed it to be nothing more than an ancient custom and therefore admissible. Only once did he express any doubt: when he realized that the act of offering posies of flowers to nobles during the old festival of Toxcatl was repeated in the ceremonials of his day, "and I also take my staff of flowers . . . and make my way reflecting on our great ignorance, for there could be evil in it" (ibid., p. 41).[9] Here Durán seems to be referring to the native courtesy accorded to all persons of import but appears to be confused as to why it should be done during a Christian religious festival. More clearly, perhaps, Durán was being included in a native framing ritual.

Also unable to find anything objectionable in the lavish deployment of flowers, Sahagún reproduced extensive commentary of native flora, transcribed *ad verbatim* from his informants' lips. These texts nevertheless demonstrate a far deeper native interest in flowers than in using them as a simple decorative tribute. The lengthy passage that "telleth how the flowers are offered" (FC11, 1963: 214–15, quoted earlier) reveals the very specific meaning and projection of their usage. The text is structured like a chant, with actions repeated over and over. Its imagery appeals primarily to the senses of smell and touch, but it is also sensuous in that the speaker who offers the flowers is completely absorbed in the flowers, while the receiver is incited, seduced, and beguiled by them. In other words, the passage adequately expresses the trancelike state sought through flowers during invocations for the presence of the sacred. Sahagún's unawareness of the underlying projections of this process is also evident in his *Psalmodia*. The native compositional style that he tried to copy certainly invoked Christian referents within a flowery world of native flora and fauna. But, as Louise Burkhart (1992: 92–93) notes, the "garden songs" probably suggested nothing more to him than the Christian's view of paradise adapted for a native audience.[10] Indeed, when compared to the bizarre dynamism of the flowery worlds of the native sacred, so clearly reenacted in prehispanic framing rituals and in the native song-poems of flowery mode,[11] Sahagún's gardens provide no easy access to the Christian sacred. They bloom and shimmer, smell sweet, and are filled with brightly colored songbirds, but they are more like a theatrical stage set within which Christian figures act out their roles. They are to be looked at, marveled at, and longed for, but they remain—like the Christian heaven—a distant promise. Their audience is denied any interaction with them in the temporal world.[12]

To a certain extent, scholars commenting on native religion after the introduction of Christianity also deny the internal value of the Indians' continuing ritual manifestations. The native religion underwent an "impoverishment" (Andrews and Hassig 1984: 24), being reduced or restricted to the private or domestic and rural arenas, which did not change with the conquest (cf. Gruzinski 1993: 146–83). Alternatively, it manifested itself in half-forgotten reenactments of rural religious traditions concerned with the cycles of life and death, medicinal cures, and agricultural and hunting practices (Carrasco 1975: 200). In short, native religion became little more than mere "folk religion" (Andrews and Hassig 1984: 24).

Two unqualified assumptions permeate these assessments of postconquest native ritual. First, while the imposition of Christianity is understood to be the main cause for the breakdown of the native religious system, it is still *Christianity*—as a defined religion in its own right—that is applied to the cases argued. Continuing "idolatry" may be attributed to the superficiality of Christian teaching, to the unsatisfactory nature of Christianity as a religion, or to the fact that its tenets were just not assimilated. But the assumption is always that the Indians understood Christianity to be a new and different religion. The traditional, yet impoverished, rituals were therefore still part of the old religion.

Second, much like the view of those working in New Spain in the sixteenth and seventeenth centuries, the assumption is that the almost daily, highly dramatized, ritual activities and cults of Tenochtitlan were typical of all native ritual expression. As observed in chapter 1, this was not the case; nor could economic and social factors ever have permitted it to be, especially in rural areas. The nature of the ritual round at the great politico-religious centers (and even then not at all of them) was the exception, not the rule. In addition, its lauded sophistication over and above the ritual structure of the private/domestic and rural worlds is misplaced, especially in regard to the rural world. "Simple" as it might appear compared to grandiose displays at the Mexica capital, rural ritual was at most times public and evidently deemed to be efficacious at the community level. Furthermore, the underlying essence of ritual as an expression of religious ideology *did* revolve everywhere around the basic pursuits of the cycles of human life and death as manifested in, and dependent on, the long-reaching ramifications of the Age of Agriculture. Urban and rural societies alike recognized this precept as fundamental to their survival.

Under these circumstances, and in a mutating form, the fundaments of the native religious system had every possibility of survival, and good evidence suggests that it did. Certainly, and despite the ruptures introduced by the Euro-Christian superimposition, the reality of the Indian world remained relatively intact. The structure and content of the native colonial literary product (the pictorial and the alphabetical), although heavily influenced by the European presence and in the main restricted to the recording of "secular" material, reveal a little-changing cosmovision. In addition, maize, the primary focus of the system and unknown to the invaders before their arrival, remained the staple foodstuff; its ancient mode of cultivation also saw no variation. (The invaders, in any case, preferred wheat.)

As a result, and in the time-honored manner, the fields were prepared for sowing in anticipation of the rainy season and the bounty of the sacred water-giving mountains. Work surrounding the crucial stages of the plant's development—the germination of the seed, the emergence of the young plant, the fertilization of its silky flowers, the appearance of the first milky kernels, the forming of the young cobs, and their maturation and harvest—was also followed through. Traditional rituals accompanied each of these stages and do not appear to have been fragmented, confused, or improvised. It seems clear, for example, that the infamous *caciques* (native rulers) of Yanhuitlan (Oaxaca), who were tried for idolatry in the 1540s, had not lost the knowledge or the wherewithal to pursue the regular and coordinated rites of the prehispanic Mixtec world (*Procesos por idolatría* 1999), although it is true that these men were high priests who had succeeded in maintaining a traditional politico-religious administration under colonial rule (Pohl 1994: 42). But the old festival of Toxcatl was celebrated publicly at Acapixtla (Morelos) in 1535 (Grijalva 1985: 59), while Totonac Indians were caught honoring the festival of Panquetzaliztli in 1540 (*Procesos de indios* 1912: 209). Durán (1984, 1:263) recorded a series of ritual activities that derived directly from prehispanic festivals. The Indians were exchanging flowers, mantles, and loincloths at the end of June, as they had done in Tecuilhuitontli. On the tenth day of Tozozontli cords hung with "little idols, or pieces of cloth, or whatever" were still being tied from tree to tree.[13] Those who did not understand the superstition (as Durán called it) believed that its purpose was to frighten birds or amuse children (ibid., p. 248). The ever-suspicious friar knew better, of course.

One important but little-cited example illustrating the continuity of organized ritual in the countryside comes in the short account entitled "Los labradores," written around 1569 by Pedro Ponce de León (1979: 126–28), parish priest of Zumpahuacan (México), to denounce persisting idolatry among his parishioners. Devoid of any syncretic interference,[14] the text traces each main stage of the maize cycle from preparation of the land to harvest. Many of the outwardly very simple and limited ritual activities taking place in the fields of postconquest Zumpahuacan across the cycle can be identified as the core of major dramatizations that had taken place at Tenochtitlan (see Wake n.d.a).[15] In addition, sixteenth-century Zumpahuacanos still invoked the power of the sacred mountains of Matlalcueye and Iztaccihuatl in their petitions for rain, along with Quetzalcoatl, the tlaloque, and Chicomecoatl, the goddess of the matured maize. Incantations directed toward this numen might well have formed the basis of the Song of Chicomecoatl sung at the capital.[16] The continuing reverence for Mother Earth as they opened her back to prepare the soil and sow the seeds of the new maize cycle is emphatic.

The salient factor to emerge from all these examples of "idolatrous" activities is that they coincided chronologically with ritual events that had taken place under the old calendar. In addition, the Indian world had no lack of specialists who could still keep track of the calendar, passing down "the count of the days, of the years, and of the ceremonies and ancient rites" to younger generations (Durán 1984, 1:218). Under the guidance of a local shaman, the Indians of Zumpahuacan were also counting the days between their rituals rather than just reenacting the same rituals when the progress of the maize crop indicated that the moment was appropriate. The practice was not restricted to Zumpahuacan. Durán (1984, 1:227) noted that the native communities to which he ministered would wait for the elders to designate the day to initiate the harvest, even if it was ready and dry beforehand and could easily ruin if left in the fields. In seventeenth-century Zola (Oaxaca) one Diego Luis, a veritable *maestro de idolatrías,* "master of idolatries," was still communicating the most propitious times to cut the first young cobs by computing the days on his fingers (Balsalobre 1900: 249). The ritual calendar was still being followed, by accurately computing the timing of corresponding activities. With the ritual sequence thus reduced, the artifacts and reenactments employed could be manipulated accordingly in order to promote the desired outcome. In sum, if these elements of prehispanic ritual survived intact, then the structure and symbolism of the rituals themselves were also in a position to do so.

The long arm of the church—firm, yet incapacitated by its lack of knowledge of the native religious system—certainly did intervene. In the private arena it denounced and prohibited any act or image that might carry a whiff of the native religious past, labeling it as non-Christian and therefore "idolatrous." In the public arena it stoically attempted to separate what was unacceptable, and therefore also "idolatrous" (pilgrimages to caves and mountains, communal ritual drunkenness, the ingestion of hallucinogens, acts of lewdness), from what was acceptable (offerings of food and flowers, singing and dancing). It also restricted these secondary rituals, carefully supervised, to church festivals; the use of food and flowers and singing and dancing at any other venue was, again, "idolatrous." But the distinction between the acceptable and the unacceptable—that is, the distinction between Christianity and the native religion on which such deliberations were ultimately founded—evidently had little meaning for the Indian world. Traditional ritual activities in both the private and public arenas persisted alongside the newly imposed Christian rituals, often invading them, and vice versa. The overlap of native artifacts and activities that came to characterize the spatial and temporal foci of colonial native religious expression, together with the early exchange and, later, wider mixing of Christian and non-Christian elements, suggests that the native peoples saw no contradictions at all. Native ritual could serve both religions; or, more precisely, native ritual could continue to serve the same religious system into which Christianity was being incorporated.

The Unacceptable

For the modern-day researcher, sixteenth- and seventeenth-century accounts describing idolatrous activities are often frustratingly lacking in detail in respect to the activities and artifacts deployed. Unlike the texts covering the prehispanic period from Sahagún or Durán, for example, which were based on native sources and therefore gave equal importance to all ritual elements, European descriptions of idolatrous activities tend to be very generalized or, if fixed on any specific aspect, highly subjective. Alcohol, hallucinogens, and human sacrifice or self-sacrifice were unacceptable on all counts and therefore most frequently noted. In many cases, however, "sacrifice" remains undefined. Here we must assume that, in the main, the term was employed in its correct sense: that is, the relinquishment of objects of practical or monetary value as offerings to the supernatural. The presence of flowers, food, pulque, mushrooms, and copal, for example, is also mentioned, as indeed are dancing and singing. But little detail is given in respect to the finer points regarding mode of use or performance. In addition, of course, few Europeans ever witnessed the reenactment of a native ritual outside the Christian arena. Usually only the telltale remains or, if it was interrupted, the odd befuddled straggler who did not manage to flee in time evidenced its having taken place. The texts of the idolatry trials occasionally offer more information; similarly, however, interrogators of witnesses or the accused inevitably sought to punish the act rather than dally over seemingly minor details. Descriptions of activities of this type nevertheless make it abundantly clear that two important elements of prehispanic ritual were retained. The old calendar was consistently adhered to, and all the ingredients required for a successful encounter with the sacred were present.

During the 1537–39 trial of the Texcocan noble Carlos Ometochtli, it was reported that a statue of the rain deity had been found smeared with liquid rubber and seeds on Cerro Tlaloc (México) (*Proceso inquisitorial* 1980: 23–24).[17] The date is not given, but we know from Durán that this mountain was the venue for the great rain-petitioning ceremonies of Hueytozoztli at the end of April in anticipation of the start of the rainy season. There the lords and principals of Tenochtitlan, Xochimilco, Tlacopan, Tlaxcala, Texcoco, and Huejotzingo made a pilgrimage to the shrine of Tlaloc at its summit (Durán 1984, 1:82–85). At the trial the configuration of the accompanying offering was identified as belonging to Huejotzingo. Recently placed offerings were also found at the water springs on the Sierra de Toluca (México) in May 1569; the offerings could be found every year if the site was visited in the same month (Sahagún 1981, 1:94). On a Palm Sunday around 1610 a large gathering of Indians was discovered at Calimaya (México), making offerings and collecting water from a mountain lake. A Christian cross erected at the site had been given a tobacco tube for smoking, while candles, copal, and braziers were left for the deity that the Indians believed resided there (La Serna 1892: 41). Trumpets (presumably of European origin) and flutes were also found at the site, indicating that songs and/or dances had been performed.

These three examples all appear to be associated with the same important festival focused on the sacred rain-mountains, which took place everywhere at the end of April and beginning of May.[18] Except, perhaps, for Sahagún, the greater part of the evangelization body believed that mountain venues were chosen as clandestine settings in which to practice the old rites undisturbed.[19] But the mountain cult, an integral part of the water-earth-fertility cult, was a fundamental aspect of prehispanic religious worship. Petitions or thanks for rain had always been made at these sites at several stages across the ritual year (Broda 1971, 1991a, 1991b, 1997a, 1997b, 2001). The Indians were pursuing the tradition not as an open act of defiance, or even as a manifestation of folk-religion, but because it was only on the sacred mountains that the water deities could be properly summoned and honored.

Examples of other (nonspecifically dated) rituals taking place on mountaintops or in mountain caves are very common across the sources. Although details are sparse, most would also have been focused on requests for rain or acknowledgment of favors granted. In the 1540s, when not coordinating rituals in their homes or the church, the caciques of Yanhuitlan carried out many of their rites at just such venues, as they had done in the past (*Procesos por idolatría* 1999: 115, 118, 120, 123, et passim). Babies and young children—the preferred prehispanic offering to the water deities—were also sacrificed (ibid., pp. 136, 170). The same caciques made tzoalli images of mountains, identified by one witness as a stepped *cu* (pyramid-platform) (ibid., p. 148).

While the slaughter of children apparently ceased,[20] the mountain rituals and associated artifacts continued. Jacinto de la Serna (1892: 53) recorded that in 1625 a Dominican friar had come across the remains of copal, balls of thread, cotton cloths, candles, and flowers on the Sierra de Toluca: clearly the sacred venue was still being honored. Elsewhere (not specified, but probably in the same area), in 1626, on the feast of Saint Michael the Archangel (September 29), the friar again found a recently placed mountain offering consisting of the same artifacts. The date of the Christian festival coincided with the end of Teotleco, "Arrival of the Gods," which nevertheless merged with Tepeilhuitl, "Festival of the Mountains" (FC2, 1981: 21, 130).[21] Torquemada (1975–83, 5:303–304) described the remains of a ritual that had taken place high in the mountains near the village of Zacatlan.[22] A pile of rocks, with a pyramidal-shaped stone placed on top, was covered with a mantle. Incense and other smaller mantles lay nearby. Still more mantles, along with copal, balls of rubber, candles, a quantity of small idols, and some Spanish coins, were unearthed as Torquemada and his companions attempted to destroy the site (ibid.). These remains echo the rituals taking place on Cerro Tlaloc in the prehispanic period, where the stone effigy of Tlaloc was surrounded with numerous smaller idols, representing all the mountains of the region, with Cerro Tlaloc at their center. The lords dressed the idols with costly jewels and quantities of mantles (Durán 1984, 1:82–84). Costly jewels would probably not have been an option for the villagers of Zacatlan, either before or after the conquest, but the newly introduced monetary system invaded society at all levels. Coins would have constituted a sacrifice of comparative value for a native community.

Colonial mountain gatherings were not intracommunity affairs either. The quantities of artifacts involved show that large numbers of Indians had congregated to make their offerings. On the Sierra de Toluca, for example, no less than fifteen villages took part in the preparations (Sahagún 1981, 1:94). In addition, framing rituals were being reenacted to summon the water deities: tobacco, copal, flowers, trumpets, and flutes were all part of the ritual paraphernalia left behind. Hernando Ruiz de Alarcón (1984: 54–57) also reported on pilgrimages made by individual penitents to mountaintops or piles of stones located in the hills; incensing and self-sacrifice was performed to attain a state of ecstasy when "they would hear, or thought they heard, words from their idol." In his own parish, tzoalli idols in the shape of a human figure were still being made at the end of the rainy season and ritually eaten in a setting of candles, incense, flowers, drumming, and song. Copious quantities of pulque were consumed until participants fell senseless (ibid., p. 53). The modeling of these figures strongly recalls the humanized tepictoton, "little molded ones," made of tzoalli in honor of the mountains in prehispanic times.

Traditional rites taking place in fields at specific moments of the agricultural cycle were also maintained. Much like the Nahuas of Zumpahuacan, the Zapotecs of Quegolani (Oaxaca) continued to honor the maize god at harvest time. In what appears to be the original version (Wake n.d.a.) of what became the great *xocotl* tree or ritual pole erected at Tenochtitlan (FC2, 1981: 111–17; Sahagún 1981, 1:184–90), they would select the largest and healthiest maize stalk in which the god was believed to be present, raise it on an altar, and dress it in clothes. Incensing, singing, and dancing followed (Burgoa 1989, 2:268). Ponce de León (1979: 128–29) also described how the "new wine" called *[h]uitzli,* "spine," produced from the fermented sap of the maguey cactus, was ritually welcomed at Zumpahuacan.[23] By 1629 Ruiz de Alarcón (1984: 121) was of the view that native invocations made to the plant were little more than superstition fueled by a pernicious desire to get drunk. But amid the plethora of metaphors that characterized the casting of the seventeenth-century incantations, the deified attributes of the maguey remained constant. The "woman . . . of eight in order/in a row" (ibid., pp. 121–23) refers to the pulque goddess, Mayahuel. Maguey was traditionally planted in rows of eight (perhaps because of the minimum of eight years required for it to mature), and its calendrical name was 8 Flint (Caso 1967: 198).[24] Similarly, the deities that the lone penitents aspired to encounter on their mountain pilgrimages were described as having "slobbery mouths" (Ruiz de Alarcón 1984: 55). This diagnostic matches the images of Tlaloc in Codex Magliabechiano, where the remains of the deity's own imbibing of the viscous pulque lie foaming on his upper lip (see fig. 6.57).

Rituals took place at a public and private level in the villages, but again the deployment of artifacts and activities associated with prehispanic framing rituals stands out. In 1539 at Ocuilan (México) mantles, copal, flowers, pulque, and food were used (*Proceso inquisitorial* 1980: 88). At Ocuituco (Morelos) artifacts included pulque, a sacrificed chicken (a replacement for the native quail), mantles and smaller cloths, food, and chocolate drink with flowers (possibly the intoxicating, deranging eloxochitl mentioned by Sahagún's informants: FC11, 1963: 201). Cristóbal of Ocuituco, the accused instigator of these forbidden activities, had also been found drunk, singing at the top of his voice, with a garland of flowers around his neck and a flower in each hand (*Procesos de indios* 1912: 143–45, 164–65). Andrés Mixcoatl of Huauchinango (Puebla) distributed mushrooms at his gatherings and asked for flowers to be brought by participants (ibid., pp. 58–65).

The unacceptable did not respect Christian space. Ritual participants at Acapixtla left their church untended in order to congregate in the atrium and celebrate the 1535 festival of Toxcatl because their cacique did not wish them to become Christians or attend their church (Grijalva 1985: 59). The caciques of Yanhuitlan burnt copal before going to church and chewed raw tobacco so as not to understand the sermon. While ordering their subjects also to attend Christian gatherings, they nevertheless directed them to worship in the area of the atrium where the prehispanic temples had stood (*Procesos por idolatría* 1999: 120, 131, 140, 151).

It is worth remembering that all these examples, which were apparently blatant acts of repudiation of Christianity where the old gods were being invoked in a traditional manner, were recorded by Europeans or under the supervision of the colonial authorities. What they saw, or understood, was not necessarily all "idolatrous." In this context, the specifically non-Christian focus of other (simultaneously occurring) rituals is much less clear. When a new house was completed at sixteenth-century Zumpahuacan, the Indians brought half the offering of tamales and pulque to the church and placed it on the altar (Ponce de León 1979: 129–30). The celebration of church holidays in the village involved the preparation of food, pulque, and rolled tobacco leaves for smoking, together with chocolate and flowers. Pulque was offered (poured) before the fire, and an equivalent amount was placed on the church altar (ibid., pp. 122–23). Were these Indians, busy invoking Quetzalcoatl, Chicomecoatl, and Matlalcueye in the fields, also honoring the prehispanic sacred site that the church now occupied? Or were they acknowledging something else (for example, that the Christian church was now also a part of their own religious world)?

Activities elsewhere suggest that the second explanation is the most probable: the Christian sacred had become a target for traditional modes of worship. Although La Serna believed that the mountain ceremonies at Calimaya were directed toward the old water deities, a Christian cross had nevertheless been erected at the site. We cannot know by whom, but the Indians did not ignore it and made it traditional offerings. In 1609 the harvest at Texcaliaca (México) was celebrated by burning maize leaves at the domestic hearth, where, together with food, jars of pulque adorned with flower garlands were offered to the fire god. These were then consumed, accompanied by the sound of drums and the words "Resplendent rose that gives light, let my heart rejoice and be uplifted before God" (La Serna 1892: 35).[25] La Serna also reported that at midnight or dawn before a saint's feast day chickens were sacrificed and cooked in the house of an Indian leader. Quantities of pulque, tobacco tubes, and chocolate drink with flowers were divided: half as an offering to the fire god and half for the church altar. To La Serna's alarm, both sets of offerings were then given to the church choir leaders as a repast and—he suspected—probably to the church ministers themselves (ibid., p. 100). In one nocturnal gathering in a private house before a particular saint's day mushrooms, pulque, and fire were placed beneath the saint's altar. Drumming and singing, along with ingestion of mushrooms and drinking of pulque, continued all night, until—as usual—the participants lost their senses (ibid., pp. 61–62).

La Serna's assumption that libations poured over the fire or offerings made with fire meant that the fire god was being invoked is typical of the obsessive manner in which native activities were so often interpreted. Among modern-day traditional groups of rural Guerrero, a ritual without fire—or at least candles—is inconceivable. Fire is considered essential to raise offerings to the designated deity or natural force (van der Loo 1987: 158–59). At Texcaliaca it was the Virgin Mary—the resplendent Christian Rose without Thorns—to whom native thanks for the harvest were raised. At Calimaya Christ's cross was petitioned at the same time as the mountain deities of old. The nocturnal gathering before the altar of the anonymous saint displayed all the characteristics of a traditional framing ritual, the object of which, it seems, was to sum-mon his presence on the eve of his feast day. Seen in this way, similar activities taking place in and around the church call for a more objective consideration of their pur-pose. Despite the Augustinian-reported defiance of the cacique of Acapixtla in 1535, the village had been a Franciscan visita since about 1528, and that order had received the support of its Indian rulers (Motolinía 1990: 82). Christianity was not, therefore, a sudden or unwelcome presence in the community. The problems encountered by the newly arrived Augustinians perhaps had more to do with indigenous reaction to the changeover of religious orders, as occurred elsewhere.[26] Grijalva (1985: 60–61) also re-corded that shortly after the Augustinians arrived at Olinalá, in the province of Tlapa (Guerrero), the lords and principals chose the atrium as a venue in which to dance and sing in honor of their old gods. But how could the chronicler, or the friars who report-ed these incidents, have been so sure that the focus of this celebration was specifically non-Christian? Perhaps predictably, they elaborate no further on their claims.

Inasmuch as the songs themselves were concerned, Durán (1984, 1:236) observed that, when a saint's day coincided with the feast of an "idol," songs were sung partly in honor of God and the saint in question and partly in the old metaphoric language, which only the devil would understand. In other words, as another sixteenth-century observer argued, the Christian god was mentioned in the songs only as a subterfuge: "they mix in songs from their pagan past and in order to hide their wicked deed they start and end with God's words, inserting their pagan words in between, lowering their voices so as not to be understood, and raising them at the beginning and end when they say 'God'" (Cervantes de Salazar 1985: 39).[27]

Despite the determination of these men to see the devil in every native act, both references strongly recall the composition and structure of the Nahua devotional song-poems contained in the late-sixteenth-century *Cantares mexicanos* collection. Although characterized by rousing and often repetitive invocations to Christian fig-ures at the beginning or end of each line or verse, the songs are based on a bewilder-ing array of imagery constructs, the precise meaning of which still evades us. It is generally agreed that some of the songs date from the prehispanic period, the names of native supernatural entities having been edited out and replaced with those of Christian figures (Bierhorst 1985a: 108–109; Lockhart 1992: 398; Burkhart 1996: 95). In the light of Durán's and Cervantes de Salazar's observations, the procedure might well appear suspicious until we come to read the songs composed in the co-lonial period. In like manner, God, Christ, the Virgin, the saints, colonial church figures, native patrons, and the church itself are plunged into the metaphorical ob-scurity and floral frenzies of the songs of old. That is, while the songs continue to invoke the presence of the bizarre, flowery world that was the Indian sacred—that vision of water, fertility, and abundance—it is now a world in which Christian fig-ures are seen to reside. Just as the prehispanic sacred approached slowly, coming closer until it touched the ritual participant's heart, so did the songs composed by native poets for the Christian sacred. They also started up slowly and quietly, with drums playing softly, then increased in volume and tempo (Torquemada 1975–83, 4:341). Words were repeated over and over until reaching a final crescendo, at which point Christian referents descend like flowers from God's home in Mexico and the worshipper is at last able to enter into his presence: "Let them be inhaled, these plume-incense flowers. They're scattered. God sets his flowers free, then takes these flowers to his home" (*CM,* f. 35r; 1985: 244–45).

In 1569 the secular priest at Churubusco (D.F.) objected to the drunken orgies into which the seven or eight Christian festivals celebrated across the year degenerated. His proselytes explained that if this custom was forbidden then their faith would be weakened (*Descripción del arzobispado* 1976: 225–26). How must we interpret this response: as manipulative defiance or complete sincerity? The priest at Churubusco would certainly have opted for the former, for drunkenness had nothing to do with Christian worship. But drunkenness had everything to do with the Indian search for the sacred. The Churubusco problem may be compared to another incident of the period. When Durán scolded an Indian for begging and then spending all the money collected on a village festival (undoubtedly another drunken orgy), the Indian replied, "Father, do not be shocked, for we are still *nepantla*" (Durán 1984, 1:237):

> [A]nd so as to understand what he meant by that word and metaphor, which means "in the middle," I insisted that he tell me exactly what they were in the middle of. He said that I should not be shocked, that because they were still not well rooted in the faith they were still neutral; they turned properly to neither one law nor the other. Or, more precisely, and this is what the abominable excuse that they were "in the middle and were neutral" meant: they believed in God and together with this turned to their old customs and rites of the devil.[28]

In religious thought, the Nahuatl morpheme *nepantla* expresses the negative concept of being "in the middle." "A place, state, figure or situation is *nepantla* when it is unstable and in transition from one status or position to another" (Elzey 1976: 324–25). Based on Durán's report, postconquest "nepantlism" has come to be defined as a confused participation in both types of rites, where Christianity is not assimilated or understood and the native religion is lost or disfigured (Klor de Alva 1982: 353–55, 1993: 181–82). But, at the level of semantics, there are questions here. The Indian translates *nepantla* as "neutral," by his own definition still not well rooted in the Christian faith and as a result adhering neither to it nor to the old beliefs in a correct manner. "Neutral," however, does not denote a state of transition but rather "in the middle" in the sense of impartiality or nonpreference for either side of the argument. It also does not imply a state of confusion. Thus, if the Indians were still not well rooted in the Christian faith, it was because they (still) could not distinguish between it and their own religion. Although Durán would not—could not—have recognized such a position as other than the nonsense he made it out to be, he certainly understood what the Indian was saying: they believed in God and "*together with this*" ("juntamente"; my emphasis) also turned to their own traditional customs and rites.[29] This, it seems to me, is what the "nahuatization" (Klor de Alva 1993) of Christianity was really all about.[30]

From this example, we can perhaps also understand how the religious spirit of the Indians of Churubusco would be compromised by acceding to their own priest's demands to abandon ritual drunkenness. For if, on the insistence of the evangelization body, the Christian sacred was made to stand on one side and the means to communicate with it stood on the other, then they would be truly *nepantla*.

Here I may be treading dangerous waters, for the whole issue of native reactions to Christianity is a hugely difficult area. As J. Jorge Klor de Alva (1982: 349) has shown, responses varied considerably; but he rightly points out that we need to avoid basing our assessments on the perceptions of others who reported on those reactions during or after the sixteenth century. It is true that some Indians wholeheartedly embraced Christianity as a new and different religion, while others merely accepted it or openly rejected it. A vast anonymous group nevertheless remains, whose diversity of responses across geography and time cannot be so easily honed down to a schema of static categories where one religion is seen to play off the other. Indian understanding of Christianity was tempered gradually across the lives of individuals, groups, and generations in accordance with a multiplicity of factors: the degree of cross-cultural communication, methodology and intensity of indoctrination, levels of permitted participation, willingness for compromise on both sides as the new laws were given and learned, and so on.

But if the evangelization body hardened or softened its attitudes to the unacceptable or the unorthodox, for it the gulf between Christianity and the native religion could never close. Men like Sahagún who attempted to understand the underlying forces of native religiousness did so in order to destroy it or at best factor out certain elements that could safely be adapted for the purposes of the conversion program. What appeared safe for them, however, was not necessarily incidental to indigenous forms of worship, and vice versa. For example, the prohibition of human sacrifice (the prerogative of rulers and the nobility) does appear to have been accepted with little dispute.[31] But where the process of reaching the sacred was dismantled through the prohibition of some of its key elements (such as ritual drunkenness), this sort of factoring out was met with resistance. In addition, the Indians were not in a position to allow it to happen. Where the projection of religious beliefs focused on the perpetuation of life in the temporal world, religious life was ongoing and ritual momentum had to be sustained. The "language" of the Christian god—the mode and image in which the omniscient giver of life now chose to manifest himself—had to be embraced quickly, with his assistants and intercessors assigned their roles and the appropriate honors paid to all. In other words (as the following chapters show), Christian figures and symbols were being incorporated as functional entities into the parameters of native religious beliefs in accordance with the Indians' understanding of Christianity and the way to approach it. If Christianity was being "nahuatized" or "reconstructed," as Inga Clendinnen (1990) has also put it, it was not as a new religion but as a working and workable form of the religious system that already existed.

The Acceptable

Although never understood as such, native framing rituals were admitted by the colonial church under two main provisos: the rituals were to coincide exclusively with formal Christian festivals and unacceptable elements (ritual drunkenness and/or the ingestion of other mind-altering substances) were not to be included. The other elements—the tributes of food, live animals, feathers, incense, embroidered mantles, song and dance, and, above all, flowers—were deemed to be acceptable expressions of native Christian devotion. Under the watchful eye of the evangelizers, they were a good thing. Commenting on how the custom of adorning the prehispanic temples with flowers had been transferred in excess to the churches, Torquemada (1975–83, 3:248–49), for example, believed that this revealed the Indians' much greater intensity of devotion as Christians.

Although many of the chroniclers of the day made observations on the native mode of Christian worship, some of the most detailed accounts of the early festivals are found in the records of Motolinía (1990: 54–58, 61–74). These were made at Tlaxcala and cover the celebration of major church festivals in general, together with Easter in 1536 and 1539, the birth of John the Baptist in 1538, Corpus Christi in 1538 and 1539, and the Annunciation in 1539. Despite this friar's efforts to emphasize the solemnity of these occasions (e.g., ibid., pp. 54, 61), it is clear that they not only were extremely lively and colorful affairs but were based very heavily on prehispanic ritual traditions and symbolism. Thus the interest of his descriptions also lies in the manner in which they begin to expose the process of syncretic beliefs taking root at that time.

Food was always a major offering, but its underlying purpose also tells us much. We might expect cooked victuals at the festival of All Saints and All Souls (November 1–2) to guide the dead back to the land of the living, but the same foods were taken to the church for Resurrection Day in 1536 (ibid., p. 56), as if to guide Christ on his (also brief) return to the world after death. The burning of incense was and is a Christian practice, of course. Sahagún (1981, 1:243) nevertheless noted that, although the type used in Europe occurred naturally in New Spain, the Indians almost always reverted back to the traditional *copalli* resin that they had used to raise offerings to their old gods. Curiously enough, this fact does not seem to have troubled him. On the part of the Indians, however, the decision to discard the new for the old would seem to suggest that the Christian sacred could be attracted in the same way as the Indian sacred: the Christian sacred also recognized the smell of native libations.

Among the offerings on Easter Sunday in 1536 the Indians included mantles of different sizes. The smaller ones (the size of hand cloths) were embroidered with an image of the cross, the Franciscan insignia of the five wounds of Christ, the names (monograms?) of Christ or Mary, or just flowers. Kneeling at the church entrance, the Indians grasped these by the corners, held them up to their faces, and raised them two or three times in the air. Then they laid them out on the church steps (Motolinía 1990: 57). The waving of mantles and cloths before the church is highly reminiscent of the paper cut-outs that are strung around modern-day ofrenda tables for the dead, like buntings. Together with food (as a symbol of the earth), drink (water), and candles (fire), they represent wind. Among today's traditional groups the wind-carriers draped over the household ofrenda are still more often than not embroidered or printed cloths and napkins. The wind preceded the coming of the rains. Easter Sunday in 1536 fell on April 16 (O'Gorman 1990: xxviii), that is, thirteen days before the special prehispanic festival of the tlaloque and the mountains, which fell on April 29–30 in Durán's correlation (1984, 1:82–85). A count of thirteen days would have been of significance to the natives of Tlaxcala, and elsewhere, for it corresponds to the constituent numbers and the parsed 20 × 13-day periods of the 260-day ritual count or *tonalpohualli*. Motolinía states that it was on the eve of Easter Sunday in 1536 and throughout that night that the inhabitants of the region started to arrive in droves with their offerings. Before dawn on the following day they processed and sang and danced. And, in that particular year, the native celebrants included what Motolinía (1990: 57–58) and his fellow Spaniards saw as another delightful Indian detail: little children—toddlers who had not left their mothers' breasts—also danced.[32] But all prehispanic rites to Tlaloc and the water deities had taken place at night (Broda 1971: 323, 1987: 72), and small children had been the primary sacrifice to these forces. Can we see the Tlaxcallan children's dance, then, as some sort of reworked, symbolic insert?[33]

Early Christian rituals among the Tlaxcallans certainly appear to have had a heavy focus on rain and fertility. Singing and dancing started up at midnight in many parts of the region and could continue for the best part of the following day (Motolinía 1990: 54). Penitential activities (usually flagellation, but also body piercing: ibid., p. 56) frequently took place after dark; "*when they lack water,* or there is sickness, or for any other need, they go from church to church with their crosses and torches, making penitence" (ibid., pp. 555–56; my emphasis).[34] On Christmas night (December 24–25) torches were placed on rooftops and around the church atria, where the Indians would sing to the sound of drums and the ringing of hand bells (ibid., p. 54). Here again, the act seems to have been to summon Christ, this time as a child-symbol of the regeneration of life. In prehispanic Tlaxcala December 26 had marked the opening of the festival of Atemoztli, "Descent of Water" (Acuña 1984c: 224, n. 282). The less than impromptu "Christmas" ritual was also not restricted to Motolinía's day, as Durán (1984, 1:287–88) tells us in his later descriptions of the same festival: "They pretended that a child came down from the sky on that day, and they called this child 'Water' . . . it was strictly ordered not to sleep all night long but to make vigil in the temple courtyard waiting for the arrival of the water . . . and so they all were . . . with fires to keep them warm, in the same manner as they now pass the whole of Christmas night."[35]

In native belief, the descending child was a water-bringer, probably one of the sacred winged beings of the Tlaxcallan people that ushered in the wind, thunder, and lightning (Muñoz Camargo 1986: 152), in other words, a tlaloque. If Muñoz Camargo did not make the connection between the tlaloque-child and the advent of Christ, Durán evidently did.[36]

The sacred Tlaxcallan water-mountain, Matlalcueye, may also have been invoked at this time of the year in both pre- and postconquest times. In the seventeenth century idolatrous offerings centered round a cave of idols maintained on the mountain by a certain Juan Coatl of Huamantla took place at Christmastide. At his trial Coatl confessed that he worshiped the mountain, invoking it under the name of the Blessed Virgin (Gruzinski 1989: 93–95). As Mother of Christ, the Virgin Mary also seems to have been incorporated into the ongoing prehispanic festival of descending water, perhaps in the role of the blue-skirted Chalchiutlicue, goddess of terrestrial water, who was the Tlaxcallan mountain and "gave birth" to water.

Here the suggestion is not that Christ came to be identified specifically as a tlaloque or the Virgin Mary as a female counterpart. But where Tlaloc was Lord of Sustenance in general ("he made that which we ate and drank—food, drink, our sustenance, our nourishment, our daily bread": FC7, 1953: 17), so at Christmas the Baby Jesus may have come to be identified as the maize seed itself. In the prehispanic era children sacrificed to the rain deity and the sacred rain mountains represented the seed that would be sown when the agricultural cycle opened (Broda 2001: 216). A Nativity song composed in 1553 suggests a syncretic manipulation of the old symbolism. Here God's creation descends to earth in Bethlehem as popcorn flowers (that is, as dried, toasted maize seeds). The Virgin Mary gives birth to these "many jewels" (*CM,* f. 37v; 1985: 254–55).

At the feast of Candlemas (February 2) in Tlaxcala the Indians brought their candles to be blessed and, after much singing and processing, retained what had not burned away for sickness and for "thunder and lightning" (Motolinía 1990: 55). In modern-day traditional communities of the central area February 2 also marks the date when shamans known as *graniceros* (rain-makers) commence their rituals to ensure a successful maize cycle, that is, the petitioning of rain and the warding off of destructive elements associated with water, such as hail (*granizo*). In villages lying southeast of Tlaxcala City, the maize seed set aside for sowing is blessed along with the candles, which are still believed to act as propitiatory agents against bad weather (González Jácome 1997: 495). The same rites and beliefs are found in Ocuilan de Arteaga, in the Valley of Toluca. Of special interest in the Toluca Valley is the perceived link with Christmas: it is acknowledged that on February 2 the Christ-child awakens, having gone to sleep on December 24 (Albores 1997: 409). The annual cycle of worship of the Niñopa, "Child-God," of Xochimilco (D.F.) also commences at Candlemas, with the blessing of the maize seeds to be sown and the candles for sickness. The cycle ends at Epiphany (*Ruta de los santuarios* 1994: 72). In addition to the purification of the Virgin Mary, Candlemas celebrates the consecration of Christ (Hall 1979: 251). Present-day Mexican associations of the sleeping Baby Jesus with the dried maize seed set aside for the next planting and the awakened Christ-child with the same seed ready for sowing thus suggest strong syncretic origins. It is as if Christ's life cycle is being paralleled with that of maize.

Although Motolinía understood acts of enflowering at major Christian festivals as decorative, it is clear that these carried all the characteristic traits of traditional framing rituals. Native paradisiacal otherworlds were also being constructed, albeit now inhabited by Christian referents. Processional routes were strewn with flowers and foliage; and, like the temples before them, the churches were carpeted with branches, blossoms, and reeds, over which aromatic herbs (*yerbabuena*) were scattered. Members of the Indian nobility danced with posies in their hands. Flowers were always sweet smelling, even if the Indians had to send to the hotlands for them (Motolinía 1990: 54, 73).

On Palm Sunday everything was embowered: the churches, the area where the palms were to be blessed, and the area where outdoor mass was to be said. Some of the palms were decorated with crosses made from brightly colored flowers of varying species or crosses with flowers grafted on, "and as the palms are green and they carry them in their raised hands, it looks like a woodland" (Motolinía 1990: 55).[37] Then they stacked them outside the church. Stacking in this case refers to the palms being arranged in an ordered pile (*un rimado*) (ibid.) as tied bundles or criss-cross frameworks of canes, which, for example, appear among ritual artifacts in the Mixtec codices.[38] Ritual manipulation of counted reed or pine bundles persists among traditional Nahua groups of modern-day Guerrero, being generally associated with petitions for a good harvest, protection from evil and disease, and auguries. Bundles of varying numbers (in accordance with the objective of the offering) are arranged in ordered stacks before the fire, with garlands of threaded leaves and flowers placed over them (van der Loo 1987: 191–93). At Tlaxcala the stacks were destined for burning on Ash Wednesday.

The elaborate and expansive Tlaxcallan celebrations surrounding Corpus Christi were remarkable to all those who witnessed them. Las Casas (1992) was so impressed with what appears to have been Motolinía's original account of the 1538 festival that he reproduced it in his *Apologética,* thereby providing further details that Motolinía changed or omitted in his final version. In that year the streets through which the procession passed were divided into three sections by freshly felled trees (Las Casas 1992: 597). To these was added a vast covering of vegetation, consisting of 10 great enflowered arches, 1,068 medium-sized ones, and 66 small ones. Nearly one-fifth of the flowers were Spanish pinks. A thousand "shields" made of flowers hung from the arches; where no shields were placed, "there were some huge flowers, made up of something like onion skins, round, very well made, and of a fine luster" (Motolinía 1990: 61–62).[39] Finally, the floor of the tree-lined processional route was covered with reeds and flowers, with spectators throwing pinks and other blossoms before the participants (ibid., p. 61). Some of the flower-throwers wore garlands of flowers across their shoulders or chests, with crowns of flowers on their heads (Las Casas 1992: 598).

Motolinía (1990: 61) states that the processional way represented a three-aisled church nave, but the very fact that he edited out his original reference to the trees suggests that the architectural likeness occurred to him later and was therefore not a native explanation of the forms being constructed. It seems clearer that these routes represented a paradisiacal woodland through which the procession carrying the Eucharist could pass. As far as flowers are concerned, the manner in which the native celebrants had appropriated and used strong-smelling Spanish flowers alongside indigenous species merits comment. Given that both the Spaniards and Indians present were counting exactly the numbers of arches and flower shields (Motolinía 1990: 62; Las Casas 1992: 597), the ratio of one-fifth Spanish pinks is probably also correct and suggests a conscious Indian computation. As supreme political leader of New Spain, the Spanish monarch would receive his Royal Fifth of riches gained from the colony; as Holy Roman Emperor, he was symbolically incorporated into the framing ritual in the same ratio. Preconquest rulers, we remember, were also treated as part of the ritual paraphernalia (Tezozómoc 1943: 104–105). The large flowers made from lustrous vegetation resembling onion skins can only refer to those still made today for religious coverings from the dried scales of the heart of the maguey cactus, that is, the inner core from which the sap is drawn.[40] Whether use of this material was a prehispanic tradition or a colonial innovation is not known. Replacement of pulque with chocolate drink (without the flowers, we must assume) in rites for the dead suggests that the Tlaxcallan Indians, at least, had renounced drunkenness at major Christian festivals; they had nevertheless inserted visual references to this powerful fertility symbol in their floral imagery.

No framing ritual could be complete without music. As the 1538 procession paused at wayside chapels, children came out singing and dancing (Motolinía 1990: 61). With the noise of the choirs, flutes, trumpets, and drums as the procession finally entered the church, "it seemed that the sky was falling in" (ibid., p. 63).[41] For some of those present, it may have done so.

The enthusiasm with which the Indians celebrated Corpus Christi and the ritual imagery and artifacts evoked and invoked at this time is again perhaps explained through native interpretations of the role of Christ in their reconstruction of the Indian sacred. The Catholic festival celebrates the presence of Christ in the Eucharist, the gift of his body as the bread and his blood as the wine, to redeem humankind. Falling on the seventh Sunday after Easter, Corpus Christi almost inevitably takes place in June.

Johanna Broda (1983: 150–51) has described two agricultural cycles a year in the prehispanic central highlands. The first was based on irrigation techniques that drew off early rainwater falling on the mountains. Sowing took place in January or February, with harvest in June and July. Two months after sowing, young maize ears may already have formed. The second cycle, dependent on the rainy season itself, involved sowing at any time between March and June, with harvest from October onward. If, as the form and timing of the sixteenth-century rituals very much imply, the birth of

Christ focused on the regeneration of the maize in the agricultural cycle commencing in January, then his presence in the Eucharist would correspond to the June harvest of that cycle. Similarly, Easter—and particularly the Resurrection—finds Christ at the start of the second cycle, when the successful outcome of sowing depends entirely on the arrival of the rainy season at the end of April. At Easter, according to the *Cantares mexicanos,* God's son has arisen and the spirit of the savior comes to earth in the form of varicolored baby maize-ear flowers (that is, the fertilized flowers that eventually develop into maize cobs): "Let him be called and be counted" (*CM,* ff. 42v–43r; 1985: 272–75). In this cycle, then, Corpus Christi would coincide with the prehispanic rituals surrounding the ripening maize ears in Tecuilhuitl (June 2–21). Corpus Christi in fact fell on June 20 in 1538 (O'Gorman 1990: xxviii).[42] Native interpretations of Christ as maize in religious art are addressed in chapter 6.

Much as at prehispanic Tenochtitlan, where urban ritual arenas were converted into artificial fields of vegetation and flowers, the Tlaxcallan celebrants of Corpus Christi in 1538 also re-created their own local landscape in front of the church. At each of the four corners of the processional route they constructed an artificial mountain with a high peak, beneath which they laid out fields of grass and flowers. The mountains were covered in trees (some carried blossoms or fruit, while others were left old and broken) as well as toadstools and mushrooms (*setas y hongos*) and moss, possibly the ritual *pachtli.*[43] Within this setting moved live birds, game animals, and serpents, some extremely venomous but made sluggish with *picietl* (powdered raw tobacco). Camouflaged in the mountains were hunters with bows and arrows who spoke a different language (Motolinía 1990: 62), identified by Las Casas (1992: 599) as Otomis. Like the later posa-chapels that stood in each corner of New World atria (see chapter 4), each mountain was dedicated to a different theme: Adam and Eve and the serpent that deceived them; the Temptation of Christ; Saint Jerome; and Saint Francis of Assisi (ibid.).

Motolinía and Las Casas give us the impression that this landscape was created on Indian initiative. Indeed, the configuration of the four mountains echoes the perceived macro- and microcosmic layout of the Indian world, with its interchangeable parameters of trees and mountains.[44] It also reflects the prehispanic organization of the province, where the four houses of the Tlaxcallan political confederacy were sited on hills overlooking the valley where the colonial city was founded. The specific identification of Otomi hunters, members of an ethnic group that occupied parts of Tlaxcallan territory as tributaries (Muñoz Camargo 1984: 78–79), is a further clue that the Corpus Christi ritual landscape represented Tlaxcala's own geography. The presentation or reenactment of the Christian story on Mexican landscapes was not to be restricted to church festivals (as later chapters show). For now, we should ponder on the inclusion of so many native symbols of abundance—trees laden with fruit and flowers, fields full of grass and flowers—on those landscapes. These appear to acknowledge and emulate the presence of the Indian sacred within those ritual arenas, summoned by way of Christian framing rituals. Visual references to the mind-altering mushrooms and powdered tobacco so often employed in those rituals apparently also were not excluded. Admittedly this is a speculative point; but given the prohibition of these substances, their presence on the paradisiacal landscape is intriguing.

The biblical Garden of Eden was also transformed into the sacred landscape of

Tlaxcala. In 1539, when the festival of the Annunciation (March 25) was pushed forward to April 16 (O'Gorman 1990: 65, n. 20) (again, thirteen days before the major prehispanic festival in honor of the tlaloque and the sacred water mountains), a special play (*auto*) reenacting the story of Adam and Eve was organized by the Indians.[45] Eden was represented with its four rivers and the *arbor vitae* or Tree of Life, surrounded by fruit-laden and flowering trees but also with quantities of live birds, rabbits and hares, and two fierce mountain cats. The whole presentation was located within a landscape of three high peaks and a large mountain range (Motolinía 1990: 66). Anyone familiar with the geography of Tlaxcala must immediately recall the three peaks of the sacred mountains (Matlalcueye, Popocatepetl, and Iztaccihuatl) that dominate the area. The large range would thus appear to refer to the chain of mountains to the northwest of Tlaxcala where Cerro Tlaloc—site of the prehispanic spring rites—lies. Described as "fertile and fresh" and filled with "all the details that can be found in April and May" (ibid.),[46] the theatrical mountain setting certainly appears to have struck a familiar chord with the non-natives who saw it.

From as early as 1524, when the first Franciscans attempted to present the work of God to the assembled nobility of Tenochtitlan, the Garden of Eden had been likened to a "flowery" place in "the interior of the precious earth" (Sahagún 1986: 192–93, 198–99).[47] It is not difficult to understand the attraction of Eden for the Indians when it was explained in this way. Certainly the Tlaxcallan Garden of Eden, with its real sacred mountains, flowers and trees, birds and game, offers a much closer image of the flowery, watery abode of the Indian sacred than do biblical descriptions of Eden. Even the birds selected for the auto—parrots of different sizes, owls, raptors, wild turkeys, and other "little birds" (hummingbirds?)—strongly recall the lineup of the *quecholtin* (sacred flyers), the constituent numbers of the Central Mexican day count but also the highest of life principles. Little wonder, then, that the Indian audience wept when Adam and Eve were expelled from the garden to take up residence in a world of cacti, brambles, and venomous snakes, finding themselves working the land in order to live (Motolinía 1990: 67).

After an equally elaborate procession to celebrate Corpus Christi in 1539, three mountains were again used as settings for three further autos (Motolinía 1990: 73–74). To the great amusement of both Spanish and native onlookers, the Indians managed to introduce Castilian wine as one of the Temptations of Christ. In the middle of Saint Francis's Sermon to the Birds, a "drunken" figure appeared on stage, "singing just like the Indians sang when they became drunk" (ibid., p. 74).[48] When this man refused to stop singing and interrupting the sermon, the usually gentle saint called on a group of demons to drag him off to burn in hell. (A few Franciscan eyebrows may have been raised at the apparent ease with which the followers of the devil were summoned by their patron.) There is no commentary on the last auto, the Sacrifice of Abraham, other than that it was short but well represented. Perhaps fortunately in this case, native initiative in playwriting seems to have run out of steam.

Despite the details, Motolinía described acceptable native ritual activities, deployment of visual imagery, and inserts drawn from the native world very much from a Western perspective. For the Europeans who witnessed them, the processions, singing, and dancing; the offering of food, mantles, and feathers; and the representations of biblical stories were theatrical performances visually enhanced by their settings and décor: the floral displays; the mountains, fields, and rivers; the flora and fauna. But from the native perspective, all these elements in combination were integral to the framing rituals. They were all "protagonists" in the great reenactment of a text that did not just invoke the sacred but was the sacred manifest.

Recent research has argued quite convincingly that the texts of the Mixtec historical codices were also scripts for live performance (King 1990, 1994; Monaghan 1990, 1994). As such, the series of artifacts, signs, and symbols contained in their graphic form—which serve as readable icons—would probably also have been utilized or reproduced as part of the live reenactment. These would have been recognizable to an audience and served, for example, to evoke community customs, agricultural practices, or prayer formulae or as direct prompts to give voice to certain words or syllables (King 1994: 115). Iconic ritual texts from the central area, such as the Codex Laud, Codex Borgia, and Codex Féjérváry, also appear to take the form of "manuals" for the performance of sacred rites.[49] We know from the chroniclers that, in dance at least, the Nahuas also acted out their own histories: heroic deeds, the lives of rulers, and the origins and actions of the gods (Durán 1984, 1:192–95; Mendieta 1973, 1:85).[50] We must therefore suppose that, in like manner, the narrative element in these performances was complemented by signs and symbols in the form of specifically designated artifacts, clothing, accessories, design motifs on costumes and skin, color, body movement, and so on.

Thus postconquest framing rituals also entailed action and the image functioning together in the live performance of the text that was the sacred. Just as the sacred knowledge, as "performed" by the sacred, was written down in the divine cosmic books, so human ritual "wrote" the sacred across real time and space. And it is through this process that we can perhaps see how the inserts of Euro-Christian symbols and figures into the native framing rituals narrated Christianity's incorporation into the Indian sacred. The acting out of the text of the Christian teoamoxtli was an activity that had very close parallels with the semitheatrical rituals of old (McAndrew 1965: 217; Burkhart 1996: 45; León-Portilla 1996: 189). But the inclusion of traditional ideas (the intimation or simulation of ritual drunkenness) and traditional actors (the sacred, as embodied in the Mexican landscape and its animate entities) is seen to impinge on the Christian sources in a manner that suggests their appropriation within native mythology. In this sense, where the ingestion of alcohol (Castilian wine, the sacred octli) and/or other mind-altering substances (psychotropic flowers, mushrooms, picietl) was not permitted in action, their images—either present physically or referred symbolically—could still adequately play out a narrative role. I do not see this mode of theatrical deployment as a form of colonial subterfuge, however. Although not prohibited, ingestion of the same substances was strictly regulated in the prehispanic period. Thus, for example, if some were permitted to drink when dancing (Códice Tudela, f. 66v), others nevertheless feigned the act and the resultant state of inebriation (Durán 1984, 1:194). As the following chapters show, native understanding of act and image—of ritual and image—as inseparable concepts (which, furthermore, could be simultaneously and nondistinctly reenacted, painted, or sung to transmit the same message) became the hallmark of native expressions of Christianity during the sixteenth century.

Throughout that first century the Indians of New Spain pursued their own lavishly accommodated framing rituals on every other important Christian occasion possible: at mass baptisms (Grijalva 1985: 101), during visits of church dignitaries (Ciudad Real 1976), and at the reception of holy relics (*Relación breve* 1995: 39–41), to give but three examples. Artificial landscapes continued to be constructed.[51] As in the pre-Christian era, they processed and danced and sang and filled their churches with heavily scented flowers and herbs (Burgoa 1989, 1:402–403, 2:28). The form and being of the Indian sacred was re-created, reenacted, and ultimately summoned to the Christian arena. The Indians even appear to have convinced the evangelization body that the Christian sacred had assumed a new and different identity. For an anonymous Jesuit, the result of native embowering of the church was "the beauty of the Glory in portrait" (*Relación breve* 1995: 42);[52] for the Augustinian Grijalva (1985: 163), "the streets were made a map of earth, water, wind, and Heaven itself."[53]

In 1531 a vision of heaven heralded the appearance of the Virgin Mary on Tepeyacac Hill. Published in 1649 by Luis Lasso de la Vega as his own work, *Nican mopohua* (1995) is perhaps the earliest known account of the miracle at Tepeyacac Hill, which laid the foundations for the later cult of the Virgin of Guadalupe. It is generally agreed, however, that the text was originally of indigenous authorship. As such, it permitted Juan Diego a brief encounter with an otherworld he would readily recognize: "there where they left it said the ancient ones, our ancestors, our grand-fathers: in the land of flowers, in the land of maize, of our flesh, our sustenance . . . in the celestial land" (*Nican mopohua* 1995: 356).[54] If the Christian heaven, abode of the Virgin of Tepeyacac, was a land of flowers and of sustenance (*in xochitlalpan in tonacatlalpan*), then it too was the abode of the Indian sacred.

CHAPTER THREE

Indoctrination and the Building of Churches

Surprisingly—for it would have been a distinct mark of success for the conversion program—we have very few accounts of Indian attendance at church services taking place outside major festivals. Sundays probably saw the best attendance; as with important feast-days, attendance was obligatory and floggings were meted out for absences (*Códice franciscano* 1941: 59).[1] Conversely, in the early years of widely dispersed populations, the impracticalities of travel to and from a village church or indoctrination center (distance, labor commitments, availability of a priest) probably also served to reduce congregations. Neither circumstance seemed to have an impact on the overwhelming response to other religious activities, however. The *autos* (dramatic representations of biblical or religious-historical themes) came to be especially popular; and, as we have seen, much time was spent singing or chanting the basic Christian litanies, such as the *Ave Maria*, the *Pater Noster,* and the Articles of the Faith, as taught by the friars. In addition, and even when reports might be exaggerated (see Mendieta 1973, 1:165–66), the rites of baptism and the use of holy water were accepted with startling enthusiasm. The expansive preparations for and celebration of important festivals in the Catholic calendar (including the honors offered by the new native *cofradías*),[2] together with the willingness with which the Indians flocked to build their new places of worship, also suggest that overall Christianity was a great success. Nevertheless, closer examination of contemporary accounts indicates that certain parts of the Christian package were being received with marked reluctance or not at all, despite possible reprisals. The Indians were actively selecting and reselecting specific elements of the imposed religious program. And it is this selectivity that gives us a much greater insight into indigenous approaches to Christianity as a functional religion and a cultural manifestation.

Indoctrination and the First Congregations

Toward the end of the 1530s the evangelization body made numerous complaints with regard to the growing indifference or outright obstinacy of the Indians when faced with the formalities of basic Christian teaching. The Indians were not only doing their best to avoid these sessions or disrupt them but continued to practice the old pagan rituals in their stead. Participation in holy rites, plays, and festivals was an acceptable part of Christianity; religious instruction was not.

Early didactic materials employed by the evangelizers for formal indoctrination of the Indians placed special emphasis on the visual image, especially at a time when language was still an obstacle for communication. One method consisted of rolled cloths (*lienzos*) painted "with pictures of the main mysteries of Our Holy Faith" (Burgoa 1989,

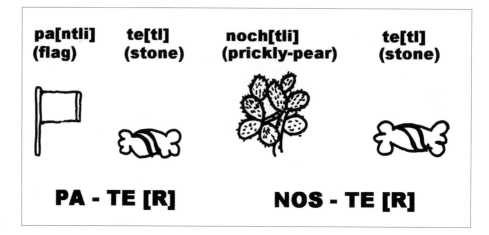

pa[ntli] **te[tl]** **noch[tli]** **te[tl]**
(flag) **(stone)** **(prickly-pear)** **(stone)**

PA - TE [R] **NOS - TE [R]**

Figure 3.1. Imaginary reconstruction of the "pantli-nochtli" writing system devised for the recital of prayers in Latin.

1: 43),[3] the meaning of which was explained through an interpreter (Torquemada 1975–83, 6:268). Reaction to this visual approach was positive, and the Indians soon responded by producing their own pinturas for confession (Mendieta 1973, 1:149; Motolinía 1990: 95). Importantly, they also created a phonetic-rebus system based on traditional native glyphs to help those who were finding difficulty in memorizing and reciting prayers in Latin (Mendieta 1973, 1:149). No examples of this system have survived; but, according to Mendieta, it employed glyphs for Nahuatl words like *pantli* (flag) and *nochtli* (fruit of the prickly-pear cactus), which, together, sounded like *pater noster* (ibid.). In the nineteenth century (from a now lost example) Joseph Aubin clarified Mendieta's description by showing that the reading was made by stringing together first syllables and included the glyph *tetl* (stone) for *pater noster* (fig. 3.1). Thus glyphs for *pa(ntli)-te(tl)-noch(tli)-te(tl)* would yield a more precise phonetic rendering of *pa-te(r)-nos-te(r)* (after Robertson 1959: 53; Glass 1975: 283). Las Casas (1992: 1456) also reported on the combination of "some figure like a spring" (*atl*, "water") with a maguey cactus (*metl*), to read as *a-me* or *amen*. At this early stage, where the friars were limited to using lienzo images as illustrations to enhance an oral explanation, the Indians were transforming European texts into phonetically readable pictographs (even though the end result in Latin probably made little sense to them).

The use of prehispanic glyphs, concepts, and even traditional reading guides was then extended to support an ideographic-mnemonic system based on predominantly Euro-Christian imagery that permitted the recital of prayers and creeds in native languages. Here some of the glyphic inserts were ideographic: for example, rectangles of dash motifs to represent the earth or a rectangle of stylized bones that would read phonetically as "place of the fleshless," the native notion of the underworld (fig. 3.2a). Others were conceptual and of marked prehispanic origin, such as the single feather ball symbolizing sacrifice (Corona Núñez 1989: 41) placed alongside the instruments of Christ's death (fig. 3.2b) or the heart that is the flower (fig. 3.2c). Any native contribution to this particular form of teaching methodology, usually attributed to the Franciscan Jacobo de Testera (Glass 1975: 281), seems to be denied. Yet, while Testera was among the first to use the painted lienzos (Torquemada 1975–83, 6:268) and it is possible that he also invented the teaching system,[4] the picture catechisms were clearly intended to be read as texts. In this respect they are so close to the prehispanic codices in structure and format that it is unlikely that a non-Indian was involved in their initial production (Galarza and Maldonado 1990: 125).[5] They are also far removed from any European equivalent of the day. Although the *Biblia pauperum* contained images for the purposes of preaching and communicating biblical stories in Europe (Anders et al. 1996: 75), prayers were not reproduced in a visual form. In addition, much of the content of the catechisms, especially figures of Indians drinking pulque ("Forgive us our trespasses") or the representations of churches as flowery places (fig. 3.2d), is also original at a graphic level in that it was not copied directly from any formal European source. The earliest examples were very possibly produced by native painter-scribes trained in the prehispanic era, such as those who, according to Juan de Tovar, brought bark-paper to indoctrination classes in order to write down Christian prayers in "figures and signs."[6]

Writing around 1589, Joseph de Acosta (1962: 290) confirmed the native origin of the picture catechisms, while at the same time giving us a hint of the process of transculturation taking place in their creation: "for this method of writing our prayers and matters of the faith was not taught to them by the Spaniards, nor could they [the Indians] have come up with it unless they had had their own specific understanding of what they were taught."[7] Native scribes were thus incorporating Christian attributes, signs, and symbols into their own writing system in accordance with their understanding of the concepts and ideas of Christianity.[8] Tovar's report also implies that they were ad-

Figure 3.2. Examples of native glyphic inserts in the picture catechisms: *a,* the earth and the place of bones or underworld (Humboldt fragment XVI; redrawn from Seler 1904); *b,* sacrificial eagle tuft (ibid.); *c,* flower-hearts or the souls of the dead (ibid.); *d,* the church as a place of flowers (Princeton MS 48; redrawn from Griffin 1968).

hering to their traditional role as scribes of the sacred: writing down the sacred words as they were spoken by the bearers of the Christian sacred knowledge. In this sense, the native scribes were recording the prayers and liturgies of Christianity in the manner of the teoamoxtli, the sacred cosmic books of the Indian world.

Picture catechisms may well have been exploited by the church in New Spain through the eighteenth and nineteenth centuries, when copies of originals were still being made for Mazahua, Otomi, and possibly Mixtec speakers. Until the extant twenty-five examples (see Glass 1975) have all been firmly dated, however, we cannot discard the possibility of a hiatus in their production during the sixteenth century that lasted through the end of the seventeenth century. No examples of painted confessions have survived (the very nature of their content would suggest immediate destruction). But as late as 1569 they were still being accepted in lieu of verbal confessions at Otomi Mixquiahuala (Hidalgo) (*Descripción del arzobispado* 1976: 187), probably as a result of the resident priest's ignorance of the Otomi language.[9] The fate of the didactic lienzos is more difficult to assess, for again no examples have survived. References to their use also imply that they were restricted to the early years, when the number of indoctrination centers was small and the missionary body was still penetrating new areas or itinerant friars were working from village to village. The success of this system in attracting the Indians to Christian teaching cannot have been lost on those friars: with the construction of permanent (that is, stone) churches and monastery complexes, didactic mural painting came to replace them.

One important change in indoctrination methodology suggests that most or all of these portable and visual teaching systems became the focus of ecclesiastical censorship. By 1537 new methods were being employed for the indoctrination of the Indians: specially prepared texts written in Spanish and/or alphabetized Indian languages, called *doctrinas*. The records of the 1537–39 idolatry trial of Carlos Ometochtli cite the accused as having made negative references not only to *cartillas* (primers, from which the alphabet, the Lord's Prayer, the Creed, and so on, were taught) but also to the doctrinas (*Proceso inquisitorial* 1980: 6, 40). With the establishment of the printing press in Mexico after 1539, numerous editions of doctrinas were published by the members of the three main orders and distributed throughout New Spain to regular and secular parishes alike. Extant examples include Pedro de Gante's *Doctrina cristiana en lengua mexicana* (1553);[10] Pedro de Córdoba's *Doctrina cristiana para instrucción y información de los indios por manera de historia* (1545: Córdoba 1945); and Juan de Zumárraga's *Doctrina Cristiana: Más cierta y verdadera para gentes sin erudición y letras* (1546).[11]

As these titles show, emphasis was placed on simplicity of teaching (in the form of stories) and the perceived nature of those who were to learn from them (people without learning and letters). In effect, these and other doctrinas of the period offer only the essentials of Christianity: prayers, the Ten Commandments, the Articles of the Faith, together with stories from the Bible to explain their meaning. Miracles and imagery of the saints are eliminated; the Mysteries of the Faith are not explained; and illustrations, if any, are kept to a minimum. As Zumárraga stipulated in the *Adiciones* to his 1546 doctrinal text, it was intended exclusively for the teachers and not for the direct use of the proselytes, the "least informed" and "most ignorant" of whom could not read (Corcuera de Mancera 1993: 211). A general appraisal of the internal structure of these printed texts also reveals that they were aimed at creating a uniform approach and methodology for the spiritual treatment of the Indians across the three orders (León-Portilla 1986a: 20–21).

These reforms, together with the preparation of the doctrinas, were formalized by the first Mexican Provincial Council in 1555. The council noted that differences in teaching methodology were a source of confusion for the Indians and ratified the elimination of the Mysteries and the "difficult things" (*cosas arduas*) of the Christian faith. The Indians were not able to understand or assimilate them and did not need to for the time being (Lorenzana 1981: 45). But the council also leaned heavily on the hitherto wide Indian participation in the indoctrination program. No further dramatic performances were to be held inside churches.[12] Church doors were to be locked at night to stop the eating, drinking, and dancing taking place there. Inappropriate responses to the Blessing were no longer to be tolerated. All religious images produced by both Indians and Spaniards, including the stories and images painted until that time, were to be placed under official censorship.[13] The numbers and use of musical instruments were to be limited; no further sermons were to be given in Indian languages (because they were not understood or were full of errors and omissions made in translation). Finally, the Indians were never to be given the texts of sermons to translate or even keep in their possession, "so that they cannot falsify or corrupt them" (ibid., pp. 82–83, 91–92, 140–41, 143–44).[14]

Before examining native reaction to these changes, it is important to understand what prompted their introduction in the first place. From the documentation available, it seems clear that Fray Juan de Zumárraga, first bishop of Mexico,[15] was partly instrumental in their instigation and that his actions resulted from a series of incidents that took place toward the end of the 1530s. The first years of Zumárraga's incumbency appeared to pass without incident. In 1531 he reported to the Franciscan General Chapter in Toulouse that all was well; like many of his contemporaries, he found the Indians to be good painters.[16] On his return from a visit to Spain in 1534, Zumárraga busied himself with a series of Indian-related projects, such as the acquisition of grammarians to assist in the learning of native languages and the establishment of the Franciscan Colegio de Tlatelolco in 1536 for the schooling of the Indian elite (Greenleaf 1992: 46; León-Portilla 1992: 54–58). Then things started to go wrong in the field, so to speak. The idolatry trial of Carlos Ometochtli opened in 1537. Zumárraga presided at the trial, which lasted for two years, and was ultimately responsible for the public execution that followed (Greenleaf 1992: 91–92). According to witnesses who were called, the Texcocan noble had openly questioned the Christian faith in relation to the beliefs of his ancestors, urging his people to continue their old practices. In addition, Ometochtli had criticized the inconsistencies in teaching among and between the secular and regular orders (*Proceso inquisitorial* 1980: 6, 40–41). This came at a time when Zumárraga was already preoccupied with the development of a similar attitude among other Indians. In November 1536 he had informed Charles V that in Ocuituco, Zumárraga's own *encomienda* (grant of Indians and tribute), young Indian girls were being secretly handed over as tribute to the caciques, "in accordance with their accursed gentile custom."[17] The caciques were hiding them away in underground locations to keep them from being exposed to Christianity (*DIHM* 1914: 61). In 1537 he reported that young Indian boys were being taken and set aside for the religion of Tezcatlipoca (ibid., p. 494). That same year we find Zumárraga writing to the Spanish Concilio Universal, complaining that many of the Indians did not come to the indoctrination center or do other things that the Christian religion required of them unless they were forced (ibid., p. 68). In undated instructions sent to Fray Juan de Osseguera and Fray Cristóbal de Alamazán for relay to the same council, he also observed: "and now they are learning how to mutter about the sermons and even stop going to listen to them; neither do they go to Mass on feast days except when they feel like it, and they say that they enjoy hearing Mass more in the [secular] clergy's churches, where they are not scolded."[18] "If they are punished in the one school they go to the other, where they speak a thousand false things" (ibid., pp. 492–93).[19]

In short, for the Indians mass was acceptable only on certain feast days.[20] Attendance at sermons was in decline or disruptive, while chastisements in the schools were prompting changes of venue. The Indians, it seems, were willing to continue participating in these activities, but under their own terms. These terms become apparent as Zumárraga continues. To remedy the problem he again recommends that the members of the religious body (that is, both secular and regular priests) should maintain uniformity not only in teaching the doctrine but also in what they permit the Indians to do. Specifically, "some do away with symbols of the devil, others admit them" (*DIHM* 1914: 493).[21]

Thus, between 1537 and 1539, Zumárraga was already identifying a series of fundamental problems in the evangelization program. Many Indians had to be forced to attend the indoctrination center; others were keeping their children away from it or taking advantage of the lack of uniformity in teaching to interpret the newly introduced religion in an erroneous manner. Still worse, some Indians appeared to be questioning the Christian doctrine itself. Ometochtli was a case in point, but the mutterings during sermons indicated to Zumárraga that the problem was not restricted to the outbursts of this man alone. Finally, the graphic imagery adopted by some of the evangelizers to get the Christian message across was evidently linked to the old religion (the "symbols of the devil") to the point that attendance at schools was being determined by the degree of concessions that the priest or friar was willing to offer (or perhaps unwittingly offered) in respect to its use.[22]

By eliminating all but the most carefully censored images in doctrinal teaching, the bishop and his contemporaries clearly hoped to correct the disturbing trend of disruptive or obstinate attitudes that was developing among the Indians in some areas of Christian teaching. In addition, the simplicity and uniformity that the doctrina texts would give to the presentation of the basic tenets of the Christian faith would ensure that teachers were not led into dangerous waters in their attempts to explain its more difficult aspects. And the Indians themselves would not question those teachings with respect to the old religion.

Zumárraga also encountered a problem with Indians who did not live in or in close proximity to an indoctrination center. In the same letter of 1537 to the Concilio Universal, he pointed out that these Indians were scattered all over the mountains, living like wild animals; there were not enough priests available to care for their souls, minister the sacraments, or indoctrinate them. Unless the Indians could be brought together, it would be a long time before Christianity and a civilized lifestyle (*la fe y la policía*) reached them, if ever (*DIHM* 1914: 490).[23]

During Zumárraga's remaining years, and on a minor scale, attempts to bring the Indians into indoctrination centers on a permanent basis were made in the 1530s and again at the beginning of the 1540s. Two major and more wide-reaching campaigns were carried out from 1550 to 1564 and 1593 to 1605 (Gerhard 1977; Torre Villar 1995). Political and economic interests were obviously an important factor in the implementation of what came to be known as the *congregaciones* (congregations). Murmurings of rebellion were always rife, but the Spaniards also wanted more land and a readily available Indian labor force to work it, especially where the workforce available had been depleted by the great epidemic of 1545–48 (Gruzinski 1993: 80).[24] Pressure to congregate also came from the church, however, and here the prime motivation was to save the conversion program. Writing to the king on this matter in May 1550, Motolinía was unhesitant in pointing out that the religious body did not know what else it could do to instruct the Indians properly in the ways of God if they could not be brought together in villages (*DIHM* 1914: 166).

Resistance on the part of the Indians was strong. In a letter dated February 7, 1554, to the Habsburg heir, Philip, viceroy Luis de Velasco explained that, since His Majesty had given the Indians liberty to chose where they could live, "to get out of the work of moving their homes to the newly laid-out villages, and so as not to be near the monasteries and churches, and in order to conceal their weaknesses [of the flesh], which are many, they are going to villages lying outside [areas of] indoctrination and conversion" (*DIHM* 1914: 204).[25] An order from Velasco for the return of the Indians to the village of Ixtepexi (Oaxaca) in March 1559 reiterated the same problem, although this time it concerned those already living in an established community: "many of the naturals and commoners of said village have gone away and absented themselves from it in other parts in order not to come together in congregation or civility or learn the Christian doctrine and be shown the way in the matters of our Holy Catholic Faith" (*Epistolario* 1939–42, 8:230).[26]

Clearly, the task of moving to a center located relatively close to the Indians' original habitat would require much less effort than moving out of a Christianized area altogether. Other factors may have been at work here, such as awareness on the part of the Indians that living in close communities was an unhealthy option. High mortality rates resulting from the epidemics would also mean extra pressure from Spanish civilians to satisfy labor and tribute demands. Kinship, ethnic identity, and age-old ties to the land and its sacred entities may have been further issues. Both examples, however, make it apparent that Velasco understood native obstinacy to be linked to the indoctrination program, and we have little reason to doubt his assessment. Ties to the land and fear of disease certainly were not the reasons for the moves noted in his first letter: here the Indians were moving away from their homes to live in other villages.

Against such resistance, the Crown was obliged to resort to brute force: farms were abandoned and Indian dwellings burnt to the ground (Gerhard 1977: 352; Gruzinski 1993: 122). Under these circumstances most Indians were left with no choice but to comply with the new system.

While these programs were by no means comprehensive, the first major campaign almost exclusively involved the creation of congregaciones around monastic centers run by one of the three regular orders present in New Spain at the time.[27] It was followed almost immediately by more calls to congregate, this time from the secular clergy. Entries in the 1570 compilation *Descripción del arzobispado de México* (1976) show that the secular camp was also experiencing difficulties with the Indians' attitudes to indoctrination. For example, the resident priest at Temazcaltepec (México), who traveled around outlying villages to indoctrinate, reported on the futility of the effort, for the Indians returned to their old ways as soon as he had moved on (ibid., p. 75). Indians living some three miles from Hueypuxtla (México) were not coming to church and refused to bring their children to be indoctrinated (ibid., p. 89). In neighboring Tequixquiac (México) the incumbent did not even dare to punish absenteeism for fear that the Indians would cut off his food supplies (ibid., p. 70).

Such reactions on the part of the Indians must be seen as quite extraordinary if we consider that in 1570 the Archbishopric of Mexico was in no way an area of uncharted waters in the spread of Christianity. More specifically, Hueypuxtla and Tequixquiac were still quite heavily populated communities lying close to the capital. Their inhabitants had been exposed to Christianity almost from the start; indeed, if they were expected to attend church services, they must also have been baptized. It is worth considering that a generation earlier other Indians also living in communities around Mexico City had actually expressed a preference for secular mass and had attended the same schools, albeit under their own terms. Thirty years later neither was an acceptable option.

The secular clergy also found themselves up against the problem of what they believed to be idolatrous activities among the Indians, especially when they were out of the range of supervision. Possibly worse, as the report (ca. 1569) from the priest at Tepozotlan (México) revealed, some Indians were celebrating their own Christian festivals in the many tiny churches and chapels scattered around the countryside and in an improper manner (*Descripción del arzobispado* 1976: 84). In sum, although the secular clergy's interest in congregation may have had other motives (competition within the church, for example, or personal gain through increased commodity tribute), the general consensus of opinion was that idolatry would cease if the Indians could be properly indoctrinated. And to achieve this the Indians had to be brought together.[28]

That view suggests that calls to congregate on the part of the secular clergy were motivated by positive results in respect to indoctrination and the elimination of unacceptable activities achieved within the congregaciones of the regular orders. This does not appear to have been the case. In 1556 (albeit as a direct attack on the regular orders) Zumárraga's successor, Alonso de Montúfar, had already complained that under the friars a great number of Indians barely knew the articles of the faith and the prayers of the church. An equally large number did not know them at all. Others repeated them parrot-fashion (*como papagayos*) and (echoing Zumárraga's own words), when questioned on their content, spoke a thousand heresies (*responden mil heregias*) (*Descripción del arzobispado* 1976: 426).

By 1565, and as part of a petition from the six bishops of New Spain to the Royal Audiencia of Mexico, we can see that even the recent congregations had not resolved the issue of persisting idolatry. Pagan practices were rife in both regular and secular communities: "as the Audiencia is well aware with what ease these Indians newly converted to our holy Catholic faith return to their idolatries, rites, sacrifices, and superstitions, and commit many and varied instances of heresy, and in order to purge these, we have great need of an overseer in each village to uncover such evils, without whom neither the preachers nor our curates, priests, or friars can uncover them" (*DIHM* 1914: 285).[29]

The situation at the end of the 1560s can be summed up as follows: noncongregated Indians were avoiding indoctrination; congregated Indians were still not indoctrinated; and both groups were pursuing native religious practices within their communities as well as without. Something had gone very wrong since the halcyon days of the first conversions, and it was affecting the whole of New Spain. Letters and reports such as those cited above do not arise from a few isolated complaints. "Idolatry," as the colonial authorities identified it, had returned with force to the villages and also had spread into the newly congregated areas. Despite careful supervision, it was operating under the very noses of the priests and friars, who were at a loss to know how it was being maintained. Clearly, however, the expense and upheavals of yet another congregation program would be pointless. What was needed was a witch-hunt.

Church-Building and the Second Congregations

In stark contrast to this dismal situation, the Indians did not lose interest in their churches. At the time when the lack of indoctrination and the resurgence of idolatry were being discussed, some from New Spain's religious fraternity were also document-ing the enthusiasm with which the Indians were building the—often enormous and architecturally complex—symbols of the new religion. Others recorded the same phe-nomenon in their later histories. Juan de Grijalva (1985: 113), for example, boasted that the Augustinian monastery complex at Epazoyucan (Hidalgo) had been completed in

TABLE 3.1

Recorded building activity at monastery sites, 1520–1620

Decade	Franciscan Order	Augustinian Order	Dominican Order	Total
1520–1530	5	0	1	6
1530–1540*	26	6	3	35
1540–1550*	22	14	4	40
1550–1560	21	21	9	51
1560–1570	27	17	12	56
1570–1580*	32	14	16	62
1580–1590*	26	5	7	38
1590–1600	10	4	6	20
1600–1610	13	9	2	24
1610–1620	2	5	1	8

* = An epidemic occurred in this decade.

Source: summarized from Kubler 1992: 66–70.

seven months and seven days, such was the eagerness of the Indians to build it. Mendieta (1973, 1:192) observed that, as the evangelization proceeded, "[i]f the monastery was not built, they did not delay in doing it [according] to the form and plan asked of them. And the speed with which they finished it was a wonderful thing, being of strong and firm stone, and they hardly took half a year."[30] Toward the end of his chronicle he exclaimed: "[W]ho but the Indians have built so many churches and monasteries as the religious have in this New Spain, with their own hands and sweat, and with the same will and joy as they built houses for themselves and their children, and begging the friars to let them construct larger ones?" (ibid., 2:45).[31] Even unfavorable working conditions did not detract from the task. In prehispanic times laborers had been provided with food and tools, but the colonial period saw the *coatequitl* (labor call-up system) transformed into a serious form of exploitation. In addition to labor, the Indians were obliged to contribute to construction costs and (as confirmed by a 1555 *Acta de cabildo*) provide themselves with food. Only in 1576 did the colonial authorities order that each village cultivate land in order to feed laborers on building projects such as palaces, churches, and monasteries (Reyes García 1979; Peterson 1993: 18–19).

Table 3.1 offers a summary of George Kubler's (1992: 66–70) listings of building activities at monastic sites between 1520 and 1620. The registered peak between 1560 and 1580 might suggest that the 1550 to 1564 congregaciones did, after all, serve to promote Indian acceptance of Christianity. Not all the monastic complexes under construction up to 1580 were included in that program, however. In addition, we should consider that hundreds—possibly thousands—of smaller, parish or visita churches and chapels were also built to serve both the regular and secular branches of the colonial church.[32] Congregated or not, and idolatrous or not, the Indians were still building their churches everywhere.

On the basis of his original listings Kubler pointed out that, paradoxically, the greatest surges in building came at a time when the Indian population was in drastic decline as a result of the epidemics of 1545–48 and 1576–81 (Kubler 1992: 60–65). He attributed this to psychological factors in that a diseased society has the effect of heightening the social conscience of a community, which, when faced with a common danger, affirms all symbols and rituals of social experience with renewed vehemence. Religious behavior suddenly assumes new and ecstatic forms of singular extravagance (ibid., pp. 57–58). If this is true, then we might also expect traditional native religious practices—frequently routed toward death and sickness (see Gruzinski 1993: 156)—to have been renewed as a response to the epidemics. Indeed, this seems to have been the case: their resurgence (at least as noted) in the mid-1530s appears to have coincided with a deadly outbreak of measles recorded for 1531. Noticeably, this date also corresponds to the greatest surge of all in Christian building activities: from work at six sites to work at thirty-five.

Church-building and the persistence of native religious practices followed a fairly even course until about 1580, when the building of churches entered into abrupt decline. The impact of the 1576–81 epidemic, followed by another in 1588,[33] evidently proved to be just too much: the momentum of Indian church-building was lost forever. But if the accumulative effect of sickness and death over some fifty years had finally crushed the religious spirit to build, it also appears to have halted non-Christian religious activities at the same time. As we shall see, these activities went underground for a period, only to reemerge at the beginning of the seventeenth century in a rather different form. Thus no continuing link exists between church-building and epidemics; much stronger is the relationship between church-building and native religious practices.

Other explanations for the extraordinary architectural achievements between 1530 and 1580 are based on the intensity of the evangelization program after 1530 (Cuevas 1946; Borges 1960; McAndrew 1965; Kubler 1992; Ricard 1994). This may also have been the case, although the program (intense or not) had not been without problems, as we have seen. Such an argument also assumes that the phenomenon of building occurred exclusively as a result of Spanish action or colonially induced circumstances. Put another way, Indian thought processes had nothing to do with the decision to build except to acknowledge Christianity as a welcome, or inescapable, fact. Yet over the same period the Indians were clearly making ongoing decisions regarding indoctrination and attendance at mass. These were not attractive activities for them; building churches was.

A more convincing explanation comes from James Lockhart (1992), for whom the attraction of church-building, at least among the Nahuas of central Mexico, can be attributed to the continuing sociopolitical importance of the prehispanic altepetl system, which had been appropriated by the colonial machine to facilitate its own geopolitical organization. Derived from the dual Nahua metaphor *in atl in tepetl,* "the water, the mountain," and registered graphically as such in toponymic glyphs (see fig. 4.4),[34] the altepetl initially defined an organization of people holding sway over a given territory. An altepetl could be of any size and consist of one political entity or a confederation; in the latter case, a dominant-subordinate hierarchy of individual altepetl gave the grouping its structure (Lockhart 1992: 14–28). After the destruction of the prehispanic temples, the church became the "central tangible symbol" of the altepetl's sovereignty and identity. The Indians would not be satisfied until each community had an edifice equivalent to that of its neighbors to represent their polity and enable them to hold up their heads when dealing with other towns (ibid., pp. 206, 421). The acknowledgment of an independent native response to the church-building program is a welcome advance on previous views, but it nevertheless suggests that the altepetl as a symbol and as a system had no religious projections and therefore that church-building had none either.

The sudden decline in religious building activities is acknowledged by most as a result of not only decreased native populations but also haphazard economic arrangements and the termination of the special dispensation accorded to the regular orders and, with it, increasing pressures of secularization (McAndrew 1965: 86–90; Weismann 1985: 38; Manrique 1990: 240; Kubler 1992: 63). This last point, however, only confirms the waning influence of the regular orders in New Spain, not the overall decline in building that occurred. Once again, none of these explanations affords the Indians a role in the decision to stop building either.

The second congregations program at the end of the century was characterized by even fiercer resistance on the part of the Indians as well as a distinct reluctance to build churches. Widespread secular congregation commenced during the early years of the 1590s and lasted until about 1605. The Indian population's determination not to submit was such that hundreds of small communities and their churches were wiped off the map (Gruzinski 1993: 122; Torre Villar 1995: 32), while order upon order was sent out between 1592 and 1599 to bring back escapees.[35] And this was at a time when labor laws had long since changed in the Indians' favor, the last epidemic had died out some five years earlier, and the exploitation of the encomienda system (abolished in 1542 on succession of two generations) was no longer a threat.[36] Even the opportunity to rebuild their churches at congregation sites using the rubble from the old churches appears not to have been an attractive proposition.[37] We see this, for example, in an order of 1592 that the Indians of Tamiahua (Veracruz) return to their center and rebuild their church (AGN, *Indios*, vol. 6: 2, exp. 515). The justification for congregation on the part of the church was again the continuing idolatry and the need for indoctrination.[38] Such reasoning appears groundless, given the noted failure in both areas during the first major campaign, unless a solution had been found along the way that now made congregation a viable option. This suggests that the roots of idolatry—understood by the colonial authorities as the main obstacle facing the indoctrination program—had at last been uncovered and steps taken to dig them up and destroy them forever.

Indoctrination and the Building of Churches

The apparent contradictions that exist between early native acceptance of Christianity and subsequent avoidance or rejection of indoctrination, combined with a simultaneous period of enthusiastic church-building and the sudden decline in building activities after 1580, can in part be explained by the relationship of all these activities to one fundamental aspect of the native world: ritual and the image as the basis of religious expression.

Where "art" (in all its forms) and religion represented a constant and inseparable element of prehispanic life, ritual and the image were the means through which religious belief was explained. Together, they served to acknowledge the presence of the sacred forces that had created and were continually re-creating the native world. The unquestioned omnipresence of the sacred maintained the spiritual link between humans and between humans and the cosmic powers. Where the Indian being was understood to be a part of the great cycles of time and nature, the sacred also penetrated every aspect of what Westerners understand to be the secular and material worlds. For this reason, no part of the day could be released from ceremonialism (Gruzinski 1993: 16–17; León-Portilla 1996: 188–89; Taylor 1996: 49; Burkhart 1998: 361), however outwardly unpretentious it might be.[39]

I believe that the coincidence of dates between the rise and fall of intensive building activities (1530 and 1580, respectively) and two developments that marked watersheds in the evangelization program pertained directly to the ongoing importance of ritual and the image as a guiding force in native life. They also concerned the overriding issue of what the ecclesiastical authorities still understood to be persisting idolatrous practices from the 1530s onward.

The 1530s witnessed the start of a noticeable native trend of selectivity toward certain elements of the Christian package. Above all, two aspects stand out. Scolding and punishment were prompting changes of venue to indoctrination centers where—we understand—misinterpretations (Zumárraga's "thousand false things") were tolerated. The content of sermons was being questioned or ignored altogether. At the same time, use of unorthodox imagery (those "symbols of the devil") to explain the Christian doctrine was determining Indians' choice of school. These reactions should not be seen as early difficulties with the indoctrination program, for, as noted, the evangelization of the heavily populated central area had been in operation for over ten years by 1537. If schools were established, then the Indians had obviously attended them at some stage. Sermons were not of recent introduction either and had been popular. As Mendieta (1973, 2:124) observed, in the early years the Indians would complain if a sermon was not given. Now they were complaining about their content (*ya aprenden a murmurar*). Besides, the Indians had also happily embraced other Christian activities (the processions, the autos, church-building) and continued to do so.

Zumárraga offers no clue as to what prompted native disaffection for the sermons, but the reason could be one of several. Perhaps, as the outspoken cacique of Texcoco had observed with regard to Christianity in general, their content was not proving spiritually satisfying or theologically acceptable. The dictates of the 1555 Provincial Council, however, tend to echo Zumárraga's earlier preoccupations and reforms in other areas: uniformity of teaching methodology; specially written, simplified doctrinas; censorship and supervision of religious imagery. It therefore seems safe to assume that the council's observations on the subject of sermons in Indian languages respond to the same source. As translated by both Indians and non-Indians, their content was full of errors and omissions.

In addition, and as Zumárraga had also recommended with respect to the doctrinas, the Indians should not have direct access to the texts of the sermons. They were, the council stated, falsifying and corrupting their content (Lorenzana 1981: 143–44). Here the council may be referring to the early missionary appropriation of Nahua terminology to explain basic Christian dogma. Given the poor equivalents that this strategy offered in conceptual terms, it was doomed to backfire (cf. Burkhart 1989: 28–45). As Burkhart also points out, the adoption of these linguistic tropes was done in a reduced and simplified manner. Many figures of speech were rarely—if ever—used, thus probably rendering the friars' sermons and teachings monotonous or repetitive and far removed from the richness of the ancient *huehuetlahtolli* oral mode (ibid., p. 190). But we are also reminded of the 1555 council's objections to "inappropriate responses" to the Blessing (Lorenzana 1981: 83). If the Indians were also scolded for making similar responses during sermons, then it was their participation that was effectively denied. The same, of course, had been true with the degree and manner of participation permitted in the early indoctrination schools and with the type of visual imagery used there. If either of these had not met with the Indians' expectations, they had decamped to another school. In other words, by attempting to dictate the procedural methodology of indoctrination, the Indians were ensuring, on the one hand, that they could participate and, on the other, that meaningful imagery was evoked.

I therefore see the change in native attitudes toward indoctrination after the introduction of the written doctrinas as a response to the denial of native participation and the elimination or censorship of the image as a didactic tool. Access to the new teaching texts was restricted to teachers. Even if some sort of reply was expected from a congregation, this could only have been repetition, for the texts do not call for opinions or answers and indeed were deliberately written to avoid prompting. Perhaps more importantly, the Indians were not even permitted to see the sacred words, much less read them and ponder over them as they had done with the picture versions. Thus, if the Indians received no visual stimulus or could not join in, they lost interest completely. This is not an entirely speculative argument, for in 1570 the Franciscans proposed (albeit unsuccessfully) a return to indoctrination by pictures on the grounds that those who had been taught under this method understood Christianity better (*Códice franciscano* 1941: 59–61). They apparently did understand the importance of the image for indigenous communication and learning.[40]

While the changes in indoctrination procedures took place formally with the dictates of the 1555 council, it is clear that they were in operation before that time. The first publication of the alphabetized doctrinas that facilitated a wide distribution of the new material was in 1539. Zumárraga, however, had clearly decided to take action in this direction before the end of the 1530s, and Ometochtli's references to what must have been handwritten prototypes confirm that the system was also in use in some areas around the same time. With the majority of Indians now not in a position to ritualize an indoctrination session, complete avoidance of the session seemed the better option. Some Indians, as we have seen, refused to attend outright, but evidence suggests that others sought to justify their absence in other ways.

In 1533 the friar ministering to the Suchimilcatzingo area (Morelos) complained that the Indians spent so much of their time quarrying and transporting great quantities of stone to Mexico City (where the marqués del Valle's rebuilding program was in full swing) that they were not even able to tend their own plots properly. This, quite naturally, was also interfering with their indoctrination into the faith (*DIHM* 1914: 48). In 1539, during his trial for idolatry, Cristóbal of Ocuituco stated that he had not been to confession since he was baptized for the simple reason that he had been too busy collecting and delivering tributes for his encomendero (*Procesos de indios* 1912: 141–75). The encomendero in question was Zumárraga. A similar excuse was recorded some three decades later when the local priest in the *cabecera* (head town of a district) of Tlalchichilpa (México) observed that the Indians were getting no indoctrination. Part of the problem was their scattered mountain dwellings, but they were also spending too much time collecting tribute for the encomendero and making "vino con raíces" (wine with roots) (*Descripción del arzobispado* 1976: 157).

The "wine with roots" to which the priest referred was of course octli (pulque), the fermented sap of the maguey, to which the hallucinogenic root *ocpactli* was added to fortify it and make the imbiber very drunk (*HM* 1979: 107; Nicholson 1991: 160). This type of pulque was specifically for ritual use. While it might well have been difficult to get time off from labor obligations to Spanish civilians to attend indoctrination classes, it seems that the Indians of Tlalchichilpa still found time to pursue ritual activities of a traditional nature.[41] If Cristóbal of Ocuituco was practicing the old rituals and at the same time fulfilling his labor obligations, then the Indians of Suchimilcatzingo might also have been occupied in pursuits other than contributing to the Spaniards' building program or attending to their plots. Motolinía (1990: 22), always to the point where the less than helpful attitudes of Spanish civilians toward the conversion program were concerned, complained: "In all the temples of the idols, if not in the burned and ruined ones of Mexico, in those of the countryside, and even in Mexico [City] itself, the devils were served and honored. The Spaniards, occupied with building Mexico and in making houses and homes for themselves, were reconciled that no public human sacrifices took place in front of them, which in secret and on the outskirts of Mexico were not lacking."[42]

These examples imply that, even though the Indians may have had no choice but to perform building or labor tasks, they still found time for their own ritual activities in preference to Christian indoctrination. Priorities had been established, and indoctrination came at the bottom of the list. Labor, it seems, was also more attractive than indoctrination for other reasons.

The rebuilding of Tenochtitlan commenced in 1522, a year after the consolidation of the political conquest. Under the direction of Ixtlilxochitl of Texcoco and the *cihuacoatl* (the administrative and judicial "snake woman" of the old Mexica capital), the ancient hierarchical call-up system of the *coatequitl* was mobilized to this effect (Kubler 1992: 75). Given the still-recognized authority of these Indian leaders, compliance on the part of the building crews would not have been at question. Nonetheless, labor in the prehispanic period had also been a ritually defined occupation, like everything else. The divisions of the work units alone conformed to the multiples of the sacred calendars.[43] We also cannot assume that the native concept of work as a ritual occupation automatically changed to the European concept of work as an unadorned necessity (see Kubler 1992: 54–55). It is clear that during the rebuilding of Mexico-Tenochtitlan the Indians were ritualizing their activities: "it is their custom to go singing and shouting, and the songs and voices hardly ceased night and day, with the great fervor that they put into the building of the town in the first years" (Motolinía 1990: 16).[44]

Later the Indians also gave voice to the new Spanish city of Puebla: "eight thousand Indians came . . . to lay out the ground plan of the new settlement . . . they came with such joy and delight at the new Catholic foundation with a variety of musical instruments, dancing and singing" (Vetancurt 1971, "Tratado de la Ciudad de la Puebla de los Angeles, y grandezas que la iluftran," f. 46).[45]

Elements of ritualization were also maintained in the area of specialized crafts. During Fray Alonso Ponce's tour of the Franciscan establishments of New Spain in the early 1580s, the metal workers and masons of Acambaro (Guanajuato) showed the important visitor how they worked to the sound of drums (Ciudad Real 1976, 2:69). Kubler (1992: 158–59) himself cited examples of ritualization of public building, noting—significantly—that activities and invocations were nevertheless directed toward the Christian supernatural.

Other types of labor for Spanish civilians—in both tribute and kind—were also heavily imposed. The numerous complaints in the 1570 *Descripción del arzobispado* (1976) regarding drunkenness among country- and city-dwelling Indians alike might suggest that life under the encomienda and later repartimiento systems became so demanding that they sought a psychological escape route. Despite its prohibition on the part of the church, civil law did not deny the Indians access to alcohol (and in the cities they could drink in their own pulque houses). But such access also facilitated ritual drunkenness. Increased consumption of alcohol in the sixteenth century probably resulted from the complete breakdown of prehispanic sumptuary laws. Linked to this, however, is the continuation of traditional rituals, where devotion was measured by the degree of intoxication. As William B. Taylor (1979: 35–39) has argued, Spanish accounts of alcohol abuse on the part of the Indians after the conquest do, in fact, mostly imply that it took place during ritual feasting.

Spanish civilians undoubtedly exploited Indian labor to a maximum; but Zumárraga's letters on the subject make it evident that a method lay behind their excessive demands. In 1533 he complained to Charles V that a certain Juan Peláez was "giving permission to the Indians to sacrifice, and taking them from the monastery and Christian doctrine . . . and ordering them to work on feast days" (*DIHM* 1914: 41).[46] In 1537 he informed the Concilio Universal that "the Spaniards permit the Indians [to carry out] heathen rites and cults of idolatry for the interest they hope [to gain] from them" (ibid., p. 68).[47] Aware that the Indians would work more productively if they were permitted to ritualize their work in some way, the Spaniards were actively encouraging these activities. It seems possible that some of them even participated in such rites. Folio 239r of Codex Tlaxcala, for example, depicts two Spaniards witnessing a heart sacrifice. Rather than showing the disapproval we might expect, they stand quietly by, holding a ritually decapitated quail in their own hands (Brotherston 1995: 42–43). Human sacrifice during encomienda labor seems most unlikely, although animal sacrifice and other activities judged by the colonial church to be offensive to God obviously did occur. Certainly, in the sixteenth-century "those that haul wood from the mountain or stones from the quarries, the laborers and travelers, mixed idolatrous rituals in the things of their work" (La Serna 1892: 25).[48] By the seventeenth century metaphorical references to European farm animals had become part of native ritual *conjuros,* "incantations" (Gruzinski 1993: 158). It is perhaps not too difficult to understand how the well-being of the sixteenth-century encomendero's sheep, cattle, or wheat fields would have prompted the early weaving of such spells.

Intensive mining appears to have been the form of enforced labor that caused greatest physical and mental distress among the Indian population. Alcoholism was indeed rife and was probably the outcome of abject despair. Alonso de Zorita (1993: 138) described how the Indians had struggled under the weight of heavy metal equipment and their terror in not being able to complete the assigned tasks.[49] In addition, in prehispanic times gold was not mined from its deep mountain veins, for these were perceived as the urine of the earth (FC11, 1963: 233). Gold came with the rain, washed into river sands, where it lay waiting to be panned (ibid.). "I excavate gold. I pulverize sand. I wash sand. I blow sand. I wash gold. I purify sand" (ibid., p. 234). Gold was a gift of the divine, made available to humans at its will. Reflecting their instigators' thirst for the end product, European mining systems would not have tolerated the reverential ritualization of the collection of divine waste. For the Indians, the act of digging gold out of the earth mother's body was probably also felt to be disturbingly profane. Alcohol or death was the only means of escape from such misery. Of direct interest in Zorita's commentary, however, is one curious remark. Duped into believing that they would be occupied in construction work (that is, ritualized occupation), many went voluntarily to the mines. Once there, they were promptly seconded to the mining crews (ibid.). Thus Spanish civilians also noted native willingness to construct edifices and took advantage of it in the usual underhanded way.

It can therefore be argued that absence from indoctrination classes may not have been motivated entirely by lack of choice on the part of the Indians. If building and agricultural labor were ritually definable, then they were preferable to what we might call the "waste of sacred time" that indoctrination supposed.

It is through an understanding of the native compulsion for ritualized occupation that we can also begin to see the Indians' particular interest in church-building. As table 3.1 shows, the initial intensity of building occurred shortly after 1530, when the new methods of indoctrination were being introduced. The surge after the implementation of the first congregations program coincides with the curb on nonacceptable ritual activities taking place outside religious communities that it entailed. Under the constant supervision of the friars and the priests and their nonparticipatory, nonvisual indoctrination sessions, little ritual stimulation could be found, whether Christian or otherwise.

Together with the devout cleaning, tending, and deployment of so many floral and other ritualized tributes that the churches or their deity appeared to inspire, the act of building the churches, at times "begging the friars to let them construct larger ones" (Mendieta 1973, 2:45), was one aspect of the Christian package that the Indians embraced wholeheartedly. The enthusiasm to build was also matched by the effort to decorate these edifices by means of sculpture and mural painting. These had been highly ritualized occupations in prehispanic times. Their product served not only to enhance ceremonial architecture visually but also to interpret it (Lockhart 1992: 419). And sixteenth-century Indian artists were also to leave their interpretive mark on the churches of New Spain.

Church-Building and the "Symbols of the Devil"

Writing around 1596, Mendieta (1973, 1:61) commented that some of the native elders still followed the named ritual periods of the old calendar: "And they have painted them in some parts; and in particular in the entrance of the monastery of Cuauhtinchan [Puebla] is painted a memory [aid] of the ancient count that they had, with these characters or signs full of superstition. And it was not correct to let them paint it; neither is it correct that that painting remains, nor that the said characters are painted anywhere else, but that they totally forget them."[50]

The importance of this passage—unique among the chronicles inasmuch as a specific set of prehispanic symbols is identified—is that it appears to confirm the suspicions of continuing idolatry voiced by the colonial authorities while at the same time pointing to the execution of similar motifs on other religious buildings of the same period (Reyes-Valerio 1989a: 75–76, 2000: 434–35). At the level of native interpretation of Christian architecture, however, it also tells us that the ancient calendar, the most fundamental of ritually associated images, had not been considered by Cuauhtinchan artists and the town's elders to be out of place on the walls of a Christian structure.

The tonalpohualli (260-day count) at Cuauhtinchan was certainly erased,[51] and to date no further traditionally executed examples of a native ritual count have been uncovered elsewhere on church architecture. Mendieta (1973, 1:61) implies that the Cuauhtinchan version had been approved at some stage ("it was not correct to let them paint it"), and evidence suggests that it was Mendieta or one of his fellow friars who actually gave the go-ahead. On the orders of the 1558 Franciscan chapter held at Huejotzingo (Puebla), Mendieta was charged with the establishment of a permanent Franciscan community at Cuauhtinchan. In addition to laying out the new *traza* (the Spanish-imposed, grid-iron street plan) of the cabecera and its *sujetos* (towns or villages subordinate to the cabecera), "he built a pleasing monastery."[52] Fray Francisco de Las Navas drew up the center's *Ordenanzas* in 1559 (Reyes García 1972) and, significantly, was later to write a study in defense of the native calendar and its signs. Thus the painted version may already have been the subject of some criticism. Indeed, Sahagún (1981, 1:371–72) reproduced Las Navas's text in the appendix to Book 4 of his *Historia general* and vehemently attacked his argument: with a count of only 260 days, this was obviously not a calendar but an aid used in the art of divination and contained "many idolatrous things, and many superstitions and many invocations of devils" (ibid., pp. 370, 372–73).[53] From this chronology we can perhaps deduce that the 260-day count was not seen as a threat to the evangelization program in some quarters, even at the end of the 1550s. Like its 360-day counterpart, it may well have been considered a secular tool. Sahagún's ethnohistorical research (from the late 1550s onward), however, had shown that the Indians' tonalpohualli was a religious tool, closely associated with the rituals and beliefs of old. At the end of the century Mendieta remembered, or was informed, that the same calendar was painted on the walls of Christian edifices.

The start of a serious purge of native imagery in general is illustrated by an account in the 1580 *Relación de Atlatlaucca y Malinaltepeque* (Oaxaca). "Ancient things" were being depicted in pinturas (here in the sense of pictographs painted on paper or animal hide), and the offending items had been "taken away from them [the Indians] because it was understood that, having them, they held the same rites and ceremonies as before" (Acuña 1984b: 49).[54] In other words, the Indians of this region had retained or rewritten a prehispanic ritual guide (probably also containing a tonalpohualli) until about 1580, at which point the colonial authorities realized that this was the reason why idolatrous rituals had persisted. It must have come as an even greater shock to discover that this same imagery had also been painted on the walls of Christian churches, but the roots of continuing idolatry were at last uncovered.

The identification and destruction of "idolatrous" imagery on the walls of sixteenth-century churches was recorded most forcefully in the 1656 writings of the secular priest Jacinto de la Serna (1892). His lengthy text on the activities of the Indians in his own day nevertheless referred back to native building activities in the previous century and how—as he saw it—those activities had also provided a means of preserving the old beliefs:

> [F]or all these things [the preservation of rituals and beliefs] it was a great help to them to have placed many of these idols as the foundations, and bases of the pillars of the cathedral, and in other houses to decorate them, and what was done just to strengthen the buildings and houses, and for street ornamentation, there were also [idols] there [in the streets] . . . and those that are on the tops of houses, and in the streets, are so that all may be preserved, where they idolatrized and made their invocations to them. (La Serna 1892: 24)[55]

La Serna is here referring to the small carved stones embedded in sixteenth-century architecture, ostensibly for the purposes of ornamentation (these are the subject of chapter 5). In addition, he mentions the larger pieces of prehispanic masonry, which, as Motolinía (1990: 22–23) also describes, were drawn from the demolished pyramid temples and reused for the foundations or other architectural features of Christian structures. Many examples of this type can still be seen today, but it is difficult to categorize them as mere rubble. At Huaquechula (Puebla) a ball-court ring was dragged several hundred yards from its prehispanic site (now beneath the monastery orchard to the extreme southeast of the huge complex—custodian, Huaquechula, pers. comm., 1991). It was embedded at ground level into the north wall of the monastery church (fig. 3.3a). Two equally large pieces of carved prehispanic masonry accompany it. The carvings on these stones are intact, as if each was cut away from its original location with care. In addition, the symmetry of their emplacement (at almost equal distances from each other and at either side of and between the two central wall buttresses) suggests a considered relocation. These stones may also, of course, have been accepted as either wall supports or ornamental detail.

Less "decorative" in projection is the relief carving of a jaguar, which had lain hidden behind the top of the facade of the monastery church at Totomiahuacan (Puebla) until the progressive decay of the edifice finally released its rump and tail at the end of the twentieth century (fig. 3.3b). The patterning of its pelt is identical to a small, three-dimensional sculpture of a jaguar that today stands on the remains of the atrium gateway. Clearly, jaguars were of some importance at prehispanic Totomiahuacan and were salvaged for colonial posterity. Bas-reliefs of the earth monster, Quilaztli-Tlaltecuhtli, can also be found on the underside of the bases of colonial stone columns (see Matos Moctezuma 1990a: 255, 1990b: 128), corresponding exactly to the traditional positioning of the image on such monumental sculptures as that of the great Coatlicue, for example. This suggests that pieces of sculpture similar to the surviving Coatlicue were also specifically selected by Indian builders to cut the bases of stone columns.

According to La Serna (1892), the revelation in the late sixteenth century that carvings taken from prehispanic buildings were still of interest to the Indians and therefore had to be related to idolatrous activities taking place around the church prompted not only a purge of the offending stonework but also the second main congregations program at the end of the century. If the roots of native idolatry had not been exposed by the first congregations program, the situation was now very different: they had at last been detected—and on the very walls of Indian-built streets and churches. La Serna (1892: 24) is very specific that the discovery of the offensive architectural details was the motivating factor behind the second main program: "for all this, the total remedy seemed to be that of the gatherings and congregations of the villages, as was done."[56] And with the congregaciones the triumphant extirpation of the roots of idolatry was imminent. The purgers smashed the stones, chipped away at them, and removed them from the places where they had been put, "either by chance, or through the malice of the same Indians who built the churches and houses, and put them there deliberately to honor them" (ibid., p. 27).[57]

Although La Serna does not give details about where the campaign of destruction took place, it could not have reached every village or indoctrination center across New Spain, for much remains today.[58] The inadequate knowledge of prehispanic symbolism at that time must have been a distinct drawback. And, if ever appointed, the village overseers who were requested by the bishops of New Spain to seek out idolatry would have needed to have been wholly converted Indians who at this late date were still able to identify those symbols for what they were. Other examples were probably not immediately obvious, in that their host stones were hidden from view (like the example at Totomiahuacan) or were inserted in unobvious places or their carvings were ambiguous in meaning.

a

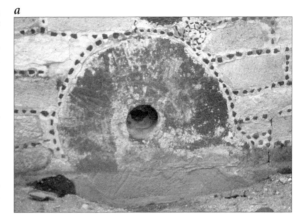

b

Figure 3.3. Two examples of the reuse of prehispanic masonry and sculpture: *a*, ball-court ring, north wall of the monastery church, San Martín Huaquechula, Puebla; *b*, jaguar rump, ex-facade of the monastery church, San Francisco Totomiahuacan, Puebla.

La Serna (1892) makes no direct reference to the formal decorative sculpture that the Indians had also taken such an active part in producing. Just as many extant examples of reused stones escaped the purge, however, examples of traditional motifs carved on facades and portals (the main areas of external architectural sculpture) still remain. Unlike mural painting, sculpture did not come under the censorship of the Provincial Councils until 1585 (Kubler 1992: 436 and n. 12). The omission suggests to me that until that date most of it had been perceived as exclusively decorative (indeed there are comparatively few examples of relief or three-dimensional sculptures of Christian themes or figures on church architecture) and would therefore not have been scrutinized very carefully, if at all. Any anomalies in this type of iconography simply had not been noticed or recognized until the 1580s. Religious mural painting was heavily thematic, however. In addition, strict guidelines governed religious representation at that time. Early censorship directed by the 1555 council at both Spanish- and Indian-executed works was therefore probably not so much concerned with possible inserts of an idolatrous nature as with the correctness of the Euro-Christian image itself.

Yet a number of surviving mural paintings dating to the second half of the century (or in some cases earlier) indicate considerable compromise with regard to how Christian themes were presented by native artists. The eagle and jaguar warriors in combat on the walls of the nave at San Miguel Arcángel Ixmiquilpan are an important example. If completed by 1572 (Estrada de Gerlero 1976), when the Augustinian chapter was held at this center (Grijalva 1985: 512), they must have raised more than a few eyebrows. Other overt examples evidencing strong native intrusions also existed elsewhere. In addition to the calendar at Cuauhtinchan, mural painters at this site included an eagle and a jaguar at either side of a representation of the Annunciation in the cloister.

The 1583 *Real Cédula* ordering preferential treatment for the secular clergy, followed by the 1585 council's official dictates on the establishment of a parochial system, may well have been another important factor in the decision to remove or wash over many mural programs (Peterson 1993: 176). Most of the large monastic centers themselves were not secularized until the mid-seventeenth century and beyond (Gerhard 1986), however, so it was perhaps also the threat of something worse that prompted the regular orders to cover them. As Jeanette Peterson (1993: 174) observes, the constant preoccupation with heresy from the 1570s onward turned into an antinative campaign to the extent that anything "native" became almost synonymous with "pagan."

But if the sixteenth-century ecclesiastical authorities believed that a purge on religious artwork in general, together with an extensive end-of-century congregations program, would rid the colonial church of the abomination of ongoing native beliefs and practices, they were to be disappointed. La Serna (1892: 32) tells us that, although this measure prompted an apparent hiatus in idolatrous activities until around 1604, it soon became clear that the Indians who were congregated had brought their idols and superstitions with them to the villages and the churches (ibid., p. 27). Even if as much attention was given to the issue of persisting idolatry in his own day as had been some seventy years earlier, he laments, the problem would still not be solved: "today . . . not even the congregations are recognized as having been a solution" (ibid., p. 237).[59]

In the context of sixteenth-century native religious activities, La Serna's remarks touch on two important points. First, they give us a more or less precise date for the discovery of the offending stonework: that is, a little over seventy years prior to 1656, when he was writing, or just before 1585, the year in which the Provincial Council formally ordered censorship of native-executed sculpture. At this point the mural paintings also started to be washed or painted over. Second, they imply that the purge of stonework was ineffectual in regard to native idolatry: "not even" the congregations program had been a solution to the problem.

Here we should note that the date of the discovery and removal of offending artwork coincided with the first abrupt decline in Indian church-building. The first great surge in construction (after 1530), we recall, had come at the point when indoctrination procedures were being drastically reformed. In other words, the initial and most noticeable increase in building activity coincided with the changeover to nonparticipatory and nonvisual doctrinal teaching; the sudden decline after 1580 followed the removal of the graphic product of those activities.

It seems possible, then, that the intensity of the evangelization program after 1530, the pressures of secularization toward the end of the century, and the shortage of native labor after 1580 were not the only reasons for the sudden changes in the pattern of sixteenth-century church-building. Deprived of the means to ritualize certain Christian activities, together with the essential visual form of communication that sustained and explained them, the Indians had found a way to retain both in their building and decorating. When the process was repeated—when the graphic results of their efforts were removed or covered over—native interest in church-building came to a halt. In regard to indigenous participation in decorative work, it is at this point that the inserts also start to disappear. Church-building, the completion of programs already commenced, and repairs and modifications certainly continued to the end of the century and the first decades of the next (Kubler 1992: 66–70). Indian labor was undoubtedly still exploited, and Indian participation in decorative work was not denied, but it remained exclusively decorative.[60] The mark of attempted Indian "participation" or initiative is very noticeably absent. The impetus to make these edifices their own ritual arenas had gone forever.

It can also be argued that these dates and events are related to the issue of native idolatry. The Spanish-noted resurgence of idolatry corresponded to the 1530s, as if provoked by the changes in indoctrination methodology but possibly also stimulated by the fervor for church-building and decorating, where the supposed "symbols of the devil" could continue to be viewed and invoked. The apparent hiatus in such activities between about 1585 and 1604 resulted from the purge of native painting and stonework and the second congregations program, although it is more correct to say that those activities went underground rather than ceased altogether. When they reemerged, they had taken on a very different form.

Writing in 1615, Torquemada (1975–83, 4:253, 5:313) recalled that some of the carved stones that the Indians had used on the corners of buildings in Mexico City were also chipped away on the orders of Archbishop García de Santa María Mendoza, that is, at some time between 1600 and 1606. The order came late in terms of the purge of the 1580s, but later still inasmuch as the removal of the stones was to be a source of consternation for the native population. As Torquemada continues, "the Indians who live [today] not only do not hold them [the stones] in esteem but do not even notice if they are there or what purpose they may have served" (ibid., p. 313).[61] Clearly, the archbishop's later gesture in respect to the presence of idols on colonial buildings was no more thorough than the earlier campaign to which La Serna refers. The difference now, however, was that the Indians had—apparently—lost interest in them. So convinced was Torquemada that this particular phase of native idolatry was over that three stones of this type (one carved with the face of Tlaloc, the rain deity) were left *in situ* on the walls of the church of Santiago Tlatelolco (D.F.) when he undertook its restoration after 1603 (see Rivas Castro and Lechuga García 1999).

The nature of renewed native practices after 1604 might support this change in Indian attitudes toward carved prehispanic masonry, but only inasmuch as its continued reuse on Christian architecture is concerned. The idols brought to the "houses, villages, and very churches" during the second congregations (La Serna 1892: 27) came to function exclusively as portable objects. They were placed, and found, inside the churches, on altars, or within the bases and platforms of statues of saints (ibid., p. 98), but the architectural or sculptural fabric of the buildings themselves was no longer a target. If it had been, La Serna would surely have made some relevant comment. We can also deduce from his text that these idols did not take the form of figurines—which he calls "idolillos" (ibid., p. 235)—but consisted of still more examples of prehispanic masonry. For La Serna, "idols" included the sun, the moon, fire, water, and "the stones in which they recognize a divinity" (ibid., p. 12).[62]

It is also apparent in the work of Serna that the objections of the colonial church authorities to the artifacts and images of the native past were more concretely focused on their continuing presence rather than on any specific siting. Within the bounds of the Christian church—and without—they were offensive because they were there. For the Indians this was not exactly the case, for the stones and their images clearly had multiple uses and meanings that were evolving or changing over time. If they had inserted them into the walls of Christian architecture in the sixteenth century, it was for a specific purpose. If they had introduced them into the interiors of the churches in the seventeenth century, it was also for a purpose, but not necessarily the same one. The reuse of old, carved stones in architecture died out over the last two decades of the sixteenth century: what was already there remained (and was in many cases maintained, as we shall see), but the practice itself was not extended to new buildings erected at new sites. As with mural painting and formal sculpture, this type of architectural detail also belonged to another Indian time and place.[63]

The new wave of idolatrous activities in the early seventeenth century shows itself to have been very firmly focused on the internal aspects of Christianity, in more than one sense of the word. The mixing of the portable idols, brought into the churches after the congregations, with the also portable images of Christ and the saints is echoed in the evidently meaningful mixing of native rites and beliefs with Catholic ones. The external manifestations—the processions, floral extravaganzas, and offerings—continued; but at this stage native shamans started to reappear in considerable numbers, openly practicing rituals in a traditional manner but frequently invoking the saints, Christ, and the Virgin along with, or in place of, their old deities. They also emulated Christian sacraments.[64] La Serna (1892: 237) understood this process as a rebirth of the cults and ceremonies of the past in acts of Christian worship. Today we know it to be a much clearer manifestation of the process of assimilating Christianity into the Indian world that gave rise to the mixed forms of worship that still exist in traditional, but nevertheless firmly Catholic, communities across Mexico today.

But the Indians' idols were also internalized physically into Christian space in the sense that their images had now penetrated the walls of the churches to stand alongside the venerated symbols of the Christian sacred within. La Serna's exasperation at this intrusion only points to an unquestionable confidence on the part of the Indians. Clearly, the figures that he saw as idols were perceived by the Indians as having attained a meaningful relationship with Christian figures in much the same way as they had been seen as appropriate in the religious architecture and decoration of the previous century. During that gray period between about 1585 and the end of the second congregaciones, when Indian spirituality again found itself thrown into confusion, a reformulation of the precepts of native religious orientation had taken place. From the Indian perspective, the result represented the shifting of Christianity from the surface of native religiousness to its core.[65] At the same time, by relocating their interpretive signs to the hallowed space that was the interior of the church, the Indians had also taken symbolic possession of the very heart of the Christian sacred.

The beginning of the seventeenth century undoubtedly marked another period in the Indian world and its accommodation of the Euro-Christian intrusion. Here, however, we should return to the sixteenth century and examine more closely the ways in which the Indians perceived their new churches and how the architectural detail and painting and sculpture of these early edifices express so well the initial process of native understanding and interpretation of Christianity.

CHAPTER FOUR

Native Perception of Churches

With few exceptions, the Christian edifices built so enthusiastically by the Indians of New Spain adhered to a fixed grouping of architectural units.[1] This consisted of a church and sometimes a smaller or larger adjoining cloister, both looking out onto a large walled courtyard or atrium. As basic elements, the atrium usually contained four chapels (posas) located at each of its corners and a central stone cross, aligned in its turn with the main atrium gateway and the church portal (fig. 4.1). The alignment served to guide the worshiper at the atrium gate along a direct line of approach to the sanctuary and main altar within. Once used as stations during processions around the atrium, surviving posas are few and today tend to be associated with large monastic

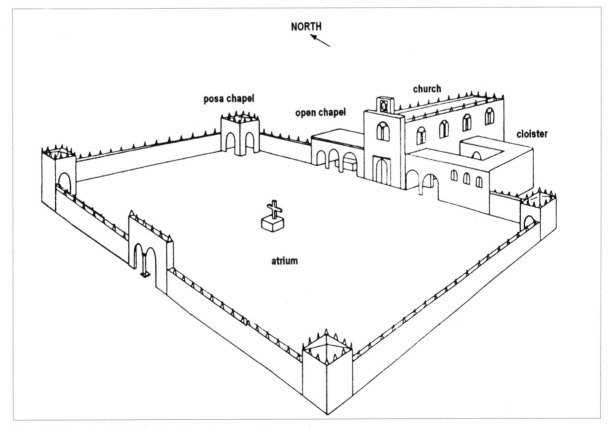

Figure 4.1. Layout of a typical sixteenth-century monastery complex
(adapted from Lockhart and Schwartz 1984).

complexes (such as Huejotzingo and Calpan). Nevertheless, they were once a standard feature of all churches and can still be found in villages where development has not encroached onto original sites (at Dominican Apoala and Chicahua in the Mixteca Alta of Oaxaca, for example). In addition, the atrium housed an open chapel from which the evangelizers preached to the congregated masses of converted and nonconverted Indians, particularly on special feast days. Of varying size, the open chapel could be free-standing, annexed to the wall of the church, or incorporated into the cloister facade at a raised or ground level. Although it was an important architectural unit, its arbitrary location within the atrium means that it cannot be seen as part of the standard configuration. The life span of these structures also varied considerably.[2]

The often vast atria, reduced cloister space, and posas and open chapels constitute New World architectural innovations designed to accommodate large Indian congregations and their comparatively small numbers of religious overseers, whose new roles as priests and evangelizers also contributed to these modifications. As such, New World architecture is indicative of the cultural change imposed on its mainstream European equivalent that resulted from the East-West encounter. The friar-architects who designed and supervised its construction, however, would have perceived it in much the same way as we do today. Mexican church and monastery complexes were symbols of the Christian religion, adhering to the architectural forms of the late medieval and early Renaissance periods. This architecture perhaps had the added connotation "Spanish" (the new dominant culture), displayed in the occasional examples of Plateresque and, much more commonly, the Spanish-appropriated Moorish style known as mudéjar. But even with such stylistic additions, the edifices nevertheless remained very firmly Euro-Christian in their intended projection and function. But if the Indians who built and congregated in and around these edifices came to recognize them as such, we cannot assume that they also perceived them in the same manner as did the friars. In what ways, for example, could this architecture reflect a native understanding of the religion it represented? Could the church, as a physical object, play any additional role that might better accommodate its presence in the Indian world?

The search for documentary evidence to shed light on native perception of their churches is not a fruitless task, for several excellent sources exist. One is the churches themselves or, more precisely, certain details pertaining to their imported or modified architectural forms and colonial siting. We can profitably conjecture on these, for the representations of Christian architecture found principally in the large corpus of area maps produced by native artist-scribes across New Spain during the sixteenth century, together with references to the Christian presence in contemporary Nahua devotional literature, support such conjectural interpretations. The maps, for example, show how Indian cartographers over several generations consistently related their churches to the temple-pyramids of old, at both a conceptual and functional level. The devotional song-poems, written down in alphabetical script, verbally support the visual representations on the maps. The remarkable homogeneity that exists between these two indigenous sources points to a common cognitive perception of the Christian church that is far removed from anything that the evangelization body could ever have imagined. It is this vision of the church that is fundamental in any assessment of native interpretations of the religion it symbolized.

The Sacred Site

On entering any town or village, the first act of the evangelizers was to demolish temples, shrines, and oratories and erect a wooden cross that, in most cases, was subsequently replaced by a small wooden chapel, later replaced in stone as a larger or smaller Christian site. The procedure—which we may call "topping" or the symbolic occupation of pagan space—was certainly not peculiar to New Spain, for it had been deployed in the West from the early days of Christianity. Where possible, pyramid-platforms were also razed to the ground, although some (with several layers of earlier constructions incorporated into the whole) were so large and structurally complex that the task proved impossible. And, as Mendieta (1973, 1:138–39) observed, with Spanish civilians occupied in building their own residences, after about 1525 the friars were left to their own devices to carry out demolition work. Native cooperation was often forthcoming, however, and the resulting masonry was often eventually used to construct the permanent church or parts of it. But motivation on the part of the Indians should perhaps not be attributed exclusively to immediate conversion to or acceptance of Christianity. Some of the prehispanic temples destroyed during the political conquest had been rebuilt once the conquistadors had passed through (ibid., p. 139). This might reflect native expectations regarding the short-term presence of the invader, but it also suggests that the sites on which the temples had stood had to be occupied architecturally.

The occupation of prehispanic religious sites began almost immediately. One of the first Franciscan arrivals, Pedro de Gante, made the decision to build over the ward temples of the four quarters of Mexico-Tenochtitlan (*Códice franciscano* 1941: 6), while Sahagún (1981, 1:210) later identified similar sites on the outskirts of the new city: at Nonoalco, Popotlan, and Mazatlan. Topping is very much in evidence today further afield. Excavations beneath the monastery entrance at Epazoyucan have revealed two levels of prehispanic staircases, indicating that at least part of the original platform remained intact after the prehispanic temple was demolished. In the Mixteca Alta of Oaxaca the church of Santiago Tilantongo stands alongside the remains of a prehispanic temple on the edge of a ravine that separates it from the locality's Black Mountain; page 22 of Codex Nuttall reproduces exactly the location of the late Postclassic temple. The Great Pyramid or *tlachiualtepec,* "handmade water-mountain," at Cholula defied even the destructive abilities of Hernán Cortés and his men. After an eventful history of erecting crosses and uncovering caches of idols at its summit, in 1594 the first chapel dedicated to Nuestra Señora de los Remedios was constructed there (Mendieta 1973, 1:185–86; Acuña 1985b: 132, 143), presumably in a final attempt to lay the native supernatural to rest.

Prehispanic temples, shrines, or oratories were frequently placed on top of natural platforms—prominent hills or ridges overlooking mountain valleys—where churches, chapels, or monasteries again replaced them. In the modern-day state of Tlaxcala the tiny neighboring villages of Totolac and Panotla are clustered on the slopes of two very prominent hills, while their comparatively large churches (sixteenth- and seventeenth-century, respectively), complete with atria, crown the summits and can be seen from miles around. Other Christian constructions are found halfway up steep hillsides or mountains, such as at Franciscan Atlixco (Puebla). Given the work of leveling and shoring up the hillside to carry the weight of the construction and its atrium, at Atlixco the natural underground spring over which they were built probably had more to do with the choice of site than the reported plagues of mosquitoes affecting the town below (see Vetancurt 1971, 4:2, f. 73). Still others stand on the edges of towns and villages, often at some distance from the main square (Yanhuitlan and Tilantongo; Tecamachalco [Puebla]; Epazoyucan, Cempoala, and Tlahuelilpa [Hidalgo]). Thus they detract from the colonial program of creating an urban nucleus within which the combined symbols of new religious and secular rule would prevail.[3] This also is the case of Asunción Tlaxcala, again built over the site of a sacred spring (Muñoz Camargo 1984: 54–55).

At the Augustinian monastery centers of Meztitlan and Molango in the High Sierra of Hidalgo the sixteenth-century buildings are perched on the edge of natural ridges, their raised atria accessed by stone ramps. Both sites boast the remains of earlier Christian buildings at nearby locations. At Meztitlan the ruins of the first monastery of La Comunidad lie partway up the path leading to the ridge. Apparently abandoned in 1539 after a flood, the remains do not present any signs of water damage, suggesting perhaps that the new site was chosen by the friars for reasons of ostentation or political importance (Victoria Asensio 1985: 84; Artigas 1989: 16). Meztitlan was a convenient stop-off point along the colonial route from Mexico City to the coast, thereby entertaining not a few prestigious visitors. But impressive as the monastery of Los Santos Reyes is, La Comunidad was also a large complex. Furthermore, the siting of the new church, cloister, and atrium again meant that the center of the urban community was physically alienated from the symbols of the new religious power. Now squeezed into a tight and very difficult topographical terrain, the complex faces toward the south (as did La Comunidad, but at a different angle of alignment [see Azcue y Mancera et al. 1940; Artigas 1989]). These are extremely unusual alignments for a Christian church (where the apse generally lies to the east, thereby orienting the congregation toward Jerusalem).

A few stones are all that are left of the first chapel at Molango (now the site of El Calvario), built at the foot of a mountain to the east of the present monastery. Grijalva (1985) recorded that the structure was built on the spot where the Augustinian Antonio de Roa, Molango's earliest evangelizer, found the Indians worshiping an image of the god Mola, tutelary deity of all the mountains in the region. According to the descendants of those Indians, Grijalva (1985: 90, my emphasis) explains, this early venue for Christian worship was later moved to the present site of the church and monastery "because it was on higher ground and *more appropriate for the siting of the village*."[4] Yet the west-facing monastic complex still finds itself on the square's north side, overlooking the ridge instead of the square. Access to its main entrance therefore requires an additional descent from the square to the ramp at the base of ridge. On-site observation suggests more clearly that the complex was directly and deliberately aligned with the early chapel to its east, built over Mola's prehispanic shrine. The shrine appears to have been focused on a massive curved peak in the High Sierra some distance to the west, which is dramatically illuminated as the sun rises over the village. The sixteenth-century complex effectively blocks the view of the mountain from the site of Mola's temple, and from the portal of the monastery church the site's free-standing belfry on the western perimeter of the atrium does the same.

The phenomenon of the alignments of the complexes at Meztitlan and Molango—two facing south, the other turned away from the urban nucleus—is not unique. If the churches of New Spain occupied the sites of prehispanic temples, they also inherited their alignments.[5] This circumstance lends an important and intriguing slant to the study of sixteenth-century Mexican religious architecture in general. In many cases, the evangelization body must have been aware that the churches followed the original alignments, especially when they faced out to the south, north, or east, as opposed to the standard west. What, then, was its purpose in permitting or ordering native builders to adhere to those alignments? Simple expediency to take advantage of extant foundations or platforms would not necessarily impinge on the internal layout of the new building, for the apse could still be placed to the east. Or was the objective to extend the topping procedure in order to take in, for example, the orientation of a native altar or some external focus of the temple-platform, as the example of Molango suggests? In other words, did the evangelizers understand the important relationship between native ceremonial architecture and the landscape?[6] The report on the orientation of the great temple at Tenochtitlan by Motolinía (1970: 24) might suggest that this was so (although he does not mention topography). But his observations on the way in which pathways running across the landscape served to enhance the importance of the temples (Motolinía 1990: 50; discussed below) would appear to deny this. Here he seems to be echoing the Euro-Christian line of vision (atrium gate–cross–church portal) described above.

The evangelizers were aware of the cult of mountain worship, however. Attempts to neutralize the sacredness of certain topographical features by obstructing them with Euro-Christian architecture or related structures (as at Molango, for example) are therefore perhaps our only clue as to why the churches inherited prehispanic alignments.[7] But it seems unlikely that they ever considered architecture to be part of the cult. In contrast, as I will show, in native perception and usage the churches, their siting, and their alignments did take over where the temples and temple-platforms left off; the relationship between the Christian edifices and the still-sacred landscape was also widely acknowledged.

The construction of Christian buildings or the erection of Christian crosses therefore took place at sites that in preconquest times were considered to be sacred and also formed part of a sacred geography. By "sacred," I mean that these were places where communication with the gods (or the natural or supernatural power that a given deity represented) was established. Whether it was architecturally accommodated or located at the site of a specific natural feature—an unusual rock formation, an underground spring, a cave, a tree—the presence of a *permanent* sacred force was recognized. The notion of permanence is evidenced, for example, in the natural cave configured as a multipetaled flower that lies beneath the Pyramid of the Sun, one of the earliest constructions at Teotihuacan. Before the architectural development of this site, the cave seems to have been a cult center that may in itself have grown out of a belief that it was a place of origin (Heyden 1983). The Mixtec historical annals record that the first ancestors were born from a sacred tree at Apoala. The tree is represented on the "landscape" pictograph of Apoala on Codex Nuttall 36, where it stands on the edge of a cliff overlooking the river valley below. The Nuttall representation of the Apoala Valley is accurate.[8] Again at a distance from the village square, the original sixteenth-century church was constructed on precisely the same site, indicating the site's continuing religious importance at the time of the conquest.[9]

The "gods" were invoked in carefully coordinated rituals that took place in architectural and naturally occurring arenas perceived to emulate the cosmic structure of the world. The teoamoxtli (divine cosmic books) frequently depict these arenas laid out in the configuration of a quatrefoil or quincunx, the title page of Codex Féjérváry being one of the finest surviving examples (fig. 4.2). Echoing the cosmic trees that, according to the mythology of creation, demarcated the terrestrial plane and separated it from the sky, the scribe placed four flowering trees at each of the petal-like corners. He also acknowledged the advent of time with sequences of the 20 day signs, the 9 lords of the night, and the 13 quecholtin running between and around the trees (Brotherston 1992: 99, 1995: 150–52). The unbroken path of footprints around the cosmic design represents the shaman's ritual journey (Brotherston 1979: 140). Pages 27–30 of Codex Borgia offer a series of ritual panels laid out in quatrefoil or quincunx. In the context of my argument here, prominent among their ritual occupants are tlaloque and wind deities (see fig. 6.76).

Figure 4.2. Title page of Codex Féjérváry. © National Museums Liverpool, World Museum Liverpool.

The creation of the terrestrial plane was also reconstructed in religious ritual. According to Durán (1984, 1:86–87), while rulers made their annual pilgrimage to the rain god's sanctuary on the summit of Cerro Tlaloc during the festival of Hueytozoztli, a miniature landscape of hills, crags, and bushes was laid out in front of the deity's temple in the ceremonial precinct. A large tree (called *tota*, "father") was erected at its center, with four smaller ones arranged around it; all were linked by ropes. Durán interpreted the ropes (made of twisted malinalli grass) as symbols of penitence, but they were more obviously a reference to the pathways of the gods flowing through the cosmos via the world trees. The rain deity's sanctuary on Cerro Tlaloc itself was an architectural equivalent of the cosmic plane, including a ritual enclosure opening at one side in the manner of many of the Borgia panels. The enclosure consisted of a square walled courtyard topped with merlons. To one side was a wooden chamber with a castellated crown where the idol of Tlaloc stood, surrounded by a series of smaller idols. The architectural layout represented Cerro Tlaloc and its surrounding mountains, all of which were associated with the rain cult (ibid., p. 82).

Archaeological survey confirms Durán's description: the chamber has long since perished, but the courtyard, with an entrance at its eastern side, remains. When the enclosure was constructed, clusters of natural boulders were left in place, corresponding to the four corners of the precinct. Other clusters of stones remaining in the center and to the east appear to repeat the assemblage of the idols inside the original chamber (Townsend 1991, 1992a). If we can understand that Tlaloc and the tlaloque were perceived as venerated mountains, the site on Cerro Tlaloc also argues that the association was extended to architectural detail. The castellated crown of Tlaloc's temple echoes the mountain-crag headdress so often depicted on images of the deity and his messengers (see fig. 1.3), while the merlons topping the enclosure's walls recall the smaller mountain-idols that surrounded him. Thus the site's architecture also emulated the idols and their mountain conceptualization. Other graphic parallels support this interpretation. The description of the festival of Tepeilhuitl in Códice Matritense del Palacio Real (f. 252r) offers a very explicit image of a deity-mountain-temple interchange in the form of a large, single hill glyph with four smaller companions, composed of the heads of the tepictoton emerging from profiled temples (fig. 4.3).

References to quatrefoil and quincuncial arrangements of prehispanic architecture are common in other sources. The *tolteca* house (the place of worship of the priests of Quetzalcoatl-Ehecatl, the wind deity) consisted of four abodes, each facing in a different cardinal direction (FC10, 1961: 166). Evidently modeled on the mythical architectural abode of the rain deities, the *ayaucalli,* "house-of-mist," consisted of four structures located on or near water, which served as shrines for water deities (Garibay 1981, 4:324), and was specifically associated with the four directional tlaloque (López Austin 1994: 180). Motolinía (1990: 26) described these structures as stepped altars arranged as a cruciform around a central spring. The association of the ayaucalli with rain mountains is also apparent, for one such group of temples was located on a mountain near Tlaxcala where sacrifices of children were made in Atlacahualo (Sahagún 1981, 1:140).

Figure 4.3. The architectural tepictoton (Códice Matritense del Palacio Real, f. 252r).

The Prehispanic Teocalli

In the immediate preconquest period not all religious architecture or ritual focused directly on the water-fertility cult, although the cult was of major importance and (together with that of the god of fire and time, Xiuhtecuhtli) extremely ancient in origin. The central Mexican cult of the mountains and its concerns with rain and fertility nevertheless pervaded all ritual to a greater or lesser degree, being interwoven with other activities directed toward ancestor-patrons; earth, sun, and maize deities; and the night, when all rites to Tlaloc were performed (see Broda 1971, 1987: 71–72, 74). A significant finding in Broda's analysis of Aztec ritual is that water cults were mainly left to the priests and the people (Broda 1982: 96). That is, water was the principal focus of ritual for the greater part of the population; as already pointed out, this focus does not seem to have changed in the postconquest era.

It is accepted today that Mexican pyramid-platforms not only were intended to emulate mountains or their interiors but also echoed the landscape itself in their spatial layout at any given site. Viewed from the south of the Street of the Dead at Teotihuacan, the so-called Pyramid of the Moon not only is aligned with Cerro Gordo to its north but also takes on its form. When viewed from that structure, the larger and older Pyramid of the Sun is seen to correspond with Cerro Xoconochco (or Patlachique) on the south side of the valley. Not surprisingly, these particular architectural replicas of mountains also echo the mythology of genesis. Excavations at the Pyramid of the Sun have shown it to be constructed of organic materials (including seeds), suggesting that it was intended to represent the mountain of sustenance (Manzanilla Naim 1999a: 25, 1999b: 81–82), which in later Nahua accounts was broken open by the deities of sun and rain to obtain food for the first humans. The *hueyteocalli,* "great temple," at Teno-chtitlan (today's Templo Mayor) evoked the Aztec conception of the universe in that its structure symbolized the three cosmic levels. Its location on an island at the center of the lake placed it at the center of the horizontal plane, at the intersection of the four sol-sticial directions (Matos Moctezuma 1987, 1988), that is, at the center of cosmic space and time. The north side of the temple, dedicated to Tlaloc, is again understood to represent the seed-filled tonacatepetl guarded by the tlaloque (Townsend 1982; Matos Moctezuma 1987, 1988). Sixteenth-century chroniclers reported that the idol of Tlaloc that stood there was full of all the seeds in the land (Cervantes de Salazar 1985: 318; Díaz del Castillo 1994: 174) or was itself molded of seeds and blood (Tapia 1980: 582). Thus Tlaloc was also an image of his own temple, the mountain of sustenance.

Broda (1987: 73–76, 112 n. 44, 1991a: 478) offers an illuminating hypothesis on the symbolism of the dual structure of the Great Temple. She proposes that it was also a representation of the dry and rainy seasons: of sun and water, of Huitzilopochtli and Tlaloc, of the day-sun and the night-sun, where this "sun" is maize. It was believed that the sacred mountains retained water within their interiors during the dry season; the water was released in the rainy season. In this sense the duality of the Great Temple seems also to have functioned as an architectural narrative of the two fundamental stages of the agricultural cycle. Aligned at 7° south of east, the point of sunrise on the horizon on the last day of Tlacaxipehualiztli (Aveni et al. 1988), which marked the close of the season of warfare and the return to agricultural labors, the edifice spe-cifically acknowledged the opening of that cycle. Its symbolism only emphasizes the continuing religious focus on the production of food—on the religious "reality"—that is so often denied the Azteca-Mexica.

Mythical associations between mountains and pyramid-platforms were further un-derscored in the metaphorical concept of *altepetl,* "water-mountain," as a territorial and political unit symbolized in the central temple-pyramid of every town and village (Lockhart 1992: 206, 421). According to Sahagún's informants, the origins of the term dated to a remote past: "they said that the mountains were only magic places, with earth, with rock on the surface; that they were only like ollas or houses; that they were filled with water which was there. . . . And hence the people called their settlements *altepetl.* They said, 'This mountain of water, this river, springs from there, the womb of the mountain. For from there Chalchiuitlicue sends it—offers it'" (FC11, 1963: 247).

A natural and permanent water source was essential in the pursuit of agricultural ac-tivities and, therefore, sustained settlement. For this reason a local mountain or hill with an underground spring or of sufficient height to attract rain clouds came to be perceived as the source of vitality of a new settlement or settlements established in its vicinity. As Sahagún's informants imply, settlements identified themselves with their own particular local mountain, whose water they appropriated or shared (Torquemada 1975–83, 3:78). The patron god was seen to reside within the mountain or to be the mountain proper; a replica of the sacred entity, the *teocalli,* "sacred-force-house," which was "just an artifi-cial mountain with levels, with steps" (FC11, 1963: 269), was placed symbolically at the heart of the community. The patron water-mountain was obviously also a mountain of sustenance, for all foodstuffs ultimately derived from its gift of water.

It is generally agreed that at the time of the Spanish conquest the graphic sign for a town or territory (altepetl) had been conventionalized in the form of a stylized mountain with a bar across its base. In turn, the base was often complemented with a shell-tipped and/or chalchihuitl-tipped water glyph, to complete the phonetic reading of "water-mountain" (fig. 4.4), or a "frill," which in some representations takes on a fang-like appearance reminiscent of the mouth of Tlaloc (Broda 1971: 302).[10] Identification of the altepetl in question was made through the addition of a toponymic glyph. But, as I posit below, the stylized mountain glyph (in contemporary usage frequently called a hill glyph) also symbolized the patron-mountain, and in many cases its graphic func-tion was not so much to designate the site of a vil-lage but to acknowledge the presence of this real and venerated feature of the locality's landscape.

Perhaps the earliest surviving representations of patron water-mountains in the central area come in the lower sections of the mural program at Tepantitla, Teotihuacan, painted circa 300–500 AD (Kubler 1984: 66) (plate 2). The predomi-nant element is the turquoise "cone" at its center. Within the cone, a bifurcated turquoise stream pours through a red-brown "arch" then flows across rectangles of irrigated fields below (Uriarte 1982: 445; Kubler 1984: 66). Placed against a red-brown background, across which tiny figures play together among flowering and fruit-laden plants and trees, the whole section represents the base of a mountain of plenty. The cone defines its watery interior; and the red-brown arch represents the

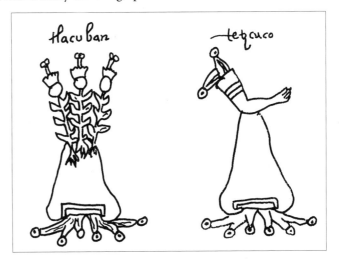

Figure 4.4. Examples of altepetl signs (Codex Osuna).

threshold of a cave or point of exit of those waters (Pasztory 1976: 166). The parallels between the configuration of the turquoise water-source and the facade of the Pyramid of the Sun (a replica of the mythical mountain of sustenance) are startling (fig. 4.5). The upper staircase divides at roughly the same point as the flowing stream in the mural, where this point also lies directly above the entrance to the cave beneath the pyramid. Archaeological excavations at the base of the Pyramid of the Sun indicate the one-time presence of a wide canal surrounding the structure on all sides, possibly for the (ritual) collection of water cascading down its slopes during the rainy season (Matos Moctezuma 2002: 189). According to Sahagún's informants, "the roads that went up the mountains were called sacred roads; they were the roads of the Tlalocs" (CMRAH, f. 54v; 1997: 201). Here, then, pyramid staircases would appear to represent "the roads of the Tlalocs," symbolic pathways that not only ascend sacred mountains but "flow" down from them.

Although I will return to the concept architecture-mountain, here it is convenient to introduce the closely related subject of chromatic symbolism. The colors employed in the Tepantitla mural are of considerable importance: the mountain is red-brown; and the interior cavelike section is turquoise blue. In the late Postclassic the combination red-blue was associated metaphorically with the entwined *atl tlachinolli*, "water-fire," a symbol for war, which had been superimposed as the ultimate "source of life" under the Mexica's bellic regime. But *atl* and *tlachinolli* name respectively the rainy and dry

Figure 4.5. West face of the Pyramid of the Sun, Teotihuacan.

seasons (Broda 1987: 105), that is, the time of the night maize-sun in the watery interior of Tlalocan and the time of the day maize-sun beneath the realm of Tonatiuh, the Sun: the blue and the red. Blue and red also define the two vital fluids that course through the cosmos: water is celestial or terrestrial blood, sustainer of the life of the landscape; blood is bodily water and the sustainer of human life (Arnold 1991: 227).[11] Likened to a beautiful landscape, Uto-Aztecan realms of the sacred are still frequently invoked in song with chromatic symbolism such as blue and crimson (Hill 1992: 117–19). Thus, as a duality of colors, I understand blue and red as a metaphor for the sacred source of life, a metaphor that originated in the context of the relationship between water and earth and was also given concrete form in the perceived physical properties of the sacred water-mountain.[12]

Pairing of the colors blue and red occurs consistently in imagery that can be firmly associated with water, fertility, and sacred mountains, and variances in its application certainly assist our reading of the imagery's conceptual relevance to the same cult complex. On page 7 of Codex Borbonicus, for example, we see Tlaloc attired in turquoise blue seated on a blue-gray hill glyph, with a red horizontal bar across its base (plate 3). Water appears to pour from the base of the hill, but a figure swimming in the opposite direction tells us that the flow is in the reverse direction. These figures may represent the human dead on their journey to the home of the rain god, but they also conceptualize Tlaloc as the universal water-mountain on which rain falls and is then absorbed or drawn into its interior. With the colors reversed—that is, with a red horizontal bar lying beneath a blue mountain, as if the (red) mountain filled with (blue) water has been turned inside-out—the suggested reading is that it describes the watery *interior* of Tlaloc's abode.

The water-mountain was also configured in other ways. Tlaloc's consort Chalchiutlicue appears dressed almost entirely in her blue-green skirts on page 5 of Codex Borbonicus (plate 4). She is seated on a red-brown bench with legs in the form of a curved, stepped design. The design pervades Mesoamerican graphic expression. As a single "leg," it may be compared to the rows of red-brown stepped motifs on a turquoise background that cover the sloping talus wall face around the base of the central courtyard of the Temple of Quetzalpapalotl, Teotihuacan. In this particular case, the upper part of each motif terminates in the curved *coliuhqui* glyph so often associated with mountains housing caves of origin.[13] With two "legs," as in the example of Chalchiutlicue's bench, the stepped component finds a notable parallel in the stepped sides of the pyramid-platforms that emulated the sacred mountains. In other words, Chalchiutlicue's bench represents the outline of a mountain or a cave opening, the exit point of an underground water source.[14] In the Borbonicus panel the goddess's blue-green, life-giving water gushes forth from beneath her seat, carrying with it two human figures. The interior of this bench is indeed a "womb of the mountain" or the womb of Chalchiutlicue herself. The analogy with the amniotic fluid that precedes human birth from deep within the body is obvious, as is, perhaps, the notion that Tlaloc as god of rain "impregnates" the mountain with water (with life), to which Chalchiutlicue then "gives birth." Her red-brown bench also carries a direct visual antecedent in the red-brown "arch" of the Tepantitla cave-mouth, from which the rivers are seen to flow out over agricultural plots.

A further example of a bench combining the conceptual aspects of the "seats" of both Tlaloc and Chalchiutlicue, and the day-sun/night-sun duality, is found on f. 9v of Codex Telleriano-Remensis. Here Tepeyollotl, "Heart-of-the-Mountain" (the jaguar manifestation of Tezcatlipoca), is seated on a turquoise-blue stepped bench with red underside that matches the color configuration of the Borbonicus Tlaloc-mountain. Where the jaguar was associated with the night, Tepeyollotl resided in the dark depths of the mountain. According to the accompanying gloss in Telleriano-Remensis, his roar reverberated in the valleys from one hill to another; Tepeyollotl was, effectively, the thunder-jaguar that heralded the coming of rain (Brotherston 1992: 65–66). Tepeyollotl's bench again represents his abode: as with Tlaloc's mountain, the application of its colors indicates that we are viewing him *within* the mountain. From the point of view of architecture, then, the red-brown outline of a mountain on a turquoise background of the Temple of Quetzalpapalotl patio frieze represents the *interior* of the mountain that the temple itself replicated.

As a combination of colors, blue and red was employed consistently throughout the pre- and postconquest codices to depict temples (plate 5). Lintels and jambs are almost always red-brown or a range of oranges or pinks; where colored, interiors are usually turquoise. On page 72 of Codex Nuttall turquoise water also pours from a red-brown temple door, with the structure itself embedded into a hill glyph.[15] Color coordination relating directly to the night-sun and day-sun hypothesis outlined above also occurs. In two images of the dual structure at Tlatelolco (Codex Mendoza, f. 10r; Codex Telleriano-Remensis, f. 36v), Tlaloc's side of the temple, with its characteristic vertically striped parapet, is detailed in blue; Huitzilopochtli's side, with its parapet of skulls, is in red.

Native representations of the old temples also display a series of consistencies in terms of architectural features and decorative elements. When represented face-on, these structures appear as stylized boxes, with the lintel, jambs, and roofs being the most prominent features (fig. 4.6a–c). Profiled temples, the commonest representational form, are most often depicted like an uppercase T, although the same emphasis on lintels, jambs, and roofs remains (fig. 4.6d–f). With very few exceptions, temple structures and/or their platforms are also seen to rest on rectangular bases (fig. 4.6b, d–e). In Codex Mendoza (fig. 4.6c) and Codex Telleriano-Remensis the base of the two temples at Tlatelolco is inferred from the elevated level of the doorways over the pyramid-platform on which they stand.

The bases of Mixtec temples and platforms in the codices regularly present a decorative frieze, often of a fretwork design, which served as a geographical substantive for *ñuu*, "town" or "place" (Smith 1973: 39). While this is a specifically regional graphic convention, decorative elements on roofs and parapets are very common in depictions of prehispanic buildings across the board. Archaeological excavations confirm that such structures were heavily decorated with sculpted or stuccoed motifs, and

Figure 4.6. Architectural characteristics of prehispanic temples: *a,* Codex Vienna 6; *b,* map of Teozacualco (1580); *c,* Codex Mendoza f. 10r, *d,* Codex Cospi 5; *e,* Codex Nuttall 68; *f,* Codex Yanhuitlan.

many were crenellated (that is, topped with merlons, which, as suggested earlier, may have replicated mountain peaks or crags). The designs on the friezes perhaps served to identify the dedication of a building and/or its specific usage. The depiction of the prehispanic temple at Yanhuitlan in the codex of the same name (fig. 4.6f) offers a double frieze of stepped motifs and four-petaled flowers.[16] Parapet friezes of concentric or single circles are also common, however, while other motifs include water/rain droplets (fig. 4.6a); a sprouting cocoa bean on the 1580 *Relaciones geográficas* map of Teozacualco (fig. 4.6b), which is not toponymic (Acuña 1984b: 143, n. 15); "lidded eye" star signs (fig. 4.6e); and a variety of geometric designs. Merlons also vary in form, although the recurrence of versions that closely resemble the shape of deities' benches, or halved versions of the same, is of interest (fig. 4.6e–f). The central Mexican site of Teotihuacan has produced a good number of merlons, including a symmetrical stepped model with a central semicircular cavity. Two examples, now in the Museo Nacional de Antropología, Mexico City, have also retained their color: the outer stepped motifs and the cavity frame are detailed in turquoise, with a red-brown wash separating the two. Chromatically, these correspond well to the mountain-cave-water elements discussed earlier. The same stylized form and coloring was still employed as a representation of a cave in the early colonial period. A native pictorial text produced during the 1539 idolatry trial of those accused of removing the idols of Tenochtitlan (AGN, *Inquisición,* v. 37) narrates how the idol of the mountain deity Tepehua was hidden in a cave. The glyphic and chromatic form of the cave echoes the Teotihuacan merlons. The entrance to this particular blue and red cave is also edged with a strip of jaguar pelt (plate 6).

Within the argument presented above, a confusion arises as to exactly which element of the temple-platform structure was supposed to represent the mountain and which the cave. Given shape and size, the association mountain/pyramid-platform is not difficult to grasp. If the earlier description of the *teocalli,* "sacred-force-house," from the Florentine Codex is presented in full, then the issue appears to be resolved, especially when compared to a second definition of *teocalli* from the same text:

> Teocalli: It means house of the god. In idolatrous times it was named *teocalli.* It is high, just an artificial mountain with levels, with steps. Some have one hundred steps. . . . And on its summit there stood two small houses, or just one; there the image of the demon, the devil, was guarded. This *teocalli* has levels, a landing, a stairway, a junction; it has a house, a house standing; it has a parapet, a column; it has columns. (FC11, 1963: 269)

> Teocalli: It means the house, not the artificial mountain; [the house] just standing on the ground. . . . It is big, high, roomy, long, wide, stretched out, long and straight, a long room, a row of rooms. It has a portal, corners, an entrance, a covering to the entrance, a stone column, a column, a door bar, a facade, a frontispiece, a wooden enclosure . . . it is high, very high, very good, surpassingly good. (ibid., pp. 269–70)

The first definition of *teocalli* clearly speaks of the architectural replica of the mountain, the pyramid-platform with its shrine or idol chamber on top. The second appears to be a description of a temple proper, such as could be found below and around the great pyramid-platforms. With its references to lintels and jambs, it also echoes those depicted in the codices. The Florentine Codex's distinction is architecturally correct, for both basic types of religious structures existed.

In the spoken and painted languages of the prehispanic peoples, places and objects often carried several names, which were complemented iconically: each variation indicated a corresponding change of ideological meaning or conceptual slant. It does not follow, therefore, that a duplication of the term *teocalli* could refer arbitrarily to such important but architecturally distinct buildings as a pyramid-platform and a temple proper. Generic names cannot occur easily when a language is written using images that may be read phonetically, ideologically, and/or conceptually. *Teocalli* must thus be understood as indicating perceptual recognition, in that it expresses the essence of the temple and pyramid-platform: specifically, a sacredness housed in or represented by the temples and platforms. Architectural distinction lay in the *teocalli*'s spoken or written definition, as listed, for example, in Book 2 of the Florentine Codex (1981: 179–93).

The first definition of *teocalli* refers to the artificial mountain with its idol chamber. Here emphasis is on the exterior aspects of the structure: the pyramid was the mountain viewed as a feature of the landscape, often with a sanctuary at the summit. The second definition, which clearly states that it was not the artificial mountain, also describes external architectural features (a portal, corners, a door bar). But it focuses on the structure's interior, placing weight on its massive proportions and layout: it is "big, high, roomy, long, wide, stretched out, long and straight, a long room, a row of rooms." If descriptive language also reflects the describer's perception of an object, then comparisons with Sahagún's informants' description of a cave suggest strong cognitive associations between the temple proper and this other important topographical feature: "[The cave of] the mountain, of the crags is extensive. It becomes long, deep; it widens, extends, narrows. . . . It is wide-mouthed; it is narrow-mouthed. It has mouths which pass through [to the other side]" (FC11, 1963: 276). Together with the consistent graphic use of turquoise or water glyphs to define the interiors of temples, the similarities between these two descriptions readily speak of a cave-temple association. Both are chamberlike, large, roomy, and stretched out; both nevertheless "widen" and "narrow" as interior space is transformed into a "row of rooms." The cave or mountain hollow (wide-mouthed; narrow-mouthed) from which the precious life-blood of the landscape emerged was the womb of the earth (Heyden 1991), with its threshold dividing the natural world from the supernatural world where the sacred forces resided. With the interiors of temples likened to water-filled caves, their exteriors—so often represented graphically with red portals and jagged walls—must also have been perceived as replicas of topography, this time as caves in their own right.

Examples of this type of religious architecture might well include the (now disappeared) temples of the earth monster Quilaztli-Cihuacoatl, which were constructed as imitations of caves (Broda 1991a: 475). Las Casas (1992: 547) described a rounded structure in the Great Temple precinct at Tenochtitlan, with an opening in the form of a monstrous reptilian mouth, a standard iconic convention to represent a cave in the codices. Temple I at the hilltop site of Malinalco (México) is perhaps the ultimate example of an artificially constructed cave-temple: with the great circular chamber cut from the bare rock, its entrance also replicates the gaping mouth of a serpent.

On the same lines, every pyramid-platform would have had a covered shrine at its summit in which the image of the idol was placed. This was also an architectural rendering of the cave (or interior of the mountain) where the patron deity resided. The 1579 *Relación geográfica* from Chinantla speaks of "a cave" on top of a pyramid-platform where idols were kept and where priests fasted (Acuña 1984a: 101). Blood from sacrificial victims was daubed on the mouths of idols and on the lintels of their chambers (Conquistador Anónimo 1980: 386), an evident allusion to a doorway also being perceived as a "mouth."

As perceived and understood by the Indians, no fundamental differences existed between the *teocalli* described as an artificial mountain and the *teocalli* that was "standing on the ground." Both types of structures conceptualized the mountain and its cave as the abode of the supernatural or the *teocalli*. Large religious precincts, such as those at Cholula, Tenochtitlan, Tlatelolco, and Texcoco, displayed a variety of *teocalli* of differing sizes and design and oriented in different directions (Torquemada 1975–83, 3:212–13). Together they must have been seen to emulate architecturally the vast expanse of the local sacred landscape, with its own corresponding topographical irregularities and openings. How, then, did the Christian churches that replaced those topographical replicas come to be perceived?

The Christian Altepetl

If "in idolatrous times" the temples and pyramids were named *teocalli* (FC11, 1963: 269), in Christian times the term was used frequently to refer to the new churches. In 1531 the inhabitants of Santo Tomás Ajusco (D.F.) may have referred to the church they were ordered to build as *teocaltzintli,* "little/venerated sacred-force-house" ("Testimonio" 1970: 211), because the exclusivity of the god it was to house was still unclear to them. As far as they were concerned, he was the same as the one they already had (ibid., pp. 200, 205–206). But in 1553 the Indian cabildo of Tlaxcala was still using *teocalli* when speaking of the churches under its own jurisdiction. It continued to do so, for the word again appears as a synonym for the Spanish *yglesia* in what are otherwise wholly Nahuatl records (see Lockhart et al. 1986: 90, 123–24).

Here we should not be too hasty in placing a non-Christian or "idolatrous" meaning on native labeling of the churches. Molina's 1571 Nahuatl-Spanish dictionary confirms that both *teocalli* and *teopan,* "sacred-force-place," were used for the architectural *yglesia* (Molina 1992, 2nd pagination, f. 100r). Both terms were also employed to refer to the temples of Tenochtitlan (FC2, 1981: 179–93), suggesting perhaps that some temples acknowledged more the locus of the sacred and others more its embodied presence. We must assume from Molina's entries, however, that, despite the observations of Sahagún's informants, the terms were accepted in ecclesiastical circles. Their adoption was probably due to the friars' own early use of Nahuatl terminology to get across the Christian message: specifically, *teotl,* which they insisted on translating as "god." "God-house" or "god-place" was thus an appropriate literal translation for the House of God.[17] But, of course, these borrowed words had belonged to the prehispanic system of religious reference, where they carried connotative rather than denotative values. This being the case, and despite architectural remodeling, to what extent did the conceptual meaning of *teocalli* and *teopan*[*tli*] change in terms of the sacred force that they defined? Was a *teocalli* or *teopan* church recognized by the Indians as the house and place of the Christian god, with the word and all its inherent associations with the sacred geography thereby having undergone a complete process of resemanticization? Or was the church perceived as a different architectural rendering of the same sacred-force-house, or sacred-force-place, that also found its origins in that sacred geography?

The hand of the Indian painter-scribe offers some evidence that, in native perception, the Christian church still adhered to the prehispanic temple naming system. The

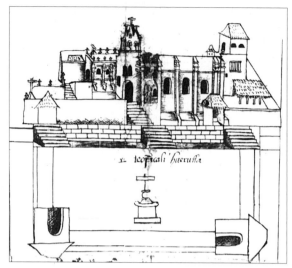

Figure 4.7. Detail from the 1580 map of Huejutla, Hidalgo, which labels its church as *teopancali,* "sacred-force-place-house." España, Ministerio de Cultura, Archivo General de Indias, MP-MEXICO 16.

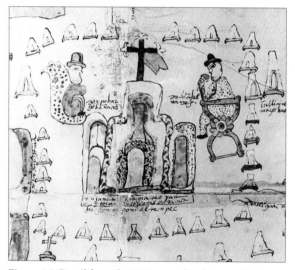

Figure 4.8. Detail from the 1579 map of Suchitepec, Oaxaca, showing its mountain-church with jaguar skin threshold. España, Ministerio de Cultura, Archivo General de Indias, MP-MEXICO 29.

1580 map of Huejutla (Hidalgo) glosses its Augustinian church as *teopa[n]cali huexutla:* that is, the edifice was qualified with the locative -*pan* to designate it not as "sacred-force-house" but "sacred-force-place-house" (fig. 4.7). In Dominican-ministered Oaxaca the five maps accompanying the 1579 *Relación de Suchitepec* (appendix B: Suchitepec group) gloss their rather strange churches as *teopan,* in conjunction with *yn santa yglesia* (Acuña 1984b: 57–72) (figs. 4.8, 4.9). Here, it seems, the Indian and Christian sacred places and/or houses were again understood to be synonymous.

As we perceive the Christian structures now occupying those ancient sacred sites, very few immediate visual parallels exist in respect to their temple-pyramid predecessors. Displaying a mixture of European architectural and decorative styles, extraordinarily thick, buttressed walls rise up vertically to be crowned with bell towers or pedimented belfries and crosses. Massive stone or wooden vaults replaced the flat-topped roofs or gabled thatching of the old temples and shrines; in most cases arched portals took over from linteled doorways.

For the Indians, some similarities between the old and the new may have been apparent. The basic principles behind public religious architecture for both cultures were, after all, not so different. Intentionally awesome in the face of the divine, architecture also served to emphasize the source of civic control. Where possible, in New Spain the Catholic Church had no intention of diverging from this long-established role. At the same time, and whether or not in emulation of the original apostles, the focus that the evangelization body placed on outdoor religious activities would also have echoed prehispanic traditions. Congregations gathered in great walled courtyards beneath towering temple-pyramids, to worship the gods, reenact rituals, process, and listen to the pronouncements of the priests and priest-rulers. But however familiar Christian space may have seemed in regard to size, ambience, and siting, Euro-Christian architecture must have been visually and ideologically alien to the Indians at a stylistic level. This would particularly have been the case for those charged with reproducing it.

Within the great enclosure of the church atrium, the posa-chapels constitute an interesting phenomenon, for they are an element of sixteenth-century New World architecture whose Old World origins remain largely undetermined, at least in a Christian architectural context (Lara 2004: 29–30). Standing as four small structures before the greater architectural mass that was the church, the posa-church ensemble echoes Códice Matritense del Palacio Real's configuration of architectural tepictoton, or mountain-tlaloque, to which the festival of Tepeilhuitl was dedicated (fig. 4.3). The pointed, pyramidal roofs (which are certainly European in origin) of some examples of posas (Huejotzingo, Calpan) also adhere partially to the native definition of mountains described in the Florentine Codex in that they are "high, pointed, pointed on top. Pointed at the summit" (FC11, 1963: 258). Coincidental as this might seem, the roof of the remaining posa at Totolapa (Morelos) rises as three peaks (not a European solution, I suspect), a form accentuated by the rows of stubby merlons around the top of the cube formed by its lower walls (McAndrew 1965: 312). Surviving posas at other sites have domed roofs, also surrounded by pyramid-shaped merlons, as at Tlapanaloya (México), for example. Thus European architectural forms could also offer openings for perceptual reinterpretation: domes and pyramids they may be to the Western eye, but how would they appear to the native eye, which had never before seen such models of roofing?

A standard feature of conversion architecture, the posas appear to have been developed as part of an ideal layout created by the friar-architects on the basis of the practical needs of converting so many Indians at the same time and of the Indians' evident interest in ritual processing. Diego Valadés (2003: 475) stated that they were used for education, as his well-published 1579 en-

Figure 4.9. Detail from the 1579 map of Tlamacazcatepec, Oaxaca, showing its mountain-church and fanged threshold. España, Ministerio de Cultura, Archivo General de Indias, MP-MEXICO 26.

graving of an idealized Franciscan mission (produced several decades after the first posas were constructed) also indicates (ibid., p. 465). But, with pathways linking them around the perimeter of the atrium and possibly diagonally from opposing corners,[18] they also undoubtedly served as stop-off points, where the Host could also be placed, during processions. As McAndrew (1965: 295) first proposed, however, it may have been the Indians themselves who gave the friars the idea of creating and siting them in this way. We remember, for example, the 1538 celebrations of Corpus Christi in Tlaxcala, where the Indians constructed miniature artificial landscapes, each with its own mountain, at the four corners of a specially designed processional route (Motolinía 1990: 62). As the painted and sculpted iconography of a number of today's remaining posas indicates, each mountain was also dedicated to a different Christian theme. Mendieta (1973, 2:50) reported on four small, covered structures placed by the Indians at the corners of another processional route, with a fifth in front of the church, from which the participants would start out.

The arrangement of four corner posas and a central cross within a walled enclosure is highly reminiscent of the configuration of the cosmic arenas depicted in the teoamoxtli. It also recalls the architectural equivalents on the summit of Cerro Tlaloc and the ayaucalli schemes. The almost intact corner posas at Huejotzingo and Calpan open on two sides, thus allowing for processions in both directions. The positioning of the remaining "bench-altars" inside the posas at Calpan, however, indicates that, in order for participants to approach the altars face-on, processions at this site must have taken place in an anticlockwise direction.[19] The orientation of the three surviving posas with one opening at Epazoyucan suggests the same directional route. This is also the case at Tezontepec (Pachuca, Hidalgo). Again, we are reminded of the ayaucalli houses, "oriented toward the four parts of the world, one toward the east, another toward the north, another toward the west, another toward the south,"[20] where four days of ritual fasting took place, one in each of the houses (Sahagún 1981, 1:164). If Sahagún's text follows the order given by his informants (east-north-west-south), then an anticlockwise route between these four temples is also implied.[21]

A detail on the pyramidal-topped posas at Huejotzingo and Calpan certainly suggests that they once offered a stunning image in stone drawn directly from the native cosmovision. The spiny, cactuslike cross with serpentine "roots" that now stands at the center of the atrium at Huejotzingo (see fig. 6.67) is all that remains of four that once topped the posas' pyramid-shaped roofs (Salazar Monroy 1944: 10; Angulo Iñiguez 1955: 202–203). The original atrial cross, also carved with spines, now stands in the town's square (fig. 6.61). Cacti also topped the posas at Calpan, the surviving example on the posa dedicated to the Virgin having been identified as an organ cactus (Angulo Iñiguez 1955: 140, 222) or as a broken example of the type found at Huejotzingo (McAndrew 1965: 327). Despite possible European intentions to render the atrium a model of the Heavenly Jerusalem (Lara 2004: 18–19), the form given to the architectural elements at these two neighboring sites must be an indigenous initiative. It constitutes an almost perfect representation of the mythical structure of the terrestrial plane, with its interchangeable parameters of sacred trees and posa-mountains and axis mundi at the center. In addition, the surviving posa-cross at Calpan takes the form of two entwined trunks that strongly evoke the twisted trunks of the cosmic trees through which flowed the divine opposing forces of the cosmos.[22]

Sixteenth-century native representations of Christian architecture rarely depict open chapels. As architectural elements that varied considerably in design, location, and life span, open chapels may have been perceived by the Indians as symbolically inconsequential within the standard atrium layout.[23] Posas, or structures echoing the configuration of the posa-cross layout, occur quite frequently, however, as if these did have an architectural value or symbolism that was meaningful on an Indian map. Figure 4.7, which represents the monastery complex of Huejutla in 1580, includes all four posas (now lost) and shows clearly that an anticlockwise route was prescribed, at least in the eyes of the mapmaker.[24] On the circa 1580 map of Huapalteopan (México) (fig. 4.10), four linteled structures are arranged in an untidy row in front of the church of San Clemente: one is upside down, another two lie on their sides. While these might represent simple dwellings, closer examination of them suggests that they were intended to be posas. From

Figure 4.10. The ca. 1580 map of Huapalteopan, México. Archivo General de la Nación 1532.

the viewer's perspective, which is from the west, and from the left (or north), they open to the south (right), east (up), north (left), and west (down), which again corresponds to the orientation of the posas at Calpan, Epazoyucan, and elsewhere.[25]

Much has been written on the subject of the "fortress churches" of early colonial Mexico, particularly the crenellated rooftops and merloned atrium walls that served as defensive elements (e.g., McAndrew 1965: 255–28; Kubler 1992: 313–15). Attacks on missions located on the fringes of Chichimec territory were a distinct reality throughout most of the sixteenth century; but by the time the churches displaying these architectural elements in the central area were completed (Cholula, Tepeaca, Tecamachalco [Puebla] and Acolman [México]), the threat of an Indian uprising was virtually nonexistent. Besides, the fragility of the Mexican fortifications is rather too evident. The purpose of these architectural details therefore remains unclear. They may, of course, be purely decorative throwbacks to the medieval churches with which the friars were familiar, but it is not impossible that they entered the New World as architectural symbols of the Catholic Church's metaphoric mission of "warfare" against the devil.[26] The Franciscans identified themselves as the "soldiers of Christ," being instructed from the outset to defend the "squadron" of the King of Heaven and to take up the "victorious struggle" against his enemies.[27] The same ideas were emphasized in communications to the native population (see Sahagún 1986: 170–75). But would the Indians have understood rooftop crenellations and merlons as architectural symbols of the Christian Good Fight, much less as a practical mode of defense? Here again the perception of visual form intercedes. As suggested earlier, the use of merlons on prehispanic ceremonial architecture

Figure 4.11. Rooftop merlons on the sixteenth-century parish church of Tlaxcoapan, Hidalgo.

probably pertained to that architecture's symbolism as a replica of the topography of the sacred landscape. In shape and form church merlons tend to echo their European counterparts, which nevertheless resemble miniature (Egyptian) pyramids. Interesting variations do occur, however. The merlons circling the tops of the nave walls at Tepeaca, for example, replicate the stepped prehispanic examples with their central cavities. The sixteenth-century parish church at Tlaxcoapan (Hidalgo) offers a selection, including both stepped and triangular varieties (fig. 4.11).

Drawing on classical forms, Spanish colonial architecture purposefully sought to employ the true arch as a cultural signifier, that is, as a symbol of European technological superiority (Fraser 1990). But here again the question must arise as to whether the Indians understood its form in the same light. Spanish reports regarding the Indians' fear of the arch as an unstable architectural innovation (Torquemada 1975–83, 5:66) may well have been exaggerated to highlight Spanish notions of cultural superiority. But native reactions may have had more to do with perception than with technique. The dark, stone-vaulted interiors, entered through arched portals, must have given the churches more than a passing resemblance to great, hollowed-out mountain caverns, where the prehispanic layperson would also have feared or have been forbidden to tread (see Burgoa 1989, 1:340).

Finally, some comment should be made on the practice of displaying traditionally or near traditionally executed glyphic toponyms of the political altepetl on the exterior or interior walls of sixteenth-century churches. Among many surviving examples we find the pot of water over the three hearthstones at Atotonilco ("Where There Is Hot Water") el Grande (Hidalgo) and the fish at Michimaloyan, "Place of Fishing" (Hidalgo) (fig. 4.12). At Mixtec Coixtlahuaca, "Serpent Plain," the wide arched entrance to the open chapel carries a double frieze of twin-headed serpents, the most usual form of the reptile found in graphic renderings of the town's toponym. In mural painting a frieze of half-moons around the walls of the monastery refectory at Meztitlan alludes to "Place of the Moon." The eagle and jaguar flanking the European Annunciation over the refectory door at Cuauhtinchan may well read as *quauhtli ychan, ocellotl ychan*, the named territory conquered by the Cuauhtinchantlaca (*HTC* 1989: 193).

Although it is not clear if the practice of displaying toponyms on religious or civic architecture followed a prehispanic tradition or was a native response to the European heraldic system, their presence on churches was evidently permitted because Europeans viewed them as a secular tool. From the native perspective, their purpose was perhaps to complement the churches' secondary function as the central symbol of the colonial altepetl's identity. Noticeable in all architectural examples of toponyms, however, is the omission of the *tepetl* hill glyph, as if the church itself represents the concept of "water-mountain" and the glyph its toponymic qualifier. An exception is found at Natividad de Nuestra Señora Tepoztlan (Morelos), where both the hill glyph and qualifier (the copper axe of the pulque deity Tepoztecatl) were carved on the church font. Here the hill glyph would read as Tepozteco, the great ridge rising to the northwest of the town (home of Tepoztecatl, its erstwhile patron deity). At a syncretic level Cerro Tepozteco's identification with the Christian sacred-water vessel is perhaps doubly emphatic.[28]

Figure 4.12. The name-glyph of Michimaloyan, "Place of Fishing," over the village church door.

The native peoples' own descriptions of their churches offer views almost parallel to those discussed above: these edifices everywhere were perceived as sacred mountains endowed with cavernous, watery interiors.

Although the *Cantares mexicanos* collection of devotional song-poems still awaits conclusive literary analysis, its texts nevertheless offer strong internal references to recognizable visual imagery. Clear references to ceremonial architecture are few but surprisingly consistent in their use of terminology. As we might expect, prehispanic architecture was likened to the cavern interiors of mountains. The "Chalcan female song" places Axayacatl's woven mat or seat of rulership "within the precious cavern house" (*quetzaloztocalco*) (*CM*, f. 72v; 1985: 386–87), while another song speaks of Tenochtitlan's "grotto house of jade" (*chalchiuhoztocalli*) (ibid., f. 52v; pp. 312–13).

But the songs containing references to postconquest figures also speak of bishops singing in cavern houses, of singer-composers arriving at cavern houses or speaking God's words within them (ibid., ff. 15r–15v; pp. 178–81). The context identifies these

venues as the house of the Christian god above (heaven) and below (the church building). His house is a "place of rain" (*quiapan*) (ibid., ff. 19r, 29r, 42v; pp. 190–91, 226–27,
272–73) and a "water palace" (*atecpan*) (ibid., f. 12r; pp. 168–69), with a garden like
"watered fields" (*acuecuentla*) (ibid., f. 52r; pp. 312–13). Ultimately the grotto house
of prehispanic Tenochtitlan also becomes his house (ibid., f. 53r; pp. 316–17).[29] An
epic song recounting a 1527–28 journey to Europe by a troupe of native dancers and
jugglers tells how God's words were given honor in the "cavern house of colors" (*tla-
papaloztocalli*) that stood at the pope's residence (ibid., f. 59v; pp. 340–41).[30] Given
the date, the cave-church in question can only be the Sistine Chapel with its recently
completed (1527) cycle of murals by Michelangelo Buonarroti. In other words, it was
not just the Indians' churches that were perceived as water-filled caves, a circumstance
that perhaps offers considerable insight into native understanding or interpretations of
Christianity as a religion.

Representations of the churches of New Spain were introduced into the area and village maps produced by Indian artists across the first century of colonial rule, ostensibly
serving as a replacement sign for the tepetl hill glyph or as an adjunct to it.[31] The source
for this new native cartographic sign was possibly early or contemporary European
maps, on which major towns and cities were often marked in the same manner.[32] Given
other options available from the same maps (an orb and cross, for example), however,
the choice does not appear to have been the result of direct imitation or adoption of
European cartographical norms.

While no itinerary maps as such have survived from the prehispanic era, we know
that they were produced and that the art of reading them was a specialist skill.[33] Indeed, if native mapping of the early colonial period is anything to go by, Indian "maps"
were more often than not complex texts offering economic, historical, political, and
religious readings as well as geographical description.[34] But I question not only the assumed colonial influence behind the representation of a church as a *sign* for an urban
settlement but also the general assumption that the hill glyph functioned only as a
sign for the geographical location of an urban settlement in the first place. As I pursue
below, a native-perceived relationship between the landscape and the church (which
physically replaced the prehispanic temple) might well explain why the church appears
to have been adopted by so many as a sign for a town or village. In addition, in numerous instances the image of a church on maps represents the real edifice or the mapmaker's perception of the same. The hill glyph, I propose, was toponymic only in that
it identified itself as the patron-mountain of its dependent community. In other words,
it did not denote the geographical location of a human settlement but, inscribed with
that settlement's glyphic name, represented the real mountain and its own geographical siting. Certainly the hill glyph was a long time in disappearing from native maps,
often being included together with an image of a church. Where it does not appear in
traditional form, in many cases it is represented naturalistically. In short, in colonial
mapping (and landscape painting—see chapter 6) church signs did not replace hill
signs. Both signs did, however, function together at an ideological level.

In most cases the image of the church as painted or drawn by Indian cartographers
varies in some way; but, as in representations of the prehispanic temple, certain common characteristics always occur.[35] Churches appear in three-dimensional form or
from one side with no suggestion of depth, often on the same map. Some are represented architecturally (or semiarchitecturally): they include European architectural

features such as domes, merlons, roof pediments, columns, capitals and pedestals, and the *alfiz* (a squared or rectangular molding that frames the Moorish arch). A number of examples in this group also constitute a very good likeness of the churches they portray (Huaxtepec [Morelos], Nopaluca [Puebla]). The most frequent representation of the church, however, is a simple stylization that takes two basic forms: flat or three-dimensional boxes or turreted cylinders, both variations usually topped with a bell tower and/or a cross (see fig. 4.15, plate 8). Multiturreted "boxes" also occur. Cylinders and turrets are one curious feature of native representations of churches, for only the early chapel of San Miguel on Chapultepec Hill (D.F.) is known to have been round.

Both architectural and stylized versions also commonly detail the church facade with a central arched (or occasionally linteled) portal and two upper windows, one at each side. The incidence of two windows at either side of the facade was unknown in sixteenth-century New Spain except in three-aisled churches (Tecali [Puebla], Cuilapan) where the configuration changes with the addition of two extra doors. A central choir window was usually the only fenestral opening in the facade of single nave churches; these were occasionally drawn in. This suggests that the sources for most representations were European. Turrets point to northern European origin (where castles of this type are common) as well as, of course, the characteristic conical spires of Gothic religious architecture. The stylized boxes, together with the facade configuration of arched portal and two lateral windows, are reminiscent of those found in the work of a number of late-fifteenth- and early-sixteenth-century engravers (Martin Wöhlgemut and Albrecht Dürer, for example). More likely sources in New Spain are the illustrations in printed books, such as Bartolomaeus Anglicus's *Libro de Proprietatibus Rerum en Romance* (published in 1520 in Toledo), or contemporary maps.

If the choice was to represent churches as depicted in European sources, then the inclusion of lateral windows is also not entirely incomprehensible, given the well-documented accuracy with which native artists could copy such material. The same sources were probably circulated widely in New Spain. Neither circumstance explains, however, why so many native mapmakers over a wide geographical area and across two or three generations *all* chose to use the same configuration, especially when it bore no resemblance to the churches they were familiar with. The choice would therefore appear to point to a common cognitive image of the building that derived from their own perception of the European versions: something about those stylizations was immediately meaningful in the native understanding of places of worship.

Native conventions governing stylization at the time of the conquest depended on a finite conceptualization of the object being depicted. Where ceremonial architecture emulated the contours of the landscape created from the body of the earth monster, temple portals were perceived as replicas of her mouths and orifices or cave entrances. By the time most of the native maps with their representations of Christian churches were painted, stone- or brick-vaulted interiors and arched portals and doorways would have been a common architectural feature across New Spain's landscape. As the *Cantares mexicanos* song-poems attest, the churches already possessed a form that likened them to mountain-caverns. E. H. Gombrich (1979: 171) reminds us that human perceptual habits are "particularly prone to project faces into any configuration remotely permitting this transformation." This habit of animation may well be the source of the portal plus lateral windows configuration, *as understood from its sources,* and if so would certainly suggest that the Indians came to perceive the Christian church as an animated object. Religious structures in prehispanic Mexico had also been animated in this way. The *chac* (rain deity) masks around temple doors in the Yucatec Maya area and the serpent-jaw portals of central Mexico offer clear evidence in this respect. These carvings were not decorative. The mountains that the temples emulated were also living entities for the Indians, and living entities have faces. A mountain with a face is identified in a monstrous cleft head on which the left-hand figure in the Palenque tablet of the Foliated Cross stands. The head represents the Maya version of the mountain of sustenance, the "first-true-mountain," which contained the maize used to mold human flesh at the Creation. Its name glyphs are found in its eyes, while maize emerges from the cleft (Freidel et al. 1993: 138–39). In the central area the tzoalli images of sacred water-mountains (the deity-temple-mountain tepictoton) were made in human form and given eyes, mouths, and teeth (FC1, 1970: 47; Durán 1984, 1:165, 279).

One extraordinary group of cartographic churches offers still clearer evidence that the Indians perceived these structures as replicas of mountains, for they in fact represented them as such. This is, admittedly, a small group across the corpus of native maps, but their churches are so distorted that they are only recognizable as architectural structures by the addition of (usually) a bell tower and/or a rooftop cross.

The 1579 maps of the Suchitepec group from southern Oaxaca (figs. 4.8 and 4.9) cover the Zapotec cabecera of Suchitepec (today's Santa María Xadani) and its four Chontal sujetos. All were painted by the same mapmaker, who created a series of church-mountains, complete with crags, peaks, and contours and in two cases (discussed below) portals resembling cave openings. In what may have been an attempt to depict vaulted roofing, the strange red-brown, "hump-backed" churches of the maps of San Pedro del Rosal (ca. 1559), San Luis de las Peras (1556), and neighboring San Jerónimo Satetlan (1559) more closely resemble rounded hills. The churches on the 1563 Mapa de Cuauhtinchan No. 4 are also only recognizable as Christian structures in that they occupy the center of the Spanish grid-iron traza used to denote the locations of villages in the Cuauhtinchan area (fig. 4.13). They take the form of the stepped mer-

lon with central cavity also deployed to depict the cave of the idol Tepehua on the 1539 painting referred earlier (plate 6). The rosy-pink church on the 1569 map of Tlahuelilpa (plate 7) boasts six "peaks" rising from a rounded mass, identifiable as a church only by its prominent bell tower.

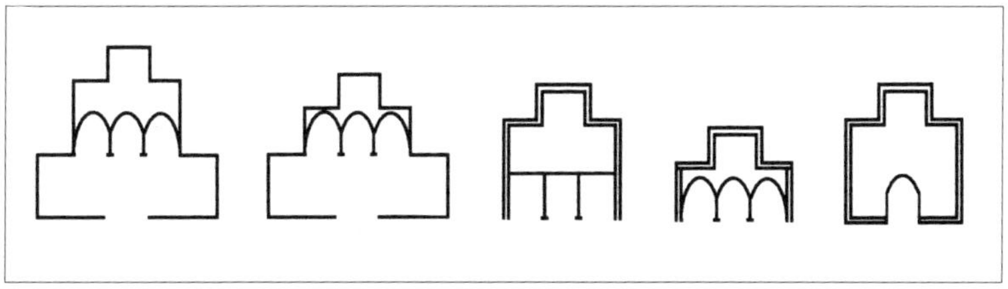

On the 1572 map of Almolonca and Maxtlatlan (Veracruz) the hill-

Figure 4.13. The merlon-like, stepped churches of the Cuauhtinchan region, as represented on Mapa de Cuauhtinchan No. 4 (based on a drawing in Yoneda 1991).

churches marking the sites of the two villages carry the curved base and horizontal bar of the traditional hill glyph but are topped with Christian crosses (fig. 4.14). One hill-church is rounded, and the other peaked. Dana Leibsohn (1995: 271) has used this map to illustrate her point that hill-church glyphs in general constitute a fusion of prehispanic and European cartographic place-signs, which acknowledge towns as being both Christian and indigenous. But, as observed earlier, the melding of architecture and topography as a single concept has prehispanic graphic precedents, also with strong religious undertones. Temples and platforms were perceived as replica sacred mountains. Small additional elements on the Almolonca-Maxtlatlan map suggest that

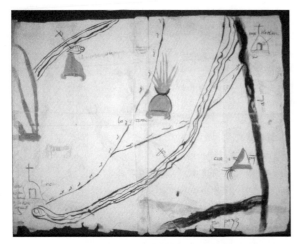

Figure 4.14. The 1572 map of Almolonca and Maxtlatlan, Veracruz. Archivo General de la Nación 1561.

the fused hill-church signs were intended to represent the actual churches of their respective villages. That is, in my interpretation of the fusion, the churches are depicted as the replica patron-mountains they were perceived to be. Both include a portal, but one is linteled and the other arched, a variation that corresponds well with the architectural reality of New Spain, where church portals did not adhere to a fixed form. The mapmaker also went to the trouble of shading in one side of the arched portal on the hill-church of Maxtlatlan, creating the effect that this particular building was aligned at a different angle than that of its neighbor.[36] Differences in alignments were also part of the reality of colonial religious architecture, and numerous indigenous cartographers acknowledged the phenomenon on their maps.

Although the source for the images was European book illustrations, the tendency toward a common stylization of cartographic Christian churches is closely aligned to the native graphic tradition, which conventionalized an object in glyphic form. More importantly, it is in the specificity of motifs or symbols to include in the glyph that the conceptual meaning of the object is expressed. In this respect, the small but consistent details that Indian mapmakers—as a group—added to their original source material can be seen to relate directly to those employed in the representation of prehispanic temples, the original replicas of sacred mountains.

A clearly defined architectural base is one feature shared by most cartographic churches. This might be seen to represent the raised, stepped esplanade that was sometimes constructed in front of the main entrance of the church and adjoining cloister. As in medieval Europe, its purpose was to raise the height of the building visually before the approaching worshiper, thereby intensifying the awe and majesty manifest in God's house. In the maps depicting three-dimensional images of churches, however, it is clear that the cartographic bases elevate the whole building (see, for example, figs. 4.15 and 4.16 and plate 8), a phenomenon that raises a number of questions. Do these bases record the continuing presence of the platforms of the old temples? If so, then this must be seen as a rather odd detail to include on a map where the image of the church ostensibly serves as a sign for a town or village and not as the real church. It also does not explain why the European cartographic sign-model underwent this modification. Or is it that all of these images—whether functioning as cartographic signs for towns and villages and/or representations of real churches—betray

Figure 4.15. The 1580 map of Cuzcatlan, Oaxaca. España, Ministerio de Cultura, Archivo General de Indias, MP-MEXICO 19.

the mapmakers' perception of the Christian church as a symbolic equivalent of the prehispanic temple and its artificial mountain platform?

What we may call "parapets" in the form of a double line across the top of facades are another common motif in both stylized and architectural representations of churches (e.g., figs. 4.15 and 4.16 and plate 8). Some are decorated with friezes of circles (as on the maps of Amoltepec, 1580, and Tornacuxtla, ca. 1599) or geometric fretworks after the Mixtec tradition (Cuquila, Mixtepec, and Chicaguastla, ca. 1595 [fig. 4.17], Nochistlan, 1581). The mountain-churches of the Suchitepec group (figs. 4.8, 4.9) also carry parapetlike details that resemble topographical contours. Such architectural detail is not European in

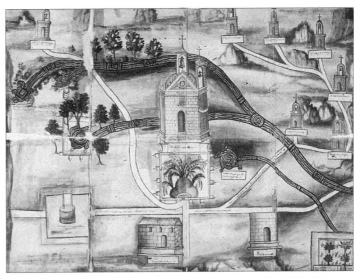

Figure 4.16. Detail from the 1580 map of Huaxtepec, Morelos (UTX JGI xxiv-3). Nettie Lee Benson Latin American Collection, University of Texas libraries, The University of Texas at Austin.

origin, being more clearly a throwback to the decorated parapets of the temples of old. Neither is it restricted to graphic representation, for it can be found across the upper facades of a number of churches or cloister buildings in the central area. The monastery-church of San Bernardino Xochimilco (D.F.) boasts a frieze of concentric circles; at Santa Cecilia Atlixco it is composed of Greek crosses.

The graphic focus on temple doorways is also reiterated in the maps, although in stylizations of churches it is usually the European arch that takes the upper hand. In sixteenth-century Mexico arched portals were employed arbitrarily for both religious and secular buildings; but where they occur as church entrances on maps, they are frequently emphasized. Size in proportion to the building is one option (the unrestrained exaggerations on the maps of Cuzcatlan [fig. 4.15] and Acapixtla [plate 9] are evident), but some are highlighted by use of a very firmly drawn double line (plates 8 and 9, fig. 4.17; Macupilco, 1579; Itztapalapa, 1580). The possibility that the arched portals of churches were perceived as cave openings has already been mooted, and several examples of native representations tend to confirm this interpretation. The mountain-church of Suchitepec (fig. 4.8) displays a heavily carved portal that probably reflects floral sculpture found commonly around sixteenth-century church entrances but that on the map more closely resembles a jaguar pelt in both color and design. The jaguar was associated with the night and the interior of the earth; the spots of the American species took the form of four- and

Figure 4.17. The ca. 1595 map of Mixtepec, Chicaguastla, and Cuquila, Oaxaca. Archivo General de la Nación 867.

five-petaled flowers. This quirk of nature was not lost on native artists when they came to depict jaguar pelts and cave portals. The murals of the net-jaguar at Tetitla, Teotihuacan, for example, include temples with floral jaguar-skin door-frames, while the cave of the idol Tepehua was depicted on the 1539 drawing with a jaguar-skin entrance (plate 6). The mapmaker of the Suchitepec group evidently still saw the portals of his own mountain-church as the entrance to the abode of the jaguar. In the map of Tlamacazcatepec from the same group (fig. 4.9), the church carries a design over its portal that closely resembles a double row of curved incisors.[37] A similar reference to a fanged cave-mouth is made on the representation of the early-sixteenth-century church at Zapotec San Miguel Tiltepec, included in the village's famous lienzo.[38] A large rectangular structure resembling a flying facade crowns the church roof and is detailed with a series of opposing diagonal lines, not unlike forward and backward slash characters:

\\\\ //// \\\\ ////

The configuration is prehispanic in origin and usually interpreted as a sky-band.[39] Closer contextual analysis, however, shows that it represents the fanged maws of the entrance to the earth (Laughton 1997: 58–75).

Graphic links between churches and local mountains are also in evidence, and here numerous formulae were deployed to emphasize the perceived association.

The circa 1595 map of Cuquila-Mixtepec-Chicaguastla (Oaxaca) (fig. 4.17) includes a raised base on both its churches and topographical features. Although the latter were drawn as rock-noduled mountain glyphs after the Mixtec tradition, their glosses identifying them as *montes* indicate that these elements represent local topography. Thus, while the churches might function as cartographic signs for the two villages, as representations of edifices they are graphically associated with the real landscape. In this map we can also note that the double lines around the church portals echo those framing the mountains.

On the 1591 map of Jocotitlan and Atlacomulco (México) (fig. 4.18) the two churches are paired with traditional hill signs, both of which carry glyphic qualifiers in the

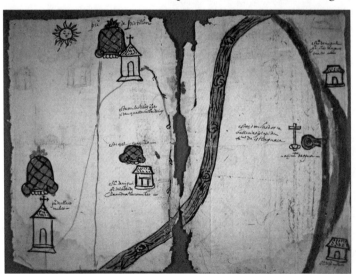

form of a stylized maguey plant. The water frill of the hill sign corresponding to Atlacomulco touches the church's rooftop cross, while that of Jocotitlan encroaches onto the fabric of the church itself.

Graphic contact in both cases might therefore represent an attempt to fuse the traditional altepetl sign with the newly adopted church sign. In fact the hill glyphs represent real mountains, by name the patron-mountains of the two towns. The qualifying maguey glyph does not correspond to either Atlacomulco or Jocotitlan, however,[40] but, rather ingeniously, to the original Franciscan establishment of San Juan Bautista Metepec ("Maguey Hill"), under whose religious ministration and indoctrination both these villages fell

Figure 4.18. The 1591 map of Jocotitlan and Atlacomulco, México. Archivo General de la Nación 1235.

until secularization between 1569 and 1575 (Gerhard 1986: 181). Cerro Metepec is a prominent mountain in the area from which the town would also have taken its original Nahuatl name. At the same time the hill glyphs denote the actual locations of the patron-mountains with which each of the two villages identified itself. With east, marked by the sun, lying toward the top left-hand corner of the map, Cerro Atlacomulco is placed correctly in respect to its namesake settlement (INEGI, *Carta topográfica* E14A17, 1997).[41] Cerro Xocotitlan lies to the immediate northeast of Jocotitlan (INEGI, *Carta topográfica* E14A27, 1998); the cartographic encroachment of the mountain onto the church is also very precise (my on-site observation). In this reading, the graphic adhesion of the village churches to Metepec speaks of Christian geo-religious organization expressed through the symbolism of patron-mountains. It is not an attempt to hybridize cartographic signs.[42]

The 1580 map of Atlatlauhca and Suchiaca (México) (fig. 4.19) presents a further alternative. The villages lie in the Valley of Matlalcingo, a rugged highland area to the east of the Nevado de Toluca, so we would expect mountains to figure prominently on this area map. The two central representations of hills covered with trees that flank Atlatlauhca, however, correspond to only two of the three important peaks surrounding the community. Where the map places south at the top, the foothills of the Nevado to the town's west (glossed *monte*) are marked to the right, while on the left Cerro Tenango (glossed *monte de Atlatlauhca*) lies to the east (see INEGI, *Carta topográfica* E14A48, 1997). Beneath Cerro Tenango (that is, to the northeast) a small church representing the town of Teotenango is depicted. Despite its prominence in the area, Cerro Tetepetl to the west of Teotenango is not included. This is very much the Atlatlauhca artist's vision of his local landscape, for, by exclusion, he referred only to the mountains that were of importance to his own village.[43] The quincuncial configuration given to Atlatlauhca's and Suchiaca's carto-

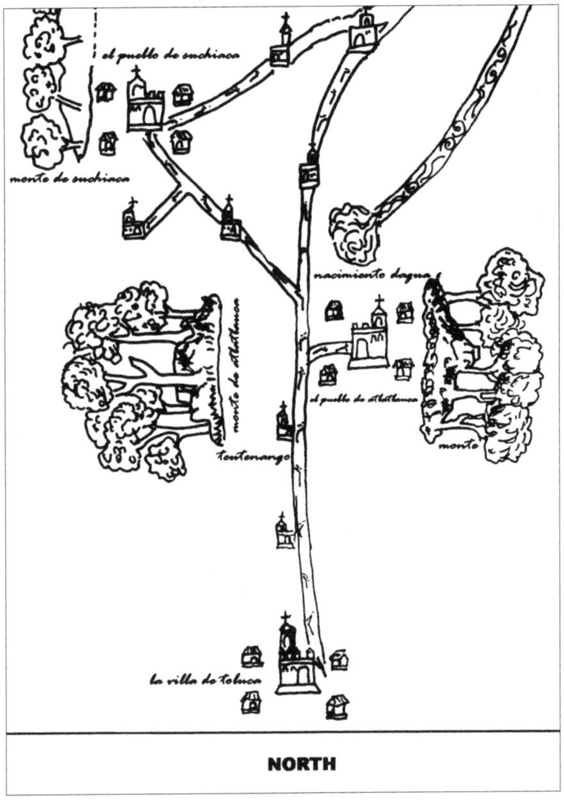

Figure 4.19. Simplified drawing of the 1580 map of Atlatlauhca, México (UTX JGI xxiii-13), showing local patron-mountains and quincuncial layout of cosmic trees.

graphic churches and four outlying structures may well represent the communities' four barrios or their barrio chapels.[44] But the mapmaker's interest in pursuing this configuration is evident, for he matched it with the arrangements of the trees on the mountains: each mountain carries five trees, but those depicted on Cerro Tenango—Atlatlauhca's mountain—are also arranged as a quincunx. In addition, Cerro Tenango is given a stepped, architectural form.

The use of color on native maps—a fundamental element of traditional writing systems—offers by far the clearest evidence of how the Indians perceived their churches as replica water-mountains.

The 1571 map of Tezontepec de Aldama, Mixquiahuala (Hidalgo) is a fine example in this respect (plate 10).[45] As glossed, the traditional hill glyph standing to one side of the stylized church represents Cerro Teçontepec (Tezontepec's own mountain), today's

Cerro Huitel to the southwest of the village (INEGI, *Carta topográfica* F14C89, 1995). Again, the hill glyph is topographical and not toponymic. While the cartographic church does denote the site of the village in relation to this mountain, it is also conceptualized as a replica of the mountain. The pink portal matches the mass of the mountain, while the facade and alfiz are chromatically paired with the deep-red horizontal bar and the surrounding yellow rim at its base. The same yellow was used for the eastern river (Río Tepeitic), while turquoise denotes the river to the west (Río Tula) *and* a second base rim. Thus the mapmaker's careful use of color effectively incorporates the image of the village's own sacred mountain into its church, together with the rivers that are fed by the mountain.[46]

Significantly, however, most colonial native mapmakers chose red or blue (or tonal variations such as pink, orange, mauve, or red-brown and turquoise or pale or deep blue) to color their churches. The choice is very consistent and far outweighs the presence of any other colors applied to this cartographic feature. Of the maps in color (listed in appendix B), the mountain-churches at Almolonca-Maxtlatlan (fig. 4.14) are outlined in red; the hill-churches of San Pedro del Rosal and San Luis de las Peras are wine-red, while the representations at Tlahuelilpa (plate 7), Tetliztaca, Minas de Zumpango, and Acambaro are pink. The church of Coatlinchan (México) on the town's two sister-maps of 1578 is pink (plate 8); in one version it boasts a deep red-pink interior, indicated by the colored infill on its portal and windows (plate 8b). On Mapa de Cuauhtinchan No. 4 the cave-church of Tepeaca is outlined in red. The predominant colors of the mountain-churches in the Suchitepec group are red, red-brown, and mauve. A red interior is implied in the upper facade windows of the church of Amoltepec, while its portal and cornice are also detailed in red and orange. Other cartographic churches present much the same features in blue. A blue interior occurs on the church of Santa María on the 1558 map of México-Tenochtitlan ("Plano en papel de maguey"); blue bells can be found on the cartographic churches of Tejupa and Itztapalapa. The cave-church of Tetela is outlined in blue on Mapa de Cuauhtinchan No. 4.

While these are all examples of the use of either red or blue, many other cartographic churches were painted as a combination of the two colors (or their tonal variations) in much the same way as their prehispanic predecessors pictured in the codices.[47] The most usual chromatic configuration is a red exterior complemented by a blue interior, although as an alternative blue bells are very common, such as in the examples of maps from Coatlinchan (plate 8a), Acapixtla (plate 9), Huaxtepec, Codex Osuna, and Nativitas and San Antonio. Native mapmakers' decision to color the interiors and exteriors of their churches in this manner leaves little doubt that they were intended to correspond directly with pre- and postconquest representations of prehispanic temples and thus the concept of the water-mountain proper.

But as in the codices, interesting variations occur. A blue church with red interior on the 1590 map of Cempoala is a chromatic reversal of the 1580 map from the same town, where the bells are red and the interiors blue. At present I can offer no real explanation for this exchange of color. Given the importance of chromatics in native expression, it is not impossible that native perception of churches mutated in accordance with circumstance or time and that cartographic color (or even lack of it) also expresses this. Blue or red church interiors might echo the rainy and dry seasons, respectively, in the two main stages of the agricultural cycle: germination/growth (blue) and maturation/harvest (red). This tentative interpretation could account for the two versions of the pink church at Coatlinchan (plate 8), dated to the same year but with a blue and a red-pink interior, respectively. Although the maps are very similar, a noticeable difference is seen in the burgeoning vegetation on the landscape in version 8b (red-pink church interior). Here some thirty-five apparently deciduous trees are depicted, as opposed to the thirteen conifers or evergreens in version 8a. In addition, the cartographer added two plots of arable land to version 8b, one with a neat quincunx of large, cob-bearing maize plants. Thus version 8a may have been painted close to or at the start of the rainy season in 1578, when the mountains still retained their water, while version 8b may be nearer harvest time, when the mountains were "empty" and the agricultural cycle was drawing to a close.

Where the *Cantares mexicanos* song-poems speak of the Christian church as a cavern-house, they also offer very consistent metaphorical descriptions of the same building as a blue and red place. God's home is a "turquoise picture house" (*xiuhamox-calli*) (*CM*, ff. 17v; 1985: 186–87) and a "house of crimson" (*tlauhcalli*) (ibid., f. 62v; pp. 352–53), a "turquoise swan seat" (*xiuhquecholycpal*) and a "roseate swan mat" (*tlauhquecholpetl*) (ibid., f. 22v; pp. 204–205). God himself is an arbor of "turquoise song flowers" (*xiuhquechol-xochinpetlacotl*) in whose home stands a "roseate altar of flowers" (*tlahuimomoz[tli]*) (ibid., ff. 17v, 22r; pp. 186–87, 202–203).

The inclusion of turquoise-blue church bells is so frequent across the corpus of maps that it must also be attributed to a native perception of the imported ecclesiastical bell that was somewhat different from the European perception. In the *Cantares mexicanos* references to the "turquoise bell" (*xiuhcoyollatoa*) at Santiago (Tlatelolco) (*CM*, f. 44r; 1985: 280–81), the "jade-gong pealing" (*chalchiuhtetzilacatzitzilicatoc*) of the bells of San Francisco (Aztapotzalco) (ibid., f. 45v; pp. 284–85), and the "jade gong" (*chalchi-uhtetzilacatl*) in God's home (ibid., f. 63r; pp. 352–53) provide a more than appropriate description of the blue bells of the cartographic church towers. Here it could be argued that native mapmakers colored their maps with the imagery of the song-poems in mind or that the Christian song-poems had a pictographic source. Both are possibilities, but I am more inclined to think that it was the song-composers' and the mapmakers' own (shared) chromatic vision of the Christian sacred that prompted their choices in both modes of expression. Hugo Nutini's informants in twentieth-century Tlaxcala understood the harmonious tones of church bells as a collective welcome for the dead who had acted as intermediaries with the masters of the sacred water-mountains Matlalcueye and Cuatlapanga (Nutini 1988: 151). This belief is not too far removed from the use of the prehispanic *ayauhchicauaztli*, "mist-rattle," which called for water from the "turquoise house" that was Tlalocan (Nicholson et al. 1997: 133, 135). Blue bells also bring to mind the remark by Mendieta (1973, 1:63) that the idols of the tlaloques were painted blue. These deities were identified as mountains, so it is not too difficult to see how a European bell could come to be perceived as a stylized water-mountain; painting turquoise bells on the maps made a clear statement of their association with water. Although red church bells are not overly common on the maps, the play with both colors may also reflect the wet/dry, water/sun metaphoric expressions suggested in the color inversions of church interiors.

Finally, the use of red and blue to link church and landscape is also fairly common. On the 1580 map of Atlatlauhca (Oaxaca) (see appendix B), which represents five churches in red and seven in blue, the pathways linking them are represented in the same colors. The same is true on the map of Cuauhuitlan, from the same area, even though its seven churches are represented in red. On the map of Tlahuelilpa (plate 7) the contrast between the pink church and the blue mountains is striking. On the map of Huaxtepec the toponymic hill glyph matches the blue and red details of the churches, while on the example from Culhuacan the interiors of the churches match both the toponym and the coloring given to Cerro Huixachtecatl, also represented on the map.

The consistency with which native mapmakers and poets referred to the churches of New Spain provides good evidence that their perception of Euro-Christian architecture was very much dictated by ongoing concerns with water and the sacred mountains as a focus of religious belief and action. Like their prehispanic predecessors, on whose sites most churches stood, each church was understood to be a replica of its community's own patron water-mountain, within which the sacred force of life resided. The chromatic detail applied to the churches also exemplifies the mapmakers' vision of the role of Christian architecture in the Indian world: the home of the Christian god had acquired the identity of the native sacred.

The Church and the Landscape

One of the most interesting aspects of many hilltop and hillside churches is their correspondence with long, straight paths or roads that run directly up the centers of their own and other mountains or hills, often linking one site to another. The pathways were common enough to be noticed in the sixteenth and seventeenth centuries. Motolinía (1990: 50) observed that "to give greater honor to the temples they laid out the pathways in a straight line, very even, of one and two leagues [long]. From the top of the main temple, it was a worthy sight to see how these pathways came in straight lines from all the smaller villages and quarters to the courtyard of the temples."[48] Referring to idolatrous activities still taking place on the slopes of mountains in the seventeenth century, Ruiz de Alarcón (1984: 54) remarked on the pathways that "rise straight up towards the summit to stop at a pile of stones or a hill of them, where they worshipped, sacrificed and prayed." According to Sahagún's informants, these pathways were "the roads of the Tlalocs" (CMRAH, f. 54v; Nicholson et al. 1997: 201).

There seems little doubt that the pathways are the vestiges of a network of sacred routes that criss-crossed the landscape. In the second half of the last century German scholar Franz Tichy carried out considerable work on the axial alignments of both prehispanic and colonial buildings. He noted that large religious and political centers, their smaller dependent settlements, pathways and tracts of land between them, and architecture itself seem to have been sited and aligned in accordance with a complex system of radial networks of imaginary sightlines that found their origins in the sacred rain mountains. In other words, the lie of the land and, in particular, the natural order of important topographical features had dictated human organization of space and movement across the landscape. As Tichy was able to confirm, sixteenth-century Christian architecture, which in so many cases physically replaced the temples of old, inherited the same alignments as its prehispanic predecessors.[49]

Drawn from Tichy's original work, with minor modifications, figure 4.20 reproduces the projections of major imaginary sightlines across the area covering the northeastern boundary of the modern-day state of México with the state of Hidalgo. The radial system out of Teotihuacan indicated on the plan also includes the siting of the

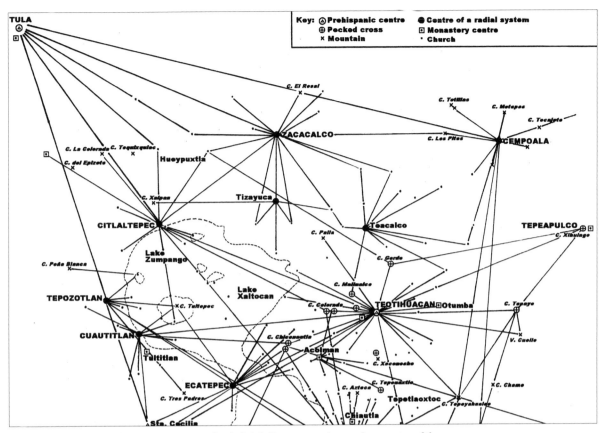

Figure 4.20. Franz Tichy's proposed system of radial sightlines across the northern sector of the Valley of Mexico (redrawn after Tichy 1991a, with modifications).

so-called pecked crosses, petroglyphs or geoglyphs associated primarily with this center that may have functioned as coordinates for a similar system of spatial organization (see Aveni 1989; Aveni et al. 1978). The relationship of the inherited alignments of churches with key mountains can be appreciated, for example, in the monastery church of Cempoala. With an azimuth of 110°—that is, a deviation angle of 20° south of east (Tichy 1992: 204; my on-site observation)—the structure faces out directly toward Cerro El Rosal to the west, itself an intermediary point on a major sightline between Cempoala and Tula. The sightline between the church and Cerro Metepec to the north of the town runs at an exact right angle to the first sightline.

With an azimuth of 106° (Tichy 1992: 204), the monastery church of Acolman faces out directly toward Cerro Chiconauhtla (see fig. 6.6b). The mountain origin of the sightline is marked by TEO14, one of two original Teotihuacan pecked crosses (Tichy 1991a: 448 and fig. 1); the line itself appears to continue onward to the east as far as Cerro Tepeyahualco, a peak also included in the Teotihuacan radial system. In addition, the monastery church is aligned at a right angle to the prehispanic site's Street of the Dead. Traced on a modern-day map (INEGI, *Carta topográfica* E14B21, 1998), it can be seen that the church's cross-axis follows a sightline north to Cerro Colorado, where pecked cross TEO16 is located on its southwestern flank. This petroglyph constituted a further coordinate of one of the visual sightlines drawn from Teotihuacan's Pyramid of the Sun to its east.

Although to date Tichy's work on the use of this system in the organization of space has remained at a hypothetical level, the work of sixteenth-century native cartographers tends to confirm that the fundaments of such a system were in place after the conquest. Therefore it seems safe to argue that the colonial references reflect a prehispanic tradition of reading and recording geography that had strong parallels with Tichy's proposed system.

Together with churches, rivers, and mountains, the networks of roads linking towns and villages also dominate the layout of sixteenth-century indigenous maps. The star-shaped configurations of cabeceras and their sujetos on the maps from Oaxaca (fig. 4.15) are perhaps the closest to the proposed system in terms of radial configurations,[50] but other cartographic pathways present features that also strongly support Tichy's observations. On contact with a church, many of them appear to pass through or under it rather than stopping at or passing by its door (fig. 4.18).[51] They also seem to pass beneath Spanish grid-iron street plans (fig. 4.21),[52] or in some cases cross them as if they did not exist at all (Teotenango [1582]; Tejupa [1579]). That is, the pathways permit no interruptions in their trajectories, as if they were a fixed element of the landscape that could not be eclipsed by any human-made structure, much less a Christian church or a Spanish traza. Other maps display pathways that stop abruptly at the foot of mountains, as if to indicate that they have arrived at their destination (plate 8).[53] In other words, in the mapmakers' perception it was not the temples or any other kind of architecture that took precedence on the landscape but the pathways that joined them. If those pathways were dictated by a system of sightlines drawn from the sacred mountains, then ultimately it was the mountains that were acknowledged and given honor by architecture. Let us look more closely at some specific examples.

As marked on the 1595 map of Nopaluca and Ixtiyuca (Puebla) (fig. 4.21), the now virtually impassable sixteenth-century track between the villages appears to originate beneath the south wall of Nopaluca's church. Emerging diagonally from the edge of the traza it then runs in a straight line toward the church of Ixtiyuca, where it is seen to disappear beneath the church's north wall. With other urban structures laid out before them, neither of these representations of churches serves as a cartographic sign for the site of its respective village.[54] The map therefore asserts that, first and foremost, the original prehispanic pathway linked specific points on the landscape beneath the churches; at the end of the sixteenth century it was still not perceived as just a communication route between the two villages.

Nopaluca and Ixtiyuca are located on the San Juan Plains to the southeast of the great Tlaxcallan volcano Matlalcueye and its smaller outcrop, Cerro Citlaltepec, today's Cerro El Pinal. To the northeast of the villages rise the twin peaks of Cerro Las

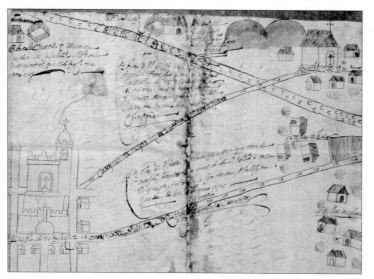

Figure 4.21. The 1595 map of Nopaluca and Santa María Ixtiyuca, Puebla. Archivo General de la Nación 2149.

Derrumbadas, included on the 1595 map even though they stand at a good distance outside the territory covered on it. Painted in bright green, together with thirteen maguey plants, they also stand out on what is otherwise a monochrome drawing. An imaginary sightline drawn between Las Derrumbadas and Citlaltepec on a modern-day map (INEGI, *Cartas topográficas* E14B44, 1995, and E14B35, 1982) is seen to run through the village of Ixtiyuca at an exact right angle to the old pathway (fig. 4.22). It seems possible, then, that the mapmaker was aware of this sightline when drawing the map.

In addition, the representations of the churches of Nopaluca and Ixtiyuca evidence the mapmaker's understanding of their alignments in respect to another important topographical features in the area: the sacred volcano of Matlalcueye. With a deviation angle of 18° south of east (Tichy 1992: 211), the church of Nopaluca faces out directly onto the volcano. Yet the cartographic church is viewed front-on, suggesting that the external viewing point from which the map was projected was in fact the great volcano. The inferred Matlalcueye-church sightline appears to be acknowledged by the visual link created between the portal and atrial crosses of Nopaluca's church and the central road running off the lower edge of the map toward the viewer. The mapmaker also acknowledged the alignment of the church of Ixtiyuca as viewed from the volcano, which at 4° north of east (azimuth 86°: ibid.) would be seen to look out toward the southwest. In addition, the mapmaker skewed the church's rooftop cross toward the volcano, apparently leaving the portal cross to echo the alignment of the church itself.[55]

The use of imaginary sightlines between mountains and churches, together with the inherited alignments of those churches, is an approach to representing geography that can also be found in a number of sixteenth-century Indian maps from other areas. Traced on INEGI's *Carta topográfica* F14C89 (1995), the 1571 map of Tezontepec de Aldama, Mixquiahuala (plate 10) also appears to have been constructed on the basis of a known sightline. This runs at a deviation angle of 20° south of east between the village church (azimuth 110°: my on-site measurement) and today's Cerro El Tejón, the mountain that therefore constitutes the external viewing point of the map (fig. 4.23). A further interesting detail on this map that emphasizes the sightline between Cerro El Tejón and the church is the way in which Cerro Teçontepec (today's

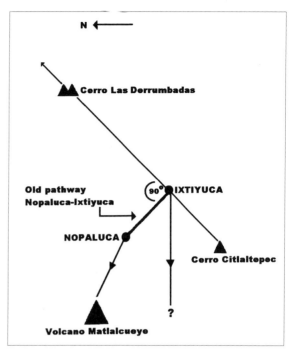

Figure 4.22. Diagram suggesting how the 1595 map of Nopaluca and Ixtiyuca was constructed. A sightline running between Cerro Las Derrumbadas and Cerro Citlaltepec cuts through Ixtiyuca at a right angle to the old pathway between the two villages. The church of Nopaluca looks out directly onto the volcano Matlalcueye, the map's external viewing point.

Figure 4.23. The geography of the 1571 map of Tezontepec de Aldama, showing the sightline between Cerro El Tejón (the viewing point of the map) and the church, which determined the structure of the map.

Cerro Huitel) is represented as splayed out on its side. Following indigenous iconic conventions, the detail explains that this is how Cerro Teçontepec appears to the eye when viewed from both Cerro El Tejón and the church.

Consistently published in portrait format, presumably because of the angle of its outsize hill glyph and gloss "Cenpoualla," the 1580 *Relaciones geográficas* map of Cempoala offers similar structural and viewing strategies. In fact this inordinately complex map affords a multiplicity of internal (and perhaps external) viewing angles that cannot be discussed in detail here. When positioned in landscape format (fig. 4.24), however, as I believe was the native artist's intention, the main external viewing point can be identified from Cempoala's frontal-facing monastery-church. Aligned at 20° south of east it looks out directly toward Cerro El Rosal to the northwest (see fig. 4.20). In other words, we are invited to "enter" Cempoala's map by way of the major sightline between Cerro El Rosal and the town's sixteenth-century church.[56] The person who drew up the 1590 map of the town (fig. 4.25) used the same sightline, this time including a pathway that follows the same trajectory.[57] Probably with the clearer purpose of orientating this map for the benefit of the Western eye, the mapmaker also added the cardinal points; their very precise positioning confirms his (or possibly her) awareness of the alignment of both church and sightline.

The very accurately portrayed church on the 1580 map of Cempoala is correctly located in relation to the actual colonial town center, marked to the church's north (left, from our perspective) as an open square with a central fountain. Cerro Metepec does indeed lie to the almost immediate north of the square (my on-site observation). Therefore, and as on the map of Tezontepec, the large hill glyph splayed out to the southwest of the church does not mark the site of Cempoala but the site of an extremely prominent mountain in the area, known today as Cerro Los Pitos (INEGI, *Carta topográfica* E14B11, 1995; my on-site observation). From the cartographic detail devoted to this hill glyph (game animals, a water source, and at its summit Cempoala's toponymic glyph) and the fact that we again are asked to view it as if from the church, we understand that the glyph represents Cempoala's patron-mountain.

Cartographic churches that face the viewer can be deceptive, however, with different ways of acknowledging the church-mountain relationship being employed in different areas. In a rich display of pink architectural representation with a central blue bell, the 1580 map of Acapixtla lays out the sites of the cabecera town and its sixteen sujetos as front-facing, stylized churches (plate 9). The monastery-church at Acapixtla is aligned at approximately 15° south of east (my on-site measurement), looking out directly toward the westernmost peak in a range of twenty mountains running from east to west to the north of the town. The peak still carries a Nahuatl name, Cempoaltepec, "Twenty-Mountain" (Maldonado Jiménez 1993: 83). The range is included on the map; Cempoaltepec (at the bottom left-hand corner) is detailed with eyes, a mouth, and an extremely prominent nose. This reads as the toponym for Acapixtla: originally Yecapixtla, "They Have Pointed Noses"/"Pointed Nose Place" (ibid., p. 73; Mundy 1996: 142). Cempoaltepec therefore appears to be Acapixtla's patron-mountain, determining the alignment of its pre- and postconquest ceremonial buildings, if not also their siting. Did the mapmaker forget all this when he painted his local geography? Closer inspection of the representations of the churches shows that their south-side walls have been carefully shaded in (they are not receiving sunlight from the east), and three-dimensionally portrayed rooftops have been added. These details

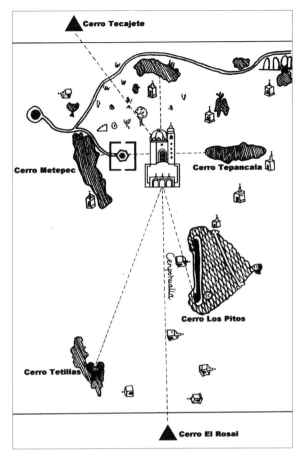

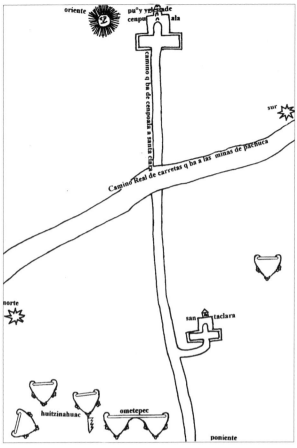

Figure 4.24. Simplified line drawing detailing the relationship of the church of Cempoala, Hidalgo, and surrounding mountains, as depicted on the town's 1580 map (UTX JGI xxv-10). The church looks out directly toward Cerro El Rosal, the map's external viewing point.

Figure 4.25. Line drawing of the 1590 map of Cempoala, Hidalgo (AGN 2152). The map's external viewing point is also Cerro El Rosal; the angle of the sightline and the orientation of the church are acknowledged in the positioning of the cardinal points. The unnamed hill glyph to the lower right represents Cerro Los Pitos.

effectively skew the alignments of the churches to the left of the map: the churches do not face the viewer at all but face northwest toward the patron-mountain.

The artist responsible for the 1581 map of Cholula (fig. 4.26) employed a graphic strategy similar to the alignment of the rooftop cross of Santa María Ixtiyuca with the volcano Matlalcueye noted above. The colonial street plan of Cholula is aligned at 26° south of east, the angle of sunrise at the winter solstice. With the great pyramid standing behind the monastery complex toward the upper right, the external viewing point of the map appears to be Cerro Zacatecas, which rises prominently on the northwest edge of the town (see González-Hermosillo and Reyes García 2002: 28–29, figs. 2, 3). Kubler (1985: 92) observed that the divergent alignments of the Franciscan monastery-church and its annexed Royal Chapel (2° north of east and 14° south of east, respectively: Tichy 1992: 212) were not acknowledged on the map. Yet we need only to look at the angles of the crosses on these two cartographic structures to see that this was not the case. Given the 26° viewing angle, the distortions of the crosses are also stunningly accurate.[58]

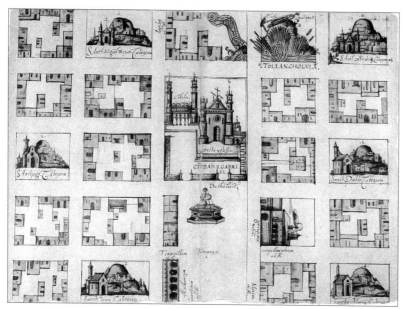

Figure 4.26. The 1581 map of Cholula, Puebla (UTX JGI xxiv-1). The mapmaker acknowledged the divergent alignments of the monastery church and royal chapel by skewing the rooftop crosses. Nettie Lee Benson Latin American Collection, University of Texas Libraries, The University of Texas at Austin.

Returning to the outwardly very simple map of Tlahuelilpa (plate 7), its mapmaker also incorporated an important sightline. The mountains delimiting Tlahuelilpa's territory are depicted around the edge of the page, with the mountain-church marking the site of the village. On this map there appears to be no external viewing point: the splayed configuration of the mountains asks us to view its geography from the center.[59] Unusually for a map with a single representation of a church, however, the edifice faces away from us toward two peaks. These can only be Cerro Xicuco (a still sacred mountain in the Mezquital Valley) and its smaller companion, Cerro Colorado, which lie to the southwest of Tlahuelilpa. The glosses *norte* and *sur* on the map confirm this, as does the form given to the mountains. With an azimuth of 78° (my on-site measurement) the church at Tlahuelilpa does face them directly (fig. 4.27). Again, the mapmaker was portraying his real church, as opposed to using the church equals village cartographical convention. He also emphasized its perceived associations with the two peaks by modeling its cartographical facade on their forms. On the south side the mapmaker painted in a high, pointed bell tower to echo Xicuco's tall, conical shape and on the north a curious architectural "stump" for the smaller, rounded Colorado. Neither detail corresponds to Tlahuelilpa's small, box-like sixteenth-century church and cloister, with its single modest bell tower attached to the south side.

Finally, the artist who painted the 1572 map of Almolonca and Maxtlatlan (fig. 4.14) may also have had a sightline in mind. Much as in the case of Atlatlauhca (fig. 4.19), only three mountains among the many that characterize this rugged highland area in the state of Veracruz (see INEGI, *Carta topográfica* E14B27, 2000) were included. These were the mountains of importance to the villages. In addition, with mountains and hill-churches configured as a quincunx, the artist appears to have drawn up his map on the basis of a locally perceived, microcosmic construction of geography.[60] Nevertheless, a faint broken line running between the hill-churches of Almolonca and Maxtlatlan via the large hill glyph at the center seems to link all three on a straight line. Our attention is also drawn to the representation of Cerro Cuetzaltepec (lower right, fig. 4.14), which lies on its side, indicating that it is to be viewed side-on, in this case from the portal of Maxtlatlan's church. On the maps of Tezontepec and Cempoala (plate 10; fig. 4.24), where this graphic convention also occurs, the lines of sight presented by the angle of the churches and the base of the hill glyphs are absolutely parallel. The additional tilting of Cerro Cuetzaltepec thus appears to be an untidy rendering of the same detail, until we note that the shaded portal of Maxtlatlan's church also skews the edifice on a parallel with the hill glyph.

The raised horizontal projections and often very naturalistic images of geography found in sixteenth-century native cartography were probably influenced by contemporary European sources, especially the imported genre of landscape painting.[61] This does not mean, however, that native mapmakers sat on the summits or slopes of local mountains to paint views of their territories, as we might expect a European landscape

artist to do. Landscape painting as a genre was very much in its infancy at the time and largely up to the imagination of the artist. Native artists would therefore not have been trained to paint landscapes from visual experience (Mundy 1996: 77). In addition, the mountain viewing points implied on the maps would in many cases have been impossible, given the distances between them and the geographical areas depicted. The maps indicate, then, that some other system of seeing and ordering geography existed, which drew on a cognitive knowledge of the lie of the land as determined by established networks of sightlines between the sacred mountains and the siting and alignments of architecture.

Figure 4.27. View from the portal of the church of San Francisco Tlahuelilpa, Hidalgo, aligned directly with Cerro Xicuco (*left*) and Cerro Colorado (*right*).

The decision of the evangelization body to appropriate the sites and alignments in the name of the Christian god effectively enabled the ancient system of spatial organization to continue. As a result, the Christian church as successor of the prehispanic temple not only came to emulate sacred topography but also stood as a physical part of its whole.

CHAPTER FIVE

Architectural Detail: Embedded Stones

We know that cut stone and rubble from the demolished pyramid-temples were used to construct Christian churches. Motolinía (1990: 22–23) commented on this valuable source of building material, and sometimes very large pieces of carved masonry can still be seen in foundations or are revealed as buildings fall into decay (fig. 3.3). Motolinía's words seem to reveal a note of triumph when he tells us that this carved masonry was also drawn from the innumerable idols that were destroyed and used for the foundations of the churches.[1] In the eyes of the evangelization body, the symbolic act of covering a pagan site with a Christian church apparently was given even greater force by raising that structure on the remains of the Indians' gods. Or as Agustín de Vetancurt (1971, "Tratado de la ciudad de Mexico, y las grandezas que la iluftran defpues que la fundaron Efpañoles," f. 17) later put it, the false gods were now obliged to support (physically) the true one.[2]

The Indians do not appear to have shared quite the same understanding of the destiny of their smashed idols. Masonry was often carefully recut so that a carved image remained intact, or pieces of considerable size were transported across large sites and positioned on specific areas of the Christian architectural ensemble. Examples such as water symbols embedded in the water trough at Tepeapulco or the Tlaltecuhtli relief carvings left intact on the bases of church columns and placed face downward after the prehispanic tradition also suggest that the conceptual associations of prehispanic imagery were retained. Although the purpose behind this particular procedure is not clear, it raises many more questions with regard to the pragmatics of construction and perceived symbolism of the churches than can be answered at present. Given the way in which Christianity found itself being absorbed into the native religious system, the Indians perhaps understood the reuse of their idols as an expression of this process. Rather than being obliterated from thought and view, they represented the conceptual foundations on which the new architectural symbol of religious life was raised.

One particular type of reused stone can be shown to be an important feature of colonial native building, although also still elusive in terms of its precise use and function. This is the series of smaller or larger stones bearing a carved motif or glyph, which were embedded into the exterior walls of chapels, churches, monastery buildings, and secular architecture of the period. Today they tend to be restricted to religious structures, because these are usually the only edifices of the time that have survived relatively intact.[3] Extant documented examples nevertheless cover a wide cultural and geographical area, from Molango in the Otomi/Huaxtec Sierra Alta of northern Hidalgo to Mixtec Tilantongo and Zapotec Zaachila in central Oaxaca. They also occur on early colonial churches in the Yucatec Maya area, although it is not included in the present survey. Not all the early churches or their surviving architectural units carry examples of these stones, but we cannot discard the possibility that they once did. Gradual decay, refurbishment, souvenir hunters, and—occasionally—the persistence of archaeologists in separating the prehispanic from the colonial have undoubtedly also taken their toll over the centuries.

Many of the stones are prehispanic in origin or carry prehispanic iconography.[4] The most common recognizable motif is the chalchihuitl symbol (usually composed of two concentric circles), but examples of stylized flowers, calendrical signs, and similar motifs are also present. Other stones were more clearly carved after the conquest, for they boast Renaissance-style designs. Floral motifs are particularly easy to identify in this context, and we must assume that they originated from earlier colonial structures. Still other stones carry Christian symbols that may also derive from earlier buildings or architectural elements or may have been prepared especially as embedded stones. It must be significant, however, that all the stones, even those of recent emplacement or replacement (see below), either are prehispanic or were produced in the sixteenth century. Thus all are probably of native manufacture.[5] In addition, all are exclusive to sixteenth-century structures or structures standing over sixteenth-century sites, although not all were placed there in the corresponding century of construction.

Little research on colonial embedded stones has been carried out to date. From an archaeological perspective, the first (and, it seems, the last) to record them as a category was the Spanish dragoon captain Guillermo Dupaix, during his early-nineteenth-century archaeological surveys of New Spain (Dupaix 1969).[6] Referring only to those he deemed to be of prehispanic origin, he observed how they had been specially prepared to lie on or slot into a wall face. Dupaix (1969: 72, 89, 96) believed that they had once been decorative features on "temples, tombs, or palaces" and also conjectured—quite astutely for the time—that they may have served as "interpreters" of those structures. We also learn from Dupaix's detailed records that embedded stones occurred in the walls of all types of early colonial buildings: private residences, commercial and industrial premises, and religious structures and substructures, such as atria walls. Further examples were found loose in Indian-occupied buildings—in an Indian shack at Mixquic, for example, and in the same village's tecpan (the seat of Indian government) (ibid., pp. 87–89). These were not just chance finds, for Dupaix writes that he was able to locate much of his material by asking local inhabitants (ibid., p. 74). Thus native peoples at the beginning of the nineteenth century continued to give house room to these old stones, or knew who did, which indicates that they still had some meaning or value at the community level. Dupaix, however, was only interested in prehispanic artifacts and did not mention whether any stones of obvious postconquest origin were also embedded into colonial walls or preserved by local inhabitants. Neither did he attempt to explain why the prehispanic stones had been reused on the walls of colonial buildings; he perhaps assumed that they were little more than the rubble of a destroyed past.

In our own times the presence of the stones was acknowledged by Kubler (1992: 432, n. 5), who nevertheless limited himself to pointing out that, with their "simple[r] Indian designs," they were an architectural element worthy of further study.[7] More recently, some examples were included in inventories of preconquest motifs in "Indo-Christian" art of the early colonial period by Reyes-Valerio (1978: 217–90, 2000: 363–68), lumped together with formal sculpture and painting. While it remains unclear what Kubler meant by "simple[r]" Indian designs and we might question Reyes-Valerio's purpose in classifying them along with formal painting and sculpture, both scholars seem to have overlooked the fact that not all the stones carry prehispanic signs, symbols, or motifs. The "designs" therefore are not all "Indian" in Kubler's sense of the word and much less "simple" in terms of the meaning of their mixed iconography. At another level, however, they are indeed "Indian," for pre- and postconquest native artisans not only must have carved them but also must have considered their juxtapositioning on the walls of colonial edifices to be appropriate and meaningful. Here, as Reyes-Valerio intuited, we can find grounds for classifying the stones along with formal native painting and sculpture, which often also carries the same mixed iconography.

A conventional approach to explaining the presence of embedded stones might be that they are indeed just part of the rubble from earlier pre- or postconquest buildings, which by chance have retained a fragment of carving. As with the carved masonry used for foundations and columns, however, these architectural details also were carefully cut to preserve as complete a motif as possible. Some are irregularly shaped or attached to walls by means of tenons and would therefore have required special preparatory work on the wall face itself. Large and bewildering as the number of stones embedded into the walls of Asunción Tetepango (Hidalgo) is (see tables 5.1 and 5.2 below), those on the north wall buttresses and the facade (which incorporates the abutted wall faces of the two bell towers) are arranged in groups corresponding to the numerals of the native calendars. At neighboring Atitalaquia two stones carrying the images of the sun and the moon on the apse wall correspond to Mesoamerican directional concepts. The sun stone lies to the south side, conceived as the place of light; the moon stone is to the north, the place of darkness. In terms of preparation and arrangement, therefore, the indication is that the stones were indeed important enough to occupy the attention of Indian stonecutters and builders.[8]

Several initial possibilities come to mind to explain the presence of embedded stones. One is that they followed the early Euro-Christian tradition of embedding images of pagan idols into the walls of churches as a reminder that the devil was always present, waiting to tempt the unwary churchgoer from the path of God. The existence of comparatively few "idols" within the Mexican stones' iconography today might be due to the sixteenth-century ecclesiastical purge of native stonework mentioned in chapter 3. But even if many more idols once existed, the high number of contextually neutral motifs such as flowers and stars, together with the colonial carvings and Christian symbols that accompanied them, would not appear to sustain this type of argument.

Flowers and the chalchihuitl, by far the commonest motifs carried by the stones, appear frequently alongside Christian imagery in the postconquest picture catechisms, where it has been suggested that they serve to express superlatives relating to the new religion. Flowers, for example, were employed as an adjective to refer to the Virgin Mary or God as "precious," "venerated," or "eternal"; the chalchihuitl reads as "great," as in "great Lord" or "great City of Rome" (León-Portilla 1979). Transferred to the walls of churches, these same motifs may have been intended to label the building itself as "precious" or "great." In this context, we might also understand the carvings of the chalchihuitl alongside spirals, conches, or the face of Tlaloc as similar glyphic renderings that marked the church as the place of water it was perceived to be. Unfortunately, the location and positioning of the stones on church walls do not support a reading along the lines of the catechisms. A chalchihuitl at ground level on an apse wall (fig. 5.1) and a barely visible flower and chalchihuitl on a high rooftop belfry

Figure 5.1. Embedded chalchihuitl, apse wall, San Juan Tlaltentli Xochimilco.

(fig. 5.2), for example, are not the most obvious places to proclaim their host structures as "great," "precious," or even "watery." In addition, the same motifs on the walls of private residences or other secular buildings must also rule out such an interpretation.

A further possibility is that the stones may have been a very literal native reworking of the classical *ars memoriae* (the art of memory) system, which the Franciscan Diego Valadés (2003) proposed in his 1579 *Rhetorica Christiana* to introduce into the New World as an aid for teaching Christianity. Based on the elements of *loci* and *imagines* (places and images), where *loci* are imprinted on the memory and each *locus* carries an image to prompt the memory, Valadés (2003: 219–93) argued that the best source of *loci* was an (imaginary) architectural structure. There is nothing to suggest that his proposal was ever taken up, however, and certainly no correspondence exists between the iconography of the stones and his mnemotechnic alphabet (ibid., pp. 242–44). Again, this is not to say that the stones did not function as reference points on the body of the structures on which they lay, but not in the sense of prompts for memory and much less clearly as an adaptation of any European system. If the Indians who placed the stones in the walls of their churches and other buildings were adhering to any colonially induced tradition or innovation—or were explaining their act as such—the practice of embedding carved stones into architecture had also been a prehispanic tradition.

Figure 5.2. View of the church and cloister buildings at Los Santos Reyes Meztitlan, Hidalgo, locating the presence of two embedded stones on a high rooftop belfry. *Inset*: Detail of the embedded chalchihuitl and flower stones.

Prehispanic Antecedents and Colonial Repercussions

The practice of embedding carved stones into architectural structures has prehispanic antecedents that also appear to have been widespread across time and geography. At Otomi Huamango (México), which flourished from the ninth to eleventh centuries AD, carved stones have been unearthed from the rubble of the ruins. Motifs include flowers, circles, spirals, and M-shaped swirls, interpreted as clouds (Folan et al. 1987). The shape and the cut of these stones suggest that they once adorned wall faces. Excavation and restoration of the post-tenth-century Tarascan site of Tzintzuntzan (Michoacán) have permitted the partial reconstruction of a row of five monuments (the so-called *yácatas*) that originally stood on the top of a high platform. The walls of these structures were covered with well-cut, polished stones of volcanic origin, some of which (with no apparent order of location and at different heights) were carved with concentric circles (the chalchihuitl), spirals, stars, and other symbols (fig. 5.3). Similar examples have also been found at nearby Ihuatzio, although none are *in situ* (Acosta 1939; Cabrera Castro 1987).

Stones carrying similar sets of motifs were also embedded into architectural structures in the central area, at least in the Postclassic period. The ruins of the earliest stage of the dual temple at Tlatelolco (D.F.) present numerous examples, among which we find concentric circles, a *xihuitl* (solar year sign) (fig. 5.4),[9] spirals, "cloud" symbols, a stylized face, and two horizontal S-shapes that I take to be the *xonecuilli,* a ritual motif that also represented a star constellation (CMPR, f. 282v), possibly Ursa Major or Ursa Minor (Angulo V. 1991: 314–15; Köhler 1991: 260; Nicholson et al. 1997: 155 and n. 12; Brotherston 2005: 51).[10] The existence of the stones *in situ* at Tlatelolco also means that a good indication of original location and positioning can be documented: restricted to the east and south walls and concentrated toward the east side on the south wall.

A number of stones were embedded into the various stages of the Great Temple at Tenochtitlan. Most are carved with dates and are possibly commemorative, although a human face accompanied by the sign 2 Rabbit (according to Matos Moctezuma 1990b: 45, the year 1390) may actually refer to the pulque deity, Ometochtli–2 Rabbit. A further example is a broken fragment carved with the "claws" or "fangs" of the earth monster. But, as Dupaix's records and modern-day archaeological collections show, relief-carved stone plaques or tenoned artifacts carved in the round were produced in large quantities in the prehispanic period.[11] All were evidently fashioned to lie on or slot into the walls of architectural structures.

Noticeable among the known prehispanic examples is the overall consistency of motifs employed. Many of

Figure 5.3. One of a series of carved stones covering the wall faces of the prehispanic yácatas at Tzintzuntzan, Michoacán. *(Photo: Valerie Fraser)*

Figure 5.4. Examples of carved stones embedded into the east wall of the prehispanic temple platform at Tlatelolco, D.F.

them (such as the xonecuilli, xihuitl, and the quartered motifs that strongly echo the pecked crosses of Teotihuacan origin) appear to be calendrical and/or astronomical in projection, while others (the chalchihuitl, cloud motifs, spirals, skulls, and flowers) refer directly to water and the fertility of the earth. Some motifs from this second group are ambiguous, however, in that they may also be calendrical and/or astronomical in reference. Spirals are associated with the interior of the conch shell, which, in cross section, is the *ecailatcozcatl,* "wind spiral jewel" (Tudela de la Orden 1980: 99) of the wind deity Quetzalcoatl-Ehecatl, invoked before the onset of rain. But the spiral (with its defined beginning and end) also evokes eras of time (Shelton 1991: 7), while both circular and squared varieties make up the stepped "tail" of the *xicalcoliuhqui* symbol, which related to the movement of the sun (Vega Sosa 1991: 522–23). Skulls were used specifically for agricultural ends in various Mesoamerican cultures, where, as representations of death, they symbolized life and the regeneration of both human and plant cycles (Baquedano 1992: 41; López Luján and Mercado 1996: 42). The skull is also a calendrical sign, occurring twice in the list of twenty day-signs: as *Miquiztli-*VI, "death," and in the form of a jawbone in *Malinalli-*XII, "twisted thing" (after a type of grass).

Flowers are ubiquitous in prehispanic iconography, where they were used as glyphs, metaphors, and symbols to be read phonetically, ideographically, and/or conceptually. Thus the image offers multiple interpretations in varying contexts (see Heyden 1983), including—as I have proposed—as a framing device for ritual and a primary symbol of the flowery world of the sacred. Where the image of the flower carries an overall abstract definition focused on the essence of life—the sacred itself—its symbolism permeated every other aspect of the world of human and plant regeneration: from the heart-flower of the sacrificial victim whose blood was exchanged for water to the arrival of that water in the springtime in confirmation of the renewal of the earth's life-giving properties (see FC2, 1981: 57). Flowers also offer calendrical and cosmological readings. Xochitl was the last of the twenty day-signs, as if to symbolize some accumulative supernatural interaction of the signs that preceded and produced it, from *Cipactli-*I (the primordial earth monster) to *Quiahuitl-*XIX (the precious rain that revitalizes the earth's body).[12]

But with the variety of graphic stylizations that the flower permits, its symbolism was extended to express a range of other associated concepts. With four petals, it is an elaboration of the basic quatrefoil or quincunx configuration: the four directions of the universe expressed through a configuration of the points of solsticial risings and settings and a center (Tichy 1990: 183; Vega Sosa 1991: 522). As evoked on the first page of the Codex Féjérváry (see fig. 4.2), the terrestrial plane was perceived as a great flower, an idealization that appropriately expresses the earth's much-sought-after eternal abundance. A multipetaled flower with concentric circles at its center represents the sun in its own right; with a central spiral, it is the sun in movement (Vega Sosa 1991: 521).

One firm reference to the prehispanic practice of embedding stones into architectural structures comes in the text of the 1537–39 trial of Don Carlos Ometochtli, a member of the Royal House of Texcoco. Among the accusations thrown at this high-ranking Indian was his use of an old house at Oztoticpac that had belonged to his grandfather Nezahualcoyotl, the great fifteenth-century Acolhua leader. A number of idols had been found on the premises, including images of Quetzalcoatl, Xipe [Totec], Tlaloc, and Chicomecoatl. One of the first witnesses testified that before the arrival of the Christians the building had been used as a house of prayer (*Proceso inquisitorial* 1980: 10–11). The images of these gods, relating primarily to water, fertility, and maize, might also perhaps imply the dedication of the preconquest building. "Indio Gabriel" from Texcoco was the next to testify in respect to the house: "asked if this witness saw the said idols in the said houses, he replied, that yes he had seen *those that were on the surface of the wall, facing outward, like broken stones placed in the wall,* and he saw nothing else" (ibid., p. 12; my emphasis).[13] Apart from the figures of idols, then, other carved images also existed, embedded in the walls of the oratory. The original question had made no reference to the embedded stones, which is crucial here for our understanding that they did carry meaning. Gabriel's unprompted response shows that he believed that they also fell under the Spaniards' definition of "idols"; that is, in some way they were associated with the native religion.

It seems that the Spaniards had not noticed the embedded stones or were not particularly interested in them, for the questioning of further witnesses was concerned only with the idols inside the house. Before Ometochtli gave his own testimony at the end of the trial, however, the inquisitorial body had evidently been back to the house to look for the stones; they found them "next to a tree, in a wall . . . and whitewashed over." Some were inside the wall and could not be seen; others were on the surface of the wall, with their carvings visible. The accused only admitted that he knew of the stones that were visible, adding that he had not ordered them to be painted over and did not know who was responsible for the act (ibid., p. 57).[14]

It seems clear from this rare reference that the practice of embedding stones into the exterior walls of temples was not restricted to great prehispanic ceremonial structures such as the dual platform at Tlatelolco; even small buildings carried them. The stones were clustered together (in the area of the tree), as at Tlatelolco. Like many of the stones on church walls today, the Oztoticpac examples also blended in well with the surrounding masonry, for the Spaniards only became aware of their presence after an Indian referred to them. In addition, between Gabriel's innocent gaffe and Ometochtli's testimony, somebody had tried to cover the stones from view. We cannot know if this was to protect the accused or the stones themselves. The latter is a distinct possibility, for a similar initiative took place at Zuni, when the Anasazi also found themselves confronted with the zealousness of the invader. In 1881 John G. Bourke recorded the presence of an old china plate on the west-facing wall of one of Zuni's tallest structures. According to an elder, it had been placed there to conceal from the Spaniards a painting of the Sun (cited by Zeilik 1989: 146).

If the practice of embedding stones into the walls of buildings was a native religious tradition that was unfamiliar to the ecclesiastical authorities of New Spain in the 1530s, it was also one that they seemed to forget very quickly.[15] Over forty years had to pass before it came to their attention again, this time in the context of the sixteenth-century purge of offensive stonework reported by Jacinto de la Serna: "and what was done just to strengthen the buildings, and houses, and for street ornamentation, there were also [idols] there [in the streets] . . . and those that are on the tops of houses, and in the streets, are so that all may be preserved, where they idolatrized and made their invocations to them" (La Serna 1892: 24).[16] As with the dubious pieces of masonry used for church foundations and columns (ibid.), these particular stones had only raised suspicion because the Indians were seen to be paying too much attention to them. Unable to hide his indignation at the duping, La Serna also noted that they had always passed as structural reinforcements

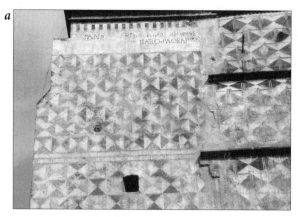

Figure 5.5. Examples of the chalchihuitl as a colonial embedded stone: *a,* west face of the bell tower, Asunción Amecameca, México; *b,* west wall of the monastery church, San Luis Obispo Tlalmanalco, México.

and/or decorative details. The remark is interesting, for it tells us that many of the stones were visible and had been so for decades. It seems unlikely, then, that they had ever carried identifiable images of native deities or other "symbols of the devil."[17]

Again the purge was no more widespread than it was exhaustive. Although there is no firm evidence in this respect, the process of destroying the stones after 1585 may have been interrupted by the Indians' own efforts to protect them, much as had been attempted at Ometochtli's house. It is easy to imagine the sixteenth-century purgers anxiously scanning the vast walls of the churches for "idols," where, with an application of wash or even a little mud, they had already been rendered invisible to the uninitiated eye. Under the pretext of removal, others may have been carried away for safekeeping until the hue and cry had died down and then returned again to their original host walls. But, given their erstwhile visibility and apparent lack of recognizably offensive imagery, it does not seem likely that any were replaced, then or later, with more "acceptable" designs. Where the church authorities were alerted to Indian interest in the embedded stones, all would have fallen under suspicion. They were therefore either removed or left in place, depending on whether ecclesiastical action was taken or not. In other words, a good number of originally placed stones, whether prehispanic or co-

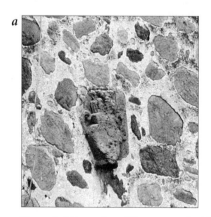

Figure 5.6. Examples of flowers as colonial embedded stones: *a,* north wall of the church of Santa María Nonoalco, Mixcoac, D.F.; *b,* church wall, San Matías Tlalancaleca, Puebla (after Heyden 1983); *c,* east face of the bell tower, San Juan Tlaltentli Xochimilco.

lonial in origin, did survive the purge and can still be seen today on the
walls of sixteenth-century edifices or those occupying sixteenth-century
architectural sites.

In sum, the colonial embedded stones also came under the suspicion
of the religious authorities in New Spain, although as an undetected
throwback to a prehispanic practice. It is open to question whether they
were actually "idolatrous," in the sense of being subversive. The records
of Ometochtli's trial and La Serna's manual for extirpation make it clear,
however, that the stones had a purpose or function that was important
enough for the Indians to attempt to conceal them from the invader.

The Iconography of Embedded Stones

Table 5.1 lists documented examples of extant embedded stones on
sixteenth-century religious structures or later replacement structures.
For the purposes of this discussion, I have divided them into seven basic
categories in accordance with the motifs or symbols they carry. Category 8 includes stones whose iconography is unclear or unidentifiable.
The categories are not intended to reflect native ideology; as a result,
my own analysis probably introduces considerable overlap in respect to
organization, identification, and interpretation of specific imagery sets
and their projected concepts.

It is clear from the table that the chalchihuitl (1), symbol of precious
water, and floral (2) and vegetal motifs (3), symbols of fertility and regeneration of the earth, predominate (figs. 5.1, 5.2, 5.5, 5.6, 5.7). In this,
they have conceptual parallels with known prehispanic examples. Such
predominance also tells us that the stones in general were selected on
the basis of iconographic requirements and not arbitrarily.

Chalchihuitl and floral motifs are often found in close association with
each other (figs. 5.2, 5.6c, 5.7c, 5.8) or as a combined motif. At Tizatlan
(Tlaxcala) (fig. 5.9) and Xochimanco (D.F.), for example, a chalchihuitl
appears at the center of a motif that resembles four and eight petals
or sepals, respectively. Two of the five examples of chalchihuitl at Tlalmanalco flank a very distinctive "flower" (figure 5.10), which takes the
form of the configuration of mushroom caps found on the pedestal of
the well-known statue of Xochipilli (see fig. 6.29). It is incidental that
Xochipilli was unearthed at Tlalmanalco, for similar flowers also occur
on several churches in Xochimilco, with further examples on the north
wall of the monastery church at Pachuca (Hidalgo) and the north face
of the bell tower of San Jacinto, San Angel (D.F.). The circular flowers
with six to nine petals found on a number of churches (figs. 5.6c, 5.8,
5.24) in urban Xochimilco are nevertheless exclusive to the town and
can be identified as the same flower depicted on the ritual mantle of
the Sun on Codex Magliabechiano 8v.[18] Some examples of "flowers,"
however, are far closer in appearance to Western graphic renderings of
stars (fig. 5.11). These may not represent stars as such but flowers and/
or schematic representations of calendrical or cosmic signs.

a

b

c
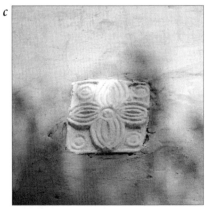

Figure 5.7. Examples of colonial embedded
stones with vegetal motifs: *a,* south wall,
Natividad de Santa María Coatepec
(Chalco), México; *b,* apse wall Santiago
Tilantongo, Oaxaca; *c,* south wall of the
later church at Tizatlan, Tlaxcala, which
now covers the south wall of the early open
chapel of San Esteban.

TABLE 5.1

Documented examples of known embedded stones on sixteenth-century religious structures by motif, site, and number of occurrences

Motif	Site	No.
1. Chalchihuitl		
	Amecameca (México)	1
	Chapatongo (Hidalgo)	1
	Chiconauhtla (México) Sta. Maria	3
	Chimalhuacan Atenco (México)	2
	Coatlinchan (México)	1
	Cuernavaca (Morelos) Capilla de Indios*	1
	Meztitlan (Hidalgo)	1
	Mixquic (D.F.)	1
	Ostoyuca (Hidalgo)	1
	Tacuba (D.F.)	1
	Tepeapulco (Hidalgo)	1
	Tequixquiac (México)	3
	Tizatlan (Tlaxcala)	1
	Tlalmanalco (México)	5
	Totolapa (Morelos)	1
	Xochimilco (D.F.) Asunción	1
	Xochimilco Dolores Xaltocan	2
	Xochimilco S. Bernardino	1
	Xochimilco S. Juan	4
2. Flowers/Stars		
	Acolman (México) S. Agustín	8
	Chimalhuacan Atenco (México)	1
	Coixtlahuaca (Oaxaca)	1
	Magdalena, Actopan (Hidalgo)	1
	Meztitlan (Hidalgo)	1
	Mixcoac (D.F.)	1
	Mixquic (D.F.)	2
	Suchixtlahuaca (Oaxaca)	1
	Tepetomatitlan (Tlaxcala)	3
	Tetepango (Hidalgo)	**
	Tilantongo (Oaxaca)	11
	Tizatlan (Tlaxcala)	2
	Tlalancaleca (Puebla)***	1
	Tlatelolco (D.F.)	1
	Tultitlan (México)*	1
	Xochimanco (D.F.)	1
	Xochimilco (D.F.) Asunción	1
	Xochimilco Dolores Xaltocan	3
	Xochimilco S. Juan	3
	Xochimilco S. Pedro	1
	Xochimilco Sta. Cruz	1

Motif	Site	No.
3. Vegetal		
	Coixtlahuaca (Oaxaca)	2
	Cuanalá (Puebla)	1
	Tepetomatitlan (Tlaxcala)	1
	Xochimilco (D.F.) Dolores Xaltocan	1
	Xochimilco S. Pedro	2
	Xochimilco Sta. Cruz	1
"mushroom" flower	Pachuca (Hidalgo)	1
	San Angel (D.F.)	1
	Tlalmanalco (México)	1
	Xochimilco S. Francisco	1
	Xochimilco S. Juan	1
	Xochimilco S. Pedro	1
maguey	Coatepec (México)	2
4. Animals/Birds		
bird	Zaachila (Oaxaca)	1
cozcacuauhtli?	Tilantongo (Oaxaca)	1
cuetzpalin	Tilantongo (Oaxaca)	1
tlacuatl/techalotl?	Tlatelolco (D.F.)	1
cuauhtli	Tultitlan (México)	1
pinauiztli?	Xochimilco (D.F.) Dolores Xaltocan	1
5. Native Various		
toponyms	Tenayuca (D.F.)	2
dot counts	Zaachila (Oaxaca)	1
chimalli	Cempoala (Hidalgo)	1
	Tultitlan (México)*	1
	Xochimilco (D.F.) S. Juan	1
xochimecatl	Tizayuca (Hidalgo)	2
spiral	Chiconauhtla (México) Sta. María	1
	Molango (Hidalgo)	1
	Xochimilco S. Bernardino	1
native head	Xochimilco S. Juan	1
	Yauhtepec (Morelos)*	1
fire-drilling	Coatlinchan (México)	1
skull	Chimalhuacan Atenco (México)	1
	Mixquic (D.F.)	3
	Yancuitlalpan (Tlaxcala) [with cross-bones]	1
	Zaachila (Oaxaca) [jawbone]	1
cloud motif?	Coatepec (México)	1

Motif	Site	No.
seated figure	Coatlinchan (México)	1
	?Xochimilco Asunción	1
idol/figurine	Atlahapa (Tlaxcala)	1
	Tlalnepantla (D.F.) Los Reyes	1
ñuhu spirit	Tilantongo (Oaxaca)	1
head of Tlaloc	Mixquic (D.F.)	1
	Tlatelolco (D.F.)	1
proto-Tlaloc?	Tlalancaleca (Puebla)	1
ecailatcozcatl	Xochimilco S. Juan	1
xihuitl	Xochimilco S. Antonio	1
oyoalli	Coatlinchan (México)	1
	Xochimilco S. Juan	2

6. Geometrics/Abstracts

	Coatlinchan (México)	1
	Tenayuca (D.F.)	2
	Tetepango (Hidalgo)	**

7. Christian Signs and Symbols

Augustinian Order

pierced heart	Acolman (México) Sta. Catarina	1
	Meztitlan (Hidalgo)	1

Dominican Order

crossbands/stars	Atitalaquia (Hidalgo)	5
	Tetepango (Hidalgo)	**
cross	Coyoacan (D.F.)	1
	Tiltepec (Oaxaca)	1
sun and moon [two stones]	Atitalaquia (Hidalgo)	1
	Tilantongo (Oaxaca)	1

Motif	Site	No.
Franciscan Order		
wounds of Christ	Cuauhtinchan (Puebla) parish church	1
angels	Coixtlahuaca (Oaxaca)	2
	Tequixquiac (México)	1
	Tilantongo (Oaxaca)	1
	Tlalnepantla (D.F.) Los Reyes	1
	Xochimilco (D.F.) Stma. Trinidad	1
Latin cross	Acatlan (D.F.) Santa Cruz	4
	Tepeapulco (Hidalgo)	1
	Tepetomatitlan (Tlaxcala)	3
	Tizayuca (Hidalgo)	1
	Tultitlan (México)*	1
	Xochimilco S. Juan	1
	Xochimilco S. Pedro	1
Lorraine cross	Xochimilco S. Antonio	1
IHS	Xochimilco Dolores Xaltocan	1
	Xochimilco S. Antonio	1
unidentified cross	Totolinga (México)	1
Other		
fragment of atrial cross	Tepetomatitlan (Tlaxcala)	1
	Tilantongo (Oaxaca)	1
crossed keys of St. Peter	Tenayuca (D.F.)	1
bishop's miter	Tizayuca (Hidalgo)	1
monogram of Virgin Mary	Xochimilco Asunción	1

8. Unidentified

[cartouche only]	Chiconauhtla (México) Sto. Tomás	1
[vegetal?]	Itzcuincuitlapilco (Hidalgo)	3
[eroded]	Tiltepec (Oaxaca)	1
[flower?]	Tlalnepantla (D.F.) Los Reyes	1

*   Reported/identified by Reyes-Valerio (1978, 2000). Other stones reported by this researcher are included here but have also been documented by the author.

**   The church at Tetepango has a total of fifty-nine embedded stones divided into three main motifs: flowers/stars, geometrical designs, and the stars and crossbands of the Dominican Order. Some stones carry a mixture of these motifs.

***   Reported by García Cook (1973) and Heyden (1983). The stones have since been removed from the church and deposited in the local site museum.

Figure 5.8. Chalchihuitl and flower together as embedded stones, east wall of the bell tower, Nuestra Señora de los Dolores Xaltocan Xochimilco.

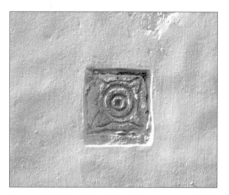

Figure 5.9. Chalchihuitl and flower combined as an embedded stone, apse wall of the open chapel of San Esteban, Tizatlan, Tlaxcala.

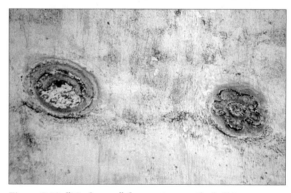

Figure 5.10. "Mushroom" flower stone on the bell tower at San Luis Obispo Tlalmanalco, México, which has strong visual parallels with the ritual configuration of mushroom caps on the pedestal of the statue of Xochipilli (see fig. 6.29).

Under category 4, there is no doubt about the identification of the lizard (*cuetzpalin*) at Tilantongo (fig. 5.12) and the eagle (*cuauhtli*) reported by Reyes-Valerio (1978, 2000) at Tultitlan, although what they refer to is far from clear. Both are of calendrical usage, representing the fourth and fifteenth of the twenty day-signs, respectively. Certainly the Tilantongo lizard, viewed laterally in a crouching position, is identical to the day-sign as it appears in the Mixtec codices. At another level, however, they may make reference to rulers or ruler-ancestors. At Tultitlan the speaking eagle alongside the shield (*chimalli*) is possibly connected with Mexica domination and/or is a reference to the famed fourteenth-century ruler of Tlatelolco, Cuauhtlahtoa, "Speaking Eagle." A Lord 1 Lizard ruled Tilantongo in the twelfth century (Kelley 1983: 169 and his table 5.1) and the stone placed high up on the north wall certainly looks out toward Cerro Montenegro, the site of the original center. Tentative identifications in this category also include the large colonial carving of a bird on the south wall of the nave at Tilantongo (fig. 5.13). This is obviously a European rendering of a peacock, but the stone was inserted into the wall upside down; in its present position it resembles the *cozcacuauhtli* vulture, the sixteenth day-sign. We note, however, that the fruit toward which the bird's head is directed carries twelve berries. A Lady 12 Vulture was mother of the first colonial ruler of Tilantongo (Kelley 1983).[19] The stone carrying a bird, jawbone, and at least three dot counts at Zaachila appears to be prehispanic in origin and may have been reused to record the date of founding or completion of the church. Apparently restricted to day-signs and slotted in rather unpretentiously on a south wall, however, it may also refer to a pre- or postconquest native ruler.[20]

At Santiago Tlatelolco a tiny animal with pointed ears and thin tail, standing on a leafy spur, may be the squirrel-like *techalotl* or possibly the *tlacuatl,* the Mesoamerican marsupial belonging to the opossum family.[21] The deity Techalotl was a god of dance, associated with the pulque deities in Codex Tudela and Codex Magliabecchiano (Tudela de la Orden 1980: 90; Boone 1983: 201); the tlacuatl was also closely associated with the pulque cult (FC11, 1963: 12; Sahagún 1981, 3:229; López Austin 1998: 18). Finally in this category, the orange "grub" on the obliquely aligned corner of the apse wall at Nuestra Señora de los Dolores Xaltocan Xochimilco is almost identical in color and form to the *pinauiztli* beetle on ritual cloaks described on Codex Tudela (f. 86r) and Codex Magliabechiano (f. 3v). It reappears on Codex Borbonicus 3 as a ritual artifact associated with the third *trecena* (thirteen-day period) of the tonalpohualli count, opening on day 1 Deer and presided over by Tlaloc.[22]

Category 5 includes all other identifiable motifs found on embedded stones that appear to be native in origin, if not prehispanic in cut. These include the skulls at Mix-

Figure 5.11. Flower-stars as embedded stones: *a,* south wall of the monastery church, Santo Domingo Chimalhuacan (Atenco), México; *b,* apse wall, San Matías Tepetomatitlan, Tlaxcala.

quic and Chimalhuacan (Atenco) (fig. 5.14); the native heads at Yauhtepec and San Juan Tlaltentli Xochimilco (fig. 5.15); and the spirals on the bell tower of San Bernardino Xochimilco (fig. 5.16). The stones carrying knotted *xochimecatl,* "flower-ropes," at Tizayuca (Hidalgo) appear originally to have been part of the bases of colonial columns and constitute an interesting reworking of the Franciscan knotted cord with a native insert.[23] The south wall at Tilantongo carries a small human form crouching within a mountain glyph (fig. 5.17), which is consistent with Mixtec representations of *ñuhu* spirits, sometimes shown emerging from the earth with the same gestures and poses accorded only to first ancestors born in a similar manner (Pohl 1994: 27–28). Tilantongo's 1579 *Relación geográfica* tells how the first lord of the community was born from a mountain of the same name (Acuña 1984b: 231), although the erosion of the stone's glyphic elements makes the image too nonspecific to be able to identify the figure as Lord 4 Alligator himself.[24] Other stones in this category are unquestionably preconquest, such as the pronged motifs from Tlalancaleca (fig. 5.6b), which date to between 500 and 100 BC (García Cook 1973), and the faces of Tlaloc on the apse wall at Santiago Tlatelolco and the bell-tower staircase at Mixquic.[25] The skull at Yancuitlalpan, however, accompanied by crossed bones, would appear to be colonial in origin.

Figure 5.12. Lizard stone, north wall of the church of Santiago Tilantongo, Oaxaca.

Figure 5.13. "Peacock" stone, inserted upside down into the south wall at Santiago Tilantongo, Oaxaca.

Complete with headdress and ear plugs, the native head at San Juan Tlaltentli Xochimilco (fig. 5.15) has its eyes closed in the native graphic convention that denotes death. We cannot exclude the possibility that it also refers to the prehispanic or postconquest native dead. In this case, the presence of a seated figure on one of the Coatlinchan stones might also be explained, the town being the original settlement and capital of the incoming Acolhua peoples before the rise of Texcoco. But the same stone

Figure 5.14. Tenoned skull inserted into the south wall at Santo Domingo Chimalhuacan (Atenco), México.

Figure 5.15. Native head mounted over a chalchihuitl, south wall of San Juan Tlaltentli Xochimilco.

Figure 5.16. Spiral stones on the west face of the bell tower, San Bernardino Xochimilco.

Figure 5.17. Mixtec ñuhu stone, south wall, Santiago Tilantongo, Oaxaca.

Figure 5.18. The xihuitl (sign of the solar year) stone, north wall of San Antonio Moyotla Xochimilco.

depicts a fire-drilling, above which appears an *oyoalli* (hollow, pear-shaped breast ornament [Nicholson et al. 1997: 101 and n. 44]) motif; as noted below, both carry strong calendrical/astronomical references. As at Tultitlan, the two circular devices resembling chimalli *s*hields at San Juan Tlaltentli and Todos Santos Cempoala may again carry political connotations. The Cempoala example, however, is strikingly similar to the "shield" motifs accompanying the sets of goggle eyes (symbols of the tlaloque) and crescent moons (symbols of the pulque cult) carved into the fabric of the sixteenth-century aqueduct that lies just south of Cempoala.

The xihuitl (sign of the solar year) at San Antonio Moyotla Xochimilco (fig. 5.18) is perhaps the only other direct calendrical or astronomical sign in this group, but again the skulls and spirals may have similar connotations. The face of Tlaloc also occurs commonly on the nineteenth day-sign (Rain). The two pronged motifs at San Matías Tlalancaleca (fig. 5.6b) each lie within a circle of flowers totaling nine and thirteen, respectively—again primary notations of the ritual sets of the Mesoamerican sacred round and, in some native sources, the numbers of levels of the celestial and subterrestrial planes.

Last but not least in this group are the two examples of pear-shaped, horizontal "droplets" on the south face of the bell tower at San Juan Tlaltentli Xochimilco (fig. 5.19), which I identify as the oyoalli ornament. The oyoalli motif was a symbol of fecundity (Tudela de la Orden 1980: 160) often associated with the pulque cult. For example, it is worn as an earring by the monkey impersonator accompanying the pulque deity Tlaltecayoa on Codex Magliabechiano 55r (fig. 5.20a).[26] Closely

Figure 5.19. Oyoalli motifs flanking a chalchihuitl, south face of the bell tower at San Juan Tlaltentli Xochimilco.

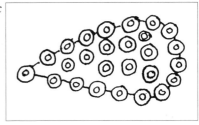

Figure 5.20. The oyoalli motif in prehispanic meaning: *a,* earring of the monkey impersonator accompanying the pulque deity Tlaltecayoa (Codex Magliabechiano 55); *b,* earring and breastplate of Xochipilli-Macuilxochitl (ibid., f. 60); *c,* the Pleiades star cluster (Códice Matritense del Palacio Real, f. 282r).

associated with the cult were the dancing gods such as Xochipilli-Macuilxochitl (fig. 5.20b) and Huehuecoyotl (Seler 1992, 3:217). Macuilxochitl wears it on Magliabechiano 60 both as earring and around his neck. Rabbit dance gods on the Bilimek pulque vessel also wear the oyoalli around their necks. As it appears on Códice Matritense del Palacio Real f. 282r, however, the same motif may have been used to represent the Pleiades star cluster (Nicholson et al. 1997: 154, n.9) (fig. 5.20c), a key constellation in the measurement of calendrical and ritual time (ibid.; and see FC4, 1979: 143). Its presence, together with a fire-drilling, on one of the embedded stones at Coatlinchan is thus particularly intriguing in respect to the stones' possible meaning and function. The fire sticks or (*mamalhuaztli*) were also named as an asterism on Códice Matritense del Palacio Real f. 282r and appear together with the Pleiades (see Nicholson et al. 1997: 154 and n. 7).

Category 7 lists Christian signs and symbols found on embedded stones to date. The most common is the Latin cross, but the insignia or other symbols of the three main regular orders also occur. Unlike other examples of insignia found on monasteries and churches connected with these orders, these stones do not form part of the formal decoration of their host buildings, although they may have found their origins in the same. The pierced heart, cap, and bell ensemble of the Augustinian order at Meztitlan lies on a buttress on the east wall of the cloister buildings (fig. 5.21); the Dominican cross of Alcántara at Coyoacan (D.F.) is placed to one side of an east-side (back) entrance to the cloister (fig. 5.22). The Dominican crossbands and stars make up twenty-four of the fifty-nine stones scattered across the walls at Tetepango and five of the embedded stones at Atitalaquia.[27] The sole example of the Franciscan five wounds of Christ is attached to the side entrance of the parish church at Cuauhtinchan. The large angel or saint rising from a

Figure 5.21. Embedded stone bearing the pierced-heart insignia of the Augustinian order, east wall buttress, Los Santos Reyes Meztitlan, Hidalgo.

Figure 5.22. Embedded stone bearing the star of the Dominican order, east-side entrance to the cloister, San Juan Bautista Coyoacan, D.F.

flower-cup may not be an original embedded stone at Tequixquiac, but it nevertheless lies on the east wall of the church at the same height as the three chalchihuitl on the adjacent bell tower.

Finally, the fragment of an atrial cross embedded at the corner of the north side of the facade at San Matías Tepetomatitlan (Tlaxcala) carries the head of Christ, with a sun and a moon, respectively, at its extremities (fig. 5.23). At Tilantongo a (possibly bearded) face may be a death mask of Christ, and I suspect that it also is part of an early stone cross.

Closer consideration of the iconography of this particular group of embedded stones must also suggest that their presence was not the result of a purge of stonework. Would the conch insignia of Quetzalcoatl on the facade of San Juan Tlaltentli Xochimilco (fig. 5.24) have survived if its Latin cross partner had replaced an offensive image? And how do we explain the monogram of the Virgin Mary on the neighboring church of Asunción Colhuacaltzingo mounted on a colonial reworking of the nahui ollin, symbol of the Fifth Sun (Reyes-Valerio 1978: 258, 2000: 313, 319)? In other words, these are original stones and not some type of subterfuge to preserve their inoffensive partners. Occurring in conjunction with native motifs, Christian signs and symbols must be understood as a meaningful part of the iconography of the stones.

The relative overall sparseness of the Christian examples across the board also means that, unlike the picture catechisms and formal painting and sculpture with native inserts, it is now the Christian symbols that appear to be part of a contextual whole that is very heavily native in projection. Can we explain this as some sort of resemanticization of Christian symbols to express native ideas? Were, for example, Christ's cross and the Dominican cross of Alcántara perceived as quartered motifs of the basic cosmic plan; the Augustinian pierced heart as the ritual *xuchimitl*, "flower-arrow"; or the Franciscan configuration of the wounds of Christ as a cosmic diagram? Or was it that Christian signs and symbols in their own right had found a meaningful place within the native iconographic

Figure 5.23. Horizontal bar of an atrial cross embedded into the church facade, San Matías Tepetomatitlan, Tlaxcala.

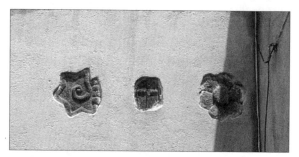

Figure 5.24. Conch insignia of Quetzalcoatl and flower flanking a Latin cross, west wall of the sacristy, San Juan Tlaltentli Xochimilco.

tradition? Neither is a completely satisfactory explanation, for the process of assimilation and utilization of Euro-Christian imagery and the continued deployment of prehispanic signs and symbols can never be so clear-cut. We are perhaps talking about a gradual resemanticization of the iconography of both cultures that reflects native attempts to reinterpret their world within Euro-Christian dimensions. In this sense, the face of Tlaloc and the conch of Quetzalcoatl were not intended as signs of the continuing presence of these deities but rather as symbols of what they represented: water and wind. Similarly, for the cross of Christ or the insignia of the Augustinian order to be meaningful on the walls of a water-filled mountain-church and placed alongside such dominant imagery as flowers, vegetation, and the chalchihuitl, their original symbolism had not so much changed as been reevaluated at an associative level. Is the Latin cross mounted on a flower on the north wall at San Francisco Tepeapulco (fig. 5.25) a "simple" Indian design that acknowledges the "preciousness" of Christianity in the native world, or does it represent a reworked native axis mundi rising from the great flower of terrestrial abundance? As with the Virgin's name in association with the symbol of the Fifth Sun—the Age of Agriculture—the iconographic mix of the stones also appears to tell the complex story of the incorporation of Christianity into the native world.

Figure 5.25. Latin cross mounted on a flower, north wall of the monastery church, San Francisco Tepeapulco, Hidalgo.

Location and Positioning of Embedded Stones

Table 5.2 lists the location, positioning, and numbers of occurrences of documented embedded stones on sixteenth-century religious structures used in this study. Location refers to the orientation of the wall or wall faces of the structure on which one or more stones are embedded, specifically in terms of the direction in which the stones are actually facing. These include the few examples of stones lying on oblique walls. Given the disparity of alignments of the churches, location and orientation are understood as referring to the general direction in which the walls and the stones face, as opposed to the precise angle of deviation. Thus the church of San Agustín Acolman might carry all eight of its stones on its north-facing wall, but these are located on the north, east, and west faces of buttresses. Its stones therefore lie on three wall faces. Conversely, Santiago Tlatelolco has two north-facing stones on its north wall, with a third on an east wall buttress that nevertheless also faces north. Its stones therefore lie on one directional wall face. Positioning refers to the actual area of wall where one or more stones are inserted. From a horizontal perspective this is divided into the center of the wall or veering toward it or at the wall ends or close to them. In like manner, but from a vertical perspective, stones lie toward the middle of a wall or on its upper or lower areas.

Of the fifty-eight structures listed in the table, thirty-eight present a stone or cluster of stones located on one directional wall face only. It is possible, of course, that stones also existed on other walls or directional wall faces at some stage in the churches' history and are now lost, but the incidence of those *in situ* on one wall today is still sufficiently high to argue that this was the overall trend. The stones on the wall at Ometochtli's house also appear to have adhered to this pattern.

Well over half of the individual stones in this first group are positioned toward or at

TABLE 5.2

Location, positioning, and total numbers of embedded stones on sixteenth-century religious structures by site.

Site	Location of Stones (wall faces)					Positioning of Stones					No.
	W	S	E	N	Oblique	Centre	End	High	Middle	Low	
Acatlan, Naucalpan		■	■			■			■	■	4
Acolman, S. Agustín	■	■	■				■		■		8
Acolman, Sta. Catarina		■					■		■		1
Amecameca	■						■		■		1
Atitalaquia		■	■				■	■			7
Atlahapa		■					■			■	1
Cempoala			■			■		■			1
Chapatongo			■				■	■			1
Chiconauhtla, Sta. María	■					■			■		4
Chiconauhtla, Sto. Tomás		■					■		■		1
Chimalhuacan Atenco		■				■	■		■		4
Coatepec		■	■				■		■		3
Coatlinchan	■					■			■		3
Coixtlahuaca				■		■			■		4
Coyoacan			■			■			■		1
Cuanalá		■					■		■		1
Cuauhtinchan (parish church)		■				■			■		1
Cuernavaca (capilla)		■					■		■		1
Itzcuincuitlapilco	■			■			■	■	■		3
Magdalena Actopan				■			■		■		1
Meztitlan		■	■				■	■	■		3
Mixcoac				■			■	■			1
Mixquic	■	■		■	nw/sw	■	■		■		7
Molango	■						■		■		1
Ostoyuca	■							■	■		1
Pachuca				■		■		■			1
San Angel				■		■		■			1
Suchixtlahuaca				■			■		■		2
Tacuba				■		■			■		1
Tenayuca	■					■			■		5
Tepeapulco	■					■	■			■	2
Tepetomatitlan	■	■	■			■			■		7
Tequixquiac		■				■		■			4
Tetepango	■	■	■	■	ne	■	■	■	■		59
Tilantongo	■	■	■	■		■	■		■		18
Tiltepec		■				■			■		2
Tizatlan		■	■			■		■	■		3
Tizayuca	■		■	■		■			■	■	4
Tlalancaleca	?					?					2
Tlalmanalco	■				sw	■	■	■	■		6
Tlalnepantla, Los Reyes		■					■	■			3
Tlatelolco				■		■			■		3
Totolapa		■				■				■	1
Totolinga				■			■		■		1
Tultitlan	?							■		■	3
Xochimanco	■						■		■		1
Xochimilco, Asunción	■	■				■	■			■	4
Xochimilco, Dolores		■	■	■	ne	■	■		■		8
Xochimilco, S. Antonio	■	■	■				■	■		■	4
Xochimilco, S. Bernardino	■						■		■		2
Xochimilco, S. Francisco	■						■		■		1
Xochimilco, S. Juan	■	■	■	■		■	■		■	■	15
Xochimilco, S. Pedro			■				■		■		5
Xochimilco, Sta. Cruz		■				■			■		2
Xochimilco, Sta. Trinidad	■						■		■		1
Yancuitlalpan				■			■		■		1
Yauhtepec	?					?					1
Zaachila		■					■		■		1

Note: Given the irregularities in the alignments of the churches, directions of wall faces are orientational only.

the extremes of walls. The remainder lie at the center of the wall or slightly off-center (for example, when they occur on or near the point that divides a monastery from its adjoining church or walled garden). In these cases, of which there are two examples on church facades proper (Sta. María Chiconauhtla [México] and Molango), they may originally have been wall-end stones, for church and cloister were rarely constructed at the same time.

Stones occur on two wall faces in eleven cases, including San Luis Obispo Tlalma-nalco (México), which carries a row of three stones on the southwest-facing, oblique corner of its bell tower (see fig. 5.26c below). Significantly, no church or monastery complex in this group carries a stone or stones located on two parallel directional walls (on a north- and south-facing wall, for example). At the same time, these stones are most often positioned toward or at the wall corner that they share (for example, Atitalaquia: east wall and east end of the north wall; Tizatlan: east wall and east end of the south wall). This corresponds well with prehispanic Tlatelolco, where the stones are also concentrated on the east wall and the east end of the south wall. Together with the end-of-wall examples on one directional wall face, a focus on specific wall corners appears to be an important factor in location and positioning, suggesting that a directional and/or structural cross-axis is being emphasized. Even in the case of Santiago Tlatelolco, where the stones on the north and east walls all face north, the face of Tlaloc lies at the north end of the east wall.

Four churches carry stones on three wall faces: San Matías Tepetomatitlan (Tlaxcala) (see fig. 5.26a); San Agustín Acolman, with its buttress stones (see fig. 5.26e); San Antonio Moyotla Xochimilco; and Nuestra Señora de Cosamaluapan Tizayuca. Again, there is an emphasis on wall corners in the latter three cases. Acolman's stones lie on the first and second buttresses from the west end. At Moyotla and Tizayuca two examples of stones lie on the north corners of the west walls.

Three churches have stones on four directional wall faces: Nuestra Señora de los Dolores Xaltocan Xochimilco (see fig. 5.26f), San Juan Tlaltentli Xochimilco, and Santiago Tilantongo. Two more carry them on five: the north- and southwest-facing stones on the oblique corners of the bell tower at San Andrés Mixquic (D.F.) (see fig. 5.26d) and the northeast-facing stones on the apse buttresses at Asunción Tetepango (Hidalgo). For the present I can offer no explanation as to why this group of churches should have been singled out to carry so many examples of stones, on all main wall faces. Perhaps within their respective geographical areas they were key edifices for whatever purpose (or purposes) the stones served.

The issue of the directional value of embedded stones and their host structures is explored in the section on spatial organization below. At this point, it remains to comment on the vertical positioning of stones. In all groups, most of the stones are found on the middle or upper areas of wall faces; in the latter category, over half are found at the top of wall faces or high up on bell towers. Differences in the size of structures mean that no correlation can be made in terms of measured heights, but it seems obvious that this was an irrelevant element in their positioning. Stones embedded into the upper and middle areas of walls would originally have been well above the height of surrounding buildings if, indeed, there were any in the immediate vicinity.[28] Both La Serna (1892) and Dupaix (1969) also observed that the stones were placed at the tops of the walls on smaller structures such as houses. The evidence therefore suggests that the stones—even those placed at ground level—were focused on, or were the focus of, some external factor.

Possible Caveats

While embedded stones on churches are generally restricted to buildings constructed in the sixteenth century, some exceptions require comment. Also, the act of placing these stones into the walls of sixteenth-century churches proper is not restricted to that century.

Stones can be found on the walls of churches formally dated after the sixteenth century, such as Santiago Tlatelolco (seventeenth century) and Nuestra Señora de los Dolores Xaltocan Xochimilco (eighteenth century). In these cases, however, we are not always talking about replacement churches but about original structures that have been partly rebuilt or heavily reformed. Research into the history of Santiago Tlatelolco shows that, although the original church started to fall down in 1603, only the baptistry and ceiling vaulting required attention (Rivas Castro and Lechuga García 1999: 3–5). Therefore the three embedded stones on the church's apse and north wall today have probably been in place since the sixteenth century. Ostensibly built over an early chapel (*Ruta de los santuarios* 1994: 71), the apse wall and north wall of Nuestra Señora de los Dolores Xaltocan bear all the hallmarks of sixteenth-century stonework, including a small flying buttress (which has now been bricked in). This suggests that the eighteenth-century structure in fact consists of an extended south wall, a remodeled facade, and an added bell tower. Apart from the stone bearing the Christian emblem "IHS" on the south wall, the remaining eight stones all lie on the wall faces of the east and north sides. It seems possible, then, that the flower and two chalchihuitl on the east-facing wall of the bell tower (fig. 5.8) were once attached to the east face of a west-end buttress over which the later bell tower was constructed.

Post-sixteenth-century preservation of stones is evident elsewhere, such as on the small extension to the north wall of the church at Santa Catarina Acolman and the church annexed to the south side of the early open chapel at Tizatlan (fig. 5.26b). Both additions correspond to the eighteenth century. But, as at Xaltocan, the original stones probably lay on sixteenth-century walls and buttresses covered by the later structures. The extension at Santa Catarina, which carries the date 1746, may have been built to serve as a parochial office for an incoming secular priest (the one-time doctrina of San Agustín Acolman itself was formally secularized in 1754); Santa Catarina became a pueblo in the same century (Gerhard 1986: 322–23). The much older stone bearing the insignia of the Augustinian order was nevertheless retained. The same seems to have occurred with the prehispanic stone on the wall of the later church at Tizatlan.

Guillermo Dupaix's 1806 archaeological report on Xochimilco (Dupaix 1969) might also suggest that not all the embedded stones on the town's churches today are sixteenth-century emplacements. Indeed, he mentioned none of them, his finds being restricted to private residences and commercial and industrial premises such as the Old Inn and the saltpeter works. Yet, littered with prehispanic fragments as early-nineteenth-century Xochimilco so evidently was, it is difficult to accept that none of its colonial religious structures carried any examples. Elsewhere (at Mixquic, for example) they certainly did.

Perhaps the obvious answer here is that by the early nineteenth century the stones on the town's churches were already covered with centuries of lime wash or plastering or hidden beneath remodeled facades. As one of the main colonial lake ports for the entry of goods into the capital (Gibson 2000: 372), Xochimilco was probably quite prosperous and could afford to maintain its churches in good condition and/or keep up with changing architectural styles. This may not have been the case in the smaller chinampa zones outside the town. Within urban Xochimilco, damage to the southwest corner of the barrio church of San Francisco Caltongo has revealed part of a roughly carved column; the style suggests that it is original to the sixteenth-century structure. The sixteenth-century facade of the chapel of San Pedro Tlalnahuac, together with its five embedded stones, was only fully uncovered at the beginning of the 1990s (Flores Marini 1993: 61). Reconditioning and decoration of the exterior walls of San Antonio Moyotla (ca. 2003) also turned up three more stones, two on the north corner of the facade and one on the west end of the south wall.[29]

A further problem arising from Dupaix's work is the possible movement of stones on Xochimilcan buildings since his visit to the town and its outskirts. That is, where he recorded stones of a certain design, these no longer exist, having apparently been replaced by other stones. Alternatively, stones reported at one site can now be found at another. Dupaix made no mention of the three stones bearing, respectively, a chalchi-huitl and two identical flowers that now lie on the bell tower of the church at Mixquic, documenting instead a much larger example carved with a spiral (Dupaix 1969: 89). Yet, as recorded by his illustrator, José Castañeda (ibid., plate 31), a stone identical to this can be seen today at the local site museum. If this is the same stone, then Dupaix may have been removing his finds from their original walls for the purposes of illus-tration; certainly, and despite Dupaix's written observations, very few of Castañeda's drawings show the stones *in situ*. Under these circumstances, subsequent movement of the stones to other sites becomes a distinct possibility.[30] The large lizard that still adorns the facade of the Old Inn in central Xochimilco (now a private residence), however, is also identical to Castañeda's rendering, although he positioned it, appar-ently *in situ*, on a wall corner (ibid., p. 72 and plate 22). Today it lies on a different area of the wall and at a different angle, as if it was returned to its host building after the survey had departed.[31] But, if this was the case, what do we make of the large xihuitl attached at ground level to the north wall of San Antonio Moyotla (fig. 5.18)? It is identical to that documented by Dupaix in the colonial residence of the Guevara fam-ily (ibid., p. 74 and plate 22). If, as Dupaix's reported itinerary implies, the Guevara residence was close to the Old Inn, then it was also close to the church of San Antonio. Is this where the stone eventually found its resting place? Or is the San Antonio stone a duplicate of the example held by the Guevara family? To extend this idea, are all these stones duplicates of those found by Dupaix?

Duplication is a strong characteristic of Xochimilco's own present-day examples of embedded stones, which leads me to believe that the look-alike stones were exclusive to Dupaix's finds and may eventually have come to form part of the collection of ar-tifacts brought together after his death, thereby being removed from Xochimilco for-ever.[32] Xochimilco has several examples of the "mushroom" flower—of which Dupaix (1969: 76 and plate 24) found one—but also the multipetaled variety of flower in two sizes, large and small (figs. 5.8, 5.24), which he did not record at all. The large, high-relief chalchihuitl (ibid., p. 76 and plate 24) occurs on San Juan Tlaltentli (figs. 5.1, 5.6c, 5.15, 5.19), Dolores Xaltocan (fig. 5.8), and Asunción Colhuacaltzingo. Thus the remains of prehispanic Xochimilco could have yielded sufficient material to comple-ment its sixteenth-century religious and secular architecture while at the same time satisfying the curiosity of its first official archaeological survey some 250 years later.

Kubler (1992: 638) described the church at Santiago Tilantongo as "modern." With its irregular stonework and heavy exterior buttressing, classicizing columns, and domed apse (a characteristic feature of early colonial Dominican architecture), it appears to belong to the seventeenth century but (like most Oaxacan churches) has undoubtedly undergone extensive later rebuilding as a result of constant seismic activity. Robert Mullen (1995: 133) observed that the ground plan nevertheless corresponds to about 1564, indicating that it was constructed over an edifice that predated the establishment of the Dominican order at Tilantongo in 1572 and the founding of their own church three years later (see Burgoa 1989, 1:373; Kubler 1992: 638). A secular priest was certainly in residence at Tilantongo from as early as 1532 (Gerhard 1986: 207; Burgoa 1989, 1:372). It seems likely, then, that the source of the stones carved with Renaissance designs at this site (figs. 5.7b, 5.13) was probably the pre-Dominican structure, while the two ostensibly prehispanic stones (figs. 5.12, 5.17) were drawn from the rubble of the Postclassic temple that the church partially covers. But Tilantongo also evidences movement and/or replacement of stones, this time in the modern era. Built on open terrain to the south side of the church and backing onto the prehispanic site, the late-twentieth-century, west-facing church offices also boast two of the early colonial stones: a floral motif and the bearded death-mask of Christ. The dusty terrain in front of the offices carries traces of the foundations of a small cloister, probably the remains of the "monastery" mentioned in Tilantongo's 1579 *Relación geográfica* (Acuña 1984b: 228). Burgoa (1989, 1:372) was accommodated in one of its cells, so the structure was still in use in the early seventeenth century. It is not impossible that these or similar stones were originally embedded into its facade. When that structure disintegrated, they were replaced on a wall at the edge of the prehispanic site or taken into safekeeping, to be incorporated much later into the facade of the new building. I am speculating, of course, but again it must be significant that, despite the chronology of extant buildings at Santiago Tilantongo, all the embedded stones are prehispanic or sixteenth-century in origin.[33]

A similar case was recorded at San Matías Tlalancaleca, where the villagers brought the two "calendrical" stones (fig. 5.6b) in 1948 from the nearby archaeological site of La Pedrera and embedded them into a wall of their handsome late-sixteenth-century church (García Cook 1973; Heyden 1983: 91–92). Labeled Elements 3 and 4, they have since been removed to the local village museum. Although it remains unclear where on the church the stones were embedded, with an azimuth of 0° (Tichy 1992: 212), the church at San Matías faces directly south. The alignment corresponds with the orientation of archaeological exhibit Element 5 (a petroglyph carved with another flower and possibly a proto-Tlaloc) found *in situ* at La Pedrera (García Cook 1973). This might suggest that the church covered a prehispanic site closely connected to the orientation of some of the main monuments at La Pedrera. Again, I can only speculate that the 1948 stones were replacements for originals that had been lost or removed by earlier archaeologists or souvenir hunters, but the twentieth-century inhabitants of Tlalancaleca also still opted for very ancient stone artifacts to embed in the walls of their church.

Finally, at San Matías Tepetomatitlan the late-nineteenth-century church stands to the north side of the original sixteenth-century chapel, the structures being separated by only a foot and a half of space. The later building has no embedded stones; neither does the north wall of the early structure that the modern church now blocks from immediate view.[34] The choice of site of the second church suggests that at the end of the nineteenth century people felt a need to keep the stones on the chapel uncovered, even though the building was perhaps no longer in use.

Overall, it would seem that the practice of embedding stones into colonial buildings—or their direct replacements—was not restricted to the sixteenth century, even though the choice of stone always belongs to that period or earlier. It is possible, therefore, that we are dealing with a still-current belief within more traditional Mexican communities that old stones have some sort of power that they transfer to their new host buildings.[35] But why that power should reside only in pre- and immediate postconquest stones is difficult to explain: perhaps they are the only ones recognized as truly and uniquely "belonging" to the native peoples. Whether or not such a belief prompted the original emplacement of stones on prehispanic and sixteenth-century architecture is also not known. But it is clear that most examples documented in this study are original to the sixteenth century. The depth at which stones lie on walls that boast multiple layers of plaster (see figs. 5.5a, 5.15, 5.16, 5.24) or are revealed as that plaster is removed is a significant detail. As I propose in the following section, the stones also manifest additional characteristics that point to their having had other or alternative meanings and functions. Possibly these too are still current today in some areas.

The Meaning and Function of Embedded Stones: A Hypothesis

Parallels in iconography and choice of location and positioning seen to exist between the prehispanic and sixteenth-century practices of embedding stones into the walls of architecture would indicate that the stones of the two eras shared the same or a very similar function. Work carried out on this particular aspect of prehispanic architecture seems to be negligible, possibly because so little remains *in situ*. Research into sixteenth-century embedded stones is also far from complete: more stones need to be found in order to build up a stronger record of their presence, while empirical knowledge of their function or functions has barely commenced. For these reasons, the following discussion is presented only at the level of hypothesis. It is also a partial hypothesis, for I suspect that the stones carry many more secrets that only time can reveal.[36]

As discussed in the previous chapter, the work of Franz Tichy (supported in part by my observations on native organization of geographical space in sixteenth-century mapping) argues that prehispanic spatial organization was founded on a complex system of visual sightlines across the landscape. The primary coordinates of this system were important rain-giving mountains. Tichy also related the same system to the measurement of time. Aerial measurement of the axial alignments of extant archaeological sites at latitude 19°N, together with early Christian structures that he suspected covered further prehispanic sites, showed that six basic groups of deviation angles existed across the board, running in the series 1–2°, 6–7°, 11–12°, 16–17°, 21–22°, and 25–26°. Large tracts of fields, the layout of villages, networks of pathways, and the geographical locations of villages in relation to a main center also followed the same axial orders. Tichy then observed that important dates during the sun's yearly cycle could be drawn from some of these groupings. For example, 25–26° corresponds to the maximum solar deviation north or south of the east-west axis or the solsticial points; 21° may be associated with the angle of the sun at the zenith passing; others may correspond to special dates in the ritual agrarian calendars. That is to say, dates deriving from these architectural calendars served not only to mark time but also to pinpoint special days in the annual ritual cycle and/or the divinatory and agricultural cycles. Structures with deviation angles of over 26° north or south of the east-west axis may have been aligned to the appearance or disappearance of other celestial bodies within the same system.[37]

Four positions of the sun on the horizon belong to each axial alignment. As we are dealing in most cases with variations of up to 26° at either side of the east-west axis, these would correspond to sunrises and sunsets that can be linked to calendrical dates once the solar declination corresponding to the structure's azimuth has been calculated. Sunrise viewed from the height of Tenochtitlan's Great Temple, for example, was aligned to the temple's axis (7° south of east) on March 4 and October 10. Correlated with Sahagún's Julian calendar of the ritual round at Tenochtitlan, these dates fall respectively on the first days of Tlacaxipehualiztli (February 22) and Tepeilhuitl (September 30) (Tichy 1988). In addition, and given that the angle of the sun at setting varies on any given day, two further dates could be computed from the same building. Sunset on the same axis falls on April 5 and September 8; these may also have corresponded to important moments in the agricultural cycle (Tichy 1990: 192–93).

Broda (1982: 94–96, 1983, 1989: 36) has followed up Tichy's work, pointing out that, as the structure of ritual activities that ran through the year was very closely connected to seasonal and agricultural cycles, the basic structure of the ritual calendar therefore derived from a combination of solar observation and the needs of those cycles. In this context, an alignment of 14–15° north of east (azimuth 75°) would correspond to the four most important dates in the maize cycle: sunrise on April 30 (the opening of the rainy season) and August 13 (the height of rainy season); and sunset on February 12 (the start of the agricultural cycle) and October 30 (the close of the agricultural cycle). Similarly, 14–15° south of east (azimuth 105°) corresponds to sunrise on February 12 and October 30 and sunset on April 30 and August 13 (Broda 2001: 221, 222 n. 59, 225).

While it is now becoming much clearer how horizon or orientation calendars functioned,[38] my interest here lies in the possibility that the wall faces of architectural structures may also have been used for the same purpose. That is, calendrical information could be read by observing the movement of the sun on and over buildings, which constituted what we might call artificial horizons, whose coordinates came in the form of stelae, platforms, or other architectural elements. Motolinía (1970: 24) recorded that on the feast of Tlacaxipehualiztli the sun rose "en medio del [templo de] Uchilobos," that is, between the shrines of Tlaloc and Huitzilopochtli on Tenochtitlan's Great Temple. He added, however, that this day coincided with the equinox, suggesting that the alignment of the temple was 90°, the angle of sunrise on the horizon at this event. In fact, the temple is aligned at 7° 6' south of the east-west axis. But as Aveni et al. (1988: 290–94) point out, in Mexica times the equinox would have taken place on March 22–23 (Sahagún's March 13), the last day of the feast of Tlacaxipehualiztli, but with sunrise at an angle of 97°6' between the two temples. The apparent contradiction here is due to the drift of the sun to the south as it climbs in the sky. Viewed from a point on the ground directly in front of temple platform, or from a lower structure directly aligned with it, the sun at the equinox appeared between the two shrines at the same angle as the temple's alignment (ibid.). Thus the Great Temple at Tenochtitlan can be seen to have recorded a series of dates, depending on the point of viewing of sunrises and sunsets. Observation of the sun on the natural horizon was one option; observation of the movement of the sun on or between the architectural elements of the temple itself was another.

At Tenochtitlan and other main ceremonial centers the presence of large numbers of temple structures all aligned differently,[39] and each with its own carefully coordinated architectural features that marked the solar-temple alignment, would have yielded a corresponding number of fixed dates. Together with observation of the movement of the sun on the horizon from the summit of these structures (or by using nearby structures as intermediary coordinates), numerous additional dates could also be computed throughout the year. In small settlements, however, often with only a single temple-pyramid, the management of such a precise calendar would have been severely restricted, for one structure alone would not easily permit the computation of key dates across the whole solar or ritual year. It also seems unlikely that in these communities labor and related ritual activities during the agricultural cycle were controlled or guided by astronomical observation made at main politico-religious centers. Agrarian calendars varied from area to area in accordance with types of terrain and climatological differences, and each community or group of communities would have had at least one resident religious leader who was trained in the complexities of calendrical computation. The skills of these leaders were certainly not lost in the postconquest period. Records point to the existence of men like Martín Tiçoc, for example, a "counter of the sun and of the feast-days of the devils," who came to the village of Ocuituco to tell "which feast-day was to which devil" (*Procesos de indios* 1912: 161).[40] Balsalobre (1900: 249–50) reported that, in seventeenth-century Zola, Diego Luis computed propitious days for agricultural and hunting activities on his fingers. Both men, however, must have been using some base date from which to reference their counts.

It is possible that by varying the alignments of temple-platforms across a group of neighboring settlements additional counts could be shared. Nevertheless, as Tichy (e.g., 1978, 1979) has shown, the alignments of churches and monasteries that followed the axes of their prehispanic predecessors tend to fall into the same or two consecutive deviation groups by area, as if each community was responsible for its own computations. That is, clusters of edifices within the same deviation group were all focused on the same area of skyline where one specific date was registered, albeit at slightly differing points. As always, there are exceptions; although it is not clear why, I might again speculate that these were in some way key structures that yielded one or more important dates that were shared by a number of communities in the same vicinity or beyond.

One obvious method of pinpointing additional dates from any building is by observing patterns of sunlight and shade on its walls. At El Zape (Durango), a site occupied from about 660 BC, some seventy-two petroglyphs have been recorded, carved on the face of a large natural rock that has been modified by the removal of certain points or the opening up of artificial cracks. Most of the glyphs are geometric in form, including squares, circles, quartered motifs, stars, and diagonal crosses but also animals and small stick figures of humans. Oriented at an angle of 25.5° south of east (that is, the point of sunrise at the winter solstice), the site is believed to have functioned as a solar observatory. The cracks permitted observation of the horizon at different angles, while the glyphs were illuminated by rays of sunlight on other special dates (Peschard Fernández et al. 1989, 1991). A similar system was followed in Anasazi territory, in the

Southwest of today's United States; for example, floral and spiral petroglyphs located behind two strategically placed slabs of stone picked up a shaft of sunlight at significant celestial intervals—the equinoxes and solstices (Folan et al. 1987). The Anasazi also kept seasonal calendars by employing architectural features as coordinates with the horizon (Zeilik 1989, 1991). At nineteenth-century Zuni the old china plate covering the face of the sun was seen to face toward a small rectangular aperture in the east wall of the building. The sun's rays passing through the opening lit up the plate around the autumn equinox.[41]

The similarity of the carved motifs at El Zape to later cosmographic glyphs of the Maya and Mixtec peoples has been noted (Peschard Fernández et al. 1991: 534). Those same glyphs, together with the spirals, flowers, and sun disks of the Anazasi, occur at Otomí Huamango, Tarascan Tzintzuntzan, and Aztec Tlatelolco and on the embedded stones of postconquest churches from the High Sierra of Hidalgo to central Oaxaca. If the peoples of El Zape and the Anazasi used these stones on strategically aligned elements (of natural or constructed origin) to compute their calendrical and seasonal cycles, then it is perhaps not unreasonable to deduce that embedded stones in the walls of later constructions to the south also served the same purpose.

The first rays of the sun emerging from behind the uneven peaks and crags of the landscape (or a closer, intermediary coordinate, such as a second building) would strike certain areas of easterly wall faces at specific moments over the course of the year. The phenomenon would be repeated at sunset on westerly walls at a different angle. The extent and area of exposure of each wall face, however, would be dependent on the width or length of the structure in question and its alignment in relation to the maximum deviation of the sun on the horizon, which at latitudes 19–20°N is between 25° and 26°. If the sun rose exactly between the twin temples at Tenochtitlan on two days of the year when viewed from below, then we should consider that aperture to be a central observation point for a solar-temple alignment on or near those days only. But before reaching the height of the central aperture, its rays would already strike points on the east wall of the platform itself, while on subsequent dates they would start to move across the walls of both the platform and temples. Eventually they would arrive at the walls' extremes, passing from there to the eastern ends of lateral walls until the sun reached its maximum deviation angle at the solstices. The closer the angle of alignment of the building is to the east-west axis, the less area of the lateral walls is open to the sun's rays. The alignment of the temple at Tlatelolco belongs to the deviation group 11–12°. At this angle, the rays of the early morning sun would strike its east-facing wall over the greater part of the year; but movement on its south wall would occur on fewer days than on its north wall. The north wall at Tlatelolco carries no embedded stones, but the myriad of tiny stones carved with a wide range of signs, symbols, and motifs covering its east wall may well have been positioned specifically to compute a series of dates and related ritual activities. This being so, the cluster of carved stones at the east end of its south wall would also correspond to dates close to and immediately after the winter solstice. Buildings aligned between 0° and 64° east of north or between 26° and 90° south of east present similar patterns; but here the lateral walls would receive most of the light of the first and last rays of the sun over the solar year. The actual alignments of these buildings may have been focused on stellar—rather than solar—observation.

The alignments of prehispanic structures in conjunction with the vertical angles of their architectural features (staircases, balustrades, talus faces) and the angle of declination of the sun on its daily path across the celestial sphere also played a key role in the marking of dates. As the sun moves over and around the volume of these structures over the course of the year, specific architectural features are illuminated or plunged into shade on certain days. The west-facing staircase of the Pyramid of the Sun at Teotihuacan (inclined at approximately 41°) in combination with the alignment of its east-west axis (15.5° south of east) is illuminated (in the modern era) by the overhead sun at a declination angle of +0.75° one or two days before the autumn equinox and after the spring equinox. At the same time, the play of light on the surrounding talus faces produces long, vertical shadows (Ponce de León 1991: 422 and n. 6). Viewed from the distance, the effect must have been spectacular, while at the same time announcing to those who were observing that the equinox had arrived (ibid., p. 426).

The potential of computing other dates by using the movement of the overhead sun is obvious, especially given the variations possible in the angles of inclination of architectural details on structures of such considerable volume as the Pyramid of the Sun at Teotihuacan or the Great Temple at Tenochtitlan. Sixteenth-century village churches may have been similar in size to the smaller prehispanic temple-platforms they replaced, yet the verticality of the greater mass of their wall face would considerably inhibit calendrical readings on the basis of coordinating geometrical angles with the sun's trajectory across the celestial sphere. Stepped, inclined, and flying buttresses, however, would offer some interesting possibilities. At Acolman four of the eight flower stones lie on the inclined faces of the two host buttresses; at Meztitlan the Augustinian insignia was embedded into the upward facing plane of a large buttress (fig. 5.21). In terms of length and height, the expanse of church and/or monastery walls would also adapt well to a system based on the angle at which the sun's first and last rays strike the building. Filtering of rays through a higher or lower and nearer or more distant coordinate (such as a range of mountain peaks on the near horizon, a neighboring architectural structure, belfries, and merlons) is another possibility.

Embedded stones therefore could well have served to mark specific points on church walls where calendrical dates could be read as they and their carvings were illuminated or crossed by the first or last rays of the sun. As the texts of both La Serna (1892) and Dupaix (1969) attest, street walls and secular buildings in urban centers also carried stones. Together with the village church or churches, these additional solar markers would provide for a fuller calendar to be computed. As the dominant theme of vegetation, water, and fertility found on the carvings of embedded stones also suggests, such a system may have served to coordinate agricultural cycles, especially the all-important stages of planting, the arrival of the first rains, and the harvest.[42] If this was the function of embedded stones, then it is perhaps not surprising that (as La Serna reported) the native peoples were seen to be paying so much attention to them.

Although no empirical work has been carried out to test this hypothesis, on-site observation of natural surroundings and the location and siting of stones provide some data for discussion.

The spiral stone near the center of the church-monastery facade at Molango (azimuth 88–89°; estimated after Kubler 1992: 259, fig. 131) would probably have been oriented toward the last rays of the sun close to the equinox. The stone faces out toward a free-standing belfry at the west side of the atrium that may have served as a coordinate to filter or deflect the rays onto the stone on that date. At Meztitlan (approximate azimuth 10°; estimated after Azcue y Mancera et al. 1940, 1:466) the two south-facing

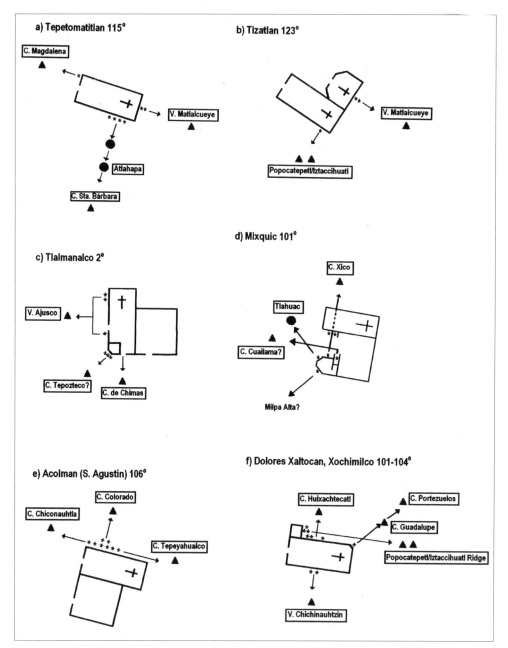

Figure 5.26. Examples of the orientational relationship of embedded stones with important topographical features, political centers, and/or neighboring villages: *a,* Tepetomatitlan; *b,* Tizatlan; *c,* Tlalmanalco; *d,* Mixquic; *e,* San Agustín Acolman; *f,* Nuestra Señora de los Dolores Xaltocan Xochimilco.

stones at the top of an east-side belfry may have been positioned to pick up rays filtered through the pedimented belfry above the church's facade, for example, at sunset on the winter solstice (fig. 5.2) and/or (given their positioning on the outer corner of the east side belfry) to be illuminated by the first rays of the sun on the same date. Alternatively, of course, the alignment of this church might also suggest that the siting of the stones marked a lookout point from the belfry to observe the movement of stars or constellations over the horizon. Indeed, they—but not the axis of the church—are aligned directly with a very prominent flat-topped peak on the south side of the valley. The surrounding area is nevertheless mountainous enough to have provided a whole series of horizon markers for this type of observation.

The church of San Matías Tepetomatitlan is aligned at 25° south of east (azimuth 115°: Tichy 1992: 215), that is, very close to the angle of sunrise at the winter solstice. The two stones positioned at the center of its apse wall (fig. 5.11b) would therefore appear to mark the solar-temple alignment, where the peak and slopes of the nearby volcano Matlalcueye would provide a more than adequate coordinate (fig. 5.26a). The stones on the east end of the south wall may have served a similar function at sunset on or near the same day. The horizontal section of an early atrial cross placed strategically at the north corner of the facade (fig. 5.23) perhaps caught the last rays of the summer solstice over Cerro Magdalena (with which the church is directly aligned) and/or other mountains to the northwest.

At San Esteban Tizatlan (fig. 5.26b) the two vertically positioned stones at the upper center of the apse wall of the open chapel (fig. 5.7c) are aligned at 33° south of east (azimuth 123°: Tichy 1992: 217), which would not correspond with any direct solar-temple alignment. It is possible that these stones may have served as an observation point for events in the night sky over the peak or slopes of Matlalcueye; one of them carries a "flower" with inverted petals that finds an iconographic partner in the native *youalnepantla* (literally "night-middle") glyph. Although pictured in the codices with a central, heavily lidded star-eye, surrounding inverted motifs represent curly darkness or night (Seler 1992, 3:290). The third stone at this site, attached to the south-side wall of the annexed nineteenth-century church, would evidently be open to solar movement on the southwest skyline, dominated as it is by the peaks of Popocatepetl and Iztaccihuatl.

Given native interest in the coordination of time and space, it also seems possible that embedded stones served a dual purpose. In almost all known examples of stones, a direct relationship with important nearby mountains is in evidence, suggesting that in addition to being "receivers" of calendrical data via their mountain coordinates they also recorded the spatial relationship between the same mountains and their host buildings and the alignments of those buildings. The open chapel at Tizatlan is one case in point, for its stones register a cross-axis of two major sightlines from the sacred mountains that appears to have determined the alignment of the chapel and probably its temple predecessor. Readings from other churches with stones on more than one directional wall face also suggest that they were purposely sited to acknowledge the existence of both primary and secondary sightlines for churches, local centers, and prominent mountains on the near or distant horizon.

With an azimuth of 2° (Tichy 1992: 208), the Franciscan monastery church at San Luis Tlalmanalco is aligned on a nearly north-south axis (fig. 5.26c). The three chalchihuitl on the lateral wall therefore face west, where they certainly could have received the last rays of the sun on dates between the equinoxes and the solstices. They also look out directly toward the volcano Ajusco.[43] The three embedded stones on the oblique corner of the church bell tower appear to record a sightline running approximately 44° west of south toward Cerro Tepozteco in the state of Morelos. In and around the Valley of Mexico and the central highlands in general, it is of course not difficult to find alignments with topographical features. Ajusco and Tepozteco are nevertheless well documented as "important" mountains in indigenous cosmogonical understanding. Indian builders at Tlalmanalco may specifically have devised the angle of the corner of the bell tower to align the stones with a further important temporal-spatial sightline.

A similar architectural manipulation may have occurred at Mixquic (fig. 5.26d). With a deviation angle of 11° south of east (Tichy 1992: 204), the complex faces out in the direction of Cerro Cuailama, a small yet important mountain where rituals continued to be carried out after the conquest (see Noguera 1972). According to J. Rafael Zimbrón Romero (1991, 1992), it was possibly a local venue for the spring rites that anticipated the start of the rainy season. Indeed, the deviation angle of the church also adheres to a solar-temple alignment common to the Xochimilco region, corresponding to sunset on April 18 (Tichy 1990: 190, 195), thirteen days before the start of the festival. During this period ritual paraphernalia for the festival per se would probably have been prepared (see Zeilik 1991: 547). The links between the prehispanic festival and Indo-Christianity are seen in the appropriation of the festival of the Holy Cross (May 2–3) to celebrate the onset of the rainy season (Broda 2001). At right angles to the main axis of Mixquic's church, the chalchihuitl on its bell tower faces toward Cerro Xico, once an island in the middle of Lake Chalco. The flower stones, located on the oblique corners of the structure, appear to point toward the centers of Milpa Alta to the southwest and Tlahuac to the northwest. Tlahuac was a major center in the Valley of Mexico radial system, oriented at the crossing point of several important mountains (including Xico), with the corresponding sightlines taking in many of the rural settlements under its control (Tichy 1983b, fig. 4, 1991a: 452, 455, fig. 2).

The two west- and two east-facing flower stones on the north wall of San Agustín Acolman (fig. 5.26e) could well have served to record special sunrises and sunsets over Cerro Chiconauhtla and Cerro Tepeyahualco, respectively. Given the angle of alignment of this church (azimuth 106°: Tichy 1992: 204), these would correspond to February 12 and October 30 (the opening and close of the agricultural cycle) and April 30 and August 13 (the opening of the rainy season and the date of its height), respectively.[44]

A final example involves the stones on the church of Nuestra Señora de los Dolores Xaltocan (fig. 5.26f). These also face out toward several important mountains, including the Popocatepetl-Iztaccihuatl ridge, one of the primary coordinates for horizon calendars in the Valley of Mexico; Cerro Huixachtecatl, site of the New Fire rites at the end of every 52-year cycle but also a focus of the cult of Tlaloc and the mountains (Durán 1984, 1:86–87; FC2, 1984: 152);[45] and Cerro Chichinauhtzin to the south, where, according to Nahua myth, pulque was invented (FC10, 1961: 193).

Inconclusive as the material presented here is, one crucial observation arising from Tichy's hypotheses concerning native systems of measurement of space and time has nevertheless led me to propose that the stones are very closely related to the same systems. This concerns the stones' apparent links with the cult of water and fertility and by extension the sacred mountains, both by far the most dominant aspects of the native religious system. The sacred mountains were given symbolic form in both pre- and postconquest ceremonial architecture, thereby reflecting humankind's acknowledgment of their precious gift of water and the means to grow food. They also furnished humans with a tool for the measurement of time with which to coordinate the cycles of cultivation and showed people how to orientate and accommodate themselves on the terrestrial plane. To put it another way, humans impressed a sacredness on the landscape by creating and structuring a spatial and temporal order out of its natural chaos. This multilayered dialogue between humankind and the sacred geography represented the framework on which the coherence of religious reality was built.

The persistence of this framework after the establishment of the new subreality is evidenced in a number of ways. We see it in ritual, where the abundance of the sacred landscape—the sacred manifest—became the focal point of manifestations directed at Christian figures. The Christian church was endowed with the ideological symbolism of the sacred water-mountains and, together with those mountains, seemingly charged with maintaining the order of geographical space. Imbued with calendrical and astronomical knowledge while at the same time consistently evoking the preoccupation with water and fertility, the iconography and positioning of embedded stones would seem to fit into this framework quite well. Indeed, as in so many cases, as we follow the silent gaze of the stones that look out from the walls of Indo-Christian architecture we inevitably find ourselves turned once again toward those eternally sacred mountains.

The stones also convey to us that Indian artisans working in the first century of colonial rule could and did employ traditional systems in the construction and treatment of their churches and placed their own signs, symbols, and motifs alongside Euro-Christian imports in a manner that was meaningful. These practices were also extended to formal art, the subject of the final two chapters.

CHAPTER SIX

Painting and Sculpture in an Indo-Christian Context

The urgency with which the evangelization body chose to establish a visual Christian presence meant that it was obliged to turn to native artisans for the construction of the new churches and related architectural elements and also their decorative programs. New Spain saw no real intake of painters and sculptors from Europe until the last decades of the sixteenth century, the few available before that time being very much occupied in the new Spanish cities. Only the occasional commission (and they were paid for their work) from an unusually generous or devout encomendero would go the way of an Indian church. We know that the friars did occasionally indulge in a little mural painting.[1] But their low numbers made it impossible to meet the demands of the conversion and the day-to-day ministration of their neophytes and still have time for the additional task of decorating the many thousands of square meters of wall-space that the monastery churches and cloisters alone once boasted (see Reyes-Valerio 1989b, 2000: 377–82). For this purpose, native artisans were trained—or retrained—in the niceties of European art forms and Christian imagery in specially established monastic workshops. Graduating students probably supervised or passed on their new knowledge to others. Some were probably never trained at all, however, having to rely on their own expertise and/or straight copying to fulfill the decorative tasks required of them.

Despite a few surviving gems (at Ixmiquilpan and Cuauhtinchan, for example), individual or original expression does not appear to have been encouraged among the native artisans, trained or untrained. In mural painting we can see only too clearly how copies of (or elements drawn from) engravings and woodcuts included in theological or similar books imported from Europe or, after 1539, printed in New Spain were simply transferred to church walls. At a technical level, direct copying of source material evidently posed few problems; the accurate scaling-up of the material to cover a large area of wall space never failed to astound (Las Casas 1992: 591–92). But the difference in native understanding of European architecture can be seen immediately in the way in which mural panels were lined or stacked up on open stretches of wall space with little or no regard for spacing, symmetry, or intervening architectural elements. Thick vertical lines or painted architectural frames such as loggia-style openings or Renaissance porticos often rather crudely divide up themes. Given their stridently classical features, the architectural frames were evidently copied from European sources, for with few exceptions sixteenth-century Mexican church architecture seldom adheres to the formality of classical architectural design. In some cases, the frames almost seem to have been added as an afterthought, possibly at the suggestion of a friar, to ensure that the saints and their stories were not merged together in crowded scenarios of unclear meaning. Indeed, for the visitor today, the divisions give the impression of walking through the orderly pages of a gigantic European Bible or similar illustrated work. Without them, the experience would be more akin to traversing the iconographic abstractness of a native pictorial text.

Outside architectural sculpture (and sometimes mural painting) is almost always heavily concentrated around doors—even secondary doors—and choir loft windows. Here native artisans seem to have been given freer license to play with European motifs and forms, or friar-architects remained indifferent to what was, in their understanding, purely decorative work. Portals often burgeon with flowers and foliage, angels and arabesques, and a myriad of other decorative motifs. Others are left plain: the rather arbitrarily selected European architectural elements employed (columns, capitals, doorjambs, arches or lintels, cornices, pediments, the Moorish *alfiz*) remain uncarved but noticeably no less isolated against the austerity of the *portada* (front, facade) walls that surround them. Yet such isolation does play on the visual senses, drawing our line of vision toward those openings as if urging us to enter and be entertained by the painted walls within. Just as those interiors remind us of Bibles and prayerbooks reprinted, as it were, in "super-folio," so the portals also carry an uncanny echo of the architecturally framed title pages of European books. Many of these included heavy decorative designs after the mode of the day. The title pages, also called *portadas* in Spanish, adhered to the European convention whereby the reader was "invited" to enter their pages as if entering a building (Fraser 1996: 286–87). As others have already suggested (see Gruzinski 1994: 20), this imported graphic convention may well have prompted or enhanced an ideological inversion in the minds of native artists: the church also came to be perceived as a "book" on whose walls the text of the Indo-Christian sacred was written.[2] Other pointers might support this idea.

The distinctive style of tequitqui carving developed by Indian sculptors in the sixteenth century and largely confined to that period is characterized by its flat, surface beveling over a roughly hewn but deep undercutting, together with the rhythmic patterning of its crowded motifs (McAndrew 1965: 198–200). Tequitqui's forms spring to life as sunlight and shadow play over them (fig. 6.1). Derived from the Nahuatl morpheme *tequitl*, "tribute," the term was originally coined in 1942 to define native sculpture executed at the behest of the conquerors and after their imposed style that nevertheless evidences "reminiscencias idolátricas" (idolatrous reminiscences) in the form of prehispanic inserts (Moreno Villa 1986: 16–19). Today the inadequacy of the term is readily apparent, both in describing the iconographic content of native artwork as a whole (on a comparative scale, it has very few "prehispanic" inserts) and in Moreno Villa's ideological pairing of tequitqui with Spanish mudéjar (ibid.).[3] Moreno Villa later extended his original definition to the "mestizo product that appears in America when the Indians interpret the images of an imported religion."[4] Whether "mestizo" still refers to the presence of "idolatrous" signs, symbols, or motifs within a Euro-Christian context or to the reworking of European imagery in a neo-Christian or syncretic context (or both), the emphasis is again on iconography rather than style. More recently, both definitions have lost focus completely: *tequitqui* is now employed arbitrarily to define any type of native-executed image copied or adapted from European sources, whether in paint or in stone, and whether or not it contains indigenous inserts.

As McAndrew (1965: 197–98) originally proposed, a more appropriate definition of tequitqui must lie exclusively in its sculptural traits. As I see it, its direct stylistic source was the European print on which it was—quite literally—based. Its flattened surface derives from paper (the medium on which the greater part of European art forms was introduced into New Spain), while the deep undercutting is simply a carved rendering of the shading and perspective in the original prints. Tequitqui—the mark of trained and untrained Indian sculptors across a wide geographical area—is, in effect, an exact copy of European book art in stone. This is an unexpected "tribute," to say the least, but one that offers a thought-provoking insight into the way in which the native eye perceived and reproduced the art of the invader.[5]

Figure 6.1. Detail of the tequitqui carved door panel of the old cabildo, Tlaxcala, Tlaxcala.

The evangelizing body probably had numerous and (by all accounts) also conflicting reasons for permitting the Indians to decorate their new churches so elaborately. The growing trend toward ostentation among the regular orders, or early competition between them and the secular priesthood to show success in the conversion mission, may have been motive enough. Complaints of over-extravagance and/or exploitation of Indian labor, most often coming from the secular authorities, were contested on two main grounds. First, the superficiality of the native character demanded emphasis on the external aspects of Christianity to hold its attention. Second, the Indians were already accustomed to this mode of spiritual uplifting:

> [T]he adornment and show of the churches [is] very necessary to raise their spirits and move them to the things of God, because their way of being, which is unfeeling and forgetful of internal things, needs to be helped with outward appearance. And this is why those who ruled them in their pre-Christian days kept them occupied most of the time in building fine temples and in adorning them with many flowers, as well as gold and silver. (*Códice franciscano* 1941: 58)[6]

Whether the friars really believed that native enthusiasm for building, decorating, and furnishing the churches was a throwback to a labor system purposefully imposed by a more spiritually focused ruling class is a matter of debate. But massive native participation in this type of work would have served the same or a similar purpose for the Christian cause. As part of the program of Indian acculturation that the colonial body as a whole embraced,[7] religious architecture, painting, and sculpture played an important role in the attempt to wipe from memory not only the native religion but also the native world. Just as the churches were intended to symbolize Hispano-Christian occupation of Indo-pagan space, so their decorated walls would function as a religious and cultural "brainwashing" for both artists and congregations alike. Wherever the Indian eye might wander, everything would be an immediate reminder of the true god and the new cultural master.

Although aware of native expertise in the visual arts and happy to exploit it, the overseers of the decorative programs at a cultural level would not have been in a position to understand the fundamental difference between what they saw as native "art" and their own. They did understand that the native system of nonverbal communication had been, and still was, pictorial;[8] but they did not recognize that the native *pinturas* constituted a developed writing system. As a result, the European distinction between "text" (specifically, alphabetical text) and "picture" held firm. Yet, whether occupied in painting, carving, featherwork, or other work, the native *tlacuilo* (artist-scribe; pl. *tlacuiloque*) had been a scribe. Preconquest populations at large probably did not have hands-on access to the "books" (although this is not to say that their contents were not performed publicly as transmitted texts).[9] The image displayed publicly was nevertheless directed toward all those who acted within its boundaries. Based on a mode of reading defined as "visual thinking" (Boone 1998b: 158), its signs, symbols, and motifs and the media on which or from which it was executed together served as comprehensive and comprehensible texts to convey the meanings of the origin, role, and destiny of humankind within the great cosmic plan. In this setting, the list of public bearers of text in native production needs to be expanded to include other modes of textual expression: the landscape, as elaborated by human intervention (geoglyphs, rock sculpture, architecture) but also in its own right; architecture, as a model of the landscape but also as a narrative; the manipulation of ritual artifacts (foodstuffs, sticks, stones, flowers) as ephemeral texts; humans and their accessories (costume, artifacts, song, dance, the synergy of movement) as texts in performance. Inextricably linked to each other, these textual forms constituted an assemblage of expressed knowledge, created by human and superhuman device. Their internal and external resonances could be read and assimilated sequentially or in combination. To put it simply: indigenous "artistic" expression served exclusively textual ends. Little or nothing was incidental or intended to embellish at the level of aesthetics.

In the light of the projection of preconquest "art" forms, therefore, we must again ask how native artists would have perceived and treated the European images they were given to copy. Training in the workshops did not necessarily mean (as the friars perhaps believed or hoped) retraining of the mind. Nor indeed, as the example of tequitqui suggests, did it mean a change in the perceived relationship between the image and the medium on or from which it was reproduced. In addition, the often very heavy influence of European art forms found in the postconquest codices indicates that the imported forms and techniques could be readily adapted to create new iconic texts that nevertheless drew on the writing and reading principles of the old system.[10] Hence we must also query the extent to which the native authors of the colonial pictorial codices and the native executors of Euro-Christian "art" may have differed in their approaches to and use of the imported forms and techniques. In terms of colonial native graphic expression, at what point can the line be drawn between text and art? Let us consider some of the implications of this question.

The introduction of Euro-Christian iconography into the native world may well have been the most disconcerting element to meet the native public eye, especially when it came to dominate. Initially, however, the images of Christian figures were perhaps not too difficult to take in; very much like the teteo of old, they were portrayed in human form and/or identified by way of specific attributes, signs, and symbols. They also inhabited landscapes of trees, mountains, and rivers and occupied ritual enclosures and temples. But what could be made of the realistic manner in which they and their world were depicted? What of the clothing and attributes they had in common: cloaks and gowns, miters and crosiers, swords and wings, halos? What of the endless trails of fanged, snarling beasts and plump, naked, and often winged children romping amid swirling vines and fruit- and flower-laden pots that so often surrounded these figures? How would the "visual thinker" interpret all this?

Musing of this type might appear fanciful, but it does underscore a further aspect of native-executed religious art of sixteenth-century Mexico. The paucity of indoctrination received by the Indians at the level of theological explanation, together with the difficulties inherent in reconciling the perception of the Indian self with the perception of the Christian self (Klor de Alva 1999), meant that native assimilation of Christianity became dependent on a fragmentary record of Christian precepts interpreted as a whole from the perspective of the function of religion in the Indian world and the framework around which it was constructed. Put another way, Christianity could only make sense in practical terms if it offered a coherent pathway to follow. Where no pathway existed, one was created on the basis of the perceived reality and spiritual needs of the Indian world. Thus, if Christianity could be explained through the imagery imposed by the colonial ecclesiastical authorities, Indo-Christianity could also be explained in the same way.

In the native-executed works in the churches, faithful copying from European sources is at least apparent, even if many of those sources are as yet unidentified. Some (perhaps many—we will never know for sure) painter-scribes, however, did change details in those sources by inserting the occasional prehispanic glyph, sign, or motif. In the past some scholars have chosen to view these inserts as early and short-lived "survivals" of an abruptly curtailed history or, as Kubler (1964) designated them, the signs of the "extinction" of a culture. Alternatively, if any native symbolic content was intended, it was soon lost through dissociation with the European contextual whole: "Unlike the glyphs in the pictographic manuscripts, they became part of a whole that was no longer Indian" (Gruzinski 1993: 39).

Regardless of the assumption here that the codices were Indian but the churches irrevocably Euro-Christian (from whose perspective?),[11] such skepticism is perhaps also initially contested by pointing out that where prehispanic inserts or themes are boldly displayed (e.g., in the mural programs at Augustinian Malinalco and Ixmiquilpan or in the eagle- and jaguar-flanked Annunciation at Franciscan Cuauhtinchan) they must have been approved by the evangelization body, whether in context or not. While this might suggest a generous dose of compromise on the part of that body, its consent was probably more firmly based on the understanding that assimilation of the Christian message was in fact facilitated by being expressed through native glyphs or themes. Some certainly adopted this methodology despite attempts to put a stop to it.[12]

Based on what has survived, native scribes more commonly appropriated European forms or configurations to produce works that might look wholly European on the surface but in fact (as I discuss later) carry a strong sense of having been "Indianized." Here we do see the native mind at work—confidently so and, I would argue, in context. Peterson (1993: 7–8) showed in her study of the Malinalco mural program that European and native elements (such as flora and fauna and some glyphic signs) can also blend together in a meaningful way, their variants being categorized at the levels of convergence or syncretism. But, as she also recognized, such a mix can give rise to numerous ambiguities. Other traditional survivals such as the chalchihuitl symbol are nevertheless viewed as juxtapositions; they function as "decorative" elements and their authenticity of meaning eludes us because of their isolation from a relevant native graphic context (ibid.).

In order to come closer to understanding early colonial native painting and sculpture, we should perhaps start by throwing out concepts such as iconographic "convergences," "juxtapositions," and "decoration." These are Western terms based on Western precepts and are therefore unlikely to reflect native usage, especially in regard to such culturally mixed imagery. In addition, our wariness in explaining the presence of prehispanic glyphs in the art of the period only belies our persistence in looking at it from a Western perspective—that is, in looking at it as "art." The pictographic catechisms successfully mix European forms and Christian symbols with conceptual and phonetic glyphs of prehispanic origin in much the same balance of content as in the mural paintings and sculpture on the churches. If we accept these inserts as an integral part of the catechisms' texts—and colonial iconic texts they surely are—why are the same type of inserts in "formal" art viewed as contextually or culturally meaningless? It seems clearer to me that many native "artists" responsible for religious mural painting and sculpture were in fact still working as scribes. They adapted or manipulated Euro-Christian art forms not only to clarify their meaning to a native audience but also to express the native world's understanding of Christianity. In doing so, they adhered to the principles of nonverbal communication of their own world. They transformed Euro-Christian art into a form of iconic text and, where necessary, supplemented it from their own iconic vocabulary. Herein, perhaps, lie the apparent ambiguities noted by Peterson. As an iconic text, this work must also open itself up to more than one reading for (possibly) more than one audience.[13] Such a process is far from carrying the stigma of survival. Rather, it proclaims the dynamics of cultural continuity and the flexibility of the native world's cultural perception as it encountered and responded to change.

Although this area requires much future research, use of color is perhaps a significant indicator that the conversion of European formal art to native text was taking place. Judging from the surviving examples of European books that found their way into New Spain's monastic libraries, most of the prints from woodcuts and engravings used by native artist-scribes as their sources would probably have been in monochrome.[14] Illuminated printed books were common in Italy and Venice by 1490 (Alexander 1995: 163) and, we must assume, in Germany, where the technology of movable type was invented (ibid.). Cost was perhaps a key reason why the mendicant groups seem to have lacked examples in their own New World collections. More significantly, the extremely high and widespread usage of red and blue (or tones thereof) for native-executed mural paintings in polychrome (see chapter 7) must indicate that native artists ignored the colors in the illuminated books even if they had access to them. That is, color applied to the murals was based on native initiative.

In the colonial period monochrome murals with tiny inserts in red or blue or both of these colors are also common. As I point out below in the case of Actopan, details in blue evidently link objects associated with water or the regeneration of life, thereby introducing conceptual readings. At Malinalco the distribution of inserts in blue and red across the so-called garden murals is yet to be analyzed. But blue is reserved for the foliage on the cloister walkway ceilings, which suggests (vis-à-vis the exclusively monochrome foliage on the walls below) that the two "gardens" are conceptually distinct and separate. Red highlights alphabetical orations or citations from the scriptures that separate these gardens, seemingly copied from sections of decorative red lettering incorporated (usually as *rubrica*) into the otherwise black-ink texts of European printed books. But at sites such as Acolman and Tepeapulco, for example, red or red-brown also tinges native-executed *images* in monochrome. By coincidence, the European combination of black and red ink equated with the dual Nahua metaphor *in tlilli in tlapalli*, "the black [ink], the red [ink],"[15] the sacred knowledge written in the divine cosmic books (see León-Portilla 1982, 1997). The friars used the same native metaphor to describe the contents of the Christian Bible (Sahagún 1986: 116–17, 140–41, 1993: 185). When indigenous artists at Acolman, Tepeapulco, and elsewhere painted their murals in black and red, is it possible that they were effectively rewriting the alphabetical text of the Christian *teomoxtli* in pictographic form?[16] Careful analysis of red or red-brown inserts in otherwise monochrome murals may well establish that they also determine reading orders or values to guide the visual thinker.[17]

The issue of interpreting European visual messages executed for a native audience takes on still broader dimensions when we consider the ideological conflict between the European understanding of art as "decorative" or "meaningful" and the native pictorial writing system, which never carried "decorative" values. We cannot assume that trained or retrained *tlacuiloque* fully assimilated this distinction any more than that they automatically took on the role of producers of images as opposed to writers of texts. Taking as an example the all too frequent incidence of emblems, signs, and symbols (Christian or pre-Christian) in the iconography of the Renaissance grotesque, the (cognizant) viewer still only receives fragmentary ideas and associations that carry meaning: here is Christ's chalice, there is an emblem for chastity, and so on. Such iconographical elements are enhanced visually—but not ideologically—by their repetition, symmetry of form, and emplacement and, more often than not, by a plethora of additional motifs such as swags of textiles, ornamental vases and urns, and floral and vegetal arabesques. From the Western viewpoint, the grotesque is an ornamental assemblage whose iconography is not invested with any overall significance. It is, and was, recognized as a purely decorative tool. But, faced with converting a printed grotesque border into a painted or sculpted frieze, how would native artists look at it? Trained or not, would they recognize it as "decorative art"? Or, still with an ingrained approach to the image as text—to "thinking" the image—would they try to "read" it or derive meaning from it and then incorporate that meaning into their own iconic version?

Again, more research is required here, but there is good evidence to show that grotesque friezes copied from European sources were being consciously—rather than erroneously—modified by native artists. The celebrated mural program in the nave of the monastery church at Ixmiquilpan is perhaps the most obvious example. Its battle narrative was modeled on two apparently quite faithfully reproduced grotesque friezes of European origin on the upper levels of the same walls (Estrada de Gerlero 1976; Fraser 1991). Although at first glance renderings of the grotesque elsewhere also seem to be the result of straight copying, they often reveal a concerted intervention by an Indian hand. Native speech scrolls and floral song glyphs abound, denoting verbal communication between the painted or sculpted protagonists or with an audience. Details such as angels with the clawed feet of a raptor (at Calpulalpan [Tlaxcala]) or the insertion of prehispanic leg bells (see fig. 7.33b) can also be found, suggesting that the original European elements have indeed been "edited" into something that carries meaning for a native audience. At Franciscan Tecali a fragment of a frieze in the area below the choir loft depicts scorpions on the trumpet-banners of two winged figures

Figure 6.2. Modifications made by native artists to a grotesque frieze: from *a*, the symmetry of mirrored scorpions, nave, Santiago Tecali, Puebla, to *b*, scorpion and crescent moon of the pulque cult, cloister, San Francisco Tepeapulco, Hidalgo.

(fig. 6.2a). Although the scorpion motifs may have been present in the original European source, the same grotesque design was repeated at Tepeapulco, this time with clear evidence of native intervention (fig. 6.2b). Defying the traditional iconographic symmetry of the grotesque, the scorpion on one of the banners remains, while the other has been replaced by the U-shaped crescent moon of Mexico. The scorpion was a prehispanic sign associated with the pulque deity Tezcatzoncatl (FC1, 1970: 51), while the crescent moon was a symbol of the cult itself. As I show below, further references to the water/pulque cult occur in native expression at Tepeapulco. Rather than being incidental, this particular aspect of the frieze therefore complements an overall theme running through the site's mural program.[18]

A further interesting example of native inserts is the use of the native slipknot, commonly depicted as a loincloth tie but also as an accouterment on the headdresses of rulers and deities. Its similarity to the decorative European swag-knot is obvious, but the context in which the knot is sometimes deployed raises questions about the native artists' intended meaning. In the remains of a frieze beneath the choir loft at Cuauhtinchan, a loincloth tied with the native knot covers the rump-end of a ferocious mythical beast of European descent (fig. 6.3). The detail certainly appears to have been added to the original of what (without the loincloth) became a fairly common motif in New Spain.[19] In the lower cloister at Cholula a remaining mural fragment depicting a group of galloping horses includes—somewhat illogically—a series of these knots tied from the animals' taut and straining reins (fig. 6.4). The prehispanic meaning of the slip-knot is unclear, but analysis of the ritual symbolism of prehispanic clothing (particularly the loincloth) aligns it with the concept of virility (Anawalt 1981: 209), which may well be in some way connected with the cult of fertility. Among other things, the tamed horse was associated in European thought with virility (Curiel Méndez

Figure 6.3. Detail from a grotesque frieze where a native slipknot has been inserted, nave, San Juan Bautista Cuauhtinchan, Puebla.

1987: 97). As a native symbol, then, it may have been used at Cholula to express a European meaning. Is this what it also means at Cuauhtinchan, although now as a native concept introduced into a European decorative panel?[20]

These brief examples must also tell us that the evolution of Euro-Christian art forms in the hands of native artists does not reflect only the cross-cultural experience in play. If European originals were modified, however slightly, and/or native signs and symbols inserted, it was because those originals did not adequately express the meaning of Christianity as understood by the native population. Just as the tenets of the imposed religion were being reconstructed to render them compatible with the native world and its religious needs, so the visual languages of Christianity and of Europe were being rewritten at a thematic level. "Editing" in the form of native inserts may also have served to communicate native concepts incorporated into the meaning of Christianity that had no European "visual" equivalent.

An exhaustive appraisal of native-executed religious artwork (I will continue to use this term for the sake of clarity) in sixteenth-century Mexico is not possible in a study of this size.

Figure 6.4. Detail of the native slipknot used on the taut reins of a galloping horse, lower cloister, San Gabriel Cholula, Puebla.

The corpus of material is so large, heterogeneous, and chronologically dispersed that superficiality would soon take the upper hand. This chapter instead concentrates on three main areas of native painting and sculpture in the Indo-Christian context where native ideas and the manipulation of Euro-Christian sources and themes to express them are in evidence: landscape painting, the attributes of certain Christian figures, and the Cross of Christ.

The decision to restrict discussion to manipulated Euro-Christian art might be viewed as selective in that it ignores the greater part of surviving native artwork of a more "orthodox" nature. But, as we will see, the orthodox itself could be manipulated. In addition, the coexistence of both types of artistic expression, at different sites or at one site, may not reflect the original decorative programs. In other words, especially in the area of mural painting, much of what once existed was removed or covered over at a very early stage as a result of changing ideas apropos their iconographic content or the aesthetics of church decoration in general.

Ample evidence shows that mural programs dating from the 1560s to the 1580s in structures raised in the 1540s or 1550s have replaced previous works. The north wall of the nave of the monastery church at San Miguel Huejotzingo once boasted a complex polychrome garden mural through which European ecclesiastical figures processed. This must have been washed over at some stage, with a monochrome decorative frieze subsequently covering the area of wall occupied by those figures (fig. 6.5). At Tepeapulco the Franciscan knotted cord across the upper area of the portraits of saints and the two representations of the Crucifixion (see figs. 6.18, 6.22) is most evidently a later addition, suggesting that the extant murals belong to an earlier period. The obliteration of Christ's head and shoulders with the cord is otherwise inexplicable. In addition to a grotesque frieze around the nave of the monastery church at Todos Santos Cempoala that was painted over, small patches of damage to the monochrome mural paintings on the apse wall indicate that they also cover an earlier, polychrome program. Juan Gerson's "orthodox" bark paintings of the Apocalypse, pasted onto the panels of the choir loft vaulting at Asunción Tecamachalco, stand in sharp contrast to the recently revealed vestiges of a mural program of cacti, bulrushes, and flowering plants standing above bright turquoise, chalchihuitl-framed rectangles (plate 11). Strongly native in style, they appear to represent irrigated agricultural or garden plots. The church was completed by 1557 and Gerson's work dates to 1562 (Camelo Arredondo et al. 1964: 14, 25–26; Kubler 1992: 578), so it is not impossible that these early paintings were almost immediately superseded by Gerson's masterpiece, perhaps because their overly "native" appearance was no longer considered aesthetically pleasing or compatible.

Figure 6.5. The remains of two different mural programs, wall of the monastery church of San Miguel Huejotzingo, Puebla.

I choose to focus on these three themes in Indo-Christian art because, while expressed differently from site to site, at an ideological level they nevertheless display an underlying consistency in respect to their interpretations of the Christian message. Original European landscapes, together with the architecture onto which they were copied, are transformed into the sacred geography of the Indian world, in which Christian figures move as naturally as the sacred forces of old. In some instances Christian figures also exhibit certain attributes that, while never openly altering their Christian identities, suggestively offer up a native reading that allots them the same roles as the supernatural entities occupying that geography. Dispossessed of his human form, Christ is perceived as the mutated Divine Provider. As the fruit of the Indian tree of trees, he is the maize that permits the native world to perpetuate.

The Sacred Landscape

Although landscape painting was a still-nascent genre in Europe at the time, its introduction into New Spain (again by means of woodcuts and engravings in imported books) was received with noticeable enthusiasm by native artists.[21] In the Old World the art form was viewed as a secondary category, employed almost exclusively as a decorative, and often specially created, background for representations of saints, the Holy Family, and other biblical and historical scenes.[22] In New Spain, as we have seen, Indian mapmakers adopted the genre as a new element of cartographic composition, often to replace the hill glyph. In mural painting native artists also reworked their source material in order to depict their own local topography.

Some examples are less obvious than others. The tall, rounded mountain rising before the rolling hills and church spires of a European countryside that backs the Crucifixion at Acolman is strangely out of place (fig. 6.6a), suggesting that it is an addition to the original engraving from which the scene was copied. At Epazoyucan the mountainous skyline to the west of the monastery complex is characterized by a

Figure 6.6. Painting local landscapes: *a,* mural painting of the Crucifixion, upper cloister, San Agustín Acolman, México (the large mountain that rises between the cross and the figure on the right is possibly a representation of Cerro Chiconauhtla); *b,* view of Cerro Chiconauhtla from the raised open chapel at Acolman.

series of peaks, the five most prominent of which were included in the landscaped background of the murals of the Crucifixion and the Deposition in the monastery's lower cloister (fig. 6.7a–b).

The monastery church at Epazoyucan is directly aligned with one of the five peaks, identifiable as Cerro Epazoyu (fig. 6.7a). According to the 1580 *Relación geográfica,* this peak stood in front of the town and gave it its name (Acuña 1985b: 89). The monastery church at Acolman is directly aligned with Cerro Chiconauhtla, which lies to its west (fig. 6.6b). From this we can perhaps deduce that the mountain inserted in the mural at this site also represents Acolman's most important local mountain. Indeed, while the positioning of the hand of the figure standing to the right of the cross

Figure 6.7. Painting local landscapes: *a,* view of the skyline from the church portal at San Andrés Epazoyucan, Hidalgo, which is directly aligned with Cerro Epazoyu; *b,* detail from the Deposition, lower cloister, Epazoyucan, with the town's own landscape as a background.

(from our perspective) represents a traditional gesture of sorrow (Hall 1979: 84), it also draws the viewer's attention to the mountain.[23] The mural paintings at both sites would therefore invoke, in whole or in part, the actual views from the two respective church portals toward local patron-mountains.

While we would expect native maps to include local topography, the decision to transform European landscapes into Mexican landscapes in religious mural painting must raise slightly different questions in respect to purpose. Why did Indian artists choose to represent the events and figures of Christian mythology against the back-drop of their own natural surroundings? To put it another way, why go to the trouble of reworking or replacing the landscaped background of an illustration copied from a book or engraving while retaining the foreground in its original form? Was this simply an attempt to retain the Indian "old" alongside the Christian "new"? Or was its purpose to explain that Christian mythology and its figures were a part of the Indian world—that a still-sacred landscape was the setting on which Christianity now acted out its own story? Although the landscape elements of the Crucifixion panels at Acolman and Epazoyucan correspond to whole or partial views of local topography as seen from the portals of their respective churches, the murals must also have been structured on the church-mountain alignment that continued to underpin native organization of geography in the colonial period. They are, in effect, reversed views along the imagi-nary mountain-church sightlines that structure the maps. At Acolman, Epazoyucan, and elsewhere a once centrally placed atrial cross would have interrupted this line of vision, although serving simultaneously as a coordinate for it.[24] But in the murals the courtyard crosses are not part of the view; they have become the real cross of Christ. At Epazoyucan the artist also skewed the upright shaft of the cross (but not the hori-zontal) in order to emphasize the intended alignment with Cerro Epazoyu. The Indo-Christian message in these paintings is twofold. Not only was Christ crucified on the sacred geography of Indian Mexico, but his Passion was in some way understood to be linked to its sacred patron-mountains.

As features of the sacred landscape, trees, caves, springs, rivers, and mountains—even large rocks, crags, and boulders (Broda 1997a: 65, 1997b: 145)—were primary manifestations of the supernatural forces that inhabited its form. These were the signs of the original and perpetual creation, as told and retold in the stories that guarded the sacred knowledge of the ancestors. And the sense of the all-pervasiveness of those forces clearly determined the way in which the landscape was perceived. Na-tive descriptions of the "eminences of the land" (FC11, 1963: 258) demand a holistic approach to their varying facets. The crag, for example, is at once jagged and smooth (ibid., p. 262); the mountain is high, low, pointed, wide, round, rocky, earthy, grassy, wet, dry; it has precipitous gorges, sloping plains (ibid., p. 258); its summit is wide, narrow (ibid., p. 261). Such contrasts might refer to topographical differences across the board, but the texts specifically refer to each eminence in the singular; in this way a second reading reflects the individuality of features that any particular crag or mountain may possess at any one moment in space and time. Central Mexican rep-resentations of a flower, for example, often attempt to include views from all angles in a single image—sometimes also with a bud and seed-pod growing simultane-ously (see Gandara n.d.). So a crag or a mountain or a cave must be considered in all its aspects. This was the special way of seeing the landscape with which the wise ones were endowed. They were the possessors of the sacred knowledge that gave them the sight of the omniscient Tloque Nahuaque, Lord of Everywhere: "O night, O wind: thou seest, thou knowest the things within the trees, the rocks . . . thou knowest, thou seest things within stones, within wood" (FC6, 1969: 25, 28). In the Maya *Popol vuh* the first four humans saw everything in the world perfectly, without any obstruction. "They didn't have to walk around before they could see what was under the sky; they just stayed where they were. . . . Their sight passed through trees, through rocks, through lakes, through seas, through mountains, through plains" (*Popol vuh* 1986: 165).

It was this vision of the landscape that prehispanic scribes were trying to explain at contact. This is illustrated, for example, on Codex Nuttall 19, 22, and 36, where three panels contain images of topography that in some ways conform to Western notions of landscape representation. Each is a composition of the specific topographical features of a particular location, and viewing appears to be on the horizontal plane. The similarities end here, however, in that any intended realism is lost to the purpose of representation. The landscape was depicted as it was perceived rather than as it was seen. Rivers complete with fish and shells are seen as rectangular containers in which water flows from side to side rather than following its natural course. Rock is glyphically defined through the use of surface nodules, while specific soil types lying beneath are described through different designs. The roots of trees and plants are all visible. Yet surface vegetation is simultaneously also recorded in vast expanses of green; on Nuttall 22 the dark form of heavily wooded Cerro Montenegro at Tilantongo is emphasized in black.

Over these sacred landscapes we see rulers, priests, and gods tracing ritual paths. Mixtec rulers claimed descent from the landscape (Pohl and Byland 1990: 116); therefore we must view their presence as part and parcel of its sacred features. The comparatively large figures of these semidivine beings vis-à-vis the landscape that they tread does not serve in the Mixtec codices to lessen the importance of that terrain but to emphasize the equal status of both. Codex Nuttall's landscapes are not "backgrounds" that set off the deeds of rulers but are an integral part of those rulers' histories. Nahua descriptions of the rituals surrounding the kindling of the New Fire at the end of each 52-year cycle give us some understanding of the act of moving across the landscape in their own world. Priests, dressed as deities, processed out from the central ceremonial precinct at Tenochtitlan toward Cerro Huixachtecatl to the south: "Very deliberately, very stately, they proceeded, went spread out, and slowly moved. It was said, 'they walk like gods'" (FC7, 1953: 27).

Three explicit examples of local topography inserted into religious painting can be found at the Augustinian monastery complexes of Culhuacan and Actopan and Franciscan Tepeapulco. As at Acolman and Epazoyucan, the paintings lie in the monastic quarters of these complexes (that is, the cloister, stairwells, and other areas occupied by the resident friars). They also share very much the same iconographic characteristics in that they manipulate European graphic sources to construct local landscapes in accordance with the native vision and/or bear strong projections of the meaning of those landscapes for the native world.[25] In the cases of Culhuacan and Actopan native perception of Euro-Christian architecture as a replica of the local patron-mountain is again clearly revealed through their artwork.

At Culhuacan it is Cerro Huixachtecatl that provides what we might initially understand to be a backdrop for two surviving landscaped murals in the lower cloister.

The hill stands some two kilometers northeast of the monastery, opening to a series of deep caves—an important qualifier of a sacred mountain, especially those dedicated to the cult of Tlaloc and the mountains (Broda 1991a: 473, 1997b: 145). In addition to witnessing the kindling of the New Fire at the end of each 52-year cycle, the mountain was evidently associated with the water cult. The tota pole raised during the feast of Hueytozoztli in the patio of the rain deity's temple (around which the four smaller trees were placed) was brought specifically from "the mountain of Culhuacan" (Durán 1984, 1:86–87). One of the amaranth dough mountain effigies made in the rain-petitioning ceremonies of Atemoztli was given its name (FC2, 1981: 152). Culhuacan's 1580 *Relación geográfica* also states that the monastery was built (probably purposefully) over a natural spring (Acuña 1986: 34), which suggests that the site was a one-time focus of the water cult.[26]

Painted around doorways at the northeast and southwest corners of the lower cloister walkway, two washes of brown, yellow, turquoise, green, and black frame a Crucifixion (plate 12) and a rendering of the *Tebaida augustiniana,* an allegorical composition of the eremitic life of the order (plate 13), respectively. Fragments indicate that similar landscapes occupied the wall areas at the two remaining corners and possibly the entire length of the lower cloister walkway. Although the colors are blended overall, concentrated patches detail large caves and trees, precisely the most sacred aspects of neighboring Cerro Huixachtecatl's topographical features. Wandering through these dense landscapes are numerous tiny figures of Augustinian monks clad in their dark habits; some converse, while others kneel in prayer. Around them, also in miniature, are a series of animals: deer, lions, and possibly a coyote or perhaps a tlacuatl, the Mexican marsupial of the opossum family associated with the pulque cult. In the upper cloister, which contains decoration in monochrome, the same deer reappear in a window niche panel alongside a second Crucifixion in miniature. Thus at one time the whole cloister program was organized as a series of Christian themes in the setting of the mountain and its flora and fauna. It is worth pointing out that the presence of animals in New Spain's landscaped mural panels is not restricted to Culhuacan.[27] Appearing so frequently in these paintings, they recall the mountain settings of the early Christian festivals celebrated at Tlaxcala and probably elsewhere (as described in chapter 2). The painted versions seem almost to be pictorial "records" of the same settings.

The immediate impact of the two remaining polychrome panels is their depth, making it clear that the landscaping is not in fact intended as a backdrop to the scenes portrayed. It rises up vertically to take us in as we also move across the slopes of the sacred mountain, around its cave entrances, and under the branches of its great trees, the source of the sacred tota poles of old. The sense of being on the actual mountain is further enhanced through use of the cloister's architectural elements. Both murals are painted over and around the arched doorways leading from the cloister to other monastic areas. That is, the walls and openings of the cloister have been incorporated into the landscapes as if to symbolize the slopes and cave mouths of the sacred mountain. In the Crucifixion the three crosses on the Hill of Golgotha stand precisely on the top of the arch, while to the right friars climb its curved form. As intermediaries between the Indians and the Christian supernatural, they now tread the old ritual paths across this watery landscape, ascending the sacred mountain "like gods."

The style of the landscaping in the murals is very close to the landscaped representation of Cerro Huixachtecatl on the 1580 map of Culhuacan, suggesting that they were painted by the same native artist, identified as Pedro de San Agustín (Mundy 1996: 65, 82–83). The use of color is similar too, but a significant detail on the map is the chromatic match of the mountain with the traditional toponym of Culhuacan (a curved coliuhqui mountain) and the portals of the stylized cartographical churches, as if the map artist was emphasizing a conceptual link between them. This concept was repeated in the murals, where the walls of the New World cloister were perceived as the slopes of Cerro Huixachtecatl.[28]

A contemporary European source for the style in which these landscapes are painted is difficult to identify. In fact, it is far closer to the wash maps produced by some Indian cartographers in the second half of the sixteenth century.[29] Despite the strong change in native artistic style, use of color was retained, particularly in the swaths of intense blue that run through the compositions, taking in trees and rocks in their path. The same blue was consistently deployed in both prehispanic and early colonial art as a symbol for water. In Culhuacan's Crucifixion panel it pushes upward past the summit of Golgotha-Huixachtecatl to link with a heavily clouded sky, echoing, it seems, the watery associations of the sacred mountain once dedicated to the cult of the rain god. "When [clouds] billowed and formed thunderheads, settled, and hung [about the mountaintops], it was said: 'The Tlalocs are already coming. Now it will rain. Now the masters of the rain will sprinkle water'" (FC7, 1953: 20).

Although in this reading the murals appear to be highly unorthodox in projection, the Culhuacan artist evidently knew the Christian source of sacred knowledge well, and it determined his choice of a series of European graphic emblems to enhance the landscape's overall message.[30] The deer was an Old World symbol of the Christian Resurrection, finding its origins as an emblem in Psalm 42, which opens: "As the hart panteth after the water brooks, so panteth my soul after thee, O God."[31] In the prehispanic world the deer was associated with Tlaloc. The Crucifixion mural depicts the animal in front of a cave entrance, an appropriate graphic reference to the source of the waters that will flow from the interior of the mountain. In his commentary on the deer in the mural paintings at the House of the Dean, Puebla, Gruzinski (1994: 162) proposes that it is the biblical reference to the desire for water that overrides the intended connotations of the Christian emblem. Its iconic meaning changes as it is included in a natural world still full of ancient divinities. The presence of an outsized date palm in the Culhuacan *Tebaida*, with a second deer running nearby, partly supports this interpretation. Unknown as a prehispanic symbol and therefore copied from a European source, the date palm was a Western emblem for the blessed person, for it flourished in wholesome and abundantly flowing waters (Psalm 1:3; Wither 1973: 172). Once more the reference to water seems to have motivated the Culhuacan artist to include the emblem in his local landscape, for the likelihood of a real date palm growing on the harsh highland terrain of Cerro Huixachtecatl is very small, even after the Spanish conquest. But its presence and size in the mural, together with the deer, strongly echo the symbolism of the great tota tree brought from the mountain of Culhuacan to stand before the rain deity's temple. Here the artist could not have been manipulating a parallel in Indian and European religious symbolism. He was not inserting prehispanic symbols for water into a Christian landscape in order to invoke ancient deities; rather, he was incorporating Christian symbols that spoke of watery abundance into a native landscape.

The several lions of African or Asian origin (which are exclusive to the *Tebaida*) must also have been drawn from Old World sources, possibly from a printed example of this typically Augustinian theme. But the *Tebaida* also contains two proportionally large cats. Plump and rather satisfied in appearance, they are outlined in profile over the turquoise water running past the date palm, with their heads turned to face the viewer. One is seated on the trunk of a small tree, with its tail extended to intertwine with the palm's fronds (fig. 6.8). Another cat occupies a fragment adjacent to the Crucifixion, suggesting that along with deer they were originally inserted at intervals across the cloister program. They might represent pumas, which probably did once roam the hills surrounding the Valley of Mexico; but again, the size and prominence of these painted felines indicate that they have an expanded importance within the Culhuacan narrative itself.

No biblical or European emblematic references to cats (as opposed to lions) that might relate to Culhuacan's Christian themes are apparent. In native ritual texts, however, large felines are seen to characterize the first rituals of the double feast of Tecuilhuitontli/Tecuilhuitl (Brotherston 2005: 62), centered around the temple of

Figure 6.8. Detail of one of the large felines in the lower cloister mural cycle at San Juan Evangelista Culhuacan, D.F.

Tlaloc and the deity Huixtoccihuatl, elder sister of the tlaloque (FC2, 1981: 13). Big cats were also an attribute of Tlaloc: their heads were often depicted on the deity's helmet, as on Codex Laud 45. The Culhuacan cats might also allude to the native thunder-jaguar, Tepeyollotl, "mountain heart," a manifestation of Tezcatlipoca, whose roar reverberated around the mountains to bring on the rain (see Codex Telleriano-Remensis, f. 9v). In the Bible the voice of God is also likened to a thunderous roar that brings rain (Job 37:2–6), a metaphor that perhaps finds an Indo-Christian reworking in a dramatic line in the *Cantares mexicanos:* "This jaguar earth is shaking, and the screaming skies begin to rip. Espíritu Santo, Life Giver [Ipalnemoani], descends" (*CM*, f. 63r; 1985: 352–53). In terms of sacred landscapes, however, a still closer interpretation might be found in Fernando de Alva Ixtlilxóchitl's description of the rock carvings surrounding an artificial pool at Cerro Tetzcotzingo, a major ritual site lying close to Cerro Tlaloc (Townsend 1995: 83): "and also a hind . . . and two jaguars at either side . . . and from there this water flowed" (Alva Ixtlilxóchitl 1985, 2:115).[32]

Covering the north wall of the *sala de profundis* (anterefectory or prayer room) at San Nicolás Tolentino Actopan, the Augustinian *Tebaida* is exceptionally dense (plate 14).[33] It is dominated by a large twisted tree laden with pears, a European emblem for abundance (Grañén Porrúa 1994: 121) but possibly also an allusion to the pear stolen by Saint Augustine when he was a young man, as recounted in the medieval text *The Golden Legend* (see Voragine 1993, 2:123). The surrounding landscape boasts smaller trees, caves, pathways, a river, and a pool and teems with tiny and not so tiny animals.

It also contains well over a hundred figures of saints, friars, and ecclesiastics. The mural was executed mainly in black outline with brown and white infill; details in blue and crimson serve to emphasize certain iconographic elements. The river, pool, sky, a bowl from which a friar washes a haloed figure's feet, the hem of that figure's robe, and the wing of a bird perched on a branch of the twisted tree are all depicted in the intense blue that symbolized water in the native tradition. Another water-blue image occurs immediately above the widest section of the river at the bottom left-hand corner of the mural: accompanied by a friar, a saintly figure appears to be ladling or filtering water that pours from the trunk of a small tree. I can find no European or biblical reference to any such activities involving trees, although New World evangelizers often performed water "miracles," undoubtedly as a tactic to promote the Christian god as controller-in-chief of this precious element.[34] Transposed to native mythology, however, the *Tebaida* image is not so far removed from the sacred bleeding tree of Tamoanchan, where, in metaphorical terms, water and blood—the blue and the red— were synonymous with the essence of life. In any case, at Actopan the precious liquid is now seen to be dispensed by the representatives of Christ.

Crimson is used for the robes of three ecclesiastical figures, including Saint Augustine preaching to a gathering of attentive friars. A large church, the saint's graphic symbol in European art, stands at some distance behind him. Above, a second figure (wearing a miter, wielding a sword, and floating within a large cloud) may represent the Eternal Father, although it too recalls Jacobus de Voragine's story of a vision of the deceased Saint Augustine descending from heaven on a shining cloud (Voragine 1993, 2:129).[35] The sword, tipped with an arrowhead, also points down toward Augustine's church.

Among the animals clearly detectable in the *Tebaida* are two deer; what might be a *tejón* (a Mexican species of badger) or possibly another opossum; and several rabbit-like creatures, depicted with short straight tails in the native manner, rather than with the usual scut of European convention. These may have been present in the print or prints from which Actopan's *Tebaida* was copied or constructed, but the presence of two American jaguars, readily identifiable by their spotted coats, must indicate a native intervention. The largest crouches inside a cave on the baseline beneath the great twisted tree.

As at Culhuacan, a number of the *Tebaida*'s animal population can be seen to play a direct role in a water-oriented reading of an Indo-Christian painted narrative. The rabbits, for example, provide an immediate reference to the pulque cult. One of the pathways originates at the pool (lower right), from which a friar is drinking. At the point where this pathway meets the river, directly beneath the figure of Augustine, a deer also laps: "the hart panteth after the water brooks," written this time very much as a pictographic text. If we can understand the Eternal Father's (or Saint Augustine's) arrow-sword as lightning and the jaguar in his mountain cave as thunder, the union of the two—rain and the regeneration of vegetation—is symbolized by the great cosmic tree of abundance that rises from the cave to pierce the sky above. In fervent prayer and visually saturating the *Tebaida*'s landscape, the friars, as messengers of the Indian Christ, will now bring the rain.

Actopan lies on a small plain to the west of the southernmost hills of the vast Sierra de Pachuca, their most distinctive feature being the series of larger and smaller rock pinnacles that crown its peaks. The two most prominent stand on what is today known as Cerro Los Frailes, immediately above the monastery center, and are visible from miles

Figure 6.9. Cerro Los Frailes and the twin crags as viewed from the site of Actopan's monastery complex.

around (fig. 6.9). These strange formations undoubtedly carried an important supernatural significance for the prehispanic inhabitants of the area. Viewed from different points around the valley, they change shape, move apart, and lean from one side to the other. Alexander von Humboldt observed in his *Vue des Cordillères* (1810) that from a distance they appear larger than when seen from close by (Holl 1996: 58). Perceived as living entities with magical powers, the hills were probably used for ritual purposes: in addition to a natural spring (the waters of which were diverted by aqueduct in 1546 to supply the monastic community), prehispanic ruins exist on the southern slopes of the peak (MacGregor 1955: 11, 55).

On the *Tebaida* two visible sets of the twin pinnacles rise at either side of the lower skyline; a third set to the extreme left is partially obscured by a representation of a church. Their craggy contours are carefully delineated through shading, with smaller rocks and boulders scattered around their base. Although they are not entirely accurate representations of this local landmark (in the sense that they have been probably been copied from a European source), their significance lies in having been selected as an iconographic tool to represent this feature on Actopan's landscape, as seen from three different angles. On-site observation suggests that the gradual change in the angle in which they lean in the *Tebaida* represents their appearance from points to the northwest, north, and northeast of the Actopan valley, as the pinnacles move from an upright position and then start to lean to the right. In other words, in a single image we are asked to look at Actopan's sacred landmark from three directions. Discrepancies in the size of human figures in the *Tebaida* support this interpretation. Compare, for example, the tiny friars in the foreground (right), the larger ones behind, and the subsequent decrease in their size as we move toward what is ostensibly a background. Moving left across that background, two more small friars are depicted outside a cave, but a larger figure is also included to their left at some distance behind them. In a manner that is utterly perplexing to the Western eye, at one level the Actopan valley is represented with a simultaneous foreground and background; at another level it is being viewed externally, from three angles simultaneously.

We cannot simply explain away this element of the mural as native difficulties in grasping the principles of perspective. In addition, if the artists responsible had wished to depict a naturalistic three-dimensional image of their landscape, a single representation of the local landmark in the *Tebaida* would have sufficed. Instead they manipulated the material drawn from their sources, perhaps to offer the viewer a glimpse of the sacred landscape as perceived by the possessors of the cosmic knowledge: those first ancestors who "didn't have to walk around before they could see what was under the sky" or the omniscient Tloque Nahuaque, who, like the Christian god, "is everywhere, sees everything . . . knows everything" (Sahagún 1986: 128–29). The *Tebaida* is a representation of Actopan's sacred landscape, as perceived through the eyes of the sacred.

The almost perfectly preserved cloister stairwell at Actopan yields other surprises in this respect. In the small vestibule at the base of the stairwell a first mural painting depicts the caciques of Actopan and neighboring Itzcuincuitlapilco to the south (fig. 6.10), accompanied by the monastery center's founder, Fray Martín de Asebedo (not pictured). According to Jorge Enciso (1935), the two Indian rulers donated the land on which the complex was founded and probably also money and labor for its construction. Behind these co-founders is a further representation of the twin pinnacles of Cerro Los Frailes, as viewed from due south, probably the direction from which the first Augustinian mission approached Actopan. A second mural, just short of the foot of the staircase proper, portrays Saint John the Good of Mantua ("S. IVAN BVENO") (fig. 6.11) standing at a loggia-style window. In the landscape beyond a leaning hill or mountain rises, which appears to represent another local landmark in the form of a giant boulder that lies between the town and Cerro Los Frailes, known today as La Peña (INEGI, *Carta topográfica* F14D71, 1992; my on-site observation). The walls of the stairwell are given over in their entirety to portraits of the doctors of the church, executed in monochrome with occasional inserts in red (fig. 6.12).[36] Each of the painted "windows" behind these figures includes a representation of La Peña.[37]

At the top of the stairwell, at roof-level, two small, squat lunettes respectively depict Mary Magdalene and Saint Jerome, a contemporary of Saint Augustine. The representation of the cave to which the Magdalene is said to have retreated in penitence for her sins (Hall 1979: 202) is dictated by the physical confines of the lunette, the saint being obliged to lie horizontally within it. Saint Jerome and his lion accommodate themselves in equally awkward poses. Two vertically extended lunettes portray Saint Nicholas of Tolentine, patron saint of Actopan (fig. 6.13),[38] and, according to Santiago Sebastián (1963: 31–32), Saint Monica, mother of Augustine (fig. 6.14).

The appearance of these four figures together corresponds well to recognized canonic relationships of the day. Their orthodoxy within Actopan's mural program is perhaps therefore not questionable, except that they are also depicted as occupying the town's sacred geography (although in a rather different way than the other examples cited in this section).

To the right (from the viewer's perspective) behind Saint Nicholas in the valley below, we can see a representation of Actopan's monastery church, identifiable by

Figure 6.10. Detail from a mural painting at the base of the stairwell at San Nicolás Tolentino Actopan, showing the two native patrons of the monastery complex. The crags to the extreme right are as viewed from the south.

Figure 6.11. Detail from the portrait of Saint John the Good of Mantua at the base of Actopan's stairwell. The "mountain" in the background probably represents a second local landmark known today as La Peña.

Figure 6.12. View of the stairwell at Actopan.

Figure 6.13. Lunette at the top of Actopan's stairwell depicting Saint Nicholas of Tolentine. *Inset:* detail of the Actopan valley behind the saint.

Figure 6.14. Lunette at the top of Actopan's stairwell depicting a hybrid Saint Monica/Mary Magdalene.

its large open chapel; the interior is detailed as ashlar-laid stonework (figs. 6.13 [inset], 6.15). The painted chapel is embedded into a mountain wall in the manner of a great vaulted cave, from which a torrent of water flows, again a rather clear image that Euro-Christian architecture was perceived as a replica of a water-filled mountain. To the right of the church and open chapel (beyond the tree) La Peña also appears. There seems little doubt that Saint Nicholas is here portrayed as standing on the site of the twin pinnacles.

Dressed in her customary wimple, Saint Monica kneels in prayer before an altar on which lie an open book and a crucifix. At her feet, in a niche cut into the side of the altar, stands an ointment pot (fig. 6.14). The setting is again a mountainous landscape, strongly reminiscent of Actopan's own, further to the north within the Sierra de Pachuca proper (my on-site observation). Yet the crucifix and open book were common medieval attributes of Mary Magdalene, depicted before her cave retreat (Apostolos-Cappadona 1998: 244); Monica usually holds the book in her hands (Hall 1979: 212). In addition, the ointment pot is the Magdalene's best-known and most traditional symbol in art.[39] The person portrayed at Actopan therefore seems to be an attempt to convert an image of Monica into Mary Magdalene or a Magdalene/Monica hybrid.

I view the image as a hybrid, for these figures do more than occupy Actopan's painted sacred geography. They were understood to form part of its reality. The sector of the Sierra de Pachuca to the east of the town was known in the colonial period as "los zerros de la Magdalena" (the Magdalene Mountains) (AGN, *Padrones* 3, ff. 27r–28r).[40] As in the case of so many local patron-mountains appropriated by the friars for their water sources or because of continuing Indian interest in them as sacred places, the change from the original prehispanic name probably took place in the early years of the Augustinian presence. That is, by the time the mural program was painted, the new name of the mountain was already established. Towns and villages were also renamed in accordance with their chosen or designated patron saints. In this respect the village of Santa Magdalena lying high up in the Sierra de Pachuca range, to the northeast of Actopan (fig. 6.16), echoes

Figure 6.15. The monastery church and open chapel at Actopan.

the presence of the horizontal image of this saint at the top of the stairwell.

Further south, directly beneath the twin pinnacles at the summit of Cerro Los Frailes, is the hamlet of San Jerónimo, corresponding to the Saint Jerome lunette at the top of the stairwell. The village of Santa Mónica, with its small church perched alone

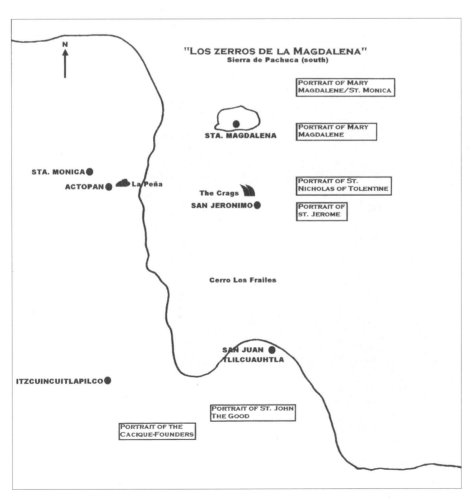

Figure 6.16. Actopan's geography, showing how the choice of murals on the walls of the cloister stairwell was determined by the Christian-imposed toponymy of Actopan's sacred landscape (not to scale).

on the top of a steep hill, lies north of Actopan. Like the portrait of Saint John of Mantua at the foot of the staircase, the town named San Juan Tlilcuauhtla lies precisely at the southern foot of the Magdalena range (INEGI, *Cartas topográficas* F14F71, 1992, and F14D81, 1998). All these communities existed with the same names in the mid-eighteenth century, as recorded on a 1750 map of the parish (AGN 4711), from which we can probably deduce that these were also their names in the sixteenth century.[41] The hybridized portrait of Monica/Magdalene would thus seem to name the village of Santa Mónica or its hilltop church, while at the same time offering the reading "Magdalena Mountains." This argument is visually supported by the figure's burgeoning robe, which extends forward over her feet in stiff ridges: this is Monica/Magdalene the mountain. Finally, Saint Nicholas of Tolentine's pose in his own roof-level lunette (fig. 6.13) is far too animated to have been copied directly from any European original. Where the Magdalene's robes have been reworked to represent the rough topography of the Magdalena range, Actopan's patron saint takes on the form of its most prominent features. Leaning backward and slightly to the right from our perspective, he and the crucifix he carries mirror the twin pinnacles as viewed from Actopan's monastery in the valley below (fig. 6.9).

Thus those responsible for Actopan's murals treated the cloister's architecture as a replica of the town's still-sacred landscape. In addition, they identified the locality's patron saints as forming part of that landscape. Actopan's murals therefore reveal a new dimension to the ways in which the native peoples perceived and interpreted Christian figures. Further examples of this type probably exist at other sites, although the difficulty in matching surviving murals with a toponymy that has undergone so much change across the centuries remains a serious obstacle for the present.

Actopan's stairwell murals raise other important issues, however. The artists responsible were not local but were sent by the Augustinian archbishop Vasco de Quiroga (MacGregor 1955: 6, 35; Kubler 1992: 68; INAH 1978: 11). What they produced there may have been on their own initiative, but it seems more likely that it resulted from consultation with the town's Indian rulers. Pablo Escalante Gonzalbo (1997) cites a similar example of manipulating Euro-Christian architecture to represent a local sacred topography at Franciscan Cuauhtinchan. Probably at the behest of Cuauhtinchan's rulers, the fountain at the center of the cloister was topped with the sculpture of an eagle, while jaguar heads lay over the mouths of its water channels. Both the fountain and the cloister walls were coated with gravel made from crushed red-brown lava stone. The ensemble therefore reads as "Place of the Eagle and the Jaguar, Red[dish] Cave of Xilote Mountain" (*Quauhtli ocellotl ychan, Tlatlauhqui tepexioztoc*), named in the *Historia tolteca-chichimeca* (1989: 193) as the original seat of government of preconquest Cuauhtinchan (Escalante Gonzalbo 1997: 221, 229–30). *Quauhtli ocellotl ychan* was in fact written glyphically in the eagle and jaguar that flank the mural painting of the Annunciation over the door leading into the refectory, thereby complementing the architectural rendering of the mountain that this cloister was also perceived to be.[42]

Restricted again to the cloister and chapter hall (today the church registry), the native-executed landscapes at San Francisco Tepeapulco follow the same conceptual patterns in terms of the perceived relationship of Christianity with an Indian sacred geography and the special way of viewing it. In addition, the native artists at Tepeapulco inserted other iconographic details that identified that geography very much as Tepeapulco's own.

Derived from the Nahuatl *tepe[tl],* "mountain," *pul/pol,* "large," and the locative *-co,* the name Tepe[a]pulco, "large mountain place," reflects the town's proximity to a large mountain (Acuña 1986: 170, 171, n. 5), which today still carries the Nahuatl name "Xihuingo" (fig. 6.17).[43] The Florentine Codex includes the peak in its list of eminences of the land, describing it as the "famed curved mountain" at Tepepulco (FC11, 1963: 260). The "curve" comes in a formation of jagged rocks on Xihuingo's southern flank, which, when viewed from the southeast, leans in a southwesterly direction toward Teotihuacan. From the southwest, the mountain is triangular-shaped and crowned with three main peaks (the highest in the center); the curved element—a small part of the mountain's total volume—appears as a rocky mass on its upper right-hand slope. As at Actopan, Xihuingo's rock face changes shape when viewed from various points on the surrounding landscape; its curve is emphasized in the mural paintings at the sixteenth-century monastery, however.

The mid-sixteenth-century Codex Xolotl (1) includes the toponym of Tepeapulco as a regularly shaped three-peaked mountain (that is, as viewed from Teotihuacan). This image of Xihuingo (together with the directional lean of its curved crag) reflects the now relatively well-documented connection between Cerro Xihuingo and Cerro Gordo, the mountain that dominates the north side of the Teotihuacan Valley. Tichy identified an important sightline between the two (see fig. 4.20). In addition to a small Teotihuacan platform at the southwestern foot of Xihuingo, numerous petroglyphs (including pecked crosses of Teotihuacan origin) on and below the mountain would appear

Figure 6.17. Cerro Xihuingo, Tepeapulco, Hidalgo, as viewed from the monastery complex of San Francisco.

to identify it as an important base for observation, computation, and storage of astronomical data of possible Teotihuacan origin (see Aveni et al. 1978; Aveni 1989; Wallrath and Rangel Ruiz 1991). The word "Xihuingo" derives from *xi[h]uitl,* "year" (Molina 1992: f. 159r, 2nd pagination; Siméon 1997: 770), and with the suffix *-co* means "Place of the Year" or place where the year is calculated or registered (Wallrath and Rangel Ruiz 1991: 298). Although we do not know what language the Teotihuacanos spoke, the mountain's Nahuatl name suggests that the observatory may still have been in use at the time of the conquest and possibly beyond. Indeed, the unique native paintings of star clusters on ff. 282r–v of Códice Matritense del Palacio Real (produced at Tepeapulco between 1559 and 1561) testify to the presence of experienced astronomers among Sahagún's native informants. It is perhaps for all these reasons that the mountain was "famed."

The surviving landscaped murals at Tepeapulco consist of three full panels on the south wall of the chapter hall and a series of portraits of saints and a Crucifixion in the cloister walkways. All were painted in monochrome with details in red. The scenes in the chapter hall depict the Nativity, the Holy Family with a Crucifixion in the background (fig. 6.18), and the Adoration of the Magi (fig. 6.19), separated from each other by vertical black lines. Remaining fragments at the adjoining corners of the east and west walls might indicate that at one time the whole room was covered with similar

Figure 6.18. Detail of the mural of the Holy Family, with the Crucifixion in the background, in the chapter hall at Tepeapulco. One of many representations of Cerro Xihuingo appears to the extreme left.

Figure 6.19. Adoration of the Magi, chapter hall, Tepeapulco. Various representations of Cerro Xihuingo appear in the background.

Figure 6.20. Fragment of a mural painting at the corner of the west wall of the chapter hall, Tepeapulco, showing a rabbit eating the leaves of a *nequametl* maguey cactus.

paintings. Each biblical scene is an interior, separated from the landscape behind by a half-wall from which rise loggia-style openings. The architectural frames are nevertheless cut off abruptly by the dividing lines, to continue in a new form in the adjoining scene. The thematic sequencing of the murals is retained in the landscaped settings behind the loggia openings, however, each of which includes two or more representations of Xihuingo's curved rock formation on the skyline. Whatever the European printed source for these murals, native artists at Tepeapulco ensured that the figures and events they portrayed were located on their own landscape.

Similar in style to the representations of Actopan's twin pinnacles, Xihuingo's curved rock mass is composed of an ensemble of rounded and elongated boulders rising upward to form a point. The crag is sometimes depicted in an upright position; at other times it leans to the left or the right. A stylized representation of a church accompanies most examples (lying to one side or the other or beneath its curve), as if also viewed from a series of different angles. From left to right (and including the representation that crosses the corner of the east and south walls), seven images of the curved rock formation occur across the three panels, with two additional examples in the fragment at the corner of the west wall (fig. 6.20). The viewing positions are (very approximately) from the southwest, northwest, west, east, west-northwest, southeast, south-southeast (south wall); and southeast and west-southwest (west wall). Some might be pinpointed more precisely: from Cerro El Rosal to the northwest or Cerro Gordo to the southwest, for example. In addition, a tree is attached to each mountain-church grouping. The multiple inclusions of the crag effectively convert the three landscapes into a single—but again perplexingly difficult—image of Tepeapulco's sacred geography. As at Actopan, it seems to express the perfect vision of the landscape as seen through the eyes of the possessors of sacred knowledge. From the northwest the right-leaning curvature of rock mass is obscured by the western flank of Xihuingo; yet it is of course still there and can be depicted, for the sight could pass through mountains. When the landscapes are viewed in this manner, it becomes evident that the giant figures of Christian referents were not intended to be foreground subjects but were superimposed over a landscape that also occupies both foreground and background.

The loggia walls in the chapter hall murals make this

mode of viewing difficult, but the fragment preserved on the south corner of the west wall and the series of panels in the cloister walkways support the argument (figs. 6.21, 6.22). In these compositions very large figures are again superimposed over the landscape, which, while evidencing some use of perspective in its background, nevertheless completely encircles them on the same plane. Several representations of the crag, again viewed from a series of angles, are present on each of the skylines but also in the foreground, standing in miniature next to the robes of the saints who tower over them. The panel depicting Saint Lawrence, for example, contains five different views of the crag: three stand on the skyline, the fourth is directly behind the saint, and the fifth is to his lower left; all, however, are exactly the same size. Other tiny details in the form of plants and rabbits (and more crags on the west wall of the chapter hall) lie under or near the feet of these figures, proportionally no larger than those that appear to be some distance behind.

In the cloister program large trees also stand alongside representations of the church, presenting the same configuration of crag-tree-church or church-tree-crag found in the chapter hall, depending on the angle of viewing. The inclusion of groups of trees, mountains, and architectural structures echoes the conceptual interchange of the cosmic trees, sacred mountain, and prehispanic temple. It also evokes the description in Durán (1984, 1:86–87) of the tota pole, made from a tall tree and erected for the Hueytozoztli rain-petitioning ceremonies in front of Tlaloc's temple on a specially constructed landscape of hills and crags. Given Aztec influence at prehispanic Tepeapulco, it is not improbable that a tota was also set up there during the same festival.[44]

While the tree at Tepeapulco was intended as a graphic link between the church and the mountain, however, in the two representations of the Crucifixion at this site it is also directly associated with Christ's cross. One example in the upper cloister stands immediately behind the cross, slightly to the left, and—following the pattern of miniaturization of the landscape over which Chris-

Figure 6.21. Portrait of Saint Lawrence, upper cloister, Tepeapulco. Note the several representations of Cerro Xihuingo's curved form in the background and foreground. *Inset:* one of several miniaturized representations of rabbits included in Tepeapulco's mural program.

tian events are portrayed—is given only half the height of the Virgin Mary and Nicodemus, who stand at either side (fig. 6.22). In the Crucifixion depicted behind the composition of the Holy Family in the chapter hall (fig. 6.18), the miniaturized tree and the cross (partially covered by a Franciscan cord) are barely distinguishable as two separate elements. Significant here is the symmetrical arrangement of the two flanking crosses and two further examples of the curved rock formation (viewed from the west and the east). Together, and with Christ's own tree-cross at their center, they form a

Figure 6.22. The Crucifixion, upper cloister, Tepeapulco. Again, three examples of Cerro Xihuingo's curved form stand on the skyline. *Inset:* another miniaturized rabbit.

laterally viewed quincuncial configuration of mountains and tree-crosses. The whole image again communicates to the viewer that it is within the native cosmic structure of interchangeable images of the tree, mountain, and temple that the Christian presence can be found.

Other details in the Tepeapulco program serve to tie its Christian themes even more closely to the local landscape. Behind the loggia columns of the Nativity on the chapter hall wall, a large red comet with an angel firmly attached to its head moves above a scene of shepherds and their flocks in the direction of a church-tree-crag group (fig. 6.23). Most obviously intended as a representation of the star of Bethlehem, it nevertheless doubles as a toponym, which in turn permits a conceptual reading of the relationship of Christ's coming to the native issue of renewal in a chronological and regenerative sense. *Xi[h]uitl* (the Nahua term for "year" from which Cerro Xihuingo takes its name) also means "comet," "turquoise," "grass," and "leaf" (Molina 1992, 2nd pagination, f. 159v; Siméon 1997: 770). The semantic relationship between these terms is clarified by the use of *xiuh-* (root: *xi[h]uitl*: Siméon 1997: 769–70; Morante López 1997: 114–15) as a prefix to express the bright green of plants in the context of freshness and newness and the turquoise of water (Morante López 1997: 114–15). In this sense the "year" is associated with the renewal of vegetation, together with the renewal of the sun's yearly cycle and water, whose arrival heralds the opening of the agricultural year. The opening of the agricultural cycle is marked by the stars, which is why *xi[h]uitl* also means "comet" (ibid.). As with the Christmastide celebrations at Motolinía's Tlaxcala, the Tepeapulco mural thus appears to associate the birth of Christ with the renewal of the agricultural cycle. At Tepeapulco-Xihuingo, however, his coming may also have been understood as the renewal of a cosmic era.

The inclusion of animals in the Tepeapulco murals is restricted to numerous images of rabbits in tiny detail across the miniature landscapes described above. The rabbits are usually pictured eating plants, many of which resemble stylized representations of the maguey cactus, a characteristic of Tepeapulco's pulque-producing terrain. Another rabbit, eating an entirely different plant, can be seen seated on a boulder at the feet of the Virgin and Child, from which sprouts a nopal or prickly-pear cactus, in flower.

If these species of flora were depicted in the murals as indicative of the countryside around Tepeapulco, we might conclude that the rabbits are representative of local fauna. They are certainly mentioned in the town's *Relación geográfica* as a main food source, but so are deer (Acuña 1986: 179), which do not appear in any of the murals. The artists' choice to include only the rabbit, then, was determined by other factors.

In pre-Christian Europe the rabbit was a symbol of rebirth, later incorporated into Christian iconography at Easter (Burkhart 1986: 125). The rabbit or hare was also commonly used to represent fecundity and lust, often pictured at the feet of virgins

to show their triumph over sexual temptation (Peterson 1993: 108). Imported images of the animal in association with these
themes may well have been the source used
by the native artists responsible for the mural program,[45] who either misunderstood
or ignored their Euro-Christian symbolism. Rabbits seem to have permeated the
whole mural program at Tepeapulco.

As a motif, the rabbit and a long-leafed
plant may also have been drawn from any
number of European graphic sources,
such as, for example, the landscaped background of an Annunciation in *Officium
B. V. Mariae,* published in Venice in 1494.[46]
The title page of the *Decem librorum Moralium Aristotelis, tres Conversiones* (Paris,
1542) again boasts a field of rabbits with
the plant. This particular book is known
to have reached New Spain, for a copy was
held in the library of San Diego, Mexico
City (Báez Macías et al. 1988: 29). If the

Figure 6.23. The star of Bethlehem, in the form of a toponymic comet (*xihuitl:* Xihuingo), soaring above the representation of Christ's Nativity, chapter hall, Tepeapulco.

Tepeapulco artists drew their rabbits from these or similar sources, they nevertheless transformed them back into the native style. The animals' fur is detailed by means of short, sharp brushstrokes, and all have the short, straight tails characteristic of na-tive representation. The Tepeapulcan rabbits are, in fact, almost identical to those that glyph the year-sign Rabbit in the 52-year count that follows the astronomical data in *Códice Matritense del Palacio Real* (ff. 283r–86r). The Tepeapulcan count com-mences with the year 1 Rabbit. As noted in chapter 1, rabbit also equates to moon in native thought, thereby possibly introducing an astronomical reading in the murals of Xihuingo. Various colonial sources record that the Fifth World Age and the first humans were created in a year 1 Rabbit and that as a result this became the day-sign of the earth deity Tlaltecuhtli-Cihuacoatl-Quilaztli. The rabbit appears next to the deity's image on the base of several prehispanic sculptures and on the Bilimek pulque ves-sel (Caso 1967: 193; Burkhart 1986: 113–17). The association persisted to at least the seventeenth century, when Ruiz de Alarcón's informants referred to the earth as "my mother earth stomper, my father one rabbit" (Burkhart 1986: 115), a metaphoric term that in turn acknowledges the dual gender of the deity.[47]

But in prehispanic Mexico the rabbit's reproductive habits were most closely associ-ated with the agricultural fertility deities of the pulque group. 1 Rabbit was the calendri-cal name of Mayahuel, the pulque goddess (Caso 1967: 193); 2 Rabbit (Ometochtli) was the supreme pulque divinity, while the 400 Rabbits, also auxiliaries to the earth-mother deities (López Austin 1994: 195–97), numbered the gods associated with the cult. As the symbolic product of the fermentation of pulque, the rabbit also represents an organ-ic process that makes way for regeneration or the passing from death to life. The rabbit is the "life" that emerges from the gestation of the maguey plant (Johansson 1996: 86).

The concentration of rabbits at Tepeapulco thus might be interpreted in the light of the region's calendrical correlation and its astronomical studies and/or as a center of pulque production, but with important religious undertones. Lying beneath Cerro Xihuingo, these multiple images therefore seem to speak of the cosmic setting of Tepeapulco's sacred geography, whose own renewal is again ensured by the birth and death of Christ.[48]

The ideas expressed in the landscaped mural paintings at Culhuacan, Actopan, Tepeapulco, and elsewhere are very consistent in that they reflect a shared native understanding of the Christian presence on and as part of a still sacred geography. The possibility that these three sites carry the work of a single group of traveling artists is also slim. There are notable stylistic and configurative differences between Augustinian Culhuacan and Actopan, and it is unlikely that the similarities in representation of sacred topography at Actopan and Franciscan Tepeapulco are the work of the same hand or hands. Competition between the orders was strong, and each would have needed a maximum input of experienced craftsmen to work on their own, often very elaborate, building programs. Hence we are talking about three separate groups of native artists who nevertheless coincided in the way in which they chose to incorporate Christian figures and symbols into local landscapes. Their work would appear to offer us a rare glimpse of the early stages of the "Indianization" of the Christian message.

The consistency of the message relayed by the landscaped mural programs is perhaps also reflected in the architectural area in which they appear—that is, the monastic buildings—as if in some way they were intended more for the friars' contemplation than for Indian congregations in general. The cloister was not off limits to the Indians, of course, but it was not a public area like the church or the atrium. Its greatly reduced size would also not be suitable for community gatherings, even after the human devastation wrought by the epidemics. Edgerton (2001: 234–35) has posited that the cloister may have hosted reenactments of religious plays and that the murals therefore served as stage backdrops; the audience would stand outside in the atrium, viewing the proceedings through specially widened cloister accesses. There are a number of problems with this proposal, however, not least the fact that landscaped murals on stairwells, within chapter halls, and in refectories would be instantly redundant. Given the examples from Culhuacan and Actopan, and in stone at Cuauhtinchan, where cloister architecture was used to replicate the sacred geography,[49] I would like to suggest a probably equally controversial interpretation of the murals' presence in cloister buildings. Through their landscape representations, were the Indians applying an architectural distinction that echoes the distinction made between the prehispanic teocalli-cave and teocalli-mountain? In other words, where the church was perceived as the cave of the mountain, did the cloister take on the role of the mountain proper?

Mutated Teteo?

The numbers of saints embraced by the Catholic Church over the calendar year, their conflation and pairing, the many manifestations and attributes of the Virgin Mary, and the varied devotional themes surrounding the life and death of Christ could all offer an open door for native reinterpretation. This is truer still if the basic roles of those figures also permitted perceived patterns of interaction with the sacred forces of old.

This is not a new idea by any means and is acknowledged by most scholars working in the field of native Mexican religious culture, past and present. The internal workings of the process of appropriation, adaptation, and change, however, are virtually impossible to follow through. Locally deified founder-ancestors or protectors who may have acquired associations with certain saints constitute one vast and impenetrable area. Within the pantheon of supernaturals controlling the universe, unstable hierarchies, diverse physical attributes, and multiple overlapping roles are as complex as the natural world from which these entities drew their being. In addition, and in their multiple aspects, the gods were interwoven in the measurement of time and space. They presided over each day and its parts, groups of days, the dry and wet seasons and their divisions, the world directions, and the levels of the universe. In short, this system determined and was determined by the native conceptualization of the world. At one level the cosmos was finite in its perceived order and all-encompassing range of action; at another, infinite in its capacity for change. If the roles, attributes, and manifestations of the saints and other holy figures were clear-cut, fixed, and unquestionable in the eyes of Christians, the continuous remolding of the teteo was an age-old fact in the native world. In the ritual codices, for example, "we see gods being consciously shaped to exist in mutual dependence on each other and on man" (Brotherston 1979: 65). The gods—and, it follows, their images, attributes, and actions—were continually mutating in accordance with prevailing circumstances. They remained the same basic entities, however. As a twentieth-century Tlapanec Indian reasoned with respect to discrepancies between the mythical family of the fire god and modern-day native explanations, it was only the circumstances that had changed: "It is the same god, but a different story" (van der Loo 1987: 199).[50]

The retelling of the "stories" of the prehispanic supernatural that the arrival of Christianity prompted, and continued to prompt across the sixteenth century and beyond, developed from the need to restructure and coordinate a world that was both changing and unchanging, at different levels and at unequal paces. Despite the tactics of the evangelizing body to insert a specific saint or other Christian referent into the seat of a perceived equivalent in the native world, the remolding of all these entities was also being made independently at a community, regional, and national level. This gave rise to a variety of reinterpretations and cross-interpretations of the same figure or symbol, whether they originated from the prehispanic or the Christian camp. The apparent ambiguities and contradictions in meaning produced by this process are readily appreciable in the native-executed art of sixteenth century. But if there are many ways to tell the same story, all would have found an internal logic within the native religious system as a whole.

A simple example of the outcome of the process of religious adoption and adaptation (and here I am piecing together snippets of information to illustrate a point rather than prove it) might be the associations made at Chiauhtempan (Tlaxcala) between Saint Anne, grandmother of Christ, and the native Toci, "Our Grandmother," in her specific aspect as Zapotlantenan (Sahagún 1981, 3:353). Within the cult theme of rain-moisture-agricultural fertility (to use the classification in Nicholson 1971), Zapotlantenan belonged to the Tlaloc complex of deities. As goddess of sweat baths and medicinal turpentine, her festival was celebrated at the opening of the ritual year (that is, between February 2 and 21), when honors and sacrifices were paid to Tlaloc and the sacred water-mountains (FC1, 1970: 17; Anderson and Dibble 1970: 17, n. 52; CMPR, f. 250r). Torquemada (1975–83, 3:357) tells us that the determining factor in choosing Saint Anne as Chiauhtempan's patron was that her festival in the Catholic calendar

(July 26) would coincide with the ancient festival, by which we must assume he meant Ochpaniztli, when the prehispanic festival of Toci proper was celebrated (FC2, 1981: 19).[51] He adds, however, that the reason for choosing Anne was not "idolatrous." As Solange Alberro (2000: 27–28) also observes, it seems clear that—much as occurred at the assumed seat of Tonantzin at Tepeyacac[52]—it was the early friars who directly appropriated Toci's shrine at Chiauhtempan in the name of Christ's grandmother.[53] Who, then, introduced Zapotlantenan into the plan, thereby placing emphasis on Anne's otherwise canonically negligible occupation as a cleanser and a healer? Was Saint Anne–Toci worshiped as grandmother of Christ in July and Saint Anne–Zapotlantenan invoked as a tlaloque and community healer and protector against sickness in February? (It was at this time that early colonial Tlaxcallans decided to keep their Candlemas candles, not only for thunder and lightning but also to ward off sickness [Motolinía 1990: 55].) Or was Saint Anne–Zapotlantenan thanked for her role in bringing rain in July, under the guise of Saint Anne–Toci?[54]

Our attempts to disentangle the entities of the native pantheon and align them with the entities of Christianity must inevitably also come face to face with the issue of interfamilial relationships and gender. In the native world the religious focus on agricultural fertility and the analogy of the cycle of food production with the process of human reproduction meant that earth, water, and maize deities had multiple familial relationships. As individuals they could also be invoked as male or female, depending on their particular roles at any given stage in the agricultural cycle. Thus, for example, Chalchiutlicue, goddess of terrestrial waters but also related to the earth-mother complex, was wife, mother, and sister of the rain deity, Tlaloc, who in turn was lord of foodstuffs in general. Earth goddess Cihuacoatl-Quilaztli was also Tlaltecuhtli, "Earth Lord," who was Tlaloc (*HMPP* 1979: 26; Nicholson 1971: 416).

Within the maize deity group, change in both role and gender reflects the stages of growth of the plant and its hermaphroditic nature. The long (male) tassels or pollen tubes at the plant's head fertilize the (female) maize silk or flowers that sprout from the stem at the points where the leaves grow. It is here, from between the plant's "limbs," so to speak, that the young maize kernels (*xilotl*) are "born" and develop into the fully matured cobs. Nahua myth inscribes the botanical makeup of the plant as it was cultivated, seemingly also acknowledging genetic modifications that resulted from the process of its domestication from the wild.[55] According to *Historia de los mexicanos por sus pinturas* (1979: 27, 33), from the first man and woman was born a son called Piltzintecuhtli, "Revered Prince Lord," a solar deity and alias of Tezcatlipoca (Olivier 2000: 104). Because he had no woman to marry, the gods created one from the hair of the earth goddess Xochiquetzal, "Flower-Plume." The product of this union was Centeotl, "Maize Cob God," also identified with Itztlacoliuhqui, god of Venus (ibid.). In this myth Piltzintecuhtli may well represent a male variety of wild maize from which the domesticated plant was developed. Crossed with a female plant (Xochiquetzal), the resulting fruit and its seed (Centeotl) produced the hermaphroditic plant that could reproduce itself in perpetuity. The name of Xochiquetzal, mother of all flowers through a process of double insemination (see chapter 1), also evokes the featherlike flower or corn silk from which the first, milky xilotl are formed.

Xochiquetzal was Xochipilli, "Flower Prince," however, a dancing god associated with the pulque cult but also with regeneration and the young maize plant (López Austin 1969; Seler 1992). The male aspect of Xochiquetzal may therefore find representation in the maize tassels, which do indeed "dance" up and down as they are caught in the breeze, permitting contact with and fertilization of the plume flowers. In *Histoyre du Méchique* (1979: 110) Xochipilli is identified as the sexual partner of Piltzintecuhtli and is therefore the mother of Centeotl. But as Guilhem Olivier (2000: 105) points out, Xochipilli is described in some native sources as maize-father or as maize itself. Maize-Venus, son of Piltzintlecuhtli-Tezcatlipoca, was also an avatar of Tezcatlipoca. In this sense there is an interesting parallel between Tezcatlipoca and Xochipilli, as both fathers of maize and maize itself.[56]

Xilonen (from *xilotl*) was goddess of the young maize ears, who, as the ears swelled and ripened, became Chicomecoatl, "Seven Serpent," fundamental maize goddess. Chicomecoatl was nevertheless a female aspect of Centeotl (Nicholson 1971: 417). In other explanations of this dual-gendered familial relationship, Centeotl, at once son and grandson of Xochiquetzal, is also her husband (Codex Telleriano Remensis f. 22v).[57]

Although in the Christian ideal the relationship of God, the Virgin Mary, and Christ is understood as fixed, the mysteries of the divine also present not a few problems for Western thought processes. God is the father of all. But as progenitor of Christ he is also the spouse of the Virgin and as God the Son he is her son. The Virgin thus becomes daughter, spouse, and mother of God but also sister and spouse of Christ.[58] Given parallel native beliefs in divine insemination and virgin births, together with the varying familial roles of their supernaturals, such apparent contradictions would probably not have been too difficult to assimilate. At very least, if the Christian Holy Family was allotted the same fundamental functions as the native Maize Family, some logic could certainly be injected. From there, gender change and exchange would be but a step away. As the following sections suggest, as Xochiquetzal, the flowery earth-fertility goddess, Mary fits in well as the spouse of Piltzintecuhtli-Tezcatlipoca or God and mother of Centeotl or Christ, where Centeotl was at once son and husband of Xochiquetzal. Centeotl-Venus was also a manifestation of Tezcatlipoca, as was Christ in his role as God the Son. As the mutated goddess of ripened maize cobs, Chicomecoatl (see Durán 1984, 1:141), Mary would also be Centeotl and therefore also maize itself.

Aided by the friars, the Christian god found identity with Tezcatlipoca in his various manifestations as the omneity Tloque Nahuaque, "Lord of Everywhere"; Ipalnemoani, "He through Whom We Live" or "Life-Giver"; and Titlacahuan, "We Are His Servants." In his 1553 exhortations against idolatry, written in Nahuatl for an Indian audience, even the no-nonsense Franciscan Andrés de Olmos (1990: 13) refers to God as Ipalnemoani and Tloque Nahuaque. Sahagún's 1564 *Coloquios* (again in Nahuatl) records the first meeting of the Franciscan mission with the priests and nobles of Tenochtitlan and consistently names the Christian god as the true Ipalnemoani–Life-Giver (Sahagún 1986). Like Tloque Nahuaque, "knower of men, seer into men's hearts and men's thoughts" (FC6, 1969: 17), the true god "is everywhere . . . sees everything . . . knows everything" (Sahagún 1986: 128–29). The Aztec priests responded by observing that the friars themselves had been touched by Tloque Nahuaque (Sahagún 1986: 146–47) in the sense that as humans they represented the native deity (León-Portilla 1986a: 147, n. 4). As Life-Giver, Tezcatlipoca was also the ultimate creator and sustainer of humanity. So too was the Christian god, who "gives you everything which there is on earth, what you drink, what you eat" (Sahagún 1986: 126–27).[59] Invisible and impalpable like the night and the wind (e.g., Sahagún 1981, 2: 55, 59; FC6, 1969: 1,

7), this aspect of Tezcatlipoca had no form: "they could only depict him as air" (*HMPP* 1979: 24),[60] while "that image of the crucified man that they saw was the image of our God, not God himself, who cannot be depicted because he is pure spirit" (Mendieta 1973, 1: 133).[61]

The assertions of the friars in this respect are shown to have taken root in the process of "editing" the *Cantares mexicanos* song-poems. Unlike references to other native deities, invocations to the native Ipalnemoani and Tloque Nahuaque were retained alongside inserts to Icelteotl, "Only Spirit," and Dios (God) of the Christian world (Reyes García 1993). The same parallel invocations occur again in the postconquest Christian songs, where the native appellations become the inserts. That is, these two entities ultimately came to be perceived as one and the same. Christian Duverger (1996: 152) asks whether the identification of the Christian god with Tloque Nahuaque was a Franciscan initiative or a native appropriation. In arguing that the omniscient native numen was, in fact, the true god "whom you had not known" (Sahagún 1986: 106–107),[62] it seems that—again—it was the Franciscans who were attempting to appropriate the native deity by identifying him as Christian. On native initiative, however, Tloque Nahuaque was reshaped to accommodate the Christian presence, as the songs in praise of both simultaneously would seem to indicate.

Although neither the Christian god nor Tloque Nahuaque had visible form, we can perhaps see the "spirit" of both in the obsidian disks once placed at the axes of many sixteenth-century atrial crosses. Although in most cases the original inserts are lost today, the cavities in which they once lay show that they boasted a variety of forms. Plain circular disks set within carvings representing the crown of thorns (fig. 6.24) are one type. Others, although also encircled by the intertwining pattern of the crown of thorns, offer more intricately worked settings resembling stars or rayed sunbursts (figs. 6.25, 6.26). A thematic association between the crown of thorns and obsidian might be found in the razorlike sharpness of the blades and splinters produced from this black volcanic glass. But the obsidian mirror, which these inserts so

Figure 6.24. The atrial cross with an obsidian insert at Taximaroa, Michoacán.   Photo: Nicholas J. Saunders

strongly resemble, was the attribute *par excellence* of the deity Tezcatlipoca, the eponymous "Smoking Mirror" (Saunders 2001: 222–23; Olivier 2006: 174). Worn around his neck, the mirror was his scryer, through which he observed the smoky images of the world and the actions of humans. As such it became a symbol of power across Mesomerica, for it was Tezcatlipoca who chose new rulers to govern in his name (Olivier 2006: 174, after FC6, 1969: 17, 24). In other words, supreme rulers were endowed with the power to view the world through Tezcatlipoca's mirror.

In the Florentine Codex the ixiptla of Tezcatlipoca-Titlacahuan, sacrificed in the May festival of Toxcatl, carries his scryer in the form of a rayed device with a central

Figure 6.25. The atrial cross at Natividad de Nuestra Señora Tepoztlan, Morelos. The cross probably once carried an obsidian insert in its central cavity.

Figure 6.26. Side "A" of the atrial cross at San Martín Alfajayuca, Hidalgo.

circle, not unlike the obsidian inserts with their carved surroundings found on the crosses (fig. 6.27). He also carries a tobacco tube, an offering made to the cross at Calimaya on Palm Sunday around 1610 (see chapter 2). For the Christian feast of Pentecost, which celebrates the descent of the Holy Spirit, the native scribe of Codex Mexicanus p. 1 employed the glyphic symbol of Tezcatlipoca's scryer to mark the day (Galarza 1979: 41, 45). Celebrated seven weeks after Easter, Pentecost falls in late May or early June, at the same time as the old festival of Toxcatl. In addition, the staff supporting the Codex Mexicanus scryer was glossed as "arbol" (tree) and, thrust upward, was made to cut through the horizontal divide between the native calendar below and the Christian calendar above, like "the tree whose sap ever rises . . . the living original of Christ's Cross" (Brotherston 2005: 80–81). Native understanding of the cross as a tree and its relationship to Christ is discussed in more detail below. But there is perhaps already an underlying sense here that the carved stone crosses' own smoking mirrors refer not only to God-Tezcatlipoca but also to his chosen one, Christ the King, designated to "rule" in his father's name.

Figure 6.27. The ixiptla of Tezcatlipoca at the festival of Toxcatl, carrying the rayed scryer of the deity (Florentine Codex, Book 2).

Native deities inhabited the flowery worlds of the Indian sacred and were invoked to emerge from them during framing rituals. This concept was also repeated in Indo-Christian artistic expression. At San Bernardino Xochimilco an early piece of relief carving (now embedded as a plaque into the wall of the upper cloister walkway) depicts four Franciscans rising from the clearly delineated petals of the native cempoalxochitl, the sweet-scented marigold that is specifically mentioned as the flower of Tlalocan (FC3, 1978: 47). At the center a great serpent entwined around a tree nevertheless

Figure 6.28. Portrait of Saint Clare, lower cloister, San Luis Obispo Tlalmanalco, México. *Inset:* detail of the psychotropic sinicuiche included in Saint Clare's floral ecstasy.

identifies this Tlalocan as the Christian Eden or, as the sixteenth-century Nahua poets reasoned, the Christian paradise of human origins that was the native *xochitlalpan,* "flower land" (*CM,* f. 41r; 1985: 248–49).

The mural program in the lower cloister at San Luis Obispo Tlalmanalco portrays Fray Martín de Valencia, one of New Spain's earliest evangelizers, and Saint Clare both rising from circles of petals. These motifs in turn give source to an elaborate, swirling arabesque of blossoming vines (fig. 6.28). Images of sacred beings emerging from

Figure 6.29. Xochipilli, "Flower Prince," unearthed in Tlalmanalco. Photos: © Michel Zabé/AZA

flowers may have been inspired by the European *Flos sanctorum* (Kubler 1992: 458), but there are also strong prehispanic precedents, as suggested in a line from one of the reworked prehispanic "orphan" songs (Brotherston 1992: 158–60), or songs that look nostalgically to the past, of the *Cantares mexicanos* collection: "God has formed you, has given you birth as a flower" (*CM*, f. 27r; 1985: 220–21). In his *Psalmodia* Sahagún (1993: 237–39) describes the virtues of Saint Clare as assistant-custodian of Saint Francis in God's flower-garden. In Tlalmanalco's rendering, however, the little virgin of Christ finds herself in the company of a native flower that Sahagún would not have been over-happy to include in that garden: the psychotropic sinicuiche (*Heimia salicifolia*) (figs. 1.7e, 6.28 inset).[63] In fact, there are striking configurative and ideological parallels between both the Tlalmanalco portraits and the statue of Xochipilli as the ecstatic "flower-prince" unearthed close to the same site (fig. 6.29). Xochipilli sits on a ritual bench sculpted in the form of a flower, whose petals, corolla, and other botanical parts spread around all four sides of the seat (Solís 2002: 425); he too rises from a flower. In addition, the flower deity carries on his body a series of images of psychotropic flowers, including the sinicuiche (Schultes and Hoffmann 1982: 62; Wasson 1982, 1983: 100–101). Like Xochipilli, Saint Clare and the saintly Martín de Valencia, now in service in the flower land of the Indo-Christian sacred, are engulfed in an ecstasy of flowers.

In sculpture, and especially on the facades of the earliest constructions, angels frequently acquire distinctively native features. The small church of Santo Tomás Tetliztaca (Hidalgo) boasts a magnificent tequitqui portal and alfiz of flowers and foliage, amid which feathery-winged angels carry emblems of the Franciscan order and the church. Round-faced, with high cheek bones and wide nostrils, and wearing the characteristic bob-haircut with which native artists represented their own people in colonial manuscripts, these angels are very clearly Indian (fig. 6.30). The angels on the monastery gate at San Miguel Coatlinchan (México) also have the same facial features and hairstyles. The interior of the portal arch of the monastery church at Nuestra Señora de Loreto Molango, in the Hidalgo High Sierra, is carved with similarly Indianized angels, again treading rich foliage (fig. 6.31). The depth of carving at the center of their eyes suggests that they may once have carried obsidian inserts. Other examples include the stern-faced warrior-angel (complete with the short, heavily shafted native spear or arrow common to the Mixtec codices) that seemingly uplifts one of the statues of saints in the church portal niches at Teposcolula (Oaxaca). The tequitqui carved chancel arch at Apasco (México) is a veritable jungle of flowers and feather-garlanded native heads, while its magnificent tequitqui portal (fig. 6.32)

Figure 6.30. Detail of the tequitqui carved portal at Santo Tomás Tetliztaca, Hidalgo, showing one of the Indian "angels."

Figure 6.31. Indian "angels" treading rich vegetation on the church portal at Nuestra Señora de Loreto Molango, Hidalgo. Note also the S-shaped xonecuilli design on the illuminated section of the jamb.

Figure 6.32. Indian "angels" presiding over rich vegetation at either side of the church portal at San Francisco Apasco, México.

boasts more of these angels formed from and presiding over heavy foliage.

Indian angels might be seen to allude to the native dead who have gone to the Christian paradise, especially where so many of them (smiling or with animated expressions on their faces) move through rich swaths of vegetation. But in the Christian tradition the souls of the faithful join the angels in heaven rather than transforming themselves into angels. In an Indo-Christian interpretation, then, they appear to have become the winged creatures of Tonatiuh Ilhuicac (the realm of the Sun) or a similar native paradise. The *Cantares mexicanos* song-poems attest to an ongoing native understanding that at death both high-ranking native figures and Spanish ecclesiastics became birds and butterflies. In a "Bird Song" archbishops and friars, together with native nobility, are all transformed into beautiful birds that depart for a watery lake-paradise called the "Flower Shore," where they will "sip jade-water flowers" (*CM*, ff. 80r–82v; 1985: 413–19). There they might possibly join legendary figures of the native past, trans-

formed into golden orioles, troupials, or quetzals (ibid., ff. 64r, 69v; pp. 356–57, 376–77). The Nahua poets also confirm that the birds in the home of God (the Indo-Christian god?) were the same as angels (ibid., f. 38r; pp. 256–57).

A flowery-watery paradise of native design was thus seen as a more appropriate destination than heaven for New Spain's winged deceased, for in an Indo-Christian context tasks still needed to be carried out in the afterlife. In the prehispanic world winged creatures were manifestations of supernatural entities such as the tlaloque, the messengers of Tlaloc, or their pulque deity cousins, both often depicted with a radiating feather or paper device on their backs (Broda 1971: 263; Nicholson 1991: 174–75) (fig. 6.33).[64] Diego Muñoz Camargo (1986: 152) observed that in colonial Tlaxcala the winged water-bringers of old became known as "angels." Ponce de León (1979: 123), secular priest at Zumpahuacan, also noted the associations between angels and tlaloque made by his parishioners. The belief persists in many traditional communities today.[65] Thus the spiritual and political leaders of New Spain's Indians became the winged messengers or intermediaries of the Indo-Christian god and were portrayed in this role on the facades of his terrestrial Water Palace.

Figure 6.33. The pulque god Tepoztecatl wearing the rayed-wing device on his back, a common diagnostic of the cult's deities (Codex Magliabechiano 49).

Clearer reworking of angels specifically as tlaloque or pulque deities is in evidence in colonial native art. The incidence of representations of angels with only one wing—a close parallel with the single radiating device on the backs of the prehispanic deities— is high. On the bell tower of Santa María Magdalena Amatlan (Morelos), erstwhile home of the pulque deity Amatecatl (see Acuña 1985a: 184), leaping angels have single wings that, curiously, also resemble the oyoalli pectorals of the pulque dancing gods (fig. 6.34). In addition, some of these creatures are depicted with crownlike motifs above their heads that recall the form of the stylized maguey plants sculpted over the church portal. A common European iconographic detail that finds intriguing prehispanic corollaries also occurs on the portal arch of the ncighboring monastery church of Natividad de Nuestra Señora Tepoztlan, seat of Tepoztecatl, a major deity of the pulque cult. Here putti are seen to suck and blow through tubes attached to stylized maguey plants (fig. 6.35), of which the church carries considerable numbers elsewhere in its decorative program.[66] The image not only evokes the piercing of the maguey heart with the *piaztecomatl* (suction tube used to extract the sap) but also brings to mind the ritual of the fivefold octli that reenacted the practice. Here priests of the cult were offered a vat of pulque, together with reed tubes through which to drink. Only one tube was hollow, however, and the winner took all (CMPR, f. 258v; 1997: 82–83).

Figure 6.34. Leaping angels on the bell tower at Santa María Magdalena Amatlan, Morelos, whose single wings emulate the form of the oyoalli pectoral worn by the dancing gods of the pulque cult.

Another frequent characteristic of sculpted native cherubs and angels is their heavily ringed eyes, reminiscent of Tlaloc's goggle eyes (figs. 6.36, 6.37, 6.38). The example in the cloister at Tlahuelilpa boasts a fine set of bared fangs, another diagnostic of the tlaloque. This particular "cherub" also has obsidian eyes. In a frieze beneath the representations of Petrarch's Triumphs in the House of the Dean of Puebla Cathedral, surprisingly unperturbed putti—this time of European stock—attempt to disentangle themselves from the grip of the ocelocoatl (jaguar-serpent) (fig. 6.39a). A ritual hybrid that occurs in similar form at the nearby archaeological site of Cacaxtla (fig. 6.39b), the ocelocoatl symbolized the thunder and lightning of Tlaloc. Its introduction into the world of the winged cherubs of Christian mythology also must be seen as significant in this respect.

These particular putti were also given wings painted in vivid turquoise blue, the chromatic symbol of precious water. This also occurs on other examples, such as in cloister lunettes at Actopan and Huejotzingo, where—dramatically emphasized on otherwise monochrome panels—they are associated directly with Christ's Passion. Such chromatic detail is notable not only for the

Figure 6.35. Detail of pulque-imbibing (?) cherubs on the portal arch of the monastery church at Natividad de Nuestra Señora Tepoztlan, Morelos.

frequency with which it occurs from site to site but also because the artists' European sources would have been in monochrome. The decision to paint angels' wings turquoise blue was therefore a native initiative that again says much about their perception of Christian angels and the theme of water.

In European art it was perhaps the Virgin Mary who (in her multiple manifestations) could carry the strongest associations with prehispanic entities, especially those juxtaposed within the great earth-mother complex under the theme of earth, fertility, and maize. It is not too difficult to understand the immediate attraction of Mary, chosen by God as the vessel of Christ's Incarnation, as an icon of fertility. Indeed, as Burkhart (1992: 101) points out, the frequent appeals to Mary in flowery terminology

Figure 6.36. The goggle-eyed, fanged face of the rain deity, Tlaloc (Codex Nuttall 2). (See plate 5a.)

Figure 6.37. Indian "angel" with heavily accentuated ringed eyes on the facade of the church at Santo Tomás Tetliztaca, Hidalgo.

Figure 6.38. Cherub of European origin depicted with heavily ringed eyes and bared teeth, cloister capital, San Francisco Tlahuelilpa, Hidalgo.

in Nahua-authored devotional texts also are more closely associated with fertility than with maidenly innocence.

Like the Virgin Mary, the great Earth Mother was a deity of multiple callings, who divided and subdivided in accordance with her different powers and attributes. Tonan, as a generic title, was "Our Mother." In her aspect as Cihuacoatl-Quilaztli, "Snake Woman–Greenery Arrives," she represented the earth in its transition from barrenness to regeneration. As Chalchiutlicue, "Jade Skirts," she was the consort of Tlaloc and goddess of terrestrial waters. Xilonen was goddess of young maize; Chicomecoatl was goddess of ripened maize and sister of Tlaloc. As Atlantonan, "Mother of the Water Place," she cured the cold of death; as Tlazolteotl, "Filth-Deity," she ate the carnal sins of humans; as Mayahuel she was the lunar goddess of the pulque cult, the virgin goddess from whose bones the maguey plant grew (Nicholson 1971; Nicholson et al. 1997; López-Austin 1994: 193–94, 208; *HM* 1979: 107).

In the chapter hall at Tepeapulco a bowl of pears, apples, and grapes alongside cherries and a half-walnut on a plinth before the Virgin and Child (fig. 6.40) directly follows the system of Euro-Christian visual symbolism with which Mary and these fruits are associated (see Hall 1979: 330).[67] But what did the Tepeapulco artist intend to say to his audience when he placed them in a native tripod vessel, with feet modeled as the taloned claws of an eagle? A shield bearing the eagle claw device is depicted on Códice Matritense de la Real Academia de Historia f. 75v (also prepared at Tepeapulco) and associated with earth-fertility goddesses (Nicholson et al. 1997: 262, n. 11). One of the insignia of the earth goddess in her aspect as Cuauhcihuatl, "Eagle Woman," or Yaocihuatl, "Warrior Woman," was an eagle claw (Seler 1963). Women in childbirth were likened to warriors in battle. Here the image of the Virgin and Child would also appear to refer more directly to Mary's biological status as a fertile woman who has successfully given birth.

On ff. 12r–13r of the native-authored *Santoral en mexicano,* Mary is described as the vessel of the spring or fount of life; her childbirth will cause honey-sweet precious rain to fall; her womb is likened to a coffer that holds jade, the quetzal plume, the turquoise. Mary is a vessel of jade-green water from which will flow the heavenly jade-green water of life; this will cause the germination of that which was frozen with the ice of sin (after Burkhart 1992: 101). These metaphorical instances emphasize one of the perceived roles of Mary's child in Indo-Christian thought, as life-bringer in the form of precious water. But the parallels between Mary and the prehispanic earth-mother deities offered in these same lines

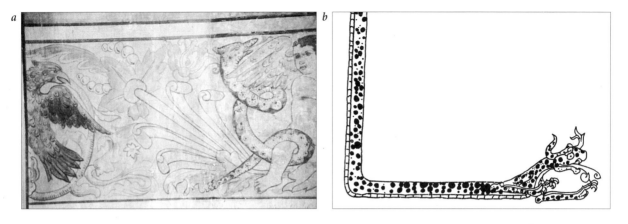

Figure 6.39. Ocelocoatl: *a,* ocelocoatl with *putto* in a painted frieze, House of the Dean, Puebla; *b,* in the mural paintings of prehispanic Cacaxtla, Tlaxcala (after CONACULTA 1990).

are startling. It was from Chalchiutlicue's womb that the life-giving jade-green water flowed; from Mayahuel's womb came the honey-sweet sap that summoned the pulque imbibers, the tlaloque; Ayopechtli, an avatar of Mayahuel, "gave birth [to] . . . begot the [jade] necklace, the quetzal feather" (CMPR, f. 278r; 1997: 143). Atlantonan cured the cold of death; Tlazolteotl ate the sins of humans. In addition, with her traditional blue cloak over a red robe (Hall 1979: 324), Mary echoes that sacred combination of colors in the prehispanic world. Blue and red are the colors of the source of life—of the place where life finds its origin. They are the colors of the life-bringing rain deities and of the maguey plant, the personification of Mayahuel, as depicted on Borgia 12 and 68, Laud 9, Nuttall 20, and elsewhere.

In European art Mary is often pictured standing on a crescent moon, an ancient symbol of chastity (Hall 1979: 325). Beneath her feet the "serpent of old" may also writhe as she symbolically vanquishes sin (ibid., pp. 285, 326). As a symbol of the Fall of Man, a serpent with an apple in its jaws is common in scenes of the Crucifixion (ibid., p. 85). In the prehispanic world the crescent moon was a major symbol of the pulque cult, worn as a nose plug by its deities and painted as a stylized U-shape on shields and vessels associated with the cult (see, for example, figs. 5.20, 6.33, 6.41). All earth-mother goddesses also display close lunar connections (Nicholson 1971: 420). A powerful fertility symbol, the serpent was an attribute of the earth-mother group, including Mayahuel. On Magliabechiano f. 58r she carries its image in her hand and on the hem of her skirt (fig. 6.41); it lies beneath her on Laud 9 (fig. 1.6) and beneath the pulque pot on Vaticanus B 56 (fig. 6.42).

The pulque cult was particularly associated with divine motherhood, for it was said that

Figure 6.40. Tripod eagle-talon bowl and Christian symbolic fruits in the mural of the Holy Family, chapter hall, San Francisco Tepeapulco, Hidalgo.

Figure 6.41. Pulque goddess Mayahuel, with serpent attributes, circular pectoral, and maguey cactus (Codex Magliabechiano 58).

Figure 6.42. Mayahuel, with flowering maguey quiote (Codex Vaticanus B 56). Her pierced heart lies beneath the pulque vat with a suction tube to the side of the eclipsing sun.

Figure 6.43. Mayahuel suckling a child (Codex Féjérváry 28).

Mayahuel had four hundred breasts (Codex Telleriano-Remensis, f. 14r). In the codices we often see her—together with other deities of the earth-mother group[68]—suckling a child (fig. 6.43), an image not far removed from the *Virgo lactans* of European origin.[69] Although nudity in sacred figures was banned by the 1545–63 Council of Trent (Hall 1979: 328–29), images of the *Virgo lactans* undoubtedly still circulated in New Spain.[70] As far as I am aware, there are no images of Mary's breasts in the surviving mural painting and architectural sculpture of the period in Mexico, though they might have been removed as a result of the prohibition. Two badly damaged examples of a seated Virgin painted in the cloisters at Acolman and Tepeapulco come to mind here. The decorative frames of these murals are well preserved, as are the paintings that lie at either side of them. In both cases the damage is concentrated in the upper area of the Virgin's body.

In the context of Mary's possible conflation with Mayahuel, the small stone figure with her back to the tomb of Christ beneath the atrial cross at Acolman (fig. 6.44) is an interesting example, especially in terms of the ambiguities inherent in its iconography. The neck, upper chest, and oversized hands of the Virgin, who is wrapped in a mantle, are the only bodily features visible. A circular disk on her breast possibly alludes to the symbol of the pierced heart of the Virgin of Sorrows. Her face (of indigenous physiognomy?) is certainly one of anguish. Beneath the figure are carved a skull (the skull of Adam and/or place sign of Golgotha); a diamond-shaped element (the folded linen cloth brought to wrap Christ?);[71] a gourd-shaped container sealed with a stopper (the jar of spices for the embalming?) (see Hall 1979: 246; John 19:38–40); and a serpent, whose head displays a bifurcated tongue flicking in the direction of the container. The iconographic assemblage is compatible with representations of the Virgin of the Seven Sorrows, although the serpent, if an allusion to the Fall, not only lacks the apple but is evidently focused on the container. The anomaly is perhaps not accidental, for strong parallels linking this scene, Mayahuel as she appears in the prehispanic codices, and other iconographical details at colonial Acolman suggest that a second, this time Indo-Christian, reading of its iconography can also be made.

In Mesoamerica the skull was a common symbol of rebirth and regeneration and therefore associated with agricultural fertility. Mayahuel, as the personification of the maguey whose heart is pierced to draw out the precious sap, is often represented in the codices wearing a circular pectoral on her chest, in the same position as the Virgin's pierced-heart disk (figs. 6.41, 6.45). The form given to the gourd's stopper is identical to native representations of the cut ends of the maguey leaves that protrude from the *zacatapayolli* hayballs after self-sacrifice was performed with their spined tips (fig. 6.46). The container at Acolman might thus be read as a pulque vessel, as depicted on Borgia 68 (fig. 6.45) and Vaticanus B 56 (fig. 6.42).

Vaticanus B 56 also depicts Mayahuel seated beneath a flowering maguey plant, with the stems of the five flowers sprouting from the quiote (the great shoot that rises from the center of the maguey cactus if its sap is not tapped) (fig. 6.47), arranged in a quasi-quincuncial configuration. Noticeably, the five flowers decorating the "INRI" inscription at the top of the Acolman cross (fig. 6.48) are not only configured in exactly the same way but offer the same pattern in terms of the number of floral types (two) and the 3:2 ratio of their appearance. In addition we note how the bifurcated tongue of Mayahuel's serpent on this and other panels from the codices echoes that of Acolman's relief-carved serpent.

On Vaticanus B 56 and Borgia 68 (figs. 6.42, 6.45) the heart of Mayahuel pierced with a suction tube is depicted. This is a rendering of the xuchimitl, the arrowed flower-heart. On Acolman's cross the two lateral arrows that pierce the heart insignia of the Augustinian order diagonally are also tipped with flowers, thereby giving a direct reading of "flower-arrow." In addition, a further xuchimitl can be found in the frame of the destroyed image of the Virgin Mary in the cloister at this site (fig. 6.49).[72] To complete these iconographic parallels, the folded linen cloth might be re-read as the ritual mat on which the pulque imbiber sits (fig. 6.42),

Figure 6.44. The sculpted Virgin of the Seven Sorrows beneath the atrial cross at San Agustín Acolman, México.

Figure 6.45. Mayahuel, with a circular pectoral and pierced heart to the side of the eclipsing sun (Codex Borgia 68).

Figure 6.46. Maguey spines and hayball (Codex Magliabechiano 79).

Figure 6.48. Detail of the head of Christ from the atrial cross at San Agustín Acolman, México. Note the two species of entwined flowers on the "INRI" inscription and the flower-tipped arrows (xuchimitl) piercing the Augustinian insignia.

Figure 6.47. Maguey cactus and shooting quiote.

although it is also similar to the "lozenge-shaped" element carried on the shields of some of the pulque deities.[73]

The viewer of the Acolman Virgin is immediately struck by her proportionally out-sized hands, crossed beneath the pectoral disk, as if the sculptor deliberately wished to draw attention to both hands and disk. Where large hands were a diagnostic of earth deities in general, one reading of Mayahuel's name—certainly a corruption of a Nahuatl original—is "round thing in the shape of a hand" (Andrews and Hassig 1984: 23), pre-

Figure 6.49. The xuchimitl (pierced flower-heart of Mayahuel) appearing in the decorative frame of a now partly destroyed portrait of the Virgin Mary at Acolman.

sumably from *ma[itl]*, "hand," + *ololoa*, "to make round" (Siméon 1997: 355). As a small postscript, then, can we read the Virgin's hands and the disk as Ma-ololoa—that is, Mayahuel? In other words, if this is an image of the Virgin of Sorrows, her heart pierced with grief at Christ's sacrifice, it is also an image of the virgin goddess, whose own heart was pierced so that humankind might survive with the gift of her honey-sap.[74]

The sacrifice of Christ was closely associated with the maguey cactus at the monastery church of San Andrés Calpan, a village lying to the northwest of Cholula (an important prehispanic center of the pulque cult).[75] It is therefore perhaps understandable that the sculptor responsible for the decoration of the church facade re-verted to imagery deriving from the maguey cactus to explain the meaning of Christ to a local audience. The plant figures heavily on the facade of the church. The choir loft window is framed with small, stylized representations, each of which carries a miniature tubelike appendage that may represent the suction tube used to extract the sap (compare fig. 6.50 with 6.42). At the level of the arch springing the columns of the portal bear two larger examples of stylized magueys at either side and, by way of capitals, immediately beneath the cornice (fig. 6.51). Most dramatically, however, the columns flanking the choir loft window are sculpted as two large, naturalistic quiote stems (fig. 6.52).

Juxtaposed with this imagery are numerous examples of the Franciscan insignia bearing the five wounds of Christ. The largest occur on the pedestals of the portal columns and above the cornice from which the quiote columns rise. The fifth example is placed centrally over the portal, carried in the manner of an escutcheon by two angels. In configuration the five insignia (and their individual motifs) form a quin-

Figure 6.50. Detail of one of the stylized maguey plants framing the choir loft window at San Andrés Calpan, Puebla, with a possible suction tube.

cunx or basic cosmic diagram, but so also do the four maguey plants on the columns when juxtaposed with the central focal design. The ostensibly European escutcheon in fact takes the shape of the *yacametztli* nose plug or stylized crescent moon insignia of the pulque cult. It is also open at the top, covered by a drape pulled down at the corners of its outwardly curving rim by the flanking angels. This unusual encasement

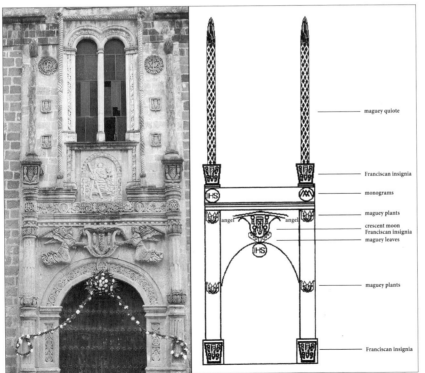

Figure 6.51. The portal of the monastery church at Calpan, which narrates the message of Christianity with symbols drawn from the native pulque cult.

Figure 6.52. Detail of one of the maguey quiote columns at Calpan, which rise from the Franciscan insignia of the Five Wounds of Christ.

of the Franciscan insignia bears a much closer resemblance to a deep vessel or container than to a European heraldic device. A further detail comes in the two stylized but clearly serrated maguey *pencas* (leaves) beneath its base (compare with Mayahuel's name glyph in fig. 6.41), which have replaced the usual European laurel branches or other sprigs of vegetation. The object is meant to be a pulque vessel. The form taken by the drape possibly represents the foaming drink at its rim (see fig. 6.42), while the angels are the mutated winged agents of the deities of water and fertility. In context they may also symbolize the "wings" so often found on prehispanic pulque vessels. The whole image rests on the IHS monogram of Christ, carved on the arch keystone. In this reading Christ's blood, as a symbol of his sacrifice, is represented as the *teoctli* (sacred "wine") of the native fertility cult.

The Calpan artist further elaborated this theme in his inclusion of the maguey quiote columns on the upper register of the church facade. The pedestals take the form of the Franciscan insignia of the five wounds, from which the quiote columns rise, nurtured by the blood of Christ as they are nurtured by the honey-sweet sap contained in the womb of Mayahuel. As the *Santoral en mexicano* states, it is this sap that will fall as precious rain when Christ is born. Mary's presence within the Calpan scheme is seen in the inclusion of her monogram beneath the south-side pedestal, juxtaposed with that of Christ on the north side.

Indo-Christian associations between Christ and pulque as symbols of fertility and regeneration of life can perhaps be more closely determined from native mythology concerning drunkenness among the gods themselves. The practice seems to have been directed toward rejuvenation or rebirth in that the gods "die" and are then "resurrected": that is, fall into a deep sleep from which they will later "resuscitate" (Olivier 2000: 114–17). In the myth of the voluntary sacrifice of the major pulque deity Ometochtli at the hands of, interestingly enough, Tezcatlipoca, the deity "dies" to make himself eternal but also so that humans can safely partake of the drink in excess (Acuña 1986: 62; also cited by Olivier 2000: 114). In other words, like the deity, humans can be eternally resurrected.

It is doubtful that this particular myth, recounted by sixteenth-century Indians at Meztitlan, "Place of the Moon," carries any influence from Christianity. Its author not only drew it from a painted source,[76] probably a ritual teoamoxtli, but also stated that such beliefs were all lies (Acuña 1986: 62). Prehispanic notions of the "resurrection" of the generic pulque deity—and his worshipers—to bring fresh "life" to the temporal world may thus explain why Christ's sacrifice and resurrection were interpreted along much the same thematic lines at Acolman and Calpan.[77] My interest in the role of Tezcatlipoca (named "principal" deity of Meztitlan) as designator of the death of Ometochtli arises from the related presence of a third major numen in Meztitlan's pantheon, in the form of the (also generic) earth-mother, Tonantzin (ibid.).[78] In other words, the basis for mutating these three supernaturals associated with the pulque cult into the "big three" of Christian mythology was already in place at Meztitlan and probably also at a number of other pulque centers. At Meztitlan (again, let us not assume the case to be unique) it was still present in a pictorial form that could be reworked into an Indo-Christian iconic text in paint or in stone.

Associations between maize, the "precious prince" (FC6, 1969: 39), and Jesus Christ are also found in native art of the period. The most dramatic image comes in the *Ecce Homo* of the Passion cycle of murals at Epazoyucan, where Christ holds a maize stalk in his arms in place of the reed scepter of the King of the Jews (fig. 6.53). The plant is readily identifiable by its alternating leaves (fig. 6.54). Maize stalks also replace the reed scepter on a number of atrial crosses (figs. 6.55, 6.56). But if the maize plant became the staff of office of the Indian Christ, it had also been a staff of office of Tlaloc. Codex Magliabechiano f. 34r depicts the rain deity in just such a pose (fig. 6.57). Durán (1984, 1:259) observed that the old sign of the month Etzalqualiztli (which in his correlation fell in June), when water was in abundance and the milky kernels of the young maize cobs were beginning to show, had been a figure "with a maize stalk in his hand, denoting fertility."[79] In the Christian calendar June is the month in which Corpus Christi is usually celebrated.

A further image proclaiming Christ's perceived associations with maize can be found in a lunette in the upper cloister at Actopan (plate 15). The crucified Christ is depicted on a hilltop overlooking a vast valley encircled by five almost identical mountains. These perhaps refer to Actopan's perceived microcosmic demarcations, for below in that valley stands what is almost certainly a further representation of the monastery complex, complete with a walled atrium and its celebrated open chapel. Toward the other side of the valley a second atrium

Figure 6.53. The *Ecce Homo* at San Andrés Epazoyucan, Hidalgo. Christ carries a maize plant in place of the reed scepter of the King of the Jews.

Figure 6.54. Maize plant, with its distinctive alternating leaves.

Figure 6.55. The atrial cross at Asunción Tlapanaloya, México. Note the upturned chalice at the base of the cross, the maize plant on its stipes, and the *tonalli* "heat" sign at the axis.

Figure 6.56. The atrial cross at San Buenaventura Cuauhtitlan, México. Note the maize plant on the stipes.

Figure 6.57. Tlaloc, Lord of Rain and Sustenance, with his staff of office, the maize plant (Codex Magliabechiano 34).

is visible, with a small church building attached to it, which may represent the adjoining settlement of Itzcuincuitlapilco, south of Actopan.

Saint Augustine stands at one side of the hilltop crucifixion. The three arrows that shoot in a straight line from the head of Christ toward the saint may be an allusion to his metaphorical affirmation that God had pierced his heart with the arrow of his love (Voragine 1993, 2: 117, 121). Precisely three arrows make up the pierced heart insignia of the Augustinian order. At the other side of the panel a strangely joyous Nicholas of Tolentine, again dressed in a starry habit and clutching his platter of reviving pigeons in his left hand, gestures toward the cross. In his right hand, outstretched toward the dying Christ, Nicholas holds a maize plant. The platter of birds and the maize plant are painted in the same vivid turquoise that also defines the monastery atrium in the valley below (perhaps a reference to the waters of the once-sacred spring on Cerro Los Frailes, diverted by aqueduct to supply the monastic community). The exclusive chromatic linking of water, maize, and reviving birds is a very clear statement regarding the nature of regeneration of life that Christ's sacrifice came to represent for the native world. At the same time, however, we should also ask if Nicholas is in fact offering the maize plant to Christ. In this extraordinary reworking of the Crucifixion theme, is it not rather the smiling patron saint of Indian Actopan who is *receiving* the gift of life from the "precious prince"?

The Christian Cross and the Native Trees of Life

Native representations of sacred trees generated considerable interest among the first Spaniards to see them, for they were immediately likened to Christian crosses. The account of the landing on the island of Cozumel by Andrés de Tapia (1980: 555–56) includes a brief description of a stuccoed "cross" standing within a walled enclosure. Grijalva (1985: 77–78) tells of the excitement of the first Augustinians to reach Meztitlan at the discovery of what must have been a geoglyph, in the form of a Tau cross, high upon a rocky outcrop. The image was accompanied by a moon, interpreted by the friars as the glyphic toponym of Meztitlan. As a result of the many crosslike images, some pondered on the possibility that the message of Christianity had already reached the New World in a distant past (ibid., p. 78).

In their commentaries on the symbolism of the Indians' "crosses" the same chroniclers also confirm that these artifacts were directly associated with water and fertility. Tapia (1980: 556) recorded that the Indians made offerings to the Cozumel cross "when they needed water, and to make it rain."[80] Later Torquemada (1975–83, 5:202) observed that the Cozumel cross was believed by the Indians to be an image of the rain god. The Meztitlan cross and its accompanying moon were painted in blue (against the white background of the rock), suggesting that in some way they were also connected with the water cult.[81]

If the Indians' tree-crosses were the object of Spanish reflection, for the native peoples the Christian cross was immediately identifiable, although not as a legacy of globe-trotting apostles. At Tlaxcala the first cross to be erected by Cortés and his men showed the native population that "the Christians worshiped the god they call Tonacaquáhuitl, which means tree of sustenance, and this is what the ancestors called it" (Alva Ixtlilxóchitl 1985, 2:214).[82] In the words of one of Ixtlilxóchitl's contemporaries, it was the tree that "feeds us and gives us life; taken from the etymology of maize, which they call *tonacayutl*, which means: of our flesh, as if to say, that which feeds our body" (Torquemada 1975–83, 5:57).[83] This was the cross they also called "Quiahutzteotlchicahualistéotl and others Tonacaquáhuitl, which means: god of rain and well-being and tree of sustenance or of life" (Alva Ixtlilxóchitl 1985, 2:8).[84]

Mendieta (1973, 1:185), who described the native reaction to the Christian cross in much the same terms, attempted to reassure his readers that the Indians only called it *tonacaquahuitl* because they did not know its proper name. As so many lines of Spanish- and native-authored texts in Nahuatl testify, its proper name—*cruz*—was soon learned and even incorporated into the Nahuatl language (sometimes in a Nahuatized form as *coloz*: see *CM*, f. 50r; 1985: 302). Yet native perception of the cruz did not change; it remained very much a tree. Paralleled with the Christian Tree of Knowledge, which in the art of the thirteenth century onward had assumed the form of a living tree (Hall 1979: 82), this was perhaps a not too serious interpretation. It is also true that in medieval legend the Christian Tree of Life, the progenitor of Christ's cross, was said to have stood at the center of the universe, its axis crossing the three cosmic regions (Sebastián 1989: 197–99),[85] as did the native arboreal axis mundi. It is clear from Indo-Christian representation, however, that the cruz remained not just as a tree but a *native* tree that symbolized physical (as opposed to spiritual) sustenance: that is, the resurrection of life on the terrestrial rather than celestial plane. In this sense, native representations of Christianity's major symbol not only succeed in communicating a holistic vision of the religion's transformation in the Indian world but also pinpoint the nuclear aspects of its conceptualization.

In painted scenes of the Crucifixion smaller and larger native inserts are apparent. At Culhuacan and Actopan the grain of the wood on the crosses was given the unusual pattern of the twisted malinalli glyph, seemingly a direct reference to the pathways of the divine essences that mingle in the sap of the native cosmic trees (see fig. 1.1). The same cross at Actopan also carried a "celestial" symbol within the crown of thorns at its axis (Reyes-Valerio 1978: 241, 2000: 279–80), which bears a strong resemblance to the lobed Venus signs found in the codices. An Indo-Christian association of Christ with Venus would fall within the parameters of native interpretations of Christianity argued here, for the planet was very closely associated with fertility, rain, and maize, specifically at the start of the rainy season (see Broda 2001: 223, 230). Although unique to Actopan, this Indo-Christian iconographical reference also brings to mind the prehispanic entity Maize-Venus (Centeotl-Itztlacoliuhqui), a name given to the product of the union of Piltzintecuhtli-Tezcatlipoca with Xochiquetzal (Olivier 2000: 104, 105). I will return to this particular idea below.

As noted earlier, rabbits frequently appear at the foot of the cross in European artistic representations of the time. In the now almost completely destroyed *Tebaida* at Meztitlan, a rabbit and a serpent could once be seen in the same location (Reyes-Valerio 2000: 268). This and other examples may be simple copies from European originals; but a rabbit is joined by a lizard at Totolapa (Morelos), while at Ocuituco the lineup consists of a rabbit, a lizard, and an eagle with a serpent in its beak (Reyes-Valerio

Figure 6.58. Detail from a frieze of Tau crosses, lower cloister, Los Santos Reyes Meztitlan, Hidalgo. Note the presence of lizards beneath the head of Christ and birds on the crossbar.

1978: 289). Echoing the prehispanic "cross" painted on the rocky outcrop, a frieze of Tau crosses in Meztitlan's monastic cloister also includes pairs of lizards gazing up at the head of the dying Christ (fig. 6.58). It would be difficult to attribute a Euro-Christian meaning to all these animals, let alone as pairs or in groups. The lizard (with or without accompanying rabbits) has no obvious Christian symbolic or emblematic relevance to the theme of the Crucifixion, and the eagle and serpent are more akin to the native tradition. Their presence together is usually associated with Aztec Tenochtitlan, although they may carry separate meanings here—as symbols of the sky and the earth, for example.[86] Together with rabbits, serpents were closely connected with the cults of water and fertility. As the fourth day-sign, the lizard was associated with the powers of generation and rain.[87] On Codex Borgia 72 and 53 it takes the form of a penis and a calendrical attachment to the same, respectively.

A second cross in the form of a prickly-pear cactus was inserted behind the main cross in the Meztitlan *Tebaida* (fig. 6.59). From the extremes of its horizontally extended branches—where the nailed, bleeding hands would be—pour two streams of colorless water, each tipped with a series of yellow droplets. On the upper area of its trunk, close to the axis, a large yellow flower bursts into bloom. As Reyes-Valerio (1978: 233–34) observed (although not in the context of this image), the nopal was a tree of sacrifice, its fruit symbolizing the heart of the sacrificial victim. A further nopal cactus was included beneath the cross in the Ocuituco mural. Its presence at both sites may thus allude to Christ's sacrifice or, perhaps more precisely, a conceptual reading of sacrifice. For the 1565 festival of Saint Sebastian (the Christian martyr shot with arrows while tied to a tree) Indian artists also produced an image of the saint tied to the same species of cactus (*Anales de Juan Bautista* 2001: 301).

The choice of water instead of blood and of the nopal that produces yellow flowers instead of red, however, argues for a different reading at Meztitlan. This reading (discussed in more detail below) relates more directly to the product of the Indo-Christ's sacrifice: water and maize. In this sense the yellow droplets flowing from the water-dripping cross at Meztitlan may in fact represent the gentle early rains falling on the newly sowed maize seeds.

But another reading of the Meztitlan cross is worth mentioning at this point, for it carries through an idea noted at many other sites. The cross stands on a great stone ridge. To one side is a representation of a Christian church and above it an image of the moon. Is this a reference to the site where the Augustinians found the geoglyph of the "cross" and the moon? In other words, did this mural also reproduce a sacred feature of Meztitlan's

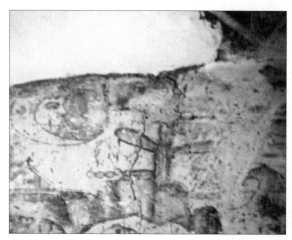

Figure 6.59. The prickly-pear cactus/cross on a ridge, with the moon and church building to one side, refectory, Los Santos Reyes Meztitlan.

own topography, reidentified by Indo-Christianity as the place where Christ died?

Together with the smaller crosses that served as architectural ornamentation (on the tops of posas, over portals, and so on), the stone-carved atrial crosses of sixteenth-century Mexico constitute some of the most unusual examples of native-executed Indo-Christian expression. As a result, they can tell us much about native interpretations of this major symbol of Christianity and the religious beliefs it came to represent. Worked in low or high relief (fig. 6.60) or in native tequitqui, the stone crosses always carry one or more symbols of the Passion. On plainer examples these might be restricted to the crown of thorns and the wounds of the nails (figs. 6.25, 6.61). At the height of elaboration, all the Passion symbols were included (figs. 6.26, 6.56, 6.60, 6.62, 6.63, 6.64, 6.65), in some cases evincing a *horror vacui* in its most concentrated form (fig. 6.66).[88]

Larger and smaller iconographical details on a number of crosses consistently evidence the Indian mind at work. The substitution of the chalchihuitl symbol for a wound on Christ's body (his hands, feet, or side) is fairly common, occurring for example, at Tlalnepantla (D.F.) and Huejotzingo (fig. 6.67). Here Christ's blood is likened to the native concept of precious water. Inserted into the side of the cross (as in the example at Tlalnepantla) the symbol provides an iconic reading of the blood and water that flowed from the wound inflicted by Longinus's spear (John 19:34).

On side "A" of the cross at Alfajayuca, above the crown of thorns, is a row of five tiny trees, each within its own niche (fig. 6.26), perhaps in allusion to the five cosmic trees that supported the sky.[89] The sum of the three dice on this cross is 11 (5 + 3 + 3), a numeral that echoes the lineup of the major pulque deities and the zodiac sky phases with which they were associated (see Brotherston 1992: 66–67). At Tecali each of the three dice is cast as 5, the quincuncial symbol of the native cosmos (fig. 6.63). The thirty pieces

Figure 6.60. One of three surviving stone crosses at San Francisco Tepeapulco, Hidalgo.

Figure 6.61. The original spiny atrial cross at San Miguel Huejotzingo, Puebla, which now stands in the town square.

Figure 6.62. Side "B" of the atrial cross at San Martín Alfajayuca, Hidalgo.

Figure 6.63. The atrial cross at Santiago Tecali, Puebla.

Figure 6.64. The atrial cross at San Matías Tepetomatitlan, Tlaxcala.

Figure 6.65. Reverse side of the atrial cross at Santiago Anaya (Tlachichilco), Hidalgo. Note the manner in which the crown of thorns is draped like a garland over the crossbar.

Figure 6.66. The atrial cross at San Mateo Huichapan (Hueychiapan), Hidalgo. Again the crown of thorns is draped over the crossbar.

Figure 6.67. The spiny churchyard cross at San Miguel Huejotzingo, Puebla, originally an architectural detail topping one of the four posas. Note the chalchihuitl-like wounds, serpentine "roots," and the carved detail of a cut stem at the tips of its "spines."

of silver, unevenly stacked in seven rows above Christ's head on the cross at Magdalena Tlatelulco (Tlaxcala), are subdivided into groups of 3, 4, and 5, key numerals in the native calendar that also carry specifically cosmic attributes (the cosmic planes, quatrefoil, and quincunx). The introduction of native calendrical counts into the art and architecture of the churches is a common occurrence (see chapter 7). Among other native manipulations of Passion symbols on the crosses, at Tlapanaloya the chalice at its base is upturned (fig. 6.55), possibly in reference to the perceived relationship between Christ's sacrifice and the fertilization of the earth.[90]

Atrial crosses were often mounted on stones carved in the prehispanic era (or in a prehispanic style) or on artifacts directly associated with prehispanic practices and beliefs. The High Sierra of Hidalgo, for example, boasts a series of crosses mounted on barrel cacti. These occur at Nonoalco (as recorded by Victoria Asensio 1985 and Lara 2004) and Molango. At Molango in 1992 a small carved barrel cactus still lay among the few remaining stones of the early church built at the foot of a mountain rising immediately to the east of the village. Cut with a deep, rectangular depression, it must once also have supported a cross. The second example at this site is the stone cross standing outside the cave of Antonio de Roa, the first Augustinian evangelizer of the locality, on the summit of the same mountain.[91] At Alfajayuca, which lies at the southern foothills of the Hidalgo High Sierra, a second atrial (or possibly posa) cross was mounted on a spherical stone that also recalls the form of the barrel cactus (fig. 6.68).[92]

Barrel cactus sacrifice possibly originated as a tradition of the Chichimecs, a people with whom the inhabitants of the High Sierra probably had contact (see Gerhard 1986: 189). It was recorded as taking place early in the Aztec migration from the north (Tira de la Peregrinación, 4), and in later times became one of the modes of death that would guarantee the victim a place in the realm of the Sun (FC3, 1978: 49). The barrel cactus was perhaps understood to be an appropriate visual explanation for the Indian Christ's sacrifice and subsequent ascent to the Christian paradise, although its indirect associations with the sun are perhaps also significant.

According to its roughly carved date, the atrial cross at Santo Tomás Ajusco was mounted on its large spherical base in the nineteenth century (fig. 6.69), although the stone is possibly of prehispanic origin.[93] A similar base is also found at Huaquechula, bearing carvings of the sun and the crescent moon (in the horizontal U-shape as it appears from Mexico) (fig. 6.70). The form and style of carving appears to be prehispanic, but a profiled face cut into the moon suggests more clearly an early influence of the European presence.[94] At Nativitas Zacapa (D.F.) the cross is mounted on a stone cube or reused Mexica stone "box." Calendrical signs are carved on its four lateral faces: the day-sign Movement, unqualified numerically (fig. 6.71a); two examples of the day-sign Death, each qualified by one dot count; and what I take to be year-date 7 Reed (fig 6.71b). The duplication of sign 1 Death must refer to the day-date and the thirteen-day period (trecena) of the tonalpohualli opening on that day and thus named after it. Perhaps not coincidentally, the Night-Lord of the first day of trecena 1 Death was Piltzintecuhtli, father of Centeotl, identified as the Sun in the context of 4 Movement, the name of the Fifth Sun (Codex Telleriano Remensis, f. 12v; Quiñones Keber 1995: 171).

Something similar is found at Mixtec San Pedro Topiltepec (Oaxaca), several hundred miles to the south, where the *stipes* (vertical shaft) of the churchyard cross consists of a carved stone that if not prehispanic in origin

Figure 6.68. The second stone cross at San Martín Alfajayuca, Hidalgo.

Figure 6.70. The original atrial cross at San Martín Huaquechula, Puebla, which now stands in the town square. Note the carvings of the sun and a section of the crescent moon on its base.

Figure 6.69. The atrial cross at Santo Tomás Ajusco, D.F. Note the three arrows emerging from the crown of thorns.

Figure 6.71. Mexica stone on which the atrial cross at Nativitas Zacapa, D.F., is mounted: *a*, the ollin or "Movement" day-sign given to the Fifth Sun; *b*, the year date 7 Reed. The day-date 1 Death appears on the remaining two faces of the stone.

certainly adheres to traditional Mixtec iconographic traditions. As noted by Maarten Jansen (1982), its iconography carries more than a passing resemblance to the image of the "Bloody Path of the Sun" on Codex Vienna, obverse 23 (fig. 6.72). The Vienna panel is understood to represent an "eclipsing event," where its accompanying calendrical date of 13 Rabbit 2 Deer (also possibly once present on the cross) reads conceptually as "genesis." The use of the same date across the Mixtec codices is inevitably associated with new beginnings (see Wake and Stokes 1997: 214–19).

In this context the date at the base of the cross at Nativitas Zacapa is worth pursuing further. In the Julian calendar 7 Reed, 1 Death, 1 Death would correspond to June 11,

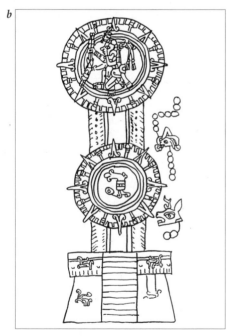

Figure 6.72. The atrial cross at San Pedro Topiltepec, Oaxaca: *a*, stipes of the cross at Topiltepec, Oaxaca, showing carvings of prehispanic glyphs that recall the iconography of the "Bloody Path of the Sun" of Codex Vienna; *b*, detail from the "Bloody Path of the Sun" (Codex Vienna, obverse 23).

1499 (www.azteccalendar.com), the year in which we might assume that the box was carved. In a Gregorian conversion this would read as June 20, 1499 (ibid.). Although this is short by one day, the closeness of the date to the summer solstice is interesting. In effect, the 1499 summer solstice fell on June 12 (Julian); in addition, Venus was close to maximum altitude as morning star and also conjuncted with Saturn (Anthony Aveni, pers. comm., 2007). As Aveni points out, this was an unusually active morning sky (ibid.). It was also probably one that was anticipated ritually the night before, thereby prompting its recording in stone. If we compute the same native date for the early colonial period (that is, one 52-year cycle later), however, the result is May 29, 1551 (Julian) and June 8, 1551 (Gregorian) (www.azteccalendar.com). I can find nothing significant about May 29, 1551, in either astronomical or historical terms; but June 8, 1499, in the Julian calendar, was the date of an annular solar eclipse, visible at sunset from Mexico (http://eclipse.gsfc.nasa.gov/5MCSEmap/1401-1500/1499-06-08.gif; Anthony Aveni, pers. comm., 2007). In other words, the eclipse took place on precisely the same day date that 1 Death, trecena 1 Death would yield for the year 1551 if calculated under the Gregorian calendar. I do not see this as mere coincidence, for the odds against such a cross-computation are quite high. Rather, it suggests some sort of recourse to the native system of "like-in-kind dates": key dates and events that recurred across different 52-year cycles (see Umberger 1981), which were still being exploited under the European calendrical adjustment. Thus, by transposing Julian and Gregorian dates, the cube selected to support the cross (evidently after 1582, when the adjustment was made) may have been intended to narrate a series of significant solar events that placed Christ's Passion in a solar and/or "eclipsing" context.

Native associations of Christ's Passion with a solar eclipse would probably have found a source in the Bible, which records Christ's death as having occurred immediately after some type of celestial phenomenon that spread darkness over the land for three hours (e.g., Matthew 27:45). And, echoing the sign for Movement on the Nativitas cube, at the moment of his death "the earth did quake" (Matthew 27:51). The evangelization body also promoted a Solar-Christ equation by transferring the Old World metaphor that likened Christ to the Sun to New World doctrinal texts (Burkhart 1988). In woodcuts and engravings imported by the mission, a solar resplendence often appears around Christ's head or body in scenes of the Nativity, during his Transfiguration, and after the Resurrection (ibid., p. 236). Some atrial crosses certainly suggest that these same images guided native sculptors: sunrays rise over Christ's head or (as we have seen in the rayed obsidian disks) appear to encircle or replace his crown of thorns. Here perhaps we can find a second reading in the sunbursts and/or crowns of thorns with obsidian inserts found at the axes of so many atrial crosses. The reflection of sunlight on the inserts can certainly produce the effect of a brilliant and shimmering rayed orb (Nicholas Saunders, pers. comm., 2003).

Other types of solar imagery found in relation to the cross tend to push the adopted Solar-Christ theme even further back into the native iconographic camp, however. At the center of the crown of thorns carved over the axis of the cross at Tlapanaloya (México) a symmetrical configuration of four small circles, the prehispanic sign for *tonalli,* was included (fig. 6.55). As applied to humans, tonalli denoted a warm vital force lodged in the back of the head, sent there at or before birth by the supreme creator (López Austin 1996a, 1: 223–28).[95] At a different level, however, the concept of tonalli related to the light or the heat of the sun, which regulated the growth of food crops (*tona, tonacayotl*) (Burkhart 1988: 239). The sign perhaps occurs in this context on the back of the headdress and pedestal of the solar-maize deity Xochipilli as he appears on the celebrated flower-trance statue (fig. 6.29). At Tlapanaloya the sign can be seen as replacing a solar-maize Christ's head; it is his tonalli that is literally the central force of the cross. The "B" side of the cross at Alfajayuca boasts a second crown of thorns (again with a sunburst element), at the center of which lies a high-relief carving of a quatrefoil formed with petal-like motifs (fig. 6.62). Further examples occur at the extremities of the horizontal bar. In its associations with the sun, the quatrefoil configuration of the prehispanic tonalli sign would appear to derive from the positioning of the four points of solsticial risings and settings on the horizon in relation to the "center." These points determined the layout of the basic cosmic diagram, which is often represented in painting and sculpture as a four-petaled flowerlike element.[96] The flower motif at Alfajayuca would therefore also appear to register Christ's sun-tonalli. Like its partner on the other side of the cross, Alfajayuca's second crown of thorns also probably once carried obsidian inserts. These would have covered the flower motif, perhaps in the sense of embedding Christ's tonalli within the "spirit" of Tezcatlipoca-God.

Another iconographic strategy may indicate that the carved and obsidian reflected sunbursts also refer directly to the Sun-Christ, although the example is unique among stone crosses. Mounted on its large orb, the atrial cross at Santo Tomás Ajusco also appears to have carried an obsidian disk within its central crown of thorns (fig. 6.69). Radiating out from the crown of thorns are three well-carved arrows. These cannot refer to the presence of the Augustinian order at Ajusco or in the area of Tlalpan (see Gerhard 1986: 102–103). A native conceptual reading is possible, however, where the arrow (as the calendar sign Reed) was associated with the eastern horizon. There the sun, moon, and planets rose in "a hurling of reed arrows" as heliacal rays (Brotherston 1992: 90). The same reading might account for the presence of the Venus-like lobes at the axis of the painted cross at Actopan: as the morning star, the planet also rises with the sun.

Thus we might speculate that the apparent allusion to the arrows of God's love that pierced Saint Augustine's heart inserted into the upper cloister Crucifixion mural at Actopan (plate 15) offers a second, indigenous reading. The manner in which these arrows originate from Christ's head at the axis of the cross is the iconographical curiosity here. As noted earlier, Jacobus de Voragine's *Golden Legend* seems to have been known to Actopan's muralists.[97] But these artists also appear to have embarked on a serious reworking of other borrowed sources for the center's painted program. Could the attraction have been more the solar aspects of the Christ-Augustine presence on Actopan's walls? Voragine (1993, 2: 117) certainly commented how Augustine came to be compared with the sun. He also cited a similarly solar-oriented invocation from the saint's celebrated *Confessions:* "When I first came to know you [Christ] you assailed my weak sight, turning your brightness blindingly upon me" (ibid., p. 119). The use of reed arrows as a glyphic sign for the blinding rays of the Sun-Christ would permit a neat conflation of Christian and Indo-Christian readings of solar metaphors.

Common to the iconography of many atrial crosses is the inclusion of floral and vegetal motifs. The cross at Acolman carries a delicate relief of flowers and foliage over its crossbar (fig. 6.73), while the reverse sides of the crosses at Chapatongo and Tecali are studded overall with flowers and vegetal arabesques, respectively.[98] At Taximaroa (Michoacán) flowering plants figure prominently on the stipes (fig. 6.24); at

Angahua (Michoacán) Christ's hands and feet are nailed to flowerlike motifs. The crosses are often also characterized by elaborately fashioned "petals" at the extremities of both the *patibulum* (the crossbar or horizontal bar) and the stipes (figs. 6.65, 6.66). At Huejotzingo (figs. 6.61, 6.67) the tips of the atrial cross proper and the example that once surmounted a posa roof consist of flower buds, each set in a calyx and opening like a whirling pinwheel. In some cases "petals" are more clearly feathers, depicted in the prehispanic graphic mode (figs. 6.62, 6.74).[99] Alternatively, the crosses bear European-styled feathers (fig. 6.56, 6.69) or three-leafed vegetal designs that resemble the European fleur-de-lis (fig. 6.25, 6.73). Finally, a number of crosses carry the crown of thorns hanging as a garland around Christ's neck or draped stolelike over the crossbar (figs. 6.65, 6.66, 6.74). Noticeably, in these examples

Figure 6.73. Upper section of the atrial cross at San Agustín Acolman, México. Note the careful floral carvings and fleur-de-lis tips.

any connotations of laceration and pain usually associated with the stiff thorn-edged crown are no longer present. This crown of thorns is not a symbol of suffering but a sculpted gesture of honor paid. The surviving posa cross at Huejotzingo carries a similarly interlaced device at its base, which nevertheless also brings to mind a serpentine root system (fig. 6.67).

In part, the inspiration behind this iconography may have been the ornamental floral buddings found at the ends of European portable metal crosses of the day (McAndrew 1965: 251). Yet, unlike the European models, the sheer exuberance of the native-executed examples often detracts from the idea of the cross as a solid, pain-accelerating instrument of torture and death. Even if they were intended as an iconographic rendering of the Christian Tree of Life, the crosses still more strongly resemble soft, sap-filled flowery and leafy vegetation. It is true that a number of stone crosses boast stipples or spines (figs. 6.61, 6.67, 6.75), again possibly introduced from Europe in the form of early portable miniatures and later engravings and woodcuts (Monterrosa Prado 1968). Yet, whether they were copied from hand-held miniatures or not, the stippled and spiny crosses still echo native cactus-trees, sturdy and bristling, but green and revitalized as their sap rises after the spring rains. The abundance of floral and vegetal imagery displayed on the crosses is also not a European constant. It therefore more clearly suggests a shared initiative on the part of native sculptors everywhere to endow the crosses with the characteristics of the flower-trees of sustenance or the native "trees of life."

Native trees of life (or, more precisely, trees and robust plants) appear to have been associated primarily with food and water. Appearing in the codices as groups or directional sequences of four, or five when a central axis mundi is evoked, they also doubled as the cosmic trees that separated the sky and the earth and determined the perceived limits of the terrestrial plane. In Codex Tudela, for example, the trees of the East, North, West, and South all rise

Figure 6.74. The church rooftop cross at San Francisco Tlahuelilpa, Hidalgo, with the crown of thorns draped over the crossbar.

Figure 6.75. The prickly or spiny atrial cross at Todos Santos Cempoala, Hidalgo.

from a receptacle containing water and, in all but one case, a pair of germinating seeds (Codex Tudela ff. 97r, 104r, 111r, 128r). In this sense the receptacles represent the earth in its regenerative cycle. Identified by their alphabetical glosses, the Codex Tudela trees are, respectively, the mesquite (*mizquitl*), the ceiba (*pochotl*), the cedar (a*huehuetl*), and the willow (*huexotl*), each prefixed with *quetzal*, which may be connotatively translated as "precious feather." The Tudela trees are therefore "feathery" in their preciousness. Although generally uncultivated, the ubiquitous mesquite, a small, thorny tree (described as having "nodules" in FC11, 1963: 120), produces a sweet edible fruit (ibid.) encased in brown pods. It is probably another example of those "life-saving" wild plants that nomadic or famine-struck populations could turn to in times of need. In the codex, however, the native emphasis is on the tree's fertilizing properties (Codex Tudela, f. 97r).[100] The ceiba is credited with producing an edible pulse (ibid., f. 104r),[101] scorned by the Aztecs (FC11, 1963: 108).[102] *Quetzalhuexotl* is the name of the tree into which the creator-serpent, Quetzalcoatl, changed in order to assist in supporting the newly created sky (*HM* 1979: 108; *HMPP* 1979: 32).

The title page of Codex Féjérváry (see fig. 4.2) presents insurmountable problems in respect to identification of its four principal and highly stylized cosmic trees. All are in flower, and it is undoubtedly significant in some way that the trees of the East (top) and North are depicted as turquoise blue; the tree of the West, white; and the tree of the South, turquoise and white. These colors also echo the painted geoglyph of the Tau cross at Meztitlan. The tree of the East has curled nodelike elements on its trunk.

Figure 6.76. Four tlaloque toting different species of ritual trees (Codex Borgia 30, simplified).

The tree of the North is covered in triangular spines, with a split bulbous formation toward its base, perhaps indicating that it is a sap-producing species of cactus. From the white trunk of the tree of the West rise what appear to be long white thorns, from which shoot smaller red thorns with white tips. The tree of the South bears cubelike nodes. From each hangs a red almond-shaped element that might be fruit or possibly droplets representing resin or sap. Viewed in this way, the trees of the West, East, and South more closely resemble cut trees, where their thorns and nodes in fact represent the shorn or hacked stumps of secondary lower branches or shoots. Significantly, none has roots. Therefore, while they may symbolize the world trees, in context they are perhaps the ritual impersonators of those trees.

The four diagonals or "sepals" of Féjérváry's flower-plane are designated as young plants, also chromatically qualified in either white or turquoise. With a yellow flower and a segmented spiny stem, the plant positioned between West and South (but qualified calendrically by the House of West) certainly recalls the prickly-pear cactus. Between South and East (that is, "calendrical" South) stands a cob-laden maize plant. With the exception of the maize plant, all the plants carry the semblance of young roots as if still growing in the ground or perhaps more recently torn from it.

On Codex Borgia 30, at each corner of a ritual enclosure composed of the bones of the skeletal earth monster, four blackened tlaloque-priests accompanying or carrying trees are depicted (fig. 6.76). Again each tree is of a different species. The only example that can be identified with some certainty is the maguey (upper right), chromatically defined on the panel, as elsewhere, by its turquoise-blue leaves tipped with red spines. The tree at the lower left of the illustration bears as its fruit a series of circular brown elements, possibly representing mesquite or other types of pod. All retain their roots, however, as if they are again the newly selected ritual trees or plants, carried to the enclosure for raising by the tlaloque-priests.

Pages 49–53 of Codex Borgia present the cosmic trees in directional order, each rising from a different manifestation of the clawed, skeletal earth deity (fig. 6.77). Each also boasts a celestial bird perched on or strutting across its branches, which, as on Féjérváry's title page, are probably drawn from the thirteen sacred quecholli (Brotherston 1992: 88,99). Echoing the lineup of identifiable tree species on Féjérváry (although not their directional associations), the spiny tree of the North is perhaps most evidently a yellow-flowering prickly-pear. The South tree again carries yellow blossoms but is thorny rather than spiny. Noticeably, its "fruit," at the tips of its branches, takes the form of large rayed disks that closely resemble representations of Tezcatlipoca's mirror-scryer. This might allude to the *tezcacuahuitl,* "tree of mirrors," into which Tezcatlipoca, the second serpent-creator deity, transformed himself in order to raise the sky over the earth (*HMPP* 1979: 32). Alternatively, the disks may be solar

WEST (maize)
Borgia 51

NORTH (cactus)
Borgia 50

CENTER (maize)
Borgia 53

SOUTH (cactus)
Borgia 52

EAST (maize)
Borgia 49

Figure 6.77. The four directional world trees, with the fifth at the center (Codex Borgia 49–53; author's reconstruction).

signs. The East, West, and Central trees are maize plants. The East tree carries *xihuitl* symbols ("greenery," "renewal," "fruits"), symbolizing the newly sprouted plant at the opening of its growth cycle. The tree of the West, with its tips laden with featherlike leaves and pollen tassels, is the young plant. As might be expected, at the center of the cosmos stands the fully matured maize plant Its horizontally extended stems display corn tassels and ripened yellow and red maize ears with their now shriveled silky protectors.[103]

Each of the Borgia world tree panels includes a temple and a look-alike secondary tree that still carries its roots, as if newly uprooted—that is, prior to being formally erected in the ritual arena. These secondary trees also echo the presence of the smaller "plants" with roots of the Féjérváry panel.

Felled and trimmed of their branches before being re-erected in ritual enclosures, trees were a fairly common artifact in prehispanic rites. The pictorial description of the eight-yearly fasting festival of Atamalqualiztli (CMPR, f. 254r; see plate 1) includes a "flowering tree," which consists of a tree or large branch whose branches or secondary shoots have been crudely lopped off. The smoothed *xocotl*, "fruit," pole erected in the festival of Xocotlhuetzi, identified as a symbol of the mature maize plant (Wake n.d.a), also started its ritual life as a very tall tree brought in from the forests (CMPR, f. 251r, Nicholson et al. 1997: 61; FC2, 1981: 111–12). Appearing in groups of four or five, the trees of the codices recall the tota tree of Hueytozoztli fame, erected together with four smaller examples in the patio of the rain deity (Durán 1984, 1:87).

None of the Borgia cosmic trees represents the maguey cactus. It must be significant, however, that all possess trunks that divide horizontally into two branches that in turn then subdivide vertically. The same is true of the nonmaguey species of the ritual trees on Borgia 30. In this they take on the very distinctive form of the maguey's quiotl in flower (see figs. 1.6, 6.42). The large circular water element backing the mature maize plant of the Center is also reminiscent of the sap-filled heart of the mature maguey. Numerous figures accompanying the five cosmic trees wear the crescent moon nose plugs of the pulque deities, thereby attesting that rituals pertaining to the cult were carried out in close association with the trees. On Borgia 49 (East) an upturned pulque jar lies at the base of the secondary xihuitl-bearing tree. The secondary tree of the North (p. 50) boasts a crescent-moon recipient at the top of its trunk. A blue and red plant, similar to the form of the maguey plant and its usual chromatic representation, is superimposed over the trunk of the tree of the West (p. 51). In short, whether defining maize plants or prickly or thorny trees, all the Borgia trees are conceptually fused with the maguey and its derivative cult artifacts and symbols.

Durán (1984) also provides a reference to the maguey as part of a fused "trinity" of native sacred trees. In the festival of Hueytozoztli, three names were given to the tota, each invoked separately but also as three in one. Durán (1984, 1:86), a proponent of the view that Christianity had reached Mexico in a distant past, immediately likened it to the Holy Trinity: "and they said *tota, topiltzin,* and *yolometl,* words that mean 'our father and our son and the heart of both [that is, the Holy Spirit].'"[104] While *tota* certainly reads as "our father" (Siméon 1997: 436) and *topiltzin* can mean "our revered child," *yolometl* reads directly as "heart-maguey" (*yolo*[*tl*], "heart," + *metl* "maguey") (ibid., pp. 199, 269).[105]

The similarities between the species of the Borgia trees and the tota group raised in Tlaloc's honor also resound in native sources that acknowledge the range of command of Tlaloc in his role as lord of foodstuffs: "Thus they said he [Tlaloc] made that which we ate and drank—food, drink, our sustenance, our nourishment, our daily bread, our maintenance. All that which grew in the summer [he made]—sprouts, fresh green sprouts, trees, amaranth, chía, squash, beans; *the maguey, the tuna [nopal] cactus;* and still others, not edible—flowers, herbs" (FC7, 1953: 17, my emphasis). In a prayer to

Tlaloc, "the trees, the maguey, the nopal, all which lieth germinating" are again named as the source of life of the common folk (FC6, 1969: 40). Thus the ritual cosmic trees of whatever species together invoke Tlaloc's realm or the terrestrial paradise of abundance. Where maize symbolized all cultivated foodstuffs in general (Nicholson 1971: 416), the references to "our sustenance . . . our daily bread" and "the trees" in these citations may also name maize at a connotative level. In this context we recall that Tlaloc carried a maize plant as his staff of office, as a symbol of fertility (Durán 1984, 1: 259). The *tonacaquahuitl,* "tree of sustenance" (Alva Ixtlilxóchitl 1985, 2:8), the tree "that feeds us and gives us life; taken from the etymology of maize, which they call *tonacayutl*" (Torquemada 1975–83, 5:57), was also recognized as "god of rain and well-being" (Alva Ixtlilxóchitl 1985, 2:8). In sum, Tlaloc, as lord of foodstuffs, was represented symbolically by way of a maize plant.

Finally, when raised in the patio of the rain deity, the tota found itself at the center of a quatrefoil of smaller trees (Durán 1984, 1:87). Also configured in quatrefoil formation beneath the sky, the tlaloque of the Tizapan lid represent the four world supports that rise from the terrestrial plane (see fig. 1.3). Thus the tota's arboreal satellites can be understood to represent the tlaloque, while the tota (the ripened maize plant, an axis mundi in more than one sense) is again Tlaloc, lord of foodstuffs or, as Sahagún's informants also defined him, the "divine provider" (FC6, 1969: 35).

It is in this fused and conceptually overlapping form that I believe we should approach an interpretation of the Indo-Christian tree crosses. At one level they certainly carry a series of iconographic details that align them very closely with the prehispanic trees of life. This is significant in terms of the possible European influences that have been attributed to the iconography of the colonial tree-crosses (see Monterrosa Prado 1968; Lara 1996). If the iconographic configurations of the Indo-Christian crosses echo written and painted medieval descriptions of the cross that may have been taken to or reported in New Spain, similar configurations already defined the cosmic trees of the native world, as seen in preconquest codices such as Borgia and Féjérváry. In this sense the introduction of the European versions would only confirm again that Christ's cross was a conceptual equivalent of the native sacred trees.

Two iconographic details of the ritualized cosmic trees in particular are common to European images of the Crucifixion. The fleshless head of the earth monster from whose body the native trees rose provides an interesting parallel to the skull of Adam or the place sign for Golgotha at the foot of the cross (figs. 6.56, 6.60, 6.63). The celestial bird poised on the native trees' upper branches must also recall the cockerel of Peter's denial, which, although usually depicted in European art on the pillar of Christ's flogging, also very frequently forms part of the crosses' iconography (for example, figs. 6.63, 6.64, 6.66). Neither the skull nor the cockerel would have been included when the first wooden crosses were erected; but where the crosses had already been identified as the tonacaquahuitl the later dissemination of printed images of the symbols of Christ's Passion could only have served to gel that initial interpretation. Although the birds that appear on the stipes of the stone crosses are often less than roosterlike in appearance, no birds of any form appear on the patibulum.[106] In the markedly "vegetal" crucifixion scene incorporated into the featherwork designs of the El Escorial miter, however, a bird is depicted in this position. Birds also sit on the crossbars of the painted Tau crosses at Meztitlan (fig. 6.58). In neither example do these flyers depict roosters.[107]

The flowery and feathery aspects of the Indo-Christian crosses are well evoked in the flowery and feathery ritual cosmic trees of the codices but also in the generic *xochiquahuitl,* "flower-tree." According to the devotional song poems, the xochiquahuitl stands in Tamoanchan: it blossoms at the place of origin, at God's home, itself a place of tassel plumes (*CM,* ff. 15r, 17v; 1985: 176–77, 186–87). The *tonacaxochiquahuitl,* "flower tree of sustenance," is also there: "There! It stands. The flower tree of sustenance. And all are pleasured. Yes, it's sprinkling dew, it's sprouting songs; it's covered in tassel plumes. Here! In Mexico!" (ibid., f. 20r; 1985: 194–95).[108] Although not synonymous, *xochiquahuitl* and *tonacaxochiquahuitl* nevertheless define the basic sequence "flower-tree to flower-food-tree," where *xochitl* also functions as a symbol of regeneration, an alternative metaphor for the essence of life. With their "tassel-plumes" (*quetzalmiahuatl*)

that complement the feathery milk corn (*quetzal[toc] xilotl*)—that is, the silky hairs protecting the newly formed kernels—"flower trees" were evidently conceived as young maize plants. At this stage in their growth cycle they were associated with the time of Christ's Passion: "Plumelike parrot milk corn comes blossoming. Parrot corn tassels are parceled out. Let's eat them. Let our souls rejoice in these—in your place of rain. . . . Rejoice. Easter has come" (ibid., f. 42v, pp. 272–73).[109]

Following this line of enquiry, Indo-Christian crosses can also be seen to carry "fruits." The large rayed disks on Borgia's South tree are one interesting example: although similar to representations of Tezcatlipoca's mirror-scryer, they also recall the rayed devices found at the axes of atrial crosses. Perhaps the most startling parallel, however, comes in the face or head of Christ at the axis (e.g., figs. 6.63, 6.64, 6.66). Of solemn or serene countenance or with eyes closed in death, the image rarely deviates from the representation of a bearded figure with shoulder-length hair common to European representation. Yet, with only an occasional iconographical reference to hands and/or feet, the head is always devoid of a body.[110] In this form it does not appear to represent part of the man who hung on the cross but rather an organic entity that is an appendage of the cross or that emerges from its interior. Lara (1996: 15, 31, and figs. 9, 24) offers evidence that the sectioning of Christ's body in this manner does have European origins, which are eschatological in nature. But again direct and clearly arboreal prehispanic parallels exist, this time more concerned with the perpetuation of life, as seen in the images of sacred maize plants in relief carving

Figure 6.78. Relief carving of the maize deity in the Temple of the Foliated Cross, Palenque, Chiapas (redrawn from Schele and Miller 1986).

at Maya Palenque (fig. 6.78) and in mural painting at Cacaxtla (plate 16). In both examples maize cobs with human facial features or as human heads sprout from between the leaves of the plants. The two cobs in the clutches of the earth monster at the base of Borgia's Center cosmic tree also have anthropomorphic faces.[111] In the Maya example the corn silk is depicted, while the face of the maize god gazes out from the axis.

In the central Mexican "Song of Xochipilli" (god of young maize), the red Centeotl,

"Maize Cob Lord," is said to stand singing at the point where the roads join (CMPR, f. 277r; Nicholson et al. 1997: 140). At harvest time the inhabitants of sixteenth-century Zumpahuacan took a fully matured maize plant with its cobs attached to a place where the road divided, offering it in thanks to the sacred mountain Matlalcueye (Ponce de León 1979: 127–28). Ripened cobs and cross-axes were evidently closely associated in native religious belief, possibly due to the perceived cosmic centrality of the fully matured maize plant. The concept of Centeotl as a maize deity also seems more directly linked with maize as food than with any particular part of the living plant: he is the product of the plant that nourishes people, that gives them continuing life.[112] Thus, if Christ's head at the axis of the crosses represents the mutated Centeotl as the ripened fruit of the maize, the cross is again likened to the maize plant or perceived as a symbol of sustenance in general. The detail of a vertical maize plant superimposed over the stipes of several examples of surviving atrial crosses in place of the reed scepter of the King of the Jews reinforces this idea. The maize plant—erstwhile staff of office of Tlaloc—became the staff of office of the Indian Christ.

Together with numerous representations of the Franciscan insignia on architecture proper (fig. 6.79) (and sometimes the crosses— see fig. 6.24), on many examples of crosses (see figs. 6.60, 6.67), the almond-shaped coagulates of Christ's blood pouring from chalchihuitl-water wounds closely resemble the form of the Mexican cintli cob as depicted in the postconquest codices (fig. 6.80). The yellow droplets falling from the painted cactus cross at Meztitlan (fig 6.59) echo the same idea. Christ's tree bleeds life on the world in the form of water and maize. These images may conflate the eucharistic elements, but an indigenous iconic reading also obtains: with the season of water come the young milky kernels; with the season of sun come the fully matured cobs.

Although the form of Europe's Latin and Tau crosses echoes the two horizontal branches of the quiote where the maguey flowers bloom, Indo-Christian crosses carry no overt iconographic references to the maguey or its cult. But they might be present in an encoded form or might once have existed on examples of crosses that have been lost to time or prohibition.[113] As we have seen at Acolman, Calpan, and elsewhere, associations of the cult with Christ were nevertheless incorporated into other areas of Indo-Christian graphic expression. Associations between Mayahuel and Centeotl in the codices also imply a perceived mother-son relationship between the pulque goddess and the maize deity (Quiñones Keber 1995: 174), a perception that accords well with the symbolism of the maize-bearing maguey quiote of the Center Borgia tree. While the *xochiquahuitl* is identifiable as a symbolic maize plant, it was also the name of the two-branched tree of Mayahuel in the myth of the Creation of Maguey; this "flower tree" eventually regrew as the maguey plant (*HM* 1979: 107). In the context of these examples, Mary's proposed occasional role as the mutated Mayahuel becomes more sustainable.[114]

Figure 6.79. Franciscan insignia from San Juan Bautista Acapixtla, Morelos, with the blood of Christ depicted in the form of maize cobs.

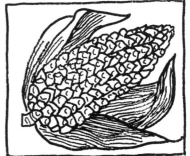

Figure 6.80. Maize cobs (cintli) as depicted in Florentine Codex, Book 11.

Finally, as with the cosmic trees depicted in the codices, the stipples or spines of the Indo-Christian crosses cannot be seen as exclusively representing these botanical elements. At the same time they may also denote the remains of secondary branches or sprouting twigs that have been cut away. This is particularly clear in the surviving posa cross at Huejotzingo that now stands in the center of the atrium (fig. 6.67), where the native sculptor included a tiny circular motif at the tip of each stipple as if to represent a cross section of a branch or twig with both bark and pith visible. I therefore propose that where the crosses symbolize the flowery trees of terrestrial regeneration they are also their ritual or ritually attired impersonators. This might also explain their carved flowers and "garlands" woven from thorns, draped gracefully over extended branches.

The iconographic fusion of so many ideas associated with water, sun, fertility and maize in the crosses of Indo-Christianity pushes them even closer to the central bleeding tree of Tamoanchan, which was the nuclear coordinate of the native world. Erected at the center of the atrium, before the house of the Indo-Christian Water-Palace-Lord, they represent the sum of the four cosmic trees and the directions of the universe. "The flower tree stands in Tamoanchan, God's home . . . God, Life-Giver whirls us four times in Tamoanchan" (*CM*, f. 15r; 1985: 176–77). The tree of Tamoanchan was also the tree that simultaneously united the sky and the earth so that life could exist but separated them so that life could continue. "O Son of God! It's you that have supported the sky, the earth!" (ibid., f. 63v; pp. 354–55).

In native representations of the cross Christ-Centeotl may also have been understood as the embodiment of the maize plant itself. Some early colonial native sources, however, suggest that within the emerging syncretic water-maize-fertility cult this role came to be attached to the Virgin Mary. On ff. 24v–25v of the native-authored *Santoral en mexicano,* for example, she is described as a "flower-food-tree" from God's "flower-food-field." Christ is her fruit, hung from the tree of life by its stalk (cited by Burkhart 1992: 103). In the seventeenth century the young maize shoot was referred to as *tonacacihuatl,* "Our Lady of Sustenance" (Ruiz de Alarcón 1984: 127). Invocations to the cross today echo these early sources. The cross is honored as "Our Most Holy Virgin" and "Our Revered Mother" (*tonantzin*) as "Our Lady of the Earth We Sow" but also as "Tree of Sustenance" (*tonacaquahuitl*) and "The Holy Cross of Our Sustenance" (Broda 2001: 196).[115] Unsurprisingly, many more variants occur, although their underlying concepts still embrace a number of the points raised by the foregoing analyses. In general, however, the cross is understood to be both male and female, thereby echoing prehispanic conceptualizations of the earth (ibid.) but also the hermaphroditic nature of the maize plant itself and the gender changes undergone by the entities associated with its growth cycles. Thus "Our Lady of the Earth We Sow" also becomes "Our Lord of the Earth We Sow" and "Our Revered Father" (*totatzin*) (ibid., pp. 196–97; Good Eshelman 2001: 293). The cross today nevertheless also still has strong associations with water because it is attributed with the power to attract rain and protect crops (Broda 2001: 197). As "Our Revered Fathers" (*totatatzitzihuan*), groups of crosses can refer to the ancestors in general or, significantly, to the sun (Broda 2001: 197; Good Eshelman 2001: 293).

While such varied notions in respect to the identity of the cross today directly reflect the diversity of evolution of Indo-Christian cult practices across geography and time, the appropriation of this major symbol of Christianity still shows itself to be far from orthodox. Crosses are attributed with special powers that relate almost exclusively to the temporal world and the necessities of those who still depend on its regenerative cycles. It seems clear that the symbolism of the cross never was wholly assimilated in accordance with the canons of the church. The carved stone crosses of sixteenth-century Indian Mexico do not represent Christian crosses with a few eccentric iconographic inserts that mark their work as indigenous. Rather, they stand as native cosmic trees with Christian iconographic inserts. They are the cosmic trees of Indo-Christianity, graphically "edited" and "updated" to express the incorporation of Christianity and its referents within what was still perceived to be and had to remain the Indian sacred.

CHAPTER SEVEN

Framing the Sacred

The framing rituals of the pre- and postconquest eras focused on summoning the sacred to the ritual arena by emulating its being through song, dance, and the manipulation of artifacts, especially flowers and vegetation. The "being" of the sacred was conceived in terms of its multiple divine forces (the teteo) and the combined impact of their actions on the native world; to employ the eloquent terminology of Inga Clendinnen (1991: 215), it was the "exemplary text" that the sacred wrote on the world. Wrought by the hand of the "divine painter" (ibid.), the exemplary text embodied the essence and the source of life, on which (through its continued renewal) the perpetuity of humankind depended. In uniting the internal dynamics of such "paradisiacal" worlds as Tlalocan-Tamoanchan and Tonatiuh Ilhuicac—even, to a degree, Mictlan, where the first sweet-smelling flowers were born—the sacred and its text took the form of a beautiful realm with flowers, trees, and vegetation, nectar-sipping birds and butterflies, and abundant water. This is what the framing rituals sought to write, as the exemplary text embodied.

The nature of the native sacred was such that the protracted efforts of the evangelization body to convert it into the Christian sacred could only flounder. The native peoples can have perceived little equivalence between the native sacred and the ideals of the Christian heaven or its promised glory. The native sacred was a place of beauty in the making, as opposed to beauty made: its elite residents worked with Life-Giver to negotiate everlasting but mortal deliverance from earthly suffering. The sacred was also an entity that mortals could and should enter, as it entered them, in order to know and acknowledge its ways.

The mode of flowery song that underpins the major part of the Nahuatl devotional texts, principally the *Cantares mexicanos* and *Romances de los Señores de la Nueva España*, can be defined by the dual Nahuatl metaphor *in xochitl in cuicatl* ("flower and song," signifying sacred words). Written down in alphabetical script in the second half of the sixteenth century, these flowery verses are littered with directions for drum cadences, suggesting that they were also performed through dance. Hence they are undoubtedly the same songs that accompanied the framing rituals of old. In Christian times songs of the same genre were composed to "frame" major Christian festivals.[1] Others, also in honor of the Christian god and his followers, were reworked from prehispanic originals, although the identity of their entourage (the flowers, the birds) remained unchanged. Rather like the landscaped mural paintings, this particular process of "editing" may have been an attempt not to remove the unacceptable but to give expression to the (also reworked) Indo-Christian sacred.

The flower-songs are more than just examples of a native literary genre, however.

Even though the precise meaning of their densely layered, metaphorical lyricism still eludes us, it is evident that at the level of verbal texture the flower-songs are also performances of framing rituals in their own right. That is, if the flower-songs served to enhance those rituals through the provision of sacred words (to be voiced through song and dance) they were also choreographed texts of the same rituals—in other words, they were also reenactments of the exemplary text.

The poets likened the act of composing and singing sacred songs to the act of painting flowers: "You're regaled with flowers: these songs that I, the singer, lift for you [Life-Giver] beside the drum are painted as flowers" (*CM*, f. 21v; 1985: 200–201). "My singer's heart is a multitude of flowers, a multitude of paintings. Yes, I'm setting free my songs" (ibid., f. 64v; pp. 358–59). The process was also like smelting or carving: "What I'm smelting is as gold: I'm carving our good songs as jades" (ibid., f. 15r; pp. 176–77). In this the poets attempt to emulate Life-Giver—the divine painter—as he writes his sacred text on the world: "With flowers he is making paintings, he, Life Giver" (ibid., f. 30r; pp. 230–31). "The flowers, Life Giver's words, are dispersed: they shower down on Anahuac. . . . The world is in Your hands. It is really You who utter them, O Life Giver" (ibid., f. 29v; pp. 228–29). And, as Life-Giver draws near, he receives his reciprocated songs: "Life Giver! . . . Your heart is pleasured, it imbibes the painted flowers. Songs are painted!" (ibid., pp. 206–207).

In the flower-songs the act of crafting or painting songs and singing flowers does not allude to the act of writing sacred songs in the glyphic mode. Rather, it anticipates the ritualization of their performance or the conjuring of flowers as they emulate the being and abode of the sacred: flower plaza, flower court, the green place, the place of rain; the cavern house of flowers and of colors, the house of pictures.[2] Like the participants in the flower rituals, the poets' words manipulate the dew-laden, flamelike, fragrant, beautiful flowers so that they descend, entwining, spreading, drizzling, sprinkling, and blossoming their way between and over the songs' lines and verses. They whirl, spin, and burn, intoxicating the songs with delirium-producing perfume and mind-altering narcotics: "From Flower Place come all the whirling flowers that make hearts spin. They themselves come scattering, come strewing flowers, whirled ones, narcotic flowers" (ibid., f. 11v, pp. 166–67).

The flowers named in these exhilarating verses correspond well with the flowers preferred by the native world for their beauty, fragrance, and other properties. Almost always paired, the densely scented cacahuaxochitl and izquixochitl make constant appearances (ibid., ff. 14v, 19r; pp. 176–77, 190–91; *RSNE* 1964: 27, 29, 53), together with Tlalocan's own flower, the cempoalxochitl (*CM*, f. 14r; pp. 174–75), and the exquisite eloxochitl and yolloxochitl (*CM*, ff. 13v, 18r; 1985: 172–73, 188–89). Psychoactive varieties include the whirling crimson huacalxochitl (*CM*, ff. 51r, 79v; pp. 306–307, 410–41) and the narcotic poyomatli (ibid., ff. 10v, 30v; pp. 162–63, 230–31, et passim), which is the calyx of the aromatic cacahuaxochitl. The frequent pairing of the pleasant but innocuous izquixochitl, "popcorn flower," with the sweet-scented but intoxicating cacahuaxochitl might also suggest that the izquixochitl is in some way weaving its own mind-altering qualities into the ritualized poetics of the songs.[3]

Amid the poetical flower-frenzy, birds of precious plumage and precious song also wing or perch or spread flowers; butterflies sing and soar. Flowers and flyers then merge as single entities, a literary strategy that underscores the tremendous and awesome forging of new life. Flowers, we recall, symbolized the essence of life; as a manifestation of Life-Giver (see Brotherston 1992: 319), the thirteen precious quecholtin symbolized its source.[4] To reinforce this understanding even further, the poets consistently tinged their poetic elements with blue and red (or tones thereof), the chromatic metaphor for the source of life and the ritual coloring of the sacred thirteen.[5] Divine turquoise and roseate birds in tandem abound (CM, ff. 1r, 17v, 19r, 22v, 28r; 1985: 186–87, 190–91, 204–205, 222–23, et passim), but also cross-matches of blue and red flower-birds: "Let there be turquoise-*quecholli* flowers, roseate-*quecholli* flowers" (ibid., ff. 35v, 53r; pp. 248–49, 314–15).[6] The frequent pairing of the blue and the red in the same line or verse to paint other counterposing elements again serves to imbue the songs with the colors of life. For example, a roseate-quecholli lord calls out to turquoise-quecholli and green-corn birds; Life-Giver descends as a turquoise-quecholli while crimson milk-corn ears blossom; and a red-crowned parrot sits in a cherry tree of turquoise quecholli (ibid., ff. 20r, 50r; 1985: 164–65, 194–95, 300–303). The mutated teteo of Indo-Christianity are not excluded: the Virgin Mary's house is filled with turquoise bracelet gems, while prayers raised to her are like red-stone plumes (ibid., f. 38r; pp. 256–57).

Gold (or golden) is often evoked, contextually associated with corn tassels, milky kernels, and the flowery tree of sustenance (ibid., ff. 3r, 12r, 20r; pp. 138–39, 168–69, 194–95) in so many cases that it can be read as maize. Elsewhere it must also metaphorically invoke the sun as the force that, in conjunction with water (blue) and earth (red), is also a source of life. Thus the blue and the crimson mix on the palette of the divine painter to produce the golden sustenance of life and its source: "These songs of Yours: I heap them up as jades. I heap them up as bracelets, gold and scarlet" (ibid., f. 34v; pp. 244–45). "Let's go gently to God Jesucristo. We'll gaze upon him in that golden hut, we'll give him jade rosary jewels. He gleams incarnadine like a roseate-*quecholli*" (ibid., f. 37v; pp. 254–57). As the poets painted their flowery songs and sang their painted flowers, they knew themselves to be writing the text of the sacred in verse: in their exquisitely textured form these verses reenact the abode of the sacred, emulate its being, and, like Life-Giver's own songs, recite it in colors (ibid., f. 69v; pp. 376–77).

Although they are preserved today in alphabetical script, the source of the flower-songs was probably the still active native oral tradition. We can be fairly sure, however, that in the prehispanic era the songs were also inscribed "in books," "on paper" (FC3, 1978: 67; Hernández 2000: 69), which themselves were understood to sing (fig. 7.1). Nevertheless, our comparatively limited knowledge (in terms of what has not survived) of prehispanic literary genres makes it extremely difficult to assess what these texts might have looked like. Flower-tipped or flower-laden speech scrolls denoting sacred song were certainly part of tlacuilolli's iconic conventions (fig. 7.2), and from very early times (see fig. 1.2), although these examples might denote that flowery words are being spoken or sung rather than textualizing the "lyrics" of the songs themselves. Codex Borbonicus 28 (fig. 7.3) depicts three figures dancing before gigantic self-supporting flower chains—perhaps a "gathering together" (*xochimamani*) of the flowers (*RSNE* 1964: 18, 37).[7] That image and the image of Xochiquetzal's descent on a blue and red flower-rope on Codex Ríos 7r are possibly the nearest we can get to the iconic words of a flower-song today. Alternatively, of course, the flowery mode of the songs may have been accommodated by a series of prompts or glyphic inventories, with actual expression left to the interpretation of those who sang and danced them (León-Portilla 1986b: 125; Lockhart 1992: 393).

Figure 7.1. The singer and his songbook (Florentine Codex, Book 10). Note that it is the songbook that is represented as singing.

Figure 7.2. Sacred flower-song (Codex Borbonicus 4).

In the colonial era the flower-songs did, nevertheless, lend themselves to pictographic representation, specifically and appropriately in the literal and metaphorical "house of paintings" that was the abode of the Indo-Christian sacred. If the songs were painted in performance to invoke the sacred before the replica patron-mountain (the cavern house, water palace, and place of rain that was the Indo-Christian church) they were also given voice within the churches. As proposed in chapter 6, colonial native artisans did not "decorate" Christian architecture any more than they "illustrated" Indo-Christianity in paint and stone. They were not artists but scribes; in addition, "decoration" was not a part of their discourse. Elements that we today refer to as "formal decoration" in paint and in stone (on portals, windows, and walls, ceilings and vaulting given over to floral designs, and the ubiquitous grotesque) were also framing rituals in performance. They framed the entities of the Indo-Christian sacred within.

As in their role as timekeepers for the feasts and prefestival preparations for the Indians' framing rituals, the (so often flowery) counts of the native calendar open the reenactment: they self-enumerate around portals and windows and permutate across cornices and up and down doorjambs. First observed by Robert J. Mullen (1983: 51–52) at the Mixteca Alta site of Santa María Tiltepec, the phenomenon of the counts of the native calendars injected into the formal decoration of the churches is in fact so common as to constitute a strong diagnostic of native-executed artwork, especially in the medium of sculpture.[8] With only the occasional motif that can be identified as a native sign or symbol set (the chalchihuitl, the xonecuilli), together with stylized flowers of uncertain identity, most of the counts are computed using European decorative motifs (coffers, Isabelline "pearls," rosettes, lilies, medallions, etc.). Some examples are fairly basic in that they are restricted to numerically asymmetrical arrangements of decorative motifs (on paired doorjambs, 6 + 5, the sky phases of the zodiac, or 6 + 7, the constituent numbers of the day count, for example). Others on arches or cornices also adhere to the same pattern or play with two or more motifs arranged in sequences that permit simple mathematical permutations. Still others are highly complex, offering possible computations of sidereal and synodic cycles of the planets, cast and counterbalanced as days/years in conjunction with the 260- and 360-day combined system. It comes as little surprise, then, that the symmetry and "phrased spacing" common to mainstream European decorative arrangement of these same motifs is almost always lost in native renderings of them (McAndrew 1965: 200). Far from revealing an inability to grasp the design aesthetics of Europe, the "calendars" on the churches of Indian Mexico are simply another example of how native sculptors could manipulate European decoration into something meaningful.[9] The conjuring had commenced.

Neither painting nor sculpture lacks images of foodstuffs, although these are usually in the form of classical urns or bowls stuffed with fruits, again drawn directly from European sources. Curious, however, is the portal arch at Santa María Altipac (México), which lays out two symmetrical sequences of foodstuffs (pineapples, legume pods [?], fish, together with forklike eating implements), mixed—somewhat disconcertingly—with rabbits, lions, turtles or frogs, and what appear to be small leg bells.

Figure 7.3. Giant self-supporting flower chains invading the ritual arena (Codex Borbonicus 28).

Figure 7.4. The doorjambs of the monastery church of Los Santos Reyes Meztitlan, Hidalgo, carved with numerically adjusted foodstuffs: *a,* west; *b,* east (the church is aligned on a north-south axis).

Figure 7.5. The arch of the portal at San Agustín Acolman, México, bearing two tiers of ritual foodstuffs: *a,* in allusion to the ritual *xuchimitl,* the top of the inner tier offers the pierced heart of the Augustinian order on a platter; *b,* the offering of a roasted piglet is made at the top of the outer tier.

One European source, probably secondhand, was nevertheless manipulated into ritual offerings of the type that the Indians would make to the Indo-Christian sacred. The ornamental dishes of fruits across the arch of the main sacristy at Seville's cathedral (Valerie Fraser, pers. comm., 1989), where so many of the evangelizers would have prayed before embarking on their long journey, were seemingly transferred to the Augustinian constructions at Meztitlan and Acolman. Here carefully arranged individual platters of food (ranging from fish and fruit to meat) frame the church doorways (figs. 7.4, 7.5). At Meztitlan (where the monastery church faces south) the four platters on the west-side doorjamb offer, respectively, three fish, one apple (possibly a quince), four peachlike fruits, and five smaller fruits, which together total thirteen (fig. 7.4a). The east side also carries four platters: the three fish are there at the base of the jamb again, but the apple has become four pears (?) and the dishes of four and five items are reversed (fig. 7.4b). Here the sum is sixteen. Thus within the symmetry of 4 + 4 dishes the asymmetry of the counts already gives 29: the average number of days in one synodic lunar cycle.

Although damaged in places, the arch of the portal at Acolman is carved with two tiers of plates of food: one depicting small, saucerlike versions (mainly bearing a single item each) and the other showing large chargers with varied content (fig. 7.5a). Of note in this figure, on the first tier (top left), is the pierced heart of the Augustinian order, neatly centered on its plate. The detail of the plate suggests yet another reworked example at this site of Mayahuel's metaphorical *xuchimitl,* "flower/heart-arrow," a ritual offering in prehispanic times in the form of a steamed maize-dough ball (*tamalli*) pierced with an arrow (Sahagún 1981, 1:59). On a dish at the top of the second tier lies a piglet, together with at least one chile pepper and possibly a knife (fig. 7.5b). Although the pig was an imported animal and therefore not a traditional food offering, its presence nevertheless recalls the (live) piglets in arms offered in the church at Tlaxcala on Easter Sunday 1536 (Motolinía 1990: 58). Where still in place, the items of food on the platters of the second tier also invoke the primary numerals of the calendar (for example, 3, 4, 7, and 11).

Other traditional offerings may not be immediately obvious, such as at Molango and Calpan. At these sites the rhythmic repetition of S-shaped motifs (figs. 6.31, 7.6) brings to mind the *xonecuilli* (Reyes-Valerio 1978: 276–77, 2000: 336), the name of the seven-star constellation but also the S-shaped or "lightning"-shaped breads prepared as ritual food offerings (Sahagún 1981, 1:50). The winglike vegetal attachments at both these sites perhaps echo the butterfly-shaped versions of the breads also named *xonecuilli* (ibid.). Their occurrence at two sites so far from each other (and under the Augustinian and Franciscan orders, respectively) might well suggest a European source. But their extensive use at both points to the sculptors' strong interest in them as a motif.

Figure 7.6. S-shaped *xonecuilli* surrounding the top of the northwest posa at San Andrés Calpan, Puebla.

Although placed under total prohibition by the evangelization body, ritual drunkenness and the ingestion of psychoactive substances were an essential part of rites to invoke the sacred, for they permitted it to enter the mind and heart in a dizzying explosion of color and light, sound and movement. Cautiously subtle references to the pulque cult and the sacred octli are (as we have seen) well represented in both sculpture and painting, in the form of rabbits, crescent moons, stylized maguey plants (or parts thereof), and the pierced heart of Mayahuel. Peterson's identification of fauna in the "garden murals" at Malinalco also yielded a tlacuatl (Peterson 1993: 102–3), the Mexican tree opossum associated with the pulque cult; a deer (ibid., pp. 106–108), a companion of Tlaloc, who imbibed the sacred drink; and more rabbits (ibid., pp.

Figure 7.7. An example of the way in which the native calendar dictates the "formal" decoration of the churches: the portal arch at Asunción Chiconcuac, Hidalgo, whose flowers and petals inscribe the 203 + 1 intervals of days associated with the pulque cult; *(inset)* the headfirst rabbit at Chiconcuac falling away from the count to cast it at precisely 203.

108–109). Finally, as might be expected, the ritual counts again come into play. The day count 203, the equivalent of 7 synodic lunar cycles (7 x 29 days), which was directly associated with the cult,[10] appears often within the calendrical permutations created in decorative iconography. One of the most ingenious examples comes on the portal of the tiny church of Asunción Chiconcuac (Hidalgo), which carries 34 flowers and 1 additional motif distributed unevenly over 7 sections of masonry that make up the portal arch (fig. 7.7). Each flower has 6 petals (34 x 6 = 204). The additional motif represents an inverted rabbit or a headfirst rabbit seen to be "falling away" from the count, thereby reducing it to 203 (fig. 7.7 inset). The same count can also be reached by multiplying the 7 sections of the arch by "rabbit," which as "moon" invokes 29.

The presence of psychoactive flora on the churches was perhaps not obvious in native artwork either, especially for those who knew little of its uses or were unable to recognize it. Stylization and Europeans' view of floral representations as ornamental must also have helped such references to remain unnoticed. Some of the examples seen on the churches do find close parallels with floral designs used in European book art of the day,[11] but this cannot automatically be attributed to straight or meaningless copying. The category of "convergence" of native and European motifs to which both Kubler (1964: 20–22) and Peterson (1993: 7–8) allude must also allow for differences in interpretation at a cultural level, not to mention the issue of what is decorative and what is meaningful. A European decorative motif is more likely to have a denotative or connotative meaning in the native world than the other way round. In addition, a European stylization of a specific flower would vary considerably from a native rendering of the same flower, assuming also that the flower was native to both hemispheres. Thus if stylizations per se were copied from European sources it was because their appearance was meaningful to the native eye rather than because they were recognizable for what they were.

This might be the case of the floral configurations that resemble sliced mushroom caps. These appear on a series of embedded stones but also in the formal decoration of churches and other religious edifices. At Santa María Tiltepec they make up a frieze of alternating flowers and caps along the base of the church facade (fig. 7.8a). Adorning the capitals and bases of the supporting pillars of the open chapel at Santa María

Figure 7.8. Configurations of "mushroom" flowers taking up their place in the framing ritual: *a*, across the base of the facade of Santa María Tiltepec, Oaxaca; *b*, at the base of the pillars of the open chapel at Santa María Tepeyanco, Tlaxcala.

a

b

Figure 7.9. Toadstool caps or possibly unopened buds of *Solandra*: *a,* across the cornice of the monastery church of Natividad de Nuestra Señora Tepoztlan, Morelos; *b,* on the doorjambs at Santos Simón y Judas Calpulalpan, Tlaxcala.

Figure 7.10. Mexica stone drum of Xochipilli-Macuilxochitl, with toadstool caps or *Solandra* buds on the deity's "cheeks." Photo: © Michel Zabé/AZA

Tepeyanco (Tlaxcala) (fig. 7.8b), they also serve as a design at the center of the chapel's rib-vaulted ceiling. Compare these examples with the same configurations that appear on the pedestal, right forearm, and knees of the statue of Xochipilli (fig. 6.29). Together with other flowers,[12] the same "flower" also figured among the prehispanic petroglyphs at the ritual site of Cerro Cuailama, Santa Cruz Acalpixca (Heyden 1983), on the outskirts of Xochimilco. A similar motif, although with a spadelike form and often a short stem or stalk, outlines the cornice and entablature of the church portal at Natividad de Nuestra Señora Tepoztlan (Morelos) (fig. 7.9a) and alternates with an unidentified blossom around the original sixteenth-century portal at Santos Simón y Judas Calpulalpan (Tlaxcala) (fig. 7.9b). Reyes-Valerio (1978: 254, 2000: 311 and photo 105) found other examples on the arch springing of the open chapel at Tlaquiltenango (Morelos), where it is combined as a four-petaled floral configuration that sprouts thick stalks

a

b

Figure 7.11. The hallucinogenic poyomatli: *a,* monkeys dancing beneath its blossoms at the House of the Dean, Puebla; *b,* as the gift of angels on the facade of the monastery church of Santiago Tecali, Puebla.

Figure 7.12. The sinicuiche putting in another possible appearance on the north door at San Gabriel Cholula, Puebla.

and foliage. While this motif might have been available in a European source, near identical examples serve as the earplugs of Xochipilli-Macuilxochitl, whose face occupies the center of a Mexica stone drum (fig. 7.10). An elongated form of this particular motif is perhaps a more naturalistic rendering of the entheogenic toadstool, although as it appears on the statue of Xochipilli proper it may also represent the bud of the psychoactive *Solandra* blossom (González Chévez n.d.). Identical examples also serve as blossoms on a tree carved on the side of a Mexica stone box (Reyes-Valerio 2000: photo 104).

A species of *Solandra* (the *tecomaxochitl*) is also found at Malinalco, together with the morning glory (*ololiuhqui* or *tlililtzin*) (Peterson 1993: 91): "Comrades are . . . spinning down as white morning glories" (*CM*, f. 10; 1985: 162–63). If monkeys dance beneath the hallucinogenic poyomatli at the House of the Dean of Puebla cathedral (Gruzinski 1994: 164) (fig. 7.11a), the frescoed angels that still survive over the church portal at nearby Tecali seem to offer it to those that cross its threshold (fig. 7.11b). At Ixmiquilpan the same blossom grows from the tail of a golden, fish-scaled equine. As at Tlalmanalco (see fig. 6.28), the north door of the monastery church at Cholula perhaps proffers another example of the sinicuiche (fig. 7.12).

A permanent presence in framing rituals, as the chronicles and codices attest (figs. 1.4, 7.13a), the distinctive blossom of the narcotic huacalxochitl (basket flower) not only invaded later important ecclesiastical festivals (fig. 7.13b) but survives in paintings at Malinalco (Peterson 1993: 93) and in sculpture at Apasco and Oztoticpac (México) (fig. 7.14a–b). "Beware of being given *these*, these offered ones, these crimson basket flowers" (*CM*, f. 51r; 1985: 306–307; original emphasis). "Would that crimson basket flowers might come whirling" (ibid., f. 79v; pp. 410–11). The presence of this easily recognizable ritual flower (traditionally mixed with raw tobacco in the smoking tubes and an important symbol of fertility in its own right) on the churches says much about the projections of colonial native religious expression.[13]

In poetry (and perhaps in dance) the whirling of the huacalxochitl refers to the effects of this powerful hallucinogen on the mind and senses, which is equaled by the effects of toloatzin, the name given to various species of *Datura* that also "spin" as their flowers open (see fig. 1.7d). It is this subtler reference to the effects of psychotropic flowers that predominates on the walls

Figure 7.13. The psychoactive huacalxochitl, also a symbol of fertility, which makes regular contact with ritual dancers: *a,* Florentine Codex, Book 9; *b,* Codex Tlatelolco. (See also fig. 1.4.)

of churches, mainly in sculpture but also in some painted examples. From a single example at Santiago Anaya (Tlachichilco) (fig. 7.15a) to a series inserted into a cornice design (at San Juan Atocpa [D.F.], for example) or a drum-march of whirlers adorning the whole portal at Jilotzingo (México) (fig. 7.15b), Indo-Christian churches proclaim themselves to be the place where whirling flower mats spin (*CM*, f. 16r; 1985: 180–81) or where hearts are made drunk with flowers (ibid., f. 2v; pp. 138–39).

Portals and windows—whether outlined by a simple string of flowers or rich with writhing foliage, graceful birds, and exotic blossoms (figs. 7.16, 7.17, 7.18, 7.19, 7.20)

Figure 7.14. The huacalxochitl in Indo-Christian sculpture: *a,* the chancel arch, San Francisco Apasco, México; *b,* cloister window, Oztoticpac, México.

a

b

Figure 7.15. Whirling flowers in Indo-Christian sculpture: *a,* the doorjambs at Santiago Anaya (Tlachichilco), Hidalgo; *b,* the church portal at Jilotzingo, México.

or choirs of Indian angels (figs. 6.31, 6.32)—draw us still nearer to the place of the Indo-Christian sacred. Within, the painter-scribe's brush pursues the theme. Pink and crimson birds sip at seed- or dew-laden flowers (plate 17); turquoise and blue birds— sometimes from the same graphic nest—tread carefully through flowers and foliage, with their heads lowered as if searching for a flower-song (plates 18, 19). Others—like the turquoise-quecholli in a side chapel at Ixmiquilpan, now hybridized as a surging acanthus vine—capture the song and let it slide from their beaks. At Cuauhtinchan

Figure 7.16. The flowery church portal at Santa Mónica, Hidalgo.

several flyers display their exquisite plumage in the early painted garden of crimson, turquoise, and gold that lies behind the church's sixteenth-century retable: a turquoise-crested, turquoise-winged warbler with crimson legs and beak (plate 20a) seemingly in company with a golden oriole, one of those "yellow birds blackened about the eyes" (plate 20b), named residents of the home of the Sun (FC3, 1978: 49). Elsewhere "feather down butterflies" descend (plate 21): "And here upon earth they came to suck from all the various flowers" (ibid.).

The churches of Indian Mexico offer much to succor the flyers: flowers drip, drizzle, and rain down from mudéjar-inspired geometrics (fig. 7.21a) or from the tips and joints of the Late Gothic star motif (fig. 7.21b). They scatter across vaulting and spread over walls and ceilings (fig. 7.21c–e): "They've reached the top. Flowers have reached

Figure 7.17. The flowery and vegetal church portal at Santiago Tequixquiac, México.

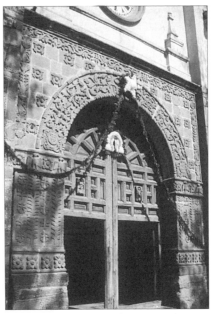

Figure 7.18. The flowery and vegetal church portal at Santa María Tulpetlac, México.

the top" (*CM*, f. 11r; 1985: 166–67). Some "dawn" in the rainy place of flowers (ibid., f. 6r; pp. 50–51) (fig. 7.22). Others, enigmatic in their turquoise and crimson petaling, hang from starry skies or stand alone (plate 22), poised as if waiting for the drums and their own blue and red painted songs to strike up.

These flowers do not wait in vain, for around them all is flower-painted song. Birds sing amid flowers and foliage but also sing flower and foliage songs (fig. 7.23). Even Old World centaurs croon blossoms that ooze nectar (plate 23) and scaled dragon-horses chant poyomatli (fig. 7.24a), while humans and leafy anthropomorphs intone other flowers (fig. 7.24b–c). At San Miguel Huejotzingo song was accompanied by flower-blaring trumpets (fig. 7.25a) and perhaps a harmonious bell tower, with its speech glyph–like architectural appendages (fig. 7.25b) (Angulo Iñiguez 1955). Clay pipes or whistles were embedded into the monastery church's rooftop merlons (Salazar Monroy 1944: 23; Lara 2004: 136). In catching the song of the wind as it heralds the onset of rain, at this site architecture itself anticipates the arrival of the sacred.

Figure 7.19. Detail of the tequitqui carved church portal at San Francisco Apasco, México, showing parrots and other creatures in rich foliage.

Figure 7.20. Detail of the flowery and vegetal, tequitqui carved church portal at San Martín Huaquechula, Puebla.

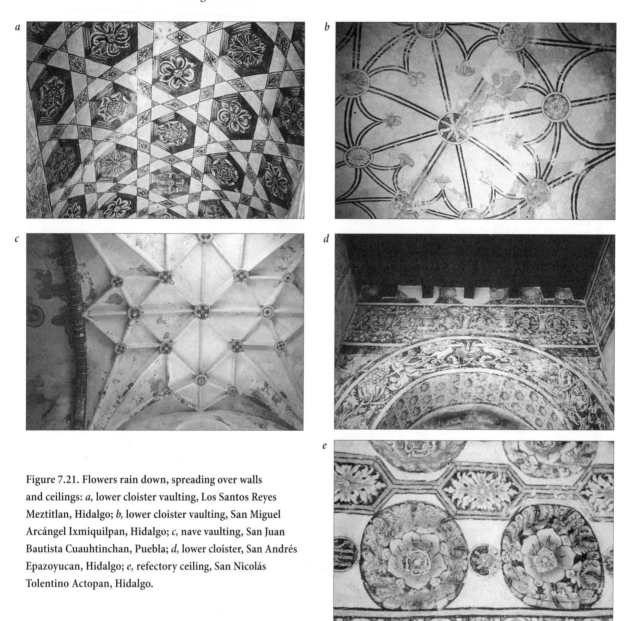

Figure 7.21. Flowers rain down, spreading over walls and ceilings: *a,* lower cloister vaulting, Los Santos Reyes Meztitlan, Hidalgo; *b,* lower cloister vaulting, San Miguel Arcángel Ixmiquilpan, Hidalgo; *c,* nave vaulting, San Juan Bautista Cuauhtinchan, Puebla; *d,* lower cloister, San Andrés Epazoyucan, Hidalgo; *e,* refectory ceiling, San Nicolás Tolentino Actopan, Hidalgo.

I strike it up. I beat the flower drum of Life Giver, and his paintings fall: these flowers. They blossom, they're spreading fragrance, they're scattering over the ground: these, God's turquoise pictures. And I offer them as well: these song marvels, these flowers. And in Your home they're strewn. . . . They're painted as pictures in Your house of crimson. (*CM*, f. 62v; 1985: 350–53)

In contrast to the flowing, melodic sequences of European linear ornament (see McAndrew 1965: 198–200), the painted and sculpted song of the Indo-Christian sacred also moves rhythmically, repetitively, and spasmodically, like a "staccato tom-tom beat" (ibid.). Abrupt changes in rhythm sometimes occur as sculpted forms step from one architectural element to another (fig. 7.26a); at other times they beat on, side by side, as if emulating overlapping cadences issuing from two or more drums (fig. 7.26b). To sustain an idea put forward by McAndrew (ibid., p. 187), the "reiterated ornamental stereotypes" that characterize both prehispanic and Indo-Christian architectural sculpture seem to have much to do with the "reiterated ritual" that took place in front of it:

Toco-toco-toti
Titico-titico-titico[14]

Figure 7.22. Flowers "dawn" in the upper cloister at San Miguel Arcángel Ixmiquilpan, Hidalgo.

Complementing those of the celebrants and those of the poets, these, then, are the churches' framing rituals. The direct parallels among the three forms of native expression reinforce the conceptual understanding of the relationship between writing the image and performing or ritualizing it. Flowers were sung—painted and crafted—in the framing rituals to reenact the exemplary text and summon its divine author to the ritual arena. They were carved and painted by the poets as the same floral frenzies—the same floral reenactments—to energize their dynamic verses in invocation of the sacred and as manifestations of its being. And they were carved and painted as framing rituals in performance on the walls of churches and related architecture where, again, they evoked and invoked the Indo-Christian sacred.

Other iconographic details support my interpretations. Peterson's close and cogent analysis of the "garden murals" at Malinalco (Peterson 1993) leads me to suggest that in a second reading (or possibly a partial reading—see below) these murals are also an excellent example of a flower-song in performance. Considerably more frenetic in

Figure 7.23. Birds sing flowery and leafy songs: *a,* monastery entrance, Santa María Guadalupe Tacubaya, D.F.; *b,* chancel arch, San Francisco Apasco, México.

Figure 7.24. Humans and leafy anthropomorphs sing flowers: *a,* south wall of the monastery church, San Miguel Arcángel Ixmiquilpan, Hidalgo; *b,* lower cloister, San Agustín Acolman, México; *c,* lower cloister, San Miguel Arcángel Ixmiquilpan, Hidalgo.

movement than the European garden tapestries to which she compares them, they are charged with the same native flora and bird species that sing their way through the devotional songs.[15] The inserts of traditionally executed flanged speech scrolls, which read as *cuicatl,* "song" (Peterson 1993: 47–49), are instructive in this respect, as are the red tinted Latin inscriptions on the upper walls and blue inserts into the vegetation covering the cloister vaulting—the same chromatic metaphors that pervade the song poems. Indeed, as Peterson observes, many of the Malinalco song scrolls are divided

Figure 7.25. The musical accompaniment at San Miguel Huejotzingo, Puebla: *a,* trumpets play flowery notes, northwest posa; *b,* the church bell tower "speaks" its pealing words.

Figure 7.26. Church walls resounding with the rhythm of drums: *a,* portal and alfiz, Santa María de la Encarnación Zacualtipan, Hidalgo; *b,* portal, San Francisco Tlanalapa, Hidalgo.

into eight sections, thereby strongly recalling the eight paired-verse sequences that characterize Nahuatl song-poems (ibid., p. 49). Although the wall murals run continuously, it is perhaps no coincidence that the vault sections, painted by a different and more traditional hand (ibid., pp. 35, 39), number sixteen,[16] arguing for a performance of two flowery songs or a repeated rendering of one.

One of the song glyphs at Malinalco carries the "day" or "feast" sign *ilhuitl,* composed of two inverted, diagonal hooks; it is accompanied by a *cillin* (small spiral shell) with two dots and a flower (Peterson 1993: 47–49) (fig. 7.27). Through comparison with more "traditional" examples, Peterson links the ilhuitl sign to the singer or music-maker and to the scribe (figs. 7.2, 7.28),[17] noting that the Malinalco frescoes may well be the first known instance in which a tlacuilo leaves the sign of his profession (ibid.). Could it not also designate the murals as the scribe's painted flower-song? As it appears on f. 43r of Codex Mendoza, the toponym of Cuicatlan, "Place of Song," in Oaxaca consists of a song scroll (also flanged) that includes the ilhuitl sign, the flower, and possibly two shells. On f. 30r of Codex Telleri-ano-Remensis a female "painter" (attached to the Aztec ruler Huitzilihuitl by a cord qualified by a flower) writes on a boxlike element marked with the ilhuitl sign and a flower. Due to glossators' corrections and apparent confusion, this and the preceding folio have defied any definitive reading to date (see Quiñones Keber 1995: 212–14). But, whether or not she is the spouse of Huitzilihuitl, as the gloss states, the female "painter" is perhaps here depicted as the re-corder of the Aztec ruler's flower-songs.[18]

Figure 7.27. The painted song scroll at Purificación y San Simón Malinalco, Morelos (redrawn after Peterson 1993).

Figure 7.28. The painter-scribe (Codex Mendoza f. 70r) (redrawn after Peterson 1993).

In addition to the painted Malinalco example, the glyphic ensemble of the ilhuitl sign, a flower, and two shells appears on the facades of San Mateo Xoloc (México) (fig. 7.29) and Santa Cecilia Atlixco (Puebla) (fig. 7.30a).[19] At Xoloc they lie beneath the relief carvings of Saints Peter and Paul that flank the church portal. At Atlixco the ilhuitl alternates with whirling flowers at the base of the northside portal jamb. The cillin glyphs seem to have been "upgraded" in honor of Saint Cecilia, who is appropriately enough the patron saint of music (Hall 1979: 60–61) and to whom the monastery complex was dedicated. The pair were divided, however, possibly to give two glyphic readings of *Ce-cil*[*lin*] ("one-shell," which sounds like Cecili[a]), and placed (again perhaps not coincidentally) at either side of the choir loft window (fig. 7.30b). Rare as these carved details might be today, as at Malinalco there is a sense that the sculptors responsible for them were indeed labeling their churches as houses of flower and song.

Edgerton (2001: 179, 211) observes that the floral friezes that often frame thematic murals recall not only the tapestries and carpets hung over balconies during European religious festivals but also the flowery carpets and décor that came to characterize the Indians' outdoor processional and dance arenas. Flower carpets and décor (not to mention garlands, crowns, posies, and the flower-songs themselves) were also prehispanic traditions, of course, and the tapestries and carpets of Europe may not have been too common a feature in most Indian churches and monastery complexes. For the evangelization body, at least, the extensive mural programs had practical as well as didactic purposes. But the floral friezes drawn from imported sources nonetheless may have acquired a perceived relationship with other flowery activities, this time on the initiative of the Indians themselves.

Where ornamental friezes or panels occur, more often than not they contain other iconographic elements within their flowery or leafy arabesques: principally (but not necessarily simultaneously) medallions, classical urns, cherubs and putti, birds, animals, and mythical monsters. The basic design stencil of a typical grotesque panel or frieze usually consists of two identical assemblages of such elements: one inverted against the other to produce a mirrored configuration, which is then repeated over and over (figs. 7.11a, 7.31, plate 24). At a structural level this overall symmetry echoes the way in which the native peoples danced and sang en masse: "with uniformity of tone and movement, mind and body alike, without variance in voice or in step" (Mendieta 1973, 1: 51).[20] The friezes are also highly rhythmic in form visually and can be perceived, like drumbeats, to increase or decrease in "speed" in accordance with the width of the panel or its particular configuration. The repetition of an arabesque across a narrow frieze, for example, is perceptibly "faster" than across a wider version of the same design (fig. 7.32).

Figure 7.29. The church at San Mateo Xoloc, México, labeled as a place of song by its sculptor.

a

b

Figure 7.30. Santa Cecilia Atlixco, Puebla, was dedicated by the sculptor to flowery song and to Cecilia as patron saint of music: *a,* the ilhuitl and flower signs at the base of the northside doorjamb; *b,* one of two shells (cillin) on the upper facade of the church.

Wider friezes, framed above and below with narrow strips (see plate 24), produce a similar visual effect. In addition, they again recall a report on how the Indians danced. They joined hands in rings, one ring inside the other: "Everyone follows the time set by the leaders, save only the outer ranks, which, because they are so far away and so many, must dance twice as fast as the others" (Gómara 1964: 147–48).

The grotesque's own visually synchronized populations of humans, semihumans, flora and fauna, and other motifs also echo the costumes and accouterments of the participants of native dances. They dressed as eagles, "lions" and "tigers," monkeys and dogs, birds and bats (Durán 1984, 1:121, 193).[21] "They carried in one hand a small shield covered with the brightest plumage" (Clavijero 1991: 244);[22] and they danced (plate 24, fig. 7.33a). Sometimes trees laden with sweet-smelling flowers were fashioned and, "[w]hile they danced, boys dressed as birds, others as butterflies, would descend. They climbed these trees and passed from branch to branch, sucking the dew from those flowers" (Durán 1984, 1:193) (fig. 7.33b).[23] "On their ankles and wrists they wore gold bells" (ibid. p. 121).[24]

Returning to my thoughts on native perception of European decorative forms, particularly the grotesque, I am proposing that the flowery friezes that—literally—frame so many orthodox images from Christianity's story were often reworked as songs and

Figure 7.31. An example of a Mexican grotesque frieze, nave wall, San Francisco Tepeapulco, Hidalgo.

Figure 7.32. The narrower the frieze, the faster its perceived rhythm (author's reconstruction).

Figure 7.33. A painted song at the Hospital de Jesús, D.F.: *a,* dancing angels with "shields" and chorusing eagles; *b,* prehispanic leg bells.

dances in performance. As such, they also formed part of the framing rituals taking place on the walls of churches. Some may even choreograph specific dances. At the Hospital de Jesús (D.F.) the gracefully leaping angels and figures carrying backpacks full of fruit (fig. 7.33b) are in many ways reminiscent of the dancing angels and gourd-laden shepherds of an Epiphany play described by Antonio de Ciudad Real (1976, 2:101) at late-sixteenth-century Tlaxomulco. The walls of the church nave and cloister of the Augustinian monastery complex at Ixmiquilpan carry the text of at least one *otoncuicatl* (Otomi warrior song), performed in the flowery mode. Here prehispanic warriors of the Sun take on the task of Saint Michael the Archangel, Ixmiquilpan's patron, in routing evil from a mutated Christian heaven (Wake 1995, 2000). Follow-up work (Wake 2002, 2003) shows that the centaurs and scaly dragon-horses are humans in costume. This painted performance also embraces at least one change of rhythm, directed by the two arabesques that structure the battle narrative on the north and south walls, respectively. In addition, the source grotesques at the top of the nave walls (retained as a wider frieze encased in two narrower ones) choreograph *and* represent the circles of dancers that fan out from the main central performance (Wake 2002, 2003).

The use of color is a final—outstandingly consistent—feature of native-executed mural painting. Monochrome examples tinged with red are one important area, for they allude to the native *in tlilli in tlapalli,* "the black, the red," the chromatic metaphor for sacred knowledge as written down in the sacred books (see chapter 6). But, as I have argued, the dual chromatic metaphor for the source of life was blue and red. Usually associated with *atl tlachinolli,* "water and fire," the metaphor for war, *atl* and *tlachinolli* also name respectively the rainy and dry seasons of the agricultural cycle. In addition, their associated colors define the two vital fluids that course through the cosmos: water and blood. As Uto-Aztecan groups of the U.S. Southwest still liken their Spirit World to a beautiful landscape that can be invoked in song through the chromatic symbolism of colors such as blue and red (Hill 1992: 117–19), the blue and the red can also be understood as the colors of the Mesoamerican sacred.

Despite the availability of an extensive range of pigments, in the prehispanic world the use of these two colors together dominates native religious expression. It pervades the codices, especially to qualify representations of prehispanic architecture as replicas of the sacred patron-mountains (red) with their watery interiors (blue) and the deities that presided over them. It is matched in the mural paintings that covered the walls of those edifices from earliest times: Teotihuacan, Cacaxtla, the Great Temple of Tenochtitlan, and, further afield, at Bonampak and the tombs of Monte Alban, for example. It also colored the statues of the deities, architectural sculpture, and other artifacts.[25]

In colonial sixteenth-century Mexico the colors of Indo-Christianity were blue and red. They dominate surviving Testerian manuscripts from that period, such as Fray Pedro de Gante's catechism (Biblioteca Nacional, Madrid) or the *Pater Noster* in Egerton MS 2898 (British Museum, London). Many ecclesiastical artifacts in Codex Tlatelolco's pictorial narrative of the founding of Mexico City's cathedral were detailed in the same colors. Perceived as the Indo-Christian replicas of the sacred mountains, the churches were also very consistently represented in native mapping as blue and red places. The pattern persisted in the overall chromatic expression of native religious mural painting. In addition to those bearing details in red, some monochrome programs were instead tinged with blue and red (Malinalco, Actopan, Alfajayuca). And there appears to be no deviation in the choice of these two colors where programs were executed wholly in polychrome, as it now seems so many originally were.[26] Almost all exhibit turquoise-blue or red-brown backgrounds, with their principal motifs in contrasting red or blue. The use of other colors of course occurs, but the overall impact of such a concentration of blue and red is what immediately strikes the eye. Closer inspection shows that the same duality of colors also extends to small, seemingly unimportant iconographic details. Just as the subtly entwined references of the poets to the blue and the red adhere to our senses as we enter their verses, so too do the solitary, delicate, blue and red flowers at the entrance to the monastery at Meztitlan and over the church portal at Cuauhtinchan (plate 22). Like sentinels, they speak as glyphic morphemes of the nature of the place we are about to access: "This is the place of the blue and the red flowers; this is the place of the source of life."

The European sources were almost exclusively book prints in monochrome, so such consistency of color can only be attributed to native initiative. The members of the evangelization body could not have been responsible for this type of chromatic synchronization. But native painters with the concept of the text of the sacred in mind could. Across at least two generations and over a wide geographical area, they instinctively, or determinedly, painted Christianity in the colors and form of the Indian sacred. In doing so, they also knew themselves to be framing the Indo-Christian sacred as it was raised and sung.

> In song I cut great stones, paint massive beams, that this, in future time when I'm gone, shall be uttered, this my song-sign that I leave behind on earth. (*CM*, f. 27v; 1985: 220–21)

I offer no lengthy conclusions here, for I have endeavored from the outset to draw a series of discursive threads through this study of the religious art and architecture of the indigenous peoples of New Spain. These ultimately weave themselves into a single pattern. Christianity attempted to impose itself over a religious *system* born of the dynamics of cultural advancement and its cosmogonical explanation rather than doctrinal requirement. Instead assimilated (often with the unwitting assistance of the evangelizing body) into the defining parameters of that system, Christianity's forms of visual expression were also subjected to reinterpretation as a result of indigenous cultural perception and address. In native expression, the ritualization of the image defined its forging, and its forging defined ritual. The image of Christianity was therefore not copied but read and rewritten, by author and audience alike, as empathic reenactments of an Indo-Christian sacred. The normally static and ponderous architecture of Christianity took up its place on a still-sacred landscape as a wholly functional apparatus within the Indian interpretation of that landscape. The churches were perceived as the living replicas of the landscape's most sacred features; therefore their orientation and architectural detail also came to coordinate Indian time and space, just as their own time and space were coordinated by the divinely imposed order of geography. In other words, within and without, that architecture was perceived as the precious life-giving image of the sacred and the text that the sacred wrote on the world. We might hear in the churches of sixteenth-century Indian Mexico the voice of a people in the process of great cultural and religious change. But we must at the same time acknowledge the ways in which those churches speak so emphatically of the continuity that accompanied that change. In the pursuit of continuity, the churches became—and in so many cases remain—the architectural and iconographical embodiment of the Indo-Christian sacred.

Churches, Chapels, Monastery Complexes, and Other Religious Buildings Visited by the Author (1991–2007)

State of Hidalgo

Acambay, San Miguel

Acatlan (Tulancingo), San Miguel

Acayuca

Acayutla, Santiago

Acelotla, San Francisco

Achichilco, San Juan

Acopinal, San Rafael Arcángel (hacienda)

Actopan, San Nicolás Tolentino

Ahuehuepan, Santa Ana

Ajacuba

Alfajayuca, San Martín

Amajac (Actopan), Santa María

Amiltepec, San Miguel

Apan

Atengo (Mixquiahuala)

Atitalaquia, San Miguel

Atotonilco de Tula, Santiago

Atotonilco el Chico, San Francisco

Atotonilco el Grande, San Agustín

Bathó, Santa María

Bella Vista (hacienda)

Casa Grande (Actopan), San José

Caxuxi (Actopan)

Cempoala, Todos Santos

Chapatongo, Santiago

Chicavasca (Actopan)

Chiconcuac, Asunción

Chilcuauhtla

Cuauhtepec (Tulancingo), San Antonio de Padua

El Durazno (Actopan)

Epazoyucan, San Andrés

Huaquilpan, San Pedro

Hueychiapan, San Mateo

Itzcuincuitlapilco

Ixmiquilpan, San Miguel Arcángel

Jala, San Antonio (hacienda)

Jaltepec, San Miguel

Juandhó

La Blanca (Actopan)

La Magdalena (Actopan)

Lolotla, Santa Catarina

Macúa (Tula), Santa María

Malpaís (hacienda)

El Mandhó, Santa Ana

Mangas

Mesquititlan, San Agustín

Meztitlan, La Comunidad

Meztitlan, Los Santos Reyes

Michimaloya, Guadalupe

Mixquiahuala, San Antonio de Padua

Molango, El Calvario

Molango, Nuestra Señora de Loreto

Munitepec

Ostoyuca, San Antonio

Pachuca, San Francisco

San Antonio (Actopan)

San Gabriel (Tepetitlan)

San Gabriel Azteca (Cempoala)

San Jerónimo (Actopan)

San Juan de Solís

San Salvador (Actopan)

Santa María Nativitas (Tulancingo)

Santa Mónica (Actopan)

Santa Mónica (Epazoyucan)

Singuilucan

Taliztacapa (Tula), San Marcos

Tecajete, Santa María

Tecajique, San Francisco

Tecomatlan, San Nicolás

Teltipan de Juárez

Temascalapa

Tenango (Mixquiahuala)

Tepa el Grande

Tepeapulco, San Francisco

Tepeitic (Mixquiahuala)

Tepemazalco, San Juan

Tepetitlan, San Bartolo

Tepeyahualco, Santiago

Tetepango, Asunción

Tetliztaca (Cempoala), Santo Tomás

Tetzahuapa, San Juan

Texcatepec

Tezontepec (Pachuca), San Pedro

Tezontepec de Aldama (Mixquiahuala)

Tezontlale, Santiago

Tizayuca, Nuestra Señora
  de Cosamaluapan

Tlachichilco, Santiago Anaya

Tlahuelilpa, San Francisco

Tlajomulco, Santiago

Tlamaco, San Gerónimo

Tlanalapa, San Francisco

Tlapacoya, Santiago

Tlaquilpan, San Pedro

Tlaxcoapan

Tlaxiaco, San Agustín

Tlilcuauhtla, San Juan

Tolcayuca

Tornacuxtla

Tula, San José

Tulancingo, San Francisco

Tunititlan

Ulapa, San Nicolás Tolentino

Venta la Cruz (hacienda)

Vixthá (Actopan)

Xochicoatlan, San Nicolás Tolentino

Xochihuacan (Cempoala)

Xochitlan (Tula), Asunción

Xoxoteco, Santa María

Zacacalco, San Francisco

Zacualtipan, Santa María
  de la Encarnación

Zapotlan (Cempoala), San Agustín

México, Distrito Federal

Acalpixca (Xochimilco), Santa Cruz

Ajusco, San Miguel

Ajusco, Santo Tomás

Atlapulco (Xochimilco), San Gregorio

Atocpa (Milpa Alta), San Juan Bautista

Atocpa (Milpa Alta), San Pedro

Atoyac, Santa Cruz

Azcapotzalco, Santos Felipe y Santiago

Aztacoalco, Santiago

Catedral Metropolitana

Churubusco, Nuestra Señora de los Angeles

Coyoacan, San Juan Bautista

Culhuacan, El Calvario

Culhuacan, San Juan Evangelista

Guadalupe, Villa de

Milpa Alta, Asunción

Mixcoac, Santa María Nonoalco

Mixquic, San Andrés

San Jacinto (San Angel)

Santo Domingo

Tacuba, San Gabriel

Tacubaya, Santa María Guadalupe
  (formerly San José)

Tecomitl (Xochimilco), Santa Ana

Tecospa (Milpa Alta), San Francisco

Tenayuca, San Bartolo

Tepalcatlalpan (Xochimilco), Santiago

Tepepan (Xochimilco), Asunción

Tlahuac, Santos Pedro y Pablo

Tlalnepantla, Corpus Christi

Tlalnepantla, Los Reyes (pueblo)

Tlalpan, San Agustín

Tlatelolco, Santiago

Xalpa (Xochimilco), San Mateo

Xochimanco (Xochimilco), San Lucas

Xochimilco, Asunción Colhuacaltzingo

Xochimilco, La Concepción

Xochimilco, Nuestra Señora de
  los Dolores Xaltocan

Xochimilco, San Antonio Moyotla

Xochimilco, San Bernadino

Xochimilco, San Esteban

Xochimilco, San Francisco Caltongo

Xochimilco, San Juan Tlaltentli

Xochimilco, San Marcos

Xochimilco, San Pedro Tlalnahuac

Xochimilco, Santa Cruz Analco

Xochimilco, Santísima Trinidad

Xochitepec (Xochimilco), Santa Cruz

Zacapa (Xochimilco), Nativitas

State of México

Acatlan (Naucalpan), Santa Cruz

Acolman, El Calvario

Acolman, San Agustín

Acolman, Santa Caterina

Acuitlapilco, San Mateo

Altipac, Santa María

Amecameca, Asunción

Apasco, San Francisco

Atlacomulco

Atlatongo, San Miguel

Chicoloapan

Chiconauhtla, Santa María

Chiconauhtla, Santo Tomás

Chimalhuacan (Atenco), Santo Domingo

Chimalhuacan (Chalco),
    San Vicente Ferrer

Coatepec (Chalco), Natividad
    de Santa María

Coatlinchan, San Miguel

Cuauhtitlan, San Buenaventura

Hueypuxtla

Huizquilucan, San Antonio

Jilotzingo, San Marcos

Jocotitlan

Mazapa (Teotihuacan), San Francisco

Nopaltepec

Occipaco (Naucalpan), Santiago

Otumba, La Concepción

Oxtoticpac

Teotihuacan, San Juan

Teotitlan, San Felipe

Tepexpa (Toluca), Santa Cruz

Tequixquiac, Santiago

Tlacoyuca, San Lorenzo

Tlahuac, Santos

Tlalmanalco, San Luis Obispo

Tlapanaloya, Asunción

Totolinga (Naucalpan), San Lorenzo

Totoltepec (Naucalpan), San Juan Bautista

Tulpetlac, Santa María

Tultitlan, San Lorenzo

Tulyhualco, Santiago

Xolco, San Miguel

Xoloc, San Lucás

Xoloc, San Mateo

State of Morelos

Acapixtla, San Juan Bautista

Amatlan, Santa María Magdalena

Atlatlauhca, La Concepción

Cuernavaca (Capilla de los Indios
  de Tamoanchan)

Ocuituco, Santiago

Tepoztlan, Natividad de Nuestra Señora

Tepoztlan, San Miguel

Tetela del Volcán

Tlayacapa, San Juan Bautista

Totolapa, San Guillermo

State of Oaxaca

Apoala, Santiago

Chacalaca, San Isidro

Chicahua, San Miguel

Chongo, San Miguel

Coixtlahuaca, San Juan Bautista

Cuilapan, Santiago

Jaltepec, Santa María Magdalena

Nochistlan, Asunción

Oaxaca, Catedral Metropolitana

Oaxaca, Santo Domingo

Suchixtlahuaca, San Cristóbal

Tejupa, Santiago

Teposcolula, Santos Pedro y Pablo

Tilantongo, Santiago

Tiltepec, Santa María

Topiltepec, San Pedro

Xadani, Asunción

Yanhuitlan, Santo Domingo

Zaachila, Natividad de Santa María

State of Puebla

Atlixco, Santa Cecilia

Calpan, San Andrés

Cholula, Capilla Real

Cholula, Nuestra Señora de los Remedios

Cholula, San Andrés

Cholula, San Gabriel

Cholula, San Juan Calvario

Cholula, San Miguel Tecpan

Cholula, San Miguel Tianguinahual

Cholula, San Pablo Tecma

Cholula, San Pedro Apóstol

Cholula, Santa María Xixitla

Cholula, Santiago Mixquitla

Cuanalá, San Mateo

Cuauhtinchan (parish church)

Cuauhtinchan, San Juan Bautista

Huaquechula, San Martín

Huauchinango, San Agustín

Huejotzingo (parish church)

Huejotzingo, San Miguel Arcángel

Ixtiyuca, Santa María

Nopaluca

Ometoxtla, San Garbiel [sic]

Puebla, Casa del Deán

Puebla, Catedral Metropolitana

Puebla, San Francisco

Tecali, Santiago

Tecamachalco, Asunción

Tepeaca, San Francisco

Tepeji, Santo Domingo

Texmelucan, San Martín

Tianguismanalco, San Juan Bautista

Tlalancaleca, San Matías

Tochimilco, Santa María

Totomiahuacan (parish church)

Totomiahuacan, San Francisco

State of Tlaxcala

Atlahapa, San Sebastián

Atlihuetzia, Concepción

Ayometla, Santa Catarina

Calpulalpan, Santos Simón y Judas

Chiauhtempan, Santa Ana

Cuauhtotoatla, San Pablo (del Monte)

Ocotelulco, San Francisco

Ocotelulco, San Pedro Tecpan

Panotla, San Nicolás

Tenancingo, San Miguel

Tepetomatitlan, San Matías

Tepeyanco, Santa María

Tizatlan, San Esteban

Tlatelulco, La Magdalena

Tlaxcala, Asunción

Tlaxcala, San José

Totolac, Los Reyes

Yancuitlalpan, Santa María Nativitas

Sample of Native Maps and Their Representations of Churches Cited in Chapter 4

Map	Date	Archive/Source
Acambaro (Guanajuato)	1580	RAH 9254/4663-x
Acapixtla (Morelos)	1580	UTX JGI xxiii-8
Almolonca/Maxtlatlan (Veracruz)	1572	AGN 1561
Amoltepec (Oaxaca)	1580	UTX JGI xxv-3
Atlatlauhca/Suchiaca (México)	1580	UTX JGI xxiii-13
Atlatlauhca/Malinaltepeque (Oaxaca)	1580	RAH 9254/4663-xxvi
Cempoala (Hidalgo)	1580	UTX JGI xxv-10
Cempoala/Santa Clara (Hidalgo)	1590	AGN 2152
Cholula (Puebla)	1581	UTX JGI xxiv-1
Coatlinchan (México) [A]	1578	AGN 1678
Coatlinchan (México) [B]	1578	AGN 1679
Cuahuitlan (Oaxaca)	1580	RAH 9254/4663-xxxi
Cuauhtinchan (Puebla), Mapa 4	1563	MNAH
Culhuacan (D.F)	1580	UTX JGI xxiii-14
Cuzcatlan (Puebla)	1580	AGI 19
Epazoyucan (Hidalgo)	1580	UTX JGI xxv-10
Huapalteopan (México)	ca. 1580	AGN 1532
Huaxtepec (Morelos)	1580	UTX JGI xxiv-3
Huejutla (Hidalgo)	1580	AGI 16
Itztapalapa (D.F.)	1580	UTX JGI xxiv-8
Jocotitlan/Atlacomulco (México)	1591	AGN 1235
Macupilco (1579 Suchitepec group) (Oaxaca)	1579	AGI 25
Mixtepec/Chicaguastla (Oaxaca)	ca. 1595	AGN 867
Nativitas/San Antonio (Hidalgo)	1602	AGN 646
Nochistlan (Oaxaca)	1581	RAH 9254/4663-xxxiii
Nochistlan Valley (Oaxaca)	1602	AGN 1082

Nopaluca/Ixtiyuca (Puebla)	1595	AGN 2149
Plano en Papel de Maguey	1558	MNAH
San Jerónimo Satetlan (México)	1559	AGN 594
San Luis de las Peras (México)	1556	AGN 1197
San Pedro Rosal (México)	ca. 1559	AGN Tierras 1871
Suchitepec (Oaxaca)	1579	AGI 29
Tejupa (Oaxaca)	1579	RAH 9254/4663-xvii
Teotenango (México)	1582	AGI 33
Teozacualco (Oaxaca)	1580	UTX JGI xxv-3
Tetliztaca (Hidalgo)	1580	UTX JGI xxv-12
Tezontepec, Mixquiahuala (Hidalgo)	1571	AGN 1240
Tlacotepec (1579 Suchitepec group) (Oaxaca)	1579	AGI 28
Tlahuelilpa (Hidalgo)	1569	AGN 1147
Tlamacazcatepec (1579 Suchitepec group) (Oaxaca)	1579	AGI 26
Tornacuxtla (Hidalgo)	ca. 1599	AGN 590
Zozopaztepec (1579 Suchitepec group) (Oaxaca)	1579	AGI 27
Zumpango, Minas de (Guerrero)	1582	RAH 9254/4663-xxxvi

Key to holding institutions: AGI (Archivo General de Indias, Seville, Maps and Plans); AGN (Archivo General de la Nación, Mexico City, Catalogue of Maps); RAH (Real Academia de la Historia, Madrid); MNAH (Museo Nacional de Antropología e Historia, Mexico City); UTX (Benson Latin American Collection, University of Texas–Austin).

Notes

INTRODUCTION

1. Authority came from the Spanish Crown by way of the 1508 *Patronato Real,* which gave the Crown special privileges in respect to the establishment of the Catholic Church in America. By special dispensation, members of these three orders elected to work in the New World were also permitted to act as parish priests (cf. Kubler 1992: 14).

2. See principally Cuevas 1946, Ricard 1994, and Borges 1960 on the conversion and Moreno Villa 1986, Kubler 1992, and Toussaint 1982 on art and architecture.

3. See the works of Elizabeth Hill Boone, Gordon Brotherston, Serge Gruzinski, Robert Haskett, Dana Leibsohn, Miguel León-Portilla, James Lockhart, Luis Reyes García, and Stephanie Wood, among many who have made great inroads into these areas.

4. See especially the work of Louise M. Burkhart, Inga Clendinnen, and J. Jorge Klor de Alva.

5. See also Reyes-Valerio 1967a, 1967b, 1967c, 1968, 1970, 1989a, 1989b.

6. Lara's (2008) follow-up work on this theme arrived too late to permit anything but the briefest of acknowledgments here. Suffice it to say that while he mainly adopts the view "from above," I take the view "from below" (cf. Lara 2008: 80 and n. 25, 81, 255–59).

7. This study focuses mainly on the area of colonial New Spain now covered by the modern-day states of Hidalgo, Morelos, Puebla, Tlaxcala, Oaxaca, México, and the Federal District (D.F.), including urban Mexico City, although some outlying central states are referred to occasionally.

8. Cf. Fraser 1990 on building in the Viceroyalty of Peru. Although an equivalent study has not been made for Mexico, colonial texts make it very clear that all building programs were intended as a statement of European cultural superiority. Cervantes de Salazar's 1554 "tour" of Mexico City (1991) is a primary example in this respect.

9. The term "cosmovision" (worldview) is from the Spanish *cosmovisión.* The Mesoamerican cosmovision is defined as the articulated grouping of interrelated ideological systems in a relatively coherent form with which, in a given historical moment, an individual or a group understands or explains the world (López Austin 1996a, 1:20). See also Broda 1991a: 462, 2001: 166.

10. The homogeneity of a pancontinental religious system based on a shared worldview is well recognized by Native Americanists today and is perhaps most strongly evidenced in Brotherston's *Book of the Fourth World* (1992). Regional or local cult practices, or variations in religious manifestations, do not point to the existence of different "religions," for these ultimately all drew, and draw, on the same system.

11. See Brotherston (1992: 50, n. 14) on the origins of this Nahuatl term.

12. While native ceremonial architecture might have provided a medium for text, it was also a text in its own right. See, for example, the numerous works of Eduardo Matos Moctezuma on the architec-

tural narratives incorporated into Tenochtitlan's Great Temple. Those same narratives were ritually reenacted on and around the structure.

13. Both these native sources were used in my dissertation (Wake 1995) and to the same end. I have also rebased some of my arguments on other native-authored texts originally written in alphabetized Nahuatl (for example, the *Santoral en mexicano,* as cited by Burkhart 1992).

14. Here I refer mainly to edited works by Beatriz Albores and/or Johanna Broda, in which they offer their own research together with that of colleagues and students (Albores and Broda 1997; Broda and Báez-Jorge 2001). Individual contributors to these excellent collections of essays or papers by others, published separately or delivered at conferences, are cited where applicable.

15. Patron-mountains filled with telephones and motor cars are one particular "updating" that comes to mind (see Medina Hernández 2001: 145, citing Pedro Pitarch, *Ch'ulel: Una etnografía de las almas tzeltales* [Mexico City: Fondo de Cultura Económica, 1996]).

16. There is one exception, for it remains unclear what the sources of its author were. Copies of my dissertation are held by the Albert Sloman Library, University of Essex, Colchester, England (since 1995); the Canning House Library at the Hispanic and Luso Brazilian Council, London; and the Instituto Nacional de Antropología e Historia, Mexico City (both since 1998).

CHAPTER 1

1. The concept of *teotl* is explained well in an early colonial account. Asked why the Indians worshiped the elements, the mountains, and other created things—why they worshiped "idols" rather than the Creator—a native informant replied that they did not worship them or hold them to be gods but that they understood their gods to exist in them (Codex Ramírez 1979: 93).

2. Water and fertility were also the fundamental preoccupation of the Mexica cult system. Further concern centered on the environmental conditions of the central highlands, with an extreme dry season and rainy season (Broda 1991a: 465).

3. "[E]llos nos dan nuestro sustento, nuestro alimento, todo cuanto se bebe, se come, lo que es nuestra carne, el maíz, el frijol, los bledos, la chía. Ellos son a quienes pedimos el agua, la lluvia, por las que se producen las cosas en la tierra." Unless otherwise stated, all translations from the original Spanish are mine.

4. Admittedly, the mythical record is fragmentary and may have been influenced by later additions, including Euro-Christian references. An overall consistency in the level of their focus nevertheless remains. Davíd Carrasco's reading of the myths of the Birth of Huitzilopochtli and the Creation of the Fifth Sun in respect to their symbolism of the center and periphery (Carrasco 1987: 132–37, 143–46), for example, reveals considerable soundness of patterning.

5. "[U]na torre, como monte."

6. See chapters 4 and 5.

7. Mendieta (1973, 1:50–51) credits Xolotl with the sacrifice of the gods, although this deity is often twinned with Quetzalcoatl, serving as his canine companion or *nahualli* (Miller and Taube 1993: 190).

8. In addition to protein, the sap of the maguey contains several vitamins (Taylor 1979: 30); the flowers can also be eaten.

9. The lunar connection also refers directly to the cultivation of the maguey cactus, which was (and still is among many traditional groups) computed by the cycles of the moon (Salinas Pedraza 1983: 283).

10. In *Histoyre du Méchique* it is Xolotl who is given the role of feeding these humans after their creation.

11. "[S]alieron Rosas q. no huelen bien . . . salieron Rosas olorosas. q. ellos llaman suchiles" (Flowers that do not smell much poured forth . . . perfumed flowers that they call *suchiles* [*xochitl*] poured forth); "y ansi tienen q. las Rosas olorosas. vinieron del otro mundo . . . y las que no huelen dizen que son naçidas desde el principio" (and so they hold that perfumed flowers came from the other world . . . and those with no smell they say are the first to be born [in this world]).

12. The Florentine Codex is hereafter cited as FC followed by Sahagún's book number and the publication date and page number(s) of Anderson and Dibble's corresponding volume (FC11, 1963: 202).

13. Códice Matritense de la Real Academia de Historia is hereafter cited as CMRAH followed by the folio number and (where the alphabetical text is used) the corresponding reference from Nicholson et al.'s 1997 translation (CMRAH, f. 84r; 1997: 177). Códice Matritense del Palacio Real (CMPR) is treated in the same way.

14. Hernando Alvarado Tezozómoc, *Crónica mexicana* (Mexico City: Editorial Leyenda, 1944), pp. 503–508, cited by López Austin 1996a, 1:384.

15. See also Broda (1991a, 1991b, 1997a, 1997b). Brotherston (1997a) discusses mountain images of Tlaloc found in other pictographic sources.

16. Brotherston (1992: 93–95) cites several examples of Native American groups who still construct their own microcosmos through a quincunx of local mountains. Ritual space is defined through use of crosses (the sacred tree of the Indo-Christian world), often in association with venerated mountains (see, for example, Vogt 1976 on rituals at Zinacantan, Chiapas; and Freidel et al. 1993 on the sacred precinct at Tixkakal Guardia, Quintana Roo).

17. A further place of destiny, this time for children, was known as "place of the tree of sustenance"; "place of the abundance of watery flowers; or "place of the nipple-tree" (FC6, 1969: 115; CMRAH f. 84v; 1997: 178 and n. 11; López Austin 1996a, 1:378). Eternity for children in their own afterworld was also conceived as a time of constant nurturing.

18. Demarest (1984) believes that human sacrifice from earliest times served as a prestige reinforcer and a signifier of legitimacy of power. Its intensification under the Azteca-Mexica is the result of a radical shift from this causal role to the role of actively motivating and eventually necessitating open-ended expansion (Demarest 1984: 235). Davíd Carrasco (1987) understands human sacrifice and incremental human sacrifice as an act of cosmic repetition for the ritual re-creation of Aztec dominance and power as established in their history. As recounted in the myths of the Fifth Sun and the Birth of Huitzilopochtli, for example, aggression against the forces of the periphery created a new world—that is, later mass sacrifice delayed a reoccurrence of cosmic disorder (see Carrasco 1987: 148, 150–56).

19. "[N]o había más cerem[oni]a [que] de quemar incienso al ídolo" (Acuña 1986: 229).

20. "[N]o había en él ceremonia señalada" (Acuña 1984a: 200).

21. Within the traditional rituals described in the *Relaciones geográficas* series and other pre- and post-conquest accounts, some close parallels with Tenochtitlan's ritual extravaganzas can certainly be identified. But they are restricted to the opening of the ritual year and the agricultural cycle, the opening of the hunting season, and the close of the ritual year. They are also greatly scaled down in terms of their levels of dramatization. In addition, a comparative analysis of all these accounts (Wake n.d.a) shows that Tenochtitlan's versions were theatrical dramatizations of the original divinatory, propitiatory, and celebratory rituals surrounding the cultivation of maize that had evolved in the fields over millennia. In other words, the Azteca-Mexica peoples adopted the stages of labor involved in the maize cycle and related ritual of the established sedentary groups in the Valley of Mexico and outlying areas for the purposes of political and economic propaganda.

22. "[Y] los que pasaban echaban sangre de las orejas o de la lengua, o echaban un poco de incienso . . . ;

otros, rosas que cogían en el camino, y cuando otra cosa no tenían, echaban un poco de yerba verde o unas pajas, y allí descansaban."

23. Both Durán (1984) and Codex Ramírez (1979) note that human sacrifice was the prerogative of rulers and nobility and was practiced as a sign of status.

24. Cf. Vogt (1976: 10–11); Brotherston (1979: 83–84).

25. In Sahagún's account, detailed descriptions of food offerings occur in eleven of the eighteen festivals and four of the movable feasts (Sahagún 1981, 1:103–277).

26. In modern-day urban Xochimilco (D.F.) the women still gather publicly to prepare foodstuffs for the patron festivals of their barrios.

27. Sahagún here seems to understand the dramatized rites of gladiatorial sacrifice as a form of entertainment, perhaps in the manner of the Roman tradition.

28. Codex Magliabechiano places tongue-piercing in Toxcatl (f. 32v) and penis-piercing in Etzalqualiztli (f. 33v), because "their god" considered it fitting to give them descendants. Diego Muñoz Camargo (1986: 162) implied that self-sacrifice related to penance for wrongdoings: the tongue was pierced for verbal offenses, the eyelids for visual offenses, and the arms if someone had been physically weak. Durán (1984, 1:170) recorded that the part of the body pierced varied by region.

29. "[L]os cantares que en aquellos areitos cantaban, tenían por oración, llevándolos en conformidad de un mismo tono y meneos, con mucho seso y peso, sin discrepar en voz ni en paso."

30. "[P]ara cuyo recibimiento tañían y bailaban toda la noche de la vigilia y comían y bebían como en las demás ocasiones acostumbraban."

31. The two female deities are identifiable from their respective images on ff. 262r and 265v of CMPR. See Nicholson et al. (1997: 110, n. 87) on the Tezcacoac Ayopechtli–Mayahuel interrelationship.

32. "Tenían delante el pulque . . . con que se enborrachavan, y bailando y bebiendo y después q[ue] se calentaban, con el sol y con el vino, se caían y los parientes y mujeres o ermanos les sacaban y llevavan y, en tornando en sí, bolvían al areyto." The same practice is still current today in traditional communities.

33. In the early days of worshiping idols at Texcoco, and before the sacrifices were introduced, Texcocans and their neighbors would "sow" the temple with flowers and dance nonstop before their gods ("Sembrándoles el templo de rosas y flores y danzando de continuo delante de ellos, tantos los de la ciudad, como los vecinos próximos") (*HM* 1979: 99).

34. Sahagún (1981, 1:182–83; FC2, 1981: 108) and his informants list seventeen different flowers. These include two varieties of the sweet-smelling marigold (*tepecempoalxochitl* and *cempoalxochitl* proper) and three more noted in Book 11 of the Florentine Codex as perfumed or fragrant (FC11, 1963: 202, 205, 213). None of the nonscented flowers classed as "useless" in the Florentine Codex appear in this list.

35. "[J]untábanlas en la casa del cu donde se hacía esta fiesta, allí se guardaban aquella noche, y luego en amaneciendo las ensartaban en sus hilos o mecatejos; teniéndolas ensartadas hacían sogas gruesas de ellas, torcidas y largas, y las tendían en el patio de aquel cu."

36. "A los tres días que andaban enramando, llegaba el dios que llamaban Telpochtli. . . . El día siguiente llegaba el dios de los mercaderes llamado Yacapitzauac o Yiacatecutli, y otro dios llamado Ixcozauhqui o Xiuhtecutli."

37. See also Torquemada (1975–83, 3:129).

38. "[Q]uita la gana del comer a los que la comen, y emborracha y enloquece perpetuamente."

39. Citations from the *Cantares mexicanos* are hereafter given as *CM* followed by the folio number and

page numbers of Bierhorst's 1985 Nahuatl to English edition (Bierhorst 1985a) (*CM,* f. 11v; 1985: 166–67).

40. For further examples of the huacalxochitl used in song and dance, see figure 7.13.

41. "[Y] con ellos estaban ojeando, como quien ojea moscas sobre las caras . . . otros metían esta yerba en las orejas. También por vía de superstición otros traían esta yerba empuñada, o apretada en el puño." Pungent sagebrush or artemisia is a member of the Asteraceae family. The Mexican variety, *Artemisia mexicana,* produces convulsions and hallucinations (Garza 2001: 98).

42. "Todos los que bailaban parecían unas flores."

43. "Perfumaban las estatuas con hierbas, flores, polvos y con varias lágrimas perfumadas de árboles y con goma de gratísimo olor."

44. The remark by Hernández, who is better known for his studies on the native pharmacopoeia, is unique among the sources. Given that he never witnessed prehispanic ritual at Tenochtitlan, we must assume that the report came from one of the native practitioners with whom he worked on his herbal treatise.

45. "[T]odas flores de muy suave olor, y de los olores y suavidades de flores estaba llena aquella iglesia."

CHAPTER 2

1. "También ofrecían gallinas y palomas, y todo en grandísima cantidad; tanto que los frailes y los españoles estaban espantados, y yo mismo fui muchas veces a mirar, y me espantaba de ver cosa tan nueva en tan viejo mundo."

2. "Double mistaken identity" occurs when "each side takes it that a given form or concept is essentially one already known to it, operating in much the same manner as in its own tradition, and hardly takes cognizance of the other side's interpretation" (Lockhart 1992: 445).

3. "Era esta tierra un traslado del infierno."

4. "[N]i de mil, ni de diez mil partes, una no hemos alcanzado a saber de la religión y particularidades della questas gentes tenían."

5. In a 1558 letter to Philip II, Pedro de Gante, one of the first Franciscans to arrive, admitted that it was the Indians' custom to dance and sing before their gods, so he encouraged the practice to attract them to Christian worship. They turned up in the thousands (*Códice franciscano* 1941: 206–207, 214).

6. "[Q]ue los cantos sean de día, y solamente los domingos y fiestas de los cristianos."

7. "[E]l bosque de la idolatría que no está talado."

8. In regard to political subversion, the classic case remains the 1537–39 trial of Carlos Ometochtli for "idolatry" (see *Proceso inquisitorial* 1980).

9. "[Y] también tomo mi báculo de rosas . . . y voy considerando la mucha ignorancia nuestra, pues podía haber en ello mal."

10. Burkhart (1992: 92–93) suggests, however, that Sahagún's native assistants were probably aware of the traditional transformational flowery world invoked by the new songs.

11. An analysis of this aspect of the flower-songs is included in chapter 7.

12. See also Anderson (1993: xxv–xxxii) on the poetic style of the *Psalmodia* in respect to the *Cantares mexicanos.*

13. "[I]dolillos, o trapos, en fin, alguna cosa."

14. The European presence is only acknowledged in the replacement of reed torches and native fowl by wax candles and domestic chickens.

15. Particularly interesting in this account is the celebration of the forming of the first young cobs (*elotes*), marked at Zumpahuacan by the sacrifice of a chicken, pulque drinking, and the roasting of a few of the cobs in honor of the fire god. At prehispanic Tenochtitlan the highlight of the same festival was the roasting of slaves dressed as young maize cobs. Their remains were also offered to the Huehueteotl.

16. Cf. FC2 1981: 241; Nicholson et al. 1997: 148.

17. The Mexican term *cerro* is used throughout this study for named hills and mountains.

18. Ciudad Real (1976, 1:22–23) observed that the Calimaya lake site was of considerable importance in the prehispanic period. The same mountain pilgrimage is still held today across rural Mexico, coinciding with the festival of the Holy Cross on May 2–3, that is, at the opening of the rainy season. Night vigils en masse on mountaintops are the norm. Although the actions and outcome of the festival appear to be Christian (crosses are erected and mass is said), the presence of traditional groups and traditional ritual elements such as pulque, incensing, offerings of food and flowers, and song and dance is notable. See Broda (2001) on this festival.

19. See Sahagún (1981, 3:354) as compared to Mendieta (1973, 1:138) and Torquemada (1975–83, 5:80, 82). Torquemada contradicts himself in this respect, for earlier in his work (3:183) he acknowledges that mountaintops and water sources were also venues for prehispanic rituals.

20. Actual reports of human sacrifice taking place in the colonial period are few. Where human sacrifice is directly referred to, it tends to fall within the earlier years, its perpetrators being almost exclusively old priests or high-ranking nobles.

21. The pairing of these prehispanic festivals is seen more clearly in Durán's naming of them. Teotleco and Tepeilhuitl are, for example, given as Pachtontli and Huey Pachtli (Durán 1984, 1:277–80) or "little" and "great" *pachtli*. *Pachtli* is a parasitic tree-moss closely associated with the fertility cult (ibid., pp. 279–80).

22. He does not state which of the several villages named Zacatlan in the central area.

23. New pulque is saturated with carbonic acid from its fermentation, which "pricks" the tongue like needles or spines (Gonçalves de Lima 1986: 199).

24. Andrews and Hassig (1984: 122–23, 349 n. 6) state that the more correct translation of *chicuetecpaciuatzin* is "Eight-flint-woman." The maguey was nevertheless conceptualized on the basis of rows of eight plants; the wording of this incantation therefore seems to incorporate a secondary pun.

25. "Rosa resplandeciente y que da luz, regocíjese, y alégrase mi corazón delante de Dios."

26. See, for example, the lengthy report by Mendieta (1973, 1:199–207) on the reactions of the inhabitants of Cuauhtinchan (Puebla) when the Dominican order attempted to take over from the Franciscan order. An unusual detail on the facade of the monastery church of San Juan Bautista Acapixtla is the presence of both the Augustinian and Franciscan insignia, suggesting that some sort of compromise was eventually reached.

27. "[M]esclan cantares de su gentilidad y para cubrir su dañada obra comienzan y acaban con palabras de Dios, interponiendo las demás gentílicas, abaxando la voz para no ser entendidos y levantándola en los principios y fines cuando dicen 'Dios.'"

28. "Padre, no te espantes, pues todavía estamos nepantla, y como entendiese lo que quería decir por aquel vocablo y metáfora, que quiere decir 'estar en medio,' torné a insistir me dijese qué medio era aquel en que estaban. Me dijo que, como no estaban aún bien arraigados en la fe, que no me espantase; de manera que aún estaban neutros; que ni bien acudían a la una ley, ni a la otra, o por mejor decir, creían en Dios y que juntamente acudían a sus costumbres antiguas y ritos del demonio, y esto quiso decir

aquel en su abominable excusa de que aún permanecían 'en medio y eran neutros.' "

29. Durán specifically chose the adverb *juntamente* and not a Spanish equivalent of "also" or "at the same time" (which, in the present context, would mean two simultaneous but ideologically separate courses of action).

30. The term *nepantla* has recently been used to describe the "language" of the invaded land, that is, the colonial texts of tlacuilolli (Brotherston 2005: 4) or the form of native iconic script that developed with the introduction of European art forms.

31. Sacrificial victims were offered by the rich and were of some value to the donor in terms of status (a war captive) or economic power (a slave bought at market). As Durán (1984, 1:141) noted, the value of a human in prehispanic times was equivalent to an offering of one, two, or three chickens in the church.

32. "[T]an chiquitos, que otros mayores que ellos aún no han dejado la teta."

33. Night rituals in the run-up to Easter continued in the central area and by 1585 had been linked to "idolatrous" activities. Hernando Ortiz de Hinojosa, a member of the Provincial Ecclesiastical Council of that year, recommended that the processions of Holy Thursday and Good Friday should not start out at night and that nocturnal visits to the (atrial?) cross during Lent should be prohibited "por evitar offensas de Dios que se hazen" (to avoid offending God as is done) ("Advertencias" 1983: 215, 218).

34. "Y cuando tienen falta de agua, o enfermedad, o por cualquiera otra necesidad, con sus cruces y lumbres se van de una iglesia a otra disciplinando."

35. "Fingían que bajaba un niño del cielo este día, y a este niño llamaban 'Agua.' . . . Había . . . riguroso mandato de no dormir toda esta noche sino estar en vela en el patio del templo, esperando la venida del agua . . . y así estaban todos . . . con lumbradas para resistir el frío, a la mesma manera que agora lo suelen estar toda la noche de Navidad."

36. See Alberro (2000: 32–33) on this same point.

37. "[Y] como los ramos son verdes y los traen alzados en las manos, parece una floresta."

38. Comparisons with Mixtec traditions are appropriate here, given the presence of Mixteca-Popoloca groups in the Tlaxcala area from earliest times (see Wake 2007).

39. "[Y] en los otros arcos que no tenían rodelas había unos florones grandes, hechos de unos como cascos de cebolla, redondos, muy bien hechos, y tienen muy buen lustre."

40. In the Mixteca Alta the scales are known as *cucharas de maguey* (maguey spoons)and are also used for eating the maize gruel *pozole*. In the central area they are often replaced today with strips of palm bark, which tend to be smaller. On the occasion of important church festivals, village churchyards are still adorned in exactly the same manner as described in Motolinía's text.

41. "[P]arecía que se venía el cielo abajo."

42. The date is doubly important, for it was the eve of the summer solstice. The early appropriation of Christian festivals to celebrate important stages of the maize cycle is still followed among traditional groups in Mexico today (see Albores 1997 and 2001 on the structure of the *cuatro fiestas en cruz,* for example). Durán (1984, 1:244–45) recorded that an old woman who remembered the "laws" of the past told him that the Indians had also celebrated Easter and Christmas and Corpus Christi and many other major Christian festivals. In other words, many important dates within the old ritual year coincided with those of the Christian calendar. This is perhaps not surprising, given Christianity's own appropriation of so many pagan festivals that also focused on the fertility of the earth and the cycles of food production. Predictably, however, the friar put the native Mexican examples down to the work of the devil (ibid.).

43. See note 21 above.

44. See chapter 1 and note 16 of that chapter.

45. From this point onward, Motolinía is citing the descriptions of the Tlaxcallan festivals from the writings of an anonymous friar (O'Gorman 1990: 63–64, n. 11).

46. "[T]odo esto lleno de cuanto se puede hallar en una sierra muy fuertil [fértil] y fresca montaña; y todas las particularidades que en abril y mayo se pueden hallar."

47. The surviving text recounting this early meeting was written some forty years later, in 1564 (Sahagún 1986). It is therefore unclear how much editing the original underwent, particularly in including details of the Indian world with which the 1524 friars would not have been familiar. Comparisons of the Christian heaven with Indian flowery otherworlds nevertheless persisted, as Sahagún's own *Psalmodia* attests.

48. "[C]antando muy al propio que los indios cantaban cuando se embeodaban."

49. See, for example, my commentary on the Codex Laud's flower-bowers in chapter 1; the "weaving" dance on Codex Borgia 39 (Gordon Brotherston, pers. comm.); or the dance steps (right, left, right, right, left) on Borgia 37.

50. These histories were probably also written down pictorially. The alphabetical texts of Sahagún's informants on the ritual round at Tenochtitlan (FC2) were certainly drawn from pictorial sources (cf. Sahagún 1981, 1:106).

51. The flower arches and props prepared for the 1577 reception of holy relics in Mexico City were also accompanied by a landscape of wooded fields, springs, and live birds.

52. "[R]etratada la hermosura de la gloria."

53. "[E]stán hechas las calles un mapa de tierra, agua, aire, y del mismo Cielo."

54. "[Y]e oncan in quitotehuaque huehuetque tachtohuan tococolhuan, in xochitlalpan in tonacatlalpan . . . ye oncan in ilhuicatlalpan." The quotation is taken from the original Nahuatl text, reproduced in Nebel (1995: 343–54, 355–67). The English translation is mine, after the 1978 Spanish version by Mario Rojas Sánchez (ibid., pp. 171–203).

CHAPTER 3

1. In this respect a 1531 Nahua testimony on the founding of Santo Tomás Ajusco (D.F.) offers an interesting insight into the fear felt by some native peoples at the manner of the early imposition of the Christian package ("Testimonio de la fundación" 1970: 199). See the analysis of this text by Stephanie Wood (1997), together with her observations on other early Nahua reactions to the conversion elsewhere (Wood 1991, 1998: 218–19).

2. The first Indian *cofradías* (sodalities) were founded around 1538 in Mexico City. Some have argued that they did not expand into other towns or rural areas until much later in the century (Sepúlveda y Herrera 1976: 6), although Motolinía (1990: 65) makes it clear that they were established in Tlaxcala (a predominantly Indian center) by 1539. The scope of my own study does not permit commentary on this particular religious activity; but given the ritualized reenactments and visual stimuli it afforded, it was also undoubtedly an attractive option.

3. "[U]nos lienzos arrollados con pinturas de los principales misterios de Nuestra Santa Fe."

4. As Matos Moctezuma (1987: 16) points out, Testera was nevertheless using a medium of native origin.

5. See also León (1900), Sentenach (1900), Seler (1904), Glass (1975), León-Portilla (1979), and Galarza (1992) for further commentary on glyphic inserts and the boustrophedon reading principles that some examples of picture catechisms utilize.

6. Juan de Tovar, *Relación de los indios* . . . (Graz: Akademische Druck, 1972), p. 5, cited by Galarza and Maldonado (1990: 126).

7. "[P]ues este modo de escrebir nuestras oraciones y cosas de la fe, ni se lo enseñaron los españoles, ni ellos pudieran salir con él, si no hicieran muy particular concepto de lo que les enseñaban." I am grateful to Jo Labanyi for providing an accurate translation of Acosta's observation.

8. See Galarza (1966, 1967, 1979) on the transformation of Christian names into phonetically readable glyphs.

9. The *Descripción del arzobispado* was based on a 1570 survey to which only the secular clergy contributed.

10. Cited by Burkhart (1989: 198). Torquemada mentions a short doctrina in Nahuatl by Motolinía, which was published. Fray Juan de Ribas prepared a catechism, Sunday sermons for the year, and a *Flos sanctorum* in Nahuatl, while similar texts were written in Tarascan, Popolocan, Matlatzincan, and Otomi, although not all were sent to press (Torquemada 1975–83, 6:123–24).

11. See Corcuera de Mancera (1993: 201–19). Between 1544 and 1548, the year of his death, Zumárraga authored, edited, or compiled at least seven more doctrinas (ibid., p. 174).

12. By 1545 Zumárraga had already prohibited these "representaciones poco honestas" (less than respectful performances) at Corpus Christi. After his death three years later, the activities were resumed (León-Portilla 1996: 194).

13. In 1552 viceroy Luis de Velasco had already ordered that native painters be examined before executing religious paintings (Lino Gómez Canedo, *La educación de los marginados durante la época colonial* [Mexico City:, Porrúa, 1982], p. 84, cited by Mundy 1996: 86).

14. "[P]orque no los puedan falsear, ni corromper."

15. Zumárraga arrived in Mexico in December 1528, having been appointed as its first bishop the previous year. He became archbishop in 1545 (Lorenzana 1981: 213–14).

16. Zumárraga's letter is reproduced in Torquemada (1975–83, 6:223–24).

17. "Según su maldita costumbre gentílica."

18. "[Y] que ya aprenden a murmurar de los sermones y aun dejan de los ir a oír, ni van a misa las fiestas sino cuando quieren y dicen que huelgan más de oír la misa en las iglesias de los clérigos, que no los reprehenden."

19. "Si en una escuela los castigan, vánse a la otra, a decir mil falsedades."

20. The majority of Indians were probably noncommunicants in the early years, although Indian nobility and their offspring were often the focus of intensive teaching and used as examples of fully fledged Christians for their subjects to follow. But by 1571 a number of other Indians were also participating in the Eucharist, as evidenced in the Ovando Series. At Nahua-Otomi Atotonilco el Grande (Hidalgo), for example, the Otomis were still not ready for communion, but the friars were making daily progress. A similar situation held at Mixquic (D.F.) (*Treinta relaciones* [1569–71], ff. 188v, 156r). Even if not participating, noncommunicants would still be required to attend, especially on important days in the Catholic calendar.

21. "[U]nos quitan algunas insignias del demonio, otros se lo conceden."

22. The "symbols of the devil" to which Zumárraga referred may well have been the glyphic system adopted for the recital of prayers.

23. Here Zumárraga is reiterating a standard line on the interdependence of the civic, civility, and Christianization. This argument is apparent from the earliest documentation concerning the native peoples in Spanish America (cf. Fraser 1990: 40–43).

24. In a letter to the Council of the Indies, dated February 2, 1554, Fray Bernardo de Albuquerque makes the point quite clear: "y para que los españoles . . . puedan tener y labrar tierras y hacer heredades y criar ganado, es necesario que S. M. mande juntar los indios como se mandó en la provincia de Guatimala para que dejasen desembarazadas las tierras baldías a los españoles" (and so that the Spaniards . . . can have and work land and build up estates and breed livestock, it is necessary that Your Majesty orders the Indians to be brought together as was done in the province of Guatemala in order to free up the uncultivated land for the Spaniards) (*DIHM* 1914: 181).

25. "[P]or excusar el trabajo de no mudar sus casas a los pueblos que se ponen en traza, y por no estar cerca de los monesterios e iglesias y por encubrir sus flaquezas que son muchas, se van a pueblos apartados de dotrina y conversión."

26. "[M]uchos naturales y macehuales del dicho pueblo se han ido y absentado del a otras partes por razón de no juntarse en congregación ni pulicía ni deprender la doctrina xriptiana y ser industriados en las cosas de nuestra sancta fé católica."

27. Gerhard (1977) cites Tepeaca, Tecamachalco, Quecholac, Acatzingo, Cholula, and Huejotzingo in modern-day Puebla; Zumpango, Calimaya, and Zinacantepec in México; Tepeapulco, Actopan, Ixmiquilpan, and Atotonilco el Grande in Hidalgo; and Teposcolula, Tlaxiaco, and Coixtlahuaca in the Mixteca Alta of Oaxaca.

28. See, for example, *Descripción del arzobispado* (1976) entries for Tetzayuhcan, Temazcaltepec, Tlalchichilpa, Nuchtepec, and Tecticpaque.

29. "[C]omo es notorio a V. A., con cuanta facilidad estos indios nuevamente convertidos a nuestra sancta fe católica, se vuelven a sus idolatrías, ritos, sacrificios y supersticiones, y cometen muchos y diversos casos de herejías, y para extirparlos tenemos gran necesidad que en cada pueblo haya un fiscal que descubra los tales males, sin el cual ni los prelados ni nuestros vicarios, curas ni religiosos los podemos descubrir."

30. "Si no tenían edificado el monasterio, no tardaban en hacerlo de la forma y traza que les querían dar. Y era cosa maravillosa la brevedad con que lo acababan, siendo de cal y canto, y apenas tardaban medio año."

31. "¿[Q]uién ha edificado tantas iglesias y monasterios como los religiosos tienen en esta Nueva España, sino los indios con sus manos y propio sudor, y con tanta voluntad y alegría como edificaron casas para sí y sus hijos, y rogando a los frailes que se las dejasen hacer mayores?"

32. See Gerhard (1986) and the *Descripción del arzobispado* (1976) on the extent of secular jurisdiction during this period.

33. The dates of the 1531 and 1588 epidemics are listed by McAndrew (1965: 14).

34. See also my argument in chapter 4 regarding the use of this sign in mapping.

35. For example, AGN, *Indios*, vol. 6: 2, exps. 759–63, 772, 817, which cover 1592 and part of 1593 alone.

36. The encomienda system was replaced by the *repartimiento,* where labor was controlled by Crown representatives, the *corregidores*. The repartimiento was open to abuse, like most colonial institutions, but right of appeal to the Crown was possible and investigative and punitive measures might be taken. Not all appeals were successful or, if so, long-term (see the 1552 case at Meztitlan in Scholes 1944), but the power of individual civilians was curbed.

37. See the surviving 1601 instructions from Viceroy Monterrey on the end-of-century congregation in Michoacán ("Instrucción que vos don Fernando de Villegas" 1995: 326–27). Instructions sent out to other provinces would have been the same or very similar.

38. See, for example, the order of January 1592 to bring in the Indians living outside Huayacocotla (Veracruz) ("porque quedasen bien doctrinados y administrados . . . como por evitar los Pecados y Ofensas de dios que cometen en los lugares Remotos" [AGN, *Indios*, vol. 6: 1, exp. 74]) or the order in July of the same year to the governor and mayor of Chicontepec (Veracruz) to bring in the Indians to the new congregation so that they could be indoctrinated (ibid., vol. 6: 2, exp. 711).

39. Klor de Alva (1999) discusses Nahua perceptions of the self in relation to imposed Christian ideals of the self. In my understanding, it is the indigenous sense of what we might call "common being" (as opposed to an individual part of a whole) that is the issue here.

40. Similarly, at the end of the seventeenth century (as a criticism of what he understood to be Indian backwardness) Agustín de Vetancurt (1971, 2:3, f. 98) commented: "[L]os Indios no tienen mas entendimiento que los ojos, creen mas por lo que vèn que por lo que entienden."

41. A number of chroniclers noted the association between ritual drunkenness and the ocpactli root added to the fermented maguey sap (Motolinía 1990: 197–98; Durán 1984, 1:200–201). Use of the root evidently continued despite a 1529 Crown order that it should cease to be cultivated (see Alonso de Zorita, *Leyes y ordenanzas reales de las Indias del Mar Océano* [1574], libro 6, título 3, ley 4, cited by Corcuera de Mancera 1993: 121).

42. "En todos los templos de los ídolos, si no era en algunos derribados y quemados de México, en los de la tierra, y aun en el mismo México, eran servidos y honrados los demonios. Ocupados los españoles en edificar a México y en hacer casas y moradas para sí, contentábanse con que no hubiese delante de ellos sacrificio de homicidio público, que a escondidos y a la redonda de México no faltaban."

43. See Rojas Rabiela (1979). The coatequitl system is known to have survived in the Valley of Mexico until 1573 (ibid.), and the ancient internal organization of task allotment, still supervised by native leaders, survived until the end of that decade (Kubler 1992: 146–47). Thus in all probability the calendrically based structure of work crews also persisted.

44. "[T]ienen de costumbre de ir cantando y dando voces, y los cantos y voces apenas cesaban de noche ni de día, por el gran hervor que traían en la edificación del pueblo los primeros años."

45. "[V]inieron ocho mil Indios . . . para hacer la planta de la nueva poblacion . . . venian con tal regozijo, y gozo de la nueva planta Catholica con diverfidad de inftrumentos de mufica baylando, y cantando."

46. "[D]ando licencia a los indios para sacrificar, y sacándolos del monesterio y doctrina cristiana . . . y mandándolos trabajar días de fiesta."

47. "[L]os españoles consienten a los indios ritos gentílicos y cultos de idolatría por el interesse que dellos esperan."

48. "[L]os que acarrean madera del monte ó piedras de las canteras, los labradores y caminantes mezclaban en las cosas de su ocupación ceremonias de su idolatría."

49. See also the short but graphic description of the horrors endured in the mines in Motolinía (1990: 17).

50. "Y los han pintado en algunas partes; y en particular en la portería del convento de Cua[uh]tinchan tienen pintada la memoria de la cuenta que ellos tenían antigua con estos caracteres o signos llenos de abusión. Y no fue acertado dejárselo pintar, ni es acertado que se conserve la tal pintura, ni que se pinten en parte alguna los dichos caracteres, sino que totalmente los olviden."

51. We have to assume it was a tonalpohualli, for the year count was not the focus of Spanish suspicion. See also my following comments on the Sahagún–Las Navas controversy.

52. "[E]dificó un gracioso monasterio" ("Cartas de religiosos de Nueva España, 1539–1594," in *Nueva colección de documentos para la historia de México,* ed. Genaro García [n.p., 1886], 1:91, cited by Kubler

1992: 563). Ricard (1994: 142) states that the monastery was actually founded between 1555 and 1557 by the Franciscan provincial Francisco de Bustamante.

53. "[M]uchas cosas de idolatría, y muchas supersticiones y muchas invocaciones de los demonios."

54. "Por pinturas demostraban estas cosas antiguas, y hánselas tomado todas porque se entendía que, por tenerlas, tenían los mismos ritos y ceremonias que de antes."

55. "Para todas estas cosas les ayudaba mucho el haber puesto muchos de estos ídolos por cimientos, y basas de los pilares de la iglesia catedral, y en otras casas para adornarlas, y lo que se hizo casualmente así por la fortaleza de los edificios y casas, y por ornato de las calles, que también los había en ellas . . . y los que están en los remates de las casas, y por las calles son para que todo lo conserven, donde idolatraban y les decían sus invocaciones."

56. "[P]or todo lo cual pareció por entonces total remedio el de las juntas y congregaciones de los pueblos, como se hizo." The congregation program that La Serna (1892: 15) refers to was that which took place from 1595 onward.

57. "[Ó] fuese casualmente, ó malicia de los mismos indios que fabricaron los templos y casas, y las pusieron allí de industria para honrarlos [*sic*]."

58. La Serna (1892: 24, 27) refers to "la iglesia catedral" (the cathedral) and to the "dioses de piedra" (gods of stone), smashed and chipped away from the churches, houses, and streets "de esta ciudad" (of this city), which might suggest that the purge was confined to Mexico City only. This offensive imagery motivated the second congregations program, however, which points to a much wider field of play.

59. "[H]oy que han pasado tantos años, como lo son más de setenta, y que no ha habido enmienda, ni se reconoce haber sido remedio el de las Congregaciones."

60. The 1585 council encouraged the use of the *grotesque* among Indian painters and sculptors, specifically to avoid misrepresentation in thematic imagery (Gruzinski 2002: 112).

61. "[L]os indios que viven no sólo no las estiman, pero ni aun advierten si están allí o de qué hubiesen servido."

62. "[L]as piedras en quienes reconocen deidad."

63. See Lockhart (1990) on the evolution of postconquest Nahua society and concepts, especially where he points out that the stone carvings and mural paintings of the sixteenth century belong to Stage 2 of the process of cultural change. Commencing around 1540, this stage is characterized by "a mixed Hispanic-indigenous style of expression . . . executed by individuals still cognisant of preconquest skills and lore, buttressed by a still strong solidarity of the altepetl. . . . Nothing comparable exists from later times" (Lockhart 1990: 111).

64. See, for example, the holy "communion" made with hallucinogenic mushrooms and pulque recorded by La Serna (1892: 61–62) or the gift of a lancet and indigenous herbs delivered in a vision to a native healer by the archangels Gabriel and Michael and the Virgin Mary, respectively (ibid., pp. 65–66). Gruzinski (1993: 146–83, 202–28) offers an insightful discussion on the Christianization of colonial idolatrous practices.

65. See Klor de Alva (1991) on the process of Nahua religious rationalization between 1560 and 1640. He proposes that this period saw a resurgence of traditional rites and beliefs, although by this time they were highly derationalized in form. Some indoctrination practices, however, such as learning by rote, provided a rationalizing base that resulted in the location of Christian religious categories in Nahua beliefs: "the Nahuas could come to know (perhaps even believe) the doctrines found in the catechisms without being committed to the ethos they implied or the worldview they asserted" (Klor de Alva 1991: 239).

CHAPTER 4

1. The early colonial architecture of Mexico has been well documented by many scholars, who also discuss variations in size, shape, plan, and architectural design existing across individual sites and between the religious groups responsible for their construction. See, for example, Azcue y Mancera et al. (1940); Angulo Iñiguez (1955); McAndrew (1965); Mullen (1975, 1995); Victoria Asensio (1985); Weismann (1985); and Kubler (1992).

2. In the Yucatán and Tlaxcala, early free-standing examples were often converted into churches through addition of a stone or adobe nave (McAndrew 1965: 522–23; Weismann 1985: 69). The practice was evidently followed elsewhere, as I have observed at Mixquiahuala (Hidalgo) and Acatlan and Occipato, Naucalpan (México). Extant examples of monastic open chapels (Actopan, Meztitlan, and Cempoala [Hidalgo]; Coixtlahuaca and Teposcolula [Oaxaca]) probably continued to be used after the church was built; but others, such as the open chapel at Huejotzingo (see Córdova Tello 1992), fell into disuse after completion of the church and were possibly demolished shortly afterward. See also Artigas (1992) on Mexican open chapels in general.

3. Fraser (1990: 51–81) offers an interesting account of the colonial urbanization program and its objectives.

4. "[P]orque es más alto, y más acomodado para el asiento del pueblo."

5. See Tichy (1992) for a listing of azimuths of colonial churches in the Valley of Mexico and the Puebla-Tlaxcala region.

6. The architecture-landscape relationship is discussed in more detail later in this chapter and in chapter 5.

7. See also Wake (2002a: 100–101) on the use of wooden crosses to obstruct the view of the landscape from the side entrances of the early atrium at San Esteban Tizatlan, Tlaxcala.

8. This observation derives from my own visit to Apoala in early 1992. Mundy (1996: 102–104) reproduces the Nuttall panel, together with an interesting schematic map of the Apoala Valley that locates its main toponyms.

9. Haskett (2005: 179–182, 253) observes the interest of the indigenous authors of Cuernavaca's Primordial Titles in acknowledging specific, and probably sacred, features of the landscape present on or near the sites of churches: springs, certain trees, or twofold and fourfold (the monastery complex itself) hillocks or ridges.

10. In the context of the tree-mountain-tlaloque interchange, it is interesting to note that the base and roots of the world trees carried by the tlaloque on Borgia 30 are depicted as the mouth and fangs of Tlaloc (see fig. 6.76).

11. Tlaloc (water) and Xiuhtecuhtli (fire), the most ancient of deities in the Mesoamerican pantheon, were probably the original givers of life. As López Austin (1994: 189) notes, in the context of the terrestrial plane, the quincunx (or basic cosmic diagram) appears frequently as a symbol of these gods.

12. For Westerners, blue, green, and turquoise are visually distinct, but in native usage color functioned at a conceptual rather than ideographic level. Quetzal green, jade green, and turquoise blue, for example, carry the same value of "richness" or "preciousness" (Galarza and Maldonado 1990: 42) and could be employed to depict both water and vegetation. This does not mean that actual usage was arbitrary within color ranges and values. The chromatics of Native American expression needs far more research than has been carried out to date. We are still unsure, for example, as to why the colors of the world directions differ slightly from source to source.

13. The curved mountain glyph in the late Postclassic read as *coliuhqui,* "curved/twisted thing" (Siméon

1997: 123), but also functioned as a homonym for *colli* or *culli,* "grandparent(s)" (ibid.), a reference to ancestors or, in the case of mountains, Culhuacan-Amecamecan-Chicomoztoc, the place of origin in the north (López Austin 1994: 214–15).

14. A symmetrical arrangement of four stepped elements reproduces the fanged opening of the cave, as employed in Mesoamerican iconic writing systems (Barbara Fash, pers. comm., 2005).

15. In the Mixtec codices water-mountain glyphs most certainly function as geographical substantives for *yucu,* "hill," in Mixtec (Smith 1973: 39). In terms of the central Mexican altepetl, their conceptual value in the Mixtec culture is unknown, although it would not be too difficult to understand that they share the same etymological origin.

16. The Yanhuitlan Codex also depicts the local prehispanic *tecpan* (seat of government). It is perhaps the frieze of circles with a central floral motif that designates it as such. The *casa de la cacica* (sixteenth-century tecpan) at Teposcolula (Oaxaca) carries a frieze of alternating concentric circles and flowers.

17. In his 1553 Nahuatl exhortations against idolatry, directed at the Indian reader or audience, the Franciscan friar Andrés de Olmos (1990: 22, 26) used *teucalli* in reference to the congregation of the church. The anonymous "Exercicio quotidiano," corrected and dated by Sahagún in 1574 (Sahagún 1997: 183), makes a clear distinction throughout between the church as an institution (*sancta yglesia*) and the church as a building (*teopan*). The main temple at Jerusalem is also referred to as the *huei teopan* (ibid., 151). It is not clear if the distinction was made by Sahagún or by the text's original author. Writing in the first decades of the seventeenth century, the devout Domingo Chimalpáhin (1998: 168) called the prehispanic teocalli "houses of devils" but also used the term occasionally in his references to Christian churches; more commonly, however, he adhered to *teopan* or *teopantli* (ibid., 202, 204, 208). Differentiation in the use of this terminology perhaps became more established only after the publication of Molina's dictionary in 1571 (Molina 1992).

18. Valadés's engraving places the church at the center of the atrium, linked to each corner with dotted lines.

19. For posas with one opening (as at Calpan, Epazoyucan, and elsewhere), an anticlockwise procession would exit the church by the west or north door and turn right to approach and make its first pause at the northeast posa, which opens to the south. From there it would continue to the northwest posa, opening to the east and the approaching procession; to the southwest posa, opening to the north and again in the face of the procession; and then to the southeast posa, which faced west toward the oncoming group. In this manner the processors could not turn their backs directly to the altar-benches and any religious artifacts placed upon them. On passing the southeast posa, they would again find themselves facing the opening and altar of the northeast posa as they proceeded toward the church door.

20. "Estaban estas casas ordenadas hacia las cuatro partes del mundo, una hacia oriente, otra hacia el septentrion, otra hacia el poniente, otra hacia el mediodía."

21. Kubler (1992: 385) observed that an anticlockwise pattern was also employed in the cloister *testera* or altar niches. See Edgerton (2001: 64–65) on the same subject. Given the extent of the phenomenon, across geography and ministering order, I am not convinced that this was an initiative on the part of the friars to attract the Indians to Christian processions. Indeed, as their chronicles confirm, processing (also a prehispanic ritual tradition) had become one of the Indians' preferred Christian activities long before the posas or cloisters were built.

22. As one reader of my original manuscript has pointed out, the entwined trunks recall the entwined trees or vines standing over the Tepantitla mountains of sustenance mentioned earlier.

23. By the time many of the maps were painted, most open chapels had also possibly fallen into disuse.

Two maps from Otomi areas close to Tula (Hidalgo) do include open chapels, however (Talistacapa 1579 [AGN 1279]; Misquiahuala, Tezontepec, and Tlahuelilpa 1580 [AGN 2136]). It is possible that these structures still played an active role in the conversion (see *Treinta relaciones*, 1569–71, which observes that the Otomi population was behind in matters of indoctrination [f. 188v]; not all would therefore have been permitted to enter the church).

24. Despite scholarly comment to the contrary, four posas are represented on this drawing. No posas remain at the site today.

25. A number of maps feature four small, identical structures arranged symmetrically around the church, but all facing in the same direction. These may allude not to posa-chapels but to the stone-built altar-chapels of village barrios located outside of the atrium. Chapels of this type still exist at San Pedro Atocpa, Milpa Alta (D.F.). On the 1580 map of Atlatlauhca (México) (see fig. 4.19), and around the churches marking the villages of San Luis, San Pedro, San Juan, and Santa María on the 1601 map of Tepexi del Río (Hidalgo) (AGN 2016), to give only one further example, edifices of this type appear as reed- or grass-covered huts.

26. Lara (2004: 36–39) comes to much the same conclusions.

27. "Patente y obediencia del General para el Padre Fray Martín y sus compañeros" (1523) (reproduced in Mendieta 1973, 1:124–26; Torquemada 1975–83, 5:35).

28. Admittedly, this is a speculative explanation for the lack of the hill glyph in church toponymy, although it is clear that the practice was not restricted to straightforward "naming" of the sociopolitical altepetl (if native toponymy can ever be straightforward). Elsewhere it served narrative purposes. In the mural program at Ixmiquilpan two examples of qualified hill glyphs (one a combined glyph that reads "*altepetl* Tenochtitlan-Ixmiquilpan") form part of an iconic rendering of a traditional warrior song (Wake 2000). The facade of San Bartolo Tenayuca (D.F.) carries Tenayuca's own toponymic glyph (without the hill sign) but also the "curved hill" of Culhuacan (D.F.), thereby referencing the conquest of the two towns by the newly established Mexica, as recorded on the title page of Codex Mendoza.

29. Bierhorst (1985a: 33) observes that in native songs written down in the colonial period the term *huehuetitlan*, "place beside the drum," refers to the church building itself, where—following his interpretation of the song-poems—ghost songs were often performed. If this is a correct reading of the metaphor, activities described in the songs were projected as taking place in the atrium. The metaphor is interesting, for the dark, barrel-vaulted interiors of sixteenth-century churches can certainly be likened to the cylindrical wooden drums of native tradition from which the rhythms of the sacred songs flowed.

30. The journey and the Indian players are mentioned in chapters 194–95 of Bernal Díaz del Castillo's *Historia de la conquista de Nueva España* (1994: 516–28). Bierhorst (1985a: 480) cites the same reference.

31. Possibly the most important study on colonial native mapping to date is Mundy (1996), an analysis of the history and sociopolitical projections of the *Relaciones geográficas* group. But see also the contributions from Gruzinski (1987), Leibsohn (1994, 1995), Brotherston (1997b), and Montes de Oca Vega et al. (2003). For in-depth analyses of the Cuauhtinchan group of maps, see Yoneda (1991, 1994, 1996, 2005) and Carrasco and Sessions (2007).

32. See, for example, the Hereford *Mapa mundi* (ca. 1280) or Nicolas Cusanus's 1491 map of Central Europe.

33. Cortés (1993: 57, 236) reported on two examples prepared for him by native rulers for further expeditions across Mesoamerica; Alva Ixtlilxóchitl (1985, 1:497) observed that some ten Indian nobles accompanied one of these maps to "give reason" to it before the corresponding expedition departed.

34. The Nahuatl and Mixtec languages had no words for "map" in the sense of a geographical diagram that permitted passage through the landscape, suggesting that what we today call maps were not distin-

guished from other types of pictographic texts (Boone 1998a: 18–19) For the sake of clarity, I continue to use the terms "map," "mapmaker," "cartography," "cartographer," and so forth.

35. Given the large corpus of native maps that has survived, the examples used in the following discussion should not be seen as exhaustive or selective. Each offers its own (very individual) detail in respect to the information it contains, but important consistencies are always present to a greater or lesser degree. This is especially true where these paintings were produced in color. The examples used here serve to collate the consistencies as shared across the board. A geographical and source listing is given in appendix B.

36. I have been unable to verify these details on the actual buildings. The church at Almolonca is modern, while the village of Maxtlatlan either has been renamed or no longer exists.

37. None of the churches represented in the Suchitepec group of maps survives in its original form.

38. The panel refers to the year 1521, although the lienzo was prepared circa 1730 (Guevara Hernández 1991).

39. See, for example, Stela 1 at Izapa or the mural paintings in Tomb 105 at Monte Alban.

40. Atlacomulco, "in the well" (Macazaga Ordoño 1979: 40; Siméon 1997: 40); Xocotitlan, "among the fruit trees" (Macazaga Ordoño 1979: 92).

41. Despite inhabiting a busy, modern town, today's Atlacomulcans still identify the mountain as their own, urging outsiders to admire its unique beauty.

42. The date of 1591 for this map is given by AGN, Mexico City, presumably after the text written on its reverse. The map may well have been produced before that year, however, when the towns still fell under the jurisdiction of Metepec. Alternatively, of course, secularization may not have been approved by the Indian communities themselves and was therefore left unacknowledged. Two further maps from Jocotitlan, attached to documents dated 1597 (AGN 2083) and 1721 (AGN 1436), reproduce hill glyphs almost identical to that of the 1591 example but without the *metl* qualifier or representations of the church. Significantly, both hill glyphs are glossed "El serro de Xocotitlan" (the mountain of Jocotitlan).

43. The exclusion may also reflect a territorial dispute between the two centers. The 1582 *Relaciones* map of Teotenango includes Cerro Tetepetl as its own mountain but glosses the mountains and hills of Cerro Tenango to its south as "comunes al Pueblo de Tenango y al de [A]tlatlauhcan" shared by the villages of Tenango and Atlatlauhcan (Acuña 1986: no pagination). The Atlatlauhca mapmaker does not appear to have agreed entirely with this claim.

44. See note 25 above.

45. Tezontepec, Mixquiahuala (today's Tezontepec de Aldama), should not be confused with the Augustinian monastic center of Tezontepec Pachuca, which lies farther to the southeast, close to the México-Hidalgo state border. Although the 1571 map is registered by AGN as belonging to Tezontepec Pachuca, when I showed a copy of it to the villagers of Tezontepec Mixquiahuala in November 1999 they immediately recognized it as their own, principally because of the configuration of the rivers. This appears to be partially acknowledged in a recent publication on the *mercedes* (land grants) maps, where the 1571 map is reproduced and attributed to the Mezquital Valley group (Montes de Oca Vega et al. 2003: 170). The same Tezontepec appears on the 1579 *Relaciones geográficas* map of Mixquiahuala and Atengo.

46. The turquoise waters of the River Tula are not echoed in the representation of Tezontepec's church. A tentative reading here might be that some of the waters flowing from Cerro Huitel feed the Río Tula but that this river's waters are not used by Tezontepec.

47. Blue and/or red churches are not restricted to cartography. In a fragment of a landscaped mural on the wall of the open chapel at Tizatlan (Tlaxcala), a blue church was included. In the monastery entrance at Atlatlauhca (Morelos) a pink church with a blue interior stands at the foot of the great Tree of Jesse that covers the south wall.

48. "[P]or honrar más sus templos sacaban los caminos muy derechos por cordel, de una y de dos leguas, que era cosa harto de ver desde lo alto del principal templo, cómo venían de todos los pueblos menores pueblos y barrios salían [*sic*] los caminos muy derechos y iban a dar al patio de los teucallis."

49. For example, Tichy (1975, 1978, 1979, 1983b). Tichy's central hypothesis is that major ceremonial and political centers were sited at the crossing points of imaginary sightlines drawn between important sacred mountains. Thus, for example, the Pyramid of the Sun at Teotihuacan was constructed on a particular point where the west-east line between Cerro Maravillas and Cerro Tepayo crossed the north-south line between Cerro Gordo and Cerro Azteca. Further south, the Acolhua capital at Texcoco was situated as an observation point toward Cerro Azteca, Cerro Tepoxtle, and Cerro Tlaloc. Villages between Texcoco and these peaks are in the main located on or close to sightlines that link the mountains with the center.

50. See also the maps of Cuauhuitlan (1580) and the Nochistlan Valley (1602) (these maps and the others cited below are listed in appendix B).

51. See also Cuauhuitlan (1580), Tetliztaca (1580), and Acambaro (1580).

52. See also Epazoyucan (1580).

53. See also Culhuacan (1580) and Epazoyucan (1580).

54. The map offers good likenesses of both churches as they still stand today. Although it has a heavily reformed facade, the small church at Ixtiyuca is little more than a rectangular box.

55. The church of Ixtiyuca does not follow the alignment of the suggested sightline between Las Derrumbadas and Citlaltepec; nor is it clear for the time being what feature of the local or more distant landscape it is focused on.

56. Here we might find another explanation for the positioning of the large gloss "Cenpoualla." Perhaps not coincidentally, it is aligned with the sightline, which, when drawn in, underscores it.

57. The pathway still exists, running in direct alignment with the church from the main atrium gateway across the countryside beyond.

58. The representations of the remaining churches on this map pose not a few problems, however. Gruzinski (2002: 139) has recently proposed that they may be individual representations viewed with the great pyramid, in the form of a landscaped hill, in the same position behind each of them. My own on-site measurements and observations suggest that this is not the case. Given native mapmakers' evident interest in mountain-church alignments, the cartographic hills might be real topographical features lying outside the urban traza. See, for example, Tucker (2001) on the greater orientation system traced out across the landscape around this important prehispanic center.

59. With respect to my argument that in the colonial era hill glyphs were sometimes transformed into a landscaped format, compare the 1569 Tlahuelilpa map with the so-called railroad maps (Robertson 1959: 179–80) of the Cuauhtinchan boundary series included, for example, in *Historia tolteca-chichimeca*. The 1569 map accurately portrays the main peaks surrounding Tlahuelilpa's territory (INEGI, *Carta topográfica* F14C89, 1995), each also identifiable by its distinctive outline. Thus the hill glyphs lined up around the edges of the Cuauhtinchan maps may well also present a panorama of the skyline surrounding that polity's territory, each representing the patron-mountain of a neighboring altepetl (which the cartographical mountain glyphically identifies) whose boundaries

adjoin those of Cuauhtinchan. In other words, the 1569 map appears to be a colonial "updating" of the "railroad" style maps, where what is usually understood to be toponymy is in fact topography. When they are read in this way, the issue of nondifferentiation between nature and culture on native maps that Leibsohn raises (1995: 269–70) can perhaps also be explained.

60. See chapter 1, note 16.

61. Horizontal projections of geography were by no means alien to prehispanic graphic conventions. See my observations on the Nuttall "landscapes" in chapter 6.

CHAPTER 5

1. See Kubler (1992: 166–67) for some colonially documented examples of prehispanic images used in this way.

2. "[F]ujetando al verdadero Dios, los Diofes fingidos que adoraban."

3. I define embedded stones as carved stones that lie isolated or in clusters on exterior wall faces and do not obviously belong to any "formal" decorative scheme or serve as recognizable architectural markers in the Euro-Christian tradition. For example, a number of churches carry a stone carved with a Latin cross placed in a central position on the upper part of the apse wall. These I take to be a standard architectural detail denoting the consecrated space that is the apse and are therefore excluded (although this is not to say that they did not serve an additional, native function). Given their size, asymmetry, or apparent arbitrariness of positioning in terms of the surrounding wall face and the presence of other embedded stones on the same building, however, other examples of Latin crosses are included. I have also included the cases of two flowers or glyphs of prehispanic origin that lie centrally on apse walls (at Tepetomatitlan and Tizatlan, respectively), for these are evidently native as far as the choice of stone and style of motif are concerned.

4. Without specialist examination it is clearly difficult to ascertain a precise date for many of the stones bearing prehispanic motifs. Not all prehispanic artisans adopted European sculptural styles, and stone tools were also still used after the conquest.

5. As is well understood, the very low number of European sculptors working in Mexico over the first century of colonial rule—particularly in the area of Indian churches—means that almost all decorative work was placed in the hands of native artisans. It perhaps goes without saying that stonemasons and laborers occupied in building the churches were also native.

6. For a history of Dupaix's work, see Alcina Franch (1969) and Estrada de Gerlero (1994).

7. Kubler's original English text refers to "rings," "star motifs," and "other simpler Indian designs" (Kubler 1972, 2:362, n. 5). In the 1992 Spanish translation this is given as "diseños indígenas sencillos."

8. For a brief commentary on the close relationship between the stones at Tetepango and Atitalaquia and a suggested date for their emplacement, see note 27 below.

9. The xihuitl sign usually takes the form of two larger concentric circles framed within a quatrefoil of smaller dots or concentric circles. See also fig. 5.18.

10. See Nicholson et al. (1997: 155, n. 12) on this and other interpretations. *Xonecuilli* was also the name given to the S-shaped maize cake made as an offering in the festival of Xochilhuitl (see chapter 1).

11. See Alcina Franch et al. (1992) for examples belonging to the Aztec period. Séjourné (1983) reproduces some interesting drawings of tenoned flowers unearthed in urban Chalco.

12. The semantic origins of the signs of the tonalpohualli count remain somewhat obscure, but see the commentary by Brotherston (1992: 60–73) on the potential of their arithmetic constructs and internal resonances of human experience.

13. "[P]reguntado si vido este testigo los dichos ídolos en las dichas casas: dixo, que sí vido los que esta-ban en la haz de la pared, hacia fuera, como piedras quebradas puestas en la pared, e no vido más."

14. "[P]reguntado, si sabía que en las dichas casas, junto á un árbol, dentro de una pared estaban otros ídolos y por encima encalados, y algunos estaban dentro, que no se parescían, y otros de fuera que se veían las figuras: dixo que nunca supo tal ni vido más de los que se veían de fuera de la pared; é que él no lo hizo encalar ni sabe quien lo encaló." That some of the stones lay inside the wall and were not visible suggests that the Spaniards had also made excavations at the site.

15. The text of Ometochtli's trial shows that his alleged idolatrous activities were not the main focus of Spanish colonial concern. His status as an Indian noble who (along with native leaders from other towns) was openly challenging the Spanish presence was a far more serious threat to the colonial pur-pose than a few idols. The activities of this man had to be curtailed quickly and under any pretext.

16. "[Y] lo que se hizo casualmente así por fortaleza de los edificios, y casas, y por ornato de las calles, que también los había en ellas . . . y los que están en los remates de las casas, y por las calles, son para que todo lo conserven, donde idolatraban y les decían sus invocaciones."

17. This is not to say that images of native deities did not exist on embedded stones, but they may well have been categorized by the invaders as different from the "decorative" variety or those used for structural support. That is, an idol embedded into a church wall—such as the face of Tlaloc on the apse of the monastery church of Santiago Tlatelolco—may have been understood as adhering to the old medieval usage noted earlier in this chapter. Spanish references to the reuse of prehispanic masonry in general are frustratingly vague in this respect.

18. Larger examples can be found on the walls of the nave at San Bernardino Xochimilco. Examples of the same flower are known to have existed at the prehispanic ritual site on nearby Cerro Cuailama (Noguera 1972; Wake n.d.c).

19. The reading is not as far-fetched as it may sound. See, for example, Brotherston (1992: 50–60) on the iconic conventions of tlacuilolli and my later observations on a third stone at Tilantongo, placed within category 5.

20. The toponyms at San Bartolo Tenayuca, which also fall under the definition of embedded stones, appear to offer a historical narrative (see chapter 4, note 28).

21. *Didelphis marsupialis* (Miller and Taube 1993: 128) or *Didelphis virginiana* (Garibay 1981, 4:361).

22. As originally documented by Reyes-Valerio (1978, 2000), a native rendering of the *ahuitzotl,* a type of otter associated with Tlaloc (FC11, 1963: 68, and note 1), can be found on the upper west face of the bell tower at Tequixquiac. He notes that Ahuitzotl was also the name of a Mexica ruler. Given its symmetrical emplacement alongside the coat of arms of Castile and Aragon, it may well be intended as a coat of arms of sorts. Again, this is not to say that it did not serve a secondary purpose, but I have chosen not to include it in the present study.

23. In painted form, the same flower-ropes occur on the walls of the area below the choir loft at Fran-ciscan Tecamachalco.

24. The possibility of reading the names of three Tilantongan rulers from embedded stones at this site seems rather more than coincidence. Representations of the last prehispanic rulers of Yanhuitlan have been identified in the formal decoration on the facade of (also Mixtec) Santa María Tiltepec (Wake and Stokes 1997: 222–27).

25. These two examples of Tlaloc's face are almost identical in configuration and the low-relief style of carving. A third identical example can be found on a shop wall in Ramírez de Castillo Street, Xochimilco. Although falling within the boundaries of colonial Xochimilco, the building is prob-ably twentieth-century. I have been unable to ascertain what occupied the site previously or if the stone belonged to it. This example is therefore not included in the present analysis.

26. The oyoalli motif represents the vulva; the breastplate may have been used as a rattle where insertion of its accompanying stick denotes entry or penetration. On Magliabechiano 55r the obscene hand gesture of European origin on the monkey's shield echoes this symbolism.

27. Tetepango and neighboring Atitalaquia are generally assumed to be Augustinian and Franciscan foundations, respectively (Azcue y Mancera et al. 1940: 129; Gerhard 1986: 307; Kubler 1992: 609). Nevertheless, a framed copy of a manuscript hanging inside the church at Tetepango refers to the residence there in 1538 of Domingo de Betanzos, head of the early Dominican mission in New Spain. Together with the iconography of the embedded stones, this would suggest that the original structure at Tetepango was Dominican. The color and style of carving of the "Dominican" stones at Atitalaquia suggest that they too came from Tetepango.

28. Early-twentieth-century photographs of Xochimilco, for example, show that the church of Dolores Xaltocan was still surrounded by open fields; this would also have been the case for the very small chapel of San Pedro, which stands close by. Tlatelolco and Coyoacan lay on the north and south fringes, respectively, of Mexico City until well into the nineteenth century. The monastery complex of San Agustín Acolman has only recently witnessed urban encroachment onto its north, south, and east sides, while the stones on the churches of Cuanalá (Puebla), Itzcuincuitlapilco (Hidalgo), and Tizatlan (Tlaxcala), which stand on high ground (in the case of Itzcuincuitlapilco, a prehispanic platform), will probably always enjoy an uninterrupted view of the distant horizon.

29. In 2003 the freshly plastered and painted barrio church of San Marcos Xochimilco displayed four stones on its west-facing bell tower: the head of a frog, a figurine, and two sets of concentric circles, one carrying a multipetaled flower at its center. All appear to be prehispanic in origin. They are stacked up one above the other in a neat vertical column, however, so their arrangement strongly suggests the intervention of a Western hand. I suspect that all four examples have been moved—possibly very recently—from their original location or locations. These stones are therefore not included in this study although as probable one-time inserts in the church's walls their iconography also reflects the notions of water and fertility associated with embedded stones in general.

30. Also prehispanic in origin, the three extant stones high up on the bell tower at Mixquic are so small and blend in so well with the surrounding masonry that it is possible Dupaix did not see them. Indeed, it was only on a later visit to the site that I noticed a second flower.

31. Because it has probably been moved from its original position (today it lies very symmetrically above the main door), the lizard stone is not included in my analysis here. As an original embedded stone, however, it is relevant to point out that lizards were associated with fertility (see chapter 6).

32. Shortly after Dupaix's death in 1818, his executor, Fausto de Elhuyar, advised Viceroy Juan Ruiz de Apodaca to order a collection of many artifacts found and recorded by Dupaix (Estrada de Gerlero 1994: 197). The collection is now dispersed, half having been taken to Europe in 1828 and the remainder lodged at the then recently established Museo Nacional de México (Bernal 1980: 104, 136). The whereabouts of the collection that remained in Mexico is unknown, although some of the more valuable pieces sent to Europe (a jade mask, for example) are traceable. For reasons of size alone, the lizard plaque housed at the Royal Museum of Art and History, Brussels, cannot be the one found by Dupaix at Xochimilco, as has been suggested.

33. It is perhaps relevant to add that Alfonso Caso and Jorge Acosta found a prehispanic stone carrying the image of the Mixtec deity 5 Death in a wall behind the church (Spores 1967: 43). Was it the removal of this stone that prompted a replacement in the form of a death mask of Christ?

34. I thank the church *fiscales* (church wardens) at San Matías Tepetomatitlan for helping me to document the stones at this site.

35. See the observations by Catherine Good Eshelman (2001: 274–76) on the religious importance of *ihcsan* (ancient or historic) stones and stony terrain among the modern-day Nahuas of the state of Guerrero. Edgerton (2001: 47) reports that the villagers of Teotitlan del Valle are still collecting fragments of prehispanic carved stones and embedding them into the walls of their seventeenth-century church. He puts the custom down to the preservation of sacred material, which gives the replacement host building the sanctity of the old. The large prehispanic stone carved with maize cobs erected in modern times in the atrium at Santo Tomás Ajusco (D.F.), however, served the purpose of revitalizing the fertility of land now under cultivation by Ajuscans (churchwarden, pers. comm., 2007). Although this is not an embedded stone, the perceived magical associations between the church's site and fertility are more than evident in this case. At Tilantongo my interest in the stones was met with considerable suspicion, but I was informed that there were more stones in the local village council office. These proved to be drawn from the same colonial source as those embedded in the church walls. Although they did not include any prehispanic examples, their presence in that office nevertheless recalls Dupaix's finds in the tecpan at Mixquic. Nobody at Tilantongo could explain why these particular stones were not also incorporated into the church walls.

36. The possibility that some stones refer also or exclusively to prehispanic rulers cannot be discarded. These might therefore have a completely different purpose on the walls of churches. Others might relate to urban ritual processing, where they served as markers for specific routes through religious complexes, or as prompts for prayers (Wake n.d.c).

37. See, for example, Tichy (1975, 1978, 1979). The deviation angle 20–21° appears in the corresponding text instead of 21–22°; but Tichy notes that the difference between each grouping is precisely 4.5°, so I take the published figure to be a misprint.

38. See, for example, Aveni (1980) and the collections of essays in Broda et al. (1991) and Broda et al. (2001).

39. "Havia en el circuito de efte Templo mayor otros quarenta Templos menores . . . [que] . . . fe diferenciaban del mayor en que no tenian la entrada al Poniente, fino vnos al Oriente, otros al Norte, y otros al Medio dia" (In the precinct of this great Temple there were some forty smaller Temples . . . that . . . differed from the great one in that they had no entrance to the West, instead some [had it] to the East, others to the North, and others to the South) (Ventancurt 1971, 2:3, f. 74).

40. "[C]ontador del sol y de las fiestas de los demonios, él les venía à decir de cual diablo era aquella fiesta."

41. John G. Bourke's *Diary* (entries for November 1881), cited by Zeilik (1989: 146).

42. Here, of course, certain motifs in the formal sculpture on buildings may also have been included. It is not impossible that some of the colonially carved embedded stones were deliberately salvaged from earlier structures because they had originally served the same function there as part of the formal decoration.

43. Had it been finished, the open chapel constructed on the west side of the church at Tlalmanalco would have blocked direct sunlight on the two north-end chalchihuitl. The present-day church dates to the second half of the sixteenth century, although an earlier version existed on the site (ca. 1532–33). The open chapel was started around 1560, with work halted some four years later (McAndrew 1965: 539; Kubler 1992: 380–81, 585–86), thereby permitting access of light to the stones on the church that followed.

44. As we have seen in the previous chapter, the cross-axis of the monastery church at Acolman, echoed by the four remaining stones, corresponds to the north-south axis of the Street of the Dead at Teotihuacan. It is also directly aligned with pecked cross TEO16 on Cerro Colorado to the north-northeast.

45. The Dominican star on the east wall of San Juan Bautista Coyoacan (fig. 5.22) also looks out toward Huixachtecatl.

CHAPTER 6

1. Mendieta is said to have painted a mural in the monastery entrance at Xochimilco (Torquemada 1975–83, 5:245). Dated 1558, one of the murals in the upper cloister at Huejotzingo was signed by a Fray Antonio Roldán (Salazar Monroy 1944: 13, 24, 1945: 11).

2. The term "Indo-Christian" is borrowed from Reyes-Valerio (1978, 2000). Objections to its being too inclusive (see Peterson 1993: 6) must depend on whether we are considering sixteenth-century native religious artwork from the point of view of style, content, or its overall projection. I use it here to define artwork that expresses native interpretations of Christianity.

3. José Moreno Villa (1986) called tequitqui the "American cousin" of mudéjar. At an ideological level, it is difficult to draw parallels between the art forms of the conqueror that were imposed on the conquered (Mexico) and the art forms of the conquered that were adopted by the conqueror (Spain).

4. "[El] producto mestizo que aparece en América al interpretar los indígenas las imágenes de una religión importada" (José Moreno Villa, *Lo mexicano en las artes plásticas* [Mexico City: Colegio de México, 1948], p. 9, cited by Camelo Arredondo et al. 1964: 45).

5. Stylistic differences in sixteenth-century tequitqui from different regions, cities, or workshops are also rare (McAndrew 1965: 197), which again supports the idea that Indian sculptors copied their European source prints exactly as they perceived them.

6. "[M]uy necesario el ornato y aparato de las iglesias para levantarles el espíritu y moverlos á las cosas de Dios, porque su natural que es tibio y olvidadizo de las cosas interiores, ha menester ser ayudado con la apariencia exterior; y á esta causa los que los gobernaban en tiempo de su infidelidad los ocupaban lo más del tiempo en edificación de sumptuosos templos, y en adornarlos mucho de rosas y flores, demás del oro y plata que tenían."

7. See Contreras García (1985) for an excellent bibliography of sources in respect to this program.

8. "[C]onforme al uso que ellos antiguamente tenían y tienen, que por falta de las letras . . . comunicaban y trataban y daban á entender todas las cosas . . . por pinturas" ([I]n accordance with the custom they had in the past and still have, [which is] that lacking writing . . . they communicated and discussed and explained everything . . . by way of pictures) (*Códice franciscano* 1941: 59).

9. See my comments on this in chapter 2.

10. Examples of the "conversion" of European art forms into meaningful iconic script are numerous. See, for example, Galarza (1966, 1967, 1979) on glyphs for European names; Aguilera (1990) on toponyms; and Harwood (2002) on the (originally) ritual text of part 3 of Codex Mendoza. Wake (2007: 232–39) discusses the various iconic meanings given to the European asterisk on Mapa de Cuauhtinchan No. 2 and other colonial pictorial manuscripts.

11. In a later work, Gruzinski (1994) nevertheless argues that the presence of these glyphs, together with other native signs and symbols, effectively speaks of a subversive appropriation of the art of the Renaissance.

12. Even Sahagún resorted to native metaphors and themes in the preparation of his *Coloquios* and the *Psalmodia*.

13. The existence of dual readings of colonial native "artwork" is admirably illustrated in the observations on part 3 of Codex Mendoza in Harwood (2002). Here the horizontal lines dividing the images into neat rows were not drawn in by the tlacuilo but by the author of the Spanish text and the glosses (the

ink is the same), apparently in order to facilitate his European-oriented interpretation of the iconic text. When these lines are removed, a different reading and a different reading order, closer to the boustrophedon conventions of the prehispanic codices, are permitted (Harwood 2002: 104–105).

14. See, for example, the collections in the Biblioteca Nacional de México, D.F., and the Biblioteca Burgoa, Oaxaca.

15. Lara (2004: 10) makes the same point.

16. Red or red-brown inserts were occasionally printed over heraldic designs or vignettes carrying the insignia of the printing house on the title pages of books or over woodcuts worked in simple outlines (see the examples reproduced in Stols 1989). The technical difficulties encountered in this process are nevertheless readily apparent.

17. A cursory examination of the black and red mural paintings at Acolman and Tepeapulco does reveal some patterning. In the Crucifixion at Acolman (fig. 6.6a) it is only the hair of the figure standing to the right of the cross that is tinted in red-brown. At Tepeapulco (figs. 6.18, 6.19, 6.21, 6.22, 6.23, 6.40) not only apparently disparate objects such as the two apples in the eagle-talon bowl and the walnut shell, the tail of the comet, and the straw in the crib of the infant Jesus were tinged with color but also the blood of Christ. But the Virgin Mary's under-robe, rims around halos (including the rayed sunburst around the head of the infant Jesus), crucifixes, books, and, interestingly, lips and eyelids are fairly consistent across the board.

18. It would seem that the same frieze also decorated the upper walls of the nave at nearby Franciscan Cempoala, although it was covered over by a later (possibly seventeenth-century) design. Although only one banner has survived, it carries the native U-shaped crescent moon. Cempoala and Tepeapulco are separated by only ten to twelve miles as the crow flies, which might suggest the continued existence of strong cult practices associated with the pulque deities. (See also my observations on Tepeapulco below and the pulque count at neighboring Chiconcuac in chapter 7.)

19. Compare figures 6.3 and 7.31. Quadrupeds tied with leads around their haunches occur in European decorative book art of the period, which might offer an ideological source for the image.

20. See also the observations on the Mexican grotesques in Gruzinski (2002: 79–132). I remain unconvinced, however, of the extent to which native artists (all native artists?) would have been initiated into the pagan origins of the grotesque's iconography, which, essentially, is the crux of his argument. The very fact that the 1585 Mexican Council encouraged Indian artists to use the grotesque in order to avoid misrepresentations in thematic religious imagery (ibid., p. 112) must surely argue against such a wide diffusion of those origins.

21. Some of the material included in this section formed part of my 1995 dissertation.

22. At the beginning of the sixteenth century the pure landscape in printmaking was an entirely new subject. Although Dürer employed the genre in much of his work, it was the artists of the Danube school—specifically Albrecht Altdorfer and Wölf Huber—who used the landscape as an image in its own right (Bartrum 1995: 192). An earlier example (composed exclusively of rocks, trees, and plants), however, can be seen in Book 14 of Bartholomaeus Anglicus's *All the Proprytees of Thynges,* published in London (Westminster) in 1495 (see Hind 1963, 2:728).

23. This figure appears to be one of the Three Marys, possibly Mary Salome, who also stood at the foot of the cross (Apostolos-Cappadona 1998: 245).

24. This is particularly clear on the 1595 map of Nopaluca-Ixtiyuca (see fig. 4.21). Although lacking the cross, the 1580 *Relaciones geográficas* map of Epazoyucan was also evidently structured on the Cerro Epazoyu–monastery sightline.

25. In the main too badly damaged to be able to identify local topography, landscaped murals can also be found in the monastic buildings at Huaquechula, Huejotzingo, and Meztitlan, to give but a few examples.

26. The monastery complex of San Juan Evangelista Culhuacan dates to the 1570s, when the once extensive program of mural painting was also executed (Kubler 1992: 448, 614–15). Juan E. Venegas and Ana Graciela Bedolla (1995) offer a brief history of prehispanic and early colonial Culhuacan.

27. Other examples include Actopan (as discussed here), the House of the Dean (Puebla), and Alfajayuca (Hidalgo).

28. In the upper cloister at Culhuacan a monochrome representation of the Adoration of the Magi appears alongside other panels narrating Christ's infancy. In the manner of the Crucifixion panels at Acolman and Epazoyucan, this boasts an interesting topographical detail in the form of a large conical mountain on the skyline, over which a great sun rises. There is little doubt that the artist responsible also intended to draw the viewer's line of vision directly toward it through the space between the Christ-child and the kneeling Magus. I therefore suspect that this is a further representation of Cerro Huixachtecatl.

29. Good examples of this cartographical style include the 1579 map of the boundaries of Mixquic, Xochimilco, and Ayotzingo (AGN 596) and the 1595 map of Chiapulco (AGN 1613).

30. Books of emblems were probably circulating in New Spain from the mid-sixteenth century onward. The 1549 Spanish version of Andrea Alciato's book of emblems (*Emblematum liber,* 1531) was possibly first taken to New Spain by Francisco Cervantes de Salazar; a Latin edition was published in Mexico in 1577 at the behest of the Jesuits, for use in their schools (Sebastián 1994: 60–61).

31. Also cited by Burkhart (1986: 126); Peterson (1993: 107–108); and Gruzinski (1994: 161).

32. "[Y] asimismo una cierva . . . y dos tigres a los lados . . . y de allí se repartía esta agua."

33. At the time of the Spanish conquest, Actopan was subjected to the rule of the Aztec Triple Alliance. The area came under the religious jurisdiction of the Augustinian order. The monastery complex of San Nicolás Tolentino was founded between 1546 and 1548, with building activity registered through 1560. The mural program has been dated to about 1579–81 (MacGregor 1955: 6; Kubler 1992: 68).

34. See, for example, Basalenque (1998: 90–91); Motolinía (1990: 82); Torquemada (1975–83, 6:161–62, 172). Burgoa (1989, 1:113–14) describes a Dominican "miracle" where water was also drawn from a tree.

35. Actopan's *Tebaida* seems to be based very heavily on Jacobus de Voragine's text on Saint Augustine. A horned devil carrying a book (in a native tumpline) and walking up the main pathway at the center of the work refers directly to another story from the saint's life in *The Golden Legend* (Voragine 1993, 2:130).

36. These figures are identified individually in Sebastián et al. (1995: 126–32).

37. So too do the remains of a painting of the Crucifixion in the monastery refectory, which is also backed by a representation of the two crags as viewed from Actopan. Again, Christ's Passion was narrated as having taken place at Actopan.

38. Nicholas of Tolentine, usually represented with a star on his breast (Hall 1979: 223), appears in several Mexican images wearing a star-covered habit. See, for example, the mural in the open chapel at Epazoyucan. In the Actopan lunette he carries a book and a bird beneath his left arm, the latter almost certainly an allusion to the legend that he restored two roasted pigeons to life (ibid., pp. 223–24).

39. See also the woodcut of the penitent Mary Magdalene on f. 117v of Sahagún's 1583 *Psalmodia* (reproduced in Burkhart 1996: 172, fig. 8), which again includes the ointment pot and the altar with open book and crucifix.

40. This useful report on Actopan is dated 1791.

41. Santa Magdalena and San Jerónimo were almost certainly existent in the sixteenth century, for both retain their original atrial crosses.

42. Escalante Gonzalbo's reading of the cloister architecture at Cuauhtinchan can be extended by observing that the cavernous indenture that was the real "reddish cave of Xilote mountain" was formed by a natural water gully sourced in the sacred Tlaxcallan volcano Matlalcueye (Yoneda 1996: 262). As included on the 1705 map of Cuauhtinchan (AGN 655; reproduced in Yoneda 1991 and in Escalante Gonzalbo 1997), a branch of this watercourse ran beneath the church and the cloister and surfaced in the monastery orchard. Antonio de Ciudad Real (1976, 1:87) recorded much the same detail in the sixteenth century. The underground stream therefore probably fed the cloister fountain, just as the stream was fed from Matlalcueye within Cuauhtinchan's sacred patron-mountain.

43. Tepeapulco, an important pilgrimage center for the cult of Tlaloc (Torquemada 1975–83, 3:79), at contact also boasted a large temple dedicated to the Mexica patron-deity Huitzilopochtli. Conversion of the area was undertaken by the Franciscan order, with little reported resistance; construction of the monastery commenced in 1530 over the site of "the demon's temple" (Motolinía 1990: 80–81). Building activity is registered for the 1530s and 1550s, with the mural paintings dating to after 1560. The monastery's most illustrious resident was probably Bernardino de Sahagún, who initiated his ethnographic research into the native past there, between 1558 and 1561. A general history of prehispanic Tepeapulco and the work of Sahagún is found in Nicholson (1973, 1974). José Gorbea Trueba (1957) provides a good description of the monastery complex.

44. On May 2 at Tepeapulco the Catholic festival of the Holy Cross (appropriated to pursue the pre–rainy season mountaintop rituals) is marked with a midday mass on Cerro Xihuingo.

45. Two rabbits appear, for example, in an illuminated Crucifixion on f. 219v of the *Preparatio ad missam pontificalem* produced in Rome in 1520 (Alexander 1995). See also the *Triumph of Chastity* from a 1488 edition of Francesco Petrarch's *Trionfi,* reproduced in Peterson (1985: fig. 149).

46. The Annunciation is reproduced in Hind (1963, 2:465, 501).

47. Andrews and Hassig (1984: 95) translate this line as "my mother, din of the earth, and you, my father, one rabbit."

48. Tepeapulco also hosts a series of big cats in its iconography (see my commentary above on Culhuacan). Lions mounted by human figures make up the main (and for a church most unusual) design over the church portal. Similar creatures romp through the frieze around the church nave (see fig. 7.31). At the town's sixteenth-century water deposit (*caja de agua*), which stands close to the monastery complex, eleven lions dispense in-flowing water from their open maws. The number is interesting not only because of its unevenness (from a European perspective) but also because it echoes the eleven sky phases of the zodiac, closely associated with the pulque deities in prehispanic religious belief.

49. The phenomenon may also exist at other sites, including Tepeapulco, but is not immediately apparent.

50. "Es el mismo dios, pero es otra historia."

51. The main participants at this festival were also medicine women and midwives (FC2, 1981: 19).

52. Here I cite Sahagún and his contemporaries. Some scholars now doubt whether Tepeyacac was a shrine to Tonantzin.

53. See also Sahagún (1981, 3:352–53) on the friars' persistence in referring to the Christian patronesses of both sites with the Nahuatl names of the old goddesses. "Idolatrous" their intentions could not have been; open to misinterpretation or reinterpretation they certainly were.

54. Saint Michael the Archangel (feastday: September 29) is saluted on churchyard buntings (*¡Viva San Miguel!*) during Day of the Dead celebrations in Tulyhualco (Xochimilco) at the beginning of November, when the sacred water-mountains are still thanked for their favors during the agricultural cycle (Nutini 1988). The saint is closely associated with the water and fertility cults (see note 65 below), possibly because his Appearance is celebrated in the Catholic calendar on May 8, at the opening of the rainy season.

55. Mesoamericans obviously had no knowledge of the science of genetic modification, the domesticated maize plant probably having resulted from centuries of attempting to grow various male and female species of wild maize together. The myths of genesis and the extraordinary interchange of role and gender among the maize deities nevertheless attest to a basic understanding of the process of cross-pollination.

56. Xochipilli appears in Codex Féjérváry and Codex Vaticanus 3773 with his leg or foot amputated (that is, as Tezcatlipoca–Smoking Mirror is commonly portrayed) (Olivier 2000: 105).

57. See also Heyden (2001: 21–22) on the dual gender of the generic maize deity.

58. Edmund Leach, *Structuralist Interpretations of Biblical Myth* (Cambridge: Cambridge University Press, 1983), cited in Gillespie (1999: 171).

59. "[O]s da todo lo que hay en la tierra, lo que se bebe, lo que se come."

60. "[N]o le sabían pintar sino como aire."

61. "[A]quella imagen que veían de hombre crucificado, era imagen de nuestro Dios, no en cuanto Dios que no se puede pintar porque es puro espíritu."

62. "[A]l que vosotros no habéis conocido."

63. With its elongated stamens, the flower also resembles *Mimosa hostilis,* another species with psychotropic properties. Sahagún also included the *tlapaltecomaxochitl* (red *Solandra* in Anderson's translation) in Saint Francis's garden (Sahagún 1993: 236; Anderson 1993: 237). The yellow *Solandra* is certainly a powerful hallucinogen, but its large bulbous blossom encasing the stamen does not correspond to Clare's flower at Tlalmanalco.

64. Numerous images of pulque deities wearing the feather/paper device occur in the codices. A primary example of a flying tlaloque comes in a stone box housed at the British Museum, London. It wears just such a device and pours both water and maize from a container as it travels through the air.

65. See Jiménez and Villela (1998: 71) on the Nahuas of Guerrero, Medina Hernández (2001: 146) on the Tzeltals of Chiapas, and Lupo (2001: 350) on the Nahuas of the Sierra de Puebla, who call Saint Michael the Archangel "son of thunder" (Lupo 2001: 351).

66. The stylized flowers at either side of the maguey plants may represent the *quioxochitl* (maguey flower), whose distinctive blossoms are crowded together in rounded formation on single stems. Similar motifs occur at Otumba, a site that also carries stylizations of the maguey plant itself, and at Calpulalpan (see fig. 7.9b).

67. The symbolic fruits occur widely throughout Renaissance art. See, for example, Joos van Cleve's *Holy Family* (sixteenth century), now housed in the Metropolitan Museum in New York, where the platter and cherry/walnut overspill occupy the foreground of a portrait of the *Virgo lactans.*

68. See also Chalchiuhtlicue, who overlaps with Mayahuel, on Féjérváry 29, Borgia 17, and Vaticanus B 42.

69. Mayahuel suckles a fish on Borgia 16, an image that would certainly find a symbolic parallel in Christian iconography.

70. An early-seventeenth-century example can be seen on the title page of Cristóforo de Castro's *Histo-*

ria Deiparae Virginis Mariae, published in Spain in 1605, a copy of which was held in the library of the monastery of San Agustín in Mexico City (Muñoz Espinosa 1999: 100, 139).

71. The diamond shape may have resulted from an attempt to depict a square or rectangular folded cloth lying on the ground and viewed from a horizontal perspective (but see below in this chapter).

72. I am grateful to Jo and Adrian Locke for bringing the painted example of the xuchimitl at Acolman to my attention. At (also Augustinian) Ixmiquilpan, a flower pierced with a flower-tipped arrow can be seen beneath one of the jaguar warrior's feet on the north wall of the nave mural program.

73. On this particular element associated with the pulque deities, see Nicholson 1991.

74. References to the iconography of pulque at Acolman are not restricted to the sculpture of the Virgin and the cross. A frieze of maguey cacti decorates the monastery entrance, while a design composed of stylized maguey spines covers the north wall of the open chapel. In both form and color, it is highly reminiscent of the maguey-spine mural painting on the wall of the temple at Atetelco, Teotihuacan. The emphasis on the hands of the Acolman Virgin also brings to mind the numerous inserts of a goddess's hands in the mural paintings at the same site. It is not impossible that the iconography of the mural paintings at Teotihuacan was already known to the sixteenth-century inhabitants of Acolman. The accurate representation of the Avenue of the Dead, with the Pyramids of the Sun and Moon but also long-buried, smaller lateral platforms, on the 1580 map of Tecciztlan, Acolman, Teotihuacan, and Tepechpan certainly suggests that they were familiar with the layout of the ancient city.

75. Cholula is best known for its shrine to Quetzalcoatl, a deity also strongly linked to the cult of water and fertility (Nicholson 1971: 428). He appears, for example, on f. 61 of Codex Magliabechiano, among the lineup of pulque deities (although not described as one of them). Quetzalcoatl in his manifestation as Ehecatl (Wind deity) was also one of the protagonists of the myth of the creation of maguey from the bones of Mayahuel (*HM* 1979: 106–107). Very early murals depicting a ritual pulque orgy occur at the site, while a number of local villages still carry the names of the cult's major deities (San Miguel Papaztac, San Garbiel [*sic*] Ometoxtla).

76. "Y, con ellos [Ometochtli and Tezcatlipoca], tenían pintada" (And, [together] with them, was a painting).

77. Modern-day Nahua groups of the Puebla highlands believe that Christ's executioners attempted to poison him with the vinegar-soaked sponge. Christ responded that the vinegar would not kill him but that his children should drink it so that they would sleep and, like him, return to life: "Y así por eso nos emborrachamos y volvemos en sí otra vez" (And so for this [reason] we get drunk and come to our senses again) (Alessandro Lupo, "Tatiochihualatzin, valores simbólicos del alcohol en la Sierra de Puebla," *Estudios de Cultura Náhuatl* 21 [1991]: 226, cited by Olivier 2000: 115).

78. "[T]enían pintada una figura de mujer, llamada HUEY TONANTZIN, que quiere decir 'n[uest]ra gran madre,' que decían madre de todos estos dioses y demonios" ([W]as a painting of the figure of a woman, named GREAT TONANTZIN, which means "our great mother," for they called all these gods and demons mother).

79. "[Y] así pintaban el signo de este día muy ufano y gallardo, con una caña de maíz en la mano, denotando fertilidad."

80. "[C]uando tenien necesidad de agua, é haciéndolo llovie."

81. The moon accompanying the Tau "cross" was not necessarily toponymic, of course. As noted above, Meztitlan appears to have been a center of the pulque cult, a primary symbol of which was the crescent moon. The villages around the modern-day town are still renowned for the quality of their pulque (local resident, pers. comm., 1992).

82. "[L]os cristianos adoraban al dios que ellos llamaron Tonacaquáhuitl, que significa árbol del substento, que así lo llamaban los antiguos."

83. "[M]adero, que da el sustento de nuestra vida; tomada de la etimología del maíz, que llaman tonacayutl, que quiere decir: cosa de nuestra carne, como quien dice, la cosa que alimenta nuestro cuerpo."

84. "[L]a cruz que llamaron Quiahutzteotlchicahualistéotl y otros Tonacaquáhuitl que quiere decir: dios de las lluvias y de la salud y árbol del sustento o de la vida."

85. Sebastián (1989: 200, citing V. Serra i Boldù, *Llibre popular del Rosari: Folk-lore del Roser* [Barcelona: Foment de Pietat Catalana, 1917], pp. 89–91) cites a third-century paleo-Christian hymn: "Este árbol que se levanta tan lejos del cielo, sube de la tierra a los cielos. Planta inmortal, se dirige al centro del cielo y de la tierra: firme sostén del universo" (This tree that grows so far from the sky rises from the earth to the heavens. Immortal plant, it places itself at the center of the sky and the earth: firm support of the universe).

86. Prehispanic Ocuituco appears to have been an independent center, with no specific allegiance to Tenochtitlan. Its only direct connection with the Mexica capital was as a regular supplier of flowers (Gerhard 1986: 93).

87. Eduard Seler, *Gesammelte Abhandlungen zur Amerikanischen Sprach- und Altertumskunde,* 5 vols. (Graz, Austria: Akademische Druck- u. Verlagsanstalt, 1960–61), 4:674–75, cited by Peterson (1993: 109).

88. In this group of crosses evincing a *horror vacui,* see also the atrial cross at the Basilica of Guadalupe (D.F.) and the smaller version that still stands in the paupers' cemetery of Santiaguito, Aztacoalco (D.F.).

89. The same detail reoccurs on the other side of this cross (see fig. 6.62) but is too eroded to be able to affirm that they also represent trees.

90. Unusually, the chalice is positioned at the base of the cross, where we might expect to see the skull of Adam or of Golgotha. I know of no symbolism related to an upturned chalice in European art. In the Counter-Reformation, however, the skull of Adam was sometimes depicted upside down, as if it were a chalice (Hall 1979: 85). But see note 113 below.

91. See Victoria Asensio (1985) and Lara (2004) for an illustration of the example at Nonoalco. During my visit to Molango in 1992, a drawing of the Augustinian Roa's mountaintop cross pasted in a shop window showed it to be of the same design.

92. See also the base of the cross as depicted on the 1580 map of Huejutla (fig. 4.7), another High Sierra site.

93. This is not the only prehispanic stone to have been brought to Santo Tomás's church in more recent times. See chapter 5, note 35.

94. The village square at Huaquechula, where the cross now stands, displays a fine collection of large pieces of carved prehispanic masonry unearthed locally. Some, however, have had Euro-Christian signs or symbols etched into them.

95. Also cited by Burkhart (1988: 239).

96. See, for example, the title page of Codex Féjérváry (fig. 4.2). The Maya *kin* sign (meaning "sun" or "day") also takes the form of a four-petaled flower.

97. See note 35 above.

98. The atrial crosses at Magdalena Tlatelulco (Tlaxcala) and San Jacinto (San Angel, D.F.), for example, also follow this iconographical pattern. These crosses are possibly not sixteenth-century but nevertheless adhere to the style of earlier versions.

99. Compare these motifs to the feathered edge of Xochipilli's headdress (fig. 6.29).

100. "Y dezían ellos q[ue] por q[ue] estavan estos árboles en las tierras las hazian fertiles" (And they said that the land was made fertile because these trees were there). The non-native glossator goes on to point out that in fact they only grow on fertile soil.

101. "Este arbol dezian estos indios q[ue] en las partes donde los avia q[ue] se cojían munchas legumbres y dezian ell[os] q[ue] por el arbol naçian" ([Of] this tree these Indians said that in areas where they grew many legumes were gathered and they said they were born of the tree).

102. Codex Tudela, one of the Magliabechiano group of postconquest texts drawn from a possibly prehispanic prototype (see Boone 1983), contains a series of later inserts that refer to the Yope Indians of Guerrero (ibid., pp. 72, 78, et passim). This would suggest that the manuscript had ties with the area. Identified also as Tlapanecs, the Yopes survived in rough, infertile terrains and were considered (at least by Sahagún's informants) to be rude and unsophisticated (Sahagún 1981, 3:205). As Brotherston (1992: 99) points out, the Tudela trees typify varieties of geography.

103. Although so highly stylized as to be barely identifiable, the tree of the East wears the same chalchihuitl-studded "bracelet" found on the trees of the West and Center, which are very clearly maize plants. In this sense, the three maize trees appear to allude to the three main stages of the plant's growth during the temporal cycle, as defined by their bracelets. I interpret the yellow bracelet of the East (with one chalchihuitl) as denoting the end of the dry season when the seedlings, germinated by the early rains, await the onset of the rainy season proper. Indeed, its thin, curling stems, dotted with small yellow circles, recall the spindly shoots and tangled root growths that sprout from the germinating seeds. The blue bracelet of the West (with an incremented number of chalchihuitl) denotes the plant during the rainy season proper. Finally, the yellow bracelet of the Center (again with one chalchihuitl) corresponds to the period of sunshine and light precipitation following the rainy season that permits maturation.

104. "[Y] decían *tota, topiltzin y yolometl,* los cuales vocablos quieren decir 'nuestro padre, y nuestro hijo y el corazón de ambos.'"

105. It seems that Durán understood *yolometl* to derive from *yol*[*otl*], "heart," and *ome,* "two," "both" (Siméon 1997: 199, 356). His misinterpretation of the native trees as references to the Trinity (which in turn led to the mistranslation) may well have been prompted by the medieval legend that Christ's cross was made of three trees seeded from the Tree of Life, which became one (Sebastián 1989: 197–99). In another version of the legend, these were identified as a cedar, a cypress, and a pine, understood to represent the Father, Son, and Holy Spirit (Mircea Eliade, *Tratado de historia de las religiones* [Madrid: Instituto de Estudios Políticos, 1954], p. 279, cited by Sebastián 1989: 199–200).

106. Although it is badly eroded, a possible exception might be to the immediate right of the representation of the sun on the remains of what appears to be a very early atrial cross embedded into the church facade at Tepetomatitlan (see fig. 5.23). If this is the rooster, its positioning not only places its crowing at sunrise (as if the iconography of the piece was in narrative form) but might also suggest that the first stone crosses did present the Christian symbol as the prehispanic celestial bird on the branch.

107. The El Escorial miter is reproduced in *Aztecs* (Royal Academy of Arts 2002: 342). According to Christian legend, a swallow tried to console Christ at the Crucifixion. The Meztitlan birds do not appear to represent swallows either.

108. See also *RSNE* (1964: 29, 32).

109. The reference to "parrot" may well allude to the last in the lineup of the thirteen quecholli flyers that make up the Mesoamerican day count. Together with the quetzal and the macaw, the parrot was a

flyer with precious feathers (Brotherston 1992: 64). In a Nahua text of the early colonial period the parrot appears as speaker for the quecholli, which it labels with the reverential epithet *ipalnemoani,* "the ones through whom we live" (ibid., pp. 318–19). In respect to other birds associated with the Indo-Christian flower-tree of sustenance in the song-poems, roosters again fail to make a contextual appearance, being usurped by the hummingbird, the golden bellbird, and the quetzal (*CM,* ff. 12, 20; 1985: 166–67, 194–95).

110. It has been observed that crosses carrying Christ's head at their axis are more typically Augustinian (Lara 1996: 9, citing Mildred Monteverde, "Sixteenth-Century Mexican Atrium Crosses" [Ph.D. diss., Los Angeles, University of California, 1972]). Given that some of the best-known examples of this type of cross are found at Franciscan establishments (Tecali, Huaquechula, Tlahuelilpa, Huichapan, Tlaxcala, the Basilica of Guadalupe, not to mention others at smaller village sites), such a pattern seems doubtful. In effect, it is difficult to detect any patterns, either by order or geographically, for this or other key iconographical features on the crosses.

111. Laurette Séjourné (1978: 117) identifies these particular cobs as sacrificial flint knives, yet each has a maize leaf appendage. Similar elements sprouting from between two leaves, often with a corn tassel attached, appear throughout Codex Borgia. The Palenque example echoes the Borgia trees in that a bird stands on the horizontally extended branches while the fleshless face of an earth deity lies at the maize plant's feet. That is, although separated by time and geography, the ancient Maya and Late Postclassic central Mexican examples represent very closely paralleled visual conceptualizations of world trees.

112. According to Molina's dictionary, *centli* (sometimes also written as *cintli*) referred to the maize cob that was "curada y seca" (Molina 1992, 2nd pagination, p. 18), in other words, the fully matured cob that had been cut and dried and was ready for shucking and storage or to be set aside for the next sowing.

113. There are two possible exceptions among surviving crosses. The upturned chalice at the base of the cross at Tlapanaloya (fig. 6.55) is reminiscent of upturned pulque pots in the codices. In this context, the tonalli sign on the same cross corresponds to one of the graphic attributes of the deity Ixtlilton, who was ritually associated with newly fermented pulque (FC1, 1970: 35–36; CMPR, f. 262v; Codex Magliabechiano, f. 63r). Crosses that display trilobed or fleur-de-lis tips may in fact evoke maguey leaves (figs. 6.25, 6.73). In Book 11 of the Florentine Codex (Anderson and Dibble 1981, illus. 749) cultivated magueys are laid out within a rectangle seemingly tied by a "decorative" motif in the form of the fleur-de-lis. A second fleur-de-lis appears between two additional plants at the base of the panel. Seen side by side, the stylized plants and the fleur-de-lis do share a visual resemblance (and the fleur-de-lis do not look out of place in the maguey patch), as if the panel is "logging" a new, European-sourced, iconic rendering of the maguey plant. Both examples of trilobed tipped crosses illustrated in this chapter (at Tepoztlan and Acolman) are found at sites with known connections to the pulque cult.

114. Mary's dual associations with maguey and maize are perhaps echoed in the crown of the Queen of Heaven sculpted on the northwest posa at Huejotzingo. As originally documented by Reyes-Valerio (1978: 258, 260, 2000: 319), the sign for precious metal (*teocuitlatl,* "excrement of the gods") was included as one of the crown's inlaid jewels. On folios 36r and 55r of Codex Magliabechiano, respectively, Xilonen, goddess of young maize, and the pulque deity, Tlaltecayoa (see fig. 5.20a), both wear the sign as a pectoral disk.

115. Broda's sources are Eustaquio Celestino Solís, "Gotas de maíz: Sistema de cargos y ritual agrícola en San Juan Tetelcingo, Guerrero" (Ph.D. diss., Universidad Nacional Autónoma de México, 1997); and Mercedes Olivera, "Huemitl de mayo en Citlala: ¿Ofrendas para Chicomecoatl o para la Santa Cruz?" in Barbro Dahlgren, *Mesoamerica: Homenaje al doctor Paul Kirchhoff* (Mexico City: INAH, 1979).

CHAPTER 7

1. See, for example, the copyist's notes at the beginning of a "children song" (*CM*, f. 46r; 1985: 286–87) and a "jewel song" (ibid., f. 37v; pp. 254–55).

2. See Bierhorst (1985b) for the naming of "paradise," as employed in *CM*. *RSNE* offers the same metaphors.

3. Certainly the *izquixochitl* is hybridized in the *Cantares mexicanos* manuscript as *cacahuaizquixochitl* ("narcotic popcorn flowers": Bierhorst 1985a: 231), while elsewhere its tree is contextually linked with *cacahuaxochinpoyon* ("narcotic cacao flowers": ibid., p. 245) (*CM*, ff. 30r, 34v; 1985: 230–31, 244–45). I can find no colonial or modern-day source to indicate that the *izquixochitl* (of the genus *Bourreria*) possesses psychoactive properties. But here a metaphorical pun may also be at work that invokes the major pulque deity Izquitecatl—one of "the four hundred rabbits, who are the substance of wine" (FC1, 1970: 51), in whose honor copious quantities of pulque were ritually imbibed (FC2, 1981: 36; FC4, 1979: 16–17). The deity's temple was very specifically located on the bank of a river at a place called Izquitlan (FC2, 1981: 145, 214.) The "illustration" of the three species of izquixochitl listed in the Florentine Codex (Anderson and Dibble 1963: 202, n. 5) depicts its trees growing between a veinlike river system around which rabbits play (see illus. 685a–c in Anderson and Dibble 1963). Like many of the (to date) over-conservatively studied images of this codex, the illustration encodes a reference to Izquitlan (see also my observations on the maguey patch in chapter 6, note 114). While in the song-poems the ritual imbibing of pulque is not directly implied, the morpheme *octli* (pulque) is nevertheless frequently employed as a suffix to denote a disturbed or deranged state (Bierhorst 1985b: 248).

4. Among the many birds admired for their song, precious plumage, or watery habitat (see Bierhorst 1985b), and together with the butterfly (*papalotl*) (7), the song-poems offer a good lineup of the thirteen flyers (quecholli): green hummingbird (*chalchiuhhuitzilin*) (2); quail (*zolin*) (4); eagle (*cuauhquecholli*) (5); owl (*tecolotl*) (10); scarlet macaw (*alotl*) (11); resplendent trogon (*quetzaltototl*) (12); and parrot (*toznene*) (13). Others may also be present, but variations in translation/species identification across sources tend to make an analysis of this type difficult. Although Bierhorst (1985a) translates *quecholli* as "swan," he nevertheless acknowledges that the term identifies the birds as divine (Bierhorst 1985b: 275–76).

5. See, for example, the blue and red quecholli and quecholli-impersonators on CMPR f. 254r (plate 1). Torquemada (1975–83, 3:403) was under the impression that the quechol was a blue- and red-plumed water bird.

6. For the sake of context, I have here replaced Bierhorst's "swan" with the Nahuatl *quecholli*.

7. Garibay (1964: 18, 37) translates this as "hilera" of flowers, although in the sense that it is the flowers that assemble themselves into a chain or garland.

8. Commentary on the extent of this phenomenon, together with an appendix of examples, is included in chapter 7 of my 1995 dissertation. Since then I have found many others. In the present study, however, this particular aspect of church iconography is restricted to its relevance to the framing rituals (but see note 9 below).

9. The use of calendrical or astronomical counts in architecture was also a prehispanic tradition, perhaps the best-known example to survive being the pyramid of 360 niches at El Tajín (Veracruz). But see Kubler (1984: 243) and Segovia (1991) on Uxmal, in the Yucatán. As counts in the formal "decoration" of the Indians' new churches, I suspect that their function was not exclusively focused on the framing rituals, for the calendar was a guiding principle of native life and the structural framework around which life operated. Good examples include "like-in-kind" historical dating (Umberger 1981); the

structure of the sacred books, and the fiscal and geographical organization of the commodities trib-ute system (Brotherston 1992: 56–73, 99, 1995: 31, 158–82, 2005: 31–39); and the divisions of the *coatequitl* (labor call-up system) (Rojas Rabiela 1979). Colonial Indian painters and sculptors would probably instinctively have arranged the invader's motifs in accordance with a model that was psycho-logically satisfying or reassuring to their world. As seen in chapter 3, however, the ritual calendar was also the target of eradication. It is not impossible that painters and sculptors may also have chosen to safeguard this knowledge by concealing it in the invader's art forms.

10. See Sahagún (1981, 1:239) on the intervals of days between rituals held at the temple of Macuilma-linalli, "five-twisted," and the number of reed "straws" placed in the "five-fold pulque" (*macuiloctli*) at the feast of Pachtecatl (ibid., p. 249), another major deity of the cult.

11. See, for example, Alexander (1995) on Renaissance book illumination between 1450 and 1550.

12. See chapter 5, note 18.

13. A magnificent preconquest relief carving of a huacalxochitl can also be found on a rocky outcrop that forms part of a one-time ritual route to the summit of Cerro Cuailama, near Xochimilco. The flower is quite rare today, but representations of it still pervade the flower murals and arches con-structed for village church festivals.

14. Drum cadences from *Cantares mexicanos* (f. 15v; 1985: 178–79).

15. The flowers at Malinalco include yolloxochitl, *xiloxochitl,* and huacalxochitl (Peterson 1993: 85–102), together with other species similar in appearance to the poyomatli and sinicuiche (ibid., figs. 27, 55, 104). Among the flying creatures are parrots, hummingbirds and eagle hawks, and, of course, butterflies (ibid. pp. 109–17). A feathery or foliaged parrot was also included on the portal panel at Apasco (México) (fig. 7.19).

16. See the diagram of the layout of the cloister murals in Peterson (1993: fig. 18).

17. Both figures are also reproduced in Peterson (1993), within the same context.

18. A Mexica stone "box" of unknown usage, also carved with the ilhuitl, a stylized butterfly, a shell and two dots, and a flower, was catalogued in Alcina Franch et al. (1992: 56) and reproduced by Reyes-Valerio (2000: photo 131). Did these boxes serve to store the books of flower-songs?

19. The Xoloc glyphs were originally documented by Reyes-Valerio (2000: 360 and photos 65, 130), al-though he identified the shells and flower as the calendrical signs Flint and Movement, respectively.

20. "[L]os cantares que en aquellos areitos cantaban, tenían por oración, llevándolos en conformidad de un mismo tono y meneos, con mucho seso y peso, sin discrepar en voz ni en paso."

21. "Llevaban por guía de su baile . . . un indio . . . vestido como pájaro o como murciélago, con sus alas y cresta de ricas y grandes plumas" (To lead the dance they brought . . . an Indian . . . dressed as a bird or a bat, with his wings and crest [made] of feathers rich and long) (p. 121). "[S]acaban diferentes trajes y atavíos de mantas y plumas y cabelleras y máscaras . . . vistiéndose unas veces como águilas, otras como tigres, y leones . . . otras veces como salvajes y como monos y perros y otros mil disfraces" (They brought out different costumes and garments [like] mantles and [made of] feathers, and long hair [wigs?] and masks . . . sometimes dressing up as eagles, at other times as tigers and lions [jaguars and pumas] . . . and at other times as wild beasts/tribes and as monkeys and dogs and a thousand other disguises) (p. 193).

22. "[Y] llevaban en una mano un pequeño escudo cubierto de las más vistosas plumas."

23. "[H]acían unos árboles a mano, muy llenos de flores olorosas. . . . Mientras bailaban, descendían unos muchachos, vestidos todos como pájaros, y otros como mariposas. . . . Subíanse por estos árboles y andaban de rama en rama chupando el rocío de aquellas rosas."

24. "En las gargantas de los pies y en las muñecas de las manos traían unos cascabeles de oro."

25. To cite only a few examples among many, see the Mexica stone sculptures of Xiuhtecuhtli and the reclining Tlaloc at the entrance to his shrine on the Templo Mayor; the blue and red merlons from Teotihuacan; the relief carvings in the interior of Tenochtitlan's Eagle Warrior precinct; the turquoise and redstone mosaic masks from Teotihuacan and Tenochtitlan; and the magnificent Mexica feathered shield depicting a blue coyote on a crimson background.

26. Polychrome murals are not restricted to the lavishness of Augustinian establishments such as Actopan, Ixmiquilpan, Meztitlan, Tezontepec (Pachuca), and Xoxoteco in the state of Hidalgo. They can also be seen or exist as faded fragments at Franciscan Cholula, Huaquechula, Huejotzingo, Tlalmanalco, Tecamachalco (including those by Gerson), Tecali, and Cuauhtinchan (Puebla), Tlahuelilpa (Hidalgo), Zinacantepec, Ozumba (México), and at Dominican Huaxtepec and Tetela del Volcán (Morelos).

Glossary of Frequently Used Nahuatl or Nahuatl-Derived Terms

altepetl: from the dual metaphor **in atl in tepetl,** "the water, the mountain." Term used for a territorial or political unit or confederation of the same.

atl tlachinolli: "water, fire," metaphor for war, but also a symbol for the rainy and dry seasons of the agricultural calendar.

ayaucalli: "mist-house," a temple or group of temples dedicated to the rain deities.

cempoalxochitl: "twenty-flower" or "many-flower" (due to its multiple petals), golden marigold (*Tagetes erecta L.*).

chalchihuitl: prized blue-green stone, a symbol for all that is precious and beautiful. In iconic script the chalchihuitl sign for precious water consists of two or more concentric circles, often in conjunction with shell motifs.

copalli: tree resin used for incensing.

huacalxochitl: "basket-flower"; red flower (now rare) with psychoactive properties, also used as a symbol of fertility (often identified as *Phyllodendrum affine* Hemsl., but disputed).

ilhuitl: "day," "feast"; the iconic sign is two inverted "hooks" (Peterson 1993).

ixiptla: impersonator of the gods destined for sacrifice.

malinalli: "twisted-thing," from *malinalli*, a type of grass, configured as two entwined elements; the twelfth of the twenty day-signs.

octli: fermented sap of the maguey cactus, more commonly known as pulque (see **teoctli**).

ollin: "movement," "rubber"; the seventeenth of the twenty day-signs.

oyoalli: hollow, pear-, or almond-shaped breast ornament frequently associated with the pulque gods; possibly used as a rattle instrument.

pachtli: parasitic tree moss associated with the pulque cult (*Tlilantia* sp.).

picietl: raw tobacco.

poyomatli: the narcotic calyx of the *cacahuaxochitl* (*Lexarza funebris*).

quecholli/quecholtin: the thirteen sacred "flyers" of the constituent day count (see **tonalpohualli**)

sinicuiche (Mexicanism, from the Nahuatl: see Santamaría 2000: 975): mountain flower with psychotropic properties (*Heimia salicifolia*)

tecpan: palace or residence of nobility, seat of Indian government.

teoamoxtli: "divine-book," containing the sacred cosmic knowledge.

teocalli: "sacred-force-house," temple.

teoctli: "sacred-*octli*," used to induce ritual drunkenness.

teotl: "sacred-force" (pl. *teteo*).

tepetl: "hill," "mountain."

tepictoton: "little molded ones," tzoalli molded effigies of the tlaloque or mountains.

tequitqui: modern-day term derived from *tequitl*, "tribute," which defines an indigenous sculptural style developed in the early colonial period.

tlacuatl: Mexican marsupial of the opossum family (*Didelphis virginiana*).

tlacuilo: painter-scribe (pl. *tlacuiloque*).

tlacuilolli: picture writing; term used today for the iconic writing system employed in central Mexico.

tlaloque: messengers of the rain deity Tlaloc.

[in] tlilli in tlapalli: "the black, the red": chromatic metaphor for writing and wisdom.

toloatzin: psychotropic flower used to provoke visual hallucinations (*Datura stramonium, Datura inoxia*).

tonacatepel: "mountain-of-sustenance," mythical mountain containing all the foodstuffs needed for humankind's survival.

tonalamatl: chapter in the ritual codices covering the counts of the tonalpohualli.

tonalpohualli: ritual calendrical count of 260 divided into 20 periods of 13 days each.

tzoalli: mixture of amaranth seed with honey or maize flour used to make effigies of deities and other sacred things.

xiuitl, xihuitl: the solar year and its corresponding iconic sign; comet, turquoise, greenery (cf. Siméon 1997: 770–71).

xochitl: flower; the last of the 20 day-signs.

[in] xochitl in cuicatl: "flower, song," dual metaphor for sacred words, spoken or sung.

xonecuilli: "twisted foot"; name given to ritual "breads," often in the shape of an S (to represent lightning) or in the shape of a butterfly; name of a star constellation.

xuchimitl: "flower-arrow," the metaphorical pierced-heart.

Bibliography

ABBREVIATIONS

ADV	Akademische Druck- und Verlagsanstalt
AGN	Archivo General de la Nación (Mexico City)
BAE	Biblioteca de Autores Españoles (Madrid, Atlas)
BUAP	Benemérita Universidad Autónoma de Puebla
CDHM	*Colección de documentos para la historia de Mexico City: Publicada por Joaquín García Icazbalceta.* 2 vols. Mexico City: Porrúa, 1980
CIESAS	Centro de Investigaciones y Estudios Superiores en Antropología Social (Mexico City)
CONACULTA	Consejo Nacional para la Cultura y las Artes (Mexico City)
CUP	Cambridge University Press
ECN	*Estudios de Cultura Náhuatl* (UNAM)
FCE	Fondo de Cultura Económica (Mexico City)
IIA	Instituto de Investigaciones Antropológicas (UNAM)
IIE	Instituto de Investigaciones Estéticas (UNAM)
IIH	Instituto de Investigaciones Históricas (UNAM)
INAH	Instituto Nacional de Antropología e Historia (Mexico City)
SEP	Secretaría de Educación Pública (Mexico City)
SHCP	Secretaría de Hacienda y Crédito Público (Mexico City)
UNAM	Universidad Nacional Autónoma de México.

PRIMARY SOURCES (PRE-1800)

Acosta, Joseph de. 1962. *Historia natural y moral de las Indias* [ca. 1589]. Mexico City: FCE.

"Advertencias del Doctor Ortiz de Hinojosa" [1585]. 1983. In *La personalidad jurídica del indio en el III Concilio Provincial Mexicano,* ed. José A. Llaguno, pp. 199–220. Mexico City: Porrúa.

Alva Ixtlilxóchitl, Fernando de. 1985. *Obras históricas* [ca. 1630]. 2 vols. Mexico City: UNAM.

Anales de Juan Bautista [1563–74]. 2001. In *¿Cómo te confundes? ¿Acaso no somos conquistados?: Anales de Juan Bautista,* trans. and ed. Luis Reyes García, pp. 131–343. Mexico City: Eco Reli Ediciones.

Balsalobre, Gonzalo de. 1900. "Relación de las idolatrías, supersticiones, y abusos en general de los naturales del Obispado de Oaxaca" [1656] and "Relación de otros casos de idolatría concernientes a los ya referidos y averiguados por el mismo Licenciado Gonçalo de Balçalobre para mayor inteligencia desta materia" [1656]. *Anales del Museo Nacional de México* 6: 237–50.

Basalenque, Diego de. 1998. *Los agustinos, aquellos misioneros hacendados: Historia de la provincia de San Nicolás de Tolentino de Michoacán* [1673]. Ed. Heriberto Moreno García. Mexico City: CONACULTA.

Burgoa, F. Francisco de. 1989. *Geográfica descripción* [1674]. 2 vols. Mexico City: Porrúa.

Cantares mexicanos. 1985. *Cantares Mexicanos: Songs of the Aztecs.* Trans. and ed. John Bierhorst. Stanford: Stanford University Press.

Cervantes de Salazar, Francisco. 1985. *Crónica de la Nueva España* [ca. 1566]. Mexico City: Porrúa.

———. 1991. "Diálogos" [1554]. In *Francisco Cervantes de Salazar. México en 1554 y Túmulo imperial,* ed. Edmundo O'Gorman, pp. 21–68. Mexico City: Porrúa.

Chimalpáhin, Domingo. 1998. "7ª Relación." In *Las ocho relaciones y el memorial de Colhuacan* [ca. 1607–37], trans. and ed. Rafael Tena, vol. 2, pp. 10–269. 2 vols. Mexico City: CONACULTA.

Ciudad Real, Antonio de. 1976. *Tratado curioso y docto de las grandezas de la Nueva España* [1584–ca. 1588]. 2 vols. Mexico City: UNAM/IIH.

Clavijero, Francisco Javier. 1991. *Historia antigua de México* [1780]. Mexico City: Porrúa.

Codex Borbonicus. 1993. *Códice Borbónico: Manuscrito mexicano de la Biblioteca del Palais Bourbon.* América Nuestra 21a. Mexico City: Siglo Veintiuno Editores S.A.

Codex Borgia. 1993. *The Codex Borgia: A Full Color Restoration of the Ancient American Manuscript.* Ed. Gisele Díaz and Alan Rodgers, with new introduction and commentary by Bruce E. Byland. New York: Dover Publications.

Codex Cospi. 1968. *Antigüedades de México, basadas en la recopilación de Lord Kingsborough.* Vol. 4. Mexico City: SHCP.

Codex Féjérváry[-Mayer]. 1968. *Antigüedades de México, basadas en la recopilación de Lord Kingsborough.* Vol. 4. Mexico City: SHCP.

Codex Laud. 1964. *Antigüedades de México, basadas en la recopilación de Lord Kingsborough.* Vol. 3. Mexico City: SHCP.

Codex Magliabechiano. 1983. *The Book of the Life of the Ancient Mexicans* [1903]. Reproduced in facsimile with introduction, translation, and commentary by Zeila Nuttall. Berkeley: University of California Press.

Codex Mendoza. 1997. *The Essential Codex Mendoza.* Ed. Frances F. Berdan and Patricia Rief Anawalt. Berkeley and Los Angeles: University of California Press.

Codex Nuttall. 1975. *Codex Nuttall: A Picture Manuscript from Ancient Mexico.* Ed. Zelia Nuttall, with new introductory text by Arthur G. Miller. New York: Dover Publications.

Codex Osuna. 1947. *Códice Osuna* [Madrid, 1878]. Reproduced in facsimile. Mexico City: Instituto Indigenista Interamericano.

Codex Ramírez. 1979. *Códice Ramírez: Relación del origen de los indios que habitaban esta Nueva España según sus historias* [ca. 1550]. Examination of the work with a Mexican chronology appended, by Lic. Manuel Orozco y Berra. Mexico City: Editorial Innovación.

Codex Ríos. 1964. *Antigüedades de México, basadas en la recopilación de Lord Kingsborough.* Vol. 3. Mexico City: SHCP.

Codex Telleriano-Remensis. 1995. *Codex Telleriano-Remensis: Ritual Divinations, and History in a Pictorial Aztec Manuscript.* Ed. Eloise Quiñones Keber. Austin: University of Texas Press.

Codex Tlatelolco. 1994. *Códice de Tlatelolco.* Ed. Perla Valle. Mexico City: INAH/BUAP.

Codex Tlaxcala. 1981. *Diego Muñoz Camargo: Descripción de la ciudad y provincia de Tlaxcala de las Indias y del mar océano para el buen gobierno y ennoblecimiento dellas* [1580–85]. Ed. René Acuña. Mexico City: UNAM.

Codex Tudela. 1980. *Códice Tudela.* Ed. José Tudela de la Orden. Madrid: Ediciones Cultura Hispánica.

Codex Vaticanus B. 1972. *Codex Vaticanus 3773.* Ed. Ferdinand Anders. Graz: ADV.

Codex Vienna. 1992. *Códice Vindobonensis.* Ed. F. Anders, M. Jansen, and G. A. Pérez Jiménez. Graz: ADV.

Codex Xolotl. 1996. *Códice Xolotl.* Ed. Charles E. Dibble. 2 vols. Mexico City: UNAM/IIH.

Codex Yanhuitlan. 1940. *Códice de Yanhuitlan.* Ed. Wigberto Jiménez Moreno and Salvador Mateos Higuera. Mexico City: SEP/INAH.

Códice franciscano. 1941. Mexico City: Salvador Chávez Hayhoe.

Códices Matritenses. 1993. *Primeros Memoriales, by Fray Bernardino de Sahagún.* Norman: University of Oklahoma Press.

Colección de documentos para la historia de México. 1980. Ed. Joaquín García Icazbalceta. 2 vols. Mexico City: Porrúa.

Conquistador Anónimo, El. 1980. "Relación de algunas cosas de la Nueva España y de la gran ciudad de Temestitán México" [n.d]. In *CDHM,* vol. 1, pp. 369–98.

Córdoba, Fray Pedro de. 1945. *Doctrina cristiana para instrucción y información de los indios por manera de historia* [1545]. Trujillo: Montalvo.

Cortés, Hernán. 1993. *Cartas de relación* [1519–26]. Mexico City: Porrúa.

Descripción del arzobispado de México hecha en 1570, y otros documentos. 1976. Ed. Luis García Pimentel. Biblioteca de Facsímiles Méxicanos 9. Guadalajara: Edmundo Aviña Levy.

Díaz del Castillo, Bernal. 1994. *Historia de la conquista de Nueva España* [ca. 1580]. Mexico City: Porrúa.

Documentos inéditos del siglo XVI para la historia de México. 1914. Ed. P. Mariano Cuevas. Mexico City: Talleres del Museo Nacional de Arqueología, Historia y Etnología.

Durán, Fray Diego. 1984. *Historia de las indias de Nueva España e islas de la Tierra Firme* [1570–79]. 2 vols. Mexico City: Porrúa.

Epistolario de Nueva España, 1505–1818. 1939–42. Ed. Francisco del Paso y Troncoso. 16 vols. Mexico City: Antigua Librería Robredo.

Florentine Codex. 1953–82. Fray Bernardino de Sahagún. *Florentine Codex; General History of the Things of New Spain.* Trans. and ed. Arthur J. O. Anderson and Charles E. Dibble. 12 vols. Salt Lake City: University of Utah Press.

Gómara, Francisco López de. 1964. *Cortés: The Life of the Conqueror by His Secretary/Istoria de la Conquista de México* [1552]. Trans. and ed. Lesley Byrd Simpson. Berkeley: University of California Press.

Grijalva, F. Juan de. 1985. *Crónica de la orden de N.P.S. Agustín en las provincias de la Nueva España* [1624]. Mexico City: Porrúa.

Hernández, Francisco. 2000. *Antigüedades de la Nueva España* [ca. 1574]. Ed. Ascensión Hernández de León-Portilla. Madrid: Dastin, S.L.

Historia de los mexicanos por sus pinturas. 1979. In *Teogonía e historia de los mexicanos: Tres opúsculos del siglo XVI,* ed. A. M. Garibay K., pp. 23–90. Mexico City: Porrúa.

Historia tolteca-chichimeca. 1989. Ed. Paul Kirchhoff, Lena Odena Güemes, and Luis Reyes García. Mexico City: FCE.

Histoyre du Méchique. 1979. In *Teogonía e historia de los mexicanos: Tres opúsculos del siglo XVI,* ed. A. M. Garibay K., pp. 91–120. Mexico City: Porrúa.

"Instrucción que vos don Fernando de Villegas, alcalde mayor de la provincia de Mechoacán, habéis de guardar en las congregaciones que de esa provincia os están cometidas" [1601]. 1995. In *Las congregaciones de los pueblos de indios, fase terminal: Aprobaciones y rectificaciones,* ed. Ernesto de la Torre Villar, pp. 313–27. Mexico City: UNAM/IIH.

Las Casas, Bartolomé de. 1992. *Apologética historia sumaria* [1550–55]. In *Bartolomé de las Casas: Obras completas.* Vols. 6–8 (consecutive page numbering). Madrid: Alianza.

La Serna, Jacinto de. 1892. "Manual de ministros de indios para el conocimiento de sus idolatrías, y extirpación de ellas" [1656]. In *Colección de documentos inéditos para la historia de España por el Marqués de la Fuensanta del Valle,* vol. 104, pp. 1–267. Madrid: n.p.

Leyenda de los soles. 1992. In *Códice Chimalpopoca: Anales de Cuauhtitlan y Leyenda de los soles* [1945], pp. 119–28. Translated from the Nahuatl by don Primo Feliciano Velázquez. Mexico City: UNAM/Instituto de Historia.

Lienzo de San Miguel Tiltepec (see Guevara Hernández 1991).

Lorenzana, Arzobispo Francisco Antonio, ed. 1981. *Concilios provinciales primero y segundo, celebrados en la muy noble, y muy leal ciudad de México* [1769]. 2 vols. Mexico City: Del Agua Impresores, S.A.

Mapa de Cuauhtinchan No. 4 [1563]. 1994. In *Cartografía y linderos en el Mapa de Cuauhtinchan núm. 4* by Keiko Yoneda. Mexico City: INAH/BUAP.

Mendieta, F. Jerónimo de. 1973. *Historia eclesiástica indiana* [ca. 1596]. 2 vols. BAE 260, 261. Madrid: Atlas.

Molina, Fray Alonso de. 1992. *Vocabulario en lengua mexicana y castellana* [1571]. Mexico City: Porrúa.

Motolinía, F. Toribio de Benavente. 1970. *Memoriales* [ca. 1549]. BAE 240. Madrid: Atlas.

———. 1990. *Historia de los indios de la Nueva España* [ca. 1550]. Mexico City: Porrúa.

Muñoz Camargo, Diego. 1984. "Descripción de la ciudad y provincia de Tlaxcala de la Nueva España e Indias del mar océano para el buen gobierno y ennoblecimie[nt]o dellas" [1580–85]. In *Relaciones geográficas del siglo XVI,* ed. René Acuña, vol. 4, 23–285. Tlaxcala I. Mexico City: UNAM.

———. 1986. *Historia de Tlaxcala* [ca. 1592–94]. Ed. Germán Vázquez. Madrid: Historia 16.

Nican mopohua ("Here is recounted"). 1995. In *Santa María Tonantzin, Virgen de Guadalupe: Continuidad y transformación religiosa en México,* ed. Richard Nebel, pp. 343–67. Mexico City: FCE.

Olmos, Fray Andrés de. 1990. *Tratado de hechicerías y sortilegios* [1553]. Ed. Georges Baudot. Mexico City: UNAM.

Ponce de León, Pedro. 1979. "Tratado de los dioses y ritos de la gentilidad" [ca. 1569]. In *Teogonía e historia de los mexicanos: Tres opúsculos del siglo XVI,* ed. A. M. Garibay K., pp. 121–41. Mexico City: Porrúa.

Popol vuh ("Book of counsel"). 1986. *Popol Vuh: The Mayan Book of the Dawn of Life.* Trans. and ed. Dennis Tedlock. New York: Simon and Schuster.

Proceso inquisitorial del cacique de Tetzcoco Don Carlos Ometochtzin (Chichimecatecotl) [1537–39]. 1980. Mexico City: Biblioteca Enciclopédica del Estado de México.

Procesos de indios idólatras y hechiceros. 1912. Ed. Luis González Obregón. Mexico City: AGN.

Procesos por idolatría al cacique, gobernadores y sacerdotes de Yanhuitlán [1544–46]. 1999. Ed. María Teresa Sepúlveda y Herrera. Mexico City: INAH.

Relación breve de la venida de los de la Compañía de Jesús a la Nueva España [1602]. 1995. In *Crónicas de la Compañía de Jesús en la Nueva España*, ed. F. González de Cassío, pp. 1–49. Mexico City: UNAM.

Relaciones geográficas del siglo XVI (see Acuña, René).

Romances de los señores de la Nueva España [1582]. 1964. In *Poesía náhuatl*, ed. A. M. Garibay K., vol. 1, pp. 1–101. Mexico City: UNAM.

Ruiz de Alarcón, Hernando. 1984. *Treatise on the Heathen Superstitions That Today Live among the Indians Native to This New Spain* [1629]. Trans. and ed. J. R. Andrews and R. Hassig. Norman: University of Oklahoma Press.

Sahagún, F. Bernardino de. 1981. *Historia de las cosas de Nueva España* [1570–80]. Ed. A. M. Garibay K. 4 vols. Mexico City: Porrúa.

———. 1986. *Coloquios y doctrina cristiana* [1564]. Ed. Miguel León-Portilla. Mexico City: UNAM/ Fundación de Investigaciones Sociales.

———. 1993. *Psalmodia Christiana* [1583]. Trans. and ed. Arthur J. O. Anderson. Salt Lake City: University of Utah Press.

———. 1997. "Exercicio quotidiano" [1574]. In *Codex Chimalpahin: Society and Politics in Mexico Tenochtitlan, Tlatelolco, Texcoco, Culhuacan and Other Nahua Altepetl in Central Mexico,* trans. and ed. Arthur J. O. Anderson and Susan Schroeder, pp. 130–83. Vol. 2. Norman: University of Oklahoma Press.

Tapia, Andrés de. 1980. "Relación sobre la conquista de México" [n.d.]. In *CDHM,* vol. 2, pp. 554–94.

"Testimonio de la fundación de Santo Tomás Ajusco" [1531/1710]. 1970. Trans. and ed. Marcelo Díaz de Salas and Luis Reyes García. *Tlalocan* 6, no. 3: 193–212.

Tezozómoc, Hernando de Alvarado. 1943. *Crónica mexicana* [ca. 1598]. Mexico City: UNAM.

Tira de la Peregrinación. 1975. *Códice Botturini: Colección de documentos conmemorativos del DCL aniversario de la fundación de Tenochtitlan, 1.* Mexico City: SEP.

Torquemada, F. Juan de. *Monarquía indiana* [1615]. 1975–83. 7 vols. Mexico City: UNAM/IIH.

Treinta relaciones de los pueblos de la Nueva España [1569–71] (Ovando Series). Archivo General de Indias (Seville, Spain), AGI Indiferente, Legajo 1529.

Valadés, Fray Diego. 2003. *Retórica cristiana* [translation of *Rhetorica Christiana,* 1579]. Mexico City: FCE.

Vetancurt, F. Agustín de. 1971. *Teatro mexicano: Descripción breve de los sucesos ejemplares, históricos y religiosos del Nuevo Mundo Occidental de las Indias* [1698]. 4 parts. Mexico City: Porrúa.

Voragine, Jacobus de. 1993. *The Golden Legend: Readings on the Saints* [ca. 1260]. Trans. William Granger Ryan. 2 vols. Princeton: Princeton University Press.

Wither, George. 1973. *A Collection of Emblemes Ancient and Moderne* [1635]. London: Scolar Press.

Zorita, Alonso de. 1993. *Los señores de la Nueva España* [1585]. Mexico City: UNAM.

SECONDARY SOURCES

Acosta, Jorge R. 1939. "Exploraciones arqueológicas realizadas en el Estado de Michoacán durante los años de 1937 y 1938." *Revista Mexicana de Estudios Antropológicos*, 3, no. 2: 85–98.

Acuña, René. 1984a. *Relaciones geográficas del siglo XVI: Antequera I.* Mexico City: UNAM.

———. 1984b. *Relaciones geográficas del siglo XVI: Antequera II.* Mexico City: UNAM.

———. 1984c. *Relaciones geográficas del siglo XVI: Tlaxcala I.* Mexico City: UNAM.

———. 1985a. *Relaciones geográficas del siglo XVI: México I.* Mexico City: UNAM.

———. 1985b. *Relaciones geográficas del siglo XVI: Tlaxcala II.* Mexico City: UNAM.

———. 1986. *Relaciones geográficas del siglo XVI: México II.* Mexico City: UNAM.

Aguilera, Carmen. 1990. "Glifos toponímicos en el Mapa de México-Tenochtitlan hacia 1550 (Area de Chiconauhtla)." *ECN* 20: 163–72.

Alberro, Solange. 2000. "Los franciscanos y la tabula rasa en la Nueva España del siglo XVI: Un cuestionamiento." In *El teatro franciscano en la Nueva España: Fuentes y ensayos para el estudio del teatro de evangelización en el siglo XVI,* ed. María Sten, pp. 21–37. Mexico City: UNAM/CONACULTA.

Albores, Beatriz. 1997. "Los quicazcles y el árbol cósmico del Olotepec, Estado de México." In *Graniceros: Cosmovisión y meteorología indígenas de Mesoamérica,* ed. Beatriz Albores and Johanna Broda, pp. 379–446. Mexico City: Colegio Mexiquense/UNAM.

———. 2001. "Ritual agrícola y cosmovisión: Las fiestas en cruz del Valle de Toluca, Estado de México." In *La montaña en el paisaje ritual,* ed. Johanna Broda, Stanislaw Iwaniszewski, and Arturo Montero, pp. 419–39. Mexico City: CONACULTA/INAH.

Albores, Beatriz, and Johanna Broda, eds. 1997. *Graniceros: Cosmovisión y meteorología indígenas de Mesoamérica.* Mexico City: Colegio Mexiquense/UNAM.

Alcina Franch, José. 1969. *Guillermo Dupaix: Expediciones acerca de los antiguos monumentos de la Nueva España, 1805–1808.* 2 vols. Madrid: José Porrúa Turanzos.

Alcina Franch, José, Miguel León-Portilla, and Eduardo Matos Moctezuma, eds. 1992. *Azteca-Mexica.* Madrid and Barcelona: Sociedad Estatal Quinto Centenario/Lunwerg Editores.

Alexander, Jonathan J. G., ed. 1995. *The Painted Page: Italian Renaissance Book Illumination 1450–1550.* London: Royal Academy of Arts/New York: Pierpont Morgan Library.

Anawalt, Patricia Rieff. 1981. *Indian Clothing before Cortés: Mesoamerican Costumes from the Codices.* Norman: University of Oklahoma Press.

Anders, Ferdinand, Maarten Jansen, and Luis Reyes García, eds. 1996. *Libro de la vida: Texto explicativo del llamado Códice Magliabechiano.* Mexico City: FCE.

Anderson, Arthur J. O., trans. and ed. 1993. *Bernardino de Sahagún's Psalmodia Cristiana (Christian Psalmody).* Salt Lake City: University of Utah Press.

Anderson, Arthur J. O., and Charles E. Dibble, trans. and eds. 1953–82. *Fray Bernardino de Sahagún: Florentine Codex; General History of the Things of New Spain* [1570–80]. 12 vols. Salt Lake City: University of Utah Press.

Andrews, J. Richard, and Ross Hassig, trans. and eds. 1984. *Hernando Ruiz de Alarcón: Treatise on the Heathen Superstitions That Today Live among the Indians Native to This New Spain* [1629]. Norman: University of Oklahoma Press.

Angulo Iñiguez, Diego. 1955. *Historia del arte hispanoamericano.* Vol. 1. Barcelona and Madrid: Salvat.

Angulo V., Jorge. 1991. "Identificación de una constelación en la pintura teotihuacana." In *Arqueoastronomía y etnoastronomía en Mesoamérica,* ed. Johanna Broda, Stanislaw Iwaniszewski, and Lucrecia Maupomé, pp. 309–27. Mexico City: UNAM/IIH.

Apostolos-Cappadona, Diane. 1998. *Dictionary of Women in Religious Art.* Oxford: Oxford University Press.

Arnold, Philip P. 1991. "Eating Landscape: Human Sacrifice and Sustenance in Aztec Mexico." In *To Change Place: Aztec Ceremonial Landscapes,* ed. Davíd Carrasco, pp. 219–32. Niwot: University of Colorado Press.

Artigas, Juan B. 1989. "Meztitlan, Hidalgo: Los edificios de la villa." *Cuadernos de Arquitectura Virreinal* 7: 9–55.

———. 1992. *Capillas abiertas aisladas de México.* Mexico City: UNAM.

Aveni, Anthony F. 1980. *Skywatchers of Ancient Mexico.* Austin: University of Texas Press.

———. 1989. "Pecked Cross Petroglyphs at Xihuingo." *Journal for the History of Astronomy* 20: 73–115.

———. 2007. "Calendar, Chronology and Cosmology in Mapa de Cuauhtinchan No. 2." In *Cave, City, and Eagle's Nest: An Interpretive Journey through the Mapa de Cuauhtinchan No. 2,* ed. Davíd Carrasco and Scott C. Sessions, pp. 147–58. Albuquerque: University of New Mexico Press.

Aveni, Anthony F., E. E. Calnek, and H. Hartung. 1988. "Myth, Environment, and the Orientation of the Templo Mayor of Tenochtitlan." *American Antiquity* 53, no. 2: 287–309.

Aveni, Anthony F., H. Hartung, and B. Buckingham. 1978. "The Pecked Cross Symbol in Ancient Mesoamerica." *Science* 202: 267–79.

Azcue y Mancera, Luis, Manuel Toussaint, and Justino Fernández. 1940. *Catálogo de construcciones religiosas del Estado de Hidalgo.* 2 vols. Mexico City: Talleres Gráficas de la Nación.

Báez Macías, E., J. Guerra Ruiz, and J. Puente León. 1988. *Libros y grabados en el fondo de origen de la Biblioteca Nacional.* Mexico City: UNAM.

Baquedano, Elizabeth. 1992. "Semejanzas entre la iconografía de los códices y de la escultura azteca o mexica." In *Azteca-Mexica,* ed. José Alcina Franch, Miguel León-Portilla, and Eduardo Matos Moctezuma, pp. 39–46. Madrid and Barcelona: Sociedad Estatal Quinto Centenario/Lunwerg Editores.

Bartrum, Giulia. 1995. *German Renaissance Prints 1490–1550.* London: British Museum Press.

Bernal, Ignacio. 1980. *A History of Mexican Archaeology: The Vanished Civilizations of Middle America.* London: Thames and Hudson.

Berrin, Kathleen, ed. 1988. *Feathered Serpents and Flowering Trees.* San Francisco: Fine Arts Museum of San Francisco.

Bierhorst, John. 1984. *Mitos y leyendas de los aztecas.* Madrid: Editorial EDAF, S.A.

———. 1985a. *Cantares Mexicanos: Songs of the Aztecs.* Stanford: Stanford University Press.

———. 1985b. *A Nahuatl-English Dictionary and Concordance to the Cantares Mexicanos with an Analytic Transcription and Grammatical Notes.* Stanford: Stanford University Press.

Boone, Elizabeth Hill. 1983. *The Codex Magliabechiano and the Lost Prototype of the Magliabechiano Group.* Berkeley: University of California Press.

———. 1998a. "Cartografía azteca: Presentaciones de geografía, historia y comunidad." *ECN* 28: 17–38.

———. 1998b. "Pictorial Documents and Visual Thinking in Postconquest Mexico." In *Native Traditions in the Postconquest World*, ed. Elizabeth Hill Boone and Tom Cummins, pp. 149–99. Washington, D.C.: Dumbarton Oaks.

———. 2000. *Stories in Red and Black: Pictorial Histories of the Aztecs and the Mixtecs.* Austin: University of Texas Press.

Borges, Pedro, O.F.M. 1960. *Métodos misionales en la cristianización de América: Siglo XVI.* Biblioteca Missionalia Hispanica 13. Madrid: Depto. de Misionología Española.

Broda, Johanna. 1971. "Las fiestas aztecas de los dioses de la lluvia." *Revista Española de Antropología Americana* 6: 245–327.

———. 1982. "Astronomy, *Cosmovisión,* and Ideology in Pre-Hispanic Mesoamerica." In *Ethnoastronomy and Archaeoastronomy in the American Tropics,* ed. Anthony F. Aveni and Gary Urton, pp. 81–110. New York: New York Academy of Sciences.

———. 1983. "Ciclos agrícolas en el culto: Un problema de la correlación del calendario mexica." In *Calendars in Mesoamerica and Peru: Native Computation of Time, Proceedings of the 44th International Congress of Americanists,* ed. Anthony F. Aveni and Gordon Brotherston, pp. 145–65. BAR International Press 174. Oxford: BAR.

———. 1987. "Templo Mayor as Ritual Space." In *The Great Temple of Tenochtitlan: Center and Periphery in the Aztec World,* ed. Johanna Broda, Davíd Carrasco, and Eduardo Matos Moctezuma, pp. 61–123. Berkeley: University of California Press.

———. 1989. "Geografía, clima y observación de la naturaleza en la Mesoamérica prehispánica." In *Las máscaras de la cueva de Santa Ana Teloxtoc,* ed. Ernesto Vargas Pacheco, pp. 35–51. Mexico City: UNAM.

———. 1991a. "Cosmovisión y observación de la naturaleza: El ejemplo del culto de los cerros en Mesoamérica." In *Arqueoastronomía y etnoastronomía en Mesoamérica,* ed. Johanna Broda, Stanislaw Iwaniszewski, and Lucrecia Maupomé, pp. 461–500. Mexico City: UNAM/IIH.

———. 1991b. "The Sacred Landscape of Aztec Calendar Festivals: Myth, Nature, and Society." In *To Change Place: Aztec Ceremonial Landscapes,* ed. Davíd Carrasco, pp. 74–120. Niwot: University of Colorado Press.

———. 1997a. "El culto mexica de los cerros de la Cuenca de México." In *Graniceros: Cosmovisión y meteorología indígenas de Mesoamérica,* ed. Beatriz Albores and Johanna Broda, pp. 49–90. Mexico City: Colegio Mexiquense/UNAM.

———. 1997b. "Lenguaje visual del paisaje ritual de la Cuenca de México." In *Códices y documentos sobre México: Segundo Simposio,* ed. Salvador Rueda Smithers, Constanza Vega Sosa, and Rodrigo Martínez Baracs, vol. 2, pp. 129–61. 2 vols. Mexico City: INAH.

———. 2001. "La etnografía de la fiesta de la Santa Cruz: Una perspectiva histórica." In *Cosmovisión, ritual e identidad de los pueblos indígenas de México,* ed. Johanna Broda and Félix Báez-Jorge, pp. 165–238. Mexico City: CONACULTA/FCE.

Broda, Johanna, and Félix Báez-Jorge, eds. 2001. *Cosmovisión, ritual e identidad de los pueblos indígenas de México.* Mexico City: CONACULTA/FCE.

Broda, Johanna, Stanislaw Iwaniszewski, and Lucrecia Maupomé, eds. 1991. *Arqueoastronomía y etnoastronomía en Mesoamérica.* Mexico City: UNAM/IIH.

Broda, Johanna, Stanislaw Iwaniszewski, and Arturo Montero, eds. 2001. *La montaña en el paisaje ritual.* Mexico City: CONACULTA/INAH.

Brotherston, Gordon. 1979. *Image of the New World.* London: Thames and Hudson.

———. 1992. *Book of the Fourth World: Reading the Native Americas through Their Literature.* Cambridge: CUP.

———. 1995. *Painted Books from Mexico: Codices in UK Collections and the World They Represent.* London: British Museum Press.

———. 1997a. "Los cerros Tlaloc: Su representación en los códices." In *Graniceros: Cosmovisión y meteorología indígenas de Mesoamérica,* ed. Beatriz Albores and Johanna Broda, pp. 25–48. Mexico City: El Colegio Mexiquense/UNAM.

———. 1997b. *Footprints through Time: Mexican Pictorial Manuscripts at the Lilly Library.* In collaboration with Galen Brokaw, Aaron Dziubisnkyj, Millie Gimmel, and Mark Morris. Bloomington: Lilly Library, Indiana University.

———. 2005. *Feather Crown: The Eighteen Feasts of the Mexica Year.* British Museum Research Publications 154. London: British Museum Press.

Burkhart, Louise M. 1986. "Moral Deviance in Sixteenth-Century Nahua and Christian Thought: The Rabbit and the Deer." *Journal of Latin American Lore* 12, no. 2: 107–39.

———. 1988. "The Solar Christ in Nahuatl Doctrinal Texts of Early Colonial Mexico." *Ethnohistory* 35, no. 3: 234–56.

———. 1989. *The Slippery Earth: Nahua-Christian Dialogue in Sixteenth-Century Mexico.* Tucson: University of Arizona Press.

———. 1992. "Flowery Heaven: The Aesthetic of Paradise in Nahuatl Devotional Literature." *RES: Anthropology and Aesthetics* 21: 88–109.

———. 1996. *Holy Wednesday: A Nahua Drama from Early Colonial Mexico.* Philadelphia: University of Pennsylvania Press.

———. 1998. "Pious Performances: Christian Pageantry and Native Identity in Early Colonial Mexico." In *Native Traditions in the Postconquest World,* ed. Elizabeth Hill Boone and Tom Cummins, pp. 361–81. Washington, D.C.: Dumbarton Oaks.

Cabrera Castro, Rubén. 1987. "Tzintzuntzan: Décima temporada de excavaciones." In *Homenaje a Román Piña Chan,* ed. Barbro Dahlgren, Carlos Navarrete, Lorenzo Ochoa, Mari Carmen Serra, and Yoko Sugiura, pp. 531–65. Mexico City: UNAM/IIA.

Camelo Arredondo, Rosa, Jorge Gurría Lacroix, and Constantino Reyes-Valerio. 1964. *Juan Gerson: Tlacuilo de Tecamachalco.* Mexico City: INAH.

Carrasco, Davíd. 1987. "Myth, Cosmic Terror, and the Templo Mayor." In *The Great Temple of Tenochtitlan: Center and Periphery in the Aztec World,* ed. Johanna Broda, Davíd Carrasco, and Eduardo Matos Moctezuma, pp. 124–62. Berkeley: University of California Press.

Carrasco, Davíd, and Scott Sessions, eds. 2007. *Cave, City, and Eagle's Nest: An Interpretive Journey through the Mapa de Cuauhtinchan No. 2.* Albuquerque: University of New Mexico Press.

Carrasco, Pedro. 1975. "La transformación de la cultura indígena durante la colonia." *Historia Mexicana* 25: 175–203.

Caso, Alfonso. 1967. *Los calendarios prehispánicos.* Mexico City: UNAM/IIE.

Clendinnen, Inga. 1990. "Ways to the Sacred: Reconstructing 'Religion' in Sixteenth-Century Mexico." *History and Anthropology* 5: 105–41.

———. 1991. *Aztecs: An Interpretation.* Cambridge: CUP.

CONACULTA. 1990. *Cacaxtla: Proyecto de investigación y conservación.* Mexico City: INAH.

Contreras García, Irma. 1985. *Bibliografía sobre la castellanización de los grupos indígenas de la República Mexicana: Siglos XVI al XX.* Mexico City: UNAM.

Corcuera de Mancera, Sonia. 1993. *El fraile, el indio y el pulque: Evangelización y embriaguez en la Nueva España (1523-1548).* Mexico City: FCE.

Córdova Tello, Mario. 1992. *El convento de San Miguel de Huejotzingo, Puebla: Arqueología histórica.* Mexico City: INAH.

Corona Núñez, José. 1989. "Correcta interpretación de jeroglíficos y algunos pasajes de códices y figuras que aparecen en la cerámica." In *I Coloquio de Documentos Pictográficos de Tradición Náhuatl,* pp. 41-47. Mexico City: UNAM/IIH.

"Correlation of Central Mexican Calendar with Julian/Gregorian Calendars." www.azteccalendar.com.

Cuevas, P. Mariano, S.J. 1946. *Historia de la iglesia en México.* Mexico City: Editorial Patria.

Curiel Méndez, Gustavo. 1987. "Escatología y psicomaquia en el programa ornamental de la capilla abierta de Tlalmanalco, México." In *Iconología y sociedad: Arte colonial hispanoamericano,* pp. 93-123. Mexico City: UNAM/IIE.

Demarest, Arthur A. 1984. "Mesoamerican Human Sacrifice in Evolutionary Perspective." In *Ritual Human Sacrifice in Mesoamerica,* ed. Elizabeth Hill Boone, pp. 227-47. Washington, D.C.: Dumbarton Oaks.

Dupaix, Guillermo. 1969. *Expediciones acerca de los antiguos monumentos de la Nueva España, 1805-1808.* Ed. José Alcina Franch. 2 vols. Madrid: José Porrúa Turanzos.

Duverger, Christian. 1996. *La conversión de los indios de Nueva España.* Mexico City: FCE. [Spanish translation of *La conversion des Indiens de Nouvelle-Espagne.* Paris: Editions du Seuil, 1987.]

Edgerton, Samuel Y. 2001. *Theaters of Conversion: Religious Architecture and Indian Artisans in Colonial Mexico.* Albuquerque: University of New Mexico Press.

Elzey, Wayne. 1976. "Some Remarks on the Space and Time of the 'Center' in Aztec Religion." *ECN* 12: 315-34.

Enciso, Jorge. 1935. "El convento de Actopan." *Archivo Español de Arte y Arqueología* 11, no. 31: 67-71.

Escalante Gonzalbo, Pablo. 1997. "El patrocinio del arte indocristiano en el siglo XVI: La iniciativa de las autoridades indígenas en Tlaxcala y Cuauhtinchan." In *Patrocinio, colección y circulación de las artes: XX Coloquio Internacional de Historia del Arte,* pp. 215-35. Mexico City: UNAM/IIE.

Estrada de Gerlero, Elena. 1976. "El friso monumental de Itzmiquilpan." In *Actes du XLIIe Congrès International des Américanistes,* Paris, September 2-9, vol. 10. Paris: Société des Américanistes.

———. 1994. «La labor anticuaria novohispana en la época de Carlos IV: Guillermo Dupaix, precursor de la historia del arte prehispánico." In *XVII Coloquio Internacional de Historia de Arte: Arte, historia e identidad en América--Visiones comparativas,* ed. Gustavo Curiel, Renato González Mello, and Juana Gutiérrez, vol. 1, pp. 191-205. 3 vols. Mexico City: UNAM/IIE.

Flores Marini, Carlos. 1993. "El arte religioso de Xochimilco: Un recorrido." *Artes de México* 20: 55-65.

Folan, William J., Lynda Florey Folan, and Antonio Ruiz Pérez. 1987. "La iconografía de Huamango, Municipio de Acambay, Estado de Mexico City: Un centro regional otomí de los siglos IX al XIII." In *Homenaje a Román Piña Chan,* ed. Barbro Dahlgren, Carlos Navarrete, Lorenzo Ochoa, Mari Carmen Serra, and Yoko Sugiura, pp. 411-53. Mexico City: UNAM/IIA.

Fraser, Valerie. 1990. *The Architecture of Conquest: Building in the Viceroyalty of Peru, 1535-1635.* Cambridge: CUP.

———. 1991. "Ixmiquilpan: From European Ornament to Mexican Pictograph." In *Altars and Idols: The Life of the Dead in Mexico,* pp. 13-16. M. A. Gallery Studies catalogue, University of Essex.

———. 1996. "The Artistry of Guaman Poma." *RES: Anthropology and Aesthetics* 29/30: 269-89.

Freidel, David, Linda Schele, and Joy Parker. 1993. *Maya Cosmos: Three Thousand Years on the Shaman's Path.* New York: William Morrow.

Furst, Peter T. 1994. *Alucinógenos y cultura.* Mexico City: FCE.

Galarza, Joaquín. 1966. "Glyphes et attributs chrétiens dans les manuscrits pictographiques mexicains du XVIe siècle." *Journal de la Société des Américanistes* 55, no. 1: 7–42.

———. 1967. «Prénoms et noms de lieux exprimés par des glyphes et des attributs chrétiens dans les manuscrits pictographiques mexicains." *Journal de la Société des Américanistes* 56, no. 2: 533–83.

———. 1979. *Estudios de escritura indígena tradicional: Azteca-nahuatl.* Mexico City: AGN.

———. 1992. *Catecismos indígenas: El Pater Noster.* Mexico City: Editorial TAVA, S.A.

Galarza, Joaquín, and Rubén Maldonado Rojas. 1990. *Amatl, amoxtli: El papel, el libro.* Mexico City: Editorial TAVA, S.A.

Gandara, Guillermo. n.d. "Flor representada en cerámica nahoa precortesiana." Offprint of issue 4 of *Anales del Instituto de Biología* (Mexico City) 1: 329–61.

García Cook, Angel. 1973. "Algunos descubrimientos en Tlalancaleca, Edo. de Puebla." *Comunicaciones, Proyecto Puebla-Tlaxcala* 9: 25–29.

Garibay K., Angel María. 1964. *Poesía náhuatl.* Vol. 1. Mexico City: UNAM.

———. ed. 1981. *Fray Bernardino de Sahagún: Historia general de las cosas de Nueva España* [1570–80]. 4 vols. Mexico City: Porrúa.

Garza, Mercedes de la. 2001. "Uso ritual de plantas psicoactivas entre los nahuas y los mayas." In *Animales y plantas en la cosmovisión mesoamericana,* ed. Yolotl González Torres, pp. 89–104. Mexico City: INAH/Plaza y Valdés Editores.

Gerhard, Peter. 1977. "Congregaciones de indios en la Nueva España antes de 1570." *Historia Mexicana* 26, no. 3: 347–95.

———. 1986. *Geografía histórica de la Nueva España, 1519–1821.* Mexico City: UNAM. [Spanish translation of *Guide to the Historical Geography of New Spain, 1519–1821.* Cambridge: CUP, 1972.]

Gibson, Charles. 2000. *Los aztecas bajo el dominio español 1519–1810.* Mexico City: Siglo Veintiuno Editores. [Spanish translation of *The Aztecs under Spanish Rule.* Stanford: Stanford University Press, 1964.]

Gillespie, Susan D. 1999. *Los reyes aztecas: La construcción del gobierno en la historia mexica.* Mexico City: Siglo Veintiuno Editores. [Spanish translation of *The Aztec Kings: The Construction of Rulership in Mexica History.* Tucson: University of Arizona Press, 1989.]

Glass, John B. 1975. "A Census of Middle American Testerian Manuscripts." In *Handbook of Middle American Indians,* vol. 14, 281–96. Austin: University of Texas Press.

Gombrich, E. H. 1979. *The Sense of Order: A Study in the Psychology of Decorative Art.* Oxford: Phaidon.

Gonçalves de Lima, Oswaldo. 1986. *El maguey y el pulque en los códices mexicanos.* Mexico City: FCE.

González Chévez, Lilian. n.d. "Hueytlacatzintli: Fragmentos de un complejo chamánico-enteogénico entre los nahuas del Norte de Guerrero." In *El uso ritual de la flor en América,* ed. Beatriz Albores. Mexico City: Colegio Mexiquense.

González-Hermosillo, Francisco, and L. Reyes García. 2002. *El códice de Cholula: La exaltación testimonial de un linaje indio.* Mexico City: INAH/CIESAS/Gobierno del Estado de Puebla.

González Jácome, Alba. 1997. "Agricultura y especialistas en ideología agrícola: Tlaxcala, México." In *Graniceros: Cosmovisión y meteorología indígenas de Mesoamérica,* ed. Beatriz Albores and Johanna Broda, pp. 467–501. Mexico City: Colegio Mexiquense/UNAM, 1997.

Good Eshelman, Catherine. 2001. "El ritual y la reproducción de la cultura: Ceremonias agrícolas, los muertos y la expresión estética entre los nahuas de Guerrero." In *Cosmovisión, ritual e identidad de los pueblos indígenas de México,* ed. Johanna Broda and Félix Báez-Jorge, pp. 239–97. Mexico City: CONACULTA/FCE.

Gorbea Trueba, José. 1957. *Tepeapulco.* Mexico City: INAH/Dirección de Monumentos Coloniales.

Grañén Porrúa, María Isabel. 1994. "El grabado libresco en la Nueva España, sus emblemas y alegorías." In *Juegos de ingenio y agudeza: La pintura emblemática de la Nueva España,* pp. 117–31. Mexico City: Museo Nacional de Arte/CONACULTA.

Greenleaf, Richard E. 1992. *Zumárraga y la inquisición mexicana, 1536–1543.* Mexico City: FCE. [Spanish translation of *Zumárraga and the Mexican Inquisition, 1536–1543.* Richmond: William Byrd Press, 1962.]

Griffin, Gillett, G. 1968. *An Otomí Catechism at Princeton.* Princeton: Princeton University Library.

Gruzinski, Serge. 1987. "Colonial Indian Maps in Sixteenth-Century Mexico: An Essay in Mixed Cartography." *RES: Anthropology and Aesthetics* 13: 46–61.

———. 1989. *Man-Gods in the Mexican Highlands: Indian Power and Colonial Society 1520–1800.* Stanford: Stanford University Press.

———. 1993. *The Conquest of Mexico: The Incorporation of Indian Societies into the Western World, 16th–18th Centuries.* Cambridge: Polity Press. [English translation of *La colonisation de l'imaginaire.* Paris: Editions Gallimard, 1988.]

———. 1994. *El Aguila y la Sibila: Frescos de indios de México.* Barcelona: Moleiro.

———. 2002. *The Mestizo Mind: The Intellectual Dynamics of Colonization and Globalization.* New York and London: Routledge. [English translation by Deke Dusinberre of *La pensée métisse.* Paris: Librairie Arthème Fayard, 1999.]

Guevara Hernández, Jorge. 1991. *El Lienzo de Tiltepec: Extinción de un señorío zapoteco.* Mexico City: INAH.

Hall, James. 1979. *Dictionary of Subjects and Symbols in Art.* New York: Harper and Row.

Harwood, Joanne. 2002. "Disguising Ritual: A Re-assessment of Part 3 of the Codex Mendoza." Doctoral thesis, University of Essex, England.

Haskett, Robert. 2005. *Visions of Paradise: Primordial Titles and Mesoamerican History in Cuernavaca.* Norman: University of Oklahoma Press.

Heyden, Doris. 1983. *Mitología y simbolismo de la flora en el México prehispánico.* Mexico City: UNAM/IIA.

———. 1991. "La matriz de la tierra." In *Arqueoastronomía y etnoastronomía en Mesoamérica,* ed. Johanna Broda, Stanislaw Iwaniszewski, and Lucrecia Maupomé, pp. 501–15. Mexico City: UNAM.

———. 2001. "El cuerpo del Dios: El maíz." In *Animales y plantas en la cosmovisión mesoamericana,* ed. Yolotl González Torres, pp. 19–37. Mexico City: Plaza y Valdés.

Hill, Jane H. 1992. "The Flower World of Old Uto-Aztecan." *Journal of Anthropological Research* 48, no. 2: 117–44.

Hind, Arthur M. 1963. *An Introduction to the History of Woodcut.* 2 vols. New York: Dover Publications.

Holl, Frank. 1996. "El viaje mexicano de Alejandro de Humboldt." In *Viajeros europeos del siglo XIX en México,* pp. 51–61. Mexico City: Fomento Cultural Banamex.

INAH. 1978. *Actopan: Guía oficial.* Mexico City: INAH/SEP.

Instituto Nacional de Estadística, Geografía e Informática (INEGI). Various dates. *Cartas topográficas.* Mexico City: Instituto Nacional de Estadística, Geografía e Informática.

Jansen, Maarten. 1982. *Huisi Tacu: Estudio interpretativo de un libro mixteco antiguo: Codex Vindobonensis Mexicanus I.* Publication 24. Amsterdam: Center for Latin American Research and Documentation.

Jiménez P., Blanca M., and Samuel L. Villela F. 1998. *Historia y cultura tras el glifo: Los códices de Guerrero.* Mexico City: INAH.

Johansson, K. Patrick. 1996. "Totochtin incuic Tezcatzoncatl: Un canto para las primicias del pulque nuevo." *ECN* 26: 69–97.

———. 1997. "Imagen y narratividad en el *Códice Xolotl.*" In *Códices y documentos sobre Mexico City: Segundo Simposio,* vol. 1, pp. 443–73. 2 vols. Mexico City: INAH/Dirección General de Publicaciones.

Kelley, David H. 1983. "The Maya Calendar Correlation Problem." In *Civilization in the Ancient Americas: Essays in Honor of Gordon R. Willey,* ed. R. M. Leventhal and A. L. Kolata, pp. 157–208. Albuquerque: University of New Mexico Press/Cambridge, Mass.: Peabody Museum of Archaeology and Ethnology/Harvard University.

King, Mark B. 1990. "Poetics and Metaphor in Mixtec Writing." *Ancient Mesoamerica* 1: 141–51.

———. 1994. "Hearing the Echoes of Verbal Art in Mixtec Writing." In *Writing without Words: Alternative Literacies in Mesoamerica and the Andes,* ed. Elizabeth Hill Boone and Walter D. Mignolo, pp. 102–36. Durham, N.C.: Duke University Press.

Klor de Alva, J. Jorge. 1982. "Spiritual Conflict and Accommodation in New Spain: Towards a Typology of Aztec Responses to Christianity." In *The Inca and Aztec States 1400–1800,* ed. G. A. Collier, R. I. Rosaldo, and J. D. Wirth, pp. 345–66. New York: Academic Press.

———. 1991. "Religious Rationalization and the Conversions of the Nahuas: Social Organization and Colonial Epistemology." In *To Change Place: Aztec Ceremonial Landscapes,* ed. Davíd Carrasco, pp. 233–45. Niwot: University of Colorado Press.

———. 1993. "Aztec Spirituality and Nahuatized Christianity." In *South and Meso-American Native Spirituality: From the Cult of the Feathered Serpent to the Theology of Liberation,* ed. Gary H. Gossen, in collaboration with Miguel León-Portilla, pp. 173–97. London: SCM Press.

———. 1999. "Telling Lives: Confessional Autobiography and the Reconstruction of the Nahua Self." In *Spiritual Encounters: Interactions between Christianity and Native Religions in Colonial America,* ed. Nicholas Griffiths and Fernando Cervantes, pp. 136–62. Birmingham: University of Birmingham Press.

Köhler, Ulrich. 1991. "Conocimientos astronómicos de indígenas contemporáneos y su contribución para identificar constelaciones aztecas." In *Arqueoastronomía y etnoastronomía en Mesoamérica,* ed. Johanna Broda, Stanislaw Iwaniszewski, and Lucrecia Maupomé, pp. 249–65. Mexico City: UNAM/IIH.

Kubler, George. 1964. "On the Colonial Extinction of the Motifs of Pre-Columbian Art." In *Essays in Pre-Columbian Art and Archaeology,* ed. Samuel K. Lothrop, pp. 14–34. Cambridge, Mass.: Harvard University Press.

———. 1972. *Mexican Architecture of the Sixteenth Century* [1948]. 2 vols. Westport, Conn.: Greenwood Press.

———. 1984. *The Art and Architecture of Ancient America.* London: Penguin.

————. 1985. "The Colonial Plan of Cholula." In *Studies in Ancient American and European Art: The Collected Essays of George Kubler,* ed. Thomas F. Reese, pp. 92–101. New Haven: Yale University Press.

————. 1992. *Arquitectura mexicana del siglo XVI.* Mexico City: FCE. [Spanish translation of *Mexican Architecture of the Sixteenth Century.* New Haven: Yale University Press, 1948.]

Lara, Jaime. 1996. "El espejo en la cruz: Una *reflexión* medieval sobre las cruces atriales mexicanas." *Anales del IIE* 69: 5–40.

————. 2004. *City, Temple, Stage: Eschatological Architecture and Liturgical Theatrics in New Spain.* Notre Dame, Ind.: University of Notre Dame Press.

————. 2008. *Christian Texts for Aztecs: Art and Liturgy in Colonial Mexico.* Notre Dame, Ind.: University of Notre Dame Press.

Laughton, Timothy B. 1997. "Sculpture on the Threshold: The Iconography of Izapa and Its Relationship to That of the Maya." Doctoral thesis, University of Essex, England.

Leibsohn, Dana. 1994. "Primers for Memory: Cartographic Histories and Nahua Identity." In *Writing without Words: Alternative Literacies in Mesoamerica and the Andes,* ed. Elizabeth Hill Boone and Walter D. Mignolo, pp. 161–87. Durham, N.C.: Duke University Press.

————. 1995. "Colony and Cartography: Shifting Signs on Indigenous Maps of New Spain." In *Reframing the Renaissance: Visual Culture in Europe and Latin America, 1450–1650,* ed. Claire Farago, pp. 265–341. New Haven: Yale University Press.

León, Nicolás. 1900. "A Mazahua Catechism in Testera-Amerind Hieroglyphics." *American Anthropologist* 2, no. 4: 722–40.

León-Portilla, Miguel. 1979. *Un catecismo náhuatl en imágenes.* Mexico City: Cartón y Papel de México.

————. 1982. *Aztec Thought and Culture: A Study of the Ancient Nahuatl Mind.* Norman: University of Oklahoma Press.

————. 1986a. "Estudio introductorio." In Fray Bernardino de Sahagún, *Coloquios y doctrina cristiana* [1564], pp. 13–29. Mexico City: UNAM/Fundación de Investigaciones Sociales.

————. 1986b. "Yancuic tlahtolli: Palabra nueva, una antología de la literatura náhuatl contemporánea." *ECN* 18: 123–41.

————. 1992. "Fray Juan de Zumárraga y las lenguas indígenas de México." In *La utopía mexicana del siglo XVI: Lo bello, lo verdadero y lo bueno,* ed. Guillermo Tovar de Teresa, Miguel León-Portilla, and Silvio Zavala, pp. 41–65. Mexico City: Azabache.

————. 1996. "¿Insertos en la 'Historia Sagrada'?: Respuesta y reacomodo de los mesoamericanos." *ECN* 20: 187–209.

————. 1997. *El destino de la palabra: De la oralidad y los códices mesoamericanos a la escritura alfabética.* Mexico City: Colegio de México/FCE.

Lockhart, James. 1990. "Postconquest Nahua Society and Concepts Viewed through Nahuatl Writings." *ECN* 20: 91–116.

————. 1992. *The Nahuas after the Conquest: A Social and Cultural History of the Indians of Central Mexico, Sixteenth through Eighteenth Centuries.* Stanford: Stanford University Press.

————. 1993. *We People Here: Nahuatl Accounts of the Conquest of Mexico.* Berkeley: University of California Press.

Lockhart, James, Frances Berdan, and Arthur J. O. Anderson, eds. 1986. *The Tlaxcalan Actas: A Compendium of the Records of the Cabildo of Tlaxcala (1545–1627).* Salt Lake City: University of Utah Press.

Lockhart, James, and Stuart B. Schwartz. 1984. *Early Latin America: A History of Colonial Spanish America and Brazil.* Cambridge: CUP.

López Austin, Alfredo, ed. 1969. *Augurios y abusiones.* Textos de los informantes de Sahagún 4. Mexico City: UNAM/IIH.

———. 1994. *Tamoanchan y Tlalocan.* Mexico City: FCE.

———. 1996a. *Cuerpo humano e ideología: Las concepciones de los antiguos nahuas.* 2 vols. Mexico City: UNAM/IIA.

———. 1996b. "Los rostros de los dioses mesoamericanos." *Arqueología Mexicana* 4, no. 20: 6–17.

———. 1998. *Los mitos del tlacuache: Camino de la mitología mesoamericana.* Mexico City: UNAM/IIA.

López Luján, Leonardo, and Vida Mercado. 1996. "Dos esculturas de Mictlantecuhtli encontradas en el recinto sagrado de México-Tenochtitlan." *ECN* 26: 41–68.

Lupo, Alessandro. 2001. "La cosmovisión de los nahuas de la Sierra de Puebla." In *Cosmovisión, ritual e identidad de los pueblos indígenas de México,* ed. Johanna Broda and Félix Báez-Jorge, pp. 335–89. Mexico City: CONACULTA/FCE.

Macazaga Ordoño, César. 1979. *Nombres geográficos de México.* Mexico City: Editorial Innovación, S.A.

MacGregor, Luis. 1955. *Actopan.* Memorias del Instituto Nacional de Antropología e Historia 4. Mexico City: INAH/SEP.

Maldonado Jiménez, Druzo. 1993. "Estudio iconográfico de la 'Pintura de Acapixtla' Morelos." *Cuadernos de Arquitectura Mesoamericana* 24: 69–86.

Manrique, Jorge Alberto. 1990. "The Progress of Art in New Spain." In *Mexico: Splendors of Thirty Centuries,* pp. 237–42. New York: Metropolitan Museum of Art.

Manzanilla Naim, Linda. 1999a. "The First Urban Developments in the Central Highlands of Mesoamerica." In *The Archaeology of Mesoamerica: Mexican and European Perspectives,* pp. 13–31. London: British Museum Press.

———. 1999b. "El inframundo en Teotihuacan." In *Chalchihuite: Homenaje a Doris Heyden,* ed. María de Jesús Rodríguez-Shadow and Beatriz Barba de Piña Chan, pp. 61–89. Mexico City: UNAM.

Matos Moctezuma, Eduardo. 1987. "The Templo Mayor of Tenochtitlan: History and Interpretation." In *The Great Temple of Tenochtitlan: Center and Periphery in the Aztec World,* ed. Johanna Broda, Davíd Carrasco, and Eduardo Matos Moctezuma, pp. 15–60. Berkeley: University of California Press.

———. 1988. *The Great Temple of the Aztecs: Treasures of Tenochtitlan.* London: Thames and Hudson.

———. 1990a. "Column Base with Earth Relief Monster." In *Mexico: Splendors of Thirty Centuries,* p. 255. New York: Metropolitan Museum of Art.

———. 1990b. *Guía oficial: Templo Mayor.* Mexico City: INAH/Salvat.

———. 2002. "From Teotihuacan to Tenochtitlan: Their Great Temples." In *Mesomerica's Classic Heritage: From Teotihuacan to the Aztecs,* ed. Davíd Carrasco, Lindsay Jones, and Scott Sessions, pp. 185–94. Boulder: University Press of Colorado.

McAndrew, John. 1965. *The Open-Air Churches of Sixteenth-Century Mexico.* Cambridge, Mass.: Harvard University Press.

Medina Hernández, Andrés. 2001. "La cosmovisión mesoamericana: Una mirada desde la etnografía." In *Cosmovisión, ritual e identidad de los pueblos indígenas de México*, ed. Johanna Broda and Félix Báez-Jorge, pp. 67–163. Mexico City: CONACULTA/FCE.

Mignolo, Walter D. 1994. "Signs and Their Transmission: The Question of the Book in the New World." In *Writing without Words: Alternative Literacies in Mesoamerica and the Andes,* ed. Elizabeth Hill Boone and Walter D. Mignolo, pp. 220–70. Durham, N.C.: Duke University Press.

Miller, Mary, and Karl Taube. 1993. *The Gods and Symbols of Ancient Mexico and the Maya: An Illustrated Dictionary of Mesoamerican Religion.* London: Thames and Hudson.

Monaghan, John. 1990. "Performance and the Structure of the Mixtec Codices." *Ancient Mesoamerica* 1: 133–40.

———. 1994. "The Text in the Body, the Body in the Text: The Embodied Sign in Mixtec Writing." In *Writing without Words: Alternative Literacies in Mesoamerica and the Andes,* ed. Elizabeth Hill Boone and Walter D. Mignolo, pp. 87–101. Durham, N.C.: Duke University Press.

Monterrosa Prado, Mariano. 1968. "Cruces cogolladas o sarmentosas." *Boletín del INAH* 34: 19–22.

Montes de Oca Vega, Mercedes, Dominique Raby, Salvador Reyes Equigas, and Adam T. Sellen. 2003. *Cartografía de tradición indígena: Mapas de mercedes de tierra siglos XVI y XVII.* With a prologue by Miguel León-Portilla. Mexico City: UNAM/AGN.

Morante López, Rubén B. 1997. "El monte Tlaloc y el calendario mexica." In *Graniceros: Cosmovisión y meteorología indígenas de Mesoamérica,* ed. Beatriz Albores and Johanna Broda, pp. 107–39. Mexico City: Colegio Mexiquense/UNAM.

Moreno Villa, José. 1986. *La escultura colonial mexicana* [1942]. Mexico City: FCE.

Mullen, Robert J. 1975. *Dominican Architecture in Sixteenth-Century Oaxaca.* Tempe: Center for Latin American Studies, Arizona State University.

———. 1983. "Santa María Tiltepec: A Masterpiece of Mixtec Vernacular Architecture." *Anales del IIE* 51: 45–58.

———. 1995. *The Architecture and Sculpture of Oaxaca, 1530s–1980s.* Tempe: Center for Latin American Studies, Arizona State University.

Mundy, Barbara E. 1996. *The Mapping of New Spain: Indigenous Cartography and the Maps of the Relaciones Geográficas.* Chicago: University of Chicago Press.

Muñoz Espinosa, María Estela. 1999. *Una muestra iconográfica de las estampas que guardan las obras que llegaron a la Nueva España.* Mexico City: INAH.

NASA eclipse website: http://eclipse.gsfc.nasa.gov/eclipse.html.

Navarrete, Federico. 1998. "Los libros quemados y los nuevos libros: Paradojas de la autenticidad en la tradición mesoamericana." In *La abolición del arte: XXI Coloquio Internacional de Historia del Arte,* pp. 53–71. Mexico City: UNAM/IIE.

Nebel, Richard. 1995. *Santa María Tonantzin, Virgen de Guadalupe: Continuidad y transformación religiosa en México.* Mexico City: FCE. [Spanish translation of *Santa María Tonantzin, Virgen de Guadalupé: Religiöse Kontinuität und Transformation in Mexiko,* published in 1992 by *Neue Zeitschrift für Missionwissenschaft.*]

Nicholson, Henry B. 1971. "Religion in Pre-Hispanic Central Mexico." In *Handbook of Middle American Indians,* vol. 10, 395–446. Austin: University of Texas Press.

———. 1973. "Bernardino de Sahagún's Primero Memoriales, Tepepolco, 1559–1561." In *Handbook of Middle American Indians,* vol. 13, 207–18. Austin: University of Texas Press.

———. 1974. "Tepepolco, the Locale of the First Stage of Fr. Bernardino de Sahagún's Great Ethnographic Project: Historical and Cultural Notes." In *Mesoamerican Archaeology: New Approaches,* ed. Norman Hammond, pp. 145–54. London: Duckworth.

———. 1991. "The Octli Cult in Late Prehispanic Central Mexico." In *To Change Place: Aztec Ceremonial Landscapes,* ed. David Carrasco, pp. 158–87. Niwot: University of Colorado Press.

Nicholson, Henry B., Arthur J. O. Anderson, Charles E. Dibble, Eloise Quiñones Keber, and Wayne Ruwet, eds. 1997. *Primeros Memoriales by Fray Bernardino de Sahagún.* Paleography of Nahuatl text and English translation by Thelma D. Sullivan. Norman: University of Oklahoma Press.

Noguera, Eduardo. 1972. "Antigüedad y significado de los relieves de Acalpixcan, México." *Anales de Antropología* 9: 77–94.

Nutini, Hugo. 1988. *Todos Santos in Rural Tlaxcala: A Syncretic, Expressive and Symbolic Analysis of the Cult of the Dead.* Princeton: Princeton University Press.

O'Gorman, Edmundo, ed. 1990 *Fray Toribio Motolinía: Historia de los indios de la Nueva España.* Mexico City: Porrúa.

Olivier, Guilhem. 2000. "Entre transgresión y renacimiento: El papel de la ebriedad en los mitos del México antiguo." In *El héroe entre el mito y la historia,* ed. Federico Navarrete and Guilhem Olivier, pp. 101–21. Mexico City: UNAM/Centro Francés de Estudios Mexicanos y Centroamericanos.

———. 2006. "Indios y españoles frente a prácticas adivinatorias y presagios durante la conquista de México." *ECN* 37: 169–92.

Pasztory, Esther. 1976. *The Murals of Tepantitla, Teotihuacan.* New York: Garland Publishing, Inc.

Peschard Fernández, A., J. Ganot Rodríguez, and J. F. Lazalde Montoya. 1989. "Cosmic Ideograms on Petroglyphs of the Mesoamerican Cultures of 'El Zape' Region in Durango, Mexico." In *World Archaeoastronomy: Selected Papers from the 2nd Oxford International Conference on Archaeoastronomy Held at Mérida, Yucatán, 13–17 January 1986,* ed. Anthony F. Aveni, pp. 300–307. Cambridge: CUP.

———. 1991. "Petroglifos de El Zape: Un calendario solar en el norte de México." In *Arqueoastronomía y etnoastronomía en Mesoamérica,* ed. Johanna Broda, Stanislaw Iwaniszewski, and Lucrecia Maupomé, pp. 529–36. Mexico City: UNAM/IIH.

Peterson, Jeanette F. 1985. "The Garden Frescoes of Malinalco: Utopia, Imperial Policy and Acculturation in Sixteenth-Century Mexico." Ph.D. diss., University of California, Los Angeles.

———. 1993. *The Paradise Garden Murals of Malinalco.* Austin: University of Texas Press.

Pohl, John M. D. 1994. *The Politics of Symbolism in the Mixtec Codices.* Publications in Anthropology 46. Nashville: Vanderbilt University.

Pohl, John M. D., and Bruce E. Byland. 1990. "Mixtec Landscape Perception and Archaeological Settlement Patterns." *Ancient Mesoamerica* 1: 113–31.

Ponce de León, Arturo. 1991. "Propiedades geométrico-astronómicas en la arquitectura prehispánica." In *Arqueoastronomía y etnoastronomía en Mesoamérica,* ed. Johanna Broda, Stanislaw Iwaniszewski, and Lucrecia Maupomé, pp. 413–46. Mexico City: UNAM/IIH.

Quiñones Keber, Eloise. 1995. *Codex Telleriano-Remensis: Ritual, Divination, and History in a Pictorial Aztec Manuscript.* Austin: University of Texas Press.

Reyes García, Luis. 1972. "Ordenanzas para el gobierno de Cuauhtinchan, año 1559." *ECN* 10: 245–313.

———. 1979. "Comentarios." In *El trabajo y los trabajadores en la historia de México,* ed. Elsa Cecilia Frost, Michael C. Meyer, and Josefina Zoraida Vázquez, pp. 66–69. Mexico City: Colegio de México/University of Arizona Press.

———. 1993. "Cantares Mexicanos: Approaching the Náhuatl Text." *Indiana Journal of Hispanic Literature* 1, no. 2: 1–8.

Reyes-Valerio, Constantino. 1967a. "El escultor indígena de Tetepango." *Boletín del INAH* 30: 9–12.

———. 1967b. "Una pintura indígena en Cuauhtinchan." *Boletín del INAH* 29: 1–6.

———. 1967c. "Las pinturas en papel de amate de Ixmiquilpan, Hidalgo." *Boletín del INAH* 27: 25–28.

———. 1968. "La pila bautismal de Zinacantepec, Estado de México." *Boletín del INAH* 31: 24–27.

———. 1970. "Los tlacuilos y tlacuicuia de Itzmiquilpan." *Boletín del INAH* 42: 9–13.

———. 1978. *Arte indocristiano: Escultura del siglo XVI en México.* Mexico City: SEP/UNAM.

———. 1989a. "Las pictografías náhuas en el arte indocristiano." In *Primer Coloquio de Documentos Pictográficos de Tradición Náhuatl,* pp. 71–77. Mexico City: UNAM/IIH.

———. 1989b. *El pintor de conventos: Los murales del siglo XVI en la Nueva España.* Mexico City: UNAM.

———. 2000. *Arte indocristiano.* Mexico City: INAH.

Ricard, Robert. 1994. *La "conquista espiritual" de México* [1947]. Mexico City: FCE.

Rivas Castro, Francisco, and Mari Carmen Lechuga García. 1999. "La lápida del Tláloc—ofidio del templo de Santiago Tlatelolco, D.F." Seminario Permanente de Iconografía, Occasional Paper 7. Mexico City: DEAS-INAH.

Robertson, Donald. 1959. *Mexican Manuscript Painting of the Early Colonial Period.* New Haven: Yale University Press.

Rojas Rabiela, Teresa. 1979. "La organización del trabajo para las obras públicas: El coatequitl y las cuadrillas de trabajadores." In *El trabajo y los trabajadores en la historia de México,* ed. Elsa Cecilia Frost, Michael C. Meyer, and Josefina Zoraida Vázquez, pp. 41–66. Mexico City: Colegio de México/University of Arizona Press.

Royal Academy of Arts. 2002. *Aztecs.* Exhibition Catalogue. London: RAA.

Ruta de los santuarios en México. 1994. Mexico City: Secretaría de Turismo.

Salazar Monroy [no first name]. 1944. *Convento franciscano de Huejotzingo.* Puebla: Imprenta López.

———. 1945. *Motivos ornamentales al fresco del Convento Franciscano de Huejotzingo.* Puebla: Imprenta López.

Salinas Pedraza, Jesús. 1983. *Etnografía del otomí.* Mexico City: Instituto Nacional Indigenista.

Santamaría, Francisco J. 2000. *Diccionario de mejicanismos* [1959]. Mexico City: Porrúa.

Saunders, Nicholas J. 2001. "A Dark Light: Reflections on Obsidian in Mesoamerica." *World Archaeology* 33, no. 2: 220–36.

Schele, Linda, and Mary Ellen Miller. 1986. *The Blood of Kings: Dynasty and Ritual in Maya Art.* Fort Worth: Kimbell Art Museum.

Scholes, Walter V. 1944. "The Diego Ramírez *Visita* in Meztitlan." *Hispanic American Historical Review* 24, no. 1: 30–38.

Schultes, Richard Evans, and Albert Hoffmann. 1982. *Plantas de los dioses: Orígenes del uso de los alucinógenos.* Mexico City: FCE. [Spanish translation of *Plants of the Gods: Origins of Hallucinogenic Use.* New York: McGraw-Hill, 1979.]

Sebastián, Santiago. 1963. "Iconología del claustro monacal de la Nueva España durante el siglo XVI." Córdoba, Universidad de Córdoba (mimeo).

———. 1989. *Contrarreforma y barroco: Lecturas iconográficas e iconológicas.* Madrid: Alianza Editorial.

———. 1994. "Los libros de emblemas: Uso y difusión en Iberoamérica." In *Juegos de ingenio y agudeza: La pintura emblemática de la Nueva España,* pp. 56–82. Mexico City: Museo Nacional de Arte/CONACULTA.

Sebastián, Santiago, Mariano Monterrosa, and José Antonio Terán, eds. 1995. *Iconografía del arte del siglo XVI en México.* Zacatecas: Universidad Autónoma de Zacatecas.

Segovia, Víctor. 1991. "La astronomía en Uxmal." In *Arqueoastronomía y etnoastronomía en Mesoamérica,* ed. Johanna Broda, Stanislaw Iwaniszewski, and Lucrecia Maupomé, pp. 61–63. Mexico City: UNAM/IIH.

Séjourné, Laurette. 1978. *Burning Water: Thought and Religion in Ancient Mexico.* London: Thames and Hudson.

———. 1983. *Arqueología e historia del Valle de Mexico City: De Xochimilco a Amecameca.* Mexico City: Siglo Veintiuno Editores.

Seler, Eduard. 1904. "Mexican Picture Writings of Alexander von Humboldt." *Bulletin of the Bureau of American Ethnology* 28: 127–229.

———. 1963. *Comentarios al Códice Borgia,* Vol. 1. Mexico City: FCE.

———. 1992. *Collected Works in Mesoamerican Linguistics and Archaeology.* Ed. Frank E. Comparato. 5 vols. Culver City: Labyrinthos. [English translation of German papers from *Gesammelte Abhandlungen zur Amerikanischen Sprach- und Altertumskunde.* Graz: ADV, 1960–67.]

Sentenach, Narciso. 1900. "Catecismos de la doctrina cristiana en jeroglíficos para la enseñanza de los indios americanos." *Revista de Archivos, Bibliotecas y Museos* 4: 599–609.

Sepúlveda y Herrera, María Teresa. 1976. "La cofradía de San Nicolas Tolentino." *Anales del INAH* 6: 5–24.

Shelton, Anthony. 1991. "Person, Time and Space: The Community of the Dead in Mexico." In *Altars and Idols: The Life of the Dead in Mexico,* pp. 7–12. M.A. Gallery Studies catalogue, University of Essex.

Siméon, Rémi. 1997. *Diccionario de la lengua náhuatl o mexicana.* Mexico City: Siglo Veintiuno Editores. [Spanish translation of *Dictionnaire de la langue nahuatl ou mexicaine.* Paris: Imprimerie Nationale, 1885.]

Smith, Mary Elizabeth. 1973. *Picture Writing from Ancient Southern Mexico.* Norman: University of Oklahoma Press.

Solís, Felipe. 2002. Catalogue entries. In *Aztecs,* pp. 400–495. London: Royal Academy of Arts.

Spores, Ronald. 1967. *The Mixtec Kings and Their People.* Norman: University of Oklahoma Press.

Stols, Alexandre A. M. 1989. *Antonio de Espinosa, el segundo impresor mexicano.* Mexico City: Biblioteca Nacional/Instituto de Investigaciones Bibliográficas/UNAM.

Taylor, William B. 1979. *Drinking, Homicide and Rebellion in Colonial Mexican Villages.* Stanford: Stanford University Press.

———. 1996. *Magistrates of the Sacred: Priests and Parishioners in Eighteenth-Century Mexico.* Stanford: Stanford University Press.

Tichy, Franz. 1975. "Explicación de las redes de poblaciones y terrenos como testimonio de la ocupación y planificación del Altiplano Central en el México antiguo." *Comunicaciones, Proyecto Puebla-Tlaxcala* 11: 41–52.

———. 1978. "El calendario solar como principio de organización del espacio para poblaciones y lugares sagrados." *Comunicaciones, Proyecto Puebla-Tlaxcala* 15: 153–60.

———. 1979. "Configuración y coordinación sistemáticas de espacio y tiempo en la visión del mundo de la América antigua: ¿Mito o realidad?" *Humboldt* 20, no. 69: 42–60.

———. 1983a. "Observaciones del sol y calendario agrícola en Mesoamérica." In *Calendars in Mesoamerica and Peru: Native Computation of Time,* ed. Anthony F. Aveni and Gordon Brotherston, pp. 135–43. Proceedings of the 44th International Congress of Americanists (Manchester, 1982). BAR International Series 174. Oxford: BAR.

———. 1983b. "Patrón de asentamientos con sistema radial en la Meseta Central de Mexico City: '¿Sistema Ceque' en Mesoamérica?" *Jahrbuch für Geschichte von Staat Wirtschaft und Gesellschaft Lateinamerikas* 20: 61–84.

———. 1988. "Measurement of Angles in Mesoamerica: Necessity and Possibility." In *New Directions in American Archaeoastronomy,* ed. Anthony F. Aveni, pp. 105–20. Proceedings of the 44th International Congress of Americanists (Amsterdam, 1988). BAR International Series 454. Oxford: BAR.

———. 1990. "Orientation Calendar in Mesoamerica: Hypothesis concerning Their Structure, Use and Distribution." *ECN* 20: 183–99.

———. 1991a. "Los cerros sagrados de la Cuenca de México en el sistema de ordenamiento del espacio y de la planeación de los poblados: ¿El sistema ceque de los Andes en Mesoamérica?" In *Arqueoastronomía y etnoastronomía en Mesoamérica,* ed. Johanna Broda, Stanislaw Iwaniszewski, and Lucrecia Maupomé, pp. 447–59. Mexico City: UNAM/IIH.

———. 1991b. "Ordenado de los pueblos indios: Un ejemplo del ordenamiento del espacio y del tiempo en el México." Mexico City: Escuela Nacional de Antropología e Historia (mimeo).

———. 1992. "Tabellenanhang 12-1: Orientierung der Kirchen im Becken von Mexico" and "Tabellenanhang 12-2: Orientierung der Kirchen im Puebla-Tlaxcala-Gebiet." In *Die geordnete Welt indianischer Völker: Ein Beispiel von Raumordnung und Zeitordnung im vorkolombischen Mexiko,* pp. 203–18. Stuttgart: Steiner.

Torre Villar, Ernesto de la. 1995. *Las congregaciones de los pueblos de indios, fase terminal: Aprobaciones y rectificaciones.* Mexico City: UNAM/IIH.

Toussaint, Manuel. 1982. *Pintura colonial en México* [1965]. Ed. Xavier Moyssen. Mexico City: UNAM.

Townsend, Richard Fraser. 1982. "Pyramid and Sacred Mountain." In *Ethnoastronomy and Archaeoastronomy in the American Tropics,* ed. Anthony F. Aveni and Gary Urton, pp. 37–62. New York: New York Academy of Sciences.

———. 1991. "The Mt. Tlaloc Project." In *To Change Place: Aztec Ceremonial Landscapes,* ed. Davíd Carrasco, pp. 26–30. Niwot: University Press of Colorado.

———. 1992a. "Landscape and Symbol." In *The Ancient Americas: Art from Sacred Landscapes,* ed. Richard F. Townsend, pp. 29–47. Munich: Art Institute of Chicago/Prestel Verlag.

———. 1992b. "The Renewal of Nature at the Temple of Tlaloc." In *The Ancient Americas: Art from Sacred Landscapes,* ed. Richard F. Townsend, pp. 171–85. Munich: Art Institute of Chicago/Prestel Verlag.

———. 1995. *The Aztecs.* London: Thames and Hudson.

Tucker, Tim. 2001. "El asentamiento prehispánico de 'Cerro Teoton': Un *axis mundi* en la región oriental del Valle Poblano." In *La montaña en el paisaje ritual,* ed. Johanna Broda, Stanislaw Iwaniszewski, and Arturo Montero, pp. 65–81. Mexico City: CONACULTA/INAH.

Tudela de la Orden, José. 1980. *Códice Tudela.* Madrid: Ediciones Cultura Hispánica.

Umberger, Emily. 1981. "The Structure of Aztec History." *Archaeoastronomy: The Bulletin of the Center for Archaeoastronomy* 4, no. 4: 10–18.

Uriarte, María Teresa. 1982. "Pintura mural en el Altiplano." *Historia del Arte Mexicano* 3: 436–56. Mexico City: SEP/Editorial Salvat.

van der Loo, Peter L. 1987. *Códices, costumbres, continuidad: Un estudio de la religión mesoamericana.* Leiden: Archeologisch Centrum Rijksuniversiteit te Leiden.

Vega Sosa, Constanza. 1991. "El curso del sol según los glifos de la cerámica azteca tardía." In *Arqueoastronomía y etnoastronomía en Mesoamérica,* ed. Johanna Broda, Stanislaw Iwaniszewski, and Lucrecia Maupomé, pp. 517–25. Mexico City: UNAM/IIH.

Venegas, Juan E., and Ana Graciela Bedolla. 1995. *Ex-Convento de Culhuacán, Estado de México.* Mexico City: INAH.

Victoria Asensio, José Guadalupe. 1985. *Arte y arquitectura en la sierra alta: Siglo XVI.* Mexico City: UNAM/IIE.

Vogt, Evon Z. 1976. *Tortillas for the Gods: A Symbolic Analysis of Zinacanteco Rituals.* Cambridge, Mass.: Harvard University Press.

Wake, Eleanor. 1995. "Framing the Sacred: Native Interpretations of Christianity in Early Colonial Mexico." Ph.D. diss., University of Essex.

———. 2000. "Sacred Books and Sacred Songs from Former Days: Sourcing the Mural Paintings at San Miguel Arcángel Ixmiquilpan." *ECN* 31: 95–121.

———. 2002a. "Codex Tlaxcala: New Insights and New Questions." *ECN* 33: 91–140.

———. 2002b. "Native Appropriation of the European Grotesque in the Art of Sixteenth-Century Mexico." Paper presented at the Association of Art Historians Annual Conference, Liverpool, England, April 5–7.

———. 2003. "Grotesque Dancing: A Further Interpretation of the Mural Paintings at San Miguel Arcángel Ixmiquilpan." Paper presented at Aztec Art and Culture: An International Symposium, Royal Academy of Arts/British Museum, London, England, March 22–23.

———. 2007. "The Serpent Road: Colonial Iconic Script and the Historical Narrative of Mapa de Cuauhtinchan No. 2." In *Cave, City, and Eagle's Nest: An Interpretive Journey through the Mapa de Cuauhtinchan No. 2,* ed. Davíd Carrasco and Scott C. Sessions, pp. 205–54. Albuquerque: University of New Mexico Press.

———. n.d.a. "The Maize Theatre: Symbolic Representations of Maize in Prehispanic Religious Rituals." In *El uso ritual de la flor (flora) en América,* ed. Beatriz Albores. Mexico City: El Colegio Mexiquense.

———. n.d.b. "Setting the New Cosmic Stage: Some Observations on Native Landscape Painting in Sixteenth-Century Mexico." In *Illegitimate Images: Studies in the Iconography of Colonial Latin American Art,* ed. Valerie Fraser. Vanderbilt University Press.

———. n.d.c. "Writing on Architecture: The Embedded Stones of Colonial Xochimilco." (ms. under revision).

Wake, Eleanor, and Phil Stokes. 1997. "Mixtec Manipulations: Pictographic History and Cultural Identity in the Art of Early Colonial Mexico." *Journal of Latin American Lore* 20, no. 2: 209–47.

Wallrath, Matthew, and Alfonso Rangel Ruiz. 1991. "Xihuingo (Tepeapulco): Un centro de observación astronómica." In *Arqueoastronomía y etnoastronomía en Mesoamérica,* ed. Johanna Broda, Stanislaw Iwaniszewski, and Lucrecia Maupomé, pp. 297–308. Mexico City: UNAM/IIH.

Wasson, R. Gordon. 1982. "Xochipilli, 'Príncipe de las Flores': Un nueva interpretación." *Revista de la Universidad de México* 11: 10–19.

———. 1983. *El hongo maravilloso teonanácatl: Micolatría en Mesoamérica.* Mexico City: FCE. [Spanish translation of *The Wondrous Mushroom: Mycolatry in Mesoamerica.* New York: McGraw-Hill, 1980.]

Weismann, Elizabeth W. 1985. *Art and Time in Mexico: From the Conquest to the Revolution.* New York: Harper and Row.

Wood, Stephanie. 1991. "Adopted Saints: Christian Images in Nahua Testaments of Late Colonial Toluca." *Americas* 47, no. 3: 259–93.

———. 1997. "The Ajusco Town Founding Document: Affinities with Documents of the Sixteenth Century." In *Códices y documentos sobre México: Segundo Simposio,* ed. Salvador Rueda Smithers, Constanza Vega Sosa, and Rodrigo Martínez Baracs, vol. 2, pp. 333–48. 2 vols. Mexico City: INAH/Dirección General de Publicaciones.

———. 1998. "The Social vs. Legal Context of Nahuatl *Títulos.*" In *Native Traditions in the Postconquest World,* ed. Elizabeth Hill Boone and Tom Cummins, pp. 201–31. Washington, D.C.: Dumbarton Oaks.

Yoneda, Keiko. 1991. *Los mapas de Cuauhtinchan y la historia cartográfica prehispánica.* Mexico City: FCE.

———. 1994. *Cartografía y linderos en el Mapa de Cuauhtinchan núm. 4.* Mexico City: INAH/BUAP.

———. 1996. *Migraciones y conquistas: Descifre global del Mapa de Cuauhtinchan núm. 3.* Mexico City: INAH.

———. 2005. *Mapa de Cuauhtinchan núm. 2.* Mexico City: CIESAS/Miguel Angel Porrúa.

Zeilik, Michael. 1989. "Keeping the Sacred and Planting Calendar: Archaeoastronomy in the Pueblo Southwest." In *World Archaeoastronomy: Selected Papers from the 2nd Oxford International Conference on Archaeoastronomy Held at Mérida, Yucatán, 13–17 January 1986,* ed. Anthony F. Aveni, pp. 143–66. Cambridge: CUP.

———. 1991. "Sunwatching and Calendars: A Southwestern Mesoamerican Contrast in a Distant, Smoky Mirror." In *Arqueoastronomía y etnoastronomía en Mesoamérica,* ed. Johanna Broda, Stanislaw Iwaniszewski, and Lucrecia Maupomé, pp. 545–56. Mexico City: UNAM/IIH.

Zimbrón Romero, J. Rafael. 1991. "La región sagrada de los xochimilcas." In *Maestrías: Historia, etnohistoria, arqueología,* pp. 16–23. Mexico City: Escuela Nacional de Antropología e Historia.

———. 1992. "Las cruces punteadas de Santa Cruz Acalpixcan, Xochimilco." *Cuadernos de Arquitectura Mesoamericana* 19: 59–74.

Index

All references to illustrations are in italic type.

Acalpixca (D.F.), 243
Acambaro (Guanajuato), 91, 128
Acapixtla (Morelos), 59, 63, 65; map, *19*, 125,
    128, 134; San Juan Bautista, 231, 270n26
Acculturation, 286n7
Acolhua peoples, 144, 151–52
Acolman (México), 45, 181, 291n74;
    San Augustín, 119, 131, 155, 157,
    165, *166*, 168, 177, 180–83, 210–12,
    214, 224–25, 231, 240, 250, 284n28,
    288n28, 291n72; Santa Catarina, 158
Acosta, Joseph de, 79
Actopan (Hidalgo), 288n33; La Peña, 189–90;
    San Nicolás Tolentino, *23, 24*, 176, 183,
    186–94, 198, 207, 215–17, 224, 248, 277n2,
    288n35, 288n37; valley/aqueduct, 188, 216
Afterlife/afterworlds, 40–42, 110, 206,
    267n17, 272n47. *See also* Mictlan;
    Tlalocan; Tonatiuh Ilhuicac
Age of Agriculture, 36–40, 59, 115,
    155. *See also* Fifth Sun; Maize
Agricultural cycles, 41–42, 45, 58–59, 63,
    71–72, 108, 128–29, 161–64. *See also* Maize;
    Mictlan; Tlalocan; Tonatiuh Ilhuicac
Ahuitzotl (Aztec ruler), 283n22
Ajusco (México), Santo Tomás, 115,
    221, 224, 272n1, 285n35
Alamazán, Cristóbal de, 82
Alberro, Solange, 200
Alcántara, cross of, 153–54
Alcoholism, 47, 61, 74, 91–92. *See also*
    Ritual drinking/drunkenness
Alfajayuca (Hidalgo), San Martín,
    203, 219–20, 224, 255
Alfiz (architectural feature), 122, 172, 205
Alligator. *See* Animals
Almolonca-Maxtlatlan (Veracruz),
    123–24, 128, 136–37, 280n36

Alphabetized texts (doctrinas), 80–81, 89–90,
    273n11. *See also* Picture catechisms
Altepetl system (*in atl in tepetl*): etymological
    origins, 278n15; evolution of native art
    style, 276n63; perception of churches,
    115–30; precolonial significance, 281n59;
    toponymy on churches, 279n28; "water-
    mountain" symbolism, 87, 108–10.
    See also Toponyms/toponymy
Altipac (México), Santa María, 239
Alva Ixtlilxóchitl, Fernando de, 186, 217
Amatecatl (pulque deity), 206
Amatlan (Morelos), Santa María
    Magdalena, 206, *207*
Amecameca (México), Asunción, *146*
Amoltepec (Oaxaca), 125, 128
Anasazi peoples, 145, 164
Angahua (Michoacán), 224
Angels, 154, 172, 177, 205–209, 213–14, 244,
    246, 252, 254. *See also* Winged beings
Anglicus, Bartolomaeus, 122
Animals, 44, 46, 49, 72, 184; alligators, 44;
    in art, 105, 148, 150, 184–87, 196–97,
    239–40, 288n37; badger, 187; bats,
    39–40, 253; cats, 73, 186; coyote, 40,
    184; deer, 185–87, 196; dogs, 253; frogs,
    49; as live offerings, 55, 67; lizard, 150;
    monkeys, 152, 244, 253; opossum, 150,
    184, 187, 241; squirrels, 150. *See also*
    Birds; Insects; Jaguars; Rabbits; Reptiles
Anne (Saint), 199–200
Annual cycles. *See* Calendars/annual cycles
Apasco (México), San Francisco,
    205, 244–45, 247, 249, 296n15
Apoala (Oaxaca), Santiago, 102
Apoala/Apoala Valley (Oaxaca),
    102, 105, 277n8
Apologética (Las Casas), 70

Arabesque, 172, 177, 204, 224, 252, 254
Architecture: creation myths and, 37; as
    cultural signifier, 119; friezes, 113; glyphic
    toponyms, 120; monastery layout and, 5,
    101–102; native and Christian parallels, 4–6,
    115–30; native perceptions of, 6, 102–103;
    "New World," 5; parapets, 111, 113, 125;
    portals and windows, 172, 245–46; as
    replica of landscape, 103, 107–109, 113–15,
    122, 192, 198; sightlines and alignments,
    5, 104–105, 108, 124, 130–37, 155, 161–68,
    181–82, 193, 281n49, 285n44, 287n24;
    as text, 256, 265n12. *See also* Churches;
    Cosmic layout/diagram; Embedded stones
Arrows, 47, 187, 211–12, 216, 221,
    224, 240. *See also* Xuchimitl
Ars memoriae, 142
Art. *See* Christian themes; Landscape
    painting; Native art
Asebedo, Fray Martín de, 189
Astronomical signs, 143–44, 147
Astronomy, 152, 169, 193, 196–98. *See also*
    Oyoalli; Xicalcoliuhqui; Xihuitl; Xonecuilli
Atitalaquia (Hidalgo), San Miguel,
    141, 153, 157, 284n27
Atlatlauhca (Morelos), La
    Concepción, *26, 30*, 281n47
Atlatlauhca-Malinaltepeque
    (Oaxaca), map, 129
Atlatlauhca-Suchiaca (México),
    127, 136, 279n25, 280n43
Atlantonan (earth mother), 208–209
Atlixco (Puebla), Santa Cecilia,
    103, 125, 252–53
Atl tlachinolli ("water-fire," symbol
    for war), 109–10, 255
Atocpa (D.F.), San Juan, 245, 279n25
Atotonilco el Grande (Hidalgo),
    San Agustín, 120, 273n20
Atrial crosses, 101, 117, 154, 182,
    202–203, 210–12, 215–33, 289n41,
    292n87, 292n98, 294n110, 294n113
Atria/patios, 5, 65, 101–102, 116–19, 232
Aubin, Joseph, 78
Augustine (Saint), 186, 189, 288n35;
    in art, *23, 24*, 187, 216, 224
Augustinian *Tebaida*, 22, 23, 184–88, 217–18
Auto/autos (religious plays), 73–75, 77, 89, 198
Aveni, Anthony, 162, 223
Axayacatl (Aztec ruler), 50, 120

Ayaucalli ("house of mist"), 107, 117–18
Ayopechtli (aspect of Mayahuel), 49, 209
Aztapotzalco (D.F.), San Francisco, 129
Aztec/Azteca-Mexica peoples, 44–47,
    108, 164, 220, 250–51, 267n18, 267n21,
    288n33. *See also* Mexica; Nahua peoples

Barrel cactus sacrifice. *See* Sacrifice
Bats, 39–40, 253
Beasts, European mythical, 32, 174–75,
    247, 252–53. *See also* Grotesque frieze
Bees, beetles, and flies. *See* Insects
Belfries (architectural feature), 165
Bells: ecclesiastical use of, 128–29, 134; in
    ritual and ceremonies, 69, 177, 239, 253–54
Biblia pauperum, 79
Birds: as angels, 206; in art, 148, 150;
    cockerels/roosters, 229, 293n106, 294n109;
    as embedded stone motif, 148; in flower-
    songs, 236–37; frieze depiction of, 26, 27,
    28; golden oriole, 246; hummingbirds,
    49, 73, 294n109, 295n4, 296n15; mural
    depiction of, 29, 246; parrots, 73, 237, 247,
    293n109, 295n4, 296n15; peacock, 150–51;
    in ritual and ceremonies, 45–46, 51, 227;
    significance of color, 49; transformation of
    dead to, 41, 206; vultures (*cozcacuauhtli*),
    150. *See also* Animals; Eagle; Sacred flyers
Bleeding hands, 218
Bleeding tree of Tamoanchan, 42, 187, 232
Blood and water, 45, 110
Body piercing. *See* Sacrifice
Bonampak (Chiapas), 255
Bones, 45, 47
Boone, Elizabeth Hill, 7
Bourke, John J., 145
Broda, Johanna, 71, 107–108, 162
Brotherston, Gordon, 7
Buonarroti, Michelangelo, 121
Burgoa, Fray Francisco de, 160
Burkhart, Louise, 58, 89, 207
Butterflies, 296n15; ceiling depiction of, 30,
    246; in flower-songs, 236–37; in grotesque
    frieze, 253; in ritual and ceremonies,
    45, 47, 49, 51, 241; transformation of
    dead to, 41, 206. *See also* Sacred flyers

Cabecera (head town), 90, 93
Cacaxtla (Tlaxcala), *25*, 207, 209, 230, 255
Cacti, 45. *See also* Maguey; Nopal; Sacrifice

Calendars/annual cycles: counts of, 46–47, 60, 91; creation of, 37–38; day-signs, 43, 106; deities' calendar names, 37, 63, 197; divinatory, 47, 68; on embedded stones, 140, 144, 147, 150, 152; 52-year cycle, 168, 183–84, 197, 233; incorporated into Christian art, 93–94, 221–23, 238–42, 295n9; keeping ceremonies and ancient rites, 60; as knowledge, 38; "like-in-kind" dates, 223; lunar cycle, 208–209, 240–41, 266n9; Night Lords, 47, 106, 221; as ordering principle, 47; as religious construct, 7; ritual cycle of festivals, 44–47, 271n42; solar imagery, 219–23; solar observation, 162–64, 193; sun's yearly cycle, 161–69, 196. *See also* Agricultural cycles; Christian festivals; Native festivals; Tonalpouhualli

Calimaya (México), 61, 64, 203

Calpan (Puebla), San Andrés, 102, 117–19, 212–14, 231, 241

Calpulalpan (Tlaxcala), Santos Simón y Judas, 177, 243, 290n66

Candles, 61–63

Cantares mexicanos, 9, 57, 65, 120–22, 129, 186, 202, 205, 206, 235

Cartillas (teaching primers), 80–81

Cartography. *See* Mappings

Castañeda, José, 159

Catechisms, 77–85. *See also* Doctrinas; Picture catechisms

Cats. *See* Animals; Jaguars

Caves, *16*, 38, 60, 62, 69, 105, 108–13, 119–22, 182, 184, 192, 220

Cave-womb, *14*, 110–11, 114

Cecilia (Saint), 252

Cempoala (Hidalgo): aqueduct, 152; maps, 128, 134–36; Todos Santos, 104, 131, 152, 179, 226, 277n2, 287n18

Censorship: of native art, 81–82, 89, 96–97, 273n13; of native ritual, 273n12

Centeotl (maize god), 42, 46, 200–201, 217, 230–32

Cerros. *See* Mountains

Cervantes de Salazar, Francisco, 65, 288n30

Chac (Mayan rain deities), 123

Chalchihuitl symbols: denoting stages of maize cycle, 293n103; as embedded stone motif, 140–48, 151, *152–53*, 154, 158–59, 167–68; as water glyph, 109, 175–76, 180, 219–20, 231, 239

Chalchiutlicue (water deity), *14*, 42–43, 69, 110–11, 155, 200, 208, 290n68

Chapatongo (Hidalgo), Santiago, 123, 224

Chapultepec (D.F.), San Miguel, 122

Charles V (Holy Roman Emperor, Charles I of Spain), 70, 81, 91

Cherubs. *See* Angels

Chicahua (Oaxaca), San Miguel, 102

Chichimec peoples, 39, 119, 220

Chicomecoatl (maize goddess), 42, 49, 60, 64, 144, 201, 208

Chiconauhtla (México), Santa María, 157

Chiconcuac (Hidalgo), Asunción, 241–42

Chimalhuacan Atenco (México), Santo Domingo, *151–52*

Chinantla (Oaxaca), 114

Chocolate drink, 63–64, 71

Cholula (Puebla), 291n75; festival of Quetzalcoatl, 50; Great Pyramid, 103, 135; map, 135–36, 281n58; Nuestra Señora de los Remedios, 103; San Gabriel, 119, 178–79, 244, 297n26

Chontal, 123

Christian crosses, 61, 64, 153–55, 181–82, 216–33. *See also* Atrial crosses; Cross of Christ; Tau crosses

Christian festivals: All Saints and All Souls (Day of the Dead), 68, 129; Annunciation, 68, 73; Ash Wednesday, 70; Candlemas, 69–70, 200; Christmas/Nativity, 69–70, 196; Corpus Christi, 68, 70–73, 117, 215; Easter, 68, 71–72, 196, 203, 241; Epiphany, 70, 254; Festival of Saint Anne, 199–200; Holy Cross, 168, 270n18, 289n44; Holy Week, 55; John the Baptist, 68; Michael the Archangel, 62; Palm Sunday, 61, 70, 203; Passion of Christ, 230; Pentecost, 203; Resurrection, 55, 68, 72, 214

Christianity: expressed in native art & architecture, 36; incorporation of native idols into, 98–99; "nahuatization" of, 67; native acceptance, 3–7, 77, 88; native adaptation to, 55–61, 256, 276n65; native religion versus, 58–60, 66–67; native understanding of, 6–7, 175. *See also* Indoctrination

Christian symbols, resemanticization of, 149, 153–55

Christian themes in art and the *autos*: Adam and Eve/Fall of Man, 72–73, 209–10;

Adoration of the Magi, 193–94, 288n28;
Annunciation, 96, 192, 197; Apocalypse,
180; Crucifixion, 22, 24, 179–82, 184–86,
193–96, 209, 215–18, 229, 287n17, 288n37;
Deposition, 181–82; *Ecce Homo*, 214–15;
Eternal Father, 187; Garden of Eden, 72–73,
203; Holy Family, 56, 180, 193–95, 209,
290n67; Nativity, 193, *197*, 223; Passion,
symbols of, 207, 214, 219–20, 223, 229;
Petrarch's triumphs, 207; Resurrection,
223; Sacrifice of Abraham, 73; Saint
Francis's Sermon to the Birds, 73; Saint
Sebastian, 218; *Tebaida augustiniana*,
22, 23; Temptation of Christ, 72–73;
Transfiguration, 223; Virgin and Child,
196, 208. *See also* individual saints
Christmas/Christ-child, 69–70
Church attendance: as evidence of
conversion, 77; religious indoctrination
and, 77–81; resistance to, 81–85
Church building: establishment of
congregaciones and, 85–88; exploitation of
Indian labor, 77, 83, 86–88; idolatry and,
97; Indian interest in, 3, 6; Indian labor
in, 87, 90–91, 173, 274n36; monastery
architecture and layout, 101–102; religious
indoctrination and, 88–93, 97; reuse
of stones in, 88, 94–96, 103, 139–42; as
ritualized occupation, 91–93; sightlines
and alignments, 130–37, 161–69. *See also*
Architecture; Color; Embedded stones
Churches: arrangement within monastery
complex, 101–102; as books, 172; built on
temple sites, 103–107; as caves, 119–22, 198,
238; as flowery places, 79; as fortresses, 119;
as mountains, 115, 120, 123–25, 127–28,
155, 190, 238, 256; mural painting, 180–98;
native artisans' decoration of, 171–80; native
epithets for, 121; native representations
of, 102, 118, 121–30, 133–36, 185, 188,
215; as places of song, 247–54, 279n29;
relationship to landscape, 121, 130–37; as
watery places, 120–21, 127, 141–42, 155,
189–90, 206, 232, 238. *See also* Sightlines
and alignments; individual named sites
Churubusco (D.F.), 66
Cihuacoatl (earth deity), 43–44, 114, 197, 200,
207–209. *See also* Quilaztli-Tlaltecuhtli
Cincalco (otherworld), 42
Ciudad Real, Antonio de, 254

Clare (Saint), 204–205
Clendinnen, Inga, 46, 67, 235
Cleve, Joos van, 290n67
Cloisters, 101–102
Cloths and mantles, ritual, 62–63, 67–68
Cloud motif, embedded stones, 143–44, 148
Coatepec (México), Natividad
de Nuestra Señora, *147*
Coatequitl (labor call-up
system), 86, 91, 275n43
Coatl, Juan, 69
Coatlicue (earth mother), 43, 92, 95, 197, 200
Coatlinchan (México): maps, *18*,
128–29; San Miguel, 151–53, 205
Codex Borbonicus, *14*, 110–11, 150, 237–39
Codex Borgia, 74, 106, 209, 211, 218,
226–31, 293n103, 294n111
Codex Cospi, 112
Codex Féjérváry, 74, 106, 144, 210, 226–29
Codex, Florentine, 39, 50, 52, 57,
113, 117, 193, 202–203, 231, 238,
245, 268n34, 294n113, 295n3
Codex Laud, 51, 74, 186, 209
Codex Magliabechiano, 39, 48, 53, 63, 147, 150,
153, 206, 209–11, 215–16, 268n28, 284n26
Codex Mendoza, 47, 111–12,
251–52, 279n28, 286n13
Codex Mexicanus, 203
Codex Nuttall, *15*, 103, 105,
111–12, 183, 208–209
Codex Osuna, 128
Codex Ríos, 40
Codex Telleriano-Remensis, 111, 186, 221, 251
Codex Tlatelolco, 245, 255
Codex Tlaxcala, 92
Codex Tudela, 150, 225–26, 293n102
Codex Vaticanus B, 209–11
Codex Vienna, 221–22
Codex Xolotl, 193
Codex Yanhuitlan, 113
Códice Matritense de la Real
Academia de Historia, 208
Códice Matritense del Palacio Real, *12*,
43, 49, 107, 116–17, 153, 193, 197
Cofradías, 77, 272n2
Coixtlahuaca (Oaxaca), San Juan Bautista, 120
Colegio de Tlatelolco, 81
Coliuhqui (glyph), 110, 277n13
Coloquios y doctrina cristiana (Sahagún), 201
Color, *15, 18, 26, 28, 29, 31*; black and red as

sacred knowledge, 38–39, 255; blue and
red as sacred source of life, 40, 49, 109–11,
113–14, 128–30, 176–77, 187, 209, 228, 237,
246–47, 249, 255, 281n47, 295n5, 297n25;
in depictions of cosmic trees, 226; in mural
painting, 184–87, 255–56, 281n47; in native
maps, 127–30; in church building, 254–56;
use of, 27, 207, 216, 277n12, 287n17, 297n26
Comets. *See* Astronomy
Concentric circles, 143–44. *See
also* Chalchihuitl symbols
Conch shell motif (*ecailatcozcatl*), 41, 154–55
Concilios provinciales (1555 &
1585), 80, 89–90, 96–97
Confessions (Augustine), 224
Congregaciones programs, 82–88, 95–97, 99
Copal (*copalli*), 56, 63, 67–68. *See
also* Incense/incensing
Córdoba, Fray Pedro de, 80
Corregidor, 274n36
Cortés, Hernán, 103, 216–17, 279n33
Cosmic books (*teoamoxtli*), 38, 74, 80,
105–106, 177. *See also* Sacred knowledge
Cosmic forces/powers, 46–54
Cosmic layout/diagram, 42, 72, 118,
154. *See also* Quatrefoil; Quincunx
Cosmic planes/levels, 108, 220; celestial, 35;
subterrestrial, 35, 152; terrestrial, 35, 38, 42–
43, 47, 106, 118, 144, 169, 225, 229, 277n11
Cosmic trees. *See* Trees
Cosmovision, 6–7, 59, 265n9
Council of Trent (1545-63), 210
Coyoacan (D.F.), San Juan Bautista,
153–54, 284n28, 286n45
Cozumel (Yucatan), 216
Creation myths, 36–44, 106, 266n4
Cross of Christ: as cactus/tree, 203, 218,
224–25, 231–32; as native ritual tree, 232
Crucifixion, *22, 24,* 179–82, 184–86, 193–96,
209, 216–18, 229, 287n17, 288n28
Cuanalá (Puebla), 284n28
Cuauhtinchan (Puebla), 120, 192, 270n26;
Mapa de Cuauhtinchan No. 4, 123, 128;
parish church, 156, 293n105; San Juan
Bautista, *29, 31,* 93, 96, 171, 175, 178–79,
198, 246, 248, 255, 289n42, 297n26
Cuauhtlatoa (Tlatelolcan ruler), 150
Cuauhuitlan (Oaxaca), map, 129
Cuauhtitlan México), San Buenaventura, 215
Cuilapan (Oaxaxa), Santiago Cuilapan, 120

Culhuacan (D.F.): map, 130, 185; San
Juan Evangelista, *22,* 130, 183–87,
198, 217, 288n26, 288n28
Cuquila, Mixtepec, Chicaguastla
(Oaxaca), map, 125–26
Cuzcatlan (Oaxaca), map, 124–25
Cycles of time, 88. *See also* Agricultural
cycles; Calendars/annual cycles

Dancing. *See* Singing and dancing
Date palm, as emblem, 185–86
*Decem librorum Moralium Aristotelis
tres Conversiones* (1542), 197
Descripción del arzobispado de México
(1570), 83–84, 91, 273n9
Devotion: acceptable ritual as evidence of,
67–68; persistence of native ritual and,
55–56; transformed native worship as, 36
Diego Luis ("master of idolatry"), 60, 163
*Doctrina cristiana en lengua
mexicana* (Gante), 80
*Doctrina cristiana más cierta y
verdadera . . .* (Zumárraga), 80
*Doctrina cristiana para instrucción
. . .* (Córdoba), 80
Doctrinas (alphabetized texts for
teaching), 80–81, 89–90, 273n11.
See also Picture catechisms
Domed roofs/apse, 117, 122, 160.
See also Architecture
Double mistaken identity, 55, 269n2
Drums/drumming, 38, 49, 63, 245, 247–49
Dupaix, Guillermo, 140, 143,
157–59, 165, 284n32
Durán, Fray Diego, 42–43, 50–51,
56–61, 65–66, 69, 106, 195, 228
Duverger, Christian, 202

Eagle (*cuauhtli*), 79, 96, 148, 150, 175,
192, 208, 253–54, 295n4, 296n15
Eagle and jaguar images, 44, 96, 120, 297n25
Eagle and serpent images, 217–18
Eagle Woman (Yaocihuatl), 208
Earth monster, 38–39, 143, 227,
229. *See also* Tlaltecuhtli
Earth mother, 43, 92, 197, 200, 207–209,
219. *See also* Coatlicue
Ecailatcozcatl ("wind spiral jewel"), 144
Eclipsing event, 222
Eden, Garden of, 73

Edgerton, Samuel, 4, 198, 252

Egerton Ms. 2898, 255

El Zape (Durango), 163–64

Embedded stones: astronomical signs, 140–44, 147, 150, 152; author's categorization of motifs, 147–55; author's hypothesis on, 161–69, 285n36; caveats to understanding, 158–61; Christian iconography, 140, 153–55; colonial iconography, 140; colonial purge of, 145–47, 154; cosmic signs, 147; defined, 282n3; list of motifs by site, 148–49; location and positioning, 155–58; meaning and function, 161–69; native iconography, 140–42, 150–53, 283n17; in prehispanic tradition, 143–46, 163–64

Enciso, Jorge, 189

Encomienda (labor system), 81, 88, 91–92, 274n36

Epazoyucan (Hidalgo), San Andrés, 85, 103–104, 118–19, 180–83, 214–15, 248, 278n19, 288n28, 288n38

Epidemics, 83, 86–88

Escalante Gonzalbo, Pablo, 192

Evangelization program: congregaciones program and, 77, 95–97, 99; destruction of native edifices, 103; first congregaciones, 82–85; second congregaciones, 87–88; selectivity and resistance toward, 88–94

Feasts/festivals. *See* Christian festivals; Native festivals

Feathers, 44, 55, 67, 225–26

Fifth Sun, creation myth, 42, 154–55, 197, 221. *See also* Age of Agriculture

52-year cycle. *See* Calendar/annual cycles

Fire, 64

Fire-drilling, 152–53

Florentine Codex. *See* Codex, Florentine

Flos sanctorum, 204

Flowers and vegetation: acuilloxochitl, 39; in atrial cross iconography, 224–33; creation myths, 39–41; as decoration, 252; as embedded stone motif, 140–44, *146*, 147–52, 154–55, 158, 165; flower and song, 40, 235; flower paths, 41; flower-ropes, 40, 50, 151, 283n23; flowery places/realms, 42, 203, 205–206; flowery water, 40–41; flowery words, 40–41, 58, 247, 249; izquixochitl, 39, 236, 295n3; painting flowers, 237–49; as ritual artifacts/framing

devices, 39–40, 44–46, 49–50, 53–54, 57–58, 60–65, 67–68, 70–74, 144, 268n34; as signs/symbols of the Sacred, 31, 45, 51, 58, 65, 75, 144, 204–205, 235–36; singing flowers, 32, 235–38; teoquauhxochitl, 40; tlalcacaloxochitl, 40; tzompanquauitl, 40; whirling flowers, 52–54, 225, 236, 244–46; xiloxochitl, 296n15; yolloxochitl, 40, 53, 236, 296n15. *See also* Psychoactive plants

Flower-songs, 53, 235–38, 246, 249, 251–52

Flyers. *See* Birds; Butterflies; Sacred flyers

Food. *See* Ritualized foodstuffs

Four directions, 35, 144, 226–27

Framing rituals, 8; art as, 238–56; Christian, 67–85; prehispanic, 46–54, 235; song-poems as, 235–38

Francis (Saint), 205

Frieze. *See* Architecture; Grotesque frieze

Gante, Fray Pedro de, 80, 103, 255

Gerson, Juan, 180

Glyphs: *altepetl*/hill signs, 109; use in picture catechisms, 77–80. *See also* Animals; Toponyms/toponymy; Writing systems

Gold (color), *27*, *29*, 237, 246

Gold (metal), 92, 173, 236

The Golden Legend (de Voragine), 186–87, 224, 288n35

Golgotha, 184–85, 210, 229

Gombrich, E. H., 122

Greek crosses, 125

Gregorian calendar, 222–23

Grijalva, Fray Juan de, 75, 85, 104, 216

Grotesque frieze, 5, 8, *33*, 177–80, 238, 252–54, 276n60, 287n20

Gruzinski, Serge, 185, 286n11

Guerrero, 70

Hallucinogenic plants. *See* Psychoactive plants

Heaven, concept of, 58, 75, 118, 121, 187, 206, 235, 272n47

Hernández, Francisco, 41, 53, 57

Hill glyphs, 109, 120–21, 130, 278n15, 279n28, 281n59. *See also* Altepetl system; Toponyms/toponymy

Historia . . . (Motolinía), 55

Historia de los mexicanos por sus pinturas, 200

Historia general... (Sahagún), 93

Historia tolteca-chichimeca, 15, 192

Histoyre du Méchique, 38, 201, 266n10

Holy Family, 56, 120, 201
Holy Family (van Cleve), 290n67
Holy Spirit, 203, 228, 293n105
Holy Trinity, 228, 293n105
Horror vacui, 45, 219, 292n88
Hospital de Jesús (D.F.), 254
House of the Dean (Puebla), 185, 207, 209, 244
Huamango (México), 143, 164
Huapalteopan (México), map, 118
Huaquechula (Puebla), 292n94; San
    Martín, 94–95, 221, 247, 288n25
Huauchinango (Puebla), 63
Huaxtec, 139
Huaxtepec (Morelos), 297n26; map,
    122, 125, 128, 130, 297n26
Huehuecoyotl (dance god), 153
Huehuetl (drum), 38. *See also*
    Drums/drumming
Huehuetlahtolli, 89
Huejotzingo (Puebla), 61, 93; San Miguel,
    102, 117–18, 179–80, 219–20, 225, 232,
    247, 250, 286n1, 288n25, 294n114, 297n26
Huejutla (Hidalgo), map, 116, 118
Hueypuxtla (México), 84
Hueyteocalli ("great temple"), 108
Huitzilihuitl (Aztec ruler), 251
Huitzilopochtli (Mexica deity), 47,
    50–51, 53, 108, 111, 162, 289n43
Huixtoccihuatl (salt deity), 53, 186
Humans, creation myths, 38–39
Human sacrifice. *See* Sacrifice
Humboldt, Alexander von, 188
Hummingbirds. *See* Birds; Sacred flyers
Hunter-gatherers, 37
Hunting, 45, 58, 72, 108, 163, 267n21

Icelteotl ("one-god"), 202
Idolatry/idolatrous activities, 7, 36, 57–58,
    60–61, 64, 84–85, 88, 92–94, 96–97,
    130, 172, 201. *See also* Native ritual
Idolatry trials, 57, 59, 61, 81, 90, 144–45, 147
Idols, 55–56, 62–63, 96, 98, 113, 141, 145–47
Ihuatzio (México), 143
Ilhuitl (day sign), 251–52
Incantations, 60, 63, 92
Incense/incensing, 45–46, 55, 61–63,
    67–68. *See also* Copal/copalli
Indio-Christian/Christianity, 6, 8, 140,
    168–69, 172, 175, 180, 187, 205–10,

214, 217–19, 224, 229–33, 237–38,
    248–49, 255–56, 286n2, 293n108
Indoctrination programs, 273n20, 279n23;
    as acculturation, 273n23; adaptation
    to, 173, 175; change of monastic order,
    65; deficiencies in, 6–7, 175; didactic
    murals, 80; native iconography in,
    82, 88, 175; native participation in,
    81–82, 88, 97; native terminology in, 89;
    resistance to, 77, 81–85, 88–93; schools
    for, 82, 89; teaching methodology,
    77–81, 89–92, 97. *See also* Auto/autos;
    Doctrinas; Lienzos; Picture catechisms
Insects, 46, 49, 150, 177–78. *See also* Butterflies
Insignia, monastic. *See* Monastic
    orders, insignia
Ipalnemoani (life giver deity), 49, 186,
    201–202, 236–37, 293n109
Itzcuincuitlapilco (Hidalgo), 189, 215, 284n28
Itztapalapa (D.F.), map, 125, 128
Itztlacoliuhqui (Venus deity), 200, 217
Ixiptla (deity impersonator), 44
Ixmiquilpan (Hidalgo), San Miguel Arcángel,
    8, *32*, 96, 171, 175, 244–50, 254, 291n72,
    297n26
Ixtepexi (Oaxaca), 83
Ixtiyuca (Puebla), Santa María, 122,
    132–33, 135, 281n50, 281nn54–55
Ixtlilton (pulque deity), 294n113
Ixtlilxochitl (snake-woman of Texcoco), 91
Izquitecatl (pulque deity), 295n3

Jaguars (*ocelotl*), 44, 94–95, 116, 120, 175,
    186–87, 192; skin/pelt, 113, 125–26;
    Spanish reference to "tigers," 253, 296n21;
    thunder-jaguar, 111. *See also* Animals
Jaguar serpent (*ocelocoatl*), 207, 209
Jaguar warriors, 44, 96
Jansen, Maarten, 221
Jerome (Saint), 189, 191
Jilotzingo (México), San Marcos, 245–46
Jocotitlan-Atlacomulco (México),
    map, 126–27, 280n42
John the Good of Mantua (Saint), 189, 192
Juan Diego, 75
Julian calendar, 222–23

Klor de Alva, Jorge, 66, 275n39, 276n65
Kubler, George, 86, 91, 141, 160, 175, 242

Labor: as ritualized occupation, 90–93; Spanish exploitation of, 274n36

Labor systems: coatequitl, 86, 91, 275n43; encomienda, 81, 88, 90–92, 274n36; repartimiento, 91, 274n36

Lady 12 Vulture (Mixtec ruler), 150

Landscape painting, 180–98

Landscapes: artificial, 72–74, 106, 117, 184, 272n51; European painting, 137, 180, 287n22; in mapping, 127–30, 132–37; in myth, 43; native painting, 180–98, 235; sacred, 38, 105–106, 115, 169, 182–83, 186, 188–90, 192, 194, 255–56

Lara, Jaime, 4, 230

Las Casas, Bartolomé de, 56, 70–72, 78, 114

La Serna, Jacinto de, 62, 64, 94–98, 145, 157, 165

Las Navas, Fray Francisco de, 93

Lasso de la Vega, Luis, 75

Latin crosses, 153–55, 231, 282n3

Lawrence (Saint), 195

Leibsohn, Dana, 123

Leyenda de los soles, 36

Libro de Proprietatibus Rerum en Romance (Anglicus), 122

Lienzos (painted cloths), 77–78

Life-Giver. *See* Ipalnemoani

Lightning, 47, 187, 241

Lions, 184, 186, 189, 239, 253, 289n48, 296n21

Lockhart, James, 55, 87, 276n63

Longinus (Saint), 219

López Austín, Alfredo, 42, 51

Lord 1 Lizard (Mixtec ruler), 150

Lord 4 Alligator (Mixtec ruler), 151

"Los labradores" (Ponce de León), 59–60

Lunar cycles. *See* Moon

Macuilxochitl ("five" deity). *See* Xochipilli-Macuilxochitl

Macupilco (Oaxaca), map, 125

Maguey cactus: association with Christ, 212–14; association with Virgin Mary, 209–12; in creation myths, 37, 40–41, 51, 231; *cuchara del maguey*, 271n40; cultivation, 266n9; deity/calendrical name, 63; fermentation and drunkenness, 71, 90, 275n41; as food/fuel, 37, 266n8; in iconography, 78, 126, 148, 227–29, 241, 290n66, 291n74, 294n113–114; on maps, 133; in murals, 194, 196–97, 270n24; quiote (*quiotl*), 211–14,

228, 231; in self-sacrifice, 48; suction tube (*piaztecomatl*), 207, 210–13. *See also* Pulque

Maize, *25*, 37, 45, 237, 240–41; association with Christ, 70, 72, 180, 214–16, 228–29, 232–33; as cosmic tree, 42, 227–29; in creation myths, 39–44, 123; cultivation cycle, 59–60, 71–72; as deity, 63, 200–201, 230–33; in native religion, 7, 59; ritual in cultivation of, 59–60, 69–70; as the Sun, 108

Malinalco (México): hilltop temple, 114; Purificación y San Simón, 4, 175–77, 241, 244, 248–49, 252, 255

Malinalli (day-sign), 144

Malinalli (twisted-grass glyph), 38, 106, 217

Mana, 35

Mappings: alignments and sightlines, 130–37; as architectural representation, 121–30; European, 121; native, 5, 8–9, 102, 180, 182, 185, 279n23, 279nn33–34; as pictographic texts, 279n34. *See also* Appendix B; *Relaciones geográficas*

Mary Magdalene, 189–90, 192

Matlalcingo, Valley (México), 127

Mayahuel (pulque goddess), 49, 63, 208–12, 214, 241, 290n69, 291n75; association with maize, 231; calendrical name, 37, 197; as maguey, 51; in native religion, 59

Mayan peoples, 139, 164, 183

Mazahua peoples, 80

McAndrew, John, 4, 117, 172, 248–49

Memoriales (Motolinía), 55

Mendieta, Fray Jerónimo de, 37–38, 48, 78, 89, 93–94, 103, 117, 129, 217, 286n1

Merlons (architectural feature), 106–107, 113, 117, 119, 122–23, 165, 247

Metepec (México), San Juan Bautista, 126–27, 280n42

Mexica, 44–45, 155, 162, 244. *See also* Aztec/Azteca-Mexica peoples

Mexico, Valley of, 37, 168, 186

Mexico-Tenochtitlan (Mexico City), 84, 90, 97, 103–104, 272n2; Cathedral, 255; Spanish building program, 90–91, 104

Mezquital Valley (Hidalgo), 136

Meztitlan (Hidalgo), 214, 216, 291n81; La Comunidad, 104; Los Santos Reyes, *27, 30, 31, 33,* 104, 120, *142,* 153, 154, 165–66, 217–18, 226, 229, 231, 239–40, 248, 255, 288n25, 297n26; prehispanic imagery, 214–16, 226

Michael the Archangel, 254, 290n54, 290n65

Michimaloyan (Hidalgo), Guadalupe, 120

Mictlan (the underworld), 39, 41, 235. *See also* Afterlife/afterworlds; Agricultural cycles

Mictlantecuhtli (Lord of the Underworld), 39

Mignolo, Walter, 7

Migration, 39, 220

Milpa Alta (D.F.), 168

Mining, 92, 275n49

Mixcoac (D.F.), Santa María Nonalco, *146*

Mixcoatl, Andrés, 63

Mixquiahuala (Hidalgo), 80, 280n45

Mixquic (D.F.), 158, 273n20; San Andrés, 150–51, 157–59, *166*, 168, 284n30

Mixteca Alta, 45, 102–103, 238

Mixtec/Mixteca, 8, 59, 74, 80, 105, 111, 120, 139, 150–51, 164, 183, 205, 221–22, 238, 278n15, 279n34

Mola (mountain deity), 104

Molango (Hidalgo), 104–105, 139, 165–66; El Calvario, 104, 220; Nuestra Señora de Loreto, 148, 156–57, 165, 205, 241

Molina, Fray Alonso de, 115

Monasteries: architecture and layout, 101–102; congregaciones as part of, 83–85; period of building activity, 85–88

Monastic orders, insignia, 68, 153, 158, 165, 205, 211, 213–14, 216, 231, 240, 270n26

Monica (Saint), 189–90, 192

Monkeys, 152, 244, 253

Monte Albán (Oaxaca), 255

Montúfar, Alonso de, 84

Moon, 45, 216, 218; in creation myth, 36–37; crescent as sign, 209, 213, 221, 228, 241, 287n19; lunar cycles, 37, 208–209; rabbit as, 37, 197, 242

Moreno Villa, José, 172, 286n3

Motolinía (Fray Toribio de Benavente), 45, 55, 68–73, 83, 90, 94, 105, 107, 130, 139, 162, 196, 272n2, 275n49

Mountain of sustenance (*tonacatepetl*): in creation myths, 39, 42, 123; Pyramid of the Sun, 107–109; Tepantitla mural, 13

Mountains (Cerros): cult of, 62, 68, 105, 107, 168, 184; ritual images of, 43; mountain tops, 45, 62–63; as sacred, 60, 128, 168–69, 182, 184; Ajusco (México), 167; Atlacomulco (México), 127; Azteca (México), 281n49; Cempoaltepec (Morelos), 134; Chichinauhtzin (México), 168; Chiconauhtla (México), 131, 168, 181;

Citlaltepec/El Pinal (Puebla), 132–33; Colorado (Hidalgo), 136–37; Colorado (México), 131; Cuailama (D.F.), 168, 243, 283n18, 296n13; Cuatlapanga (Tlaxcala), 129; Cuetzaltepec (Veracruz), 136–37; El Rosal (Hidalgo), 131, 134–35, 194; El Tejón (Hidalgo), 133–34; Epazoyu (Hidalgo), 181–82; Gordo (México), 107, 193–94, 281n49; Huitel/Teçontepec Hidalgo), 127–28, 133–34, 280n46; Huixachtecatl (D.F.), 130, 168, 183–85, 286n45, 288n28; Iztaccihuatl (México), 60, 73, 167–68; Las Derrumbadas (Puebla), 132–33, 281n55; Los Frailes (Hidalgo), 187–89, 191, 216; Los Pitos (Hidalgo), 134–35; Magdalena (Tlaxcala), 167; Maravillas (México), 281n49; Matlalcueye (Tlaxcala/Puebla), 42, 60, 64, 69, 73, 129, 132–33, 135, 167, 231, 289n42; Metepec (Hidalgo), 131, 134; Metepec (México), 127; Montenegro (Oaxaca), 103, 150, 183; Nevado de Toluca (México), 61–62, 127; Popocatepetl (México/Puebla), 73, 167–68; Tenango (México), 127, 280n43; Tepayo (México), 281n49; Tepeyahualco (México), 131, 168; Tepoxtle (México), 281n49; Tepozteco (Morelos), 120; Tetepetl (México), 127, 280n43; Tetzcotzingo (México), 186; Tlaloc (México), 61–62, 73, 106–107, 117, 186, 281n49; Xico (D.F.), 168; Xicuco (Hidalgo), 136–37; Xihuingo (Hidalgo), 193, 196–97; Xoconochco/Patlachique (México), 107; Xocotitlan (México), 127; Zacatecas (Puebla), 135. *See also* Caves; Patron mountains; Rain mountains; Sierra (mountain range); Water-Mountains

Movement (day sign), 43, 221

M-shaped swirl motif, embedded stones, 143, 148

Mudéjar (architectural style), 5, 102, 172, 246, 286n3

Mullen, Robert, 160, 238

Muñoz, Camargo, Diego, 51, 69, 206, 268n28

Mural paintings: censorship and destruction, 96–97; landscape representations, 180–98; native artisans and, 171–80; use of color, 254–56. *See also* Color

Mushrooms (*teonanacatl*). *See* Psychoactive plants

Myths. *See* Creation myths

Nahua: altepetl system, 87; creation
　myths, 36–44, 168, 200; ideals of self,
　175, 275n39; peoples, 41, 183. *See
　also* Aztec/Azteca-Mexica peoples
Nahua devotional literature/poetry, 9, 65,
　102, 203, 207, 229. *See also Cantares
　mexicanos*; *Romances de los señores de la
　Nueva España*; *Santoral en mexicano*
Nahuatl language: alphabetization of, 8–9,
　80; as "civilizing," 39; flower-songs and
　metaphor in, 235–37; glossary of terms,
　299–300; missionary appropriation,
　89. *See also* Writing systems
Nahui ollin. *See* Movement
Nanahuatzin (deity who became
　the Sun), 36–37, 39
Native art: adaptation of Euro-Christian art to,
　4–5, 175–76, 179; colonial mural painting,
　93, 96, 171–72, 297n26; colonial sculpture,
　93, 96, 172–73; colonial sources, 176, 180;
　decorative vs. meaningful, 177; evolution
　of, 276n63, 286n13; as framing rituals,
　238–56; Indio-Christianity expressed in,
　198–233; mediums/"sign carriers," 7–8,
　174; prehispanic inserts in, 3–4, 78–79,
　172, 175–79; purge of, 82, 94, 96–97; as
　text, 7–8, 78–80, 173–77, 214, 235–38,
　253–54, 256, 286n10. *See also* Calendars/
　annual cycles; Censorship; Embedded
　stones; Landscape painting; Mappings;
　Mural paintings; Picture catechisms; Ritual
　and the image; "Symbols of the devil"
Native artists (*tlacuilo/tlacuiloque*):
　colonial training, 171, 174; expertise
　of, 3, 171, 173; as scribes, 7–8, 78–80,
　173–76, 183, 238; use of, 171, 173
Native caciques, 77, 81, 189, 192
Native calendars. *See* Calendars/annual cycles
Native cults: the dead/ancestors, 40–41, 68;
　Sun, 44; warrior, 44; water-earth-fertility,
　62, 107, 168, 184. *See also* Pulque
Native festivals: Atamalqualiztli, 12, 49,
　228; Atemoztli, 43, 69, 184; Atlcahualo,
　107; Etzalqualiztli, 46, 50, 53, 215;
　Hueytecuilhuitl, 53; Hueytozoztli,
　46, 61, 106, 184, 195, 228; Izcalli, 47;
　Ochpaniztli, 200; Panquetzaliztli, 59;
　of Quetzalcoatl, 50; Tecuilhuitl, 186;
　Tecuilhuitontli, 59, 72, 186; Teotleco, 46,
　48, 62, 270n21; Tepeilhuitl, 43, 47, 62,

107, 117, 162, 270n21; Tlacaxipehualiztli,
　46, 108, 162; Tlaxochimaco, 46, 50; of
　Toci, 199–200; Toxcatl, 47, 50, 57–59,
　63, 202–203; Tozozontli, 59; Xochilhuitl,
　46, 50; Xochipaina, 53; Xocotlhuetzi,
　228. *See also* Calendars/annual cycles
Native religious system, 7, 35–36, 43, 45,
　256, 265n10, 285n35; adaptation of
　Christianity, 61, 67, 254–56; attempted
　eradication of, 56; colonial ignorance of,
　6, 56, 60; deities and deity complexes, 7,
　199–200. *See also* Religious ideology
Native ritual, 267n21, 270n15, 271n33;
　adaption to Christianity, 55–58; church
　building and, 87, 90–92; deemed acceptable,
　7, 67–75; deemed unacceptable, 7,
　60–67; prehispanic, 40, 44–46; survival
　within Christianity, 59–61, 86. *See
　also* Calendars/annual cycles; Framing
　rituals; Idolatry; The Sacred
Native sacred. *See* The Sacred, concept of
Native symbols, as embedded
　stone motif, 148–49
Native trees of life, 216–33
Nativitas (Hidalgo), map, 128
Nativitas Zacapa (D.F.), 221–23
Nepantla ("in the middle"), 66, 271n30
New fire ceremony, 168, 183–84.
　See also Fire-drilling
Nezahualcoyotl (Acolhua ruler), 144
Nican mopohua (Lasso de la Vega), 75
Nicholas of Tolentine (Saint), *24,*
　189–90, 192, 216, 288n38
Nicodemus (Saint), 195
Nochistlan (Oaxaca), 125
Nonoalco (Hidalgo), 220
Nopal cactus (prickly pear), 196, 218, 226–28
Nopaluca (Puebla), 132–33; Santa María
　Ixtiyuca, 122, 135, 281nn54–55
Ñuhu (Mixtec earth spirit), 151
Nutini, Hugo, 129

Ocelocoatl (jaguar-serpent), 207, 207–209
Ocpactli (hallucinogenic root), 90, 275n41
Octli/teoctli. *See* Pulque
Ocuilan (México), 63, 70
Ocuituco (Morelos), 63, 81,
　292n86; Santiago, 217–18
Ocuituco, Cristóbal de, 63, 90
Offerings: food as, 68, 239–41; in

native ritual, 55–57; shared by church and native gods, 64–66

Officium B. V. Mariae (1494), 197

Olinalá (Guerrero), 65

Olivier, Guilhem, 201

Olmos, Fray Andrés de, 201

Ometochtli (pulque deity), 143, 197, 214

Ometochtli, Carlos, 61, 80–82, 89–90, 144–47, 155, 283n15

Open chapels, 5, 101–102, 118–19, 190–91, 277n2, 278n23, 279n23, 281n47

Opochtli (a *tlaloc*), 50

Osseguera, Fray Juan de, 82

Otomi peoples, 72, 80, 139, 143, 164, 254, 273n20, 279n23

Otumba (México), La Concepción, 290n66

Oyoalli: in art, 206–207; breast ornament, 206, 284n26; embedded stone motif, 152–53; as Pleiades star cluster, 153

Oztoticpac (México), 144–45, 244–45

Pachtli (tree moss), 72, 270n21

Pachuca (Hidalgo), 147

Painted murals. *See* Mural paintings

Painted song. *See* Flowers and vegetation

Palenque (Chiapas), 123, 130

Panotla (Tlaxcala), 103

Pantli-nochtli writing system, 78

Papaztac (pulque deity), 36–37

Parrots. *See* Birds

Passion of Christ, 207, 214–15, 219–20, 223, 229–30, 288n37. *See also* Crucifixion

Patron mountains, 109, 121, 124, 126–27, 134–35, 182–83, 191, 238, 255, 281n59, 289n42

Paul (Saint), 252

Peacock. *See* Birds

Pear tree, as emblem, 186

Pecked crosses, 130–31, 144, 193

Peláez, Juan, 91

Peter (Saint), 229, 252

Peterson, Jeanette F., 4, 96, 175, 241–42, 249–51

Petroglyphs, 131, 160, 163–64, 174, 193, 216, 218, 226, 243

Peyote, 52–53

Philip II (king of Spain), 41, 83, 269n5

Picietl (powdered tobacco), 52, 72, 74. *See also* Tobacco

Pictographic texts. *See* Writing systems

Picture catechisms, 80, 141, 154, 176,

255, 272n5. *See also* Doctrinas

Pilgrimages, 60–61, 63, 106, 270n18, 289n43

Piltzintecuhtli (maize deity), 200–201, 217, 221

"Pinturas," 55–56, 78, 94, 174

Places of origin/destiny. *See* Mictlan; Tamoanchan; Tlalocan; Tonatiuh-Ilhuicac

Ponce, Fray Alonso, 91

Ponce de León, Pedro, 60, 63–64, 206

Popol vuh, 183

Posas (chapels), 5, 101–102, 116–19. *See also* Architecture

Prayer: doctrinal teaching, 79–81; Indian lack of knowledge, 84; "pantli-nochtli" system, 77–79

Processions, 8, 44, 55–56, 68, 70–71, 75, 89, 98, 117–18, 271n33, 278n19, 278n21

Provincial councils. *See* Concilios provinciales

Psalmodia Christiana (Sahagún), 57–58, 203, 205, 249–51, 269n10, 272n47

Psychoactive plants, 51–55, 60–61, 67, 204–205, 290n63; datura, 52, 244; huacalxochitl, 48, 52–53, 236, 244–45, 296n13, 296n15; mushrooms, 52–53, 63–64, 72, 74, 147, 159, 242–43, 276n64; ocpactli, 90, 275n41; ololiuhqui, 52, 244; peyote, 52–53; poyomatli, 52, 236, 244, 247, 296n15; sagebrush, 53; sinicuiche, 53, 205, 296n15; solandra, 243–44, 290n57; tlapatl, 52; tliiltzin, 52, 244; toloatzin, 53; "whirling" flowers, 52–54, 225, 236, 244–46. *See also* Tobacco

Puebla de los Angeles (Puebla), 91

Pulque (*octli/teoctli*), 51, 61, 63, 71, 168, 198, 270n23, 291n74; association with Christ, 214; cult, 150, 152, 178, 184, 187, 197, 207–209, 211–14, 228, 231, 241; deities, 206, 211, 219, 228, 290n64; given to mortals by the gods, 37–38; in ritual and ceremonies, 46–49, 90. *See also* Maguey cactus; Ritual drinking/drunkenness

Pumas, 186, 296n21. *See also* Jaguars

Putti. *See* Angels

Pyramid of the Sun/Moon. *See* Teotihuacan

Quartered motifs, 144, 163

Quatrefoil, 42, 106–107, 144, 220, 224, 229, 282n9. *See also* Cosmic layout/diagram; Quincunx

Quecholtin/quecholli. *See* Birds; Sacred flyers

Quegolani (Oaxaca), 63

Quetzalcoatl (creator deity), 38–40, 50, 60, 64, 154–55, 226, 266n7, 291n75

Quetzalcoatl-Ehecatl (wind deity), 37, 107, 144, 291n75

Quilaztli-Tlaltecuhtli (earth deity), 38–39, 43, 95, 114, 197, 200, 208. *See also* Cihuacoatl; Tlaltecuhtli

Quincunx, 42, 106–107, 127, 129, 136, 144, 196, 211, 213, 267n16, 277n11. *See also* Cosmic layout/diagram; Quatrefoil

Quiote. *See* Maguey cactus

Quiroga, Vasco de (Bishop), 192

Rabbit: as calendar name, 37, 197; as calendar sign, 143, 197, 222; as deity, 45, 48, 153, 295n3; in European art, 196–97, 298n45; in iconography, 187, 194–98, 217–18, 239, 241–42; as moon, 37, 197, 242; in myth, 37; as pulque symbol, 37

Rain: in creation myths, 108–10; deities, 228–29; petitioning, 61–62, 70; unacceptable rituals, 61–63, 69. *See also* Tlaloc; Tlaloque

Rain mountains, 47, 61–62, 69, 107–108, 127–30. *See also* Water-mountains

Relaciones geográficas, 151, 160, 181, 184, 196, 267n21

Relaciones geográficas maps, 113, 134

Religious art. *See* Native art

Religious conversion. *See* Christianity

Religious ideology. *See* Idolatry/idolatrous activities; Native religious system

Religious indoctrination. *See* Indoctrination program

Religious plays. *See* Auto/autos

Reptiles: lizards (*cuetzpalin*), 150, *151*, 159, 217–18; serpents, 45–46, 49, 72, 203, 210–11, 217–18

Resurrection, 72, 185, 214, 217, 223

Reyes-Valerio, Constantino, v, xix, 4, 6, 9, 140–41, 149–50, 218, 286n2

Rhetorica Christiana (Valadés), 142

Ritual and the image, 8, 45, 73–74, 88–90, 256. *See also* Native ritual

Ritual drinking/drunkenness, 45, 55, 60, 66–67, 74, 90–91, 241, 275n41, 291n75. *See also* Alcoholism; Pulque

Ritualized foodstuffs, 44, 46–47, 55, 60–61, 63, 67–68, 239–41, 268n25

Ritual processionals. *See* Processions

Roa, Fray Antonio de, 104, 220

Rock formations, 105, 182, 187–88, 193

Roldán, Fray Antonio, 286n1

Romances de los señores de la Nueva España, 9, 57, 235

Roosters. *See* Birds

Ruiz de Alarcón, Hernando, 63, 130, 197

The Sacred, concept of, 35; Christian, 64–65, 68, 75, 205; framing the sacred, 46–54, 67–85, 235–56; Indian, 8, 43–44, 46, 48–49, 53–54, 65, 68, 75, 88, 130, 172, 203, 235–36, 245–46; Indio-Christian, 205, 235–36, 238, 248, 255–56. *See also* Color

Sacred flyers, 47, 49, 73, 236–37, 246, 293n109, 295n4. *See also* Birds; Butterflies

Sacred forces, 88, 105. *See also* Teotl/teteo

Sacred knowledge, 38, 177, 182–83, 185, 188, 194. *See also* Color; Cosmic books

Sacred landscapes/geography. *See* Landscapes; Mountains

Sacred mountains, 128, 184–85, 195, 231. *See also* Patron mountains; Rain mountains; Water-mountains

Sacred places/sites, 44–45, 103–107

Sacrifice: barrel cactus, 220–21; in creation myth, 36–38; human, 44, 55, 61–62, 67–69, 90, 267n18, 268n23, 270n20, 271n31; nopal cactus, 218, 220–21; other/non-human, 49, 92; self (body piercing), 45, 48, 55, 61, 63, 69, 268n28

Sahagún, Fray Bernardino de, 36, 41, 46–58, 61–63, 67–68, 93, 103, 108–109, 114–15, 118, 130, 162, 193, 201, 205, 229, 289n43

San Antonio (Hidalgo), map, 128

San Augustín, Pedro de, 185

San Jacinto, San Angel (D.F.), 147, 292n98

San Jerónimo, Actopan (Hidalgo), 191, 289n41

San Jerónimo Satetlan (México), 123

San Juan Tlilcuauhtla (Hidalgo), 192

San Lucas Xochimanco (D.F.), 147

San Luis de las Peras (México), map, 123, 128

San Mateo Xoloc (México), 252

San Pedro del Rosal (México), map, 123, 128

Santa Ana Chiauhtempan (Tlaxcala), 199–200

Santa Magdalena, Actopan (Hidalgo), 191, 289n41

Santa María Ixtiyuca (Puebla), 281n50. *See also* Nopaluca, Santa María Ixtiyuca

Santa María Mendoza, García de (archbishop), 97

Santa María Xadani (Oaxaca).
    See Suchitepec (Oaxaca)
Santa Mónica, Actopan (Hidalgo), 191–92, 246
Santiago Anaya/Tlachichilco
    (Hidalgo), 220, 245–46
Santoral en mexicano, 208, 214, 232
Saturn, 223
Sculpture. *See* Native art
Sebastian (Saint), 218
Sebastián, Santiago, 189
Self-sacrifice. *See* Sacrifice
Sermons, 81–82, 88–89
Serpents/snakes. *See* Reptiles
Seville cathedral, 240
Shamans/wise ones, 52, 60, 70, 98, 182–83
Shells/conch shells, 44–45, 141, 154–55, 252
Shields, 47, 150, 152, 208, 253–54
Sickness. *See* Epidemics
Sierra (mountain range): Alta de
    Hidalgo, 104, 139, 164, 205, 220; de La
    Magdalena (Hidalgo), 192; de Pachuca
    (Hidalgo), 187, 190–92; de Toluca
    (México), 62. *See also* Mountains
Sightlines and alignments. *See*
    Architecture; Churches; Temples
"Sign carriers," 7–8, 174
Singing and dancing, 38, 44–45, 51,
    60–61, 65, 252–53, 269n5; in Christian
    ritual, 67–68, 71; flower-songs, 53,
    235–38, 246, 249, 251–52; framing rituals,
    48–49, 235; in native ritual, 56–57
Sistine Chapel, 121
Skulls as art and symbol, 44–45, 144,
    150–52, 210, 229, 292n90
Slipknot, 178–79
Spiral motif, embedded stones, 141,
    143–44, 148–49, 151–52, 165
Spirit Land, 43–44, 255
Stars, as embedded stone motif, 143,
    147–48, *151*, 153, *154*, 163
Suchiaca (México). *See* Atlatlauhca-Suchiaca
Suchimilcatzingo (Morelos), 90
Suchitepec (Oaxaca), maps, 116,
    123, 125–26, 128, 280n37
Sujeto (subordinate village), 93, 134
Sun: association with Christ, 223–24; as
    celestial body, 45, 145, 162, 221; creation
    myth, 36–37, 39; eclipse, 211, 223;
    as maize, 108; mantle of, 147; realm
    of, 41–42, 221; yearly cycle, 161–69,

196. *See also* Tonatiuh-Ilhuicac
Supernatural forces, 35, 61
Sustenance (food). *See* Mountain of sustenance
Symbolism, of myth and reality, 36–44
"Symbols of the devil," 88, 93, 146, 273n22
Syncretism, early manifestations: native and
    Christian artifacts, 60–61, 99, 276n64;
    native and Christian iconography,
    4, 141, 175–76; native and Christian
    referents, 64–65, 198–212; native and
    Christian ritual, 60–61, 67, 98, 276n64

Tacuba (D.F.), 61
Tacubaya (D.F.), Santa María Guadalupe, 249
Tamoanchan, 38–39, 42–43, 51,
    187, 229–30, 232, 235
Tapia, Andrés de, 216
Tarascan peoples, 143, 164
Tau crosses, 216–18, 226, 229, 231, 291n81
Taximaroa (Michoacán), 202, 223
Taylor, William B., 91
Tebaida augustiniana, 22, 23, 184–88, 217–18
Tecali (Puebla), Santiago, 122,
    177–78, 219, 224, 244, 279n26
Tecamachalco (Puebla), Asunción, *21*,
    104, 119, 180, 283n23, 297n26
Techalotl (pulque deity), 150
Tecuciztecatl (deity who became
    the Moon), 36–37
Tejupa (Oaxaca), map, 128, 132
Telpochtli (deity), 50
Temazcaltepec (México), 83
Temples, 15; architectural characteristics,
    111–15; as caves, 114–15, 120, 122; churches
    built on the site of, 64, 103–107; native
    representations of, 111–13; reuse in church
    construction, 94–99, 139–42; sightlines
    and alignments, 130–31, 161–69; Spanish
    destruction of, 56, 103. *See also* Architecture
Tenayuca (D.F.), San Bartolo, 283n20
Tenochtitlan: eagle and serpent as symbol
    of, 218; idols of, 16, 113; Plano en Papel de
    Maguey, 128; rebuilding of, 91; ritual at,
    44–54, 59–60, 63, 72, 183, 267n21, 270n15;
    Templo Mayor, 105, 108, 114–15, 162–64.
    See also Aztec/Azteca-Mexica peoples
Teoamoxtli. *See* Cosmic books
Teocalli (sacred force-house), 107–16,
    198, 278n17. *See also* Temples
Teotenango (México), 127, 132

Teotihuacan/Teotihuacan Valley: Atetelco, 291n74; in creation myths, 36; Pyramid of the Moon, 107, 291n74; Pyramid of the Sun, 105–10, 131–32, 164–65; sightlines, 130–31, 193, 281n49; Street of the Dead, 107, 131; Techinantitla, 40; Temple of Quetzalpapalotl, 110–11; Tepantitla, *13*, 40, 109, 111, 278n22; Tetitla, 126; Tlacuilapaxco, 40–41

Teotitlan del Camino (Oaxaca), 45, 285n35

Teotl/teteo: Christian figures and, 115, 174–75, 198–216, 237; concept of, 35–36, 224, 229–30, 232, 235, 266n1; in myth, 38, 40

Teozacualco (Oaxaca), map, 112–13

Tepeaca (Puebla), San Francisco, 119, 128

Tepeapulco (Hidalgo), 192–96, 289n43; San Francisco, 139, 155, 177–80, 183, 192–98, 208–10, 219, 253, 287n17–18, 289n48; water storage tank (caja de agua), 298n48

Tepehua (mountain deity), *16*, 113, 123, 126

Tepetomatitlan (Tlaxcala), San Matías, 154, 157, 160–61, *166*, 167, 220, 293n106

Tepexi del Río (Hidalgo), map, 279n25

Tepeyacac Hill, 75, 200, 289n52

Tepeyanco (Tlaxcala), Santa María, 242–43

Tepeyollotl (mountain deity), 111, 186

Tepictoton (molded effigies), 43, 49, 63, 107, 116–17, 123

Teponaztli, 38. *See also* Drums/drumming

Teposcolula (Oaxaca), San Pedro y Pablo, 205

Tepozotlan (México), 84

Tepoztecatl (pulque deity), 120, *206*, 207

Tepoztlan (Morelos), Natividad de Nuestra Señora, 120, 203, 206–207, 243–44, 294n113

Tequitqui carving, 172–74, 205–206, 219, 247, 286n3, 286n5

Tequixquiac (México), 84; Santiago, 154, 247

Testera, Fray Jacobo de, 78, 272n4

Testerian manuscripts. *See* Picture catechisms

Tetela (Puebla), 128

Tetela del Volcán (Morelos), 297n26

Tetepango (Hidalgo), Asunción, 141, 149, 153, 157, 284n27

Tetliztaca (Hidalgo): map, 128; Santo Tomás, 205, 208

Texcaliaca (México), 64

Texcoco (México), 61, 89, 91, 115, 144–45, 151, 268n33, 281n49

Tezcatlipoca (omnipotent deity), 38, 50, 81, 111, 186, 200–203, 214, 217, 224, 227, 230

Tezcatzoncatl (pulque deity), 178

Tezontepec de Aldama (Hidalgo), *20*, 46, 118, 127–28, 133–34, 136, 280nn45–46

Tezontepec Pachuca Hidalgo), 280n45; San Pedro, 118, 297n26

Tezozómoc, Hernando de Alvarado, 42, 51

Tichy, Franz, 5, 130–31, 135, 161, 168

Tiçoc, Martín, 163

Tigers. *See* Jaguars

Tilantongo (Oaxaca), 183, 283n25; Santiago, 103–104, 139, *147*, 150–51, *152*, 154, 157, 160, 283n24

Tiltepec (Oaxaca), San Miguel, lienzo of 126

Tiltepec (Oaxaca), Santa Mariá, 149, 238, 242, 283n24

Titlacahua (aspect of Tezcatlipoca), 201–202

Tizapan (D.F.), 229

Tizatlan (Tlaxcala), San Esteban, 147, *150*, 157–58, *166*, 167, 277n7, 281n47, 284n28

Tizayuca (México), Nuestra Señora de Cosamaluapan, 151, 157

Tlachichilco (Hidalgo). *See* Santiago Anaya/Tlachichilco

Tlacopan (Tacuba, D.F.), 61

Tlacuilolli, 7–8, 237, 265n11, 273n8, 283n19

Tlahuac (D.F.), 168

Tlahuelilpa (Hildago): map, *17*, 123, 128, 130, 136; San Francisco, 104, 136–37, 207–208, 225, 297n26

Tlalancaleca (Puebla): La Pedrera (archaeological site), 151, 160; San Matías, *146*, 152, 160

Tlalchichilpa (México), 90

Tlalmanalco (México), San Luis Obispo, *146*, 147–48, *150*, *166*, 167–68, *204*, 205, 244, 285n43, 297n26

Tlalnepantla (D.F.), Corpus Christi, 219

Tlaloc (rain deity), *14*, 49, 51–53, 60–63, 68–69, 98, 107–11, 141, 144, 150–52, 155, 157, 162, 168, 184–86, 195, 199–200, 206–208, 241, 277n11, 283n25; as architecture/replica mountain, 106–108; as mountain, 62, 106; as source of sustenance, 41–43, 215–16, 228–29, 231

Tlalocan (home of rain deities), 41–44, 110, 129, 203–204, 235. *See also* Afterlife/afterworlds; Agricultural cycles

Tlaloque (water deities), 39, 42, 68–69, 73, 106–108, 116–17, 129–30, 152, 186, 200, 206–207, 209, 226–27, 229, 290n64

Tlalpan (D.F.), 224

Tlaltecayoa (pulque deity), 152, *153*, 294n114

Tlaltecuhtli ("Earth Lord"), 38, 42–43, 95, 139, 197, 200

Tlamacazcatepec (Oaxaca), map, 117, 126

Tlanalapa (Hidalgo), San Francisco, 251

Tlapanaloya (México), Asunción, 117, 215, 220, 223–24, 294n113

Tlapanec peoples, 199

Tlaquiltenango (Morelos), 243

Tlatelolco (D.F.), 57, 115, 150, 157, 284n28; Colegio de Tlatelolco, 81; prehispanic platform, 111, 143, 145, 164; Santiago, 98, 129, 151, 155, 157–58

Tlatelulco (Tlaxcala), Magdalena, 219, 292n98

Tlaxcala (Tlaxcala), 51, 55, 61, 107, 115, 117, 129, 173, 184, 196, 199, 206, 216, 241, 272n24; Asunción, 104

Tlaxcallan peoples, 49, 68–73, 200

Tlaxcoapan (Hidalgo), 119

Tlaxomulco (Xalapa), 254

Tlazolteotl (earth mother), 208–209

Tloque Nahuaque (deity, "Lord of Everywhere"), 183, 188, 201–202. *See also* Tezcatlipoca

Tobacco, 52, 64, 77, 244. *See also* Picietl; Psychoactive plants

Toci (earth mother), 53, 199–200

Tolteca house, 107

Toluca Valley, 70

Tonacatepetl. *See* Mountain of sustenance

Tonalli (life force), 223–24

Tonalpohualli (divinatory calendar), 93–94, 150, 221, 275n51, 282n12

Tonantzin/Tonan (earth mother), 200, 208, 214

Tonatiuh-Ilhuicac (realm of the Sun), 41, 110, 206, 235. *See also* Afterlife/ afterworlds; Agricultural cycles; Sun

Topiltepec (Oaxaca), San Pedro, 221, 223

Toponyms/toponymy, 87, 109, 120–21, 126–27, 134, 185, 192, 216, 251, 279n28, 280n40, 283n20

Topping (occupation of pagan space), 5, 103–105

Tornacuxtla (Hidalgo), 125

Torquemada, Fray Juan de, 48–49, 53, 62, 97–98, 199–200, 216, 270n19

Tota/tota pole (ritualized tree), 106, 184–85, 195, 228–29

Totochtin (rabbit deity). *See* Rabbit

Totolac (Tlaxcala), 103

Totolapa (Morelos), San Guillermo, *28*, 117, 148, 156, 217

Totomiahuacan (Puebla), San Francisco, 95

Totonac peoples, 59

Toulouse, 81

Tovar, Juan de, 79

Traza (urban plan), 93, 104, 132

Trees: in art, 185–87, 195; association with Christ, 195, 203, 229–33; bleeding, 42, 187, 231–32; Christian Tree of Knowledge, 217; Christian Tree of Life, 73, 217, 225, 293n105; cosmic, 38, 42–43, 106, 118, 187, 219, 225–26, 228, 231–33, 293n103; flower-trees, 229–31, 237; of life, 225–29; in ritual, 49, 51, 63, 70, 227–28; as sacred features, 105, 182; of sustenance, 216–17, 225–33; tree crosses, 216

Trumpets, 61, 247

Tula (Hidalgo), 131

Tulpetlac (México), 247

Tultitlan (México), San Lorenzo, 150, 152

Tulyhualco, Xochimilco (D.F.), 290n54

Tututetepango (Oaxaca), 45

Tzintzuntzan (Michoacán), 143, 164

Tzoalli, 43, 47, 62–63, 123, 184

Uto-Aztecan peoples, 43, 110, 255

Valadés, Diego, 117, 142

Valderrama, Jerónimo, 57

Valencia, Fray Martín de, 204–205

Vegetation. *See* Flowers and vegetation

Velasco, Luis de, 83

Venus, 201, 217, 224

Vetancurt, Agustín de, 139

Vicaría church, 207

Virgin Mary, 64, 69–70, 141, 198, 201, 231–32, 237, 287n17; in art, 94n114, 154–55, 195–96, 207–12, 214, 290n67

Virgin of Guadalupe, 75

Virgo lactans, 210

Visita church, 9, 65

Visual sightlines. *See* Sightlines and alignments

Visual thinking/thinker, 7–8, 174–75, 177

Vogt, Evon, 35

Volcanoes. *See* Mountains

Voragine, Jacobus de, 187, 224

Vue des Cordillères (Humboldt), 188

Vulture. *See* Birds

Water: in creation myths, 108–10;
    in Mesoamerican ritual, 36
Water deities, 37, 39, 42–43, 45,
    62–63, 107. *See also* Tlaloque
Water miracles, 187, 288n34
Water-mountains, 15, 73, 103, 110–11,
    120, 123, 169, 199, 290n54. *See also*
    Altepetl system; Rain mountains
Wind deity. *See* Quetzalcoatl-Ehecatl
Winged beings, 69, 175, 206, 214,
    290n64. *See also* Angels
World directions, 43
Writing systems/pictographic texts,
    5, 7–8, 74, 77, 79, 94, 113–14, 129,
    174, 273n8, 279n34. *See also* Glyphs;
    Tlacuilolli; Visual thinking/thinker

Xaltepetongo (Oaxaca), 45
Xicalcoliuhqui (tailed step glyph), 144
Xihuitl (solar year sign), 143–44,
    152, 159, 227–28, 282n9
Xilonen (maize deity), 201, 208, 294n114
Xipe-Totec (flaying deity), 144
Xiuhtecuhtli (fire and time deity), 37,
    47, 64, 107, 277n11, 297n25
Xochimilco (D.F.): Asunción Colhuacaltzingo,
    154, 159; Nuestra Señora de los Dolores
    Xaltocan, 150, 157–59, *166*, 168, 284n28;
    Old Inn, 158–59, 284n31; San Antonio
    Moyotla, 152, 157, 159; San Bernardino,
    125, 151–52, 203, 283n18, 286n1; San
    Francisco Caltongo, 159; San Juan Tlaltentli,
    142, *146*, 151–52, *153*, 154, 157, 159; San
    Marcos, 284n29; San Pedro Tlanahuac, 159
Xochipilli (maize/dance deity), 147, 200–201,
    204, 205, 223–24, 230, 243, 290n56
Xochipilli-Macuilxochitl ("five"
    deity), 46, *153*, 244

Xochiquetzal (flower/fertility deity),
    39–40, 42, 50–51, 200–201, 217, 237
Xochitlalpan ("flower-place"), 203–204
Xocotl (ritual tree), 63
Xolotl (canine deity), 37, 266n7, 266n10
Xonecuilli: as motif, 143–44, 239;
    as ritual food, 47, 241; as star
    constellation, 143–44, 241, 282n10
Xoxoteco (Hidalgo), Santa María, 297n26
Xuchimitl ("flower-arrow"), 46,
    154, 211–12, 240, 291n72

Yacametztli (nose plug). *See* Moon
Yácatas (monument), 143
Yancuitlalpan (Tlaxcala), Santa
    María Nativitas, 151
Yanhuitlan (Oaxaca), 283n24; caciques,
    59, 62–63; prehispanic temple,
    113; Santo Domingo, 104
Yauhtepec (Morelos), 151
Youalnepantla (midnight glyph), 167
Yucatec Maya, 123, 139–40

Zaachila (Oaxaca), Natividad
    de Santa María, 150
Zacatlan, 62
Zacualtipan (Hidalgo), Santa María
    de la Encarnación, 251
Zapotec peoples, 63, 123, 126, 139
Zapotlantenan (healing deity), 199–200
Zimbrón Romero, J. Rafael, 168
Zinacantepec (México), 297
Zola (Oaxaca), 60, 163
Zorita, Alonso de, 92
Zumárraga, Fray Juan de, 80–82,
    84, 88–91, 273n15
Zumpahuacan (México), 60, 63–64
Zumpango (México), map, 128
Zuni peoples, 145, 164